365 Must-Know Talks of All Time

Caroline Berglund

365 Must-Know Talks of All Time

Copyright © 2022 by Caroline Berglund

Any reference to historical events, real people, or real places are used at the author's discretion and for the use of self-help.

Some characters and events in this book are fictitious. Any similarity to real person, living or dead, is coincidental and not intended by the author.

All rights reserved. No part of this book may be reproduced or used in any manner without written permission of the copyright owner except for the use of quotations in a book review.
For more information, address: caroline@talktalk.ca.

First paperback edition January 2022.

Edited by Diane Bolt
Book design by Creative Capture

ISBN (Paperback) 978-1-7780305-0-5
ISBN (ebook) 978-1-7780305-1-2

www.talktalk.com

Blog   2010

JANUARY: Category   tip

- #365 - Albert Einstein   - war   - conviction
- #364 - Al Gore   - science   - tell a story!
- #363 - Arthur Schopenhauer - philosophy   - Be yourself!
- #362 - Douglas Adams   - politics   - be relevant / enthusiasm
- #361 - Tony Blair   - politics   - keep it simple!
- #360 - Steven Hawking   - music   - provoke new thought
- #359 - Confucius   - philosophy   - Be humble!
- #358 - Liberace   Be entertaining
- #357 - Bill Clinton   Be truthful
- #356 - Ronald Reagan   Be prepared for the impromptu talk
- #355 - Immanuel Kant   Be accessible
- #354 - Ann Richards   Set the tone w/ start preparing
- #353 - Pierre Trudeau   Have an opinion
- #352 - Sally Field   Speak from your ♡ / prepare
- #351 - Robin Williams   Live, laugh, cry, play
- #350 - Steve Jobs   Be theatrical!
- #349 - Lou Gehrig   Be Grateful
- #348 - Conan O'Brian   Be funny!
- #347 - Peter Pan   Believe & you will achieve
- #346 - Ken Robinson   Do schools kill creativity (TED) / know more about your audience
- #345 - Heraclitus   Learn the art of self feedback
- #344 - ~~Clairee Brown~~   ~~Use all your senses~~
- #343 - George Bernard Shaw Be Daring!
- #342 - Keith Barry   Be interactive
- #341 - Dale Carnegie   Take the spotlight off yourself!
- #340 - Anthony Synott
- #339 - Michel de Montaigne
- #338 - Jacques Barzun
- #337 - Lao Tsu
- #336 - J.K. Rowling   the highlight/fringe benefits of failure.
- #335 - Elizabeth Gilbert   Hilroy

Foreword

A little more than a decade ago, I launched an idea on my blog, a countdown of 365 must-know talks of all time—one for each day of the year. On day 365, I revealed my #1 talk. This monumental collection of exploration and analysis of the spoken word—from ancient history, religion, philosophy, science and politics to sports, war, love and medicine—includes excerpts from presentations, essays, monologues, dialogue from books, film, and TV, and everything in-between. And yes, I know excerpts from books and movie dialogue are not technically speeches or talks per se, but I've taken some liberties with the written word, and there will be some works of fiction included here and there that I can visualize being spoken, so work with me here!

I feel like the luckiest person in the world to have found what I love to do and to have had the chance to immerse myself in it for an entire year. I enjoyed every minute, and I hope you will too.

My gratitude goes to those who followed my daily blog in 2010. Your encouragement, support, and contributions were invaluable.

To my girls (you know who you are) for continually checking in on progress, but also for the mockery and insistence that no one could possibly read the blog because it was "far too deep." Thank you for laughing and celebrating with me along the way.

And, to my Mom, my most avid follower who tuned in and offered feedback almost every day in person or via reply posts (118 replies), emails, and telephone calls. And encouraged all her friends to check out the blog's home, talktalk.ca. Your feedback spanned the gamut from showering posts with praise (#201: the girl giving herself a motivational talk in the bathroom mirror, which has since been removed in this edition) to complete disagreement (#40: Jesse Jackson) to adoring and fawning (#191: her hero, Tina Turner) to anger at racial discrimination (#27: Malcolm X) to highlighting grammatical errors and sharing your presentation advice. Thank you for talking about it to anyone who would listen and for telling me how great it was, even when it still needed work. I dedicate this epic project to you. Thank you.

And so, it has come to this. I have found what I love to do and was given the chance to study it for a year back in 2010. Now more than a decade later, I'm attempting a refresh. Replacing some of the original posts with more recent content, as a lot has happened in the public speaking realm during the last 10 years. What a great excuse to immerse myself in my own public speaking university yet again!

Whether you're a professional keynote speaker or a novice talker, I hope the tips in this book will help you take to the stage with confidence.

Contents

Web Links to Video References 465
Photo Sources. 467

#365 - Albert Einstein. 11
#364 - Al Gore 12
#363 - Arthur Schopenhauer 12
#362 - Douglas Adams 13
#361 - Tony Blair 14
#360 - Stephen Hawking 14
#359 - Confucius 15
#358 - Liberace. 16
#357 - Bill Clinton. 16
#356 - Ronald Reagan 17
#355 - Immanuel Kant 19
#354 - Ann Richards 20
#353 - Pierre Trudeau 21
#352 - Sally Field 21
#351 - Robin William as Sean in *Good Will Hunting* 22
#350 - Steve Jobs. 23
#349 - Lou Gehrig 25
#348 - Conan O' Brian 26
#347 - Peter Pan 27
#346 - Ken Robinson 28
#345 - Heraclitus 29
#344 - Charlie Brown 30
#343 - George Bernard Shaw 31
#342 - Keith Barry 32
#341 - Dale Carnegie 33
#340 - Anthony Synnott. 33
#339 - Michel de Montaigne. 34
#338 - Jacques Barzun. 35
#337 - Lao Tsu. 36
#336 - Elizabeth Gilbert 37
#335 - Percy Bysshe Shelley. 38
#334 - Emmeline Pankhurst 39
#333 - William Shakespeare. 40
#332 - Margaret Thatcher. 42
#331 - Tim Brown. 43
#330 - Chip & Dale. 44
#329 - Salvidor Dali 45
#328 - The Tin Man, The Lion, The Scarecrow and Dorothy . . 46
#327 - Paul Potts 47

#326 - David Peebles 49
#325 - Yoda 49
#324 - David Logan. 50
#323 - Stephen Duneier 51
#322 - Leo Tolstoy 54
#321 - Romeo & Juliet 55
#320 - Don McMillan 56
#319 - Noam Chomsky 58
#318 - Judson Laippley 58
#317 - George Orwell 59
#316 - Isabel Allende 60
#315 - Hans Rosling. 62
#314 - Napoleon Bonaparte 63
#313 - Doug Zongker. 64
#312 - Tina Fey 65
#311 - Francis Frei 67
#310 - Jon Stewart. 69
#309 - Greta Thunberg 70
#308 - Brené Brown 72
#307 - Roberto Benigni 74
#306 - Duke Ellington and Erving Mills. 75
#305 - Muhammad Ali 77
#304 - Temple Grandin 77
#303 - Pyotr Ilyich Tchaikovsky 78
#302 - Arthur Benjamin. 79
#301 - Jiddu Krishnamurti 81
#300 - Jesse Owens 82
#299 - Bobby McFerrin 83
#298 - Tom Wujec. 84
#297 - Susan Blackmore 85
#296 - Ben Aeck and Matt Damon. 87
#295 - Gloria Steinem 87
#294 - James Cameron 88
#293 - Matthieu Ricard 89
#292 - Stuart Brown 90
#291 - Jacinda Ardern 91
#290 - Gary Vaynerchuk 93
#289 - Tim Urban. 93
#288 - Shekhar Kapur. 96
#287 - Lakshmi Pratury 97
#286 - Robert Waldinger 98
#285 - Jamie Oliver 100

#284 - Mohandas K. Gandhi 102	#239 - Jon Stewart 150
#283 - Benjamin Zander 102	#238 - Lloyd Jones 152
#282 - Apollo Robbins 103	#237 - Nicholas Christakis 152
#281 - Robert Gupta 105	#236 - Dan Meyer 154
#280 - Andy Warhol 106	#235 - Viktor Frankl 155
#279 - Ricky Gervais 106	#234 - Gretchen Rubin 156
#278 - Kiran Bir Sethi 108	#233 - Calvin Coolidge 157
#277 - Poet, John Rives 109	#232 - Judy Garland 157
#276 - Al Pacino 110	#231 - George Clooney 159
#275 - Tom Rielly 112	#230 - Joe Rogan 160
#274 - Galileo Galiliei 112	#229 - Michelle Obama 161
#273 - Plato 113	#228 - Jean de la Bruyère 163
#272 - Susan Cain 114	#227 - Dan Buettner 163
#271 - Julian Treasure 116	#226 - Neil Armstrong 165
#270 - Dalai Lama 118	#225 - William Blake 166
#269 - Alain de Botton 119	#224 - Amy Tan 167
#268 - Carmen Agra Deedy 120	#223 - William Golding 168
#267 - Erin McKean 121	#222 - Golan Levin 168
#266 - Abraham Lincoln 122	#221 - Adlai Stevenson II 170
#265 - Malcolm Gladwell 122	#220 - Amy Cuddy 170
#264 - Bhagavad Gita 123	#219 - Jean Piaget 173
#263 - Becky Blanton 125	#218 - Kevin Spacey 174
#262 - Dan Ariely 126	#217 - Sojourner Truth 175
#261 - Gustave Flaubert 127	#216 - Kelly McGonigal 176
#260 Sarah Jones 128	#215 - Dr. Seuss 178
#259 - Sir John Mortimer 130	#214 - David Byrne 181
#258 - Geronimo 131	#213 - Dan Pink 182
#257 - Anthony Bourdain 132	#212 - Christopher Poole 183
#256 - Fran Lebowitz 133	#211 - Mike Rowe 184
#255 - Eve Ensler 135	#210 - Jamiroquai 185
#254 - Hillary Clinton 136	#209 - Ralph Waldo Emerson 188
#253 - C.S. Lewis 137	#208 - Mark Twain 188
#252 - Geena Davis 138	#207 - Paulo Coelho 190
#251 - Jimi Hendrix 138	#206 - Rory Sutherland 191
#250 - Dan Gilbert 140	#205 - Stefan Sagmeister 192
#249 - Peter O'Toole 141	#204 - Baltasar Gracián 194
#248 - Ben Stein 142	#203 - Stephen King 194
#247 - Chevy Chase 142	#202 - Napoleon Hill 196
#246 - Natalie Merchant 143	#201 - Monica Lewinsky 197
#245 - Marcus du Sautoy 144	#200 - Elizabeth Hardwick 199
#244 - Joseph Priestly 146	#199 - Anish Kapoor 200
#243 - Simon Sinek 147	#198 - Yogi Bear 201
#242 - Philip II of Macedon 148	#197 - Wayne Dyer 201
#241 - Diana, Princess of Wales 149	#196 - Siegfried Woldhek 202
#240 - Jesus Christ 150	#195 - Malcolm X 203

#194 - Marcus Aurelius 204
#193 - James Lipton 206
#192 - William Arthur Ward 208
#191 - Tina Turner 209
#190 - Stuart Brown 210
#189 - Albert Einstein... 212
#188 - Adam Grant 213
#187 - Hippocrates 215
#186 - J.K. Rowling 216
#185 - Daniel Goleman 217
#184 - George Eliot... 219
#183 - Ronald Reagan 221
#182 - Douglas Englebart... 221
#181 - John Cleese 222
#180 - Dale Carnegie 222
#179 - Julia Child 224
#178 - William E. Hickson 224
#177 - Warren Buett 225
#176 - Theodore Roosevelt 226
#175 - Michael Pollan 227
#174 - Matt Damon... 228
#173 - Ludwig van Beethoven 229
#172 - Richard Dreyfus... 230
#171 - The Fun Theory... 231
#170 - Julie Andrews 231
#169 - Pericles.. 233
#168 - Jeff Bezos.. 234
#167 - Carlos Castaneda 236
#166 - Severn Cullis-Suzuki 237
#165 - Muammar al-Gadda 238
#164 - Elie Wiesel.. 239
#163 - Elizabeth Barrett Browning 243
#162 - Sebastian Wernicke.. 244
#161 - Antoine de Saint-Exupery................................ 245
#160 - Clark Gable.. 246
#159 - William Shakespeare.. 247
#158 - Oscar Wilde 248
#157 - Jean-Jacques Rousseau 249
#156 - Tony Robbins 249
#155 - Dr. Seuss... 251
#154 - Robin Williams.. 251
#153 - Al Pacino 252
#152 - James Veitch 253
#151 - Lia Mills.. 254
#150 - Spiderman 255

#149 - Anthony Michael Hall...................................... 256
#148 - Conan O'Brien.. 256
#147 - Voltaire 257
#146 - John Mayer... 258
#145 - Steve Ballmer... 259
#144 - Robert Pio Hajjar 260
#143 - Jonathan Macoy.. 261
#142 - George H.W. Bush 261
#141 - Abraham Lincoln 262
#140 - Jennifer Buchanan.. 263
#139 - Barack Obama 264
#138 - Pablo Picasso... 266
#137 - Oprah Winfrey... 266
#136 - Simone De Beauvoir 267
#135 - Bob Geldof 268
#134 - Richard Nixon 269
#133 - Harry S. Truman.. 272
#132 - Dean Furness... 273
#131 - Leon Trotsky.. 275
#130 - Tom Lehrer 276
#129 - Eldridge Cleaver 277
#128 - Eric Miller.. 278
#127 - Henry Miller 280
#126 - Jeremy Rifkin... 281
#125 - Kelli Jean Drinkwater 282
#124 - Derek Sivers 285
#123 - Charles Darwin 286
#122 - Isaac Newton... 287
#121 - Patrick Henry 288
#120 - Franklin D. Roosevelt 290
#119 - 14th Dalai Lama of Tibet 291
#118 - James Stewart.. 292
#117 - Earl Spencer 293
#116 - Sylvester Stallone.. 294
#115 - John Keats.. 295
#114 - Nahda Media 297
#113 - Confucius... 299
#112 - Bill Clinton 299
#111 - Jason Sudeikis 300
#110 - Steven Johnson.. 301
#109 - Rene Descartes.. 303
#108 - Sebastian Seung 304
#107 - Archimedes 306
#106 - J.K. Rowling 306
#105 - Caecilius Statius 307

#104 - Saint Augustine	308
#103 - Michelangelo di Lodovico Buonarroti Simoni	309
#102 - William Lyon Phelps	309
#101 - Charles Dickens	311
#100 - Meryl Streep	312
#99 - Jesse Jackson	313
#98 - Charlie Chaplin	315
#97 - Naguib Mahfouz	315
#96 - Frank Morgan	317
#95 - Louis Armstrong	318
#94 - Linus Van Pelt (Charles Schulz)	319
#93 - Alec Baldwin	320
#92 - Bono	321
#91 - Gerald Huther	324
#90 - Chelsey Sullenberger & Patrick Harten	326
#89 - Godfrey Hardy	329
#88 - Barbara Charline Jordan	331
#87 - A.A. Milne	333
#86 - Blake Mycoskie	334
#85 - Seth Godin	335
#84 - Cinderella	337
#83 - William Boughton Pitkin	338
#82 - Anna Quindlen	340
#81 - Jill Tarter	341
#80 - Harvey Milk	343
#79 - Bill Stewart	343
#78 - Luc de Clapiers, marquis de Vauvenargue	345
#77 - Jimmy Carter	346
#76 - Brothers Grimm	347
#75 - Alfred Adler	349
#74 - Benjamin Franklin	350
#73 - Heribert Watzke	351
#72 - David Icke	352
#71 - Gerda Weissmann Klein	353
#70 - Bert Lahr	353
#69 - Melinda French Gates	355
#68 - Richard St. John	355
#67 - Wayne Gretzky	356
#66 - Scott Berkun	357
#65 - Pat Carroll	358
#64 - Matt Ridley	360
#63 - Carl Jung	361
#62 - Tiany Shlain	363
#61 - Lewis Carroll	363
#60 - Barak Obama	365

#59 - Ryan Hreljac	367
#58 - Leonardo DaVinci	368
#57 - Richard Bach	369
#56 - Pema Chödrön	371
#55 - Harry S. Truman	372
#54 - Lucius Annaeus Seneca	372
#53 - Ellen DeGeneres	374
#52 - Aristotle	375
#51 - Ho Chi Minh	377
#50 - George Berkeley	378
#49 - Moses	379
#48 - Clarence Darrow	381
#47 - Mother Teresa	383
#46 - Ronald Reagan	389
#45 - George W. Bush	390
#44 - Queen Elizabeth I	392
#43 - George Washington	394
#42 - Nelson Mandela	396
#41 - James Carville	397
#40 - Jesse Jackson	398
#39 - William Faulkner	400
#38 - Edward (Teddy) Kennedy	401
#37 - Steve Jobs	402
#36 - Winston Churchill	404
#35 - Susan B. Anthony	405
#34 - Margaret Thatcher	407
#33 - Sidney Poitier	408
#32 - Demosthenes	409
#31 - Alexander the Great	410
#30 - John F. Kennedy	412
#29 - William Shakespeare	413
#28 - Sally Field	415
#27 - Malcolm X	416
#26 - Pierre Elliot Trudeau	417
#25 - St. Francis of Assisi	421
#24 - Virginia Woolf	422
#23 - Aristotle	425
#22 - Ray Nagin	427
#21 - Marie Curie	429
#20 - Maya Angelou	431
#19 - Rudolph the Red-Nosed Reindeer	435
#18 - Colin Powell	436
#17 - Graeme Taylor	437
#16 - Frederick Douglass	438
#15 - Rosa Parks	441

#14 - Carrie Fisher 442
#13 - Barack Obama 443
#12 - Judy Garland 444
#11 - Plato 445
#10 - John F. Kennedy 447
#9 - Leonardo DaVinci 448
#8 - Helen Keller 449

#7 - Martin Luther King Jr. 450
#6 - Aristotle 451
#5 - Socrates 452
#4 - Gandhi 454
#3 - Leo Tolstoy 457
#2 - Randy Pausch 459
#1 - Atticus Finch 462

#365 Must-Know Talks…

We'll begin at #365, of course!

#365 – Albert Einstein

1879–1955

Context – At an address in Princeton in November 1946, the year following the dropping of the atomic bomb in Hiroshima, Japan – 'The Social Task of the Scientist in the Atomic Era, A Symposium' by the Emergency Committee of Atomic Scientist.

"The position in which we are now is a very strange one which in general political life never happened. Namely, the thing that I refer to is this: To have security against atomic bombs and against the other biological weapons, we have to prevent war, for if we cannot prevent war, every nation will use every means that is at their disposal; and in spite of all promises they make, they will do it. At the same time, so long as war is not prevented, all the governments of the nations have to prepare for war, and if you have to prepare for war, then you are in a state where you cannot abolish war. This is really the cornerstone of our situation. Now, I believe what we should try to bring about is the general conviction that the first thing you have to abolish is war at all costs, and every other point of view must be of secondary importance."

Analysis – What makes a talk memorable? Is it content? Is it body language? Is it the character of the speaker? Is it the ideas the speaker espouses? Or is it something more? Here we see Einstein exude conviction. Conviction is of primary importance to almost any talk, arguably it is a person's conviction that encourages others to act. Einstein is firm and uncompromising in his choice of words; "…we have to prevent war, for if we cannot prevent war every nation will use every means that is at their disposal… they will do it." I can envision his fists pumping in the air, a strong tone and inflection, a firm stance. These physical attributes aid a talk and come naturally when one speaks with conviction.

Tip – Speak with conviction.

#364 – Al Gore

(1948)

Context – From the opening monologue of the documentary *An Inconvenient Truth*

"You look at that river gently flowing by. You notice the leaves rustling in the wind. You hear the birds; you hear the tree frogs. In the distance, you hear a cow. You feel the grass. The mud gives a little bit on the riverbank. It's quiet; it's peaceful. And all of a sudden, it's a gear shift inside you. And it's like taking a deep breath and going…
'Oh yeah, I forgot about this.'"

Analysis – Whether you believe in global warming or think it's a bunch of bunk, you cannot deny the facts in the opening of this film, and you cannot deny its success. A variety of things are happening here; one is that Gore grabs your attention immediately. How? By telling you a story. You are immediately thrown into the world of nature's tranquility as you hear these words. The entire point of any talk is to get others to listen to what you have to say, to ignite action and educate and that just isn't going to happen if you've put your audience to sleep. Oh, and if you look out into the audience and your participants are asleep, it is no one's fault but your own. Gore could've started with innumerable statistics about temperatures and ice caps, instead he waits to do that until the belly of his talk when you are already invested, and he has your attention. Keep your audience engaged by telling them a story to bring them into your world.

Tip – Tell a story.

#363 – Arthur Schopenhauer

1788–1860

Context – Taken from Chapter XXII, "Thinking For Oneself "in Parerga and Paralipomena: Short Philosophical Essays, Volume 2 (1851). This collection of Schopenhauer's works that gives insights into the German philosopher's, often pessimistic, point of view. (Warning: Schopenhauer's philosophical musings are not light reading, and it's certainly not all sunshine and puppies!)

"Truth that has been merely learned is like an artificial limb, a false tooth, a waxen nose; at best, like a nose made out of another's flesh; it adheres to us only because it is put on. But truth acquired by thinking of our *own is like a natural limb; it alone really belongs to us. This is the fundamental difference between the thinker and the mere man of learning. The intellectual attainments of a man who thinks for himself resemble a fine painting, where the light and shade are correct, the tone sustained, the colour perfectly harmonized; it is true to life. On the other hand, the intellectual attainments of the mere man of learning are like a large palette, full of all sorts of colours, which at most are systematically arranged, but devoid of harmony, connection, and meaning."*

Analysis – When I read Arthur Schopenhauer's works, I can't help but think that his mother, the novelist Johanna Schopenhauer, had a lot to do with his pessimism (yes, very Freudian, I know, and I'll get to that later). His mother was a novelist and operated a literary salon, which is much like a book club meets library. Even as a young boy, Schopenhauer would pontificate to his mother's guests about the futility of existence, which apparently drove them away and ultimately was the reason for his mother and Arthur not talking for nearly 25 years. It sounds all very sad, but it really isn't. Do not pity Schopenhauer because he learned one of the most valuable lessons in life and certainly a valuable lesson in giving a talk. Don't emulate others. Be yourself! There is nothing worse than watching someone give a talk as they put on the cloak or mask of another. Speak of what you believe, what you know – not what others believe or know. It is transparent and, frankly, hard to watch. This type of speaker is my least favourite but, unfortunately, the most plentiful. Find a way to be yourself, which usually comes with a lot of introspection, deep thinking, and plenty of practice.

Tip – Be yourself.

#362 – Douglas Adams

1952–2001

Context – From Adams' book, *The Restaurant at the End of the Universe* (1980), the second book in the Hitchhiker's Guide to the Galaxy comedy, science fiction series.

"The major problem, one of the major problems, for there are several, with governing people is that of who you get to do it. Or, rather of who manages to get people to let them do it to them. To summarize: it is a well-known and much-lamented fact that those people who most want to rule people are, ipso facto, those least suited to do it. To summarize the summary: anyone who is capable of getting themselves made President should on no account be allowed to do the job. To summarize the summary of the summary: people are a problem."

Analysis – Ah yes, you've gotta love Douglas Adams. Here, Adams captures the mood of the time. *The Restaurant at the End of the Universe* was published in 1980 following Richard Nixon's U.S. presidency, which ended with an eruption of general discontent. Oh, then throw in Ford and Carter, and Reagan who was elected in '80, and you get why many believed the American government to be more than a little shady. Adams, albeit in a satirical way, captures an important component in giving an effective talk – be relevant and know your audience! On more than one occasion I've listened as a speaker voiced an irrelevant topic at an inappropriate time. Doing a talk right is a much more complex task than most people really digest (or perhaps they know this, and that is the reason public speaking is one of the most feared experience that is not even trumped by death!) It takes research and a ton of work upfront, including the much over-looked relevancy component. While preparing your talk, ask yourself: Does my audience want to hear this? Will it make sense to them? Will this topic keep them engaged?

Tip – Be relevant.

#361 – Tony Blair

(1953)

Context – 1998, British Prime Minister Tony Blair oversees negotiations between the British and Irish governments over Northern Ireland.

"A day like today is not a day for soundbites, really. We can leave them at home, but I feel the hand of history upon our shoulders. I really do."

Analysis – There are times in a talk that one needs to get to the point and keep it simple. Here, Blair illustrates this consideration audibly. Although Blair immediately offers a soundbite after warning against them, he also deftly illustrates that there are times that one needs to simply make the point and move on.

Negotiations regarding the conflict in Northern Ireland had been underway for years, and there had already been plenty of discussion and debate. On this day in 1998, it was the final negotiations and time to conclude the previous years of talks with the signing of the Good Friday Agreement.

There had been plenty of discussion; there had been plenty of debate. On this day in 1998, it was the final negotiations and a wrap-up of all this work. In my practice and in observing others, I've noticed that, for some, keeping it simple is a monumental task. You know the type who likes to pontificate ad nauseam long after the participants have stopped listening. Watch your audience. Is it time to re-cap and move on? Is it time to get to the point? If you are doing a longer talk, you may not be able to go from one simple statement to the next. But peppering your talk with bold, simple statements ensures recollection and digestion. And isn't that the function of a talk?

Tip – Keep it simple.

#360 – Stephen Hawking

1942–2018

Context – Hawking did several public talks or lectures. This excerpt is taken from "Life in the Universe."

"In this talk I would like to speculate a little on the development of life in the universe, and in particular the development of intelligent life. I shall take this to include the human race, even though much of its behaviour throughout history has been pretty stupid and not calculated to aid the survival of the species. Two questions I shall discuss are: what is the probability of life existing elsewhere in the universe, and how may life develop in the future."

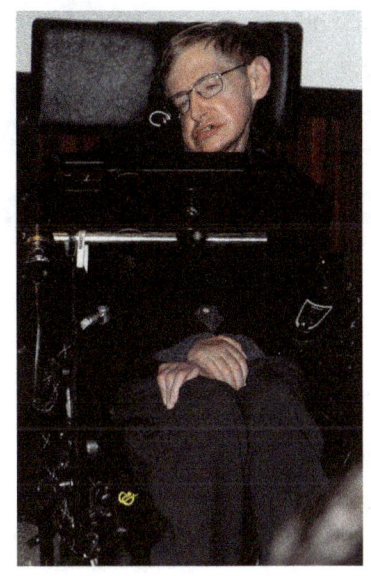

Analysis – Well, I certainly don't claim to be a very good student of quantum physics or applied math, but I don't believe one needs to be when listening to Hawking speak. That said, I get serious brain freeze when I try to understand his concepts around time. But there is little doubt that Hawking elicits thought. Whether you agree with what he is saying or not, you can't deny that he can make you think in new and interesting ways. One of the many reasons one is asked to give a talk is not only to share their point of view but to get the audience to think of something in a new and fresh way. A speaker's dream is hearing, "I never thought of it that way" or "really? I didn't know that!" A talk should rarely reiterate what someone already knows. That would be a colossal waste of everyone's time (there are some exceptions, which we'll discuss later).

There are many reasons to give or to invite someone to give a talk, and these can be distilled into the following categories: to inform, to persuade, or to entertain. I would argue that all three require thought provocation to be successful.

Tip – Provoke thought.

#359 – Confucius

551–479 BCE

Context – Confucius, the famous Chinese philosopher, is attributed with hundreds, if not thousands, of witty and profound sayings. His disciples compiled all of his teachings after his death into the *Analects of Confucius* (Much like Plato penned Socrates' work). The following is derived from that compilation.

"He knows most who says he knows least."

Analysis – Apparently, Confucius was infamous for spouting these words (although one can't really know since it is like playing a game of telephone) repeatedly. It shows the monumental difference between being a good speaker and being a superb one. Speakers who recognize that they have much to learn from the world and certainly from their participants bring an aura of wanting to learn even though they are the ones teaching.! This type of speaker listens at what I call 'Level 1' listening. They will listen with their whole being, digest what is being said or asked, and will not think about a rebuttal until the speaker has finished their thought. They are engaged; they are humble.

I really enjoy watching a speaker when a question is posed by the audience. Many will rush into the corners of their brain to respond with something that sounds good, fancy, and articulate, often leaving the person who asked the question, as well as the rest of the audience, puzzled. The speaker will move on at a rapid pace so as not to shed light on the fact that the question hasn't been answered. Or the speaker will say something like, 'Make sense?' and the person who had asked the original question feels compelled to slowly nod their head up and down. A superb speaker will rightfully admit that they don't have the answer, but they'll also commit to finding it out. Credibility means a lot when you've been asked to do a talk, and the foundation of credibility comes from being humble.

Tip – Be humble.

#358 – Liberace

1919–1987

Context – This quote is from a letter Liberace sent to a critic in response to an unfavourable review in 1954.

"When the reviews are bad I tell my staff they can join me in crying all the way to the bank."

Analysis – Liberace was not exactly critically acclaimed, and he was maligned by many for being too flamboyant and extremely highly paid for his act. I disagree. Liberace knew what he was good at, and that was to entertain. I don't think I'm alone in that either. In the early '50s, he had a fan club in excess of a million members and he made a lot of loot from his act in Las Vegas. Those statistics don't sway me either way, but obviously, there was something about Liberace (kinda like there was 'Something about Mary') that made people flock to see him. He was fun to watch; he was entertaining, enjoyable, and good for a few laughs. In sum, he was delightful. Liberace shows us an essential component in giving an effective talk. I don't care if you're talking about networking languages, sales strategies, or car insurance you need to find a way to be entertaining. That can come from a variety of mediums, but the trick to doing it well is to stay within the boundaries of your personality.

Tip – Be entertaining.

#357 – Bill Clinton

(1946)

Context – On August 17, 1998, Bill Clinton gave one of the most famous (or infamous) speeches and I remember watching it in real time. In this short, terse speech, Clinton finally admitted he had engaged in an improper relationship with former White House intern Monica Lewinsky. The admission occurred several months after a much-publicized dramatic denial by the President. That denial had been staunchly defended by First Lady Hillary Rodham Clinton, White House staffers, and various friends and supporters of the President.

"This afternoon in this room, from this chair, I testified before the Office of Independent Counsel and the grand jury. I answered their questions truthfully, including questions about my private life, questions no American citizen would ever want to answer. Still, I must take complete responsibility for all my actions, both public and private. And that is why I am speaking to you tonight. As you know, in a deposition in January, I was asked questions about my relationship with Monica Lewinsky. While my answers were legally accurate, I did not volunteer information. Indeed, I did have a relationship with Ms. Lewinsky that

was not appropriate. In fact, it was wrong. It constituted a critical lapse in judgment and a personal failure on my part for which I am solely and completely responsible. But I told the grand jury today, and I say to you now that at no time did I ask anyone to lie. To hide or destroy evidence or to take any other unlawful action. I know that my public comments and my silence about the matter gave a false impression. I misled people, including even my wife. I deeply regret that…"

Analysis – It is amazing to me that folks seem to have forgotten this whole mess. Clinton is a liar and untruthful. There, I said it. Yeah, yeah, there are those of you who'll say, "oh, but his policy and execution were phenomenal; what he did behind closed doors ain't none of our business." Sorry, but I don't buy it. It's about integrity and you either have it in all aspects of your life, or you don't. Clinton shows us what happens when you get tangled up in lies and then try to talk your way out of it. From a speech perspective, he certainly does his job here. He speaks to his answers being 'legally accurate' so as to save his ass, he talks about the sorrow he feels for misleading his wife, and for giving a false impression. If you have a chance to watch Clinton's speech, I highly recommend doing so as it provides a firm lesson on body language and subtle lying cues.

When you're giving a talk, I urge you to not be weaselly or duplicitous. Seriously, I'm not just saying that to be fun or cute. Weaselly people aren't fun to watch on stage. You can pick 'em out, and often you can't quite put your finger on it, but you know something is up, something is wrong, something just isn't jiving. Generally, that is your intuition kicking in, telling you that the person you're listening to isn't being truthful.

Tip – Be truthful.

#356 – Ronald Reagan

1911–2004

Context – The Space Shuttle *Challenger* disintegrated into a ball of fire 73 seconds after liftoff. Instead of the State of the Union Address scheduled for that evening, Reagan paid tribute to the seven astronauts on the shuttle.

"Ladies and gentlemen, I'd planned to speak to you tonight to report on the state of the Union, but the events of earlier today have led me to change those plans. Today is a day for mourning and remembering. Nancy and I are pained to the core by the tragedy of the shuttle Challenger. We know we share this pain with all of the

people of our country. This is truly a national loss.

Nineteen years ago, almost to the day, we lost three astronauts in a terrible accident on the ground. But we've never lost an astronaut in flight; we've never had a tragedy like this. And perhaps we've forgotten the courage it took for the crew of the shuttle. But they, the Challenger Seven, were aware of the dangers, but overcame them and did their jobs brilliantly. We mourn seven heroes….We mourn their loss as a nation together…"

Analysis – There are few things I know for sure, but one is Murphy's Law—if it can go wrong, it will. As a speaker, whether you are doing so professionally or as a novice doing your very first talk, I urge you to think of at least three things that may go wrong with your presentation. I was in sales for ten years before I launched into the consulting profession, and while I was at a sales meeting in Toronto, the 9/11 tragedy occurred. There were 200 or so sales personnel sitting in a conference room listening to various department heads speak. Marketing got up to tell us about the upcoming plans, the sales VP got up to talk about the numbers for the previous year and the vision for the year ahead. I will never forget watching as the President got up after a break, and you could tell from his body language there was something really wrong. Prior to this the mood of the meeting had been upbeat and fun, but as he walked up to the mic with his head pointed south and his shoulders down, he didn't meet anyone's eyes. He announced, "I have some news. For the first time in American history, American air space is a no-fly zone." I remember those words verbatim and much of the speech that followed. It's probably the only talk I can recount pretty closely word for word. What made this talk impactful? Much like Reagan's, it certainly wasn't a practiced talk, albeit Reagan had a speechwriter. It was the fact that he was prepared for an impromptu talk. Both these men were able to maintain their composure at a very difficult time and deliver. Impromptu speeches can only come when one has the ability to go outside themselves, be humble, be caring, and focus on delivering a message. In order to do this type of talk, you must always be prepared for Murphy's Law and recognize that you have become a caveat for delivering the message. You are no longer there to entertain, and you must be genuinely humble and empathetic (and if you can't, then be willing to find someone who can).

Beyond the emotional element of this talk, you must be prepared with a formula. Write down the following questions so you are prepared for an impromptu situation:

1. What is the situation?

2. What are my thoughts?

3. What are some examples of someone overcoming adversity/challenges in history (within your history or history in general)

4. What will I do, and how will I react?

If you tie in a bit of practice and organization with genuine and heartfelt caring, you too will be prepared for the difficult impromptu talk.

Tip – Be prepared for the difficult Impromptu talk.

#355 – Immanuel Kant

1724–1804

Context – Kant was a professor of Logic and Metaphysics at the University of Konigsberg. The quote below came from answering arguably one of the biggest questions; 'What is Enlightenment?'

"Enlightenment is man's emergence from his self-incurred immaturity. Immaturity is the inability to use one's own understanding without the guidance of another. This immaturity is self-incurred in its cause is not lack of understanding, but lack of resolution and courage to use it without the guidance of another. The motto of enlightenment is therefore: Sapere aude (latin for 'Dare to know.') Have courage to use your own understanding!

"Laziness and cowardice are the reasons why such a large proportion of men, even when nature has long emancipated them from alien guidance nevertheless gladly remain immature for life. For the same reasons, it is all too easy for others to set themselves up as their guardians. It is so convenient to be immature! If I have a book to have understanding in place of me, a spiritual adviser to have a conscience for me, a doctor to judge my diet for me, and so on, I need not make any efforts at all. I need not think so long as I can pay; others will soon enough take the tiresome job over for me.

"The guardians who have kindly taken upon themselves the work of supervision will soon see to it that by far the largest part of mankind (including the entire fair sex) should consider the step forward to maturity not only as difficult but also as highly dangerous. Having first infatuated their domesticated animals, and carefully prevented the docile creatures from daring to take a single step without the leading strings to which they are tied, they next show them the danger which threatens them if they try to walk unaided. Now this danger is not, in fact, so very great, for they would certainly learn to walk eventually after a few falls. But an example of this kind is intimidating and usually frightens them off from further attempts.

"Thus, it is difficult for each separate individual to work his way out of the immaturity, which has become almost second nature to him. He has even grown fond of it and is really incapable for the time being of using his own understanding because he was never allowed to make the attempt."

Analysis – Wittgenstein (another philosopher) once said that reading philosophy is a kind of agony. And for me, there are some philosophers where that sentiment holds true. To know that I have struggled with many of the philosophers in history, including Mr. Kant, one needs only look at my copy of *Philosophy for Dummies*, which I purchased many moons ago. As I stare at it while writing this, I can see the post-it notes seeping from every available space. Kant is the one that resurrected (in the Western world, that is) the notion of enlightenment. He had enjoyed a great career of public lecture on a vast number of topics for many years and then abruptly stopped for some ten years to ponder the topic enlightenment. My point is, if you feel lost in the above quote, you are not alone. Kant has to be one of the most influential yet unreadable and difficult to digest of all the theoretical philosophers. So, I can imagine sitting in one of his lectures, eyes glazed, wondering what the heck he was talking about but also knowing that the content must be good. Have you ever sat in a talk or speech and you knew the speaker was incredibly knowledgeable in his/her topic, yet you couldn't digest what they were saying (unless of course you'd had ten years to ponder the subject in a corner somewhere)? I don't care how brilliant you are; if you can't find a way to make what you're saying accessible to your audience, then don't bother! It will simply fall on deaf ears.

Tip – Be accessible.

#354 – Ann Richards

1933–2006

Context –Democratic National Convention Address by Ann Richards (Texas State Treasurer and former Governor). Keynote Address July 18, 1988

"Good evening, ladies and gentlemen. Buenas noches, mis amigos! I am delighted to be here with you this evening because after listening to George Bush all these years, I figured you needed to know what a real Texas accent sounds like. Twelve years ago, (former Rep.) Barbara (C.) Jordan, another Texas woman, made the keynote address to this convention – and two women in 160 years is about par for the course. But, if you give us a chance, we can perform. After all, Ginger Rogers did everything that Fred Astaire did. She just did it backwards and in high heels.

I want to announce to this nation that in a little more than 100 days, the Reagan-Meese-Deaver-Nofziger- Poindexter-North- Weinberger-Watt-Gorsuch-Lavelle-Stockman-Haig-Bork-Noriega- George Bush era will be over. You know, tonight I feel a little like I did when I played basketball in the eighth grade. I thought I looked real cute in my uniform, and then I heard a boy yell from the bleachers, "Make that basket, bird legs." My greatest fear is that same guy is somewhere in the audience tonight, and he's going to cut me down to size. Where I grew up, there really wasn't much tolerance for self-importance, people who put on airs…"

Analysis – What a fun, funny, and interesting keynote address. I've only included the introduction because it shows the importance of having that part of the talk practiced. Not only practiced, but I would suggest knowing the opening of your presentation backwards, forwards, and inside out! It helps if you include humour and enthusiasm as Richards has done here. Even if you've never seen this keynote address, you'll likely be familiar with that opening line, *"Good evening, ladies and gentlemen. Buenas noches, mis amigos! I am delighted to be here with you this evening because after listening to George Bush all these years, I figured you needed to know what a real Texas accent sounds like."* These words could not have been said in a sullen, flat tone but an upbeat and enthusiastic one, which includes the use of inflection! Yes, inflection—a change in modulation of intonation in the voice. The words rise and fall to create interest. Set the tone of what is to follow in your talk by grabbing your audience's attention using humour, enthusiasm, and having practiced, practiced, practiced!

Tip – Set the tone with your introduction.

#353 – Pierre Trudeau

1919–2000

Context – Comment in the Canadian House of Commons on the decriminalization of homosexuality (1967)

"We take the position that there is no place for the state in the bedrooms of the nation. What's done in private between adults doesn't concern the criminal code"

Analysis – Anyone who knows me knows that I think Trudeau senior is a pretty cool dude. And his speech in the House of Commons on the decriminalization of homosexuality in 1967 serves as a perfect illustration of how one should always have an opinion. A thoughtful opinion is key to generating a superb talk. Your participants will inevitably ask, "so, what do you think?" And it is up to you to be well-read enough and have researched enough to provide it. In 1967 there were all kinds of attitudes, if not controversy, surrounding being gay, but Trudeau didn't care about that; he offered his opinion and it's an important one. Some would say that you have to be politically correct, I say it depends on the audience, but one should most often answer truthfully regarding their own beliefs. How you go about offering your opinion is of equal importance: Be respectful to everyone in your audience. Respect that others may have opinions that are the polar opposite of yours. That's okay but find a way to communicate what you believe so that others may hear it, digest it and contemplate it. Perhaps you will be able to position your opinion in a way that they haven't heard before and vice versa. The foundation for this tip is respect.

If you're able to do it respectfully, then go ahead and share your opinion!

Tip – Have an opinion!

#352 – Sally Field

(1946)

Context – The acceptance speech given by Sally Field at the Academy Awards in 1984 for her role in *Places in the Heart*.

"This means so much more to me this time, I don't know why. I think the first time I hardly felt it because it was all too new. But I want to say 'thank you' to you. I haven't had an orthodox career. And I've wanted more than anything to have your respect. The first time I didn't feel it. But this time I feel it. And I can't deny the fact that you like me… right now… you really like me. Thank you."

Analysis – You can feel the emotion jumping from the page as you read this acceptance speech. True emotion. Not fabricated, not contrived. But good ol' fashion heartfelt gratitude. I really like this speech because it proves what one should do in giving a talk of thanks or gratitude. You should absolutely think about and possibly practice what you are going to say, in the event that you are in a position to extend gratitude, BUT—and this is a biggie—be prepared to throw it all away in the moment and get swept away in what you are feeling at the time. When you're preparing, you can't possibly know how you will feel at that particular moment, nor should you. I always say that one should prepare but toss it all aside and allow the winds of emotion transport you into heartfelt thanks.

Tip – Speak from your heart.

#351 – Robin Williams as Dr. Sean Maguire in *Good Will Hunting*

1951–2014

Context – 1997 delivered one of my favourite movies of all time, *Good Will Hunting*. In the below, Maquire (played by Robin Williams) tells Will Hunting (Matt Damon) a thing or two about what he's learned in life.

"So, if I asked you about art, you'd probably give me the skinny… on every art book ever written. Michelangelo? You know a lot about him. Life's work, political aspirations. Him and the pope. Sexual orientation. The whole works, right? I bet you can't tell me what it smells like in the Sistine Chapel. You never actually stood there and looked up at that beautiful ceiling. Seeing that. If I ask you about women, you'll probably give me a syllabus of your personal favorites. You may have even been laid a few times. But you can't tell me what it feels like to wake up next to a woman… and feel truly happy. You're a tough kid. I ask you about war; you'd probably ah throw Shakespeare at me, right? "Once more into the breach, dear friends." But you've never been near one. You've never held your best friend's head in your lap… and watched him gasp his last breath lookin' to you for help. If I asked you about love, you'd probably quote me a sonnet, but you've never looked at a woman and been totally vulnerable. Known someone that could level you with her eyes. Feelin' like God put an angel on Earth just for you, who could rescue you from the depths of hell. And you wouldn't know what it's like to be her angel, to have that love for her be there forever. Through anything. Through cancer. And you wouldn't know about sleepin' sittin' up in a hospital room… for two months, holding her hand, because the doctors could see in your eyes… that the terms "visiting hours" don't apply to you. You don't know about real loss, 'cause that only occurs when you love something more than you love yourself. I doubt you've ever dared to love anybody that much. I look at you. I don't see an intelligent, confident man. I see a cocky, scared shitless kid. But you're a genius, Will. No one denies that. No one could possibly understand the depths of you. But you presume to know everything about me because you saw a painting of mine. You ripped my fuckin' life apart. You're an orphan, right? Do you think that I'd know the first thing about how hard your life has been – how you feel, who you are – because I read Oliver Twist? Does that encapsulate you? Personally, I don't give a shit about all that because – You know what? I can't learn anything from you… I can't read in some fuckin' book. Unless you wanna talk about you who you are. And I'm fascinated. I'm in. But you don't wanna do that, do you sport? You're terrified of what you might say. Your move, chief. "

Analysis – I love this soliloquy. It's both well written, and beautifully delivered. Robin Williams' character, you may remember, had been working on getting through to Matt Damon's character with no success. Hunting has a genius IQ and is showing it off, to Maguire, his therapist. A superb talk is always elevated when you have a wealth of life experience. That doesn't mean that you need to be 80 years old to deliver a great talk. It simply means that you have to soak up what life has to offer; laugh, play, cry, and live. It's easy to be 'book smart,' just pick up a book, read and digest. It is much more difficult to be life smart. Have you ever listened to a speaker talk, and that speaker just shows you his or her 'book smart' side? It is dry, boring, and one-note. Now, when someone throws in their life's journey, we get something that is interesting and engaging. Remember to sprinkle in your life experience, both good and bad, into the core of your speech.

Tip – Live, laugh, cry, play!

#350 – Steve Jobs

1955–2001

Context – 1984 launch of the Macintosh computer at Apple's annual shareholders meeting.

"Welcome to Apple's 1984 Annual Shareholders meeting. I'd like to begin by reading part of an old poem by Dylan, that's Bob Dylan. Steve flashed a big smile as he started to recite the second verse of "The Times They Are A-Changin," stretching an occasional vowel in a Dylanesque fashion:

Come writers and critics
Who prophesies with your pen
And keep your eyes wide,
The chance won't come again
And don't speak too soon
For the wheel's still in spin
And there's no tellin' who that it's namin'.
For the loser now
Will be later to win

For the times they are a-changin'.
and later on in the presentation…

And later on in the presentation…Jobs walks over to a lone Macintosh that has been sitting in its canvas carrying case near the centre of the stage. He carefully opens it up, revealing the Mac to his audience and the world for the very first time. The Mac introduces itself,

"Hello, I am Macintosh. It sure is great to get out of that bag!

Unaccustomed as I am to public speaking, I'd like to share with you a maxim I thought of the first time I met an IBM mainframe: Never trust a computer that you can't lift! Obviously, I can talk, but right now, I'd like to sit back and listen. So, it is with considerable pride that I introduce a man who has been like a father to me…Steve Jobs!"

Analysis – Be forewarned, Jobs appears on this list a few times. Jobs has the ability to get a crowd into a frenzy about a new product and have them sitting on the edge of their seats waiting patiently for him to unveil a new product (the iPhone, iPod and iPad). For this presentation, Apple rented the Light-Valve, a powerful video projector that projected the Mac display brighter and larger than anything had done before. It is amazing how far we've come as I sneak a peek at my beloved 'Ben-Q' projector, which is the size of a Hilory notepad or my portable mini projector that is tucked into my briefcase. The projector they used the day they unveiled the Macintosh computer was very temperamental, and if you watch the presentation online, you'll see that it repeatedly shuts down for no apparent reason. But this doesn't distract from anything! The auditorium where they unveiled the Mac, was packed to its 2,500-person capacity. The software team usually didn't show up to the office 'til 10 am, but on this morning they filled the first and second rows. The lights dim, Jobs appears at the podium in his signature his black suit and bow tie; he's nervous and that is okay with me because it shows that he cares. In fact, I'd be alarmed if I watched that video, read the transcript, and didn't detect monumental nerves. Jobs' opening is well rehearsed, artfully constructed, and incredibly effective. Jobs has the audience eating out of the palm of his hand. It is palpable. By the time he gets to the computer demo, it's pandemonium! The audience and Jobs are so thrilled with what has transpired. You can see real emotion emanating from Jobs' face, and he is fighting back tears. There are many tips that I could extrapolate from this famous presentation, but it comes down to this: If you love your presentation topic, and are really passionate about it, you will find ways to make the content digestible and interesting to the audience by seeking out innovative and, theatrical ways to communicate your message. Perhaps you too will quote Bob Dylan, or find a new and better projector, make a computer talk, get emotional, and whatever it takes to make your audience jazzed about what you have to say.

Tip – Be theatrical.

#349 – Lou Gehrig

1903–1941

Context – On July 4, 1939 the Yankees held a ceremony to honour Lou Gehrig, who retired uniform #4, due to being diagnosed with a crippling disease that now bears his name. The following speech, titled 'The Luckiest Man on the Face of the Earth', comes from that ceremony.

"Fans, for the past two weeks you have been reading about a bad break I got. Yet today I consider myself the luckiest man on the face of the earth. I have been in ballparks for seventeen years and have never received anything but kindness and encouragement from you fans. Look at these grand men. Which of you wouldn't consider it the highlight of his career to associate with them for even one day?

Sure, I'm lucky. Who wouldn't consider it an honor to have known Jacob Ruppert – also the builder of baseball's greatest empire, Ed Barrow – to have spent the next nine years with that wonderful little fellow Miller Huggins – then to have spent the next nine years with that outstanding leader, that smart student of psychology – the best manager in baseball today, Joe McCarthy!

Sure, I'm lucky. When the New York Giants, a team you would give your right arm to beat, and vice versa, sends you a gift, that's something! When everybody down to the groundskeepers and those boys in white coats remember you with trophies, that's something. When you have a wonderful mother-in-law, who takes sides with you in squabbles against her own daughter, that's something. When you have a father and mother who work all their lives so that you can have an education and build your body, it's a blessing! When you have a wife who has been a tower of strength and shown more courage than you dreamed existed, that's the finest I know. So I close in saying that I might have had a tough break – but I have an awful lot to live for!"

Analysis – Nicknamed the Iron Horse for his commitment to the game of baseball, after 2,130 consecutive games, Gehrig's career came to a grinding halt as a result of the disease we all recognize today as Lou Gehrig's disease, which is how Amyotrophic Lateral Sclerosis (ALS) is more commonly known.

What strikes me about Gehrig is, he is the antithesis of a whiner, or the all too familiar pity party thrower. He does not take this opportunity to wallow in self-pity. Instead, in the face of what will be the fight for his life, he extends his gratitude to his teammates, his family, and his wife. Before you go into your next presentation, talk, or speech, ask yourself, 'am I the type to complain?' There are some who will complain even at the metaphorical podium and the drive is to elicit pity. I'm unclear why one would attempt to elicit pity from anyone. It is a useless and completely selfish emotion. If you are apt to behave in this way, recognize it and change it to gratitude. You will be much more appealing not only in your talk but in your life.

Tip – Be grateful.

#348 – Conan O' Brian

(1963)

Context – Commencement Speech to the Harvard Class of 2000

"I'd like to thank the Class Marshals for inviting me here today. The last time I was invited to Harvard, it cost me $110,000, so you'll forgive me if I'm a bit suspicious. I'd like to announce upfront that I have one goal this afternoon: to be half as funny as tomorrow's Commencement Speaker, Moral Philosopher and Economist, Amartya Sen. Must get more laughs than seminal wage/price theoretician.

"Students of the Harvard Class of 2000, fifteen years ago I sat where you sit now, and I thought exactly what you are now thinking: What's going to happen to me? Will I find my place in the world? Am I really graduating a virgin? I still have 24 hours, and my roommate's Mom is hot. I swear she was checking me out. Being here today is very special for me. I miss this place. I especially miss Harvard Square – it's so unique. Nowhere else in the world will you find a man with a turban wearing a Red Sox jacket and working in a lesbian bookstore. Hey, I'm just glad my dad's working.

"It's particularly sweet for me to be here today because when I graduated, I wanted very badly to be a Class Day Speaker. Unfortunately, my speech was rejected. So, if you'll indulge me, I'd like to read a portion of that speech from fifteen years ago: 'Fellow students, as we sit here today listening to the classic Ah-ha tune which will definitely stand the test of time, I would like to make several predictions about what the future will hold: 'I believe that one day a simple Governor from a small Southern State will rise to the highest office in the land. He will lack political skill but will lead on the sheer strength of his moral authority. I believe that Justice will prevail, and on the day, the Berlin Wall will crumble, uniting East and West Berlin forever under Communist rule. I believe that one day a high-speed network of interconnected computers will spring up worldwide so enriching people that they will lose their interest in idle chit chat and pornography. And finally, I believe that one day, I will have a television show on a major network, seen by millions of people a night, which I will use to re-enact crimes and help catch at large criminals. And then there's some stuff about the death of Wall Street, which I don't think we need to get into…The point is that, although you see me as a celebrity, a member of the cultural elite, a kind of demigod, I was actually, a student here once, much like you."

Analysis – O'Brian has had a myriad of late-night talk shows over the years including a brief stint at The Tonight Show, Late Night with Conan O'Brian and most recently a self-titled TBS show. But it is a very funny transcript from a very funny commencement speech that stands out in his body of work. You can see O'Brian's hair bobbing in the wind as he delivers these lines. I am not suggesting for you to be a comedian when delivering a talk, particularly if you're not funny. Come on, you know the type, a little awkward, and the punch line is met with a resounding thump. There are very few things as uncomfortable as watching someone trying desperately to be funny, when they're not (insert bad best man speech at a wedding). What I am suggesting is that we can all find levity and humour in almost (I said almost) any talk. And I've yet to meet anyone who has zero sense of humour. So find yours is and try it out. It is even more effective to include humour when you are doing a difficult talk, one latent with numbers, statistics, one that requires perhaps some concentration (well, perhaps I'm speaking for my numbered-challenged self, but you get the point).

To reach all types of learners in the room, try including some levity. Anyone who has attended one of my workshops has most likely heard the terms red, yellow, green, and blue to describe different personality types (with acknowledgement to DiSC and Insights, which I will discuss in more detail later), but for now, we can break it down into left-brain, logical and fact-based (green/blue) and right brain, intuitive and feeling-based (red/yellow).

I promise, if you don't include some humour, some fun, and some levity into your talk, you will lose your right-brainers. If you've lost half your audience, then I ask you, what is the point of doing the talk at all?

Tip – Be funny (within your own personality…please).

#347 – Peter Pan

1904

Context – The character of Peter Pan first appeared in a section of *The Little White Bird*, in 1902 to which the following quote is extracted.

"Everytime a child says 'I don't believe in fairies,' there's a little fairy somewhere that falls down dead."

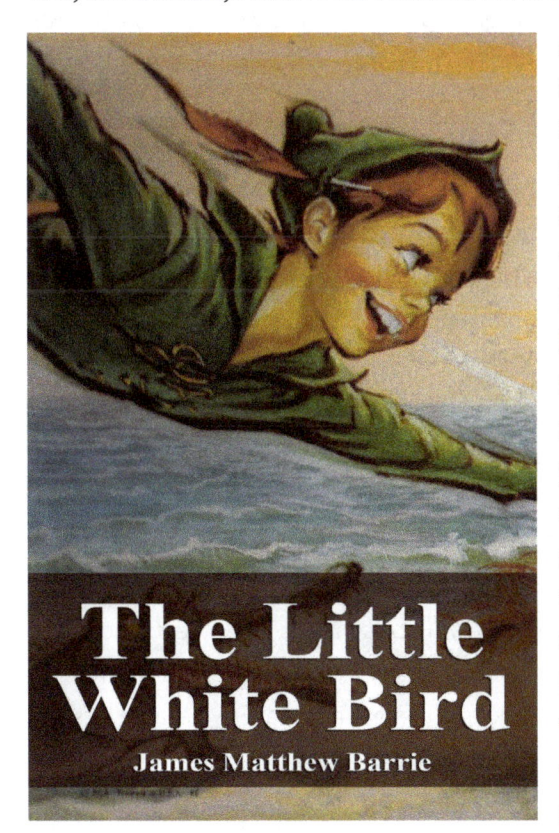

Analysis – I love *Peter Pan*. The book, the movies, the characters, the setting, the prose, the fun, all of it. The creativity that author J.M.Barrie demonstrates is so plentiful, it could be an entire semester class at a university—fiction writer professors, get on that, would you? In the context of a talk or a speech, Peter Pan shows us the power of belief. If you believe you won't do well or succeed in your talk, then you won't. It's as simple as that. I could get all metaphysical on you with a long diatribe about how your thoughts create real energy and that you create negative energy when your pep talk is de-motivating, i.e., "I'm gonna suck, I can't believe I have to do this, I don't know how to give a speech, oh, Gawd I should've prepared", etc. (okay, maybe I did launch into a little diatribe there.) But it's important to understand that your thoughts are the currencies with which you exchange energy with the universe, so it has no choice but to manifest what you're thinking. Scientists are just beginning to accept the idea of thought energy. Energy never dies so simply meditating on one idea or thing, can change the physical world. Sounds crazy? Try it. Next time you want something to change in your own personal universe, meditate and ruminate on it. These thoughts are throwing energy out to the world. See what happens.

It has been my own experience that if I believe that I will do well and create an entire pep talk around that notion before going on 'stage' then I am always pleased with the results. That said, you can't simply 'will' yourself to do a great talk through the power of belief; you must earn that right. You have to put in the practice. A little piece of trivia that has proved to be invaluable is allowing a 'bare minimum' benchmark that for every hour you are in front of an audience you should practice and prepare for a minimum of three hours. Frankly, more is always better when it comes to practice. Believe you will do a great talk, prepare and practice and you will greatly increase your chances that it will be so.

Tip – Believe and you will achieve.

#346 – Ken Robinson

1950–2020

Context – Ken Robinson, in his TED Talk, "Do Schools Kill Creativity?" says schools do kill creativity at a conference in 2006 in Monterey, California

"My contention is that creativity now is as important in education as literacy, and we should treat it with the same status. I heard a great story recently – I love telling it – of a little girl who was in a drawing lesson. She was six, and she was at the back, drawing, and the teacher said this little girl hardly ever paid attention, and in this drawing lesson, she did. The teacher was fascinated, and she went over to her, and she said, "What are you drawing?" And the girl said, "I'm drawing a picture of God." And the teacher said, "But nobody knows what God looks like." And the girl said, "They will in a minute." Kids will take a chance. If they don't know, they'll have a go. Am I right? They're not frightened of being wrong. Now, I don't mean to say that being wrong is the same thing as being creative. What we do know is, if you're not prepared to be wrong, you'll never come up with anything original—if you're not prepared to be wrong. And by the time they get to be adults, most kids have lost that capacity. They have become frightened of being wrong. And we run our companies like this, by the way. We stigmatize mistakes. And we're now running national education systems where mistakes are the worst thing you can make."

Analysis – It takes 20 minutes to watch this TEDTalk. Robinson argues that we've been educated to become good workers rather than creative thinkers. Students with restless minds and bodies—far from being cultivated for their energy and curiosity—are ignored or even stigmatized, with terrible consequences. "We are educating people out of their creativity," Robinson says. The content is gold, and his delivery is superb. Notice how he shares a mix of personal stories, stories he's heard, and his own opinion. His talk is well thought out and practiced, but it doesn't come across that way because he's 'in the moment.' Meaning, he is free at any point to read the crowd and tell a sidebar joke or another story that he perhaps didn't include in his preparation. He knows far more about his topic than he has the time to divulge in his talk. This is the key; get yourself a massive reservoir of reserve material when delivering any talk so that you are free to switch things up. This will ensure a less 'robotic' delivery and one where we can see you.

Robinson is funny; he's articulate; he's imaginative and innovative. Let's be honest, though, it takes many hours in front of an audience to become as relaxed and natural with your delivery as Robinson. There's no question in my mind about that. Being a superb speaker won't come from your first and, even your fiftieth talk (at least for most, but I have seen some pull it off much sooner). It takes practice at the craft of public speaking to become this good, and few reach the realms of expert because it is hard work. Much of that hard work comes in the form of extensive research on your topic and developing your reserve.

Tip – Know far more about your topic than you have time to divulge.

#345 – Heraclitus

540 BCE–475 BCE

Context – Heraclitus text survives in fragments, below is a quote from one.

"Although this Logos is eternally vali, yet men are unable to understand it-Not only before hearing it, but even after they have heard it for the first time…though all things come to pass in accordance with this Logos, men seem to be quite without any experience of it…My own method is to distinguish each thing according to its nature, and to specify how it heaves; other men, on the contrary, are as forgetful and heeless in their waking moment of what is going on around and within them as they are during sleep."

Analysis – Heraclitus talks in mystical paradoxes in a way that, for some, is completely unfamiliar. I wonder if Heraclitus lived during a different time, he wouldn't have been revered for being an enlightened one. Heraclitus was known as "Heraclitus the Riddling" for the obscure riddles that he pontificated in verbal and written form. He lived in Greece at the time of Pythagoras and Socrates. All three of these philosophers didn't fit into the philosophic tradition of the time. One of the reasons Heraclitus has a bad rap is because if you've read up on Aristotle, you'll know that he was a major antagonist of Heraclitus. In fact, Aristotle didn't like him one bit, and because Aristotle is so revered, they sweep Heraclitus to the side, giving way to Aristotle's more popular opposing views.

Heraclitus's words ring so true in the above quote. Superb speakers are not afraid of listening to the truth and eliciting feedback. Both good and not-so-good feedback. Superb speakers will often plant their mentors in the audience several times during the year, people that they admire and aspire to be perhaps, just for their feedback. It sounds cliché, but constructive feedback is a gift. Superb speakers demand feedback from all audience members continually, and really digest it. They get to a point where they can provide themselves with real, valid feedback. Superb speakers know with certainty if they don't demand this of themselves and those around them then they will never get better. In many of my workshops, I use the technique of videotaping. Some are horrified to find a video camera set up when they walk into the room. A video camera is an integral tool to providing valuable feedback. And this doesn't include self-loathing. It allows the speaker to get to a place where they can objectively view themselves and acknowledge what is working and what they need to change.

Tip – Learn the art of self-feedback.

#344 – Charlie Brown

Charlie Brown's birth occurs in the comic strip published on October 30, 1950.

Context – Charlie Brown is the principal character of author Charles M. Schultz's comic strip, *Peanuts*. Here is the transcript between Lucy and Charlie in *A Charlie Brown Christmas*.

Lucy Van Pelt: Are you afraid of responsibility? If you are, then you have hypengyophobia.

Charlie Brown: I don't think that's quite it.

Lucy Van Pelt: How about cats? If you're afraid of cats, you have ailurophasia.

Charlie Brown: Well, sort of, but I'm not sure.

Lucy Van Pelt: Are you afraid of staircases? If you are, then you have climacaphobia. Maybe you have thalassophobia. This is fear of the ocean, or gephyrobia, which is the fear of crossing bridges. Or maybe you have pantophobia. Do you think you have pantophobia?

Charlie Brown: What's pantophobia?

Lucy Van Pelt: The fear of everything.

Charlie Brown: THAT'S IT!

Analysis – We love this show in our house. Everyone gets pretty jazzed when it comes on. We have the Vince Guaraldi playlists, which inspires us to remember this great show. In a mere 30 minutes, Schulz covers some pretty big value and moral issues. The meaning of Christmas is questioned by Charlie, and he becomes depressed as a result. He is disgusted by how commercial the entire event has become. Lucy and Snoopy are obsessed with presents and decorations, Schroeder is obsessed with the pageant and everyone else in a frenzy about Christmas cards, letters to Santa, etc. Charlie is anointed finally with the task of picking out a tree for the pageant, and he selects one that he thinks needs him; a scrawny little tree that (helps everyone, including Linus (I love Linus), to ultimately understand the true meaning of Christmas.

I find the above quote fantastic for two reasons: one is our need to label everyone. And this is no exception for a speaker. ("She's animated, he's funny, she's smart, he's boring.") We tend to label speakers into one group or another and also allow others to define us by labels. I encourage all speakers—from novices to professionals—to work hard at developing the sides of themselves that don't come naturally so they can shake off some of those labels. Often labels arise out of your natural way of being. In order to be a superb speaker, you need to be able to access many aspects of the human spirit, including things you may find challenging.

My other observation is the notion of fear. We've all heard that "Public Speaking is America's (insert Canada here too) #1 fear." I tackle this idea more than a few times during the course of this countdown, but for today I would like to throw out a definition from Wikipedia: Fear is an emotional response to a perceived threat. The operative word is perceived. Fear is an innate emotion that we all have, and it comes in handy, say, if a rhinoceros is chasing you. It pumps up your adrenaline, gets that cortisol going, and activates the flight or fight response. When it comes to public speaking, fear can work to your advantage if you learn how to harness it. I read a study many years ago that indicated adrenaline and cortisol are active each time we give a presentation. These stress hormones realize their power to such a degree that it is the equivalent of consuming seven cups of coffee! No wonder so many of us experience serious jitters right before we take centre stage. Now, the release of these hormones is determined by how much practice you've had in the art of presenting and how comfortable you are. For the well-practiced presentation guru, it may only be the equivalent of one cup of coffee, but for the seriously nervous novice, it could be as much as twelve.

It's okay to be nervous before a presentation. I would say it's a requirement to be highly effective. Being nervous, in its simplest form, just means you care. You care about the content, and the delivery of your audience is absorbing the content, etc. There is nothing awful about admitting to that. If you're one to get nervous at the say, a seven-cups-of-coffee level, I say, good! Then, with practice and perhaps some new tools in your presentation toolbox, we can bring that down to a level of six cups or maybe even five. It's important to harness your nerves and butterflies as you prepare, then deliver your presentation. But aligning those butterflies and getting them to fly in formation does take practice.

Tip – If you're nervous, good.

#343 – George Bernard Shaw

1856–1950

Context – The below quote is from one of Shaw's many writings.

"Tell 'em what you're gonna tell 'em. Tell 'em. Then tell 'em what you told 'em."

Analysis – Interesting fella, this George Bernard Shaw. He wasn't a fan of organized training, and his education was irregular as a result. This is probably one of the most overused 'help me give a presentation quotes' out there. But I do like it. It reminds us of a couple of things, first and most obvious the power of show and tell. Leave the lecturing to professors and avoid standing at podium pontificating ad nauseam. There is no room for that in a superb talk. Use all your senses to communicate in a daring way. Yup, I said, *daring*. New learning rarely comes from staying within your comfort zone. Your audience learns from all their senses, not simply their ears. Use props, visual aids, and your body language. Use stories, analogies, quotes, your creativity and mix it up!

Giving a presentation is not rocket science, but it is an art form. I promise, Leonardo da Vinci, Picasso, and Michelangelo all practiced their art much like Mozart, Tchaikovsky and Chopin practiced their instrument. Remember, developing this skill is a process, not an event, and it takes practice and a sprinkling of daring.

Tip – Be daring.

#342 – Keith Barry (1976)

Context – In his TED Talk, "Brain Magic." Keith explores what brain magic is and how it is dissimilar to traditional magic with the use of a sixth sense.

"Brain magic. What's brain magic all about? Brain magic, to me, indicates that area of magic dealing with psychological and mind-reading effects. So, unlike traditional magic, it uses the power of words, linguistic deception, non-verbal communication, and various other techniques to create the illusion of a sixth sense. Now, I'm going to show you all how easy it is to manipulate the human mind once you know-how. And I want everybody downstairs also to join in with me and everybody here. I want everybody to put out your hands like this for me, first of all. OK, clap them together once. OK, reverse your hands. Now follow my actions exactly. Now about half, the audience has their left hand up. Why is that? OK, swap them around, put your right hand up. OK, now, cross your hands over, so your right-hand goes over, interlace your fingers like this, then make sure your right thumb is outside your left thumb—that's very important. Yours is the other way around, so swap it around. Excellent, OK. Extend your fingers like this for me. All right. Tap them together once. OK, now, if you did not allow me to deceive your minds, you would all be able to do this. (Laughter) So, now you can see how easy it is for me to manipulate the human mind once you know-how. (Laughter)

"Now, I remember when I was about 15, I read a copy of Life magazine, which detailed a story about a 75-year-old blind Russian woman who could sense printed letters—there's still people trying to do it here—(Laughter) —who could sense printed letters and even sense colors, just by touch. And she was completely blind. She could also read the serial numbers on bills when they were placed, face down, on a hard surface. Now, I was fascinated, but at the same time, skeptical. How could somebody read using their fingertips? You know, if you actually think about it, if somebody is totally blind – a guy yesterday did a demonstration in one of the rooms where people had to close their eyes, and they could just hear things. And it's just a really weird thing to try and figure out, how could somebody read using their fingertips? Now earlier on, as part of a TV show that I have coming up on MTV; I attempted to give a similar demonstration of what is now known as second sight. So, let's take a look."

Analysis – One of the best ways to sway your audience when presenting a new or conversational concept is through interaction and active participation. Lecturing your audience about your new ideas is pointless. There are times that words should simply aid your talk and delivering your message happens effortlessly while interacting with your audience. If you have 20 minutes to spare, read the above transcript, then see how watching the video of Barry's TED Talk compares. The experience relating to the digestion of Barry's concept, mystic, fun, and recollection changes dramatically in every way. Try it on your next talk by including audience interaction and see what happens!

Tip – Interact with your audience.

#341 – Dale Carnegie

1888–1955

Context – From Dale Carnegie's 1936 book, How to Win Friends and Influence People, a self-help book having sold over 30 million copies worldwide and continues to surface as one of the bestselling books of all time over the years.

"You can make more friends in two months by becoming more interested in other people than you can in two years by trying to get people interested in you."

Analysis – I've spent many years studying Dale Carnegie. I took his workshop, became a graduate assistant and went through the instructor program. It was an invaluable learning experience as I navigated how to stand comfortably in front of an audience and deliver a message that I hoped would help people. I was in my early 20s, full of piss and vinegar when I took the instructor program. During this program, the master instructor, whom I still consider to be one of the greatest speakers I've ever met, gave me the single best advice I've learned to date. At the culmination of the training week, each student was given the opportunity to facilitate a section of the program. I was up first and had practiced verbatim what I was going to say and the gestures I'd use. I got up, did my section, and returned to my seat at the back of the class while another of the trainees got up to do their section. I thought I'd done a fantastic job. I was sitting in the headspace of, "Wow, did that ever go well? I'm really cut out for this." The master instructor approached me, leaned in and gently said, "Who are trying to impress?" I was horrified! And even though there was much discussion about her statement and analysis, I didn't digest what she was saying to me for many years to come. It came to me one day as I observed a speaker during a training session. The speaker was putting on a show, eager to let her audience see how knowledgeable she was, while not being terribly interested in getting her message digested by her audience. Suddenly what the master instructor meant, and what she was trying to teach me became clean. It was simple in theory but incredibly difficult to execute. When you're doing a talk (whether facilitating or speaking) it is not about you. It is about the audience. If you get up to the front of the room thinking you're all that and a bag of chips, with an air of arrogance then you'll be doing a disservice to your audience. The entire function of any speech is to transmit your ideas so that your audience will hear and digest them. They won't hear your ideas if you're pontificating about how great you are or if you're in your little bubble and not observing your audience and reading their reactions. It is only when you take the spotlight off yourself that you can begin observing your audience, interacting with them, learning about them, and ensuring that they have heard and digested what you have to say.

Tip – Put the spotlight on your audience where it belongs.

#340 – Anthony Synnott (1940)

Context – Okay, this is perhaps an odd addition to my list as Anthony Synnott was a university professor of mine from my time at Concordia University some (gulp) 28 years ago. His class was my favourite, and I still look at my notes from that class. Synnott also wrote the text for his class entitled "The Body Social" which contains the following quote.

"The conceptual and existential significance of the sensorium is obvious. We are social beings, and we communicate in and with and through our senses. Long before we are rational beings, humans are sensing beings. Life without the senses does not make sense."

Analysis – I would argue and add to the above that doing a talk without fully utilizing all the senses doesn't make sense either. There is much debate on exactly how many senses there are; it seems that Aristotle was the first to determine five. Zen Buddhists say there is a sixth sense, Darwin thought there were 12 and some other notable researchers and philosophers indicate there are 17. Recently, Barry Smith a professor of the Institute of Philosophy of Advanced study at the University of London says there could be as many as 22 and up to 33.

When you're giving a talk, utilizing words accesses hearing, using a PowerPoint slideshow engages the sense of sight, and for most, it stops there. If we use Aristotle's five senses; touch, taste, smell, hearing, and sight, that narrows our view of some others that may be impactful in giving a talk. Granted, sometimes it isn't easy to integrate all of them into one talk, but I have found the talks I have been a participant in that involve all five are the most memorable. Several years ago, I attended a workshop in which the facilitator had music playing while we walked into the room. While in the room, we were greeted by coffee and light snacks. He had put out lemons on everyone's table and created a game that encouraged each of us to introduce ourselves to all the other participants before the class began. He had posters askew all over the room, back and front. He had a PowerPoint slide up. He didn't stand at a podium but moved freely and with purpose throughout the room. He was flooding the senses! He created an environment that every single participant with varying learning styles could digest. By the way, the lemons came in later as he bridged to an analogy, which was fantastic!

Now some people attending your talk may have one or more senses absent. If you're unaware of this beforehand, then if you make it a common practice to utilize all five senses, you are ensuring they too are digesting your message. I once attended an information seminar and as I sat in my seat at the back of the room, I notice that the person seated next to me was signing to her neighbour, so it appeared she was hard of hearing. The session had some 40 people in attendance, and the speaker sat at the front of the room for the duration of the seminar and my neighbour, therefore, couldn't absorb the information being shared. Please, always be conscious that you may have someone in the room who has a sensory impairment and think about how to best reach these participants before your talk begins.

Tip – Be conscious of your participants' senses when delivering your talk.

#339 – Michel de Montaigne

1533–1592

Context – Montaigne, a French philosopher, retired at a young age to read, write and reflect. The result was *The Complete Essays* (1580) and the below quote is found in Book One, Chapter 26, "Of the Education of Children."

"I quote others only the better to express myself."

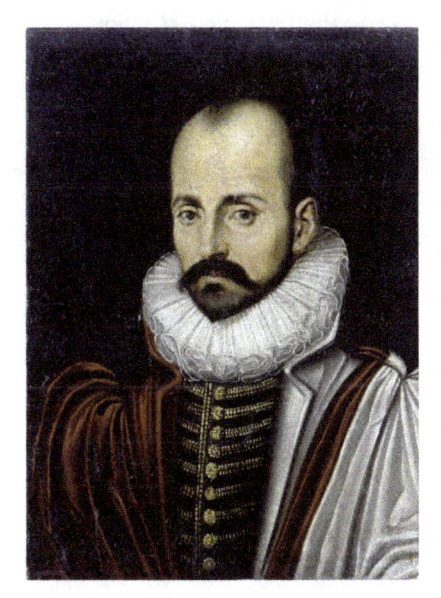

Analysis – I love a great quote. My good friends will buy me books on quotes for my birthday. They will ensure there are quotes included in the greeting card. They will drop quotes in my presence just to get a rise outta me and it works. I believe that if you can't find the words yourself, research and find a great quote by some fancy author or speaker, and your audience will listen a little harder. That said, the quote has to have a purpose, and it should operate as a springboard or foundation for further thought. There is something intriguing about throwing out something Picasso, Martin Luther King Jr. or President Nixon said that will get the attention of your audience. It's like your audience will say 'yeah, oh yeah, what did Socrates say about that?' Don't believe me? Try it. Next time you are to give a talk, set up one of your points with a quote, watch the body language of your audience, those who were looking down, jotting down notes, whispering to their neighbour or checking their crackberry will focus and if you've set it up well, with an air of anticipation and weight, and tell them you're going to quote from someone, and then dangle it in front of them like a carrot, I promise, you will have everyone's undivided attention. The trick here is not to blow it! There is nothing worse than quoting someone important and messing it up with, 'Whoops! forgot it, let me check my notes' or 'Oh, how does it start again?' You must have your chosen quote memorized verbatim; word for word, no excuses. If used right, a great quote can act as a pivotal point for your audience in terms of recollection.

Tip – Use quotes.

#338 – Jacques Barzun

1907–2012

Context – Believed to come from *Teacher in America* and *The House of Intellect*.

"Convince yourself that you are working in clay, not marble, on paper not eternal bronze: Let that first sentence be as stupid as it wishes. No one will rush out and print it as it stands. Just put it down, then another. Your whole first paragraph or first page may have to be guillotined in any case after your piece is finished: it is a kind of forebirth."

Analysis – While I was at the University of Manitoba many moons ago, I enrolled in a class called Political Geography. During the first class, the professor stood at the front of the room and declared that this class would have no exams while the 60 or so students all stared at each other wondering if this was joke, or cause for serious celebration? The professor re-emphasized that no, there would be no exam, but that 100 percent of our mark would be a presentation. We chose a country, and, with the format he provided, talked for 45 minutes on the politics of that country. The professor had an entire rotation system in place. How many of those students do you think showed up to the second class? Seriously, take a guess. About 30. So, half of the prospective students thought they'd rather have had the exam, and that a presentation was just too much to handle. Well, this was my second year, and I had never done a presentation before in my entire life. I have no clue why I chose to stay; even to this day, I think about it, and I'm confused why I didn't drop the class. Two months went by as I watched my fellow students take their turn giving their presentations. It was one of the best classes I ever took. The professor stood in the wings, kind of like a safety net just in case, but for the most part, everyone rose to the occasion, and with only two exceptions, there were no actual bombs. Then, it was my turn. I'd researched, I'd practiced, I'd used everything in my presentation arsenal (which wasn't much at the time), and where do you think you could find me five minutes before I was to go on? Yup, the bathroom where I was, let's say 'forcefully releasing my breakfast via my mouth.' Yup, I was literally, not figuratively, sick to my stomach. Somehow, I got it together, got to class and started to deliver the presentation that I had worked so tirelessly on. What I didn't anticipate was the physiological reactions I would have. I stood there, still queasy, with a flush on my cheeks that I'm sure could've been seen from outer space, with sweat pouring from my armpits and an unusual shake that started at my fingertips and slowly crept its way into the meat of my limbs. I'm sure it was a sight to see. I will talk about physiological reactions to giving a presentation several times during this list, but for today suffice it to say that if you are witnessing a presentation where someone is turning red, sweating, shaking, never bring it to their attention. "Look how RED Peggy Sue is getting!" Believe me; she knows and highlighting it will only make it worse. If you are the one experiencing the physiological reaction, tell yourself white lies and convince yourself that it's not that bad.

I tell this story often in my workshops because had you told me then that one day, I would be giving presentations for a living, I would have not believed you and placed some hardy bets on the matter. Many of us need to bomb many times before we can learn what works and what doesn't. Building the confidence to speak well in front of a group of people takes years to develop, and you can't expect to reach the height of a superb speaker without a few bumps and bruises along the way. Pick yourself up, dust yourself off, and don't shy away from doing it again. Seek out ways to continue to practice. Be the one who volunteers to give the presentation before it gets assigned; keep practicing, even when you don't want to. (I got a B+ in that class, and it was the best B+ I ever earned.)

Tip – Keep on trying even after you've bombed.

#337 – Lao Tsu

Unknown specific birth and death, and there is some controversy as to when he lived – either in the 4th or the 6th century BCE.

Context – Unknown (but it is said to have been found in the *Records of the Historian*).

"Without going beyond his own nature, one cannot achieve ultimate wisdom."

Analysis – I believe that all new learning comes from outside of your comfort zone. You know the mental home in which you live. So, you get up in the morning and stop the alarm clock at exactly 6:05. You jump in the shower, make a cup of coffee, and you are always amazed that the clock reads 6:57 am when you leave the house. You arrive at the office, say 'hi' to the receptionist, wave to your colleague in the far-off corner office who is always there at 6:30 a.m. sharp, turn on your computer and start reading through your emails. Lunch is always at 11:55 am when your work buddy comes by to pick you up…yada yada yada. Every day can seem like the last if you don't force yourself out of your comfort zone. To be an exemplary speaker, you must consistently and regularly force yourself to speak. And, even for those who enjoy the process, there is a bit of mental gymnastics that you must go through to accept giving a talk because it is a lot of work. I will discuss comfort zone as it relates to the actual presentation in another post, but for today, focus on accepting, volunteering, and seeking opportunities to speak even if, as Tsu says, it is beyond your nature.

Tip – Stretch the limits of your comfort zone.

#336 – Elizabeth Gilbert

(1969)

Context – Elizabeth Gilbert (author of *Eat Pray Love*) talks to an audience at TED in 2009 on nurturing creativity.

"I am a writer. Writing books is my profession, but it's more than that, of course. It is also my great lifelong love and fascination. And I don't expect that that's ever going to change. But, that said, something kind of peculiar has happened recently in my life and in my career, which has caused me to have to re-calibrate my whole relationship with this work. And the peculiar thing is that I recently wrote this book, this memoir called "Eat, Pray,

Love," which, decidedly unlike any of my previous books, went out in the world for some reason and became this big, mega-sensation, international bestseller thing. The result of which is that everywhere I go now, people treat me like I'm doomed. Seriously – doomed, doomed! Like, they come up to me now all worried and they essay, "Aren't you afraid – aren't you afraid you're never going to be able to top that? Aren't you afraid you're going to keep writing for your whole life, and you're never again going to create a book that anybody in the world cares about it all, ever again?"

Analysis – I am a pretty darn big fan of Elizabeth Gilbert. I read her book long before she made it to the 'Oprah temple.' It reads like Gilbert speaks. Warm, calm, sarcastic, and natural. She has somehow figured out a way to translate her easy-going hippy-like nature onto the written page. It's quite the feat if you ask me. If you have the time, I'd encourage you to watch her speak at TED to see her natural movement; she gestures with purpose, which further punctuates her points, and she is naturally witty. For today however, I'd like to home in on this topic of fear, as per the above quote. We've already addressed the fact that most people fear giving a speech. And that fear is why many people will dodge the work presentation, why some don't volunteer to give the best man speech, why others conveniently and quietly leave the boardroom when it is time to introduce themselves etc. I encourage you, if you are one of the folks out there who are plagued with this debilitating fear, to tackle it head-on. It is critically important to tell yourself and visualize what a great job you will do. All thought is energy, and by putting out that energy you suppress your fear and elevate your ability to deliver one superb talk.

Tip – Use your fear.

#335 – Percy Bysshe Shelley

1792–1822

Context – Shelley is the first poet to hit my list. Known as one of the major English Romantic Poets. The below is from one of his long, visionary anthologies.

"A man, to be greatly good, must imagine intensely and comprehensively; he must put himself in the place of another and of many others; the pleasures and pains of his species must become his own."

Analysis – I could easily get into a massive philosophical discussion on what the golden rule actually means. "Do unto others" can be transposed onto Shelley's quote as similar. Does it mean that we must impose our wishes onto other people? Does it mean that we should treat others the way we want to be treated rather than as they want to be treated? It can be a complex notion. However, for the purposes of this book, let's take the golden rule in its most traditional format: Putting ourselves into the place of the people affected by our actions. To break it down to its most simplistic form, we should take our self-interest out of the formula and look only at the other person's interest. This notion or concept is fabulous in any part of one's life, but it's even better when we discuss and observe the art of giving a talk. Those who can earn the respect of their audiences through being prepared, presenting quality information and delivering it with a firm understanding of the golden rule or by removing their self-interest, are a rare breed. As I reflect on the most impactful talks I've seen, it is without question when the speakers could shine when appropriate, but also take a back seat when needed. These speakers listen with intensity, watch the body language of their audience, and as a result, are able to present in a way that their audience want to hear. They most certainly had a predetermined thought about how the presentation was going to go, but because they had the ability to take the *self* out of the mix they were able to alter their presentation when needed, in the moment, right before your eyes.

Tip – Remember The Golden Rule.

#334 – Emmeline Pankhurst

1858–1928

Context – On November 13, 1913 British political activist Emmeline Pankhurst delivered a speech in Hartford, Connecticut.

"When women asked questions in political meetings and failed to get answers, they were not doing anything militant. In Great Britain it is a custom, a time-honoured one, to ask questions of candidates for parliament and ask questions of members of the government. No man was ever put out of a public meeting for asking a question. The first people who were put out of a political meeting for asking questions, were women; they were brutally ill-used; they found themselves in jail before 24 hours had expired…"Put them in prison," they said, "that will stop it." But it didn't stop it at all: instead of the women giving it up, more women did it, and more and more and more women did it until there were 300 women at a time, who had not broken a single law, only "made a nuisance of themselves" as the politicians say."

Analysis – No question about it, Emmeline Pankhurst was a spitfire. In 1999, Time magazine named her one of the 100 most important people of all time. I couldn't agree more and frankly am saddened that so few women, especially women from my generation, have even heard of her. Time said, "she shaped an idea of women for our time; she shook society into a new pattern from which there could be no going back." Pankhurst was the leader of the British suffragette movement, which won women the right to vote. Certainly, a monumental task, and as we see in the above quote, a task that came with serious consequences. There are pictures of Pankhurst speaking in Trafalgar Square in London, and you can see in her body language, fists pumping in the air, big open stance, big burly frowned brows—that she was beyond passionate about her topic. You get the sense in reading her story that she would've done anything to get her message across. I find it incredibly difficult to watch a speaker who doesn't speak with conviction and passion; those qualities don't just fall out of the sky; they are beckoned only when you have a firm point of view. Many people like to ride the fence, stay in the middle, and be politically correct. All of those things certainly have their place, and sometimes they are warranted. However, the most interesting characters, and the most interesting speakers are the ones who can stand for something that they believe in.

Tip – Have a point of view.

#333 – William Shakespeare

1564–1616

Context – *Hamlet* (written between 1599 and 1601)

Hamlet – Act 3, Scene 1:
"To be, or not to be : that is the question:
Whether 'tis nobler in the mind to suffer
The slings and arrows of outrageous fortune,
Or to take arms against a sea of troubles, And by opposing end them? To die: to sleep;
No more; and by a sleep to say we end
The heart-ache and the thousand natural shocks
That flesh is heir to, 'tis a consummation
Devoutly to be wish'd. To die, to sleep;
To sleep: perchance to dream: ay, there's the rub;
For in that sleep of death what dreams may come
When we have shuffled off this mortal coil,
Must give us pause: there's the respect
That makes calamity of so long life;
For who would bear the whips and scorns of time,
The oppressor's wrong, the proud man's contumely,
The pangs of despised love, the law's delay,
The insolence of office and the spurns
That patient merit of the unworthy takes,
When he himself might his quietus make
With a bare bodkin? who would fardels bear,
To grunt and sweat under a weary life,
But that the dread of something after death,
The undiscover'd country from whose bourn

No traveller returns, puzzles the will

And makes us rather bear those ills we have

Than fly to others that we know not of?

Thus conscience does make cowards of us all;

And thus the native hue of resolution

Is sicklied o'er with the pale cast of thought,

And enterprises of great pith and moment

With this regard their currents turn awry,

And lose the name of action.–Soft you now!

The fair Ophelia! Nymph, in thy orisons

Be all my sins remember'd."

Analysis – Should I or shouldn't I kill myself? That is the question that Hamlet is asking, but Shakespeare delivers this line with gusto, brilliance and it gets your attention immediately. With the exception of King Lear, I previously didn't get Shakespeare at all. But as I am reading fervently and vastly to add to this list every day, I have gained a new and profound respect for the Bard's words. I read recently that the above speech 'To be or not to be' has similarities with the clash song "Should I Stay, or Should I Go" with the words "if I stay there will be trouble, if I go it will be double," I love that. The lyrics in this punk-rock classic also form great contrasts as Shakespeare does. And both get your attention.

When one is preparing to give a talk, there should be a disproportionate amount of time spent thinking about what will be said in those first two minutes. Even if your talk is scheduled to be a lengthy one (say, over 45 minutes). A lot is going on in the first two minutes. Namely, first impressions and nerves. And I'm not exaggerating when I say that one must know the script for those opening minutes so well that it could be stated it backwards, forwards, and inside out. Even the most experienced speaker can get caught up in the wave of fuzzy head due to nerves. The only way to eloquently and articulately pull yourself out of it, without sounding like a blubbering idiot, is to be well rehearsed with those first two minutes. That said, it's important to add some pizzazz so as not to seem robotic; like Shakespeare shows us here through Hamlet. Some zip, some 'hey…did I get your attention with that?' In fact, if you think of some of your favourite novels, they too likely make an amazing first impressions in the first few lines or paragraphs too:

- Call me Ishmael. —Herman Melville, *Moby-Dick* (1851)

- It was a bright cold day in April and the clocks were striking thirteen. —George Orwell, *1984* (1949)

- It was the best of times, it was the worst of times, it was the age of wisdom, it was the age of foolishness, it was the epoch of belief, it was the epoch of incredulity, it was the season of Light, it was the season of Darkness, it was the spring of hope, it was the winter of despair. —Charles Dickens, *A Tale of Two Cities* (1859)

- If you really want to hear about it; the first thing you'll probably want to know is where I was born, and what my lousy childhood was like, and how my parents were occupied and all before they had me, and all that David Copperfield kind of crap, but I don't feel like going into it if you want to know the truth. —J. D. Salinger, *The Catcher in the Rye* (1951)

- My name is Salmon, like the fish. First name: Susie. I was 14 when I was murdered on December 6, 1976. —Alice Sebold, *The Lovely Bones* (2002)

Great first lines are not reserved for great novels as a great first two minutes is also essential to beginning a superb talk!

Tip – Get your audience's attention immediately.

#332 – Margaret Thatcher

1925–2013

Context – In a 1984 interview with the BBC's political editor, John Cole, Margaret Thatcher responded to a question about how she saw relations with the man who looked likely to be the successor of the Soviet Union's ailing General Secretary. Mikhail Sergeyevich Gorbachev became General Secretary in 1985.

"I am cautiously optimistic. I like Mr.Gorbachev. We can do business together. We both believe in our own political systems. He firmly believes in his; I firmly believe in mine. We are never going to change one another. So that is not in doubt, but we have two great interests in common; that we should both do everything we can to see that war never starts again, and therefore we go into the disarmament talks determined to make them succeed. And secondly, I think we both believe that they are the more likely to succeed if we can build up confidence in one another and trust in one another about each other's approach, and therefore, we believe in cooperating on trade matters, on cultural matters, on quite a lot of contacts between politicians from the two sides of the divide."

Analysis – So, you are fully prepared for your presentation. You have practiced, customized the content to the audience, and know the techniques to use once on stage. But how do you handle the tough questions and challenges that you know will be coming at the end? The above quote is in response to a question that Thatcher was asked, and how she answers it is a lesson indeed. She starts by being optimistic but doesn't sugar coat that the two leaders have very distinct ways of looking at things where they can "agree to disagree." Thatcher ties it up nicely by showing interests or common ground. But what if you've been asked a question at the end of your presentation that is not only difficult and challenging, but the person asking is putting up a fight? If a person in the audience is insisting on arguing a point with you or other members of the audience, it can start out passionately but can easily get out of control. You, as the presenter, have a responsibility to control what is going on in the room. You are the one that has elicited a response, so it is your responsibility to diffuse it, resolve it, or change direction. Here are a few ideas that I have found helpful when confronted by an audience member who I like to call the fighter:

- Get other audience members involved, ask them what they think and see if you can find common ground.
- Acknowledge and appreciate the passion being demonstrated.
- Keep the people involved focused on the topic, rather than on the person.
- Remain calm. It is not your position to engage in the fight.
- There are times when it is absolutely appropriate to commit to discussing the topic outside of the room when the presentation is done (this is if you can detect the audience as a whole is ready to move on).
- The situation may require that the individuals engaged in the heated debate agree to disagree; however, it is of critical importance to respect the opinions of both sides.

Tip – Agree to disagree.

#331 – Tim Brown (1962)

Context – Tim Brown, CEO of the innovation and design firm, IDEO, talks on creativity and play (May 2008 at TED)

"So, this guy, this guy is a guy named Bob McKim. And he was a creativity researcher in the '60s and '70s and also led the Stanford design program. And in fact, my friend and IDEO founder, David Kelley, who's out there somewhere, studied under him at Stanford. And he liked to do an exercise with his students where he got them to take a piece of paper and draw the person sat next to them, their neighbor, very quickly, just as quickly as they could.

"And in fact, we're going to do that exercise right now. You all have a piece of cardboard and a piece of paper. It's actually got a bunch of circles on it. I need you to turn that piece of paper over; you should find it's blank on *the other side, OK? And there should be a pencil. And I want you to pick somebody that's sat next to you, and when I say, go, you've got 30 seconds to draw your neighbor, OK? So, everybody ready? OK. Off you go. You've got 30 seconds; you'd better be fast. Come on, those masterpieces. OK? Stop. All right, now."*

Analysis – The TED Talk clip from which the above quote is taken is 27 minutes long. If you don't have the time to watch all 27 minutes, please take two minutes to watch Brown walk through the above text. Great talks aren't just reserved for historical figures, politicians, writers, and famous people. Brown is a CEO and, like many of my clients, he is active in the real corporate world. There are two things I'd like to bring to your attention that happen in the first two minutes of this speech. Brown starts with an audience exercise right off the bat. Often people will say to me, 'but my audience is far too large for audience participation.' Nope, audience size is not an excuse. Whether you are presenting in front of one person or a crowd of 1,000 or more, you can always involve your audience. Always. As soon as Brown announces the draw your neighbour exercise, listen and watch to what is happening with the audience and to Tim. The audience is smiling, they're talking, there's a buzz in the room, and when the participants show one another what they've drawn, there is a burst of laughter and a fun, lively energy in the room. The second thing I want to point out from this presentation is that Brown settles in too while the audience is going through the exercise. He feeds off the energy in the audience; you can read it in his body language. He begins to move around the stage more naturally. Brown becomes a much better speaker the more he interacts with his audience; he laughs, takes pictures, and the quality of his performance increases significantly. When you get the audience involved, it maintains the audience's interest and relieves you of some of the talk time. For best results, every presentation should involve audience participation at some point. And sometimes it is more than acceptable to have it happen multiple times if it supports the end goal of your presentation.

Tip – Get the audience involved.

#330 – *Chip 'n' Dale*

Characters created by animator Jack Hannah in 1943.

Context – *Chip 'n' Dale* drop their acorns in a chicken farm and go in after them. Inside, Dale mistakes the eggs for walnuts. He meets a hatched chick and is then forced to impersonate a chick to hide from the cockerel. His cover is almost blown, and it looks like he may get stuck in the nest.

Analysis – There are no actual words in this classic 1951 *Chip 'n' Dale* episode (save for an occasional, "no, no," or "chirp, chirp") so you may ask, 'How can this possibly be one of my *#365 Must-Know Talks*? Talking, per se, is so much more than the spoken or written word. The fact that this entire episode has few to no words shows that you can tell a story rather brilliantly using just body language and gesturing. I'm reminded of a time when I was on a global sales team and taught a workshop in Cuernavaca, Mexico. We had translators at the back of the room who would translate what I was saying into the headsets of the participants in real time. I noticed on the third day of this workshop that the translators were gesturing madly with their arms, contorting their faces, and occasionally jumping up and down from their booth at the back of the class. The translators were doing real-time translation and translating word for word as I was speaking, which is a very complicated thing to do. When we had a break, I was intrigued, so I asked one of the translators, "What are you guys doing in the booth? It looks like you're having a party!" The translator laughed rather heartily and explained, "We are mimicking you!" "What?" I said. The translator went on to say that words are useless if they could not match my enthusiastic intonation. "Words are simply words,'" she explained. "Our job is to translate all of your messages so that the participants hear them." So, all of the partying they were doing was to match what I was doing at the front of the room. It was fascinating for me to watch the next two days as I knew they were matching what I was doing. I had no idea until then how animated I had become during that session. What I was unconsciously doing was over-animating my body because of the language barrier. So, the translators taught me a lesson I will never forget, your body language impacts all aspects of your communication and is integral in having your message understood. Here is a little fact you may want to remember the next time you're asked to give a talk: Human communication consists of 93 percent body language and paralinguistic cues, and only seven percent words.

Tip – Use your body to communicate.

#329 – Salvidor Dali

1904–1984

Context – *People* magazine (1976)

"Drawing is the honesty of the art. There is no possibility of cheating. It is either good or bad."

Analysis – Ah, yes, Dali… arguably one of the most eccentric artists there ever was. Probably his most famous piece, *The Persistence of Memory*, has become a reference in popular culture. You know the one, melting pocket watches cascading over various objects. It has been claimed that the piece symbolizes the irrelevance of time. In my love of quotes, I came across the above quote many years ago and often thought that it could easily speak to other professions as well, including the art of public speaking. You cannot cheat when you're up at the front of the room giving a presentation. You are, at the end of the day, either good or bad. It sounds pretty black and white, because, frankly, it is. It is rare that upon reflection, I'll think a speaker was okay, or give them a C+. It's generally an A+ or an F, period. Most of the great talks are great simply because the presenter has invested adequate preparation time and the bad ones haven't. It is baffling to me during introductions in my workshop on presentation skills that I'll ask the participants to share why they are there, and one will inevitably answer, "my boss sent me here, but I think the less preparation I do, the better, I'm much better when I wing it."

I couldn't disagree more. I can tell in a millisecond who is winging it and who has put in the preparation time. Preparation, in short, can make the difference between a presentation hit and a presentation fiasco. The audience knows whether you are prepared—it shows in your knowledge, confidence, and in your ability to articulately answer questions.

Tip – If you're winging it, you'll stink!

#328 – The Tin Man, The Lion, The Scarecrow and Dorothy

(1939)

Context – From *The Wizard of Oz*

Cowardly Lion: I'd be brave as a blizzard.

Tin Woodsman: I'd be gentle as a lizard.

Scarecrow: I'd be clever as a gizzard.

Dorothy: If the Wizard is a wizard who will serve.

Scarecrow: Then I'm sure to get a brain.

Tin Woodsman: A heart.

Dorothy: A home.

Cowardly Lion: The nerve!

Analysis – My favourite movie of all time, The Wizard of Oz, will rear its head several times during this list. The above song lyric speaks to looking to outside forces to fix us. Missing a heart? A home? Courage? A brain? Or perhaps, the ability to speak in public? Well, just get yourself to someone smart, and in this case, it's the wizard, and he will fix it all up for you. It is a great metaphor for life because I think we all look to outside forces to make us whole, to make us happy, to improve a skill when in reality we know (and soon Dorothy and the others learn too) that the fix is always found within. The same can be true of public speaking. So many of the people I work with are exceptional at speaking in front of groups, they have so much to say, are incredibly intelligent, have a distinct and profound message, but they allow themselves to think that what they are lacking in their presentations can be found in a book or a workshop. That somehow, the author or the facilitator will wave a magic wand, and poof, they will have the power to deliver brilliant presentations. The truth is a book, or a workshop facilitator cannot do that for you. What they can do (if they are any good) is highlight your strengths and allow a portal for you to see the things you may need to work on and provide you with some tried and tested techniques. But you will only get good once you develop the confidence (not arrogance) from time spent presenting in front of a group. I have found time and time again, if you focus on the message and not your fear, then this singular component can be a solid platform for improving your confidence and you'll be able to cease seeking outside validation or help. Once you've established a true sense of confidence then you will be able to provide yourself with feedback and absorb feedback from others in a way that catapults your public speaking abilities. So, develop your foundation; focus on your message, not yourself (or your fear), and true confidence will follow.

Tip – Focus on your message.

#327 – Paul Potts

(1970)

Context – A mobile phone salesman from South Wales has a dream of becoming an Opera singer and auditioned on *Britain's Got Talent*, a competition show that people showcase their talents ranging from mundane to the extraordinary:

No sleep, no sleep
Nessun dorma, nessun dorma

You too, o, Princess
Tu pure, o, Principessa

In your cold room
Nella tua fredda stanza

Look at the stars that tremble
Guardi le stelle che tremano

Of love and hope
D'amore e di speranza

But my mystery is closed in me
Ma il mio mistero e chiuso in me

No one will know my name
Il nome mio nessun saprà

No, no, I'll say it on your mouth

No, no, sulla tua bocca lo dirò

When the light shine
Quando la luce splenderà

And my kiss will break the silence
Ed il mio bacio scioglierà il silenzio

That makes you mine
Che ti fa mia

(No one will know his name)
(Il nome suo nessun saprà)

(And we must, alas, die, die)
(E noi dovrem, ahimé, morir, morir)

Vanish, o night
Dilegua, o notte

Set, stars
Tramontate, stelle

Set, stars
Tramontate, stelle

I'll win at dawn
All'alba vincerò

I will win
Vincerò

I will win
Vincerò

Analysis – I know, this is a song but it's more than just a song. From my vantage point, it is a fabulous story that reads like one of the best talks I've ever heard. I use this video in nearly every single workshop and keynote speech I do. I love it that much. I encourage you to find the clip (it is four minutes long) from beginning to end. The beginning is the most interesting part. They interview Potts for a few seconds in the clip before he sings. Watch his body language; shoulders low, nervous hand pulling, looking down, pacing. Potts says, "Confidence has always been a difficult thing for me; I've always found it difficult to be confident in myself." This low self-esteem permeates to everyone around him. As soon as Potts walks out onto the stage, one of the competition judges, Piers Morgan gives the other judges a look that says, "This is going to be a waste of time." Simon Cowell, another of the show's judges, sighs deeply as if to say, "Let's get this over with." And members of the audience roll their eyes with disdain. It is remarkable. Potts hasn't uttered a single word, phrase or gesture and already he's been written off. But, when Potts begins singing, Cowell looks up, pen in mouth with a look that is nothing short of astonishment. Amanda Holden another judge, is almost crying, and they pan out to reveal the audience some of the whom are also in tears. No one expected Potts to belt out "Nessun Dorma" as well as he does. At the end of the song, the audience explodes with cheer, and Cowell exclaims, "You work at a Car Phone Warehouse, and you do this! I wasn't expecting this." Was Potts lucky? Nope, it was nothing to do with luck. I read some background on Potts, and apparently, he had been taking lessons for many years leading up to this moment. He had worked hard honing his craft, not for fame and fortune, but for the love of opera. Even though confidence had evaded him up until this point, he still pushed himself out of his comfort zone and auditioned. Even with the risk of embarrassment. As with presentations or speaking in public, work hard, accept opportunities to speak (even when you are afraid to or don't want to invest the energy), practice, practice, practice, push the boundaries of your comfort zone. When opportunities come up, they are yours for the taking. Who knows how those opportunities will unfold for you?

Tip – Opportunity will always meet preparation.

#326 – David Peebles

1525-1579

Context – This quote is attributed to David Peebles who was a Scottish composer of religious music.

"The depth of conviction counts more than the height of logic, and enthusiasm is worth more than knowledge."

Analysis – Not much is known (or perhaps it is just me and my research) of David Peebles. What I do know is that he was a composer of religious music in Scotland. I've collected quotes for years, scribbling into journals and books, I've amassed quite the collect, the above is one of my most referenced.

If you're not excited and enthusiastic about your topic, then how the heck can you expect your audience to be? I know, some of you are saying, "but my presentation is on numbers, statistics or is really technical—how can I possibly be enthusiastic about it?" Find a way. You must find something in your topic that will get your creativity flowing. If you don't, your audience will not only be bored, but they won't retain what you've said. And this is the sole purpose of any presentation. To communicate what you have to say in such a way that your audience will understand the information and retain it. Your audience will retain more if they are enjoying themselves, relaxed, and they see you are also having fun with it.

Tip – Enthusiasm is infectious!

#325 – Yoda

(896) BBY

Context – *Star Wars*, Episode V: *The Empire Strikes Back*

"You must unlearn what you have learned…Do or not do, there is no try"

Analysis – I must admit I'm not the biggest *Star Wars* fan, but I do like the movies. I remember watching *Star Wars* as a kid and not understanding it. Now that I've gone back as an adult and watched all the films again, I can see what all the fuss is about. Yoda is hands down my favourite part of the original trilogy. It is interesting to me that Yoda's name is derived from the Sanskrit word yodha, meaning warrior. And a warrior he is. As an experienced Jedi master and while training the young Luke Skywalker in the ways of the Jedi, he drops some incredible nuggets of brilliance, even on par with some of the wisest there are. The trick with his teachings is, one needs to decode them, and really think about them.

There is a monumental difference between trying and doing. In the scene that features the above quote, Luke says, "We'll never get it out now." But, as Yoda coaxes Luke on, Luke relents and says, "Okay, I'll try." Which unleashes Yoda's famous reaction, "Do or do not, there is no try." It reminds me of the many people I've encountered in my life who wish for something to happen but don't attempt it. These are the folks who talk of their hopes and dreams and feel that simply talking about it is somehow trying. We all know the types, those that try to improve or change, or whatever, and those that just get it done. No chitter-chatter, no pontifications of grandeur, as they are too busy executing. Life is a challenge in many ways, and in my estimation, the difference between living a life that is fulfilling and living a life of existing is the difference between as Yoda says, "Doing or not doing."

The same can be true when giving a presentation. It is a challenging and even a monumental obstacle for many, but the action of doing is the only way you will improve. Life, in so many ways, is a challenge—for many this includes getting up in front of an audience and sharing what is on your mind. So, as the Nike ad says, Just Do It! If you take Yoda's quote as your new mantra for all aspects of your life, imagine what may unfold.

Tip – Life (including giving a presentation) is a challenge; meet it head on.

#324 – David Logan

(1956)

Context – After a ten-year study and more than 24,000 people polled, David Logan, a business professor, speaks on the five kinds of tribes that humans naturally form. Those in schools, workplaces and even the driver's license bureau.

"What we're really here to talk about is the "how?" Okay, so how exactly do we create this world-shattering, if you will, innovation? Now, I want to tell you a quick story. We'll go back a little more than a year. In fact, the date—I'm curious to know if any of you know what happened on this momentous date? It was February 3rd, 2008. Anyone remember what happened, February 3rd, 2008? Super Bowl. I heard it over here. It was the date of the Super Bowl.

And the reason that this date was so momentous is what my colleagues, John King and Hailey Fischer-Wright, and I noticed as we began to debrief various Super Bowl parties, is that it seemed to us that across the United States if you will, tribal councils had convened. And they had discussed things of great national importance. Like, "Do we like the Budweiser commercial?" And "Do we like the nachos?" And "Who is going to win?" But they also talked about which candidate they were going to support….

So, I'd like to leave you with these thoughts. First of all: we all form tribes, all of us. You're in tribes here.

Hopefully, you're extending the reach of the tribes that you have. But the question on the table is this. What kind of an impact are the tribes that you are in making? You're hearing one presentation after another, often representing a group of people, a tribe, about how they have changed the world. If you do what we've talked about, you listen for how people actually communicate in the tribes that you're in. And you don't leave them where they are. You nudge them forward. You remember to talk all five culture stages. Because we've got people in all five, around us. And the question that I'd like to leave you with is this: Will your tribes change the world? Thank you very much." [Applause]

Analysis – In the consultant community, this TED Talk, "Tribal Leadership" has been all the rage for years. "Yeah, yeah, we should get a life," I can hear you saying. But many of us are trying to figure out the meaning of life, and that in itself can be the making of a great life. "The unexamined life isn't worth living," Socrates said (oh, how I adore Socrates and he makes this list, so stay tuned). The content of this video is interesting and fun to listen to. Logan dissects five tribes and helps the audience ascertain which tribe they fall into. From stage 1; Life Sucks to stage 5; Life Is Great. The stories and analogies that he weaves in are perfect, too, and he hits perfectly each time.

Presenters and speakers need to remember that the audience loves to think about and put themselves in your presentation. The more you can get your audience thinking, "Where do I fit?" or "What would happen if I got there?" the more they will remember and absorb your content, and the more fun they will have. In many of my workshops, I go through personality or behaviour assessments. There are zillions out there now: Myers Briggs, DiSC, HBDI, Firo-B, CLI, etc. I do this very consciously to provide my audience time to gain introspection and figure out:

- #1 where they currently are
- #2 where the people around them are (family, friends, work relationships) and
- #3 where they want to be (what is the vision, the ultimate goal)

You don't have to go through a lengthy and detailed personality or behaviour assessment to get your audience involved. It could be as simple as asking a question (as Logan does at the beginning and the end of his presentation) to elicit thought of where one is and where they want to be. Asking questions is a brilliant tool to allow your audience into the belly of your presentation. Asking questions takes your audience from merely watching your presentation to becoming a part of your presentation. When you afford your audience the time to be introspective, you'll notice the entire environment change, and there will be laughter, fun, energy and most importantly, learning!

Tip – Great presenters provide their audience time to be introspective!

#323 – Stephen Duneier

(1967)

Context – In his 2017 TED Talk "How to Achieve Your Most Ambitious Goals," Duneier shares his approach to decision making and how the small, seemingly insignificant decisions that we make each day can edge you closer to achieving your most ambitious dreams. Duneier is an investment manager, strategy consultant, speaker, author, artist, and Guinness world record holder—in 2016 he crocheted the world's largest granny square.

"By a show of hands, how many of you believe you could replicate this image of Brad Pitt with just a pencil and piece of paper? Well, I'm going to show you how to do this.

And in so doing, I'm going to give you the skill necessary to become a world-class artist. And it shouldn't take more than about 15 seconds. But before I do that, how many of you believe you could replicate this image of a solid grey square? Every one of us. And if you can make one grey square, you can make two, three, nine.

Truth of the matter is, if you could make just one grey square, it'd be very difficult to argue that you couldn't make every grey square necessary to replicate the image in its entirety. And there you have it. I've just given you the skills necessary to become a world-class artist. I know what you're thinking, "That's not real art certainly wouldn't make me a world-class artist."

So let me introduce you to Chuck Close. He's one of the highest-earning artists in the entire world for decades, and he creates his art using this exact technique. You see, what stands between us and achieving even our most ambitious dreams has far less to do with possessing some magical skill or talent and far more to do with how we approach problems and make decisions to solve them.

…From kindergarten all the way through to my high school graduation… yes, that's high school graduation for me… every one of my report cards basically said the same thing: Stephen is a very bright young boy, if only he would just settle down and focus. What they didn't realize was I wanted that even more than they wanted it for me. I just couldn't. And so, from kindergarten straight through the 2nd year of college, I was a really consistent C, C- student.

But then, going into my junior year, I'd had enough. I thought I want to make a change. I'm going to make a marginal adjustment, and I'm going to stop being a spectator of my decision-making and start becoming an active participant. And so, that year, instead of pretending, again, that I would suddenly be able to settle down and focus on things for more than five or ten minutes at a time, I decided to assume I wouldn't.

And so, if I wanted to achieve the type of outcome that I desire—doing well in school—I was going to actually have to change my approach. And so, I made a marginal adjustment. If I would get an assignment, let's say, read five chapters in a book, I wouldn't think of it as five chapters. I wouldn't even think of it as one chapter. I would break it down into these tasks that I could achieve that would require me to focus for just five or ten minutes at a time. So, maybe three or four paragraphs. That's it.

I would do that, and when I was done with those five or ten minutes, I would get up. I'd go shoot some hoops, do a little drawing, maybe play video games for a few minutes, and then I'd come back. Not necessarily to the same assignment, not even necessarily to the same subject, but just to another task that required just five to ten minutes of my attention.

From that point forward, all the way through to graduation, I was a straight-A student, Dean's List, President's Honor Roll, every semester. I then went on to one of the top graduate programs in the world for finance and economics. Same approach, same results.

So then, I graduate, I start my career, and I'm thinking, this worked really well for me. You know you take these big concepts, these complex ideas, these big assignments, you break them down to much more manageable tasks, and then along the way, you make a marginal improvement to the process that ups the odds of success in your favour. I'm going to try and do this in my career…."

Analysis – Lean in, folks! This talk is incredibly inspiring, so much so that when I initially saw it, I watched it three times in quick succession and it immediately spurred me into action. I have since watched it dozens of times. This talk spoke to me at such a visceral level and convinced me that if I followed Duneier's advice, I too could achieve my most ambitious goals. Whoa! Isn't that what a talk should do? Make you want to watch it over and over and inspire you to change your behaviour.

I watched this talk on December 31, 2019, and on January 1, 2020, I created a list inspired by this talk. I made a 50 to 50 list. The list mapped out 25 things I wanted to learn and 25 things I wanted to do before my 50th birthday. As I write this, I only have a couple of months to go, and I am only about halfway through the list, so I need to get moving! Watching this talk again today made me believe that I still have a shot.

Achieving your most ambitious goals is not a magical skill, but how you approach problems and decisions is, says Duneier. Marginal improvement can produce tremendous results. From art to sports to his own life experiences, Duneier shows us that we may not be setting our goals high enough. That just marginal improvements are achievable in all aspects of our lives, academically, professionally or personally. Imagine learning how to speak German instead of listening to music on your daily commute and after ten months surprising your family with a trip to Germany and speaking the language fluently with the locals to the bewilderment and awe of your children! Imagine choosing to make small decisions every single day that lead to you getting your auto racing or helicopter licences, or learning how to rock climb, skydive, hike 33 trails, run a half marathon, read 50 books. Imagine learning how to knit with such proficiency and focus that you know what *yarn bombing* is (art or graffiti that employs colourful knitted yarn rather than paint). Imagine crocheting a granny square so large that you are awarded a spot in the Guinness World Records. Well, Duneier did, it all.

Duneier's talk is engaging, funny, awe-inspiring. The same content delivered by another might ignite jealousy, but when it comes from Duneier it does not. It elicits a feeling of marvel and a desire to turn off the TV and put down my phone, so I can ring out as much of life's nectar as possible.

I'll finish this entry with a few more of Duneier's words in the hopes that they will spur you to write your own list:

"I'm still that C minus student. I'm still that kid who can't settle down or focus for more than five or ten minutes at a time. And I remain a guy who possesses no special gift or talent or skill. All I do is take huge, ambitious projects that people seem to marvel at, break them down to their simplest form and then make marginal improvements along the way to improve my odds of achieving them."

Tip – Use your own stories to inspire others.

#322 – Leo Tolstoy

1828–1910

Context – The below quote doesn't come from *War and Peace*, *Anna Karenina*, or my favourite Tolstoy classic, *The Death of Ivan Ilych*. It comes from a simple discussion that was documented from Tolstoy's diaries (Diaries Volume 2: 1895-1920.)

"Memory? How often people take memory for intelligence. And they don't see that memory excludes intelligence, is incompatible with intelligence – intelligence which solves problem in an original manner. The one is a substitute for the other."

Analysis – A discussion with Leo Tolstoy.

I have often felt the same way as Tolstoy's testament. Our school system nurtures a regurgitation of what the curriculum and teachers want. If you're new to my writing, I encourage you to check out entry #346, where Ken Robinson discusses the notion of schools killing creativity. For today's purposes, though, I'd like to bring to the fore the idea that memory, and how good you are at memorizing, should have very little do with giving a great talk. I often work with clients who say, "That is a lot of stuff to remember if I have to talk for an hour!'" The truth is that you should have practiced your talk, and this, for further clarification and emphasis, does not mean memorizing your talk. Again, practicing does not equal memorization. If you sit back and think of the best talk you've ever heard it's most likely a talk that was delivered without copious notes and it was certainly not delivered robotically. Often people get hung up on memorizing a talk because that is what they learned to do during their school years, but honestly, it is one of the worst things you can do for delivering a great talk. If you think about the best talk you've ever heard, I'm sure it was conversational amongst a laundry list of other things. The only way you will come across as having a conversation is if you have prepared in advance but have not memorize. So, you may ask, "how the heck do I do that? "Well, it is as simple as talking to yourself out loud. While preparing for a talk, I will start the process several weeks and sometimes months in advance; getting my slides together, my flip charts, putting together my research, sourcing out great analogies, etc., and as the date approaches, I begin the process of talking to myself. Door closed, talking it out loud, going through the talk over and over until I hit what I refer to as readiness. Some talks just take longer than others to get to that point.

Your ability to memorize, too, will not help you with answering and fielding questions! You certainly may prepare for what questions may arise, but you cannot (or shouldn't anyway) go through a stack of 3x5 cards that you have brought with possible questions. I've seen this before. An audience member asks a question, and the speaker undergoes a painful waiting period as she goes through her cards to find the one that has the answer. The audience didn't come to hear you read to them. If they wanted that, they would've bought an audio book!

There is a small component of memorization involved in giving a talk. I've used something called *stacking* for years. I learned part of my technique from Dale Carnegie and part of my technique from a comedian that I once met. In its simplest form, it is about breaking your talk out into sections by topic. Think of your talk as a novel, and each chapter is a component of your talk. For each chapter start at the bottom of the piece of paper and include the topic headings. Break each chapter out into subsections and allow a few word prompts to spill out from that main topic to the right side. For today, simply work on not memorizing your talk.

Tip – Never memorize a talk word for word.

#321 – Romeo and Juliet

Published 1597

Context – Written by William Shakespeare, Juliet says the below in *Romeo and Juliet*.

"A rose by any other name would smell as sweet."

Analysis – Today happens to be Valentine's Day that I write this, so it is only natural that I would choose a quote from Shakespeare's Romeo and Juliet to demonstrate the need for analogies in a talk. Okay, so I hear you out there, "What's an analogy again?" An analogy is comparable to a metaphor and simile in that it shows how two different things are similar. Rather than a figure of speech, an analogy is more of a logical argument. The presenter of a metaphor will often demonstrate how two things are alike by pointing out shared characteristics, with the goal of showing that if two things are similar in some ways, they are similar in other ways as well. Okay, that sounds all fancy, but in its simplest form, it is a way to bridge the gap for your audience. Often when we are asked to give a talk or presentation, we tackle some challenging concepts or ideas. An analogy used at the right time, in the right way, will light a bulb over many of your audience's heads. "Oh, I get it!" Please don't underestimate the power of a great analogy. In Shakespeare's quote, Juliet uses a metaphor when she says, "A rose by any other name would smell as sweet." Her point is that Romeo's surname, Montague, shouldn't matter. If a rose were called a cabbage or cheese or whatever, it would still smell sweet. Even though Romeo's name is the name of her family's enemy, to her he's still wonderful. Okay, maybe that was a challenging one to start with, but here are some other famous analogies:

1. Act like yesterday's lunch: Go down and out the back.

2. Busy as a button on a back house door.

3. Hanging in there like stink on a stockyard boot.

4. Make like diarrhea and run.
5. Make like Houdini and disappear.
6. Make like Levi's and fade away.
7. Make like Linda Lovelace and blow.
8. Make like Michael Jackson and "Beat it!"
9. Make like Pablo and Cruise.
10. Make like Santa Claus and leave your presents.
11. Make like Tom and Cruise.
12. Make like Bill Clinton and blow.
13. Make like a Catholic and pull out.
14. Make like a Hewlett Packard laser printer and jet.
15. Make like a nut and bolt.
16. Make like a bakery truck and haul buns outta' here.
17. Make like a banana and split.
18. Make like a baseball player and home-run

Tip – Use analogies.

#320 – Don McMillan

(1959)

Context – In his comedy sketch, "Life After Death by PowerPoint" McMillan demonstrates how not to use PowerPoint.

McMillan starts his sketch by pulling up a PowerPoint on a screen and reads the word-littered slide verbatim. "Most common PowerPoint Mistakes. People tend to put every word they are going to say on their PowerPoint slides. Although this eliminates the need to memorize your talk, ultimately this makes your slides crowded, wordy, and boring. You will lose your audience's attention before you even reach the bottom of your…" He clicks his page turner to reveal a slide with the words, (continued) …first slide

Analysis – Those aspiring to be better speakers can learn a thing or two from comedians. Their delivery, cadence, intonation, well-timed pauses, comedic pacing and unique voice. It's interesting to watch how the comedian behaves when the joke hits well and what they do when it bombs.

Whether using PowerPoint, Keynote or whatever presentation app you have access to, find a presentation software that you are comfortable using, then get really good at it, and I mean really good at it. The PowerPoint (Microsoft) vs Keynote (Mac) debate has been around for ages, I've used both extensively and can say there are advantages and disadvantages of both. Keynote is slicker and has better looking themes but nowadays you can access all kinds of sites to help develop cool content such as Canva or Visme. If you can think of something creatively, the tools to build them exist.

All right, now let's talk slides. Oh, yes, this will come up a lot. Today, let's focus on the single most significant presentation infraction I see—staring at slides. Slides are a crutch. A speaker gets nervous, and boom, you'll find them fixated on the slide. So, there you are, in the audience, staring at the back of someone's head! Give yourself some honest feedback and ask yourself if you do this. It's okay to admit it, but, once you do, let's fix it. Paring down all of your slides and mixing it up with other presentation aids (flip charts, pictures, quotes, etc.) is a great way to turn your attention away from the slides.

You can also tell a lot about the speaker by how they have constructed the slides: Too wordy? Poor font design or size? Wrong colours? A reliance only on PowerPoint and no other presentation aides?

Here are some ideas that you may want to try:

- Allow six words maximum per slide. Your audience should look at the slide and be intrigued rather than know exactly what you will say. They should look at the slide and require more explanation. Never read a slide word for word. Again, if your audience wanted to hear you read, they would've gone to a reading, not a presentation or a talk.

- Font size. Often, a small font size is chosen to fit as much information as possible. If you find yourself choosing anything less than 16 point as your font size, you likely have too much content on the slide.

- You have to consider colours when constructing a presentation. I came across an article many years ago written by a psychologist. His theory for using colours when writing was based on the research used to figure out the best colour for jail cells. As it turns out blue is the optimum colour, and many correctional facilities use colour to influence the behaviours of its inmates. I continue to refer to his article when I construct my own PowerPoints presentations.

1. Black sets a neutral tone.
2. Blue promotes creativity; calms the mind.
3. Green fosters harmony.
4. Purple gives power and inspiration.
5. Red stimulates and provides excitement.
6. Brown suggests balance and warmth.
7. Orange is useful for positive thinking.
8. Yellow helps the digestion of ideas.

Tip – Use slides as an aid, rather than the focus.

#319 – Noam Chomsky

(1928)

Context – Noam Chomsky is a Professor of linguistics and philosophy at the Massachusetts Institute of Technology. The below is from *Chomsky on Anarchism*, a book he wrote in 2005.

"Language is a process of free creation; its laws and principles are fixed, but the manner in which the principles of generation are used is free and infinitely varied. Even the interpretation and use of words involves a process of free creation."

Analysis – Chomsky is known for his presentation style, which is informal, has great dissection, and immense documentation. Some have even called him ruthless at times. I like him a lot. His views are well thought out, detailed and complex. I've previously used the above quote in workshops to see if my audience can interpret it and have welcomed a variety of interpretations. For me, the quote is about the varied aspects of language—how we use it and how it is interpreted. Here's an example; I've taken a few fiction writing classes over the years, and often there is a reading of a novel, a short story, or a poem etc., and we are then invited to interpret its meaning. Sometimes the interpretation is significantly different from person to person, and sometimes we all share the same understanding of the piece. Perhaps you have had a similar experience when discussing a book or a movie? The same can be said when you are giving a talk. If you have a solid message that you are trying to communicate, then orchestrate your language in a way that leaves a narrowing in the interpretation. Recognize that your audience brings their life experience to their listening abilities. Your words will be shaped and molded depending on their experiences. It is essential that you communicate to all members of your audience at all times and mix up your language so that your message can be heard and digested in the way you intended.

Tip – Use your language consciously.

#318 – Judson Laipply

(1976)

Context – Judson is a motivational speaker and dancer. He is best known for his performance in "The Evolution of Dance" which went viral.

Analysis – Never heard of Judson Laipply? Me neither! Until I saw the video. Laipply is a comedian and enjoyed some fame as a result of his sketch 'Evolution of Dance.' It makes me smile, and by the time he gets to his rendition of *Ice, Ice, Baby* by Vanilla Ice, I'm laughing out loud and eager and interested to see what song and corresponding dance will surface next. Please note that there isn't a single word uttered here, yet he tells a complete story with a beginning, a middle, and an end. Words are great. Anyone who knows me knows that I love the spoken word, the cadence, the intonation, the articulation. But there is so much more to the art of communicating. It reminds me of when my fiction writing teacher kept telling me repeatedly to, "show me, don't tell me!" What I'm learning as a writer can be transferred to the speaker: the more you can *show* what you're trying to convey, the more deeply you will impact your audience.

What Laipply demonstrates so brilliantly is the art of show rather than tell. When preparing a talk, I encourage you to do the same. Is there a way to show your audience the concept and message you're trying to convey? If you were a piano teacher, you wouldn't talk ad nauseam about the brilliance of C major or the allegro of Minuet in G. You would teach by showing. You might play the piece for your student first, so they understand the melody, the rise, and fall of the tone. The same can be said for doing a talk. There are plenty of times that one can show rather than tell. If you were giving a presentation on a fancy new Excel spreadsheet, you'd have a screen up and support the visual with words, but the real show is the example. If you were talking about communication conflict, you might encourage a role play to show the right way and wrong way. There are so many ways of showing rather than telling, and I encourage you to stretch the boundaries of your comfort zone and put a little show into your talk.

Tip – Don't just tell me, show me.

#317 – George Orwell

1903–1950

Context – Big Brother is a fictional character and symbol in George Orwell's dystopian 1949 novel *Nineteen Eighty-Four*.

"Big Brother is watching you."

Analysis – I once did a small keynote address to a class at one of Calgary's local colleges. At some point, I mentioned the quote, "Big Brother is watching you" and was shocked when one of the students wrongly assumed I was referring to the the reality TV show that was created in 1997, you know the one where a bunch of people voluntarily lock themselves in a house, are videotaped 24/7, and make utter fools of themselves as they are watched by viewers with insatiable voyeuristic appetites. Intrigued, I proclaimed, hands in the air and with a smirk said, "Please, oh, please, *1984*?" Nope, I was met with a vacant and dumbfounded gaze. I suppose one can't blame this student entirely for not having heard of Orwell's classic book, and, later, film 1984. In my experience as a student, English teachers choose the most utterly painful books as part of their curriculum insert, *Tess of the D'Urbervilles*, instead of what I would say was a non-negotiable in the literary world (and for the record; *To Kill a Mockingbird* and *Lord of the Flies* are on my non-negotiable list too).

It may have taken a little longer than he predicted, but Orwell's vision of a society where cameras and computers spy on a person's every movement is here. I don't think one needs to be a conspiracy theorist to believe that we are being monitored at all times, from social networking pages and emails, websites and blogs, to whenever you swipe your air miles, preferred customer and loyalty cards, and credit cards. No doubt about it, Big Brother is here. The above quote is a brilliant reminder for those preparing, doing, and exiting the talk stage. Your audience will be watching you like a hawk! Never forget that. I once hired a consultant for a very large fee to conduct a workshop (I had worked with her while I was at a company). She did a fantastic job, as she had prepared, and worked tirelessly throughout the entire day. The feedback from the participants was brilliant. I had stayed behind to recap with her and heard her say on her cell phone what a horrible, exhausting day it had been, and how her audience couldn't grasp any concepts, and she was glad it was over. Did I hire her again? Nope, I did not. You may ask, "why not?" She did her job well after all. I didn't hire her again for a few reasons; she wasn't authentic, and that eventually would start permeating out to the audience. One cannot sustain acting for extended periods, and she was merely acting the role of caring trainer. It wasn't professional either. Please learn from her mistakes (I know I certainly did!) If your audience is not familiar with you, once they do get to know you, you will feel them looking at you. You have been asked to speak because you have something of value to contribute, and so whether you are a formal leader or not, you must behave like one. If your audience does know you, they will watch you before the talk to assess where you're at, and they will watch you after and everywhere in between. The point is you should behave as if you are a presenter (and a leader) even when you are not physically on stage.

Tip – Behave as a presenter on and off the stage.

#316 – Isabel Allende

(1942)

Context – In her 2014 TED Talk: "How to Live Passionately – No Matter Your Age", Isabel Allende, a Chilean writer, talks about her fears as she gets older and offers her perspective on living passionately indefinitely.

"Hi, kids.

I'm 71. My husband is 76. My parents are in their late 90s, and Olivia, the dog, is 16. So, let's talk about aging.

Let me tell you how I feel when I see my wrinkles in the mirror, and I realize that some parts of me have dropped, and I can't find them down there.

Mary Oliver says in one of her poems, "Tell me, what is it that you plan to do with your one wild and precious life?"

Me, I intend to live passionately.

When do we start aging? Society decides when we are old, usually around 65, when we get Medicare, but we really start aging at birth. We are aging right now, and we all experience it differently. We all feel younger than our real age because the spirit never ages. I am still 17. Sophia Loren. Look at her. She says that everything you see she owes to spaghetti. I tried it and gained 10 pounds in the wrong places. But attitude, aging is also attitude and health. But my real mentor in this journey of aging is Olga Murray. This California girl, at 60, started working in Nepal to save young girls from domestic bondage. At 88, she has saved 12,000 girls and she has changed the culture in the country. (Applause) Now it is illegal for fathers to sell their daughters into servitude. She has also founded orphanages and nutritional clinics. She is always happy and eternally young.

What have I lost in the last decades? People, of course, places, and the boundless energy of my youth, and I'm beginning to lose independence, and that scares me. Ram Dass says that dependency hurts, but if you accept it, there is less suffering. After a very bad stroke, his ageless soul watches the changes in the body with tenderness, and he is grateful to the people who help him.

What have I gained? Freedom: I don't have to prove anything anymore. I'm not stuck in the idea of who I was, who I want to be, or what other people expect me to be. I don't have to please men anymore, only animals. I keep telling my superego to back off and let me enjoy what I still have. My body may be falling apart, but my brain is not yet. I love my brain. I feel lighter. I don't carry grudges, ambition, vanity, none of the deadly sins that are not even worth the trouble. It's great to let go. I should have started sooner. And I also feel softer because I'm not scared of being vulnerable. I don't see it as weakness anymore. And I've gained spirituality. I'm aware that before, death was in the neighborhood. Now, it's next door, or in my house. I try to live mindfully and be present in the moment. By the way, the Dalai Lama is someone who has aged beautifully, but who wants to be vegetarian and celibate?"

Analysis – "I should have started sooner," Allende says in her talk about living passionately at any age. She is funny, joyful and her inner light shines through her self-effacing, buoyant energy. This talk is only eight minutes long, but you want her to go on! Wait, aren't TED Talks supposed to be 19 minutes? "You can't finish yet!" I hear myself saying out loud.

"Tell me, what is it that you plan to do with your one wild and precious life?" Allende recites from Mary Oliver's poems. It's a good question. For Allende, it is the intent to live passionately.

Allende says yes to everything that comes her way in her pursuit of a passionate life. She says yes to drama, comedy, tragedy, love, death, losses. She says yes to life, but the real lesson in her talk, and something that I've heard from others in the +70 crowd, is to let go of the deadly sins. Let go of vanity and ambition. Seek to live mindfully so that you can gain freedom and become lighter.

It is interesting to me the vulnerable way Allende presents herself. At one point during the talk, she calls herself a vain female and shares how it is hard to age in this culture. Hallelujah, Isabel! It sure is. Think about the diet culture that has existed forever, the existence of any pharmaceutical pill that will numb anything, slim you, burn fat, the Botox culture that we now live in. Celebrity culture coupled with social media trends leave people reaching for unobtainable and unrealistic ideals and Barbie-like standards that are ridiculous and sad. I was talking to a friend who is in her 30s recently, who was telling me that she was saving up for cool sculpting—a non-surgical fat removal technique. What the hell is that? She doesn't own a house, car, or even a bike, yet she's saving-up for cool sculpting!

I can relate to the struggle of aging that Allende is referring to; a feeling that death is lingering in the room and there is little runway left. While she does not use the words existential angst, this is what she appears to be talking about. What has the purpose of this life been and in our last chapters of life who do we want to be, what do we want to do, how do we want to be remembered. She talks about becoming invisible as she ages and that she wants to be the centre of attention. Drawing on her friends experiences she shows how they have circumvented their invisibility cloaks in their own ways.

While Allende is certainly in touch with her vulnerable side, which gently draws her audience in, she is equally adept at being funny—she shares her fantasies about Antonio Banderas and notes that although the Dalai Lama has aged beautifully, would anyone really want to be vegetarian or celibate? This mix of vulnerability and fun creates a joyful environment where the audience is hanging on her every word eager to learn her secrets to living a passion-filled life and how to unlock the secret door in their own lives. It's almost as though she knows far more than she is relinquishing in this talk. It creates a mystical quality to this talk that I'm not sure can be taught until you arrive at the same point of understanding as Allende.

Tip – Vulnerability + humour = a joyful talk.

#315 – Hans Rosling

1948–2017

Context – Hans Rosling shows in his 2006 TED Talk, "The Best Stats You've Ever Seen". A professor of global health at Sweden's Karolinska Institute, his current work focuses on dispelling common myths about the developing world, which he says is no longer worlds away from the West. In fact, most of the Third World is on the same trajectory toward health and prosperity, and many countries are moving twice as fast as the developed world.

"About ten years ago, I took on the task to teach global development to Swedish under-graduate students. That was after having spent about 20 years together with African institutions studying hunger in Africa, so I was sort of expected to know a little about the world. And I started in our medical university, Karolinska Institute, an undergraduate course called Global Health. But when you get that opportunity, you get a little nervous. I thought, these students coming to us actually have the highest grade you can get in Swedish college systems —so maybe they know everything I'm going to teach them about. So, I did a pre-test when they came. And one of the questions from which I learnt a lot was this one: "Which country has the highest child mortality of these five pairs?" And I put them together so that in each pair of country, one has twice the child mortality of the other. And this means that it's much bigger a difference than the uncertainty of the data. I won't put you at a test here, but it's Turkey, which is highest there, Poland, Russia, Pakistan, and South Africa. And these were the results of the Swedish students. I did it, so I got the confidence interval, which is pretty narrow, and I got happy, of course: a 1.8 right answer out of five possible. That means that there was a place for a professor of international health —[Laughter] and for my course. But one late night, when I was compiling the report, I really realized my discovery. I have shown that the Swedish top students know statistically significantly less about the world than the chimpanzees. [Laughter] Because the chimpanzee would score half right if I gave them two bananas with Sri Lanka and Turkey. They would be right half of the cases.

But the students are not there. The problem for me was not ignorance: it was preconceived ideas.

I did also an unethical study of the professors of the Karolinska Institute [Laughter]—that hands out the Nobel

Prize in Medicine and they are on par with the chimpanzee there. [Laughter] This is where I realized that there was really a need to communicate because the data of what's happening in the world and the child health of every country is very well aware."

Analysis – It is at about a minute and a half into his talk when Rosling gets going and states the need for a professor in his new class after doing a pre-test. In it, the students do poorly, and he recognizes that there is a need for him to teach global health, and he is pretty excited about that notion. He adores what he does. You can see it; you can feel it. Normally I wouldn't recommend putting up a graph or chart with lots of data on a slide, but you'll notice how the cadence of his voice changes as soon as the slide is shown (at around the four-minute mark, for those of you who look up this talk) Rosling starts talking slightly faster, he gets animated, pumping his arms up and down, and his excitement gets the crowd engrossed, laughing and having fun—they are excited about data and numbers! He proclaims at the end of the slide that we have a completely new world.

Whenever I say in a workshop that to be a superb speaker you must enjoy what you're talking about (in fact, if you can love it, then love it), the following question often surfaces, "But what if I'm talking numbers? Like budget stuff or sales forecasts or, or, or?" My answer is always the same: if you're not passionate about what you're discussing, or if you are nonchalant about it, your audience will be too. It is your role to find a way to get excited about your topic, to extract nuggets from it that will get your enthusiastic juices flowing. What Rosling illustrates so well is that data or topics that others may find boring are in the eye of the beholder and it can be fascinating to anyone if the speaker is jazzed about it. In short, energy, either good or bad, is contagious.

Tip – If you love the topic; they will love it too.

#314 – Napoleon Bonaparte

1769–1821

Context – There is some controversy over who first coined the below phrase. Some say it's a Chinese proverb, and some say Fred Barnard, some say Ivan Turgenev, or a few others. I like the interpretation of Napoleon Bonaparte, so have chosen to recognize him as the original author, while noting that plenty of others have claimed it too.

"A picture is worth a thousand words."

(With appreciation to 'Adbusters' for the graphics)

Analysis – Your right brain audience member will adore you if you sprinkle your talk with vivid, thought-provoking, and even funny pictures. Yes, I know, some believe that the terms right and left brain are incredibly archaic, and I'm apt to agree, but many of us understand what is meant by the terms so it is difficult to not embed them into mass generalizations. Right equals creative, wordy, artistic, intuitive, random, macro. Left equals numerical, methodical, rational, logical, micro. It is your job as a speaker to be able to speak to both sides. I would argue there are four sides that a presenter needs to pay attention to. If you adopt any personality of behaviour profile to help navigate different natural personalities as a barometer of whether you're appealing to each person that is observing or participating in your talk. If we adopt the DiSC or Insights for observing various personalities that we all hold, the right brain is broken out into two colours; red and yellow, and the left brain is broken out into two colours; blue and green. Each colour is distinct and unique. And the theory is that we all have a natural way of behaving, and we also have an adaptive way of behaving. Our natural way of behaving is where we are most comfortable, and most ourselves. The adaptive way of behaving is often uncomfortable, particularly if it is in the opposite pole of your nature. During a talk, the goal as a speaker is to speak fluently to all four quadrants. It sounds rather like adopting four split personalities, and honestly, it is a little like that. If you are on the right side, you need to adopt left side behaviours for your message to be heard and vice versa. And yes, for my right brain extroverts, that means taking it down a few notches and sitting in pauses instead of filling up every millisecond with words.

Another way to not always use words is by utilizing imagery. The notion of today's quote refers to the idea that complex concepts can be described in a single image. Look at the picture I respectfully attained from AdBusters. I don't even need to use words here to dissect what the images mean. Each is clear and doesn't require any explanation. Introducing pictures or images is a terrific way to approach difficult and complex issues in a talk. It is also a way to bring levity to the longer talk. No matter how you use pictures in your talk, your audience, and all the personalities within your audience, will not only enjoy them, but they will also be able to better understand the message you are conveying. In fact, the direct translation of Bonaparte's quote: "Un bon croquis vaut mieux au'un long discours" is "A good sketch is better than a long speech" (and this is where the translation of a picture is worth a thousand words is derived).

Tip – Use visuals such as pictures, photos, and graphics.

#313 – Doug Zongker

Context – Doug Zongker, a software engineer, gave a scientific presentation "Chicken Chicken Chicken" at the AAAS humour session.

"Chicken chicken chicken chicken chicken..."

Analysis – Can a speaker use only one word for the entirety of a four-minute presentation? Well, not one word but the same word repeatedly? Let's say that it can be done, and the chosen word is, *chicken*. It can be done! In fact, it can be done very well, as Zongker shows us in the video. What makes it so funny and entertaining? Is it because he essentially mocks the typical PowerPoint presentations that we've all seen countless times? The ones that use the PowerPoint appointed template and utilize too many graduated bullets with graphs that are impossible to read. One of the reasons we find this session amusing is that we can relate and are all tired of seeing the same old presentation over and over in meetings. We, as the audience, hunger for something more, something interesting, something to wake us up, and most importantly, we hunger to learn something. For me, what is so fascinating about this video is the use of one word, chicken, and how it is said differently each time. Intonation is the key! Notice too, which is even more fascinating to someone who studies presentations for a living, that he stands behind a podium, no real gestures to be seen, and he relies on just two components; his voice and the slides (this is not something I'd generally recommend, but it works here, and I'm open to exceptions to every rule). Most of us will be familiar with the statistic that 80 percent of our communication is nonverbal and just 20 percent is verbal (words). Well, here, the stat would still be the same, but, boy, does it demonstrate itself differently.

I once attended a workshop on how infants and children learn to communicate. This presentation brings me to what the trainer called *pre-linguistic* communication, or communication that precedes the use of true language. It's a stage in speech development that is characterized by the use of strings of speech sounds in vocal play such as, "ga-ga-ga, ba-ba-ba," or "chicken." Zongker is not using the word chicken in its true context, so it could fall within the definition of pre-linguistic communication. However, it is entertaining to watch four minutes of a successful presentation filled with a single word. Much like communicating with someone just learning how to speak, to be effective, you have to vary the rise and fall, the emphasis, the tone, the pitch, and the cadence to elicit a response (in this case, laughter). A baby will not coo back at you unless you do those things, and your audience won't respond to you unless you use the same methodology.

Tip – Intonation is key.

#312 – Tina Fey

(1970)

Context – The scene in which Liz Lemon, played by Tina Fey, reels off a laundry list of buzzwords in the hit TV show, *30 Rock*.

"Cross promotional, deal mechanics, revenue streams, jargon, synergy."

"That's the best presentation I've ever heard; get started right away."

Analysis – The scene takes 12 seconds to watch, so I encourage you to track it down on YouTube and watch it. I love *30 Rock*, mostly because of Alec Baldwin. His response to Fey's 12-second list of corporate buzzwords (above) has me on the floor laughing. Call it 'acting hot,' or 'I'm emulating my boss,' or 'I fit into the corporate world,' whatever you want to call it, corporate buzzwords will drive at least 96 percent of your audience plain crazy, two percent will be the folk that use them, and the final two percent will be searching for a dictionary desperately trying to crack the buzzword code. As soon as I hear the first glimmer of a buzzword, I start to feel my skin crawl. I get hives. Okay, maybe not actual hives, but I feel like I'm about to jump out of my skin and say, "would you just say what you want to say and stop trying desperately to fit in." I once worked for a man who lived on Steven Covey-isms, or whatever the latest buzzwords were. If you want to psychoanalyze, that is probably where my disdain for this section of vocabulary most likely originates. What I could tell from him is he genuinely struggled to have an original thought, and so to sound articulate, well-read, and well-versed in the topic at hand, he would throw in buzzwords. These buzzwords didn't show a vast knowledge base or business acumen. It highlighted a lack of originality, and it felt phony, fake, copycat-like—he was plagiarizing another's words. The entire message then became difficult to digest. Like a piece of popcorn lodged in your windpipe. You desperately try to choke it down, but even after a couple of hard swallows, it just won't budge. It's one thing to have a one-on-one conversation with a buzzword junkie, but it's entirely different to listen to one in a presentation. The latter quickly becomes unpalatable. Let's have an honest moment, just you and me. Are you one of the buzzword junkies out there? The first step is to admit you have a problem; the second step is: Just stop it! Simply speak as you. Don't emulate some self-help book guru, or Betty Sue in the corner office, or your boss. Just be yourself. Let your language fall naturally. I promise people will infinitely appreciate you more in the end. Yes, we have stumbled on one of my pet peeves. In my workshops, I'll often talk about my genuine and inherent dislike of corporate buzzwords. Synergy FYI is the one that tops my list. Here are some others that drive me plain batty:

- Employee engagement (who's getting engaged? Oh, does this mean that we will elicit opinions? Oh, then why not say that?)
- Out of the box (Jack or Charlie?)
- Paradigm shift (sounds other earthly to me)
- Going forward (Oh, thanks, I thought we were going to go backwards?)
- Does that make sense? (you'd better agree with me! Never, I mean never say this in a talk. Instead, ask, "What questions do you have?" Assume your audience has questions. Asking if something makes sense will only elicit a head nod up and down, and you'll never get your audience to open up and participate.
- Set them up for success (Wow, I thought we were going to set them up for failure)
- Rightsizing (Whoops, we hired too many people)
- Reskilling (Your skills are no longer of value)
- Push-back (Someone who has a different opinion)
- Take it to the next level (What level? Level 10 on my Donkey Kong Atari game circa 1983?)
- Tee it up! (With or without a caddy?)
- It's gone viral! (What?)
- Metric (Should have just said measurement, but now people think I am so smart)
- Proactive (Actually doing your job versus the status quo)
- Organic growth (Business is bad, so we need to scale back our original forecast growth projections)
- Incentivize (Formerly known as getting a raise for a job well done)

- Touch base (Does this mean that we are going to talk?)
- Circle back (I have no idea what the answer to your question is, so let me just say I'll circle back to you at a later time)

Tip – Stop the buzzword craze.

#311 – Francis Frei

Context – In this 2018 TED Talk, Francis Frei, a Harvard Business School professor, delivers an eye-opening talk that digs into the topic of trust and how to build and rebuild it.

"I want to talk to you about how to build and rebuild trust, because it's my belief that trust is the foundation for everything we do, and that if we can learn to trust one another more, we can have unprecedented human progress.

But what if trust is broken? What if your CEO is caught on video disparaging an employee? What if your employees experience a culture of bias, exclusion and worse? What if there's a data breach, and it feels an awful lot like a cover-up than seriously addressing it? And most tragically, what if a technological fail leads to the loss of human life?

If I was giving this talk six months ago, I would have been wearing an Uber T-shirt. I'm a Harvard Business School professor, but I was super attracted to going to an organization that was metaphorically and perhaps quite literally on fire. I had read everything that was written in the newspaper, and that was precisely what drew me to the organization. This was an organization that had lost trust with every constituent that mattered.

But there's a word about me that I should share. My favourite trait is redemption. I believe that there is a better version of us around every corner, and I have seen firsthand how organizations and communities, and individuals change at breathtaking speed.

I went to Uber with the hopes that a turnaround there could give license to the rest of us who might have narrower versions of their challenges. But when I got to Uber, I made a really big mistake. I publicly committed to wearing an Uber T-shirt every day until every other employee was wearing an Uber T-shirt. I had clearly not thought that through.

It was 250 days of wearing an Uber T-shirt. Now I am liberated from that commitment, as I am back at HBS, and what I'd like to do is share with you how far I have taken that liberty, which, it's baby steps, but I would say I'm on my way.

Now, trust, if we're going to rebuild it, we have to understand its component parts. The component parts of trust are super well understood. There're three things about trust. If you sense that I am being authentic, you are much more likely to trust me. If you sense that I have real rigour in my logic, you are far more likely to trust me. And if you believe that my empathy is directed towards you, you are far more likely to trust me. When all three of these things are working, we have great trust. But if any one of these three gets shaky, if any one of these three wobbles, trust is threatened.

Now here's what I'd like to do. I want each of us to be able to engender more trust tomorrow, literally tomorrow, than we do today. And the way to do that is to understand where trust wobbles for ourselves and have a ready-made prescription to overcome it. So that's what I would like to do together."

Analysis – I don't think it would be an understatement to say that the topic of trust has been an obsession of mine for decades. I've devoured books, talks, articles, and trust models on the subject, and I continue to develop my own perspective. Take how Frei starts this talk, "I want to talk to you about how to build and rebuild trust because I believe that trust is the foundation for everything we do and that if we can learn to trust one another more, we can have unprecedented human progress." That is one bold statement, and I couldn't agree more. Trust is the foundation of all our relationships.

The topic of trust has been explored by many. In Patrick Lencioni's book, *The Five Dysfunctions of a Team*, he explores how the absence of trust creates an unwillingness to be vulnerable, which can be damaging as it sets the tone for a second dysfunction: fear of conflict. His model is borrowed from Maslow's Hierarchy of Needs (physiological, safety, love and belonging, esteem, and self-actualization). Much like a foundation to a house, it is necessary to have a solid psychological base—food, water, shelter, warmth—prior to building safety, love and belonging, esteem, and finally self-actualization. Amy Edmundson, a Harvard Business school professor, coined the term *psychological safety* which is a belief that one will not be punished or humiliated for speaking up with ideas, questions, concerns and mistakes. Frei's view is not earth-shatteringly new, but her stories and delivery offer a novel slant.

Frei sought to work with Uber, an organization that was metaphorically and literally on fire from a trust perspective. Her goal: to help improve the decline in their culture as it relates to trust. Frei looked at three components of trust—authenticity, logic, and empathy. Based on Frei's components of trust and her recommendations, Uber began to:

- Demonstrate increased empathy, deeply immerse yourselves with the other person. A good start is to turn off your cell phone.

- Demonstrate logic. Start with your point in a crisp half-sentence, and then give your supporting evidence, this means that people will be able to get access to our awesome ideas, and if you get cut off before you're done, you still get credit for the idea, as opposed to someone else coming in and snatching it from you. And she shows her logic for starting this talk precisely this way.

- Demonstrate authenticity.

There is something delightfully soothing about this talk. Frei is being herself, and that is why it is both easy-listening and captivating. So often, when we listen to others give a talk, it can feel disingenuous or inauthentic. Frei is real, and we connect with that authenticity at a physical level. As Frei says, "You can sniff inauthenticity out in a moment." Frei's components of trust, authenticity, logic, and empathy are evident throughout this talk. She tells us about these components, offers examples and stories and shows us those qualities in her talk.

Tip – Be authentic, logical, and empathetic in your talks.

#310 – Jon Stewart

(1962)

Context – Jon Stewart's is a comedian, writer, political commentator, actor and tv host. Here in a statement to the house judiciary committee on the September 11th victim compensation fund Stewart delivers an impassioned plea for permanent health care for the first responders.

"I want to thank Mr. Collins and Mr. Nadler for putting this together. But, as I sit here today, I can't help but think what an incredible metaphor this room is for the entire process that getting health care and benefits for 9/11 first responders has come to.

Behind me: a filled room of 9/11 first responders.

And in front of me: a nearly empty Congress.

Sick and dying, they brought themselves down here to speak—to no one.

It's shameful.

It's an embarrassment to the country.

And it is a stain on this institution.

And you should be ashamed of yourselves for those that aren't here, but you won't be because accountability doesn't appear to be something that occurs in this chamber.

We don't want to be here. Lu [Detective Luis Alvarez] doesn't want to be here. None of these people want to be here. But they are, and they're not here for themselves. They're here to continue fighting for what's right. Lu's going to go back for his 69th chemo. The great Ray Pfeiffer would come down here, his body riddled with cancer and pain, where he couldn't walk; and the disrespect shown to him and to the other lobbyists on this bill is utterly unacceptable.

You know, I used to get...I would be so angry at the latest injustice that's done to these men and women and, you know, another business card thrown our way as a way of shooing us away like children trick-or-treating, rather than the heroes that they are and will always be.

Ray would stay, "Calm down, Johnny. Calm down. I got all the cards I need." And he would tap his pocket, where he kept the prayer cards of 343 firefighters. The official FDNY response time to 911 was five seconds. Five seconds! That's how long it took for FDNY, for NYPD, for Port Authority, for EMS to respond to an urgent need from the public.

Five seconds.

Hundreds died in an instant. Thousands more poured in to continue to fight for their brothers and sisters.

The breathing problems started almost immediately. And they were told they weren't sick—they were crazy. And then, as the illnesses got worse and things became more apparent, "Well, okay, you're sick, but it's not from the pile." And then, when the science became irrefutable, "Okay, it's the pile—but this is a New York issue. I don't know if we have the money."

And I'm sorry if I sound angry and undiplomatic, but I'm angry—and you should be too, and they're all angry as well. And they have every justification to be that way. There is not a person here, there is not an empty chair on that stage that didn't tweet out, never forget the heroes of 9/11; never forget their bravery; never forget what they did, what they gave to this country.

Well, here they are! And where are they? And it would be one thing if their callous indifference and rank hypocrisy were benign. But it's not. Your indifference cost these men and women their most valuable commodity: time. It's the one thing they're running out of…"

Analysis – This is an emotional talk. There are several points when Stewart is choking back tears and pausing to collect himself so that he can get his precious words out. His language is pointed, strong and clear. In the last line of his speech Stewart says, "They responded in five seconds. They did their jobs with courage, grace, tenacity, humility. Eighteen years later, do yours!" As I watch and read the transcript of this talk, I too am enraged. I didn't know that in 2019, the year Stewart gave this speech, the 9/11 first responders were being denied health care and benefits, and, as Stewart says, it is utterly unacceptable.

Stewart is not giving this talk to enhance his celebrity. You can feel his anger, compassion, and empathy. You can feel his desire for change and, as he tears into Congress and urges them to act, I find myself audibly cheering him on.

So many talks on this list are impassioned pleas for change. Some of the greatest speeches of all time come from a deep desire for change. "The pen is mightier than the sword," as Edward Bulwer-Lytton said in 1839. While Bulwer-Lytton was referring to the written word, the spoken word is also a more effective communication tool than violence. Speeches like Stewart's help to shape the world as we know it today and into the future. "I Have a Dream", "Quit India", "We Shall Fight on the Beaches", "Give Me Liberty or Give Me Death" are a few other examples that are so deeply ingrained in our culture. For me, Stewart's monologue at Congress should be entitled, "I Am Angry, and You Should Be Too," and should serve as an addition to the most powerful impassioned pleas of this century.

Tip – If you're angry about an injustice, use your voice to be a catalyst for change.

#309 – Greta Thunberg

(2003)

Context – Greta Thunberg is an environmental activist, the 2019 TIME person of the year. Here is the four-and-a-half-minute speech she delivered at the 2019 U.N. climate action summit that has come to be known as "How dare you." This speech garnered her global popularity and went viral immediately. Thunberg helped to spark a climate movement within the younger generation.

"My message is that we'll be watching you. This is all wrong. I shouldn't be up here. I should be back in school on the other side of the ocean. Yet you all come to us young people for hope. How dare you!

You have stolen my dreams and my childhood with your empty words. And yet, I'm one of the lucky ones. People are suffering. People are dying. Entire ecosystems are collapsing. We are in the beginning of a mass extinction, and all you can talk about is money and fairy tales of eternal economic growth. How dare you!

For more than 30 years, the science has been crystal clear. How dare you continue to look away and come here saying that you're doing enough, when the politics and solutions needed are still nowhere in sight.

You say you hear us and that you understand the urgency. But no matter how sad and angry I am, I do not want to believe that. Because if you really understood the situation and still kept on failing to act, then you would be evil. And that I refuse to believe…"

Analysis – Oh, Greta! Go Greta! When I initially saw Thunberg deliver this speech, I was thrown that she was only sixteen years old. I no longer see her age. I am simply captivated by her messages. This speech is stinging, and she does not mince her words. Thunberg predicts that the summit will not deliver new plans to avoid catastrophic climate breakdown. "You have stolen my dreams and my childhood with your empty words," she says. Her words are heavy with emotion and fueled by anger. As President Donald Trump arrives at the summit to attend another speech, there is a famous photo of Thunberg giving him a hard stare of utter disgust.

Now eighteen years old, Thunberg has given dozens of speeches, led marches, and spoken at summits and conferences. She uses powerful, abrasive, blunt, scientific language in the hopes of inciting action. Below are excerpts from some of Thunberg's other talks that show her unwavering spirit, and all of them could be included in this list of 365 talks:

"Adults keep saying: 'We owe it to the young people to give them hope.' But I don't want your hope. I don't want you to be hopeful. I want you to panic. I want you to feel the fear I feel every day. And then I want you to act. I want you to act as you would in a crisis. I want you to act as if our house is on fire. Because it is."

- "Deforestation of our great rain forests, toxic air pollution, loss of insects and wildlife, these are all disastrous trends being accelerated by a way of life that we in our financially fortunate part of the world see as our right to simply carry on."

- "We should not be the ones who are fighting for the future, and yet, here we are. We will rise to the challenge. We will hold those who are most responsible for this crisis responsible, and we will make the world leaders act"

- "What I'm telling you to do is act because no one is too small to make a difference. See you on the streets."

- "Can you hear me? Is my microphone on? Is my English okay? Because I'm beginning to wonder."

- "I agree with you; I'm too young to do this. We children shouldn't have to do this. But since almost no one is doing anything, and our very future is at risk, we feel like we have to continue."

- "If you still say we are wasting valuable lesson time, then let me remind you that our political leaders have wasted decades through denial and inaction."

- "Where celebrities, film and pop stars who have stood up against all sorts of injustices will not stand up for our environment and climate justice because that would impact on their right to fly around the world visiting their favourite restaurants, beaches and yoga retreats."

Thunberg has had to be explicit that she writes her own speeches. There has been skepticism that she is being paid or has someone behind her forcing her into activism. Her parents were not climate activists, she said, until they were made aware of the situation. She is independent and represents herself.

I find her endearing, intriguing, intense and admirable. In August 2018, armed with just a sign, Thunberg went on strike from school and that was the beginning of many subsequent school strikes. Thunberg has been open about her Asperger's diagnosis. "Some people mock me for my diagnosis. But Asperger's is not a disease. It's a gift." I love that. For those who know anyone on the autism spectrum, including Asperger's, this is a beautiful way to view being on the spectrum. Some are simply born with a wise soul and can see the world as it is and see their role in making the world a better place. Some, like Thunberg are compelled to speak. Thunberg's sense of worldly duty is equivalent to eating and breathing, and she feels she must do it.

Check out the last line in her speech to the U.N. climate action summit; "We will not let you get away with this. Right here, right now, is where we draw the line. The world is waking up. And change is coming, whether you like it or not." Thunberg speaks so powerfully that people are compelled to listen. Where do I sign up?

Tip – No one is too small to make a difference and use their voice, so I'll see you on the streets of justice.

#308 – Brené Brown

(1965)

Context – Brené Brown is a professor, lecturer, author, and researcher. She has studied topics such as courage, vulnerability, empathy, and shame. Her 2011 TEDx Houston talk, "The Power of Vulnerability" has been watched 40 million times. In her 2019 one hour and 16-minute Netflix special, *The Call to Courage*, Brown discusses what it takes to choose courage over comfort in a culture defined by scarcity, fear and uncertainty. Below are some of the show's most powerful excerpts.

- *"…If your team isn't willing to create a culture that's vulnerable, it will become a team unable to create. It isn't that being brave might lead to failure; it's that being brave most certainly will lead to failure. But there's a catch. Feedback and criticism should be sought from those who value you because of your imperfections and assume you're doing the best you can, while feedback from those unwilling to get into the arena, to be brave, to be vulnerable, isn't worth a minute of your time. You cannot take criticism or feedback from people who are not being brave with their lives."*

- *"You spend half your time at work, and not being vulnerable will eat you alive. It's time to show up, be seen, and lean in."*

- *"First, some inspiration:*

    I'm going to live in the arena.

    I'm going to be brave with my life.

I'm gonna show up.

I'm going to take chances.

- *Second, a realization:*

Vulnerability is not about winning. It's not about losing. It's having the courage to show up when you can't control the outcome.

- *Third, a declaration:*

If you are not in the arena getting your ass kicked on occasion because you were being brave, I am not interested in or open to your feedback about my work. Period. You can't take feedback and criticism from those who are not brave with their lives. It will crush you."

Analysis – *The Call to Courage* is a funny, lighthearted, personal, and, yes, vulnerable documentary. It has one big message interspersed between its stories, lessons, and anecdotes. Her style is relatable yet substantial. Her message, "Today, I'll choose courage over comfort. I can't make commitments for tomorrow, but today I'm gonna choose to be brave, and I know what that means." Or, more succinctly, "Answer the call to courage."

Brown was invited to talk at TEDx Houston in 2011. When she asked the organizers what they would like her to talk about, they came back and said, "Whatever you want. Go crush it." Brown was on a return flight from a client trip in Maui. She had been helping her CEO clients understand the importance of vulnerability in their leadership roles. Houston bound she turned to her husband and announced that she would not do her usual talk with heavily laden statistics and data, but she would instead be consciously vulnerable. She had spent four days working with CEOs and asking them to be vulnerable. So, she had to put this into practice. It ended up being the worst talk she'd ever given. Although devastated at her performance, Brown's embarrassment was lessened by the fact that there were only a few hundred people in the audience, so she figured her poor performance would blow over. Then a video of her talk was posted on YouTube, and then it showed up on the TED website. She reassured herself that no one would watch the video, but she couldn't have been more wrong. One or two views suddenly turned into a million. Brown talks about having the worst vulnerability hangover imaginable. She began reading the hateful comments, which ranged from her appearance to death threats. In her angst, she poured herself into the tv show, *Downton Abbey* and her go-to snack, peanut butter and binge-watched all the episodes without moving from the sofa. When it was over, she continued to want to escape the real world, so she started googling the cast of *Downton Abbey* and who the president was during the era in which the show is set and so on. And it was while exploring this rabbit hole that she unearthed a speech from Theodore Roosevelt:

"…It is not the critic who counts; not the man who points out how the strong man stumbles or where the doer of deeds could have done them better. The credit belongs to the man who is actually in the arena, whose face is marred by dust and sweat and blood; who strives valiantly; who errs, who comes short again and again…who at the best knows, in the end, the triumph of high achievement, and who at the worst, if he fails, at least fails while daring greatly." *Theodore Roosevelt, The Man in the Arena, April 23, 1910.*

Brown talks about her life before discovering that quote and how it has changed her life since. If you're going to be brave with your life, and you choose to live in the arena, you *will* get your ass kicked. You *will* fail. You *will* need to choose courage over comfort because you are going to know failure.

I remember giving a talk about ten years ago to several hundred people at a gala event. The audience included my peers, clients, and my manager at the time. I completely bombed. I was standing on this grand stage while my audience dined on fine lunchables and sipped champagne, and my mind went fuzzy. I couldn't remember what I was supposed to be saying, I lost my place, and I was unable to recover. It was a living nightmare. I was a self-anointed public speaking expert, and I found myself on stage, exposed. I was utterly devasted. Oh boy, did I have some critics that day, but I didn't need them. I knew I'd screwed up and I didn't need any naysayers pointing this out to me. The criticism and feedback poured in that day, and it continued in the days and weeks that followed.

I remember thinking almost immediately that I needed that experience. That might sound bizarre, but I had been getting too comfortable. The butterflies had stopped flying in my stomach before giving a talk. I had started to prepare less and less for presentations. Since that day, every time I give a larger talk, I think back to that moment on the stage when I tanked. I don't do this to psych myself out but to remember that even though I speak frequently, and I continue to write about public speaking, that I too am infallible and can fail. Most of all, I'm do it to remind myself that I am turning up to live in the arena. And as Brown says in her documentary, "I want to be in the arena. I want to be brave with my life. And when we choose to dare greatly, we sign up to get our asses kicked. We can choose courage, or we can choose comfort, but we can't have both. Not at the same time."

Tip – Be prepared to fail and only accept feedback from those who are also risking it all and getting their asses kicked in the arena.

#307 – Roberto Benigni

(1952)

Context – 71st Academy Awards, Best Leading Actor and Best Foreign Language Film, Roberto Benigni who goes wild when he learns of the film's win.

Famously joyful after *Life is Beautiful* was announced as the Best Foreign Language Film, Benigni climbed over and then stood on the backs of the seats in front of him and applauded the audience before proceeding to the stage.

"This is a moment of joy! I want to dive into this ocean of generosity!"

Analysis – These are the words Benigni proclaims after climbing to the tops of the audience seats to get to the microphone on stage. You feel his abundant enthusiasm and joy. You do feel as though he is about to jump out of his skin. What you don't feel is someone afraid of expressing himself, someone who is nervous, someone who cares about what others think of him. What you sense is he is genuine and honest. I can't help but have a look at Sophia Loren in the background, too who is overcome with happiness for Benigni; hands at her mouth, tears streaming down her face. She feels it too and is overcome with genuine and heartfelt joy. See, when you are authentic and when you are speaking in front of a group, your audience will receive a wonderful gift, a portal into your emotions. Genuine emotion is contagious. If you choose to stand in front of a group and concern yourself about how you look, or how others perceive you, then you may end up wondering why you were not well received. Even if your audience can't quite put their finger on it, they can feel the incongruence between your words and your actions, and the result is a lack of trust. Yup, it becomes that serious. Your audience won't trust you if they can't consciously or unconsciously see a rhythm between what you're saying, your actions, and the emotion you are putting forward. It's like watching an infomercial on QVC or the Shopping Channel. The host will spew words in the hopes of selling the product, but very rarely can you feel that they believe in what they are selling. Can I prove it quantifiably? Nope. I can just feel it.

Tip – Allow your words and emotion to match authentically.

#306 – Duke Ellington and Irving Mills

1899–1974 and 1894–1985

Context – Duke Ellington sings "It Don't Mean a Thing" (1943). Lyrics by Irving Mills.

It don't mean a thing, if it ain't got that swing
(doo-ah, doo-ah, doo-ah, doo-ah, doo-ah, doo-ah, doo-ah, doo-ah, doo-ah)

It don't mean a thing all you got to do is sin
(doo-ah, doo-ah, doo-ah, doo-ah, doo-ah, doo-ah, doo-ah, doo-ah, doo-ah)
It makes no difference
If it's sweet or hot
Just give that rhythm

Everything you've got
It don't mean a thing, if it ain't got that swin
(doo-ah, doo-ah, doo-ah, doo-ah, doo-ah, doo-ah, doo-ah, doo-ah, doo-ah)
It don't mean a thing all you got to do is sing
(doo-ah, doo-ah, doo-ah, doo-ah, doo-ah, doo-ah, doo-ah, doo-ah, doo-ah)
It makes no difference
If it's sweet or hot
Just give that rhythm

Everything you've got

It don't mean a thing, if it ain't got that swing

(doo-ah, doo-ah, doo-ah, doo-ah, doo-ah, doo-ah, doo-ah, doo-ah, doo-ah)

It makes no difference

If it's sweet or hot

Just give that rhythm

Everything you've got

It don't mean a thing if it ain't got that swing

It don't mean a thing all you got to do is sing

(doo-ah)

It makes no difference

If it's sweet or hot

Just give that rhythm

Everything you've got

Don't mean a thing all you've gotta do is swing

It don't mean a thing all you've gotta do is sing

It makes no difference

If it's sweet or hot

Give that rhythm

Everything you've got

It don't mean a thing if it ain't got that swing

(doo-ah, dooooo-aaaaah)

Don't mean a thing

Analysis – Go ahead, sing along! It's okay, no one's watching so have some fun. (I've posted the lyrics for you too, but, come on, who doesn't already know them?). This may not be a talk in the traditional sense, but its message is transferable to giving a superb talk. I've spent some time doing curriculum design for a client. That's part of what I do. I talk to companies, hear what their desired results are and help them get there by conducting various workshops. So, I'm looking at the long list from one of my clients and I started the process of dissecting those pieces and putting them back together in a way that enables each team member to attain their vision and the organization's vision. It's a fun process, kind of like putting together a puzzle. What's difficult to translate, though, is what the environment will be in those workshops. The environment is one of those intangibles that can't be written down in the proposal, as it can only be experienced. Those workshops won't mean a thing if *I ain't got my swing*. Meaning, if I don't bring all of those 'intangibles with me; enthusiasm, passion, listening skills, storytelling, entertaining, humour, etc., then the entire series of workshops, won't mean a thing, 'cause it simply won't be digested by the participants.

Tip - It won't mean a thing, if you ain't got your swing.

#305 – Muhammad Ali

(1942)

Context – Ali said the below so many times it became his trademark speech.

"Float like a butterfly. Sting like a bee. Your hands can't hit what your eyes can't see."

Analysis – Well, let me just metaphorically throw out this punch. I am not suggesting that one needs to start boxing or fighting to execute a superb talk. If you do so then it'll likely be your final talk, and if it's your final talk, then there would be no need for my book. So, no boxing in the presentation room, please.

There are so many comparisons in those words with doing a great talk, and the reason it has hit my list of the *365 Must-Know Talks*. Ali's height and reach made headshots a better option than body shots. Ali developed a unique boxing style, which was aptly named the Ali shuffle and could be likened to a dance. He would rise and fall on the balls of his feet, floating like a butterfly, the sting of the headshot, hands at the ready, eye on the prize. I like the rhythm of these words as it relates to the importance of looking at your audience while doing a great presentation. Like Ali says, "your hands can't hit, what your eyes can't see" and in the presentation room, your words can't have an impact without your eyes observing every single participant in the room. Watch your audience. Are they yawning? Sleeping? If they are then that's not good at all! It's time for a break or to switch it up. Start getting your audience involved. Are they talking to their neighbour? Having a sidebar conversation? Then it's time to get up and move around the room. There's no rule that says you have to present at the front of the room next to your slides. I give you permission to stroll about the room; I dare you! The point is your barometer for how you are doing is in front of you while you're giving your presentation so watch your audience and react accordingly.

Tip – Watch your audience.

#304 – Temple Grandin

(1947)

Context – Temple Grandin, diagnosed with autism as a child gives a talk titled, "The World Needs All Kinds of Minds" at TED 2010.

Analysis – I am a huge fan of Temple Grandin. I've read the books, watched the 2010 movie by her name, and am compelled to watch whenever she is interviewed. I've also had the privilege of watching her in a presentation setting. I've been holding onto a bunch of talks so that I can reserve them 'til higher up on my countdown list of *365*

Must-Know Talks, but I just couldn't wait to share this one. This presentation is simply one of my favourites. One of the best that I've ever seen, and I would go so far as to say that it should be used to demonstrate how to do a superb presentation in workshops. I've certainly added it to my roster. Through a variety of experiences that are too plentiful to name here, Grandin learned how to navigate the world brilliantly. In this talk, she describes how her brain thinks differently than the neurotypical brain…and how that's actually a good thing! "The world needs people on the autism spectrum; visual thinkers, pattern thinkers, verbal thinkers, and all kinds of smart geeky kids." I say, "Hallelujah." I adore this talk. Grandin uses humour, fun, storytelling, pictures, clean and uncluttered slides, passion—all the ingredients needed for a superb talk—but what resonates most with me, is her message. Often, when a child and then an adult is different from the norm, we avoid, as we are afraid, and we are uncertain how to interact, so we don't. But what Grandin teaches us, not only in this talk but in all that she does, is that we are all massively different, unique individuals, and we should take a moment to thank the universe for that. I can assure you. I would not want to interact with a mirror image of myself as I navigate through life. What makes living interesting is our differences. The trick is to digest that notion in its truest form. It is not our differences that will divide us, but our inherent inability to recognize, accept and celebrate those differences. Remember that the next time you stand in front of an audience giving a talk. Your message should be able to cross over to all the wonderfully unique and different individuals looking at you.

Tip – Believe in your message, and your audience will believe in you.

#303 – Pyotr Ilyich Tchaikovsky

1840–1893

Context – "Dance of the Sugar Plum Fairy" in the 1940 film *Fantasia* was Disney's animated ode to classical music. Sparkling lights, fairies spreading their fairy dust in a mesmerizing dance that includes a magical awakening of various flowers coming alive with Tchaikovsky's Dance of the Sugar Plum Fairy musical classic offered as a lead character in the movie, *Fantasia*.

Analysis – I went to the Philharmonic Orchestra to hear my beloved Pyotr Ilyich Tchaikovsky at the Tchaikovsky festival. I feel like we know each other personally as I've spent so many hours listening to him that I've adopted a warmer and somewhat informal way of talking about him. There is something about this composer that allows me to tap into every single emotion I possess, all within an hour or two. I've chosen the above quote as it showcases Tchaikovsky's *The Nutcracker Suite* in *Fantasia*. If you've never seen it before, stop what you're doing and watch it! If you haven't seen it in a long time, I suggest taking a ten-minute break from whatever you are doing to refamiliarize yourself with it. It will sweep you away into another world. A vivid, magical one. (By the way, the mushrooms have always been my favourite part). So, what does Tchaikovsky, *The Nutcracker Suite*, and *Fantasia* have to do with presentations and doing talks? I don't think it would be a stretch to say there are great similarities between being a composer and being a presenter. The composer must sit down and artfully construct a piece, utilizing all of their being, creating a rise and fall in notes that will evoke strong emotion. It is true of being a presenter as well. I don't think many people sit back and really consider what it means to give a presentation artfully—one that elicits the same response to hearing a great song, or one that you'd happily listen to over and over again. Creating magic in a song must be a feat for the composer, and I know it takes patience, emotion, and diligence to do the same in a talk. So, my tip for you today is certainly the most challenging of all, put magic, charm, and fascination into your words while giving a talk, and your audience will be swept away.

Tip – Pepper a little magic into your talks.

#302 – Arthur Benjamin

(1961)

Context – Arthur Benjamin is an American mathematician who specializes in combinatorics (an area of mathematics primarily concerned with counting). In this 2005 TED Talk, "A Performance of 'Mathemagic'" Arthur races a team of calculators to solve massive mental equations.

"Good morning ladies and gentlemen. My name is Art Benjamin, and I am a 'mathemagician.' What that means is, I combine my loves of math and magic to do something I call 'mathemagics.'

Before I get started, I have a quick question for the audience. By any chance, did anyone happen to bring with them this morning a calculator? Seriously, if you have a calculator with you, raise your hand. Raise your hand. Did your hand go up? Now bring it out, bring it out. Anybody else? I see, I see one way in the back. You sir, that's three. And anybody on this side here? OK, over there on the aisle. Would the four of you please bring out your calculators, then join me up on stage. Let's give them a nice round of applause.

That's right. Now, since I haven't had the chance to work with these calculators, I need to make sure that they are all working properly. Would somebody get us started by giving us a two-digit number, please? How about a two-digit number?

Audience: *22*

AB: *And another two-digit number, sir?*

AB: *Multiply 22 times 47, make sure you get 1,034 or the calculators are not working.*
Do all of you get 1,034? 1,034?

Volunteer: *No*

AB: *594. Let's give three of them a nice round of applause there.*

Would you like to try a more standard calculator, just in case? OK, great. What I'm going to try and do then – I notice it took some of you a little bit of time to get your answer. That's OK. I'll give you a shortcut for multiplying even faster on the calculator. There is something called the square of a number, which most of you know is taking a number and multiplying it by itself. For instance, five squared would be?

Audience: *37*

AB: *37 squared, OK.*

Audience: *23.*

AB: *23 squared, OK."*

Analysis – What a lively, fun, and informative talk! A few years ago, I consciously stopped saying, "I'm awful at math." I believed that putting that out into the ether perpetuated the notion. Instead, I changed my narrative to, "I simply wasn't taught the basics of math very well in my formative years." Now, I'm not prepared to push all of my past insecurities around numbers onto my elementary, junior and high school teachers, but I do believe that had any one of them tried to find my learning style and worked with that, then calculus, algebra and quantum physics wouldn't have been such a monumentally daunting task. If they had ignited a passion within me to find out more, to learn more, to try and fail, I wouldn't have been plagued by my weaknesses surrounding math. I saw a PBS documentary several years ago that turned it all around for me. I remember it vividly as it talked about quite challenging (well, for me anyway) formulas and various math problems (like the popular $E=MC^2$), but I watched the entire two hours and I understood how they arrived at their answers because the information was presented in my learning style. There are as many learning styles models as there are behavioural analysis models (i.e., Myers Briggs, DiSC, EQ, Firo B, HBDI) but I've always liked the simple one based on Fleming's VARK model:

1. Visual learners think in pictures, visual aids, diagrams, handouts etc.

2. Auditory learners learn through listening; lectures, discussions, tapes, etc.

3. Reading/writing preference learners learn through introspective reading and writing exercises.

4. Tactile learners and kinesthetic learners learn via experience – moving, touching, and doing.

All teachers (and presenters and speakers are teachers) must tap into each learning style throughout their time in front of a group. Most people are a combination of learning styles. I'm a visual/auditory learner and occasionally tactile/reading learner depending on the topic. What my teachers didn't do was tackle these difficult concepts by painting a picture of why we were learning the stuff we were learning. What the documentary did for me was go through a history of the individuals that came up with the formulas and explained why they constructed the formulas the way that they did. It gave me a 'macro' scope on why we were messing about with the numbers anyway. I needed that. I need a macro picture on pretty much any topic before I can go micro, and I find it very difficult to go vice versa.

I enjoyed the above link by Arthur Benjamin because he included all of the four learning styles in his presentation, and this is why I was able to understand it. Recognize too that your learning style will most likely be different to your audience members. Always include elements from all four learning styles in your talks.

Tip – Take tough concepts and make them easy to learn by including all four learning styles.

#301 – Jiddu Krishnamurti

1895–1986

Context – Born in South India, Jiddu Krishnamurti was a philosopher, speaker and writer. *Think on These Things* is a compilation of material contained into volumes. The book was originally presented in the form of talks to students, teachers and parents in India. In it, Krishnamurti examines culture, education, religion, politics and tradition. He also explores emotions such as ambition, greed and envy, security and power. As author and aviator Anne Marrow Lindbergh said, "To listen to him or to read his thoughts is to face oneself and the world with an astonishing morning freshness."

"The highest form of human intelligence is to observe yourself without judgement."

Analysis – The average person thinks sixty-thousand thoughts per day. Ninety-five percent, unfortunately, are the same thoughts as yesterday. How you talk to yourself is more important than you think. Not good enough? Not successful enough? Not a good speaker? How does having these thoughts impact our reality? Is there a correlation between our internal dialogue and our external reality?

Krishnamurti, the great Indian philosopher, said, "the highest form of human intelligence is the ability to observe yourself and not judge yourself." As you read this, I encourage you to observe yourself without judgement to unlock areas in your internal dialogue that are prohibiting you from doing what you want to do in your career and in the presentations that you've been asked to do.

Take a moment right now to jot down three thoughts you've had today. Any three thoughts. Now, jot down one time you can think of in your life that you set a goal for yourself and accomplished it. Write it down. Come on, I see you wavering on pulling out a piece of paper and finding a pen. You've taken the time to pick up my book, and it will only take a minute to do this exercise. Good. Now put this note aside as we'll reference it later.

Your thoughts create your future; your now. Your internal pep talk is far more critical than you may think. By taking responsibility for yourself and your thinking process, you can make your life more positive and uplifting and reduce or negate the influence of any negative energy you may encounter.

To help navigate my internal pep talk, I constructed five ideas or ways to improve being more conscious of this process. Today I'll unfold one of them. Perhaps it will help you too.

#1. Understand the emotional brain and not the anatomy of your brain.

I was once trying to figure out how to work the new stereo I got for my office when I finally pulled out the instruction manual. I read it line by line, and poof, several hours had passed by before I realized I finally had the stereo figured out. I invested the time because I wanted it to work but also because I had spent a good amount of money on it. A thought came to me as I was doing this, we often don't spend even an eighth the amount of time trying to unlock the instructions for our brain. The more complicated and expensive the equipment, the more carefully we study the instruction manual. If we could put a price on our brains, it would likely be the most expensive piece of hardware that we possess.

After birth, your brain nerve cells no longer divide (with few exceptions). So, you have the brain that, in essence, you were born with. Do you assume then that your brain was already working properly all on its own fro the moment you were born? I suggest not. You must learn how to use your brain and for what purposes. Your brain is malleable to a great degree, even in adulthood. I am not a scientist doing brain research or even close to this, but I have studied the brain in some detail. Many scientists would have us believe that the amygdala is the source of fear, the hippocampus is the source of learning, the cerebral cortex is the source of thinking, and so on. I suggest that if you've heard of any of this stuff, you could promptly disregard it as an essential part of your internal dialogue or internal pep talk.

I was reading a book on the brain the other day and it struck me how important it is to at least look at the fundamentals of the brain physiology to understand our internal dialogue. There are no genes for laziness, intelligence, melancholy, addiction, or egotism. Indeed, there may exist a character predisposition or specific vulnerabilities to some of the ills in our lives but there are no specific genes.

Our internal dialogue, or how we talk to ourselves, cannot be found in physical brain matter but rather in the spaces in between. For example, we've heard of right-brain vs. left-brain thinking. Right being creative, left being more analytical. These centers can't be touched; they simply are. To start the process of changing how we talk to ourselves we must first become aware. Consider your brain as an emotionally intelligent centre for all you do, including giving a talk. Everything you do starts from this vantage point.

We should be kind and honest when we talk to ourselves and we should be peaceful, particularly as we prepare to give a talk. Our pep-talk should bolster enthusiasm and our morale, and not bring us down. If our pep talk is horrid, how can we expect our outward being to be anything different? That said, who wants to listen to a speaker who is struggling with a negative internal dialogue? No one.

Now, go back to the three thoughts that you wrote down. Would you consider them to be disposable or garbage? How about the goal that you set for yourself and accomplished? How was that one different? More often than not, it is a matter of our internal pep talk. We are often less kind to our internal psyche than we would be to our own worst enemy. Next time you catch yourself judging too harshly or thinking negative thoughts, stop and remember to be conscious of your internal dialogue well before you take the presentation stage.

Tip – Be mindful of your internal dialogue before you step foot on the stage.

#300 – Jesse Owens 1913–1980

Context – Jesse Owens has said the below quote far too many times to cite just one place.

"We all have dreams. But in order to make dreams come into reality, it takes an awful lot of determination, dedication, self-discipline and effort."

Analysis – Owens was a part of the 1936 Olympic games held in Berlin, Germany during the reign of the dictator Aldolf Hitler who intended to make use of the games to underline the superiority of the Aryan race. Owens was an American sprinter. After Owens won four gold medals during those Olympic games, Hitler stayed true to his promise and apparently refused to shake Owens' hand. Owens responded to the media buzz around this by saying he hadn't been invited to shake the American President's hand either (he finally got the opportunity to do so in 1976). Owens showed a strong strength of character in his refusal to let Hitler, or any racists get him down during what was an incredible period in his life.

I really do love Owens' quote, and he didn't simply spew them; he lived them. Owens worked three jobs while he attended University and trained for the Olympics! It was amazing how so many people today talk about how busy they are. Jesse was busy! Executing a superb talk is similar to being a great athlete. Many of the ingredients are the same: determination, dedication, self-discipline, and effort. Owens would never have reached the Olympics without all of those ingredients. He wouldn't have dreamed of showing up at the starting line without years of practice and an awful lot of training. So too is the life of the superb presenter.

Tip – Remember the ingredients: determination, dedication, self-discipline and effort.

#299 – Bobby McFerrin (1950)

Context – Bobby McFerrin hacks your brain with music at the World Science Festival 2009 with "Notes & Neurons: In Search of a Common Chorus."

"Talking about expectations, expectations. What is interesting to me about that, regardless of where I'm at, anywhere, every audience gets that. It doesn't matter, it's the pentatonic scale."

Analysis – In his fun, three-minute performance from the World Science Festival, musician Bobby McFerrin (you know, the guy who sang "Don't Worry, Be Happy") uses the pentatonic scale to reveal a surprising result of how our brains are wired. A pentatonic scale is a musical scale with five pitches per octave, in contrast to a heptatonic or seven-note scale such as the major scale and minor scale. Whew! Not up on your music theory? The pentatonic scales were developed by many civilizations and are still used, the bagpipes are a great illustration of the pentatonic scale, as is most jazz, blues, and Celtic music.

The first time I saw this presentation, I was intrigued because there are so many messages that you can extract from it from a presentation perspective:

- the use of non-verbal behaviours
- how rhythm is embedded in each of us
- harmonization with your audience
- setting audience expectations that they will meet and exceed
- how we must remember that the human mind is playful and creative

However, the message or tip that really resonates with me is how music can unite a crowd. Are you using music in your presentations? If not, why not? Music is a much-overlooked component of a great talk. Music not only connects you to your audience but can also help to connect your audience members to one another. Now that is an experience.

Tip – The crowd can be your presentation instrument.

#298 – Tom Wujec

(1959)

Context – From Tom Wujec's talk titled, "The Three Ways the Brain Creates Meaning."

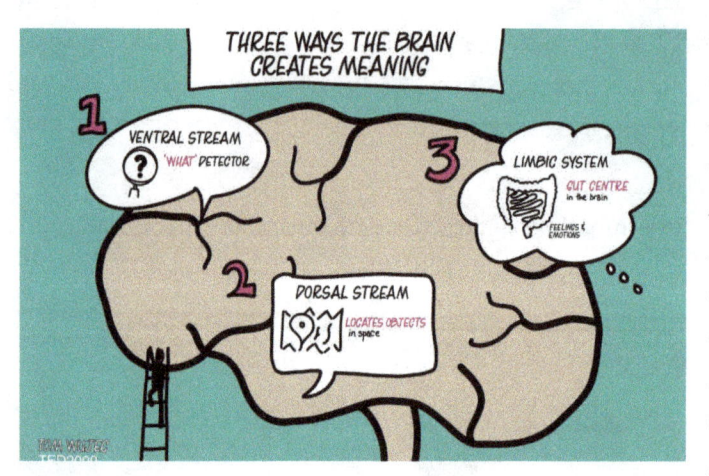

"Last year at TED we aimed to try to clarify the overwhelming complexity and richness that we experience at the conference in a project called Big Viz. And the Big Viz is a collection of 650 sketches that were made by two visual artists. David Sibbet from The Grove, and Kevin Richards, from Autodesk, made 650 sketches that strive to capture the essence of each presenter's ideas. And the consensus was: it really worked. These sketches brought to life the key ideas, the portraits, the magic moments that we all experienced last year.

"This year we were thinking, "Why does it work?" What is it about animation, graphics, illustrations, that create meaning? And this is an important question to ask and answer because the more we understand how the brain creates meaning, the better we can communicate, and, I also think, the better we can think and collaborate together. So, this year we're going to visualize how the brain visualizes.

"Cognitive psychologists now tell us that the brain doesn't actually see the world as it is, but instead, creates a series of mental models through a collection of "Ah-ha moments," or moments of discovery, through various processes."

Analysis – I selected this talk not because Wujec is an incredible speaker—he's got a long way to go on that goal—but because his talk has such engaging content. This is the first time I'm picking content over delivery and it will, most likely, be my last. Great talks are all about the delivery. However, this talk is valuable enough to include here even when the speaker has difficulty translating. We're several entries in now so, once you have watched the clip, how do you think Wujec could've improved his delivery? How is the cadence and speed of his voice? Is he making sure his audience is picking up the concepts? What else do you see that could use improvement? Start the process of harnessing some of what you've been learning and practice the art of feedback.

I like this talk because it delves deeper into utilizing images (animation, pictures, graphics, etc.) into talks and presentations. But we should be conscious of *how* we use images. Wujec talks about areas of the brain that are targeted when viewing an image, which is quite interesting:

1. Ventral Stream – the *What?* detector (i.e., the book)

2. Dorsal Stream – locates object in physical space (i.e., the book is on the shelf)

3. Limbic System – feels (i.e., I love that book)

While this is a good conversations starter for the next cocktail party, it doesn't tell me what or how I should manipulate images so they are more effective. What Wujec does show is a strategic vision session —Managers in a room with Post-it notes, creating a vision for their organization. Later, we'll discuss a topic called mind-mapping, which is another useful image tool in the presenter's tool kit. By getting bums up and out of their chairs, Wujec hits the three main components of using an image effectively:

- Use images to clarify ideas.

- Make images interactive so that the audience can engage more fully.

- Augment memory by creating a visual persistence.

Tip – Use images and make them meaningful.

#297 – Susan Blackmore

(1951)

Context – Susan Blackmore, is a writer, lecturer and broadcaster. In this talk entitled "Memes and Temes" Blackmore explores memes and what she believes is a new form called a "teme."

"Cultural evolution is a dangerous child for any species to let loose on its planet. By the time you realize what's happening, the child is a toddler, up and causing havoc, and it's too late to put it back. We humans are Earth's Pandoran species. We're the ones who let the second replicator out of its box, and we can't push it back in. We're seeing the consequences all around us.

Now that, I suggest, is the view that comes out of taking memetics seriously. And it gives us a new way of thinking about not only what's going on on our planet, but what might be going on elsewhere in the cosmos. So first of all, I'd like to say something about memetics and the theory of memes, and secondly, how this might answer questions about who's out there, if indeed anyone is.

So, memetics: memetics is founded on the principle of Universal Darwinism. Darwin had this amazing idea. Indeed, some people say it's the best idea anybody ever had. Isn't that a wonderful thought, that there could be such a thing as a best idea anybody ever had? Do you think there could? Audience: No. Someone says no, very loudly, from over there. Well, I say yes, and if there is, I give the prize to Darwin.

Why? Because the idea was so simple, and yet it explains all design in the universe. I would say not just biological design, but all of the design that we think of as human design. It's all just the same thing happening.

What did Darwin say? I know you know the idea, natural selection, but let me just paraphrase "The Origin of Species," 1859, in a few sentences.

What Darwin said was something like this: if you have creatures that vary, and that can't be doubted—I've been to the Galapagos, and I've measured the size of the beaks and the size of the turtle shells and so on, and so on. And 100 pages later. (Laughter) And if there is a struggle for life, such that nearly all of these creatures die—and this can't be doubted, I've read Malthus and I've calculated how long it would take for elephants to cover the whole world if they bred unrestricted, and so on and so on. And another 100 pages later. And if the very few that survive pass onto their offspring whatever it was that helped them survive, then those offspring must be better adapted to the circumstances in which all this happened than their parents were.

You see the idea? If, if, if, then. He had no concept of the idea of an algorithm, but that's what he described in that book, and this is what we now know as the evolutionary algorithm. The principle is you just need those three things -- variation, selection and heredity. And as Dan Dennett puts it, if you have those, then you must get evolution. Or design out of chaos, without the aid of mind..."

Analysis – I'm certainly not a conspiracy theorist, nor will I admit or deny whether there is such a thing as Darwinism (yup, surprise, surprise I've got some opinions on that too, but this is not the time nor place to get into all that jazz). What is fantastic about this talk is the fervor with which Blackmore communicates. It's palpable. It's wickedly interesting, whether you agree or disagree with Blackmore and her theories, I'd imagine that individuals would be vehement either way. From a presentation perspective, watch Blackmore's body language, and in particular, her hands and arms. She is one of the best examples I've seen in a while of what I call, moving with purpose. It is what happens when you're in the zone—that sweet spot when you hit your groove while giving a presentation. Blackmore is so engrossed in what she is communicating, I'd bet she has no idea the amount her arms are moving and naturally punctuating her every thought. It's not distracting because it's authentic. It's a thing of beauty (at least for those of us who teach the art of presentation skills) to observe. When you see someone punctuating their thoughts, utilizing their body in some capacity (some walk and punctuate), it signals their deep desire to translate their ideas to their audience. This only comes when you are engrossed in your topic. If you want to see the opposite of moving with purpose, observe pretty much any politician. Bill Clinton comes to mind with fingers folded into his palm, thumb laying on top, and that whole mess is pumping up in the air, or more accurately, in front of him. It is so unnatural. Clearly, he has been coached to do this—to not point is my guess. But it comes across as disingenuous and distracting. That thumb pumping he does—Obama and Bush had the same coaches. Thank goodness our Canadian politicians don't hire the same public speaking consultants—if you are giving a talk and don't punctuate a thought with authenticity (such as the case with thumb pumping), your audience will know that something is off, which for me translates into a lack of trust. Yup, it's that big. So, let your body move naturally while giving presentations, and your audience will digest your message.

Tip – Allow your body to move naturally while giving a talk.

#296 – Ben Affleck and Matt Damon

(1972 and 1970)

Context – Affleck and Damon's 2008 Academy Award acceptance speech on winning an Academy Award for *Good Will Hunting*.

"I just said to Matt, losing would suck and winning would be really scary. It's really, really scary. We're just really two young guys who were fortunate enough to be involved with a lot of great people whom it's incumbent upon us – there's no way we're doing this in less than twenty seconds – upon whom it's incumbent of us to thank. Harvey Weinstein, who believed in us and made this movie. Gus Van Sant, for brilliant direction. Robin Williams, who delivered such great lines. Minnie Driver, whose performance was brilliant. Stellan Skarsgard, who was great. (Your brother.) My brother Casey, who's brilliant in the movie. (Cole Hauser.) Cole Hauser. My mother (Jon Gordon) and Matt's mother, (my mom) the most beautiful women here. (My dad right over there. Jack said hi to you. Alright!) Shhh... (Jon Gordon from Miramax.) Jon Gordon. Chris Moore (Chris Moore!), who produced the movie (Chris Moore!). Patrick Whitesell, the best agent in Hollywood! (Yeah! Patrick Whitesell!) And Cuba Gooding, for showing us how to give [an] alright acceptance speech! (All our friends and family! And everybody back in Boston watching us tonight!) And thank you so much to the city of Boston... And I know we're forgetting somebody. (Whoever we forgot we love you! We love you!) Thank you! Thank you so much!"

Analysis – I'm not going to go into a long diatribe about what makes this speech such a joy to watch. It comes down to one simple notion, speak from your heart, and your audience will experience what you are experiencing. They talk over one another, they shout out names, they don't follow any kind of script. But you know what? The audience couldn't care less because the speech is so genuine, and so heartfelt; you feel what they are feeling. Remember this, particularly if you have the opportunity to give a speech of acceptance..

Tip – Speak from your heart.

#295 – Gloria Steinem

(1934)

Context – This motto appeared in 1977 on T-shirts distributed by *Ms.* magazine and is attributed to Gloria Steinem.

"A woman without a man is like a fish without a bicycle."

Analysis – I don't believe this statement at all. I find it brash. That said, I was born in 1971, so was a teenager and young woman in the late 80s early 90s, which was a *very* different time to what my mother's generation contended with as it relates to the Women's Liberation Movement. For many of the women's libbers of the day, a little brashness was required, so I don't begrudge the statement one bit because it was appropriate, for the times. A woman needs a man like a fish needs a bicycle is another way of framing this quote. Of course, one doesn't need a man or vice versa, and one person can certainly not *complete* another, but to share your life with someone can make life's journey more enjoyable ☺.

Okay, enough of the politics and my view on all that. Let's discuss this statement as it relates to doing a talk or a presentation. Be bold and daring in your statements. Presenters who aren't wishy-washy and make bold statements—with the caveat that they are not downright degrading, inciting hate, or belligerent—are interesting and informative speakers. Even if you find yourself in the audience flagrantly disagreeing, if the presenter has evoked emotion within you and has charged you with thinking then they are doing something right. Yes, I said, thinking. Often, we sit in a presentation, checking the clock, and desperately counting down the hours, minutes, and seconds until we can be excused…kind of like school. Speak on topics that are interesting to you and that evoke strong emotions within the bowels of your being. Be bold; be daring and your audience will listen.

Tip – Be bold. Be daring. Your audience will listen.

#294 – James Cameron

(1954)

Context – James Cameron's 2010 TED presentation, "Before Avatar…a curious boy."

"I grew up on a steady diet of science fiction. In high school, I took a bus to school an hour each way every day. And I was always absorbed in a book, science fiction book, which took my mind to other worlds, and satisfied, in a narrative form, this insatiable sense of curiosity that I had.

"And, you know, that curiosity also manifested itself in the fact that whenever I wasn't in school, I was out in the woods, hiking and taking "samples" – frogs and snakes and bugs and pond water – and bringing it back, looking at it under the microscope. You know, I was a real science geek. But it was all about trying to understand the world, understand the limits of possibility.

"And my love of science fiction actually seemed mirrored in the world around me, because what was happening, this was in the late '60s, we were going to the moon, we were exploring the deep oceans. Jacques Cousteau was coming into our living rooms with his amazing specials that showed us animals and places and a wondrous world that we could never really have previously imagined. So, that seemed to resonate with the whole science fiction part of it.

"And I was an artist. I could draw. I could paint. And I found that because there weren't video games and this saturation of CG movies and all of this imagery in the media landscape, I had to create these images in my head. You know, we all did, as kids having to read a book, and through the author's description, put something on the movie screen in our heads. And so, my response to this was to paint, to draw alien creatures, alien worlds, robots, spaceships, all that stuff. I was endlessly getting busted in math class doodling behind the textbook. That was – the creativity had to find its outlet somehow…"

Analysis – We are all born with a deep curiosity. A baby will explore and explore and learn and learn. They become little scientists and experiment with everyone and everything in their environment. But sadly, we are coached out of this natural desire as we grow. Questions like, 'Why are we here? Or 'Why was I born?' are cute and fun when asked by a five-year-old child but these questions can become monumentally more complex to answer when being asked by an adult. It's one of the reasons I love Leonardo da Vinci. The famous Italian artist and engineer once said that *curiosita* or having an insatiable appetite for curiosity was the key to life, and I couldn't agree more. As we progress towards the #1 spot on this list of *365 Must-Know Talks* you'll read more and more about da Vinci.

This TED Talk by James Cameron is horrible. If you watch the talk, you'll see he's arrogant and boring. The camera pans the audience, and they're bored. Although if you read the above excerpt, you may not pick up on that, as the words are decent enough. I picked this talk, however, because *Avatar*, Cameron's gazillion-dollar movie, was incredibly popular at the time (especially at the Oscar's that year) and was brimming with newness. The movie contained new technology, new concepts, new everything, all fueled by curiosity. Without Cameron's curiosity the film would never have been made. Had Cameron not been interested in all the books and science fiction literature that he discusses in this talk; the film wouldn't have been possible. Think about all the presentations that you can jazz up with just a bit of curiosity. Think about that sales presentation, that marketing presentation, that whatever presentation you're currently preparing for. Sit back, close your eyes and open your mind, open your spirit to being curious and see what direction that will take you. You may be sitting on a gold mine.

Tip – Be curious and encourage curiosity in your audience.

#293 – Matthieu Ricard

(1946)

Context – In "The Habits of Happiness" TED Talk in 2004 Mathieu Ricard's answers the question, "What is happiness?"

"So, I guess it is a result of globalization that you can find Coca-Cola tins on top of Everest and a Buddhist monk in Monterey.

And so I just came, two days ago, from the Himalayas to your kind invitation. So, I would like to invite you, also, for a while, to the Himalayas themselves. And to show the place where meditators, like me, who began with being a molecular biologist in Pasteur Institute, and found their way to the mountains.

So, these are a few images I was lucky to take and be there. There's Mount Kailash in Eastern Tibet – wonderful setting. This is from Marlboro country.

This is a turquoise lake. A meditator. This is the hottest day of the year somewhere in Eastern Tibet, on August 1. And the night before, we camped, and my Tibetan friends said, "We are going to sleep outside." And I said, "Why? We have enough space in the tent." They said, "Yes, but it's summertime."

So now, we are going to speak of happiness. As a Frenchman, I must say that there are a lot of French intellectuals that think happiness is not at all interesting.

I just wrote an essay on happiness, and there was a controversy. And someone wrote an article saying, "Don't impose on us the dirty work of happiness."

We don't care about being happy. We need to live with passion. We like the ups and downs of life. We like our suffering because it's so good when it ceases for a while…."

Analysis – Matthieu Ricard is fantastic! Funny and happy. He emanates joy from every pore of his body. Let's not confuse funny and happy with unbounded enthusiasm as the two aren't mutually exclusive, although they may fall into one another's lap. But true happiness looks like Ricard. Calm, confident, at peace, and wrapped up in a bundle of energy. I've been preparing for a bunch of upcoming workshops myself, throw in personal commitments, some wickedly tight timelines, and as I sat down to work tonight, my shoulders found familiar territory—clenching and making their way up to my ears! So, as I watched Ricard and closed out my day, it is a firm reminder that stress in any form is futile energy. Happiness is a decision, not a destination. So, I've made the decision tonight to remove those stressors that were tensing up my shoulders and taking the brunt of my burden. My mentor always told me, you teach what you need to learn, and today is no exception.

Pour true and authentic happiness into your next talk. Your audience will be enveloped by it and will want to hear more.

Tip – Emanate joy and happiness.

#292 – Stuart Brown

Context – Stuart Brown's TED Talk "Play is More Than Fun" was delivered in 2008 and links play to human development and intelligence.

"If its purpose is more important than the act of doing it then it is probably not play."

Analysis – Stuart Brown is one helluva storyteller! He's composed, and has a relaxed presentation style, that comes from a wealth of experience and many hours standing in front of a group. I find Brown mesmerizing to watch, and very intriguing. He walks the stage to and fro; it's natural. The content of his talk is exciting for me too. As adults, we often lose the art of play. In our day-to-day lives we are coached out of the foundations of play: curiosity, exploration, and imagination. Think back to the last time you read something or did something out of sheer curiosity or exploration with no hidden agendas, but simply because you were intrigued—can you recall? When was the last time you daydreamed? The more you allow yourself the freedom to play as you navigate your interests, the more fulfilled and recharged you will feel.

Weave play into your presentations. I'm looking at my bookshelf right now, and there is one called *Games Trainers Play* that is dog eared, ripped, and covered in tags and Post-It Notes. The book is at least 13 or 14 years old and feels like an old friend. I can tell you what is on page 65 (a fun ESP icebreaker that I've used a gazillion times before and that always elicits great laughter), or on page 209, which is ripped from its original home and tucked behind the cover (a listening game that uses a newspaper clipping) and more.... I'm not kidding, and I haven't even cracked it. I just know it that well. I had been a participant in a few workshops that included many games to bring levity to the room after a long, difficult section. I saw early on the magic of play and always include it in my presentations. So, I speak from experience when I suggest you do the same.

Tip – Use play in your talks.

#291 – Jacinda Ardern

(1980)

Context – On March 15, 2019, an Australian man walked into the Al-Noor Mosque in Christchurch, New Zealand and began shooting at the congregation with a semi-automatic rifle. He massacred 50 people. In the aftermath of the shooting, Prime Minister Jacinda Arden provided comfort to the Muslim community, the city of Christchurch and the nation in an address to New Zealand parliament. In this speech, she promised that the country's gun laws would change, and they did.

"I wish to make a ministerial statement relating to the Christchurch mosques terror attacks.

Assalam alaikum (translation: peace be upon you), peace be upon you, and peace be upon all of us.

The 15th of March will now be forever a day etched in our collective memories. On a quiet Friday afternoon, a man stormed into a place of peaceful worship and took away the lives of 50 people. That quiet Friday afternoon has become our darkest of days. But for the families, it was more than that. It was the day that the simple act of prayer, practising their Muslim faith and religion, led to the loss of their loved ones' lives. Those loved ones were brothers, daughters, fathers, and children. They were New Zealanders. They are us. And because they are us, we, as a nation, we mourn them. We feel a huge duty of care to them, and we have so much we feel the need to say and to do.

We walk with you.

One of the roles I never anticipated having—and hoped never to have—was to voice the grief of a nation At this time, it has been second only to securing the care of those affected and the safety of everyone. In this role, I wanted to speak directly to the families. We cannot know your grief, but we can walk with you at every stage. We can and will surround you with aroha, manaakitanga, and all that makes us, us. Our hearts are heavy, but our spirit is strong.

…He will remain nameless.

There is one person at the centre of this terror attack against our Muslim community in New Zealand. A 28-year-old man, an Australian citizen, has been charged with one count of murder; other charges will follow. He will face the full force of the law in New Zealand. The families of the fallen will have justice. He sought many things from his act of terror, but one was notoriety, and that is why you will never hear me mention his name. He is a terrorist, he is a criminal, he is an extremist, but he will, when I speak, be nameless, and to others, I implore you: speak the names of those who were lost rather than the name of the man who took them. He may have sought notoriety, but we in New Zealand will give him nothing—not even his name.

We will also look at the role social media played and what steps we can take, including on the international stage and in unison with our partners. There is no question that ideas and language of division and hate have existed for decades, but their form of distribution, the tools of organization—they are new. We cannot simply sit back and accept that these platforms just exist and that what is said on them is not the responsibility of the place where they are published. They are the publisher, not just the postman. There cannot be a case of all profit, no responsibility."

Analysis – World leaders should take note; this is how a competent leader deals with a crisis. Ardern immediately implemented swift practical new gun legislation, showed empathy for the survivors, and refused to tolerate anti-Islamic rhetoric. I am a massive fan of Ardern. Imagine a world leader who is not robotic but authentic. Imagine a world leader who is so authentic that she can deeply hug those in mourning without a shred of self-consciousness as she too is mourning. Unfortunately, her response is rare and unfamiliar.

Ardern wore the hijab post-event as a symbol of solidarity and said, "If in wearing the hijab as I did gave them a sense of security to continue to practice their faith, then I'm very pleased I did." Many people in New Zealand followed Ardern's lead and wore the hijab, and public support on the streets and schools followed. You see, Ardern set the tone with her words and actions as if to say, "This is how we behave here; we love one another, and we cry and empathize when part of our community is hurting." Beyond her behaviour is the fact that she changed gun legislation. No lip service, no parliamentary nonsense of arguing parties making any legislation impossible to garner support. Nope, she just set out what she planned to do and then did it.

In a world where governments in Europe and in the United States are either brazenly anti-Muslim and xenophobic or at best silent on the matter of immigration and Islam, Ardern's response was comprehensive, well thought out and genuine. She is a moral politician with a no-frills leadership style.

My favourite part of Ardern's speech to parliament is when she vows never to say the gunman's name. "He is a terrorist, he is a criminal, he is an extremist, but he will, when I speak, be nameless, and to others, I implore you: speak the names of those who were lost rather than the name of the man who took them." The gunman's desire for attention was made clear in a manifesto sent to Ardern's office and others before the massacre. While he may have sought notoriety, Ardern made sure that in New Zealand and beyond he was given nothing—not least his name.

Tip – If asked to give a talk in the wake of a tragedy, be swift, be empathetic, be action-oriented, be authentic and honest, but above all else, follow through and deliver on your promises.

#290 – Gary Vaynerchuk

(1975)

Context – Gary Vaynerchuk's talk "Gary Vaynerchuk: Building Personal Brand Within the Social Media Landscape - Web 2.0 Expo NY.

"Hey, so first and foremost, I really want to thank everyone, this is outrageous and humbling, every single person that is here, since you are here, there is no doubt in my mind that you are going to kill it. This is what I want to talk about today, PP. Patience and Passion. Passion, there is way too many people doing what they hate, stop doing that. There is no reason in 2008 to do shit you hate, none. Promise me you won't. Because you can lose just as much money being happy as hell. Clap that off cause it's the real shit…"

Analysis – Too much! Oh, way too much! I picked this speech with the assumption that it was picked for the book, not because it is brilliant, but because it's worth considering that the point of doing a fantastic talk is to translate your message so that your audience cannot only hear it but digest it—Vaynerchuk's message is a fantastic one, but his delivery overshadows it, and his onstage persona becomes the main focus. I watched the video a few times, and I find it disturbing. Vaynerchuk describes himself as "a loud, obnoxious, east coast guy." I know he's making fun of himself because he's created an onstage character. There are times that I don't mind his delivery—when he is being more himself—but every few seconds, that loud, obnoxious guy rears his head once again. At the beginning, a woman introduces Vaynerchuk and begins exiting the stage as he enters. She asks him a question, "you don't want this do you?" referencing the microphone she is trying to give him, and he all but ignores her. You know what, I know exactly why that happened. Vaynerchuk was hyper-focused and perhaps a little nervous. Many might watch this and say, "Oh, he's not nervous, just the opposite, he looks confident." But nerves play out in different ways for different people, and some hide their nerves by enveloping themselves in a character and taking on a role but the character he's manifested in this talk is rather difficult to listen to for an extended time.

I have followed Gary since this talk, as he has grown tremendously as a speaker and shows less of the "loud, obnoxious, east coast guy" and more of himself. A terrific lesson that we are all growing and evolving as people and as speakers.

Tip – Don't put on an act. Just be.

#289 – Tim Urban

1981

Context – In his 2016 TED Talk, Ted Urban, a writer, and blogger, talks about the instant gratification monkey in a talk entitled, "Inside the Mind of a Master Procrastination."

"So, in college, I was a government major, which means I had to write a lot of papers. When a normal student writes a paper, they might spread the work out a little like this. So, you know, you get started maybe a little slowly, but you get enough done in the first week that, with some heavier days, later on, everything gets done, things stay civil.

And I would want to do that like that. That would be the plan. I would have it ready to go, but then, actually, the paper would come along, and then I would kind of do this. (Here, Urban references a chart that tracked the work needed per day until the paper is due.)

And that would happen every single paper.

But then came my 90-page senior thesis, a paper you're supposed to spend a year on. And I knew for a paper like that, my normal workflow was not an option. It was way too big a project. So, I planned things out, and I decided I kind of had to go something like this (Urban again references a chart tracking the work per day toward the thesis due date). *This is how the year would go. So, I'd start off light, and I'd bump it up in the middle months, and then at the end, I would kick it up into high gear just like a little staircase. How hard could it be to walk up the stairs? No big deal, right?*

But then, the funniest thing happened. Those first few months? They came and went, and I couldn't quite do stuff. So, we had an awesome new revised plan.

And then…
(Here, Urban references the same chart with a revised new plan with more condensed timelines.)

But then those middle months actually went by, and I didn't really write words, and so we were here (chart shows even tighter timelines to get the thesis done). And then two months turned into one month, which turned into two weeks. And one day I woke up with three days until the deadline, still not having written a word, and so I did the only thing I could: I wrote 90 pages over 72 hours, pulling not one, but two all-nighters—humans are not supposed to pull two all-nighters—sprinted across campus, dove in slow motion, and got it in just at the deadline.

I thought that was the end of everything. But a week later, I get a call, and it's the school. And they say, 'Is this Tim Urban?' And I say, 'Yeah.' And they say, 'We need to talk about your thesis.' And I say, 'Okay.' And they say, 'It's the best one we've ever seen' That did not happen. It was a very, very bad thesis…I just wanted to enjoy that one moment when all of you thought, 'this guy is amazing!'"

Analysis – Let's start at the beginning and discuss the use of a conjunction such as *so* at the start of a sentence. Many would say that the word *so* shouldn't be used to start your speech as it makes for a weak opening and is far too casual. I strongly disagree. In writing or speaking, using a conjunction at the start of a sentence is not only okay but encouraged in my book. The word *so* does impart a casualness that I kinda dig. Some compare starting a speech with *so* to beginning with *um* or *like*, but I disagree entirely. *So* is a deliberate word whereas *um* or *like* are more akin to annoying ticks. Some may regard *so* as a weasel word—words that are ambiguous or misleading, think of *but, however, probably, somewhat, usually, almost* etc. Nope, once again, I disagree. If used correctly, *so* can give your speech personality. It's almost like that little word is making sure the audience is sitting comfortably and ready to begin.

A 90-Year Human Life in Months

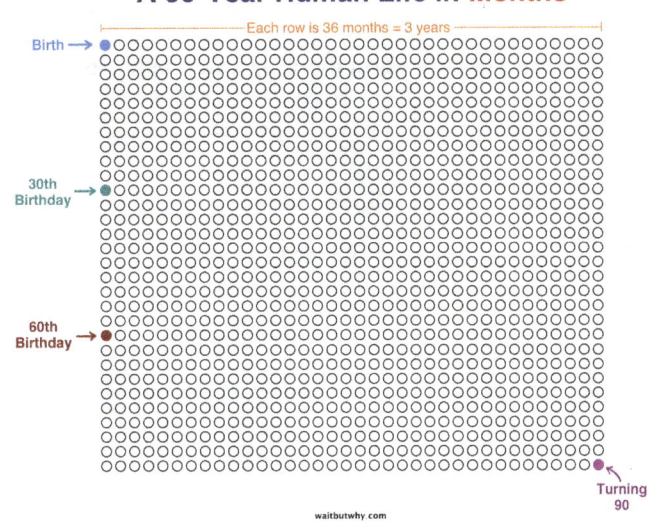

So can be used to announce a new topic or set up a joke. In Urban's case, it sets up a college anecdote. Heck, the last line of *The Great Gatsby*, which many consider to be one of the most important lines in any novel, reads, "So, we beat on, boats against the current, borne back ceaselessly into the past." If it's good enough for F. Scott Fitzgerald, it's good enough for me. So, I encourage my readers to test out using *so* at the beginning or even as the first word of the final sentence of their talks.

Now in terms of Urban's content and delivery. What a fun talk. Who hasn't struggled with procrastination? From Urban's perspective, we are all procrastinators, yup, you too. You'll want to check the full version of his TED Talk. With over 54 million views, you'll see why. Urban uses very basic charts and stick figures such as the instant gratification monkey and the panic monster. His witty banter with the audience and his funny, self-effacing vulnerability is endearing.

Urban says we have both the rational decision-maker and the instant gratification monkey within us all. That instant gratification monkey will find a way to do anything but the task at hand— I once read the entire Wikipedia page devoted to the Nancy Kerrigan/Tonya Harding scandal instead of focusing on my deadline. The shame of taking unearned breaks, to aimlessly wander the internet is a feeling most of us can relate to.

This intense procrastination frustration can be divided into two categories: commitments with deadlines and those without. Deadline-centric procrastinations are clear; projects at work, preparing for a marathon, preparing for a talk. Commitments without deadlines are less tangible—these deadlines are more ambiguous such as creative projects, entrepreneurial endeavours, family time, exercising, and working on your relationship. Urban talks about how long-term procrastination is often not discussed and this really resonated with me. Many people I work with in my coaching practice often feel as though they have become spectators in their own lives. Because of this long-term procrastination, they become focused on the day-to-day tasks—one day, I will finish that painting, or deliver that talk becomes, I wish I would have, or I've missed that boat. Urban's illustration of what he dubs the Life Calendar is brilliant. He shows us visually that one box for every week of a 90-year life is not that many boxes. Urban encourages us to take a long hard look at our own Life Calendar and figure out what we are really procrastinating on and to stay away from the instant gratification monkey at all costs.

Tip – Stay away from the instant gratification monkey and crush those deadlines.

#288 – Shekhar Kapur (1945)

Context – TED India Hollywood/Bollywood director Shekhar Kapur (Elizabeth and Mr. India) in his 2009 talk "We Are the Stories We Tell Ourselves."

"So, I was just asked to go and shoot this film called "Elizabeth." And we're all talking about this great English icon and saying, "She's a fantastic woman, she does everything. How are we going to introduce her?" So, we went around the table with the studio and the producers and the writer, and they came to me and said, "Shekhar, what do you think?"

And I said, "I think she's dancing."

And I could see everybody looked at me, somebody said, "Bollywood."

The other said, "How much did we hire him for?"

And the third said, "Let's find another director."

I thought I had better change. So, we had a lot of discussion on how to introduce Elizabeth, and I said, "OK, maybe I am too Bollywood. Maybe Elizabeth, this great icon, dancing? What are you talking about?" So I rethought the whole thing, and then we all came to a consensus. And here was the introduction of this great British icon called "Elizabeth…"

Analysis – There is something fascinating about this guy, that compels people to watch him. Is he a phenomenal public speaker because he follows all the rules? Nope. He breaks all the public speaking rules, but that is just fine with me because he knows himself so well. He's honest with his emotions and deep with his message. I went back and listened to sections a few times to digest the content, which isn't the most favourable environment to create when giving a presentation, but I'm not going to be harsh with Kapur. I have a fondness for him, and so I make allowances for his somewhat unorthodox presentation methods—I hope you will too. The audience will often excuse a great deal if they are enjoying the presenter's character.

Finding moments of what Kapur calls "organic truths" in the film is the goal. "If you can get five moments like that in your film, then it is all worthwhile," says Kapur. He then walks us through how to harness organic moments; through panic, visual storytelling, not measuring. But for me, the key to his message comes down to how we talk to ourselves. If you've been reading this book in a linear fashion, you'll know what I mean by the term pep talk and that I consider a positive internal dialogue as one of the keys to doing a superb talk (and, I might add, is the key to life, the universe, and everything—shout out to all the Hitchhiker fans).

It is not the physical brain that guides our inner dialogue. It is our experiences and how we view those experiences through our internal voice. The experiences a person has had in life become firmly anchored in our brain and become the foundation for current and future behaviours. This, in essence, is what Kapur is saying. Our experiences define our expectations; they steer our attention in very specific directions, and they determine the value we put on our lives and how we react to our surroundings. These individually acquired experiences, and how we house them internally, are the most valuable treasures a person possesses.

These experiences become viewing portals. We've all met people who consider themselves indispensable, or people with low opinions of themselves, or people who think they are godlike or omnipotent, or people who are controlling, or small, or power-hungry, or who have narcissistic tendencies, etc. These behaviours have a direct correlation to one's experiences. Allow your experiences to act as a springboard to teach others and make a difference in their lives. Recognize, too, that our experiences are a nucleus for how we talk to ourselves in our internal world. Begin the process of recognizing that your experiences are the foundation of your internal conversations. This is rather important if you plan to have conversations with others, especially in a crowd—aka the presentation. (Whoa! This post hurt my head. You?)

Tip – Use your experiences to teach others.

#287 – Lakshmi Pratury

Context – Lakshmi Pratury's inspires her audience to break out a pen and paper in her TED Talk in 2007 on "The Lost art of letter-writing."

"So, I thought, I will talk about death." Seemed to be the passion today. Actually, it's not about death. It's inevitable, terrible, but really what I want to talk about is, I'm just fascinated by the legacy people leave when they die. That's what I want to talk about.

So, Art Buchwald left his legacy of humor with a video that appeared soon after he died, saying, "Hi! I'm Art Buchwald, and I just died." And Mike, who I met at Galapagos, a trip which I won at TED, is leaving notes on cyberspace where he is chronicling his journey through cancer. And my father left me a legacy of his handwriting through letters and a notebook. In the last two years of his life, when he was sick, he filled a notebook with his thoughts about me. He wrote about my strengths, weaknesses, and gentle suggestions for improvement, quoting specific incidents, and held a mirror to my life.

After he died, I realized that no one writes to me anymore. Handwriting is a disappearing art. I'm all for email and thinking while typing, but why give up old habits for new? Why can't we have letter writing and email exchange in our lives? There are times when I want to trade all those years that I was too busy to sit with my dad and chat with him, and trade all those years for one hug. But too late. But that's when I take out his letters and I read them, and the paper that touched his hand is in mine, and I feel connected to him.

So maybe we all need to leave our children with a value legacy, and not a financial one. A value for things with a personal touch—an autographed book, a soul-searching letter. If a fraction of this powerful TED audience could be inspired to buy a beautiful paper—John, it'll be a recycled one—and write a beautiful letter to someone they love, we actually may start a revolution where our children may go to penmanship classes…"

Analysis – I don't know about you, but the entire notion of texting makes me, well, just plain sick. I was in a meeting last week with the CEO of an organization. I gathered more information before giving a presentation and ensured I had all the details down correctly. Mid thought—Boom! He pulls out his blackberry phone and starts typing away, all the while pretending to still listen to me and be engaged with me. Pretending is the operative word because we all know when one is tuning in and out of a conversation. The whole mess is rude! Every workshop I do, every keynote talk, it comes up, and I am saddened that I have to teach adults basic protocols. I cannot stand texting in any form or the technological devices that house them. We've lost so many art forms, as Lakshmi so eloquently points out, and the art of letter writing is, in my estimation, a beautiful way to communicate. It's relaxed, not chaotic, and it is thoughtful—the opposite of the text. So, I encourage you to reignite this lost art form and begin by giving thanks to those who help you in your presentations. Did someone assist you with the equipment set up? Did someone make photocopies for you? Did someone volunteer to be your practice partner? These are important people to thank, and if you do it with a handwritten note, it will have meaning and be kept, unlike a text that will most assuredly find its way into the trash folder. Be inspired by this video to write a beautiful letter. Be inspired to reignite the lost art of letter writing in your personal lives, as well as your business lives.

Tip – After your talk, send handwritten Thank You cards to anyone who assisted you.

#286 – Robert Waldinger

1951

Context – In this 2015 TED Talk, Robert Waldinger, the fourth director of the Harvard Study of Adult Development, talks about one of the most comprehensive longitudinal studies in history in his talk, "What Makes a Good Life?"

"What keeps us healthy and happy as we go through life? If you were going to invest now in your future best self, where would you put your time and your energy? There was a recent survey of millennials asking them what their most important life goals were, and over 80 percent said that a major life goal for them was to get rich. And another 50 percent of those same young adults said that another major life goal was to become famous.

And we're constantly told to lean in to work, to push harder, and achieve more. We're given the impression that these are the things that we need to go after in order to have a good life. Pictures of entire lives, of the choices that people make and how those choices work out for them, those pictures are almost impossible to get.

Most of what we know about human life we know from asking people to remember the past, and as we know, hindsight is anything but 20/20. We forget vast amounts of what happens to us in life, and sometimes memory is downright creative.

But what if we could watch entire lives as they unfold through time? What if we could study people from the time that they were teenagers all the way into old age to see what really keeps people happy and healthy?

We did that. The Harvard Study of Adult Development may be the longest study of adult life that's ever been done. For 75 years, we've tracked the lives of 724 men, year after year, asking about their work, their home lives, their health, and of course, asking all along the way without knowing how their life stories were going to turn out.

Studies like this are exceedingly rare. Almost all projects of this kind fall apart within a decade because too many people drop out of the study, or funding for the research dries up, or the researchers get distracted, or they die, and nobody moves the ball further down the field. But through a combination of luck and the persistence of several generations of researchers, this study has survived. About 60 of our original 724 men are still alive, still participating in the study, most of them in their 90s. And we are now beginning to study the more than 2,000 children of these men. And I'm the fourth director of the study."

Analysis – This talk is beautiful. It is well crafted and delivered with such calmness and intention that it moves the audience to reflect on their own lives. Waldinger talks about his insights as the fourth director of a 75-year study into what keeps people happy and healthy. Each year, the study checks in on the lives of 724 men, split into two groups—one group made up of sophomores from Harvard College and the second group consisting of boys from Boston's poorest neighbourhoods. The test subjects were given questionnaires and interviewed by the researchers to get a clear picture of their lives. The researchers looked at medical records, scanned the men's brains, and talked to their children and their wives.

"So, what have we learned? What are the lessons that come from the tens of thousands of pages of information that we've generated in these lives? Well, the lessons aren't about wealth or fame or working harder and harder. The clearest message that we get from this 75-year study is this: good relationships keep us happier and healthier. Period."

Waldinger tells us that the study has exposed three big lessons about relationships. First is the importance of social connections. Second is the quality of your close relationships because it matters. Third, good relationships don't just protect our bodies but also our brains.

As I reflect on my own life, I agree that good relationships do keep us happier and healthier. I have made many decisions over my 50 years on this planet that have been based on relationships—choosing a divorce many years ago, choosing new friends, choosing to depart old friendships that were no longer healthy, choosing more connections, choosing to leave toxic workplaces, choosing entrepreneurship. These decisions, whether conscious or unconscious, were made to pursue relationships that would contribute to a happier life.

This past year, some of my greatest joys have been when collaborating with people whom I have deep, trusting, psychologically safe relationships. Some of what we have produced has been the most creative, invigorating work I've ever produced. I met a person on a plane several years ago. I used to be that person on the plane who was laser-focused on where I was going and why. So, if I was on a plane, 99 percent of the time it was for work. So I'd settle into my seat and after take off, and begin preparing for whatever client work was ahead of me. One day, however, I was stuck on the tarmac amidst a snowstorm, waiting for the ground crew to de-ice the wings, which involves removing snow, ice, and frost from the wings of the plane. After waiting out the storm's intensity on the ground, I had completed enough of my tasks and decided to treat myself to a few pages from the book I had picked up at the airport. As I began to read, the person seated next to me said in delight, "I know that book's author; he's a friend!"

And so began one of the most interesting conversations I've had. My seat neighbour and I talked about his leadership business and my leadership work, he shared his philosophies on work, life, and I shared mine, and then we moved on to our love of art and the written and spoken word. Several hours later, a lifelong friendship was born. We've since met for lunches to continue our chats. When the pandemic broke, we scheduled regular zoom chats to continue to explore our philosophies, and boom, one day, an idea was born for a book, and we've been collaborating on that project for more than a year now. The funny thing is the book is not about fame or infamy but creativity, collaboration, and exploration. We've been very clear on that intention right from the start. It's probably why we'll still be writing that book ten years from now! There are no deadlines set, and there are no expectations. I've learned so much from this relationship. Now when I board a plane, I'm not as intent on my work tasks because I am more open to just chatting with the person sitting beside me.

Giving a talk may feel like a solo act, but all your good, and even bad, relationships contribute to your talk. I had a speaking engagement coming up and, as I started to create the skeleton of the talk, I was reminded of all the good relationships I have in my life and how they could contribute to the talk's content, so I started calling people in my friends and family circle as they came to mind and asking what they thought of my topic. The richness and differing points of view were unbelievable. My talk became more robust with so many more layers and much more well thought out because I invited those around me who I admire and adore to weigh in with their contributions.

Waldinger finishes his talk with a Mark Twain quote, which seems to sum up the secret to a happy life, "There isn't time, so brief is life, for bickerings, apologies, heart burnings, callings to account. There is only time for loving, and but an instant, so to speak, for that."

Tip – Replace screen time with people time. Develop your next talk in collaboration with those you love.

#285 – Jamie Oliver

(1975)

Context – Jamie Oliver's Award-winning 2010 TED speech, "Teach every child about food," inspires his audience to break out of our cluelessness about food.

"Sadly, in the next 18 minutes when I do our chat, four Americans will be dead through the food that they eat. My name is Jamie Oliver; I'm 34 years old. I'm from Essex in England, and for the last seven years, I've worked fairly tirelessly to save lives in my own way. I'm not a doctor. I'm a chef; I don't have expensive equipment or medicine. I use information, education. I profoundly believe that the power of food has a primal place in our homes that binds us to the best bits of life. We have an awful, awful reality right now. America, you're at the top of your game. This is one of the most unhealthy countries in the world.

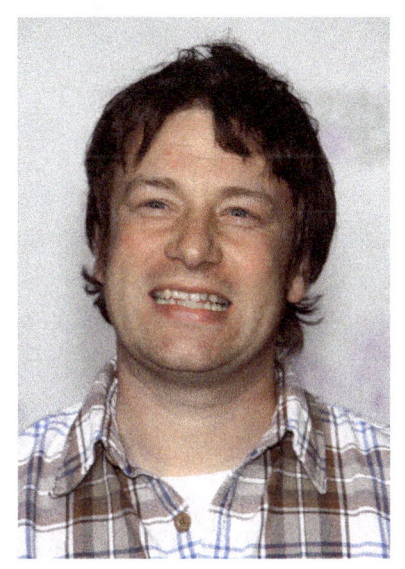

"Can I please just see a raise of hands for how many of you have children in this room today? Put your hands up. You can continue to put your hands up, aunties and uncles as well. Most of you. OK. We, the adults of the last four generations, have blessed our children with the destiny of a shorter lifespan than their own parents. Your child will live a life ten years younger than you because of the landscape of food that we've built around them. Two-thirds of this room, today, in America, are statistically overweight or obese. You lot, you're all right, but we'll get you eventually, don't worry…"

Analysis – This is one of the best openings I've heard in a very long time. Why so good? It grabs your attention immediately with a startling statistic before Oliver even introduces himself. It is my favourite type of opening. Start with a fact, a joke, a statistic, and then, once you've got your audience's attention, introduce yourself.

Oliver is articulate; he's serious, he's funny, he's passionate, he's informative and I am surprised! Here I thought I was going to watch a nice little video clip from Jamie Oliver, the *pukka* guy who has a spot on my cooking bookshelf and the young pup that I watched faithfully hosting his very first cooking show, *The Naked Chef*. Yeah, I knew he had done some stuff with the school lunch programs in England, but I had no idea to what extent and I no idea that he could be so incredibly persuasive in an artfully constructed, well-practiced, superb talk. He uses his slides perfectly; they are not cluttered with text. He uses pictures of people to support his argument. He walks to and fro rather passionately, which I like —and, no, I don't think he's pacing it is much too purposeful—and he punctuates his points. He uses alarmingly scary clips of families that are obese including toddlers, children, adults and the death sentences that result, which further demonstrates his point. He is funny with near perfect comedic timing coupled with the gusto of an impassioned activist. Bravo, Jamie! Bravo!

*I almost wish I could hold onto this one to the top 100 of my list but, I was too excited and had to share it with you now.

Tip – Start with a fact, a statistic, a joke, and grab your audience's attention before you introduce yourself.

#284 – Mohandas K. Gandhi

1869–1948

Context – Gandhi's list of seven social sins is engraved on the wall of his memorial, modestly ignoring capital letters.

"politics without principles
wealth without work
pleasure without conscience
knowledge without character
commerce without morality
science without humanity
worship without sacrifice."

Analysis – Ghandi served two years before being released from a six-year prison sentence for sedition (conduct or speech inciting people to rebel against authority) between 1922-1924, Gandhi steered clear of active politics for a few years, concentrating instead on social and human rights issues. His seven social sins is a blueprint for what he perceived was wrong with life in India at the time. Each sin suggests an ideal opposite. I adore them. Each is moving and fitting. To be a superb speaker, I would argue that his fourth sin is the most applicable: knowledge without character. Just because you know something or have learned something doesn't give you the right to present it. You need principled character. Character that shows your values such as integrity, honesty, fairness, respect, justice etc. Intellectual presentations without character are hollow.

Tip – Allow your character to shine through in your talks.

#283 – Benjamin Zander

(1939)

Context – Benjamin Zander has been the conductor of the Boston Philharmonic since 1979. This is an excerpt from his 2012 TED Talk on music and passion.

"Probably a lot of you know the story of the two salesmen who went down to Africa in the 1900s. They were sent down to find if there was any opportunity for selling shoes, and they wrote telegrams back to Manchester. And one of them wrote, 'Situation hopeless. Stop. They don't wear shoes.' And the other one wrote, 'Glorious opportunity. They don't have any shoes yet.'

Now, there's a similar situation in the classical music world, because there are some people who think that classical music is dying. And there are some of us who think you ain't seen nothing yet. And rather than go into statistics and trends, and tell you about all the orchestras that are closing, and the record companies that are folding, I thought we should do an experiment tonight. Actually, it's not really an experiment, because I know the outcome. But it's like an experiment.

Now, before we start—before we start, I need to do two things. One is I want to remind you of what a seven-year-old child sounds like when he plays the piano. Maybe you have this child at home. He sounds something like this.

I see some of you recognize this child. Now, if he practices for a year and takes lessons, he's now eight and he sounds like this..."

Analysis – In his talk, Zander shows how each child—the six-year-old, the eight-year-old, the nine-year-old, and finally the ten-year-old—learns to play the piano and the differences and progression shown each year. And if the child hangs in there, they will inevitably realize the beauty of classical music and understand the impulses and cadence of music. If I had had him as a teacher, I certainly would have! He makes classical music accessible by taking out the pretense. His unbridled passion and enthusiasm make your ears perk up, and your eyes follow him as he joyfully shuffles across the stage. He is beyond a good teacher; he is fantastic. I had begrudgingly spent countless years in piano lessons as a child, with a teacher who didn't provide me with even a droplet of inspiration, unlike Zander, who inspires all who come into his sphere. Watching this should be a prerequisite for all music teachers!

There is nothing about this guy that I don't like, not one thing. Laughter, excitement, enthusiasm, music, compassion, humility, intuition, fun, and talent all rolled into a 20-minute presentation of sheer delight. My cheeks are taut with a gigantic smile as I type this.

Zander is having a ball doing this presentation, and it shows. He interacts with his audience so well and is unquestionably the most intuitive presenter I've ever seen. He seems to read the minds of his audience brilliantly—which, is a requirement if you have aspirations to be a superb public speaker.

My tip for today relates to both music or to the art of presentation—the more you practice, the more you will understand the cadence of notes or words. As a result, you will be more entertaining, and therefore your audience will digest the information you are sharing and remember you. Practice does not make perfect (perfection does not exist, in any form!) Practice makes permanent.

Tip – Practice makes permanent *not* **perfect!**

#282 – Apollo Robbins

(1974)

Context – Apollo Robbins is hailed as the greatest pickpocket in the world, and Forbes once called him "an artful manipulator of awareness." In his 2013 TED Talk, "The Art of Misdirection," Robbins studies human behaviour in an unorthodox way.

"Do you think it's possible to control someone's attention? Even more than that, what about predicting human behaviour? I think those are interesting ideas. For me, that would be the perfect superpower, actually kind of an evil way of approaching it. But for myself, in the past, I've spent the last 20 years studying human behaviour from a rather unorthodox way: picking pockets. When we think of misdirection, we think of something as

looking off to the side, when actually the things right in front of us are often the hardest to see, the things that you look at every day that you're blinded to.

For example, how many of you still have your cell phones on you right now? Great. Double-check. Make sure you still have them. I was doing some shopping before.

You've looked at them a few times today, but I'll ask you a question. Without looking at it directly yet, can you remember the icon in the bottom right corner? Bring them out, check and see how accurate you were. How'd you do? Show of hands. Did we get it?

Now that you're done, close them down. Every phone has something in common. No matter how you organize the icons, you still have a clock on the front. So, without looking at your phone, what time was it? You just looked at your clock, right? Interesting idea. Let's take that a step further with a game of trust. Close your eyes.
I realize I'm asking you to do that while you just heard there's a pickpocket in the room but close your eyes.

Now, you've been watching me for about 30 seconds. With your eyes closed, what am I wearing? Make your best guess. What colour is my shirt? What colour is my tie? Now open your eyes. Show of hands, were you right? Interesting, isn't it?

Some of us are a little bit more perceptive than others, it seems that way. But I have a different theory about that model of attention. They have fancy models of attention, Posner's trinity model of attention. For me, I like to think of it very simple, like a surveillance system. It's kind of like you have all these fancy sensors, and inside your brain is a little security guard. For me, I like to call him Frank. So Frank is sitting at a desk. He's got lots of cool information in front of him, high-tech equipment, he's got cameras, he's got a little phone that he can pick up, listen to the ears, all these senses, all these perceptions. But attention is what steers your perceptions; it's what controls your reality. It's the gateway to the mind. If you don't attend to something, you can't be aware of it. But ironically, you can attend to something without being aware of it. For example, the cocktail effect: You're in a party, having conversations with someone, and yet you can recognize your name without realizing you were listening to that.

Now, for my job, I have to play with techniques to exploit this, to play with your attention as a limited resource. So, if I could control how you spend your attention and if I could maybe steal your attention through a distraction. Now, instead of doing it like misdirection and throwing it off to the side, instead, what I choose to focus on is Frank, to be able to play with the Frank inside your head, your security guard, and get you, instead of focusing on your external senses, just to go internal for a second."

Analysis – My guess is that Robbins has delivered this talk dozens of times and it fits him like a comfortable pair of slippers. The delivery is effortless, which it needs to because it's likened to a magician's performance. In only nine minutes, Robbins demonstrates the theory of distracting attention—Posner's attention model—and then shows us the art of misdirection with a volunteer from the audience. Before he brings the volunteer up onto the stage, he goes into the audience and starts *fanning*. In an interview with *The New Yorker* magazine, Robbins explained fanning, which is when he lets his fingertips graze someone's pocket and says, "What I'm doing is taking inventory and making sight maps and getting a feel for who these people are and what I'm going to do with them. I'm a jazz performer—I have to improvise with what I'm given...A lot of magic is designed to appeal to people visually, but what I'm trying to affect is their minds, moods, and perception. My goal isn't to hurt them or to bewilder them with a puzzle but to challenge their maps of reality."

Robbins is so interesting and mystical that after watching this talk a few times, I began reading articles and watching tutorials and videos on how to be a master pickpocket and anything else I could find to unlock Robbins' secrets and how he's does what he does. Sleight of hand is a thing, and you see Robbins' dexterity and quick fingers as he misdirects his subject's attention. It is fascinating as you watch his hands move in this well-choreographed pickpocket dance.

He collaborated with two neuroscientists on a book called, *Sleights of Mind: What the Neuroscience of Magic Reveals about Our Everyday Deceptions*. They coin the phrase *Neuromagic*, a discipline aimed at the interaction between brain science and the art of magic. Understanding how the mind perceives magic and perception and cognition in general. Recently psychiatrists, neuroscientists and the military have studied Robbins' methods for what they reveal about the nature of human attention. Robbins has also consulted for the department of defence on the military applications of pickpocketing, behavioural influence, and con games. I bet Robbins would never have guessed that he would have such a strong influence in helping others understand human behaviour when his older brothers taught him how to pickpocket at a young age.

In his talk, Robbins says, "Things that you look at every day are often the hardest to see" and then blows the audience's mind when while suitably distracted with his volunteer demonstration, he changed his clothes, and the audience doesn't even notice. I leave this talk thinking differently, more conscious of looking at everyday things, a little more discerning and intrigued to learn more.

Robbins question in the last line in his talk is a good one to ponder, "If you could control someone's attention, what would you do with it?"

Tip – Think about how you will hold your audience's attention while giving a talk.

#281 – Robert Gupta

(1987)

Context – Robert Gupta 2010 TED Talk, "Music is Medicine, Music is Sanity". Robert is a violinist with the Los Angeles Philharmonic and talks about a violin lesson he once gave..

"Music is medicine, music is sanity."

Analysis – Violinist Robert Gupta joined the Los Angeles Philharmonic at the age of 19 and also has a passionate interest in neurobiology and mental health issues. He's a great storyteller! He shares one of the best messages I've heard in a while. Nurture others, recognize others' brilliance, understand the transformational power of tapping into one's passion, respect others, make friends outside of your 'norm,' discrimination has no role in life.

Music is sanity for Nathan, the individual that Gupta discusses for nine and a half minutes of his presentation. I saw a piece on *60 Minutes* a few months ago about Nathan, and I remember Gupta from that piece too. In the *60 Minutes* piece, they show Gupta playing violin with Nathan, and their interaction is so pure and respectful. We can all learn a thing or ten from both Nathan and Gupta. Welcome others into your life, and help them if they need it, encourage them if they want it, and allow them to teach you.

Tip – Allow your audience to teach you.

#280 – Andy Warhol

1928–1987

"In the future, everybody will be world-famous for 15 minutes."

Context – New evidence suggests that Warhol never actually uttered the above quote. According to *Smithsonian Magazine*, the quote seems to date back to a program distributed at one of Warhol's exhibitions held in Sweden in 1968. Warhol was rumoured to have weighed in on the debate in 1980, and admitted he never said it. But it was too late, and the line continues to be attributed to him to this day.

Analysis – A successful commercial artist in the 50s, Warhol shot to fame in the 60s as a leader in the field of pop art. You may recall the famous image of the Campbell's soup cans or the colourful images of Marilyn Monroe (I'm such a fan of this imagery that I copied this template for my son's first-year photo. Not a traditional portrait for a one-year-old, but I suppose I'm not what one would consider traditional). Warhol spent time at the famous studio 54 during this time, and it is said that the quote originates from this location. In the context of my list of *365 Must-Know Talks*, I find it a wonderful reminder to anyone asked or volunteering to give a presentation or talk. Be cautious of what you say and ensure, in particular with your Q&As, that you have thought about all challenges and objections that may arise, and that you have already articulated how you will respond before the question is posed. That, or insert a pause to give you time to think of an appropriate and thoughtful response, or simply say that you don't know! There is nothing wrong with admitting that you don't have the answer to a question instead of digging yourself a hole and being famous (or perhaps infamous) for a response that you didn't intend. That said, if you can't answer a question, commit to finding out the answer and getting back to the person who posed it.

Tip – It's okay to say you don't have the answer.

#279 – Ricky Gervais

(1961)

Context – Excerpts from Ricky Gervais' opening monologue "No One Cares about Movies Anymore," given at the 77th annual Golden Globes in 2020.

"You'll be pleased to know this is the last time I'm hosting these awards, so I don't care anymore. I'm joking. I never did. NBC clearly don't care either—fifth time. I mean, Kevin Hart was fired from the Oscars because of some offensive tweets—hello?

Lucky for me, the Hollywood Foreign Press can barely speak English, and they've no idea what Twitter is, so I got offered this gig by fax. Let's go out with a bang. Let's have a laugh at your expense. Remember, they're just jokes. We're all gonna die soon, and there's no sequel, so remember that.

But you all look lovely, all dolled up. You came here in your limos. I came here in a limo tonight, and the license plate was made by Felicity Huffman. No, shush. It's her daughter I feel sorry for. OK? That must be the most embarrassing thing that's ever happened to her. And her dad was in Wild Hogs…

…No one cares about movies anymore. No one goes to the cinema. No one really watches network TV. Everyone's watching Netflix. This show should just be me coming out, going, "Well done, Netflix. You win everything. Goodnight." But no, we got to drag it out for three hours. You could binge-watch the entire first season of Afterlife instead of watching this show. That's a show about a man who wants to kill himself because his wife dies of cancer, and it's still more fun than this. Spoiler alert, season two is on the way, so in the end, he obviously didn't kill himself, just like Jeffrey Epstein. Shut up. I know he's your friend, but I don't care…

…So, if you do win an award tonight, don't use it as a platform to make a political speech. You're in no position to lecture the public about anything. You know nothing about the real world. Most of you spent less time in school than Greta Thunberg.

So, if you win, come up, accept your little award, thank your agent and your God, and fuck off, OK? It's already three hours long. Right, let's do the first award."

Analysis – Full disclosure, I'm a massive Ricky Gervais fan. His Netflix show, *Afterlife*, is one of the finest pieces of screenwriting I've ever seen. My partner is British, and he often tells me that North Americans don't get British humour. Sarcasm, insults, self-deprecation, taboo subjects, wit, and innuendo form the foundation of British humour. And Gervais checks all these boxes in his monologue.

Watching the audience during this monologue is fascinating! Some raise their eyebrows and some struggle with how to react at all. Fake Hollywood exposed. From my perspective, there are four types of people in the audience; those who are laughing because it's funny, those who are laughing or smiling because the camera is on them, those who are laughing because they think Gervais is talking about everyone else, and Tom Hanks. The camera pans to Hanks a few times, and his face is contorted in mass discomfort. When Gervais is booed rather frequently, it only strengthens his resolve, "Your boos mean nothing to me; I've seen what makes you cheer." Gervais' speech is brave and bold.

Would I have the *kahunas* to deliver a talk like this? Hell no. But I'm glad that Gervais exists to fulfil this role. He tackles racism and the trappings of Hollywood celebrity and makes clear that he doesn't care what this elite, overpaid, over-appreciated segment of society have to say. The speech is brutal, and honest. Comedians are brilliant because, for many, their jokes come from truth—after all, many a true word is spoken in jest.

This approach is polarizing. You'll either love it, as I do, or you'll hate it. Nothing in between. But what can those studying presentations skills glean from this monologue? I believe that for many, we construct and deliver talks that are plain vanilla. We skirt around issues so as not to offend anyone and, in doing so, we remove much of what we believe. I started a video podcast earlier this year with a colleague. It's interesting to see the progression from pretty darn vanilla delivery versus today, where the mask of societal norms is slowly being removed. In our podcast, my colleague and we have given ourselves the permission and freedom to use taboo language and speak our truths through our stories. It's a much more enjoyable watching two people interact without rules and expressing themselves freely.

Social norms are those unwritten rules of behaviour considered acceptable by society or a group. These norms, of course, vary based on culture, situation, and behaviour. What if the next time you prepared your talk, you expressed exactly how you felt without editing yourself to ensure acceptance by your peers? What if you developed a daring point of view on a topic and presented it with no filter? Would it create a better talk? It just might.

Tip – Try freeing yourself from social norms in the development of your talk and just express yourself.

#278 – Kiran Bir Sethi

(1966)

Context – In her 2009 TED Talk, Kiran Bir Sethi teaches kids to take charge.

Contagious is a good word. Even in the times of H1N1, I like the word. Laughter is contagious. Passion is contagious. Inspiration is contagious. We've heard some remarkable stories from some remarkable speakers. But for me, what was contagious about all of them was that they were infected by something I call the "I Can" bug.

So, the question is, why only them? In a country of a billion people and some, why so few? Is it luck? Is it chance? Can we all not systematically and consciously get infected? So, in the next eight minutes I would like to share with you my story. I got infected when I was 17, when, as a student of the design college, I encountered adults who actually believed in my ideas, challenged me and had lots of cups of chai with me.

And I was struck by just how wonderful it felt, and how contagious that feeling was. I also realized I should have got infected when I was seven. So, when I started Riverside school 10 years ago it became a lab, a lab to prototype and refine a design process that could consciously infect the mind with the "I Can" bug. And I uncovered that if learning is embedded in real-world context, that if you blur the boundaries between school and life, then children go through a journey of "aware," where they can see the change, "enable," be changed, and then "empower," lead the change. And that directly increased student wellbeing. Children became more competent, and less helpless. But this was all common sense.

So, I'd like to show you a little glimpse of what common practice looks like at Riverside. A little background: when my grade five was learning about child rights, they were made to roll incense sticks, agarbattis, for eight hours to experience what it means to be a child laborer. It transformed them. What you will see is their journey, and then their utter conviction that they could go out and change the world.

Analysis – Sethi is the best natural speaker I've ever laid eyes on, period. She emanates what she speaks of; her smile is contagious, and her natural charm engages the audience in a magnetic way. She is easy, her delivery humble. The talk is truly a thing of beauty. Perhaps my shine for her is also because of the fantastic role she has created for herself and the changes she's making in her community and the world. She starts with talking about the children of riverside school (in India); "Laughter is contagious, passion is contagious, inspiration is contagious…they were infected by something called an "I can" bug…why? Luck, chance?" Sethi talks about a learning model that North American school administrators should ponder if learning is embedded into a real-world scenario context. You begin the process of blurring the boundaries between school and life. With that, the students then go through a process: aware (feel), enable (imagine), empower (leading the change). So, the children of Riverside School in India go from "the teacher told me to" to "I can do it." And they move mountains.

As I watched this video, I was inspired by Sethi's contagious energy. The same can be true of adults. Adults attend workshops (schools), but often there are very few real-world analogies embedded in the curriculum. If facilitators and trainers can blur the lines between classrooms and the real world and have a powerful message to communicate, we too could empower our students to move mountains. So, this post is for my fellow professional public speakers out there. Empower your students with an 'I can' attitude and inspire them to change their communities and the world. Now get to work!

Tip – Inspire a can-do attitude.

#277 – John Rives

(1968)

Context – In a 2007 TED presentation Rives, a poet, unpacks "The 4 a.m Mystery." He later resurrected the talk in 2014 with "The Museum of 4 a.m."

Analysis – Comics, music, quotes, newspaper clips, pictures of stamps, *The Simpson's* videos, songs, conspiracy theories, pictures of sculptures, Google search pics—are all tools that Rives uses in his nine-minute presentation on what happens at 4 in the morning. Rives uses his slides brilliantly. So, if you're looking for new ways to play with your slides, he shows some interesting techniques that I know I'll be weaving into my work (for example showing an overview picture then zoom in on the detail in another slide). His presentation topic is unique, to say the least, and for that, I would've opened it up to start watching, but it isn't why I stayed glued to the screen. Rives shows us that 4 a.m. has become a kind of meme, and the worst possible time to be awake. It's a time of inconvenience, mishaps, yearnings. It's a time for plotting—think whacking the chief of police in the movie *The Godfather*. In his script, Francis Ford Coppola writes that these guys are exhausted, in shirtsleeves in 4 a.m. in the morning. Rives goes on to untangle why 4 a.m. has such a bad rap. "The Palace at 4 a.m.," which is a 1932 sculpture developed by Alberto Giacometti. Rives weaves between theories to distill this bad rap to this single sculpture.

He unpacks his theory on 4 a.m. in such a fun rhythmical way. Rives pays particular attention to his cadence, he is a poet and boy does it show. This is the primary reason I love this presentation. Rives has the cadence and the smooth delivery of a poet in a smoldering club, complete with a French beret, lit cigarette, and faint 'finger snaps' in the background. It is lyrical origami. It is mesmerizing. I enjoy Rives and found myself watching this presentation several times in a row. I've never seen anything like it.

So, my tip for today is simple; pepper your delivery with the cadence of a poet and see how your audience reacts.

Tip – Throw a little poetry into your delivery.

#276 – Al Pacino

(1940)

Context – Al Pacino's ending speech in *Scent of a Woman*, a 1992 film which tells the story of a preparatory school student who takes a job as an assistant to a retired, blind army officer.

Mr. Trask: I'm going to recommend to the disciplinary committee that you be expelled, Mr. Sims. You are a cover-up artist, and you are a liar.

Frank Slade: But not a snitch.

Trask: Excuse me?

Slade: No, I don't think I will.

Trask: Mr. Slade.

Slade: This is such a crock of shit.

Trask: Please watch your language, Mr. Slade. You are in the Baird School not a barracks. Mr. Sims, I will give you one final opportunity to speak up.

Slade: Mr. Sims doesn't want it. He doesn't need to label: "Still worthy of being a 'Baird Man.'" What the hell is that? What is your motto here? "Boys, inform on your classmates, save your hide" – anything short of that we're gonna burn you at the stake? Well, gentlemen, when the shit hits the fan, some guys run, and some guys stay. Here's Charlie facing the fire; and there's George hidin' in big Daddy's pocket. And what are you doin'? You're gonna reward George and destroy Charlie.

Trask: Are you finished, Mr. Slade?

Slade: No, I'm just gettin' warmed up. I don't know who went to this place, William Howard Taft, William Jennings Bryan, William Tell – whoever. Their spirit is dead – if they ever had one – it's gone. You're building a rat ship here. A vessel for sea goin' snitches. And if you think you're preparing these minnows for manhood you better think again. Because I say you are killing the very spirit this institution proclaims it instills! What a sham. What kind of a show are you guys puttin' on here today? I mean, the only class in this act is sittin' next to me. And I'm here to tell ya this boy's soul is intact. It's non-negotiable. You know how I know? Someone here – and I'm not gonna say who – offered to buy it. Only Charlie here wasn't sellin'.

Trask: Sir, you are out of order!

Slade?????????? Outta order? I'll show you outta order! You don't know what outta order is, Mr. Trask! I'd show you but I'm too old; I'm too tired; I'm too fuckin' blind. If I were the man, I was five years ago I'd take a FLAME-THROWER to this place! Outta order. Who the hell you think you're talkin' to? I've been around, you know. There was a time I could see. And I have seen boys like these, younger than these, their arms torn out, their legs ripped off. But there isn't nothin' like the sight of an amputated spirit; there is no prosthetic for that. You think you're merely sendin' this splendid foot-soldier back home to Oregon with his tail between his legs, but I say you are executin' his SOUL!! And why?! Because he's not a Baird man! Baird men, ya hurt this boy, you're going to be Baird Bums, the lot of ya. And Harry, Jimmy, Trent, wherever you are out there, FUCK YOU, too!

Trask: Stand down, Mr. Slade!

Slade: I'm not finished! As I came in here, I heard those words, "cradle of leadership." Well, when the bough breaks, the cradle will fall. And it has fallen here; it has fallen. Makers of men; creators of leaders; be careful what kind of leaders you're producin' here. I don't know if Charlie's silence here today is right or wrong.

I'm not a judge or jury. But I can tell you this: he won't sell anybody out to buy his future!! And that, my friends, is called integrity! That's called courage! Now that's the stuff leaders should be made of. Now I have come to the crossroads in my life. I always knew what the right path was. Without exception, I knew. But I never took it. You know why? It was too damn hard. Now here's Charlie. He's come to the crossroads. He has chosen a path. It's the right path. It's a path made of principle—that leads to character. Let him continue on his journey.

Analysis – It is a good speech, that's for sure! It isn't a presentation exactly, but any person about to launch into a presentation can learn a thing or two by watching Pacino deliver the speech in the last nine minutes of the movie, Scent of a Woman. It conjures up a ton of emotion and it ends with the students' resounding applause. The speech has conviction, power and tone. It evokes emotion, and that is what a good presentation, too, will do. To be clear, I am not suggesting you put on an act in front of your audience, as a speech needs to be authentic, but the use of emotion is essential. I'm sure you've seen the robotic delivery of a speech before, you heard the words but feel absolutely nothing. There is a reason you have been asked to deliver this talk and that a printed article wasn't sent to your audience, they want to hear from you, and for you to do this effectively requires injecting emotion into your talk. Granted, it may not be as impassioned as Pacino, but it does need to leave your audience wanting more.

Tip – Bring out the actor in you, and evoke emotion in your presentation.

#275 – Tom Rielly

(1964)

Context – Tom Rielly delivers the close at the TED 2006 conference with an 18-minute monologue he called "A Sharp Intake of Death."

"I just want to give you a quick overview. First of all, please remember I'm completely politically correct, and I mean everything with great affection. If any of you have sensitive stomachs or are feeling queasy, now is the time to check your Blackberry."

Analysis – Manic? Yes. Frenetic? Yes. Wild? Yes. Funny? Yes. Rielly knows his job for this speech is to leave his audience laughing. At first, I find myself watching and wondering what the hell is going on. And then, about four minutes in, I find myself enjoying the frenzy. At one point, Rielly's microphone isn't working, and he doesn't miss a beat as the technician tries to fix it. He continues to do his thing. He's in some crazy bubble of energy with seemingly no direction. But he does have direction and a very real focus. His presentation is prepared, and quite organized when you start peeling back the layers of his frenetic onion. His job is to summarize all the other TED speakers during the convention. And he does it this with great humour and brilliant visual aids (from a chart graph used creatively, to Barbie dolls, to fruit roll-ups, to a 'granola house' and everything in between). As presenters, we are often so conscious of so many trivial things: how we look, how we move about the stage if we drink or don't drink water, where our aids should be placed after we are finished. But Rielly doesn't give a poop about any of that, which doesn't affect how much his audience digests and enjoys his message. Now, could everyone pull this off? I doubt it. But most of us would be able to pull it off in our way, within our senses of humour, and personalities. I've decided to give myself (and you) permission to act a little manic and frenetic when giving a presentation. You, and your audience, may just enjoy it.

Tip – Allow your frenetic side to (occasionally) jump into your presentation.

#274 – Galileo Galilei

1564–1642

Context – 1615, Italy. The church condemned Galileo for discussing the sun-centered model of the solar system as a fact. This is his response.

"…I do not feel obliged to believe that the same God who has endowed us with senses, reason and intellect has intended to forgo their use and by some other means to give us knowledge which we can attain by them."

Analysis – Galileo, the Italian astronomer, was the first to construct a telescope and study the sky. In 1610, he discovered that the planet Jupiter had four satellites orbiting around it as the moon does around the Earth. This was in direct opposition to Aristotle's version, where Earth was the center of the cosmos, and all the other planets orbited Earth. Galileo was a deeply religious man and found himself in an interesting predicament as this idea was in direct opposition to any Church ideas or teachings. He inevitably drew the conclusion found in the above quote, which in essence means that God wouldn't have given us brains if he hadn't intended us to use them. This made me think about whom I might choose for my blog today and immediately thought of historical religious figures and, for me, up popped Galileo.

As presenters, we often get stuck in a rut where we stop learning, stop adding new tools and techniques to our toolbox. Beyond just the nuts and bolts of presenting what makes a presenter interesting is the multifaceted nature of a complex personality. Like an onion, a presenter may only show you the first few layers, but in my estimation, you need to have dozens, even hundreds of complex layers that have come from thoughtful exploration in many areas; from science to nature to war to humanity and everywhere and everything in between. That is why it takes a lifetime to get good at the art of storytelling (and presenting falls into this art) because it takes a lifetime to amass as much knowledge as possible, and as Galileo said, "God wouldn't have given us brains if he hadn't intended us to use them!"

Tip – Include thoughtful exploration into everything in your quest to become a superb presenter!

#273 – Plato

c. 428–348 BCE

Context – Plato was the student of Socrates, and Aristotle was the student of Plato.

"Until philosophers are kings, or the kings and princes of this world have the spirit and power of philosophy, and political greatness and wisdom meet in one, and those commoner natures who pursue either to the exclusion of the other are compelled to stand aside, cities will never have rest from their evils, nor the human race, as I believe, and then only will this our State have a possibility of life and behold the light of the day."

Analysis – I'm excited to get to a point in this list where I get to discuss my beloved Greek philosophers. I am a fan of Plato (albeit he's lower down on the list and he's no Socrates or Aristotle, but hey, he said some cool stuff, including the above quote). He wrote *The Republic*, which was based on Socrates' teachings. I've often wondered if we'd even know about Socrates if it had not been for Plato's writings. He was so in awe and inspired by Socrates that he felt compelled to write it down. Few would admit it but many of us would love to be so adored by our students. *The Republic* is one of Plato's Socratic dialogues—fictionalized accounts of discussion between Greek philosophers. There is a section on political philosophy where there is a discussion between Socrates and Glaucius, and they debate what kind of people are fit to rule. In Athens at the time, rulers tended to be a select few who got their way through clever persuasion and clever use of words rather than wisdom. So, how they said something was more important than the content. And that is the essence of Plato's above quote. It made me think about my blog and if I have, I put too much emphasis on how one should present and too little emphasis on what the meat of the presentation is, or the content. I have pondered this question for a while and believe that as it relates to rulers, Plato is on to something. It is fascinating to me that the rulers in 380 BCE behave much like modern-day politicians, but I digress. As it relates to presentations, though, I would suggest that I may be on a good path. Our body language, our tone of voice, our fine attention to detail and delivery is important, it is essential, but the content has to be interesting, entertaining and knowledgeable too. I shift back and forth on the percentages of which is more important, the content or the vehicle of communication. So, my tip for today will simply be to focus on both equally, the how and the what (that sounds rather 'politician' like of me…I promise I'll stop that!)

Tip – Concentrate on the how and what of your presentation!

#272 – Susan Cain

(1968)

Context – Susan Cain is a writer, lecturer, lawyer and author of the 2012 nonfiction book, *Quiet: The Power of Introverts in a World That Can't Stop Talking*. The book presents the argument that our culture misunderstands and undervalues the traits and capabilities of introverts. Cain's 2012 TED Talk, which has garnered millions of views, celebrates and encourages the power and glory of introverts.

"When I was nine years old, I went off to summer camp for the first time. And my mother packed me a suitcase full of books, which to me seemed like a perfectly natural thing to do. Because in my family, reading was the primary group activity. And this might sound antisocial to you, but for us, it was really just a different way of being social. You have the animal warmth of your family sitting right next to you, but you are also free to go roaming around the Adventureland inside your own mind. And I had this idea that camp was going to be just like this, but better.

I had a vision of 10 girls sitting in a cabin cosily reading books in their matching nightgowns.

Camp was more like a keg party without any alcohol. And on the very first day, our counselor gathered us all together, and she taught us a cheer that she said we would be doing every day for the rest of the summer to instil camp spirit. And it went like this: "R-O-W-D-I-E, that's the way we spell rowdie. Rowdie, rowdie, let's get rowdie."

Yeah. So, I couldn't figure out for the life of me why we were supposed to be so rowdy or why we had to spell this word incorrectly.

But I recited a cheer. I recited a cheer along with everybody else. I did my best. And I just waited for the time that I could go off and read my books.

But the first time that I took my book out of my suitcase, the coolest girl in the bunk came up to me, and she asked me, "Why are you being so mellow?" -- mellow, of course, being the exact opposite of R-O-W-D-I-E. And then the second time I tried it, the counselor came up to me with a concerned expression on her face, and she repeated the point about camp spirit and said we should all work very hard to be outgoing.

And so, I put my books away, back in their suitcase, and I put them under my bed, and there they stayed for the rest of the summer. And I felt kind of guilty about this. I felt as if the books needed me somehow, and they were calling out to me, and I was forsaking them. But I did forsake them, and I didn't open that suitcase again until I was back home with my family at the end of the summer.

Now, I tell you this story about summer camp. I could have told you 50 others just like it—all the time that I got the message that somehow my quiet and introverted style of being was not necessarily the right way to go, that I should be trying to pass as more of an extrovert. And I always sensed deep down that this was wrong and that introverts were pretty excellent just as they were. But for years, I denied this intuition, and so I became a Wall Street lawyer, of all things, instead of the writer that I had always longed to be—partly because I needed to prove to myself that I could be bold and assertive too. And I was always going off to crowded bars when I really would have preferred to just have a nice dinner with friends. And I made these self-negating choices so reflexively that I wasn't even aware that I was making them.

Now, this is what many introverts do, and it's our loss for sure, but it is also our colleagues' loss and our communities' loss. And at the risk of sounding grandiose, it is the world's loss. Because when it comes to creativity and to leadership, we need introverts doing what they do best. A third to a half of the population are introverts—a third to a half. So that's one out of every two or three people you know. So even if you're an extrovert yourself, I'm talking about your coworkers and your spouses and your children and the person sitting next to you right now -- all of them subject to this bias that is pretty deep and real in our society. We all internalize it from a very early age without even having a language for what we're doing…"

Analysis – I'm a full-blown extrovert, and when I saw this talk in 2012, I immediately ran out to buy Cain's book, *Quiet*. I've been deeply fascinated by introversion for a long time because it is so opposite to who I am, and I have a palpable appetite for understanding my Yang to my Yin.

Cain reports that at least one third of the people we know are introverts—those who prefer quiet reflection, small group activities, listening to speaking, and reading to partying. Carl Jung, the founder of analytical psychology, was famous for coining the phrase, and Cain builds on this by adding there is no such thing as a pure introvert or a pure extrovert. A newish phrase, *ambiverts* are people at the centre of introversion and extroversion who can switch between the two depending on their mood, situation, and environment.

Cain argues that historically introverted leaders have been some of the most transformative. Eleanor Roosevelt, Rosa Parks, and Gandhi are explored in this talk as examples of those who have described themselves as quiet and softly spoken or even shy. And they all took the spotlight, even though "every bone in their bodies was telling them not to." Their drive to be at the helm came not from wanting to be in the spotlight but because they felt they had no choice but to do what they thought was right despite the discomfort. This idea of freeing yourself from group dynamics, going away in solitude, and creating your own ideas resonates. It reminds me of a quote by Rasheed Ogunlaru, "If you listen quietly enough, life will whisper its secrets to you." Gandhi believed that restraint was one of his greatest assets. "I have naturally formed the habit of restraining my thoughts. A thoughtless word hardly ever escaped my tongue or pen. Experience has taught me that silence is part of the spiritual discipline of a votary of truth. We find so many people impatient to talk. All this talking can hardly be said to be of any benefit to the world. It is so much a waste of time. My shyness has been my shield and buckler. It has allowed me to grow. It has helped me in my discernment of truth."

Having always wanted to be a writer, Cain instead ended up as a Wall Street lawyer as she tried to adhere to societal norms that favoured extroverted professions. She continued making these self-negating choices so reflexively, that she wasn't even aware that she was making them. Schools and workplaces are designed primarily for extroverts, and extroverts need lots of stimulation. The act of working alone is considered a problem. Pre-COVID, we have designed open-plan offices, where collaborative spaces were coupled with constant noise.

In schools, we used to have student's desks in rows, and now students are in groups or pods where the desks are pulled together to face one another. What strikes me about Cain's talk is when she touches on the need for solitude, "Solitude is a crucial ingredient to creativity." I agree with this 100 percent! Even the process of writing this book has required me to spend hundreds if not thousands of hours alone. When I write a talk or develop a workshop, most of this work is done at my desk or alone in meditation, on a walk or painting. Da Vinci talked about *Curiosita*, an insatiable curious approach to life and an unrelenting quest for continuous learning. This creativity, this curious approach to life, is often self-work and cannot be done in groups.

Cain's talk is animated, funny, and enlightening. As the audience, we immediately get a sense of who Cain is because she starts her talk by sharing a story about being away at camp and describes it as "a keg party without alcohol." She is vulnerable when delivering this talk, indicating that her book took seven years to write and, for her, "that seven years was total bliss because I was reading, I was writing, I was thinking, I was researching…but now all of a sudden my job is very different, and my job is to be out here talking about it, talking about introversion. And that's a lot harder for me because as honoured as I am to be here with all of you right now, this is not my natural milieu." Cain talks about the importance of practising public speaking every chance she could and refers to her time spent promoting her book as a "year of speaking dangerously."

Tip – Challenge your inner introvert and spend a year speaking dangerously.

#271 – Julian Treasure

(1958)

Context – Julian Treasure and his 2009 TED Talk, "The Four Ways Sound Affects Us."

"Over the next five minutes, my intention is to transform your relationship with sound. Let me start with the observation that most of the sound around us is accidental; much of it is unpleasant. (Traffic noise) We stand on street corners, shouting over noise like this, pretending it doesn't exist. This habit of suppressing sound has

meant that our relationship with sound has become largely unconscious.

There are four major ways sound is affecting you all the time, and I'd like to raise them in your consciousness today. The first is physiological. (Alarm clocks ring.)

Sorry about that. I just gave you a shot of cortisol, your fight-flight hormone. Sounds are affecting your hormone secretions all the time, but also your breathing, heart rate – which I just also did – and your brainwaves.

It's not just unpleasant sounds like that that do it. This is surf. (Ocean waves) It has the frequency of roughly 12 cycles per minute. Most people find that very soothing, and, interestingly, 12 cycles per minute is roughly the frequency of the breathing of a sleeping human, so there is a deep resonance with being at rest. We also associate it with being stress-free and on holiday.

The second way in which sound affects you is psychological. Music is the most powerful form of sound that we know that affects our emotional state. (Albinoni's Adagio) This is guaranteed to make most of you feel pretty sad if I leave it on. Music is not the only kind of sound, however, which affects your emotions.

Natural sound can do that, too. Birdsong, for example, is a sound which most people find reassuring. There's a reason: over hundreds of thousands of years we've learned that when the birds are singing, things are safe. It's when they stop you need to be worried..."

Analysis – Sound affects us in the following four ways:

1. Physiological (where Julian gives us a shot of cortisol – the stress hormone)
2. Physical (music, bird song)
3. Cognitive (two people talking at once)
4. Behavioural (driving while listening to music).

What an incredibly effective talk! One I will not ever forget. That is a measure of great content hitting excellent delivery. Most of the sound is accidental and unpleasant, Julian says, "we all need to work to move away from unpleasant sound to more pleasant sound." In fact, it is even bad for your health! He is an expert, a subject matter expert on sound. Julian has earned the right to talk on this subject because you can tell, even without looking at his bio, that he is well-versed. You get the sense that he has a foundation of knowledge that he could never cover in a five-minute talk. There is something comforting about that. When you hear a presenter speak, you want them to be the expert, and as an audience member, you want to learn something. I learned more than a few things in a short period of time from this talk:

1. Open space offices reduce productivity by 66 percent. I didn't know that, but it is a compelling and exciting idea. Once Treasure plays the soundtrack from an open plan office, you can understand why productivity would go down rather dramatically. This explains why intuitively, many of us will throw headphones on our ears in these environments.

2. Use sound in your presentation. As I watched Treasure's presentation, I recognize how little I utilize this component in my talks. Sure, I have music playing as my audience arrives; occasionally, I'll have a little music at the end. But I rarely use sound to punctuate a point. It may be worth investing in a portable set of speakers because Treasure's presentation has shown me the highly effective nature of sound.

Tip – Use sound in your presentations.

270 – Dalai Lama

(1935)

Context – The Dalai Lama speaks on compassion in 2007.

"Genuine compassion is unbiased."

Analysis – Let me begin by saying it is not my role to push any religion, spiritual practice, or way of life. That said, I am deeply interested in all these things but don't necessarily subscribe to any one dogma. Buddhism is fascinating to me, much like other religions and spiritualities. I was watching a PBS documentary tonight called *The Buddha* and it is certainly not my first exposure to the Dharma, the disciples of Buddhism, or Buddha himself. I have read a little on the topic, and there is something about this way of life that I enjoy exploring. Each time I've read or watched something on Buddhism, it makes me want to do better, live better, be a better person. I feel inspired. And isn't that what a 'teaching' of any kind should do? As a result of the documentary, something surfaced for me more so than before, and that is the topic of compassion. The Dalai Lama says, "Genuine compassion is unbiased. We are all sentient beings who have feelings, oneself and other—no difference, friend or enemy— all are sentient beings, and all have similar experiences in this world." How true is that! We often forget this as we lead our ego-driven/centered lives. While watching the documentary and again while watching a short Dalai Lama clip, I wondered how this can translate into giving a talk or a presentation. Frankly, it is the base camp, the foundation for reaching the summit of superb presentation and teaching skills.

I remember teaching a workshop with about 20 participants, and if you've ever attended or taught a workshop before, you know that emotions can often come to the surface (if you're doing your job well that is): anger, frustration, enthusiasm, fun, jubilation, despair, sadness. Hopefully, the negative emotions aren't directed at any one person in the room, but how that participant may be feeling about a certain aspect of their life (i.e., work) other dialogues and thoughts come to the surface. During the workshop, I found myself drawn to one participant in particular. Throughout the day, I kept thinking, "Is she okay?" She had shown no outward signs of being in distress; in fact, she was laughing and being rather jovial. At one point during the day, we broke out into small groups and I spend time as an observer in each group ensuring everyone understood the activity and that the discussion stayed on track and was rich in content. When I sat in with the group with this particular individual, she started discussing how unhappy she was in her current work environment, and after a lengthy download, she looked as though she was about to cry. It was not the appropriate time for her to unleash so to give her a chance to gather her thoughts, I quickly changed the subject. I did speak to her at the break, at which time her emotions came to the surface. The point is I intuitively knew something was going on with her, although she had given no real outward signs. This is not unique to me as we all have the ability to tap into what others are feeling and to feel compassion toward them. I believe particularly for the professional speakers who read this blog, that compassion for all your participants—I mean genuine compassion, unbiased compassion—is what will make you feel like you are creating real value. I love to teach, I really do. But that comes with a genuine desire to recognize that we all bring a personal story to the classroom. We all experience pain, sadness, and suffering. How, then, could you possibly teach from any other vantage point? Imagine if your point of view required shifting into a more compassionate direction, and how that may improve not only teaching in the classroom but outside of the classroom too.

Tip – Compassion is the base camp for teaching others.

#269 – Alain de Botton

(1969)

Context – Alain de Botton 2009 TED Talk, "A Kinder, Gentler Philosophy of Success."

"Next time you see someone driving a Ferrari, don't think this is someone who is greedy, think this is someone incredibly vulnerable and in need of love, feel sympathy, instead of contempt."

Analysis – In his talk, de Botton explores snobbery, envy, the impossibility of pure meritocracy or justice, the end of God, the adoration of nature, and father/mother figures. He speaks with wit, charm, and a rapid cadence that will keep your ears on their metaphorical toes. I am in awe of this presentation and this doesn't happen often. I'm struck with how de Botton can deliver such heavy content with such lightness and effervescence. If you read the above quote on the page without de Botton's delivery, you miss half of the equation; the words feel cold and judgmental, but his delivery is witty, fun, and cunning.

I've spent more time pondering success and failure than I'd care to admit. What defines success? Money, achievement? de Botton and I are in complete agreement; you can't be successful at everything. Some think that you can have it all, but the truth is you can't. It is nonsense to think otherwise. Perfection does not exist either, so its pursuit is futile. Such is the same for presentation skills. The pursuit of being the perfect presenter is ridiculous. I've not yet met a perfect anyone, much less a presenter. What we can do in the pursuit of betterment is to define what success for us looks like, individually. Through that process, we get better, learn more, and are more compassionate as presenters, we are more engaging, and thus our audience digests our concepts and is moved to take action.

Tip – Be the author of your definition of success.

#268 – Carmen Agra Deedy

(1960)

Context – Carmen Agra Deedy spins stories at TED 2005 in her talk, "Once upon a time, my mother…"

"When I knew I was going to come to speak to you, I thought, "I gotta call my mother." I have a little Cuban mother—she's about that big. Four feet. Nothing larger than the sum of her figurative parts.
You still with me? (Laughter)

I called her up.

"Hello, how're you doing, baby?"

"Hey, ma, I got to talk to you."

"You're talking to me already. What's the matter?"

I said, "I've got to talk to a bunch of nice people."

"You're always talking to nice people, except when you went to the White House."

"Ma, don't start!"

And I told her I was coming to TED.

And she said, "What's the problem?"

And I said, "Well, I'm not sure." I said, "I have to talk to them about stories. It's 'Technology, Entertainment and Design.'"

And she said, "Well, you design a story when you make it up, it's entertainment when you tell it, and you're going to use a microphone." (Laughter)

I said, "You're a peach, ma. Pop there?" "What's the matter? The pearls of wisdom leaping from my lips like lemmings is no good for you?" (Laughter)

"Crafting a great story is telling a story someone wants to hear. Great storytelling is the art of letting go."

Analysis – What a storyteller! Deedy spins a funny, wise, and electric tale of parents and their kids.

We all have the desire to tell our story, and have it heard, and it is my experience that sprinkling personal tales into your presentations will help your audience listen, digest, and enjoy themselves. Deedy tells a story about her Mom that winds down narrow side streets, main thoroughfares, overpasses, underpasses, and every emotion in between. It reminds me of a presentation skills class I did a while back. In the class, there were all levels of participants some had never stood in front of a group to give a presentation, some intermediate, and one participant who was what I'd consider incredibly experienced—he had given more than 200 presentations in his career. Hands down, the most challenged of all 15 participants were the most experienced and the ones who had logged the most hours speaking in front of people. Sure, the most experienced of the group was polished and articulate, and his content was interesting (a marketing professional), but his presentations felt flat. The delivery was robotic, unemotional, and there was no sense of who he was as a person; it felt like instead of listening to a presentation, I was reading information from a textbook. His presentations were one-dimensional, both literally and figuratively. He lacked what Deedy demonstrates in her talk, the ability to tell a story. Not any story, but a personal story. I'm not suggesting that your presentation is an opportunity to pontificate your life's story—unless, of course, that is the subject of your talk. I'm suggesting that at least half of your audience will require authenticity from you for them to continue to listen. Yup, at least half, the other half couldn't care less, but a solid 50 percent will need you to connect on an emotional level to continue to listen, absorb and learn. Does it have to be an earth-shattering story? Nope, but your stories need to give your audience insight into who you are.

Tip – Throw personal stories in your presentations.

#267 – Erin McKean

(1971)

Context – Erin McKean, in her 2007 TED, talks about redefining the dictionary in her talk, "The Joy of Lexicography."

"Now, have any of y'all ever looked up this word? You know, in a dictionary? (Laughter) Yeah, that's what I thought. How about this word? Here, I'll show it to you. Lexicography: the practice of compiling dictionaries. Notice – we're very specific – that word "compile." The dictionary is not carved out of a piece of granite, out of a lump of rock. It's made up of lots of little bits. It's little discrete – that's spelled D-I-S-C-R-E-T-E – bits. And those bits are words.

"Now one of the perks of being a lexicographer—besides getting to come to TED—is that you get to say really fun words, like lexicographical. Lexicographical has this great pattern: it's called a double dactyl. And just by saying double dactyl, I've sent the geek needle all the way into the red. (Laughter and Applause) But "lexicographical" is the same pattern as "higgledy-piggledy." Right? It's a fun word to say, and I get to say it a lot. Now, one of the non-perks of being a lexicographer is that people don't usually have a kind of warm, fuzzy, snuggly image of the dictionary. Right? Nobody hugs their dictionaries. But what people really often think about the dictionary is, they think more like this. Just to let you know, I do not have a lexicographical whistle. But people think that my job is to let the good words make that difficult left-hand turn into the dictionary and keep the bad words out."

Analysis – Here is a brilliant example for all my former and current students who have said, "my content is boring. There is no way I can make it interesting!" Yeah, this lexicographer walks you through her profession of compiling a dictionary. McKean is exuberant, fun and uses her slides brilliantly. She sprinkles in personal stories, wit, charm, and a whole lot of passion. Watch and learn my leery friends :)

Tip – Not all content can be fascinating, but it is your job to find a way to make it so.

#266 – Abraham Lincoln

1809–1865

Context – September 8th, 1854. Lincoln is reported to have said the below at a senatorial campaign meeting in Illinois.

"If you once forfeit the confidence of your fellow citizens, you can never regain their respect and esteem. You may fool all the people some of the times; you can even fool some of the people all the time; but you can't fool all of the people all of the time."

Analysis – Lincoln made it clear that he favoured giving equal rights to slaves, and this speech was reported to have been refuting an attack by his democrat rival for the senate seat. I've seen these words plenty of times but hadn't, until recently, pondered the immensity of them. Now that I understand them in their proper context relating to slavery, they are even more powerful.

As it relates to presentation skills, it couldn't be any more accurate. If you aren't able to develop and gain respect from your audience, you won't be able to move your audience to action. This is something that can't be bought or cajoled. It is not a popularity contest. It is a process that requires you to be knowledgeable on your topic, be able to express that knowledge, and then help your audience understand how to apply that knowledge into a skill or changed behaviour. And the process of attaining trust and respect begins with giving trust and respect. Truly respecing your audience, listening to what they have to say, and accepting their feedback. Take the time to build a solid foundation of trust and respect with your audience, and you will have them hanging on your every word.

Tip – Develop trust and respect with your audience.

#265 – Malcolm Gladwell

(1963)

Context – Gladwell's 2004 TED Talk, "What We Can Learn from Spaghetti Sauce?" Gladwell is the author of the *Tipping Point* and *Blink*.

"I think I was supposed to talk about my new book, which is called Blink, and it's about snap judgments and first impressions. And it comes out in January, and I hope you all buy it in triplicate.

"But I was thinking about this, and I realized that although my new book makes me happy, and I think would make my mother happy, it's not really about happiness. So, I decided instead, I would talk about someone who I think has done as much to make Americans happy as perhaps anyone over the last 20 years, a man who is a great personal hero of mine: someone by the name of Howard Moskowitz, who is most famous for reinventing spaghetti sauce.

"Howard's about this high, and he's round, and he's in his 60s, and he has big huge glasses and thinning gray hair, and he has a kind of wonderful exuberance and vitality, and he has a parrot, and he loves the opera, and he's a great aficionado of medieval history. And by profession, he's a psychophysicist. Now, I should tell you that I have no idea what psychophysics is, although at some point in my life, I dated a girl for two years who was getting her doctorate in psychophysics. Which should tell you something about that relationship…."

Analysis – If you've read any of Gladwell's books, you won't need me to convert you into a fan, as, most likely, you already are. If you've never heard of him nor read any of his books, let me forewarn, Gladwell's writing and presentation styles are that of a calm, analogy-driven, story-loaded/driven methodology. You have to stick with him to get his message in either of his venues. It's like investing time upfront into a great plot or ending of a novel. You know the kind of books, the ones that take forever to get moving, and end up tucked away onto a bookshelf never to be re-open again. I have a rule that if I pick up a book, I have to finish it. The two exceptions to this rule are Anna Karenina and Lisey's Story—a Stephen King book. Of the hundreds of books I've read, those were the only two that I just couldn't finish no matter how hard I tried. I'm sure you've got a list too. Sometimes, (just like with some authors) you have to stick with a presenter. Sure, Gladwell could spice it up at the beginning and be more compelling. But I still enjoy this talk because he finishes with a bang, and he talks about spaghetti sauce for 18 minutes! Which is no easy feat! To be fair, he's not only talking about spaghetti sauce but the food industry as a whole.

Today's tip is to build a crescendo in your talks, build and build until the very end. It's also worth noting that Gladwell doesn't use a single slide, so listen up PowerPoint junkies!

Tip – Experiment with no slides.

#264 – Bhagavad Gita

Written between 400 BCE and 200 CE. 5th-century BCE is only a guess as to the inception of this book. No one knows!

Context – *Bhagavad Gita* means 'The Song of the Blessed One' and is book six of India's national epic, Mahabharata.

"Although you mean well, Arjuna
your sorrow is sheer delusion.
Wise men do not grieve
for the dead or for the living.
Never was there a tim
when I did not exist, or you,

or these kings; nor will there come a time when we cease to be
Just as, in this body, the Self
passes through childhood, youth
and old age, so after death
it passes to another body.
Physical sensations—cold
and heat, pleaser and pain –
are transient: they come and go;
so bear them patiently; Arjuna.
Only the man who is unmoved by any sensations, the wise man
indifferent to pleasure, to pain,
is fit for becoming deathless.
Nonbeing can never be;
being can never not be.
Both these statements are obvious
to those who have seen the truth."

Analysis – This 264th entry, takes us in a new direction: Hindu scripture. There are thousands and thousands of pages of scripture that one could pour themselves into. Vedas, Upanishads, Mahabharata, amongst others. Please don't get the impression that I am well studied on any of them. Frankly, whenever I try to unfold these books, my head feel like a spinning top. I wonder if even the most devoted Hindus occasionally feel the same way. My guess is they do. But it doesn't stop me from trying to unfold the most accessible in terms of the Hindu scripture, the *Bhagavad Gita*. The Gita is one short part of the *Mahabharata*, a much longer text with some 13,000 pages! It is a very long poem. For those poets out there, imagine that the *Mahabharata* is eight times the length of the *Iliad* and the *Odyssey* combined! It tells the story of a war between two clans of a royal family in India. The Gita takes place on the battlefield at the beginning of the war. Arjuna, the central character, receives lessons from Krishna. These lessons surface from Arjuna's complete dread about the deaths of so many brave warriors. He refuses to fight. So, begins Krishna's lessons on life, death, love, spirituality, non-attachment, and everything in between. Oh, and Krishna happens to be the Lord Supreme God of All Things.

So, the primary question of the Gita is, 'How should we live?' Or, more applicable, 'How should I live?' Arjuna stands eager for illumination in front of Krishna, much like the reader, and Krishna is not only patient and kind but uses a superior form of teaching. He doesn't use a systematic manual approach but rather a circular pattern constructed into the poetic rhythms. He can teach the most versed reader and the novice who is unaware of the importance of the scripture and has picked it up because it was on some best sellers list. Now, I'll attempt to bridge this important book with presentation skills. It is your job as a presenter to present, and re-present again and again until your audience has understood what has been said. However, to be able to switch it up so that you present from a new angle each time. To do so, you must remove your ego from the equation so that you can genuinely observe what is transpiring with your audience. If you are inwardly thinking about yourself—your nerves, your delivery, your wardrobe choices, etc., you will never get your attention on the people that matter the most in a presentation scenario, your audience. Your audience is the reason you are there, so watch them and engage with them. Are they digesting? Krishna was immensely patient with Arjuna:

"Let go."
What does that mean?
"It means this."
I don't get it.
"It means that."
I still don't get it.
"Then let me paint you a picture."
But how do I let go?
"Just act in this way."
But I can't.
"All right, then act in this way."
But what if I can't do that either?
"All right, here's still another approach."
The presenter's job is to be patient with their audience and gently guide them to a place of understanding. Om Shanti. (peace be with you)

Tip – Have unabashed patience with your audience as you work with them to help them understand your message.

#263 – Becky Blanton

(1955)

Context – Becky Blanton's 2009 talk, "The year I was homeless." Blanton is a writer and journalist.

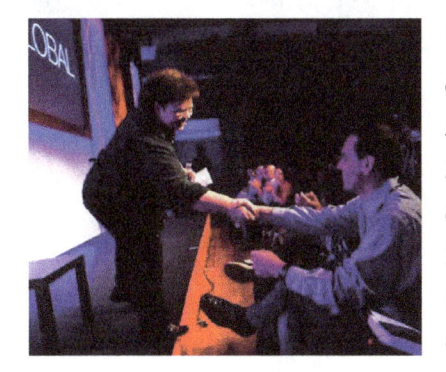

"My I.Q. hadn't dropped. My talent, my integrity, my values, everything about me remained the same. But I had changed somehow. I spiraled deeper and deeper into a depression…The human spirit can overcome everything if they have hope! People are not where they live, where they sleep, or what their life situation is at any given time. Three years ago, I was living in a van in a Walmart parking lot. And today, I'm speaking at TED. Hope always always finds a way."

Analysis – Maybe I still have the *Bhagavad Gita* on the brain from a recent post (it was a bit of a head hurter, no?), but I'm feeling rather grateful today to have watched this excellent presentation from Blanton. Here is a woman who, after some difficult circumstances, finds herself living in her car. She's a respected writer, photographer, and journalist. She communicates with a genuine humbleness that I wish all my corporate clients would adopt. I can't teach this and that is why I've found myself occasionally inserting different spiritual and otherworldly genres into my work. It is in the hopes that we can all take a little of what Blanton demonstrates for us today. Compassion, kindness and hope toward ourselves and to others. If we do that as presenters, we cannot help but inspire others and perhaps provide them with a little hope too.

Tip – Be compassionate to yourself and others.

#262 – Dan Ariely

(1967)

Context – In his 2008 TED Talk, Dan Ariely asks, "Are We in Control of Our Own Decisions?"

"Academic papers are not that fun to read and often not fun to write. So I decided to try and write something more fun. And I came up with an idea that I will write a cookbook."

Analysis – No one wanted to publish Ariely's cookbook, but there was a suggestion: publish a book on your research, then you'll have the opportunity to publish something else, perhaps the cookbook. And so he wrote a book on his research, *Predictably Irrational*. Ariely's pursuit is to answer questions such as:

- Why are we convinced that *sizing up* at our favourite burger joint is a good idea, even when we're not that hungry?

- Why are our phone lists cluttered with numbers we never call?

- Why does your grocery store run out of your favourite flavour of ice cream?

His presentation style is one of my favourites. He strings together a series of examples to support his idea, but those examples are told in a storytelling format. Peppered with a good balance of slides, humour, and wit. In Ariely's presentation, which I hope you take the 17 minutes to watch, he goes through a few examples of how our emotional states, moral codes, and peer pressure can affect our ability to make rational and often crucial decisions in our daily lives with both professional and personal choices. There is a wonderment behind each of the examples, a metaphorical gasp when he gets to the punch line, it is delivered with the cadence of a great symphony; rise and falls, crescendos, and everything in between.

Here are the examples he uses:

- When Dan gets to the part of his presentation on organ donation, it punctuates his point on the illusion of decisions brilliantly.

- He tells a story that has the following characters: Piroxicam, Ibuprofen, and hip replacement surgery. Not to be missed!

- Rome with or without coffee. What do you think?
- *The Economist* subscription centre newsprint example
- Will ugly Jerry and Tom help the brothers?

Notice how these examples are one dimensional and confusing when you don't have a story behind them.

Behavioural economy is interesting and it's exciting! And I never even heard the term before I watched this presentation. That, my friends, is what you call a powerful presentation. I wonder though, Ariely, if human beings are perhaps not fundamentally irrational, but rather that there are hidden elements that influence our decision making unconsciously. Hmmm :)

Tip – Use the element of surprise and wonder in your talks. Make your audience say, "Hmmm."

#261 – Gustave Flaubert

1821–1880

Context – Gustave Flaubert, a French writer, is said to have been one of the greatest Western novelists. His novel, *Madame Bovary*, is perhaps his most famous piece.

"…they write criticism because they are unable to be artists, just as a man unfit to bear arms becomes a police spy…I'd like to know what poets throughout the ages could have in common with the critics who have analyzed their work…Criticism occupies the lowest place in the literary hierarchy: as regards form, almost always and as regards 'moral value,' incontestably. It comes after rhyming games and acrostics, which at least require a certain inventiveness."

Analysis – Although Flaubert's quote is blunt, I agree with it wholeheartedly both from his vantage point of literary work but also as it relates to presentation skills. The other day, one of my students asked me why I rarely, if ever, provide constructive criticism. It's simple. I believe that if I (or anyone else for that matter) highlights strengths as they relate to presentation skills, then those are the skills that will be remembered and duplicated. If, by contrast, I provide negative feedback, then those are the skills that will be at the nucleus of one's mind, and it will be a monumental task to override them. That said, I may point out certain elements of a presentation that are overwhelmingly apparent and need to be addressed in order for the audience to focus on the message. For fun, a few years back, I participated in a well-known presentation skills workshop. The facilitator had each of us go to the front of the room and give a presentation. She'd stop each one of us as she saw us doing something wrong. My error was that I like to have a Sharpie clipped onto my belt so that I can get to a flip chart and have it at the ready. For a solid year after that, I questioned that stupid Sharpie; I obsessed about it and didn't have it on my belt but put it on the table. Then I'd scurry about looking for it while I tried to find my way to the flip chart. It broke up my rhythm, threatened my confidence and made me flustered. I know the other participants must've had the same aftershock experiences with their so-called errors. Some other examples from that class included: jiggling pocket change, pen clicking, hair tossing, getting flushed or blushing. To all of these,

I say 'Bologna!' From that day forward in my classes, I made the conscious decision never to call out what I consider insignificant wrongs and I focus instead on the presenters' strengths. Focusing on one's strengths builds confidence, encourages positive behaviour, and frankly, it feels good to give and receive a compliment. That said, the compliments are always $20 compliments vs. 20-cent compliments. A 20-cent compliment looks something like this: Good job, and I love your shirt. A $20 compliment looks something like this: You have the ability through your words to inspire others. As a result of your presentation today, I will <insert specific examples>. You have changed the way I've viewed this topic, and I will forever remember it. See the difference. So, my tip for today, take other's constructive criticisms with a grain of salt. Learn the art of providing yourself with honest feedback and use that as your barometer for success.

Tip – Be cautious of the criticism you get from others.

#260 – Sarah Jones

(1973)

Context – Sarah Jones in her 2009 TED Talk, "A One-Woman Global Village."

"I should tell you that when I was asked to be here, I thought to myself that well, it's TED. And these TEDsters are—you know, as innocent as that name sounds—these are the philanthropists and artists and scientists who sort of shape our world. And what could I possibly have to say that would be distinguished enough to justify my participation in something like that? And so, I thought perhaps a really civilized-sounding British accent might help things a bit.

"And then I thought no, no. I should just get up there and be myself and just talk the way I really talk because, after all, this is the great unveiling. And so, I thought I'd come up here and unveil my real voice to you. Although many of you already know that I do speak the Queen's English because I am from Queens, New York. (Laughter) But the theme of this session, of course, is invention. And while I don't have any patents that I'm aware of, you will be meeting a few of my inventions today. I suppose it's fair to say that I am interested in the invention of self or selves. We're all born into certain circumstances with particular physical traits, unique developmental experiences, geographical and historical contexts. But then what? To what extent do we self-construct, do we self-invent? How do we self-identify and how mutable is that identity? Like, what if one could be anyone at any time? Well, my characters, like the ones in my shows, allow me to play with the spaces between those questions. And so, I've brought a couple of *them with me. And well, they're very excited. What I should tell you – what I should tell you is that they've each prepared their own little TED Talks. So, feel free to think of this as Sarah University. (Laughter)"*

Analysis – Jones is what one calls a monologist, which, by definition, is a person who makes long speeches, often monopolizing a conversation. It is not a stretch to say that actors and presenters share a lot in common; actors often have to do the same role for months and years. How do Broadway plays stay fresh? The same question can be asked of presenters. Many of the individuals I work with do the same presentation repeatedly (i.e., sales, marketing, etc.) Quite often, we focus our attention on the nervous presenter, but what about the presenters out there who have lost his/her butterflies (which is a very worrisome sign to me, because being nervous means you care.)

Here are a few tips to help keep your well-worn presentation fresh, which I've borrowed from my acting friends:

1. Improvise. This doesn't mean wing it. It means letting go and allowing yourself to be in the moment. You've earned the right since you've done your talk so many times. Allow your audience to throw your talk out of sync. If a question or comment comes up and you have that embedded in your talk, go there instead of saying, "I will get to that later in my talk." Presenting on the fly is not for the faint of heart, you have to know what you're doing and know your presentation backwards, forwards, inside out, and standing on your head.

2. Be theatrical. Actors try to keep it real, whether on the movie screen or the stage. However, on stage, there is a need for a heightened form of action. Reality would be boring to watch on stage! Even subtle performances have a flash of theatrics thrown in. So, be slightly larger than life! This means being more animated. Now, I'm not saying to put on an act per se. What I'm saying is, be yourself, just a little bit bigger.

3. Vary each scene. Anything that goes on for too long or belabours the point becomes tedious. Even a funny comedian who doesn't change it up will become boring. The same is true of presentations. Just because that introduction was successful due to the well-placed cartoon slide doesn't mean that you should repeat it for your entire 20 minutes on stage. I have a general format I worked to whenever I deliver a presentation: story, lecture, transition, activity, major point, another story, and repeat. This is a guideline I use as I'm developing a talk to ensure I change scenes often and frequently.

4. Keep your stories personal. Your job as presenter is to ensure that you memorize the experience, the emotion of your stories, not the words. Relive the experience as you retell it, see it, feel it. If you can't visualize the story as you're telling it, your audience won't either. Think about your favourite actors, I bet the reason you like them is that they are able to tell you about an experience in which they pour real and strong emotion into, they tell it in such a way that transports you in time and place.

Tip – Break a leg.

#259 – Sir John Mortimer

1923–2009

Context – Sir John Mortimer is a writer best known for the TV shows *Rumpole of the Bailey* and *Brideshead Revisited*.

"The difference…between the person who say he 'wishes to be a writer' and the person who says he 'wishes to write.' The former desires to be pointed out at cocktail parties, the latter is prepared for the long, solitary hours at a desk; the former desires a status; the latter a process; the former desire to be, the latter to do."

Analysis – Alongside my presentation career, I have had a private writing life for nearly 20 years. So, I can completely identify with this quote from Mortimer. I have people in my life that don't understand. They can't comprehend why, if I have a few hours spare or the opportunity to have a few days off, I gravitated to my little (okay, not so little at 80,000 words) novel, which I worked on for nearly two-years before its completion. Gravitate is the operative word, I was driven to it like a magnet drawn to its other half. I committed to myself that I would finish *365 Must-Know Talks of All Time*, but before that I made a much larger commitment to develop my writing as a creative outlet, and, if I continued to enjoy it, do it until the literal and metaphorical end. Except for three editors and one writing teacher, no one has read anything of mine (and what has been read has been only snippets at that). I haven't received recognition, and only a handful of my closest friends know that my novel exists. I write for the sheer delight and the utter angst it brings me. Both are mine. I promise I'm not relinquishing this fact to sound fancy—like a cocktail party citation. I share this to help identify two camps of people; there are doers, and there are talkers. That's why I like this quote so much. Please, don't go around telling others how much you want to be or do something, just do it (shamelessly quoting Nike). There will be obstacles, there will be days that you'll want to throw in the towel, there will be days that you can't figure how you got yourself into that mess, but ask youself, "Are you one of those talkers? Will you regret the decision not to act on your ideas when you're on your death bed?" I am of the firm belief that there is no success without some risk.

The same can be said of presentations. Many folks when they hear what I do as a profession say, "A talker? You mean you stand up and talk to a bunch of people? I could never do that! I'm horrible at public speaking!" (Perhaps not verbatim but pretty darn close). The truth is many people aspire to be able to develop this skill in a way that would bring both them and their audiences joy. We all have a story to tell, and we all want to be heard. Giving a talk in a public venue is one way of reaching out to and significantly impacting large groups. Developing presentation skills is not an act of hope (i.e., "I wish I could")—it is a conscious act of doing. So, get out there. Force yourself to stop talking about doing it and commit to it. It's time to roll up your sleeves and just do it!

Tip – Just do it!

#258 – Geronimo

1829–1909

Context – Geronimo was a leader and medicine man from the Bedonkohe band of the Apache tribe

"I cannot think that we are useless, or God would not have created us. There is one God looking down on us all. We are all the children of one God. The sun, the darkness, the winds are all listening to what we have to say….I was warmed by the sun, rocked by the winds, and sheltered by the trees as other Indian babes. I was living peaceably when people began to speak bad of me. Now I can eat well, sleep well and be glad. I can go everywhere with a good feeling…"

Analysis – While on a plane on my way back from Phoenix, Arizona, I was thinking about my 365 entries and who I might choose to represent the state. It became apparent that Geronimo, the prominent native American leader and medicine man who fought against Mexico and the United States, was a perfect choice. Although he was born in what is known today as New Mexico territory.

Geronimo's parents raised him according to Apache traditions. In 1858, a company of 400 Mexican soldiers from Sonora attacked Geronimo's camp. Among those killed were Geronimo's wife, his three children, and his mother. Although he was never a chief, he was a military leader, known to have special powers of telepathy and telekinesis. He survived many gunshots and was wounded numerous times. The Apache men chose to follow him for his powers and his abilities to survive insurmountable odds. He represented the Apache values of aggressiveness and courage in the face of difficulty.

I began to research Geronimo and came across the above quotes. And it made me think of the incredible discrimination that Geronimo and his community experienced. Discrimination that still exists today. It made me expand the boundaries of prejudice to include all people that have encountered such horrible acts of violence simply due to identifying with a different culture or having a different skin colour. As I re-read Geronimo's quote, I realized it could also include anyone that doesn't fit nicely into societal norms; people with disabilities, intellectual impairments, gender inequality, ageism, etc. Unfortunately, my heart is heavy because these ideologies of superiority that existed hundreds of years ago during Geronimo's time still exist today. Geronimo was correct when he said, "I cannot think that we are useless, or God would not have created us. There is one God looking down on us all. We are all the children of one God. The sun, the darkness, the winds are all listening to what we have to say." We are all equal, and it is dumbfounding that anyone would think differently. We all have purpose. I struggle to find the words to express my despair to those that have difficulty seeing this. I feel the weight of this deeply and hope that if you don't, you'll explore your thought processes, widen your horizons, stretch the boundaries of your comfort zone, and open up your world to everyone within it. My hope is that you will feel the weight of what those who are discriminated against have to endure. Then and only then, you can identify with Geronimo when his says, "the winds are all listening to what you have to say." It is so much more than identifying with and agreeing with a statement. It is the morals and values you take into everything you do. It is not enough to agree that discrimination is horrible. When encountering discrimination, regardless of whether it is aimed at you or others, it is of paramount importance to act on it even when it isn't comfortable or doesn't fit within society's social graces.

So, what does this all have to do with presentation skills? Simply if you think that you are superior in any way to anyone in your audience or anyone else in society, then I beg you, please close your mouth and leave the stage! You are not equipped to teach others. I remember teaching a presentation skills class many years ago. Each participant was asked to do a short three-minute talk at the front of the class. One participant thought it was appropriate to make a racial slur that he referred to as "a joke." I rarely get angry in the classroom, certainly not when I'm teaching. But, on this occasion, I halted the class, asked him to join me outside, and informed him he was no longer welcome in my class. He tried to rationalize his behaviour saying, "That's just how I was raised." But this is not an excuse. Just because you are raised poorly doesn't give you license to perpetuate hate. Even now, all these years later, it still sickens me to think about it. When I returned to the class, I explained to the other participants what had happened and that the rules for my classroom were to respect others and that this type of behaviour would not be tolerated. As presenter, it is your role to stamp out hideous behaviour. If it happens, you must address it immediately. Too often, I'll watch a presenter ignore a disrespectful or racist comment from an audience member. Even if they disagree with the comment, they let it slide because they don't know how to address it—make no mistake, to do so makes you complicit. You, as presenter, are the one in control of the room. It is your responsibility to indicate your disapproval and act on what has happened. How else will this world ever change? If you want to live in a world of acceptance for all human beings, I plead with you to make a difference and adopt the Apache values of aggressiveness and courage in the face of adversity. If you observe discrimination, be prepared to act immediately.

Tip – Address inappropriate behaviour immediately.

#257 – Anthony Bourdain

1956–2018

Context – Anthony Bourdain, *No Reservations*. The below quote is from his book, by the same name as his show (which, of course, I've read).

"My whole life, cooking has been about control. Travelling and eating are about letting things happen."

Analysis – If I have the television on, it's likely tuned into the food network, or alternatively I will channel surf to PBS or any other locale that is hosting a food show. There is something about watching the culinary arts that relaxes me. As a kid, I was plastered to the television watching *Julia Child*, then later, *Molto Mario*, *Emeril Live*. Today, I'm hooked on baking shows. I'm drawn to the fact that a cooking show is, essentially, a teaching show. There are good cooking teachers and not-so-good cooking teachers (Naturally, Julia Child has her spot on this list but today is not her day). Possibly my favourite of all the food-inspired shows is anything to do with Anthony Bourdain. Sadly, Bourdain died in 2018 and is a big miss on all my beloved food shows.

Okay, so Bourdain was one cool guy. He had some heated dispute with the Food Network and left, but you can find him on the travel network now hosting his show, *No Reservations*. Born in France, he lived in New York. Yeah, I could talk about his quick wit, his sarcastic cadence, his bold opinions, his quest for the perfect meal, his attempts to cook the perfect meal, but I won't. Instead, I'd like to shine a light on what I believe is his most awe-inspiring quality, which is apparent in each episode of his show; his utmost respect for the cultures he visits. From Japan to Greece to the Middle East to the U.S. to Mexico and everywhere in between, he always showed great respect for everyone and every tradition he encountered. He showed that while you may arrive in a new place and feel a little uncomfortable, you can quickly win friends by being eager to learn about what another culture offers. This may sound like a line pulled from an episode of *Pollyanna*, and I'm chuckling as I write this because Bourdain was anything but a goody-goody, but he was always open to learn and fully immerse himself into other cultures while staying within the realm of his unique personality.

There is a lot to be said for letting things happen when giving a presentation. There is no way you can anticipate all that will happen while you are doing it. You can prepare and prepare and prepare. But much of that preparation is so you can relinquish control, let things evolve organically in the room and feel comfortable as it happens around you. Preparation allows you to engage with your audience, teach in a natural way and allow the room to be its own living thing. When you are travelling, you can prepare a flight plan, book a hotel, even plan an itinerary, but none of that can prepare you for the actual experience —that will only happen when you are there. So, as you prepare for your presentations, show respect for your audience as if travelling to a new country, but once you are in the room, just let things happen.

Tip – Let things just happen.

#256 – Fran Lebowitz

(1950)

Context – *Public Speaking* is a 2010 HBO documentary that follows writer Fran Lebowitz who is known for her unique perspectives. The documentary was directed and produced by Martin Scorsese and contains clips from Lebowitz's various speaking engagements and interviews. Scorsese and Lebowitz teamed up in 2021 for another film entitled *Pretend it's a City*, which is somewhat of a love letter to New York City. Lebowitz wrote *The Metropolitan Life* (a book of comic essays) in 1978 when she was 27 and the book became a best-seller. *Social Studies*, a collection of comedic essays, followed in 1981 and was also a best seller. Lebowitz hasn't published anything for more than 20 years and has become famous (or infamous) for having writers' block so severe that many writers joke that they have taken a break in sympathy. Her last publication was a children's picture book, *Mr. Chas & Lisa Sue Meet the Pandas*. She makes her living talking about politics and New York City and teaming with Scorsese, who has said of his friend, "She's my inspiration." Her perspective on Scorsese? "He's promising," she says.

"When I was young, it was called talking back. Now it is called 'public speaking,' but it's really the same. The thing I used to get punished for at home and in school and get bad marks for then I ended up getting paid and rewarded for it."

Analysis – Lebowitz is the definition of wit. In contrast to humour, wit can be cold, and judgemental and makes assumptions. Humour is safer and is used to provoke laughter and provide amusement. Lebowitz is not safe. She is one of the most charming and witty talkers on the planet. She also personifies New York City, having lived there much of her life. She's brash and she moves fast. She speaks fast, with a cigarette hanging from her mouth. She says of her addiction to cigarettes, "People act now like smoking is a moral failure, it's an addiction. I could be starving to death; I wouldn't leave my apartment at 3 a.m. in a snowstorm but for cigarettes. If you told me at 14 that the most deviant behaviour I would possess is smoking, I would have had a whole different adolescence." She doesn't beat around the bush, that's for sure!

I could listen to Lebowitz forever. She has such an original perspective on the world. There are few people who I would follow down every rabbit hole, but I have spent many hours devouring Lebowitz-related videos and books. It's no wonder the game show Jeopardy honoured her with her very own category, The Quotable Fran Leibowitz. The best way to wrap your brain around Lebowitz, if you're unfamiliar with her work, is to listen to her own words. Here are some of my favourite quotes:

- Great people talk about ideas, average people talk about things, and small people talk about wine.
- All God's children are not beautiful. Most of God's children are, in fact, barely presentable.
- In real life, I assure you, there is no such thing as algebra.
- Life is something that happens when you can't get to sleep.
- The opposite of talking isn't listening. The opposite of talking is waiting.
- As a teenager, you are at the last stage in your life when you will be happy to hear that the phone is for you.
- Success didn't spoil me; I've always been insufferable.
- No animal should ever jump up on the dining-room furniture unless absolutely certain that he can hold his own in the conversation.
- Ask your child what he wants for dinner only if he's buying.
- You're only as good as your last haircut.
- There is no such thing as inner peace. There is only nervousness and death.
- There's always something to complain about.
- The difference between children and adults is when children don't get what they want, they ask. When adults don't get what they want, they become republicans.
- As I'm sitting on the subway, I often think that the next person to enter it would be a better President than Trump.

- I believe in the freedom of not listening to others, my second amendment.

- I could be a Supreme Court judge because you don't need a law degree. The cases are so easy. I don't know what takes them so long. I could decide all of them in two seconds. Slow judgements mean there is corruption.

- Don't boo me; I'm not even getting paid.

Public Speaking is interspersed with interviews and public speaking engagements with Leibowitz's giving her perspective on a vast array of topics. She recounts a New Yorkers opinion of Times Square. In the 1970s, the city was losing money so Times Square was created to attract tourists to the city. Like many New Yorkers, Leibowitz's doesn't like tourists. If a New Yorker bumps into another New Yorker in Times Square, they'll each come up with every conceivable excuse as to why the hell they are there—"I'm on my way somewhere else," or "I'm doing research." I find myself pausing the documentary several times as I'm laughing so hard, and I don't want to miss a millisecond.

Gender, politics, sexuality, race, no topics are off-limits. There is nothing gray about Leibowitz's world. It is black or white. It's refreshing. Leibowitz is a thinker who talks. For those seeking to improve their public speaking skills, I would not suggest emulating anyone and certainly not Leibowitz. What I glean from this documentary and researching Leibowitz is that she has many areas of knowledge. She is interested in and knows a lot about many things. Leibowitz is a modern-day Renaissance woman! Having in depth knowledge on an array of topics is incredibly important to deliver interesting talks. This helps develop a unique voice. Beyond knowing a lot about many different things, being bold can add an additional dimension. I can't help but think why most of us fear taking big, bold perspectives on topics—fear of Imposter Syndrome or of not being liked or conflict or being booed off the stage by the audience. Tell you what, I'm preparing for a talk right now, and I will channel Leibowitz, her documentary and my own advice. I'm going big, bold, and original.

Tip – Be bold and original and tap into your inner New York City persona.

#255 – Eve Ensler

(1953)

Context – Even Ensler, American playwright, performer, feminist, activist, and creator of "The Vagina Monologues", talks about "Finding Happiness in Body and Soul" in this 2007 TED Talk.

"I was worried. That's why I began this piece. I was worried about vaginas. I was worried what we think about vaginas and even more worried that we don't think about them. I was worried about my own vagina. It needed a context, a culture, a community of other vaginas. There is so much darkness and secrecy surrounding them. Like the Bermuda Triangle, nobody ever reports back from there."

Analysis – Ensler is known for her hugely successful and groundbreaking play *The Vagina Monologues*. Inspired by intimate conversations with friends, the play shares a series of stories from women about their bodies and experiences. It first hit the stage in 1996, and since then has been translated into more the 45 languages, performed in more than 120 countries and has been re-created as an HBO film. One woman, sitting on a stool, telling stories from her body, as Ensler describes it, and not her head. This single, lone female character tells a string of stories that makes the message real. From *The Vagina Monologues* comes 'V-Day,' a movement to stop violence against women and girls.

I bring this play to the fore as it relates to presentation skills. Ensler's presentation style in comfortable and easy-going, with the tranquility of a casual and calm narrator. You can tell Ensler's has talked in front of myriad audiences in a public speaking venue. Her ease is palpable. As a result, the audience is relaxed and can tackle and perhaps digest more of what many would find a somewhat embarrassing topic. If you find yourself giving a presentation on a topic that will make your audience (and maybe you) a little uncomfortable, Ensler teaches two essential lessons: Be at ease, and your audience will be at ease and utilize a storytelling approach rather than a technical one.

Tip – Be at ease and your audience will be at ease too.

#254 – Hillary Clinton

(1947)

Context – Democratic Debate 2008 with Clinton and Obama.

"Everyone here knows that I've lived through some crisis and some challenges, and I am grateful for the support and the prayers of countless Americans. How can you keep going, people ask me? I shake my head in wonderment because of all the challenges I have had; they are nothing in relation to the Americans I see every day."

Analysis – A political debate reminds me so much of the question-and-answer segment that generally follows a presentation. You better believe you're going to get grilled on your subject material, so take some time to think about and even document the questions that you may be asked following your presentation. It is critical that you formulate hypothetical responses. Much like how you'd prepare for a job interview, you need to anticipate the questions that will be asked and have a firm understanding of how you'll answer them. Clinton does this well. I've watched her in at least a dozen debates, and she is better at the debate than giving a speech. She's magnificent on the spot. She starts with a tongue-in-cheek response that elicits laughter and applause, such as: "Everyone here knows that I've lived through some challenges…" but then she'll humbly take her answer to a more appropriate place and speak of others that have survived much more significant challenges than she has faced.

Tip – Anticipate the questions that will come your way and prepare your answers in advance.

#253 – C.S. Lewis

1898–1963

Context – From C.S. Lewis' book, *Mere Christianity*

"Very often the only way to get a quality in reality is to start behaving as if you had it already. That is why children's games are so important. They are always pretending to be grown-ups—playing soldiers, playing shop. But all the time, they are hardening their muscles and sharpening their wits, so that the pretence of being grown-up helps them to grow up in earnest"

Analysis – Inner attitude is often the most important key to outer results, which we've discussed several times. As we try to acquire any new skill, we must have an upfront faith that we will accomplish it. We need a belief in our competence. Otherwise, it would prove to be an utterly worthless endeavour. We often need to work hard to cultivate inner confidence.

The average person thinks sixty-thousand thoughts per day. Ninety-five percent, unfortunately, are the same thoughts as yesterday. How you talk to yourself is more important than you think! "I'm not good enough, successful enough." These negative thoughts impact our reality. Is there a correlation between our internal dialogue and our external reality?

Your thoughts create your future. Your internal pep talk is far more critical than you may think. By taking responsibility for yourself and your thought process, you can make your life more positive and uplifting and reduce or negate the influence of negative energy.

Causation is the act of causing or producing an effect. Every action has a reaction, including our thought process and how we talk to ourselves. If we speak to ourselves unkindly, the outcome will be the same. If we constantly tell ourselves, we won't or can't be happy or that we will perform badly during our presentation, then that's the result we will manifest. Be very careful how you think because it is much more powerful than we are taught to believe.

The same can be true of timelines. There is a past, a present, and a future, right? We are taught that things happen one at a time. We walk from here to there, from one location to another, and a timeline is created. The world does not work like this though. It is synchronistic; it is coincidental. Things happens simultaneously. It is the process of infinite correlation—the ability to do an infinite number of things and correlate them with one another simultaneously. A great example is the human body. One cell does not say to another, "Listen, I'm going to digest some food right now. I need you to wait while I do some thinking." It happens at the same time. Another example is the entire cosmos, the symphony of the universe continues at the same time. The earth, moon, planets, and stars continue to do what they do simultaneously while you and I sit here. We are all connected to this, and it happens with or without our consciousness. Why not be conscious? Especially as it relates to how you think. Be aware that your thoughts and your internal pep talk always affects your external world.

Tip – Your thoughts are far more important than you think. So, train yourself to think positively.

#252 – Geena Davis

(1956)

Context – Movie star, Geena Davis became quite philosophical in a magazine interview, and said the below.

"Listen to me talk about the meaning of life. I'm only trying to say that I view life as a journey. It's not so much having some goal and getting to it. It's taking the journey itself that matters. The process, each step along the way, is the important thing—the moment you're in right now. Taking seriously the opportunity to be responsible for yourself as a person, for who you are and what you believe. I don't think life is about arriving somewhere and then just hanging out. It's expanding and expanding and trying and trying to get somewhere new and never stopping. It's getting out your colours and showing them."

Analysis – This quote could easily have been said by a world-renowned and revered philosopher, but it's not, it's said by the actor Geena Davis who caught herself beginning to wax philosophical. I couldn't agree more. Most of us will be familiar with the phrase, it's not the destination but the journey that is of utmost importance in human life. Yes, life is a process. If you aren't enjoying the process of your life as it is, then you need to make a change. Only then will you be positioning yourself for the most satisfying, and enduring forms of success. The more you enjoy the process, the easier it will be to set and define goals. Confidence will arrive naturally. It will be easier to focus your concentration, and things will begin to get accomplished. If you enjoy the process, issues of character will not be as tricky to manage. Sounds simple, yes? It is. If we look to presentation skills as our analogy, we can see how simple this concept is. If you're giving a presentation in the future, and you are dreading the process or feeling overwhelmed because the material, audience or content is new to you, whatever the reason try looking at teh process of preparation as you would diving into writing a novel. Start with the best first sentence ever, follow up with a captivating introduction, break the content out into chapters, and finish with a powerful ending. Set your mind to enjoy each stage of the process, much as you would enjoy flipping through the pages of your favourite novel.

Tip – Enjoy the journey.

#251 – Jimi Hendrix

1942–1970

Context – Jimi Hendrix said this many times in various places.

"Knowledge speaks, but wisdom listens."

Analysis – Good ol' Hendrix needs no introduction. However, for those living under a rock, Hendrix was an American guitarist, singer, and songwriter. Considered by some to be the best at his craft. I've seen the above quote many times before and it's not only accurate but should be a quote that all presenters read, digest, and adopt.

In my presentation workshops, I talk about the three levels of listening. Level 3 is completely tuned out. So, you walk into someone's office, they are on the phone, on the computer, you sit down to talk to them, and they continue to talk on the phone and type away on the computer. Sure, they look at you and nod now and again, but this person is not listening.

In the same scenario, with Level 2 listening the person will hang up the phone, turn away from the computer and look at you. What happens next though is what I call mental vacations. You are listening, but then you are stopped in your tracks with random thoughts like, "Oh boy, don't forget to pick up milk on your way home," or "Oh, goody, American Idol is on tonight," or "What am I going to make for dinner?" This constant barrage of intrusive thoughts that don't pertain to the conversation is something we all experience. Can we tell when someone has taken a mental vacation? You bet we can. Glazed eyes and the appropriate, "yups, ah huhs," and head nods. If anyone reading this has a spouse or partner, you likely be familiar with being on the receiving end of Level 2 listening. You've told an entire story, but you can tell that your partner hasn't been listening, so you call them out, and they say, "Sorry, I wasn't listening." Level 2 is tuning in and out of the conversation.

Level 1 listening is by far the hardest place to stay in for an extended time. In the same scenario, you notice something refreshing. The person is listening to digest not to respond, and they are using their body to communicate with you, head nods. You feel as though you are being heard, perhaps the first time all day. Your words are being met with intense concentration and complete attention. Level 1 listening is when you are completely tuned in to the conversation.

As the receiver or sender of communication which level is best? Obviously, Level 1. But Level 1 listening takes an exorbitant amount of energy. Try it for a full day or even just an hour. You'll be exhausted. That is why if you've ever done a long presentation, you may find yourself a little tuckered out at the end. As a presenter, you are not afforded the luxury of Level 2 listening, where most of us often find ourselves, and certainly not Level 3. You must stay at Level 1 for the entire presentation. Have you ever been in the audience and the presenter had been asked a question, they answer, and you and everyone else in the room say to yourselves, "Huh, that didn't answer the question at all!" This will most likely be because the presenter took a little mental vacation

Tip – As Hendrix says, the wise person is a listening person. Listen to learn from your audience and appreciated that you are not the only teacher in the room.

#250 – Dan Gilbert

(1962)

Context – The author of *Stumbling on Happiness*, Dan Gilbert in his 2007 TED Talk, "Why Are We Happy? Why Aren't We Happy?"

"When you have 21 minutes to speak, two million years seems like a really long time. But evolutionarily, two million years is nothing. And yet in two million years, the human brain has nearly tripled in mass, going from the one-and-a-quarter pound brain of our ancestor here, Habilis, to the almost three-pound meatloaf that everybody here has between their ears.

What is it about a big brain that nature was so eager for every one of us to have one? Well, it turns out when brains triple in size, they don't just get three times bigger; they gain new structures. And one of the main reasons that our brain got so big is because it got a new part, called the frontal lobe, particularly, a part called the pre-frontal cortex. Now what does a pre-frontal cortex do for you that should justify the entire architectural overhaul of the human skull in the blink of evolutionary time? Well it turns out the pre-frontal cortex does lots of things, but one of the most important things it does is an experience simulator. Pilots practice in flight simulators so that they don't make real mistakes in planes. Human beings have this marvelous adaptation that they can actually have experiences in their heads before they try them out in real life. This is a trick that none of our ancestors could do, and that no other animal can do quite like we can. It's a marvelous adaptation. It's up there with opposable thumbs and standing upright and language as one of the things that got our species out of the trees and into the shopping mall."

Analysis – The prefrontal cortex does lots of things. At the fore, it is an experience simulator. Gilbert discusses the anatomy of certain parts of the human brain and how they relate to happiness. He also discusses that human beings can have experiences in their heads before they action them. I couldn't agree more. I love to daydream, which is a perfect example. His example: Ben and Jerry's doesn't have a liver and onions flavoured ice cream but you can simulate that taste experience and say, "Yuck" therefore Ben and Jerry's doesn't make that flavour! Another example he uses is two individuals; one wins the lottery; another individual becomes a paraplegic. Gilbert suggests that a year after winning the lottery and a year after losing the use of their legs, both are equally happy. I believe that because it has to do with our choice to be happy or not be happy. It's as simple as that. Gilbert calls it; synthetic happiness vs. natural happiness. He suggests that synthetic happiness is inferior in our minds. And that synthetic happiness is every bit as real as the natural joy that you may happen upon.

This is the point that keeps on coming up. If you are going to give a presentation, it is a requirement and a foundation, that you bring the right attitude. The right attitude is often happiness. That you are happy and honoured to have been asked to present. I was once asked to watch a presenter give a presentation. The content was there, along with the correct tone, intonation, inflection, and body language. But something was missing. I sat back, turned my chair slightly so as not to get caught, and closed my eyes for a few minutes to try to feel out what was incongruent. I knew something was off. The audience was bored stiff, falling asleep, chatting with their neighbours, and one audience member was trying desperately to take over the presentation, probably in a last-ditch hope of staying engaged. So, there I am, eye's closed, chair turned around and, about 20 seconds in, I figured it out. This presenter was not interesting because he had the wrong attitude. His presentation topic was light, even though it had some technical detail, but there was no *pizzazz*, no underlying joy in the delivery. And that, my friends, is what every single audience member was unconsciously picking up on. Everything else was there. That is why I spend only a small portion of time in my presentation skills workshops on the *what* and instead focus on the *how*. The presentation's design means absolutely nothing if you cannot deliver it in a way that your audience will hear. It is a fine balance of gentle coaching and content, because I know that we are led to believe that content is so important. The truth is content is only as important as the delivery. So, if you're about to give a presentation, be happy to have been asked to do it. If you can't get there naturally, do what Gilbert suggests and synthesize it!

Tip – If you're not happy before a presentation, synthesize it!

#249 - Peter O'Toole

1932–2013

Context – Esteemed actor, Peter O'Toole, as the voice of Anton Ego in the movie *Ratatouille* (2007)

"In many ways, the work of a critic is easy. We risk very little yet enjoy a position over those who offer their work and themselves to our judgment. We thrive on negative criticism, which is fun to write and to read. But the bitter truth we critics must face is that in the grand scheme of things, the average piece of junk is probably more meaningful than our criticism designating it so. But there are times when a critic truly risks something, and that is in the discovery and defence of the new. The world is often unkind to new talent, new creations. The new needs friends. Last night, I experienced something new, an extraordinary meal from a singularly unexpected source. To say that both the meal and its maker have challenged my preconceptions about fine cooking is a gross understatement. They have rocked me to my core. In the past, I have made no secret of my disdain for Chef Gusteau's famous motto: Anyone can cook. But I realize, only now do I truly understand what he meant. Not everyone can become a great artist, but a great artist can come from anywhere. It is difficult to imagine more humble origins than those of the genius now cooking at Gusteau's, who is, in this critic's opinion, nothing less than the finest chef in France. I will be returning to Gusteau's soon, hungry for more."

Analysis – After learning the ratatouille served at Gusteau's restaurant had been prepared by Remy, a bluish-grey country rat (voiced by Patton Oswalt), the snobbish, hard-to-please, and unapologetically harsh food critic Anton Ego (voiced by Peter O'Toole), wrote the above glowing, self-actualizing review. Peter O'Toole is brilliantly cast as the voice of the aptly named Ego. At first blush, Ego is pompous and thick with superiority. As you listen to the words from this scene in *Ratatouille*, you are left with a new way of looking at criticism and new talent. Ego talks about the discovery of a new talent and that the world is often unkind to new talent, and new creations. Ego was talking about the fabulous meal that he had even though he went into the restaurant with a disdain for the chef but the meal simply rocks him to the core. This is because his old ways of looking at things are challenged, and he is forced to change his opinion. It made me think about early in my career and how I had a small group of people who were kind to any talent that I showed. I was full of piss and vinegar—well, let's be honest, I still am, but it has been diluted. Had I not been surrounded by some key individuals who nurtured me, encouraged me, and believed in me, I would not have had many of the opportunities I have had so far. As Ego says, "The new needs friends." So often, when we meet or work with someone young and fresh, we discount them as not knowing as much, as lacking wisdom and experience. Truthfully some of the wisest individuals I've met have been younger than me. This thought process often permeates into the boundaries of giving a presentation. I saw a young woman give a presentation recently that frankly rocked my world. She was articulate, intelligent, prepared, funny, interesting and the way she communicated was fresh, lively, and invigorating. As I panned the audience, I noticed that she did not appear to garner the same level of attention that the senior individuals who went before and after her, as if they were somehow more worthy of respect simply because of the badges and titles behind their names.

This young woman was by far the best presenter of eight in the room, including the president of the organization. I wondered if she would get the accolades that she had so rightfully earned? If someone would nurture her talents or ask her to teach her skills? So, my tip for today is simple; recognize nurture and coach talent regardless of status and title. The world can be unkind to new talent.

Tip – Recognize, nurture and coach new talent.

#248 – Ben Stein

(1944)

Context – Actor Ben Stein plays droning and dry economics teacher in *Ferris Bueller's Day Off*, 1986

"In 1930, the Republican-controlled House of Representatives, in an effort to alleviate the effects of the… Anyone? Anyone? The Great Depression passed the…Anyone? Anyone? The tariff bill? The Hawley-Smoot Tariff Act? Which, anyone? Raised or lowered?… Raised tariffs in an effort to collect more revenue for the federal government. Did it work? Anyone? Anyone know the effects? It did not work, and the United States sank deeper into the Great Depression. Today we have a similar debate over this. Anyone know what this is? Class? Anyone? Anyone? Anyone seen this before? The Laffer Curve. Anyone know what this says? It says that at this point on the revenue curve, you will get exactly the same amount of revenue as at this point. This is very controversial. Does anyone know what Vice President Bush called this in 1980? Anyone? Something-d-o-o economics. 'Voodoo' Economics."

Analysis – I love this movie. But this entry is more a guide of what not to do. As the inception of my blog, I knew that I would have Ben Stein's monologue on the list. It is without question a must-know talk because all anyone has to do is utter one word in the same cadence as Stein's character, and most people will be able to pick out exactly what movie it is from. *Anyone? Anyone?* Notice how Stein has absolutely no regard for whether what he is saying is being digested. Notice how his audience is falling asleep, disinterested, and waiting for it all to be over. Notice how there is no tone or inflection in his voice. I had a teacher like this for Grade 11, English. I bet you too had a teacher like this. I can't remember a single thing that he taught in that class, and I probably would've been caught drooling on my desk too. If you are preparing to give a presentation, watch this fun video then do the exact opposite.

Tip – Find the worst presentation and do the opposite.

#247 – Chevy Chase

(1943)

Context – *National Lampoon's Vacation* – Chevy Chase "It's a quest for fun" scene, 1983.

"I think you're all f–ked in the head. We're ten hours from the f–kin' fun park and you want to bail out! Well, I'll tell you somethin'. This is no longer a vacation. It's a quest. It's a quest for fun. I'm gonna have fun and you're gonna have fun. We're all gonna have so much f–kin' fun we'll need plastic surgery to remove our god-damn smiles. You'll be whistling 'Zip-A-Dee Doo-Dah' out of your assholes! I gotta be crazy! I'm on a pilgrimage to see a moose. Praise Marty Moose! Holy S–t!"

Analysis – The above is the deranged foul-mouthed exhortation and rant from half-crazed Clark Griswold (Chevy Chase) to his beleaguered family to press on to Wally World. Warning: this post is littered with profanity. It is so funny, though, and I knew I had to include it as it is certainly one of the most memorable speeches I've ever heard. Griswold has lost his marbles. He's on the vacation from hell with his family. His two kids and wife are ready to pack it all in and go home early even though they are a mere ten hours from their destination, Wally World. Even though Griswold is pretty darn close to losing his mind, he teaches us an important lesson. Life and life circumstances may get hard, really hard, but you have to keep on keeping on. You will encounter people who will pressure you to take the easy route, and although it may be tempting, there are no shortcuts (yes, this is the post of clichés, sorry not sorry). As it relates to presentation skills, preparing and giving a presentation is hard work. There is no doubt about that. It takes me weeks and sometimes months to prepare for a single presentation. There are times when I'm asked to give a presentation that is brand new to me, and when I agree to do it, I know it will be an exorbitant amount of work. I know because I've done it countless times now. I'll have to pep talk myself out of all kinds of challenges and obstacles. That is life. Life, including giving a presentation superbly, is work. Get over it and get to work!

Tip – Get over it and get to work!

#246 – Natalie Merchant

(1963)

Context – American singer-songwriter Natalie Merchant's career spans three decades. She is known for being the leader of the alternative rock band 10,000 Maniacs as well as her solo work. Here at TED, in 2010, she adapts well-known poetry into songs.

"I suppose I owe you an explanation. I been working on a project for the last six years adapting children's poetry to music. And that's a poem by Charles Edward Carryl, who was a stockbroker in New York City for 45 years, but in the evenings, he wrote nonsense for his children. And this book was one of the most famous books in America for about 35 years. "The Sleepy Giant," which is the song that I just sang, is one of his poems. Now, we're going to do other poems for you. And here's a preview of some of the poets. This is Rachel Field, Robert Graves, a very young Robert Graves, Christina Rossetti. Ghosts, right, have nothing to say to us. Obsolete. Gone. Not so. What I really enjoyed about this project is reviving these people's words, taking them off the dead, flat pages, bringing them to life, bringing them to light. So, what we're going to do next is a poem that was written by Nathalia Crane. Nathalia Crane was a little girl from Brooklyn. When she was ten years old, in 1927, she published her first book of poems called "The Janitor's Boy." Here she is. And here's her poem."

Analysis – A friend of mine sent me this link to include on the list. At first blush, I said, "But this isn't a talk at all; this is a bunch of songs!" But now that I understand the context around these songs, I understand why my friend suggested I include it. What Merchant has done is adapt children's poetry to music. She breathed new life into old poems, some that have laid dormant, and some that are still popular today.

These poems have been put through a new creative process and turned into music. Some are haunting, some fun, some uplifting. Each poem started beautifully without melody, but something happens to a string of words when thrown through this creative process. It's probably why I like poetry so much and why I admire the greats. If you've ever had the opportunity to watch a poet recite their works, it can be mesmerizing, spellbinding, awe-inspiring as they rock a cadence (check out "The Museum of Four in the Morning" TED Talk by Rives, who has been called "the first 2.0 Poet," using video, tech and images!)

Tip – Don't be afraid to rework your presentations and turn a poem into a song.

#245 – Marcus du Sautoy

(1965)

Context – Marcus du Sautoy talks about symmetry, TED 2009

"…And I think Galileo summed up, very nicely, the power of mathematics to understand the scientific world around us. He wrote, "The universe cannot be read until we have learnt the language and become familiar with the characters in which it is written. It is written in mathematical language, and the letters are triangles, circles and other geometric figures, without which means it is humanly impossible to comprehend a single word.

But it's not just scientists who are interested in symmetry. Artists too love to play around with symmetry. They also have a slightly more ambiguous relationship with it. Here is Thomas Mann talking about symmetry in "The Magic Mountain." He has a character describing the snowflake, and he says he "shuddered at its perfect precision, found it deathly, the very marrow of death.

But what artists like to do is to set up expectations of symmetry and then break them. And a beautiful example of this I found, actually, when I visited a colleague of mine in Japan, Professor Kurokawa. And he took me up to the temples in Nikko. And just after this photo was taken, we walked up the stairs. And the gateway you see behind has eight columns, with beautiful symmetrical designs on them. Seven of them are exactly the same, and the eighth one is turned upside down.

And I said to Professor Kurokawa, "Wow, the architects must have really been kicking themselves when they realized that they'd made a mistake and put this one upside down." And he said, "No, no, no. It was a very deliberate act." And he referred me to this lovely quote from the Japanese "Essays in Idleness" from the 14th century, in which the essayist wrote, "In everything, uniformity is undesirable. Leaving something incomplete makes it interesting and gives one the feeling that there is room for growth." Even when building the Imperial Palace, they always leave one place unfinished.

But if I had to choose one building in the world to be cast out on a desert island, to live the rest of my life, being an addict of symmetry, I would probably choose the Alhambra in Granada. This is a palace celebrating symmetry. Recently I took my family – we do these rather kind of nerdy mathematical trips, which my family love. This is my son Tamer. You can see he's really enjoying our mathematical trip to the Alhambra. But I wanted to try and enrich him. I think one of the problems about school mathematics is it doesn't look at how mathematics is embedded in the world we live in. So, I wanted to open his eyes up to how much symmetry is running through the Alhambra…."

Analysis – Symmetry deals with pictures in conjunction with numbers, and I can naturally gravitate to the pictures to guide me to understand the numbers. I enjoy watching these types of presentations, and du Sautoy is one of my favourites because he speaks and intersperses the real world to ground his presentation (the historical figures and Rubik's cube, in particular, resonate with me). If this presentation did not include the real-world examples, the tangible and the people, it would be like a helium balloon through a child's fingers, flying away into the abyss.

One of my clients asked me to develop a complete leadership package of six classes. Each workshop embodies components of what it is to be an exceptional leader. So, we have all the natural insertions; people, communication, strategy, operations, and the numbers part of the model; finance.
I have stopped pigeon-holing myself as a total right-brain thinker, but I must admit even though I teach very introductory finance classes, numbers always leave me a bit nervous. Call me your *Accounting for Dummies* expert. I believe, though, that since I don't naturally gravitate to a mathematical theorem or quantum physics, it gives me an edge in teaching basic finance. Yes, there will be some of you out there who will disagree with me, but please note that I'm not lecturing at Harvard on this particular topic. My students don't demand a Harvard economics Ph.D. from me. They need to learn how to explain that the income statement is the one that has the bottom line on it as opposed to the balance sheet. The income statement determines profit or loss also known as the P&L to those in the know. No earth-shattering

quadratic equations or cracking the universe's codes here. Just a little finance understanding for the emerging leader is all. I work hard on all my presentations, but I work doubly hard on financial presentations. My natural tendency is to think in pictures, not numbers, so it takes more time for me to hit my groove in my preparation. I need to dissect the information into manageable parts and painstakingly go through the theory and exercises until I fully understand. Once I have the basics to a level that I'm comfortable with, I start layering on top of it and that brings the presentation to life for me. The job of the presenter is to see the teaching and learning process from every angle. Does everyone need pictures to learn numbers? Nope, not at all, but many do. It is our job to ensure all the participants have digested and retained the information being presented. The point is this: We all have natural tendencies in everything we do, but when we give a presentation in topics that don't come naturally, we have to work hard not only to understand the content but also to find a new way, perhaps a new language, to communicate what we are teaching.

According to de Sautoy, "Math is not a spectator sport!" and I shout, "Yes! Yes!" Often when we are lacking a skill in a certain area, we shy away from it and would never volunteer to give a presentation in that area. I encourage you, though, whether it be a business plan or *Accounting for Dummies*, take on the task. You'll be shocked at how much you will learn in the preparation process and how beneficial it can be to expand on your typical presentation language to teach others what you've learned. It is never too late to learn something new.

Tip – Branch out and teach something new.

#244 – Joseph Priestley

1733–1804

Context – Joseph Priestly was an 18th-century English theologian and a philosopher who published over 150 works. He was rather famous for trying to fuse Enlightenment rationalism with Christian theism.

"The more elaborate our means of communication, the less we communicate."

Analysis – I once had the opportunity to observe a speech session at a children's hospital. What a fabulous task when you communicate for a living. A speech therapist sits down with a child, observes where they are in terms of verbal and non-verbal cues and places them on a fancy graph called Speech Milestones. If the child isn't performing within their peer group, they are placed at a lower level on the graph, if they are performing at higher levels than their peer group, then they are plotted accordingly on that graph as well. The child's parent or guardian are asked a string of questions. Through the entire process, the child is labeled as either delayed or advanced. I recognize that some children need to be evaluated to determine if additional help is needed, I get that. What I find disturbing, as Priestley says, is that the more articulate we are, the less we are able to communicate. So, as this relates to presentation skills, an individual being fancy with their words risks alienating their audience. Communication is a delicate process. The speech therapist cannot decipher in her graphs and questionnaire the subtle cues between parent and child. Even though there is no discernible language being bounced to and fro, there are real and tangible cues that can't be measured on a chart—such as gesturing, head nodding, and positive affirmations, amongst others. A gentle glare, a raised eyebrow, a finger tap, these more subtle cues are often overlooked as important communication methods. This experience made me realize that labeling continues until we are dead. I'm so tired of labels. It's time to look at the individual in front of us and adjust our skills to better communication with them. The same needs to be done in the classroom. Look at your audience, speak naturally and from the heart with a genuine desire to deliver your message. If you do that, you will be brilliant.

Tip – Speak from the heart not from the dictionary.

#243 – Simon Sinek

(1973)

Context – Simon Sinek: "How great leaders inspire action," TED 2009

"How do you explain when things don't go as we assume? Or better, how do you explain when others are able to achieve things that seem to defy all the assumptions? For example: Why is Apple so innovative? Year after year, after year, they're more innovative than all their competition. And yet, they're just a computer company. They're just like everyone else. They have the same access to the same talent, the same agencies, the same consultants, the same media. Then why is it that they seem to have something different? Why is it that Martin Luther King led the Civil Rights Movement? He wasn't the only man who suffered in pre-civil rights America, and he certainly wasn't the only great orator of the day. Why him? And why is it that the Wright brothers were able to figure out controlled, powered man flight when there were certainly other teams who were better qualified, better funded – and they didn't achieve powered man flight, and the Wright brothers beat them to it. There's something else at play here.

About three and a half years ago, I made a discovery. And this discovery profoundly changed my view on how I thought the world worked, and it even profoundly changed the way in which I operate in it. As it turns out, there's a pattern. As it turns out, all the great inspiring leaders and organizations in the world, whether it's Apple or Martin Luther King or the Wright brothers, they all think, act and communicate the exact same way. And it's the complete opposite to everyone else. All I did was codify it, and it's probably the world's simplest idea. I call it the golden circle.

Why? How? What? This little idea explains why some organizations and some leaders are able to inspire where others aren't. Let me define the terms really quickly. Every single person, every single organization on the planet knows what they do, 100 percent. Some know how they do it, whether you call it your differentiated value proposition or your proprietary process or your USP. But very, very few people or organizations know why they do what

they do. And by 'why' I don't mean 'to make a profit.' That's a result. It's always a result. By 'why,' I mean: What's your purpose? What's your cause? What's your belief? Why does your organization exist? Why do you get out of bed in the morning? And why should anyone care? As a result, the way we think, we act, the way we communicate is from the outside in, it's obvious. We go from the clearest thing to the fuzziest thing. But the inspired leaders and the inspired organizations – regardless of their size, regardless of their industry – all think, act and communicate from the inside out. ..."

Analysis – Why did I start my blog on January 1st, 2011? Because I wanted to transfer some of the presentation skills and knowledge that I had acquired over the years.Sound pretty straightforward, right? But, I never thought that I'd be arriving at some of the conclusions that I've come to on how to communicate and what makes a superb presentation. This is a portal into my thought process (and is somewhat evident in the last dozen or so posts). Language, the words, are much less important in a presentation than everything else; the intangible, the non-verbal cues, body language, participation from the audience, storytelling, enthusiasm and passion, cadence, and intonation, etc., but most importantly, what is emerging is the transfer of feeling and emotion that sets an okay presentation apart from a superb one. In any presentation, there is a purpose; to sell, to inspire, to inform and within those parameters, there are real emotions that can be tied to any one of them; to inspire, to create positive energy and happiness, to influence, to motivate, and the list goes on. It is our jobs as the presenters to get to the root of those feelings or emotions and to find a way to lay it on the laps of our audience.

I adore Sinek's talk for so many reasons. First, on a technical level, it's great to see a presenter do an entire 20-minute presentation with a flip chart and sharpie. I'm a massive fan of creating graphs in real-time with the audience. Sinek does it well, first with the Golden Circle explaining the Why, the How and the What, then with the law of diffusion of innovation. Beware, novice presenters, you'll need to know your material beyond well to do this, so practice in advance. Second, on a conceptual level, the presentation is fresh, identifiable, and engaging. Third, from a storytelling perspective, it is magic. Sinek's cadence and tone are mesmerizing. Finally, and the point of this post, after I watched his presentation, I felt moved. As a result of these 20 minutes, I too want to decipher my own, "Why?" statement (or perhaps my own "I have a dream..." statement), I'm moved to change the way I do things, how I deliver my presentations, I'm moved to do better and be better. Now that is a talk! Bravo!

Tip – At the core of your presentation, transfer and evoke feeling.

#242 – Philip II of Macedon

382 BCE – 336 BCE

Context – Plutharch was a Greek historian and among his works is the *Opera Moralia*. In the third volume is a collection of sayings from Greek and Roman kings and commanders, where you will find the below.

"Macedonians... hath not the with to call a spade by any other name than a spade."

Analysis – You may have heard this quote before, and you may have even used it (to call a spade a spade) but it is always fascinating to see a quote or a speeches roots, and to understand how it came to be. One of the stories is about when the Macedonians conquered their former ally Olynthia after Philip II bribed two leading citizens—Lasthenes and Euthycrates—to surrender as traitors, so they complained to Philip, who retorted with the above statement, which meant that his soldiers were too rough and stupid to tell anything but the truth.

As we ponder this quote in today's society, to call a spade a spade is to speak honestly and directly about a topic, specifically topics that others may avoid talking about due to sensitivity or embarrassment. One dictionary definition reads: "To be outspoken, blunt, even to the point of rudeness; to call things by their proper names without any beating about the bush." (*Brewer's Dictionary of Phrase and Fable*, 1913.) As this quote relates to presentation skills, to go on and on belabouring the point is a form of torture for your audience. Practice your presentation to avoid long-winded, directionless presentations. Get to the point!

Tip – Get to the point.

#241 – Diana, Princess of Wales

1961–1997

Context – A BBC interview for Panorama with Princess Diana conducted by Martin Bashir in 1995.

"I'd like to be a queen of people's hearts, in people's hearts, but I don't see myself being Queen of this country. I don't think many people will want me to be Queen. Actually, when I say many people I mean the establishment that I married into, because they have decided that I'm a non-starter."

Analysis – I remember this interview vividly. It led to increased sympathy for Princess Diana. At this point, Diana had become incredibly skilled at dealing with the media and knew how to get her point across—a far cry from where she had started as the naive 19-year-old who married Prince Charles in 1981. As a result of this interview, the Queen intervened and decided that it would be best for everybody concerned if the couple divorced, so they did, but Diana had no intention of fading into the background.

Today's point is simple: when you are giving a presentation, recognize that the number of people you have in the audience is the number of life stories. Every person sitting in the audience has amassed a life story, including positive parts and perhaps some challenges. You, as a presenter, have no idea what that audience member is going through at any given moment. So, give people the benefit of the doubt, treat people with respect and empathy be the Queen or King of people's hearts in the classroom!

Tip – Treat your audience with empathy.

#240 – Jesus Christ

c. 7–4 BCE – AD 26–36

Context – In chapters 5–7 of St. Matthew's Gospel, the passage known as the Sermon on the Mount.

"Our Father which art in Heaven, Hallowed be thy name. Thy kingdom come, thy will be done on Earth, as it is in Heaven. Give us this day our daily bread. And forgive us our debts, as we forgive our debtors. And lead us not into temptation but deliver us from evil: For thine is the kingdom, and the power, and the glory, forever."

Analysis – Let's start first by saying again that I am not analyzing religion. I am analyzing people and their speeches. My blog included the words of many religious and spiritual leaders. I am not here to enlighten anyone as it relates to the choices they've made around religion, whether it be Christianity, Buddhism, Hinduism, or wherever you fall.

Christ expresses here what would become one of the foundations of Christianity, the Lord's Prayer. Perhaps the best-known prayer in Christianity. I must admit that, until now, I've never really studied this prayer, but doing so has shed light on its meaning. My drive, however, is to look at Christ as a teacher. This prayer comes from the passage known as the Sermon on the Mount. It made me think again, why so many people stopped to hear what Christ had to say? Why did He garner such a following not only then but 2000 years later? For me, it is about truth. Christ spoke out of what was for Him, His truth. People felt and heard that and followed his teachings. It sounds straightforward, and I could go into a long diatribe about why I believe people want to follow and listen to others, but I won't. Suffice to say, the Lord's Prayer is a perfect illustration for those seeking superb presenters. Speak from a place of truth, create meaning and substance in your talks, and people will listen.

Tip – Speak from a place of truth.

#239 – Jon Stewart

(1967)

Context – On June 11, 2019, the former late-night host and 9/11 first responders advocate, Jon Stewart slammed Congress over the heath care of first responders to the September 11 terrorist attacks.

I want to thank Mr. Collins and Mr. Nadler for putting this together. But, as I sit here today, I can't help but think what an incredible metaphor this room is for the entire process that getting health care and benefits for 9/11 first responders has come to.

Behind me: a filled room of 9/11 first responders.

And in front of me: a nearly empty Congress.

Sick and dying, they brought themselves down here to speak – to no one.

It's shameful.

It's an embarrassment to the country.

And it is a stain on this institution.

And you should be ashamed of yourselves for those that aren't here, but you won't be because accountability doesn't appear to be something that occurs in this chamber.

We don't want to be here. Lu [Detective Luis Alvarez] doesn't want to be here. None of these people want to be here. But they are, and they're not here for themselves. They're here to continue fighting for what's right. Lu's going to go back for his 69th chemo. The great Ray Pfeiffer would come down here, his body riddled with cancer and pain, where he couldn't walk; and the disrespect shown to him and to the other lobbyists on this bill is utterly unacceptable.

You know, I used to get...I would be so angry at the latest injustice that's done to these men and women and, you know, another business card thrown our way as a way of shooing us away like children trick-or-treating, rather than the heroes that they are and will always be.

Ray would stay, "Calm down, Johnny. Calm down." "I got all the cards I need." And he would tap his pocket... where he kept the prayer cards of 343 firefighters. The official FDNY response time to 911 was five seconds. Five seconds! That's how long it took for FDNY, for NYPD, for Port Authority, for EMS to respond to an urgent need from the public.

Five seconds.

Hundreds died in an instant. Thousands more poured in to continue to fight for their brothers and sisters.

The breathing problems started almost immediately. And they were told they weren't sick – they were crazy. And then, as the illnesses got worse and things became more apparent, "Well, okay, you're sick but it's not from the pile." And then, when the science became irrefutable, "Okay, it's the pile – but this is a New York issue." I don't know if we "have the money."

And I'm sorry if I sound angry and undiplomatic, but I'm angry – and you should be too; and they're all angry as well. And they have every justification to be that way. There is not a person here, there is not an empty chair on that stage that didn't tweet out, "Never forget" the heroes of 9/11; never forget their bravery; never forget what they did, what they gave to this country.

Well here they are! And where are they? And it would be one thing if their callous indifference and rank hypocrisy were benign. But it's not. Your indifference cost these men and women their most valuable commodity: time. It's the one thing they're running out of..."

Analysis – "Angry and undiplomatic," Stewart says as he addresses Congress in 2019. Emotional, moving, eloquent and yes, angry, and undiplomatic. I've always liked Stewart but even more so now that I've seen this clip and his initial reactions post 9/11 when he had *The Jon Stewart Show*. He is fearless in showing his grief and anger. In doing so, he shines a much-needed spotlight on the lack of accountability for the men and women who became sick, continue to battle illness and those who lost their lives in the aftermath of 9/11. My tip today; be fearless in sharing your genuine feelings with your audience in your presentations and your message will be heard and felt.

Tip – Share your emotions with your audience.

#238 – Lloyd Jones

(1955)

Context – From Jones' novel, *Mister Pip*, published in 2006.

"I had found a new friend. The surprising thing is where I'd found him—not up a tree or sulking in the shade, or splashing around in one of the hill streams, but in a book. No one had told us kids to look there for a friend. Or that you could slip inside the skin of another. Or travel to another place with marshes, and where, to our ears, the bad people spoke like pirates."

Analysis – Have you read *Mister Pip*? My sister gave me this book a many years ago. The first time I read it slowly so that I wouldn't waste it. I would let myself read just a few pages each night so that it would last and last. The story takes place on the Pacific Island of Bougainville, part of Papua New Guinea. *Mister Pip* is a novel about a novel. Pip is the name of the main character in *Great Expectations* by Charles Dickens. I would argue that *Great Expectations* becomes one of the main characters in *Mister Pip*, as *Great Expectations* serves as much of the plot for Jones' work. At its core, *Mister Pip* is about how literature can create and open up a brand-new world to people. Writing is one venue to open up a new world to others, but so is the art of storytelling or speaking. A well-crafted presentation can elicit the same emotion as a great book. It can have people on the edge of their seats, and it can have them mesmerized. In *Mister Pip*, *"You cannot pretend to read a book. Your eyes will give you away. So, will your breathing. A person entranced by a book simply forgets to breathe. The house can catch alight, and a reader deep in a book will not look up until the wallpaper is in flames."* I believe the same can be said of listening to a great presenter. You can feel the presenter's attention when they are doing their job well. You could hear a pin drop, and you can envision the rapture in the audience's eyes. They hang on every word with bated breath. Indeed, if you have your audience feeling what you are saying, they may not even notice until the wallpaper is in flames.

Tip – Engulf your audience and show them a new world through your presentations.

#237 – Nicholas Christakis

(1962)

Context – Greek-American sociologist, physician and professor, Nikolas Christakis discusses "The Hidden Influence of Social Networks" in his 2010 TED Talk.

"For me, this story begins about 15 years ago, when I was a hospice doctor at the University of Chicago. And I was taking care of people who were dying and their families in the South Side of Chicago. And I was observing what happened to people and their families over the course of their terminal illness. And in my lab, I was studying the widower effect, which is a very old idea in the social sciences, going back 150 years, known as "dying of a broken heart." So, when I die, my wife's risk of death can double, for instance, in the first year. And I had gone to take care of one particular patient, a woman who was dying of dementia. And in this case, unlike this couple, she was being cared for by her daughter. And the daughter was exhausted from caring for her mother. And the daughter's husband, he also was sick from his wife's exhaustion. And I was driving home one day, and I get a phone call from the husband's friend, calling me because he was depressed about what was

happening to his friend. So here I get this call from this random guy that's having an experience that's being influenced by people at some social distance.

And so, I suddenly realized two very simple things: First, the widowhood effect was not restricted to husbands and wives. And second, it was not restricted to pairs of people. And I started to see the world in a whole new way, like pairs of people connected to each other. And then I realized that these individuals would be connected into foursomes with other pairs of people nearby. And then, in fact, these people were embedded in other sorts of relationships: marriage and spousal and friendship and other sorts of ties. And that, in fact, these connections were vast and that we were all embedded in this broad set of connections with each other. So, I started to see the world in a completely new way, and I became obsessed with this. I became obsessed with how it might be that we're embedded in these social networks, and how they affect our lives. So, social networks are these intricate things of beauty, and they're so elaborate and so complex and so ubiquitous, in fact, that one has to ask what purpose they serve. Why are we embedded in social networks? I mean, how do they form? How do they operate? And how do they affect us?..."

Analysis – Professors need to be passionate, interesting, engaging, and intelligent. I guess that's why it is so costly to attend Ivy League universities. Each time I see a professor from one of these schools, it seems from the outside to be worth the price of admission. Christakis talks about how people live not in groups, but in networks. Like a tree, we have branches that trace our friendships, work ties, family, and interconnect to hundreds or even thousands of people, most of whom we don't know. What intrigues me about this talk, is not just Christakis' delivery, but his style. I can focus on why I pressed the play button in the first place, the content. Christakis goes through several examples of our impact on others and the impact others have on us. He discusses the widowhood effect—when one spouse dies shortly after their partner—and how it extends beyond the boundaries of that relationship. He discusses obesity (which is fascinating) and pitches the theory that if your friends are obese, your chances of being obese go up. Christakis discusses; smoking, altruism, ideas, emotions, how each of us can stand alone and be contagious not only to the people we know but to the people they know too, and so on. Fascinating.

This topic reminds me of energy takers and energy givers. Time spent with an energy taker leaves you feeling drained, exhausted, maybe even sad, but the opposite is true of time spent with energy givers where you're charged with enthusiasm and joy. I don't need a sociological study to know giving energy is contagious, especially when giving a presentation. You, as a presenter, must find a way to become an energy giver in the room. It is the only way your message will be heard. You are the person at the front of the room with all eyes on you. (No pressure!) However, the people participating in your presentation will catch the energy virus you are emitting. Think of your energy (and everything else for that matter) like a virus your audience will catch. Whatever you have thrown out into the environment, I would suggest that all your energy be of the positive variety: happiness, altruism, idea generating, fun, passionate. Make your positivity and joy contagious, and this is the energy you will attract back.

Tip – Be an energy giver.

#236 – Dan Meyer

(1957)

Context – Dan Meyer is now part of the team at Desmos, which offers a free suite of math software tools. In his 2010 TED Talk, Meyer talks about how "Math Class Needs a Makeover."

"Can I ask you to please recall a time when you really loved something – a movie, an album, a song or a book – and you recommended it wholeheartedly to someone you also really liked, and you anticipated that reaction, you waited for it, and it came back, and the person hated it? So, by way of introduction, that is the exact same state in which I spent every working day of the last six years. (Laughter) I teach high school math. I sell a product to a market that doesn't want it but is forced by law to buy it. I mean, it's just a losing proposition.

So, there's a useful stereotype about students that I see, a useful stereotype about you all. I could give you guys an algebra-two final exam, and I would expect no higher than a 25 percent pass rate. And both of these facts say less about you or my students than they do about what we call math education in the U.S. today.

To start with, I'd like to break math down into two categories. One is computation; this is the stuff you've forgotten. For example, factoring quadratics with leading coefficients greater than one. This stuff is also really easy to relearn, provided you have a really strong grounding in reasoning. Math reasoning – we'll call it the application of math processes to the world around us – this is hard to teach. This is what we would love students to retain, even if they don't go into mathematical fields. This is also something that, the way we teach it in the U.S. all but ensures they won't retain it. So, I'd like to talk about why that is, why that's such a calamity for society, what we can do about it and, to close with, why this is an amazing time to be a math teacher.

So first, five symptoms that you're doing math reasoning wrong in your classroom. One is a lack of initiative; your students don't self-start. You finish your lecture block and immediately you have five hands going up asking you to re-explain the entire thing at their desks. Students lack perseverance. They lack retention; you find yourself re-explaining concepts three months later, wholesale. There's an aversion to word problems, which describes 99 percent of my students. And then the other one percent is eagerly looking for the formula to apply in that situation. This is really destructive."

Analysis – I wish I had this guy as my math teacher in high school. I was not a great math student but the teachers I had were monotone, boring and certainly not passionate about teaching despite likely being passionate about math. I follow Meyer's blog faithfully now that I know it exists so I can learn from him (blog.mrmeyer.com).

I adore this talk, and I hope that you'll take the 11 minutes to watch it. Meyer talks about today's math curriculum in high school and describes it as paint-by-numbers classwork, designed in such a way that it robs kids of formulating and solving problems. He credits Einstein with the theory and quotes him as saying, "The formulation of the problem is more important than the solution."

My head spontaneously nods aggressively during certain sections of this talk, and that is what you want from your audience whether they are sitting alone at a laptop or watching you live on stage. Myer talks about the school kid who is intimidated by math, the kid who would never shout out an answer or a theory, and the one who would never raise their hand to ask a question. This kid has most likely fallen so far behind that he is embarrassed to say anything and is at a loss as to what to do. The challenge is monumental. I adore that Meyer levels the playing field and I hope this is what you can glean from him too. In the classroom, Meyer strips problems down so that they are no longer foreign to all in the room from the kid who is brilliant at math to the kid I just described. Meyer makes the problem visual, uses multimedia, encourages intuition, and as a teacher, he becomes incredibly helpful in the process. All these attributes work brilliantly in a presenter's room too. You, too, will incite members of your audience members, who would not usually participate in presentation discussions, to join in. It is your job as a presenter to level the playing field, so that every member of your audience is naturally drawn to contribute and participate.

Tip – Level the playing field.

#235 – Viktor Frankl

1905–1997

Context – In a clip from 1972, Holocaust survivor and psychiatrist, Viktor Frankl delivers a powerful message about the human search for meaning and the most important gift we can give others. Below is a beautiful excerpt.

"If we take man as he really is, we make him worse, but if we overestimate him …. If we seem to be idealists and are overestimating, overrating man, and looking at him that high, here above, you know what happens? We promote him to what he really can be.

So, we have to be idealists in a way because then we wind up as the true, the real realists.

Do you know who has said this? "If we take man as he is, we make you worse, but if we take man, as he should be, we make him capable of becoming what he can be." This was not my flight instructor. This was not me. This was Goethe. He said this verbally.

Now you will understand why I, in one of my writings once said this is the most apt maxim and motto for any psychotherapeutic activity. If you don't recognize a young man's way to meaning, man's search for meaning, you'll make it worse, you'll make him dull, you'll make him frustrated. You still add and contribute to his frustration.

While, if you presuppose in this man in this so-called criminal law, juvenile delinquent, or drug abuse and so forth, there must be a… What we call? Spark. Yeah, a spark of search for meaning. Let's recognize this. Let's presuppose it and then you will elicit it from him, if you will make him become what he, in principle, is capable of becoming."

Analysis – Frankl wrote 39 books, his best known, *Man's Search for Meaning* is a must-read. I'd never seen Frankl before, I'd only read some of his books, and you know, it wasn't surprising to me when I stumbled on this clip to see that he was as charismatic in person as he is on the page. It is funny how a writer can pour themselves into their words, clearly revealing their personalities and personae to readers who may never have laid eyes on them. In his retro talk, Frankl is funny and makes fun of himself, which is endearing; *"I know why I'm speaking a marvelous accent without the slightest English."* He is charming, and his message of what a man could be is worth repeating, particularly for those gearing up to give a presentation or looking to adopt more tools and techniques in their presentation skills toolbox. Frankl says, *"Consider what a man could be—not what he is."* So, have high expectations of yourself and your audience. I know I try harder when others have higher expectations of me. If you go into a presentation with high expectations on your performance, you'll likely live up to that vision. The same is true of the reverse.

Tip – Set high expectations of yourself.

#234 – Gretchen Rubin

(1965)

Context – Excerpt from the New York Times self-help best-seller list book, *The Happiness Project*.

"The belief that unhappiness is selfless and happiness is selfish is misguided. It's more selfless to act happy. It takes energy, generosity, and discipline to be unfailingly lighthearted, yet everyone takes the happy person for granted. No one is careful of his feelings or tries to keep his spirits high. He seems self-sufficient; he becomes a cushion for others. And because happiness seems unforced, that person usually gets no credit."

Analysis – I bought *The Happiness Project* many years ago and devoured it quickly. When I came upon the above quote, I realized that Rubin was onto something.

It is more selfless to act happy than not. It does take energy and generosity, and discipline to bring levity to all that you do. It's true, the happiest person I know, a dear friend, is probably someone who is taken for granted more than any other person I know. Most of her friends just think that she's good. She rarely, if ever complains, she always puts a silver lining on any dark cloud. She gives energy and rarely takes it. She's happy, period. She never needs cheering up as she's already cheerful. She never gets credit for consciously deciding to assume this role every day. As I read the above quote, I thought of my bubbly friend immediately and wondered how she maintains her cheerful disposition? So, I picked up the phone and asked her. Her response, with a jovial chuckle "it feels better to be happy than the alternative."
I adore that. It does indeed feel better to be happy than sad, angry, selfish, or melancholy. As it relates to presentation skills, no one wants to see an angry presenter. Choose to be happy long before you hit play on your PowerPoint slideshow, and that energy will permeate your audience.

Tip – Choose happiness.

#233 – Calvin Coolidge

1872–1933

Context – Calvin Coolidge was the 30th president of the United States. Coolidge believed persistence was the most important attribute you can have and is famous for the below quote.

"Education will not take the place of persistence; the world is full of educated derelicts. Persistence and determination alone are omnipotent. The slogan 'press on' has solved and always will solve the problems of the human race."

Analysis – I had an experience today that shone a bright light on the topic of persistence. I thought immediately of this quote from Coolidge. I had read the quote hundreds of times but didn't understand its weight until today. Isn't it funny how that happens? You can ponder a theory, quote, book, or teaching, but you don't fully understand its power until you experience it. Persistence is a characteristic, a quality that develops over time. It takes confidence to be persistent. Coolidge suggests that by pressing on, even in the face of adversity, the challenges faced by humanity can be solved. Believing what you are saying or doing is essential and will give you the drive to continue even when others think you should throw in the metaphorical towel. After my experience today, I did a little self-reflection. Wouldn't you know it, almost every obstacle I've overcome and every success I've experienced in my life has been due in part to my persistent attitude. The same can be true of developing presentation skills. When I gave my first presentation many decades ago, I had a tough time stringing together a semi-articulate sentence.

I got flustered. I exhibited every physiological manifestation of nervousness. I was a presentation catastrophe. Had you told me as I exited the lecture hall of my political geography class following that first attempt at public speaking that I would one day speak for a living, I would've thought you were clinically insane. There was no way I was going to do that again. I did, though. When I left university, I got a sales job and public speaking was a part of the package, you had to do presentations. Instead of continuing to flounder, though, I enrolled in an evening class to help me with presenting. I ended up teaching that same evening class. Anyone out there who can relate, please know that if you persist and get some tangible skills to help calm your nerves and elevate your confidence, you will not only live through the experience of giving a presentation, but you could find that you love it. You might even take what you've learned and teach others.

Tip – Be persistent.

#232 – Judy Garland

1922–1969

Context – Judy Garland sings "Somewhere Over the Rainbow" in the 1939 film, *The Wizard of Oz*.

Somewhere over the rainbow
Way up high,

*There's a land that I heard
Once in a lullaby.*

*Somewhere over the rainbow
Skies are blue
And the dreams that you dare to dream
Really do come true.*

*Someday I'll wish upon a star
And wake up where the clouds are far
Behind me.*

*Where troubles melt like lemon drops
Away above the chimney tops
That's where you'll find me.*

*Somewhere over the rainbo
Bluebirds fly.
Birds fly over the rainbow.
Why then, oh why can't I?*

*If happy little bluebirds fly
Beyond the rainbow
Why, oh why can't I?*

Analysis – It is no surprise to anyone who knows me to find Judy Garland hitting this list. Sure, it's not a talk per se but these lyrics evoke the emotion of one of the best talks I've ever heard, and so, as captain of this project, it is included. Sure, Garland has a beautiful voice, her tone and inflection are brilliant, but that is not what makes me well up each time I hear this song (play time must be into the thousands by now)! Garland sings with her heart, not her head. She feels the words, and as such we feel them too. My brain is at home with this song and this movie. It is a rather strange sensation and only one other movie does this for me (oh, the other movie will be revealed in a later post). This song is bright, and its cup is filled with joy and cheer. Yet, it has a quiet delivery and Garland tells the story perfectly. Have you ever really listened to the lyrics? 'And the dreams that you dare to dream do come true. Someday I'll wish upon a star and wake up where the clouds are far behind me. Where troubles melt like lemon drops…" She describes what many of us aspire to and that is to have our dreams realized and our troubles left behind. This song is a stunning masterpiece. With a view on presentation skills, notice Garland makes the song; the song doesn't make Garland. The same is true for you.

Tip – You make the presentation, the presentation doesn't make you.

#231 – George Clooney

(1961)

Context – In the 2009 movie *Up in the Air*, George Clooney delivers the below monologue as Ryan Bingham, a corporate downsizing expert who travels around the U.S. gutlessly firing people whilst living out of a suitcase.

"How much does your life weigh? Imagine for a second that you're carrying a backpack. Now, I want you to pack it with all the stuff you have in your life. You start with the little things: the shelves and drawers and nicknacks. Then you start adding larger stuff: clothes, tabletop appliances, lamps, your TV… Your backpack should be getting pretty heavy now. You go bigger. Your couch, your car, your home. I want you to stuff it all into that backpack. Now, I want you to fill it with people. Start with casual acquaintances, friends of friends, folks around the office. Then you move into the people that you trust with your most intimate secrets. Brothers, your sisters, your parents, your children. And finally, your husband, your wife, your boyfriend, your girlfriend. You get them into that backpack. Feel the weight of that bag. Your relationships are the heaviest components of your life. All those negotiations and arguments and secrets and compromises. The slower we move, the faster we die. Moving is living. Some animals were meant to carry each other, to live symbiotically over a lifetime: star-crossed lovers, monogamous swans. We. Are. Not. Swans. We're sharks."

Analysis – I've been trying to locate one of the presentations that Clooney delivers in *Up in the Air*, but alas, the trailer is all I can find. It serves the purpose, though. Close your eyes and listen to the cadence of Clooney's voice as he talks about life fitting into a backpack. Notice how his words feel; hollow and eerie, yet I'm compelled to keep listening. The movie has many themes, but at its forefront, it is a film examining the philosophy of choosing to live with nothing and nobody.

If you showed up to hear a presenter speak and a metaphorical George Clooney showed up and delivered this talk, would you listen? I know I would. It's dark; it's different; it's compelling. Clooney paints a picture. A vivid picture. It is the antithesis of a pumped-up fire-walking Tony Robbins seminar with all the showy grandeur. The above speech is now commonly known as "What's In Your Backpack?" It is both subtle and harsh, but it is compelling.

Tip – Be compelling.

#230 – Joe Rogan

(1967)

Context – Joe Rogan is a comedian, podcaster, and UFC commentator. The Boston native who now lives in Los Angeles hosts the podcast, *The Joe Rogan Experience*, in which he encourages his audience to live their best life.

"Most men live lives of quiet desperation. It' one of my favourite quotes ever because it is true. You live in this world where you can't wait to run away. But I think one of the reasons why these people have this deep-seated anger and resentment is there are a bunch of people out there that have these lives that are deeply unsatisfying because I think there are so many people that are working all day long doing something that is deeply unsatisfying and almost painful soul-killing, they're stuck in traffic all day, and then they're stuck in a cubical after that they relish in the fact that they take a shit in the bathroom and look at their phone I mean they literally do that that's a highlight of someone's day they get in traffic on the way home, they get home after that they're watching television, and they're fucked. If people have a regular day job, if you could just find some one thing that you do as a passion project and just keep building on it, just keep at it, keep watering, keep adding fertilizer, keep giving it attention, keep giving it focus and you can escape, you can escape, and you can be self-serving you can be okay you're gonna be okay for making furniture. Making furniture feels good, if you make furniture you make furniture for a living and you feel a great satisfaction of that you sell that furniture look man if you can do that you could cut those corners perfectly and sand everything down nice and stain it and then it's done you get this satisfied and you sell it to someone, and that pays your bills that is infinitely more satisfying than being stuck in some fucking cubicle working for someone that you don't want to work for, having to have these stupid fucking office meetings, talking to people in human resources sitting down with your supervisor where they evaluate your job performance, and you know you really you need to be enthusiastic about this company this company is your future…kill me now! There's a lot of people out there that would way rather do something else, and I hope they understand that they can, and people that are trapped in bad situations, one of the problems is you feel like this is your future. You feel like you can't get out of that there's no hope there's no light at the end of the tunnel, there's no rainbow, and if you feel like that, that alone can be incredibly defining and limiting, but if you can look at if you look at yourself objectively and say okay I kind of am fucked here I'm in credit card debt, I'm working in a shitty job I don't like, I don't like what I'm doing, but I have some ideas I need to feed those fucking ideas, and I need to feed them and water them, and I need to set aside a certain amount of time every day to just try to make those things happen, You can do that! Everyone has a different personality. They have different interests' different things that they would be really satisfied pursuing that's not encouraged. What's encouraged is go find a job. What's encouraged is, go find someplace that you can shove yourself into, go find a square hole so you can stick your round peg and just jam it in there and shave down the top and the bottom, so you slide in with all this extra space on the sides and finish for the rest of your life because you need a job because you're in debt because you have credit cards because you have student loans because that's what everybody does and so you do it too that what's wrong…."

Analysis – This isn't a speech; it's a call to action. Rogan's words are laced with so much authenticity, that I'm inspired to act. His words make me think hard and ask myself some big questions. Am I living a purpose-driven life? Am I creating meaning in my life? Am I doing enough?

About a year ago, I made a massive life change. I exited the corporate rat race, resurrected my company, Talk Talk and started realising my ideas and ideals. It's scary and daunting, but this talk, this 22 minutes and 14 seconds, reaffirmed my trajectory and resolve to pursue my goals.

A day that begins with being stuck in traffic, then sitting in a cubicle all day, listening to a manager who doesn't understand humanity or leadership, then dealing with office politics, jealously and passive-aggressive conflict, only to come home and veg out in front of the boob tube until numb in quiet desperation seems like a life sentence in proverbial hell. So many people I know are stuck in this unending cycle of untapped potential. It makes me weep. Making a shift to live a more purpose-driven life changes you mentally, psychically, emotionally, and spiritually. You begin to see the world differently, more positively, more optimistically. You attract different people into your sphere, people who share your energy, have similar ideas, have other ideas but are eager and open to exploring. You vibrate at a different frequency, and those who no longer serve your purpose or calling fade away and those who you need in this next chapter show up. What happens is that you marvel at where or how they came to be at precisely the right moment to contribute to your cause. If you are stuck in this propagated societal norm of what you think you are *supposed* to be doing, this is the post for you.

Some of you may say that you enjoy living life in *The Truman Show* and that you don't aspire for anything more—I call bullshit. In the 1998 movie, *The Truman Show*, everyone lives a predetermined, automatic life where a routine, rinse and repeat existence is revered. This hits the nail on its head when it questions truth and explores awakening. Of course, you aspire to live your highest purpose, and you're not going to find it pushing paper in some crappy cubicle or office driving profits for someone else's already swollen corporate bank account.

You need a kick in the ass. Read the excerpt above again or invest 22 minutes and watch the clip.

Rogan's talk is filled with fervour and mounting intensity. Is it scripted? Not a single word. He's tapping into a deep desire to share what he's learned. Why don't we all aspire to share what we've learned in such a way that it spurs those around us to act? Why wouldn't we scream from the rooftops what we've learned so that others may benefit from our experiences? The easy answer is the safety of our comfort zone plus our fear of rejection. As humans we want to be liked but, in that pursuit, we don't push ourselves to live bravely. Many of us fear dipping our toes outside our comfort zones that we live a life of vanilla. Watching this talk was like refilling my motivational gas tank with premium fuel.

Tip – Push yourself outside the limits of your comfort zone and challenge your fear of rejection.

#229 – Michelle Obama

(1964)

Context – 2008 Democratic National Convention, Denver.

"As you might imagine for Barak running for President is nothing compared to that first game of basketball

with my brother Craig. I can't tell you how much it means to have Craig and my mom here tonight. Like Craig, I can feel my dad looking down on us, just as I've felt his presence in every grace-filled moment of my life.

And at six-foot-six, I've often felt like Craig was looking down on me, too, literally. But the truth is, both when we were kids and today, Craig wasn't looking down on me; he was watching over me. And he has been there for me...

Every step of the way since that clear day, February, 19 months ago, when, with little more than our faith in each other and a hunger for change, we joined my husband, Barack Obama, on the improbable journey that has led us to this moment.

But each of us comes here also by way of our own improbable journey.

I come here tonight as a sister, blessed with a brother who is my mentor, my protector, and my lifelong friend. And I come here as a wife who loves my husband and believes he will be an extraordinary president.

Analysis – So you think you're nervous about preparing for an upcoming presentation? Let's put this into perspective. In this 2008 talk, Michelle Obama delivers a speech to more than 38 million viewers—several hundred in the crowd and millions more watching on television. Back then she hadn't delivered hundreds or thousands of talks, she was still in 'speaker infancy'. Whenever I get nervous, I imagine all the folks out there who have ever prepared to deliver a talk to a massive crowd. Sure, Obama most certainly had help, whether it was a scriptwriter or direction with regard to delivery, but we're talking 38 million people! I would amass a team to provide as much feedback as possible to get prepped for that. I watched this speech live in 2008, and since then many, more times. I've paused it, rewound it, fast-forwarded it, and I cannot find a hint of nervousness. How is this possible? It would be one thing if Obama was a callous woman who didn't care about connecting with her audience, but she does care, and she still delivers brilliantly. She is warm, funny, personable and simply endearing. I especially love the part where she talks about her older brother. This is a highlight for me in terms of her role as FLOTUS (First Lady of the United States), before she had as much practice in the public realm as she does today, with all the pressure associated with it. I wish it were a simple answer, and in previous posts, I've outlined simple tips by saying, "If you practice, you'll succeed." Sure, practice is part of it, but Obama is a beautiful combination of a hundred things going right in a talk: she is well-read and articulate, she has love in her heart, she shows emotion, is charismatic and confident, and she exudes integrity. Simply, Michelle Obama is a great storyteller, and yes, she most certainly practiced.

Tip – Let your presentations showcase your character.

#228 – Jean de la Bruyère

1645–1696

Context – French essayist and moralist, Jean de la Bruyère is attributed to the below quote in his only work, *Les Caracteres* (1688).

"There are certain things in which mediocrity is not to be endured, such as poetry, music, painting, public speaking."

Analysis – Speaking in front of a group of people used to be considered an art form. Frankly, I still believe that to be true, and it is why I love the sentiment that Jean de la Bruyère brings when he says that mediocrity is not to be endured in poetry, music, painting, and public speaking. Public speaking is an art. It is why I dedicated a year of my life to this project. It is why I've chosen public speaking as a profession. I respect it. I adore it and want others to recognize that it is one of the highest forms of self-expression. When done well, an audience participating in a presentation can be moved as much as someone viewing da Vinci's *Mona Lisa* or Monet's *Lily Pond* or Picasso's *Self Portrait* or Van Gogh's *Starry Night* or Warhol's *Campbell's Soup Can* or someone watching Shakespeare's *Romeo and Juliet* play out on the stage or listening to Bob Marley's "Get Up Stand Up." Words cannot encompass how I feel about the art of public speaking. So, I am saddened when some abuse the profession and use it simply as a platform for their ego. You can imagine the number of videos I've poured over. It's well into the thousands now, as I search for the expression of the spoken word to demonstrate my point. I've watched some of the most spectacular demonstrations of public speaking ever. I've also watched plenty of what I call, ego driven talks. They usually take the form of someone who has dubbed themselves to be a motivational or inspirational speaker. There are some wonderful motivational and inspirational speakers out there. Some of my mentors fall within this category. However, some people take the title of motivational and inspirational speakers but are nothing more than salespeople. It could be a book, another talk, or some new fad but whatever it is, they are there to sell you something and use the motivational talk platform as a disguise. It makes me sad because it is a flagrant abuse of the art of public speaking. It all comes down to intent. I wonder if other artists feel the same way when individuals, who have no business being there, creep into their worlds. Mmmmm.

Tip – Public speaking is an art, that takes time, energy, and commitment to develop.

#227 – Dan Buettner

(1960)

Context – Dan Buettner 2009 TED Talk, "How to Live to Be 100+."

"Something called the Danish Twin Study established that only about 10 percent of how long the average person lives, within certain biological limits, is dictated by our genes. The other 90 percent is dictated by our lifestyle. So the premise of Blue Zones: if we can find the optimal lifestyle of longevity we can come up with a de facto formula for longevity.

But if you ask the average American what the optimal formula of longevity is, they probably couldn't tell you. They've probably heard of the South Beach Diet, or the Atkins Diet. You have the USDA food pyramid. There is what Oprah tells us. There is what Doctor Oz tells us.

The fact of the matter is there is a lot of confusion around what really helps us live longer better. Should you be running marathons or doing yoga? Should you eat organic meats or should you be eating tofu? When it comes to supplements, should you be taking them? How about these hormones or resveratrol? And does purpose play into it? Spirituality? And how about how we socialize? "

Analysis – Ninety percent of our life span is determined by lifestyle, not genes. I must tell you that this erupted into one of the most enjoyable talks I've seen in quite a while. It is nearly 20 minutes long, and I was shocked how quickly the time passed and saddened when it came to an end. Buettner, a *National Geographic* writer, and explorer discusses why those in some cultures live longer than ours and how they do it. Buettner distills it down into something he calls, "blue zones" or areas with people that live the longest:

1. Sardinia, Italy
2. Okinawa, Japan
3. Adventists culture (Loma Linda, California).

He discusses what those in each culture eats, how they view life, the types of relationships they have, and their exercise routines. Fascinating! He tells one story within the Blue Zone of Okinawa that is permanently etched in my brain. Buettner explains that in Okinawa, you are born with half a dozen friends that travel through life with you. He draws a comparison to North American culture where he describes people as, "friendship deprived." Most have only one close friend. "What are the implications of that?" he asks. In Okinawa, this group of a half dozen friends is called a *Moai*. Your Moai is gifted to you at birth. So, when you encounter a bounty of luck, you share. When your child gets sick or a parent dies, your Moai help you to carry burden. Buettner shows a picture of a Moai that have been together for 97 years, and the average age in the group is 102. It's funny that the day I watched this video I had spoken to a friend earlier on the same day and we had discussed the topic of disconnectedness. (She is a dear friend that I can philosophize with, and neither of us thinks the other is insane for our universal theories. She is undoubtedly part of my Moai). Once again, isn't it interesting how life unfolds; you ask a question, and the answers present themselves to you later. Again, fascinating! But I digress. So, what do the people living in these three cultures (or blue zones) have in common?

1. They all move naturally.
2. They all have an optimistic outlook.
3. They all eat well (which, for some Sardinians includes a daily dip into Cannonau wine, more commonly known as Grenache, which I will be buying by the case tomorrow).
4. They all connect.

I am beyond jazzed about this presentation. I won't dissect Buettner's delivery as it relates to the presentation. It doesn't need it. He did his job gloriously well. He made me think, he told me stories I will never forget, and he taught me a few things. That is one helluva presentation.

Tip – Teach your audience.

#226 – Neil Armstrong

1930–2012

Context – At 10:56 pm Eastern Time on July 20, 1969, astronaut Neil Armstrong put his left foot on the lunar surface and famously delivered the below quote.

"That's one small step for a man, one giant leap for mankind."

Analysis – In a list of 365 Must-Know Talks, it is evident that Armstrong's words would have to show up somewhere. Now, let's get this out. There are all types of conspiracy theories out there as to whether Armstrong even walked on the moon or not, but for today's purposes, we'll simple explore the gravity (pun intended) of the words he spoke that day in 1969. Some six and a half hours after landing on the moon, Armstrong headed down the lunar module's ladder. As he took the final large step, he spoke the words above. There are mixed opinions on whether Armstrong included the *a* in his quote and instead said, "That's one small step for man, one giant leap for mankind," which basically means the same thing. One theory is that he'd rehearsed saying, "That's one small step for a man, one giant leap for mankind," which makes more sense frankly, but he either messed up or the *a* was drown out on the audio (we've all experienced technical issues, right?). In any event, he became the first human to step onto the surface of anything not of this Earth. While on the surface for some two and a half hours, Armstrong and Aldrin planted the US flag, took some notes and photographs, and then returned to the module. What I'd like to bring to the fore as it relates to presentation skills is Armstrong knew it was going to be a monumental day and started preparations months in advance, which included rehearsing what he was going to say. Even with this preparation, what came out of his mouth was either slightly different from what he had planned or was heard globally as something else. The winds of emotion will sweep you away when you're talking during a monumental event, and what you had planned might end up looking, or sounding, a little different. Be prepared for the unexpected and roll with those punches!

Tip – Be prepared for the winds of emotion to alter your original plans.

#225 – William Blake

1757–1827

Context – William Blake was an English poet, painter, and printmaker. Blake went largely unrecognized during his lifetime but is now considered the innovator of the poetry of the romanticism era.

"In seed time learn, in harvest teach, in winter enjoy."

Analysis – Life has a cyclical pattern to it, and each year we can witness this pattern through the seasons. This is why I've always loved this quote from Blake. There is summer, fall, winter, and spring. In our learning patterns, there is a parallel universe. There is a time to plant, a time to nurture, and a time to harvest. You may think that this type of theory can only be set to the confines of farming or gardening. Not so. Your learning behaviour can utilize the same language. From my vantage point, learning can be broken out into four stages, and below I've played with Blake's sentiment:

Stage One: Plant the seeds of learning (Summer)

Stage Two: Nurture your new skills (Fall)

Stage Three: Hunker down and play with what you have learned. Ruminate on it! Enjoy! (Winter)

Stage Four: Harvest time. Now is the time to teach! (Spring)

Stage One: Plant the Learning Seed – There is a time to plant – new ideas and new concepts. Stretch your comfort zone. Think back to a time when you were in school, be it elementary, junior, high school, or even university. A time when a teacher or professor sparked your interest in a topic. You got what they were saying, you were driven to learn more. In Grade 10, I was taking geography with Mr. Headen. Here was a man deeply interested in his topic and it showed. He had written the textbook for the course for of the love of it. His enthusiasm was contagious! I learned about developed countries and under-developed countries. More than twenty years later, I can still vividly recall many of Headen's lectures and looking down on the questions on the landscape printed paper as I wrote the year-end exam in a fluorescently lit classroom. I read the first question and legitimately, for the first time in my fifteen years of schooling, I not only knew the answer but was eager to craft my answer. I remember finishing the exam and not even thinking about how I had done or what mark I would get. I was just excited to have comprehended what had been presented. I got an A. But unlike the other As I had received, this one was different. It felt like an accomplishment. Even then, I recognized it. You see, what Mr. Headen had done for me was plant the seed for learning. Through his enthusiasm and encouragement I nurtured that seed all semester-long, watering it with an insatiable thirst for geography, and at the exam, I had the wonderful opportunity to harvest it. Many of us will have a story of when we immersed ourselves into a new idea or concept that was presented to us. But in this time-starved culture, when was the last time you sought out a brand-new shiny seed? If you never plant because you are waiting for the conditions to be just right, you will never experience the joy of the harvest.

Stage 2: Learning is not an event; but a process that needs to be nurtured. A process that requires new seeds every year. But planting the seed is the easiest part of the four-stage process. Nurturing takes time and commitment. How often do we read something or take a workshop but fail to implement the action plan?

Stage 3: Play with it. Ruminate on it. And enjoy! If you've ever baked or cooked, you know that for the end product to produce the tastiest results, you need to let it simmer, rest, or rise. You need to enjoy the process, maybe get a glass of wine or put on some music. A great spaghetti sauce needs time for the flavours to develop, a ball of dough needs time to rise, and a sugar cookie needs time to chill. Much is the same with learning—you've put the ingredients in a bowl, stirred it up, and kneaded it. Now you must let it rest and soak in all of the flavours!

Stage 4: Harvest time! Teach! – I was in a meeting many years ago that I'll never forget. The meeting had stopped for lunch. Fifteen sales executives were sitting at a table chit-chatting when the conversation turned to education. Each person bragged about the outstanding education they received. One by one, they shared what degree they had and where they went to school. When it got to me, I turned to the most boisterous voice in the group, a vice president, and asked her what year it was that she'd received her commerce degree. Stunned, she responded, that it was seventeen years ago. It is incredible how people cling to a harvest they achieved light years ago. One should seek out new learning opportunities each year. Harvest time is one of the best times of the year. You have the chance to take what you've learned during the last year and teach those around you.

Don't judge yourself by the result but by the seeds you plant. With summer just around the corner, think of the seeds you will plant so that when you are ready to harvest, and therefore teach, you will have something of value to share.

Tip – Plant new seeds.

#224 – Amy Tan

(1952)

Context – Amy Tan talks on creativity at TED 2008. Tan is the author of *The Joy Luck Club*, *The Hundred Secret Senses*, and *The Valley of Amazement*.

Analysis – WOW! Tan is one of the most naturally charismatic speakers I've seen. Her talk is funny, poignant, sad, foreboding, intelligent, enlightening, and joyful all mixed together into 22 minutes. A fun section I'd like to highlight happens in the first minute; Amy talks about the TED Commandments, which isn't really a part of the talk on creativity, but because I post so many TED videos, it's appropriate to include here:

TED Commandments

1. Rehearse but act spontaneously!
2. Provide revelations!
3. Show vulnerability!

4. Is Al Gore in the audience?

5. Don't be tedious!

6. Change the world!

7. Don't use bullet points!

Funny and true. Read and re-read those TED Commandments. They offer real and tangible advice on how to deliver a superb presentation.

For today I won't pour over the details of Tan's talk. I'd ask that you do that on your own. It is beyond worthwhile to sit back, watch and digest. Today's tip is an analogy: developing your presentation skills is like baking a cake. All cakes are unique and different. There is vanilla, chocolate, red velvet, German chocolate, cheesecake, black forest, carrot, coffee, pound, chiffon, gingerbread, lemon, pineapple upside-down. Okay, so I like cake! Presenters, like cakes, are all unique. Each of the above-mentioned cakes requires certain ingredients to create the tastiest and most delicious version. The same can be true of presenters. Tan has a set of unique characteristics that allow her to deliver the best talk that she can.

My characteristics are very different from hers. We have two distinct presentation styles. You need to nurture your unique style to give the best presentation you can.

Tip – Develop your unique characteristics in order to give the best presentation you can.

#223 – William Golding

1911–1993

Context – Excerpt from, *The Lord of the Flies*, published in 1954.

'Shut up,' said Ralph absently. He lifted the conch. 'Seems to me we ought to have a chief to decide things.'

'A chief! A chief!'

'I ought to be chief,' said Jack with simple arrogance, 'because I'm chapter chorister and head boy. I can sing C sharp.'

Another buzz.

'Well then,' said Jack, 'I-'

He hesitated. The dark boy, Roger, stirred at last and spoke up.

'Let's have a vote.' 'Yes!'

'Vote for a chief!' 'Let's vote-'

Analysis – Jack's desire for power is not a result of the island. This is a character trait he brought with him to the island. I've adored this book since first reading it in junior high school. The analogies that one could bridge to the real world are endless (I probably do this far too often). Take one of the stars of the novel, the conch shell. The conch shell represents the need for someone to take on the leadership role. Someone who will ultimately make the final decisions and can be relied on for guidance. I'll often talk about the conch shell in my presentation skills workshops. Presentations are, an opportunity for you to tell a story to an audience. As a presenter, you are the one holding the metaphorical conch shell. You are the one in the leadership role. You have been asked to give a presentation because you have something to contribute. You are the one who sets the tone of the room and creates order and balance. Respect this role and take it seriously.

Tip – Hold the conch shell with integrity!

#222 – Golan Levin

(1972)

Context – Golan Levin "Makes Art That Looks Back at You" in his 2004 TED Talk.

Analysis – Levin created quite a big buzz at TED in 2004 when he discussed that software or code is art. That, a separate discussion, but for the record, one that I wholeheartedly agree with. Here Levin shows through a series of interactive and, at times, live demonstrations how art can look back at you. I find this rather interesting from a presentation perspective, but also from a sociological and philosophical angle too.

Levin explores full-body art with a cool interactive program to detect what he calls, "negative imaging." He discusses voice as part of art or phonesthesia, which is an obscure branch of linguistics that refers to the idea that vocal sounds have meaning. He discusses how eyes, or a gaze relate to each other with a live demonstration that is rather wild. Every time Levin blinks, he creates a program with an eye-tracking system, so whenever he blinks, a live image of his eyes would pop on the screen. Akin to typing with your eyes. The larger and more profound question he's asking is, "What if art was aware that we were looking at it?" An interesting question to ponder.

I'd like to highlight something Levin does brilliantly during his presentation—he uses interactive visual aids. His version may be much more advanced than the rest of us would (or could) implement. But we can certainly observe how well live interaction works in a presentation setting. With that, it is another reminder to ensure the use of good visual aids, or more significantly, three-dimensional props, those that your audience can hold and touch. If your audience has a multi-sensory experience, rather than simply listening to the spoken word or reading words on a PowerPoint slide, their recollection almost triples. Over the years I've used a slew of different three-dimensional aids to demonstrate key points, usually through an analogy. I've used sunglasses to illustrate the art of true observation. I've mobbed the dollar store for feathers, construction paper, stickers, glue sticks, and anything else I could find for an activity on developing a personal mission statement. I've worn a hard hat to illustrate coming prepared for the job at hand. I've used binoculars to illustrate what the competitors are doing or to project a company's vision in five years' time. I've used a bag of lemons and asked my audience to smell their fresh scent and then bridged this to the program's objectives. Almost anything can be brought into the objective of a presentation. Use interactive aids in all your presentations.

Tip – Be creative with your use of three-dimensional props and aids.

#221 – Adlai Stevenson II

1900–1965

Context – Adlai Stevenson II, US statesman and was often revered for his quick wit. He ran for President twice in 1952 and 1956 against Dwight Eisenhower. During his campaign he was seen by many as a egghead intellectual, a term associated with academics sympathetic to Communism. The below quote is attributed to Stevenson.

"Flattery is all right so long as you don't inhale".

Analysis – Yes, quite often, after a presentation, the presenter basks in the glow of good reviews. I caution my students as well as myself to take that flattery with a grain of salt. Don't get me wrong. I, like anyone, enjoys it when someone pats me on the back and tells me I've done a good job. But the presenters that I've enjoyed the most, are the ones in a league of their own, and they are always humble. They take in the praise but rely more on self-feedback, than what other say. One of the worst characteristics, especially in a presenter, is arrogance. They haven't studied the craft per se but have learned how to get the most accolades. Being humble means that you have so much more to learn, and if harness that when standing at the front of the room, your audience will appreciate your candor and your willingness for learning to flow both ways.

Tip – Learn how to take praise from yourself, not others.

#220 – Amy Cuddy

(1972)

Context – In her 2012 TED Talk, "Your Body Language May Shape Who You Are," social psychologist, author, and speaker Amy Cuddy, reveals that we can change other people's perceptions and even our own body chemistry by simply changing our body positions.

"So, I want to start by offering you a free no-tech life hack, and all it requires of you is this: that you change your posture for two minutes. But before I give it away, I want to ask you to right now do a little audit of your body and what you're doing with your body. So, how many of you are sort of making yourselves smaller? Maybe you're hunching, crossing your legs, maybe wrapping your ankles. Sometimes we hold onto our arms like this. Sometimes we spread out. (Laughter) I see you. So, I want you to pay attention to what you're doing right now. We're going to come back to that in a few minutes, and I'm hoping that if you learn to tweak this a little bit, it could significantly change the way your life unfolds.

So, we're really fascinated with body language, and we're particularly interested in other people's body language. You know, we're interested in, like, you know—(Laughter)—an awkward interaction, or a smile, or a contemptuous glance, or maybe a very awkward wink, or maybe even something like a handshake.

(Video inserted here of the President of the U.S shaking the hand of the security guard and the Prime Minister of the U.K ignoring the security guard) Narrator: Here they are, arriving at Number 10.This lucky policeman gets to shake hands with the President of the United States. Here comes the Prime Minister – No.

So, a handshake, or the lack of a handshake, can have us talking for weeks and weeks and weeks—even the BBC and The New York Times. So obviously, when we think about nonverbal behaviour or body language—but we call it nonverbals as social scientists—it's language, so we think about communication. When we think about communication, we think about interactions. So, what is your body language communicating to me? What's mine communicating to you?

And there's a lot of reason to believe that this is a valid way to look at this. So social scientists have spent a lot of time looking at the effects of our body language, or other people's body language, on judgments. And we make sweeping judgments and inferences from body language. And those judgments can predict really meaningful life outcomes like who we hire or promote, who we ask out on a date. For example, Nalini Ambady, a researcher at Tufts University, shows that when people watch 30-second soundless clips of real physician-patient interactions, their judgments of the physician's niceness predict whether or not that physician will be sued. So, it doesn't have to do so much with whether or not that physician was incompetent, but do we like that person and how they interacted? Even more dramatic, Alex Todorov at Princeton has shown us that judgments of political candidates' faces in just one second predict 70 percent of U.S. Senate and gubernatorial race outcomes, and even, let's go digital, emoticons used well in online negotiations can lead you to claim more value from that negotiation. If you use them poorly, bad idea. Right?

So, when we think of nonverbals, we think of how we judge others, how they judge us and what the outcomes are. We tend to forget, though, the other audience that's influenced by our nonverbals, and that's ourselves. We are also influenced by our nonverbals, our thoughts and our feelings and our physiology.

So, what nonverbals am I talking about? I'm a social psychologist. I study prejudice, and I teach at a competitive business school, so it was inevitable that I would become interested in power dynamics. I became especially interested in nonverbal expressions of power and dominance.

And what are nonverbal expressions of power and dominance? Well, this is what they are. So, in the animal kingdom, they are about expanding. So, you make yourself big; you stretch out, you take up space, you're basically opening up. It's about opening up. And this is true across the animal kingdom. It's not just limited to primates. And humans do the same thing. (Laughter) So they do this both when they have power, sort of chronically, and also when they're feeling powerful in the moment. And this one is especially interesting because it really shows us how universal and old these expressions of power are. This expression, which is known as pride, Jessica Tracy has studied. She shows that people who are born with sight and people who are congenitally blind do this when they win at a physical competition. So, when they cross the finish line, and they've won, it doesn't matter if they've never seen anyone do it. They do this. So, the arms up in the V, the chin is slightly lifted.

What do we do when we feel powerless? We do exactly the opposite. We close up. We wrap ourselves up. We make ourselves small. We don't want to bump into the person next to us. So again, both animals and humans do the same thing. And this is what happens when you put together high and low power. So, what we tend to do when it comes to power is that we complement the other's nonverbals. So, if someone is being really powerful with us, we tend to make ourselves smaller. We don't mirror them. We do the opposite of them...."

Analysis – Cuddy creates a very compelling argument for the much-used phrase, fake it 'til you make it in a talk that quickly went viral. When faced with stressful situations, Cuddy suggests that we can increase our testosterone levels and decrease cortisol levels through what she calls power poses. Cuddy talks about natural power poses such as when an athlete finishes first in a race and punctuates their excitement with a fist-pump, arms raised into a V-shape, and chin slightly lifted pose. When confronted, animals will often make themselves big, so they take up more space which immediately makes me think of gorillas standing tall and pounding their chests.

Cuddy's proclamation seems brazen, but her research is correct—even slightly tweaking our body's shape to reflect a power position can change the way a situation unfolds. A cool section of Cuddy's talk is when she discusses the job interview experiment. Along with her fellow researchers, Cuddy brought several participants into her lab to play the role of the job interviewee, while Cuddy's group acted as the interviewers. The researchers created a complex environment: the interviewers were instructed to maintain a neutral expression and not provide any verbal cues or feedback. Think about it, when you were last interviewed for a job, what were you doing in the waiting room? Were you posing small, on the phone, hunched over, stressed out and anxious or were you posing big, shoulders back, confident, strong, visualising how great you were going to be?

Cuddy suggests that by assuming these power poses our bodies can shape our minds and we can elevate our testosterone levels and lower our cortisol levels. Whether musing about an interview or delivering a talk, the same principle applies. I often give myself a pep talk backstage, accompanied by pacing. I get my mind prepped by doing two things: reviewing the first line of my intro repeatedly and then telling myself how the talk will be informative, engaging and fun. My body naturally finds the power pose even, at times, unconsciously standing in one of the most well-known and versatile high-power poses, The Wonder Woman—legs shoulder-width apart, chest out and hands on hips.

Our bodies change our minds, our minds change our behaviours, and our behaviours can change our outcomes. Some may say, adopting or pretending to be more powerful than we feel is fake. The Imposter Experience is all about feelings of self-doubt, being exposed as a fraud, and low self-esteem and is a substantial behavioural health condition that impairs professional performance and contributes to burnout. If that feels like you, you're not alone! A quick google search yields more than five million results. Even highly successful people suffer from this condition. Sheryl Sandberg, the COO of Facebook and the author of *Lean In* is quoted as saying, "And every time I didn't embarrass myself—or even excelled—I believed that I fooled everyone yet again. One day soon, the jig would be up." Tina Fey said, "The beauty of Imposter Syndrome is you vacillate between extreme egomania and a feeling of, 'I'm a fraud!' Oh, God, they're on to me! I'm a fraud!'" And Lady Gaga and Tom Hanks have made similar admissions.

Cuddy becomes emotional as she recounts her own imposter within experiences after a severe car accident resulted in a head injury that dropped her IQ by two standard deviations. Her personal journey of shedding the Imposter Experience didn't come until she was able to teach one of her students to overcome their feelings of inadequacy. She empowered her student by telling her that she deserved to be there. That it was okay to fake it until she became it and in doing so she gave herself permission to do the same.

Tiny tweaks result in significant changes. When preparing for your next talk, try striking a power pose to get your testosterone up and your cortisol down.

Tip – Fake it 'til you become it.

#219 – Jean Piaget

1896–1980

Context – Jean Piaget was a Swiss epistemologist (the theory of knowledge) and well known for his epistemological studies with children.

"Play teaches children to master the world."

Analysis – Ever watch a child at play? Children are passionate about everything. They are natural explorers and experimenters. They'll reach out for anything; a ladybug, a hand, an animal, they'll splash in puddles to see the effects and soak up the joy of their creation. As presenters we can learn a lot from observing children. When a child is bored, they don't do the socially accepted thing and sit with it. They let you (and anyone else within range) know about it. They remove politeness and will simply announce they are bored and move on to a more exciting task. This teaches a child that they should continue to seek out only those activities that bring them joy. Imagine if you were presenting to a room of children? Would they be interested? Or would they seek out a new task or toy?

Children also teach us that when confronted with the unfamiliar or unknown you shouldn't turn the other cheek. You should explore it, until you figure it out. They'll touch, poke, shake, and study until they have a handle on what is in front of them. Adults, by contrast, will look at a thing, place a label on it and say that we already know what it is and what it is for. When was the last time you looked at a familiar object in an unfamiliar way? This is where great visual props come from. Look at the everyday objects around you and see if you can bring anything into your presentations to bolster your point.

Children also place great prestige on their dreams. They talk about them as though they are real. They have tremendous confidence in the attainment of those dreams and will share with anyone who'll listen. What are your dreams about? What do they look like? Create a vision for yourself, talk about it, practice it, believe it will come true.

Finally, as the Piaget quote says, "Children play to understand and master the world." Children can make a game out of just about anything. They can create entire worlds to play in from their imaginations alone. They don't get hung up on whether or not any of it is accurate. There is no tangible goal it simply what is driving them that day. Creativity is the nucleus of any great presentation. Play with your presentation, step outside the bounds of accuracy for a moment, and let it be pure fun.

Tip – Observe children to master your presentations.

#218 – Kevin Spacey

(1959)

Context – Kevin Spacey stars in *American Beauty*, 1999. As the film comes to an end, Lester Burnham (Spacey) delivers a voiceover at the moment of his death. He describes some of the experiences of his life in the below monologue.

"I had always heard your entire life flashes in front of your eyes the second before you die. First of all, that one second isn't a second at all. It stretches on forever, like an ocean of time. For me, it was lying on my back at Boy Scout camp, watching falling stars. (gunshot) And yellow leaves from the maple trees that lined our street. (gunshot) Or my grandmother's hands and the way her skin seemed like paper. (distant gunshot) And the first time I saw my cousin Tony's brand-new Firebird. And Janie. And Janie. And Carolyn. I guess I could be pretty pissed off about what happened to me, but it's hard to stay mad when there's so much beauty in the world. Sometimes I feel like I'm seeing it all at once and it's too much. My heart fills up like a balloon that's about to burst. And then I remember to relax and stop trying to hold on to it. And then it flows through me like rain, and I can't feel anything but gratitude for every single moment of my stupid little life. You have no idea what I'm talking about, I'm sure. But don't worry, you will someday."

Analysis – Kevin Spacey stars in the film *American Beauty* as Lester Burnham, a 42-year-old office worker who becomes infatuated with his teenage daughter's best friend. As I watch this clip, I'm struck by how similar the story is to some of the great classics. For example, one my favourite pieces of literature in the entire world; *The Death of Ivan Ilych*. This is Leo Tolstoy, the wonderful Russian writer, at his finest. Written in 1886, The *Death of Ivan Ilych* centers around a character in his 40s, who asks some substantial questions about life. Many more movies, pieces of literature, poetry, etc., can be traced back to meaning-of-life themes. These two fictional pieces deal with being escaping imprisonment. Everything is grey.
As you watch the clip of Burnham, notice the monotone delivery, the onerous weight of his voice, the

matter-of-fact nature of isolation and loneliness. The responsible life in the banality of the suburbs is one that Spacey's character comes to despise, and thus the arrival of a fresh young girl reawakens him. My hope is this project will reignite or ignite a passion for my readers. This post is addressed to those readers who dread the upcoming business presentation. Perhaps it is a sales review, or a year-end recap, or any presentation where you are forced to stick to a tired and uninspiring 'standardized template. Listen, there are presentations that feel like you've been handed a prison sentence when you've been asked to do it, but it is all how you look at it. Take that damn template and jazz it up, go ahead and follow it because you must, but there is no reason you can't do all the other things that will ignite a passion for what you've been asked to do. Add music or video into that boring template. Insert visual aids. Hire a damn juggler to illustrate your point? Spacey's character in *American Beauty* chose his grey existence in everything he did. What colour are your presentations, Technicolour or Pantone Grey?

Tip – Make your presentations colourful.

#217 – Sojourner Truth

1797–1883

Context – The below is an excerpt from a speech delivered by Sojourner Truth in 1851 at the Women's Convention in Akron, Ohio.

"Well, children, where there is so much racket, there must be something out of kilter. I think that 'twixt the negroes of the South and the women at the North, all talking about rights, the white men will be in a fix pretty soon. But what's all this here talking about?

That man over there says that women need to be helped into carriages, and lifted over ditches, and to have the best place everywhere. Nobody ever helps me into carriages, or over mud-puddles, or gives me any best place! And ain't I a woman? Look at me! Look at my arm! I have ploughed and planted and gathered into barns, and no man could head me! And ain't I a woman? I could work as much and eat as much as a man—when I could get it—and bear the lash as well! And ain't I a woman? I have borne thirteen children and seen most all sold off to slavery, and when I cried out with my mother's grief, none but Jesus heard me! And ain't I a woman?

Then they talk about this thing in the head; what's this they call it? [member of audience whispers, "intellect"]

That's it, honey. What's that got to do with women's rights or negroes' rights? If my cup won't hold, but a pint and yours holds a quart, wouldn't you be mean not to let me have my little half measure full?

Then that little man in black there, he says women can't have as many rights as men, 'cause Christ wasn't a woman! Where did your Christ come from? Where did your Christ come from? From God and a woman! Man had nothing to do with Him.

If the first woman God ever made was strong enough to turn the world upside down all alone, these women together ought to be able to turn it back and get it right side up again! And now they is asking to do it, the men better let them.

Obliged to you for hearing me, and now old Sojourner ain't got nothing more to say."

Analysis – Sojourner Truth was the name taken by an American born into slavery who became a noted speaker for both the Abolitionist Movement and the Women's Rights Movement. Her original name was Isabella Baumfree. "Ain't I a Woman?" is simply spectacular! I've read it, re-read it, and soaked in the words. I can feel the delivery, the cadence, the conviction. The question: "Ain't I a woman?" is repeated over and over again and the impact is palpable. Can you feel this speech? Can you feel the power behind it? The importance of it? I can.

Tip – Speak to change the world.

#216 – Kelly McGonical

(1977)

Contex – In her 2013 TED Talk, "How to Make Stress Your Friend," psychologist Kelly McGonigal provides us with a positive perspective on stress.

"I have a confession to make. But first, I want you to make a little confession to me. In the past year, I want you to just raise your hand if you've experienced relatively little stress. Anyone?

How about a moderate amount of stress?

Who has experienced a lot of stress? Yeah, me too.

But that is not my confession. My confession is this: I am a health psychologist, and my mission is to help people be happier and healthier. But I fear that something I've been teaching for the last ten years is doing more harm than good, and it has to do with stress. For years I've been telling people, stress makes you sick. It increases the risk of everything from the common cold to cardiovascular disease. Basically, I've turned stress into the enemy. But I have changed my mind about stress, and today, I want to change yours.

Let me start with the study that made me rethink my whole approach to stress. This study tracked 30,000 adults in the United States for eight years, and they started by asking people, "How much stress have you experienced in the last year?" They also asked, "Do you believe that stress is harmful for your health?" And then, they used public death records to find out who died.

Okay, some bad news first. People who experienced a lot of stress in the previous year had a 43 percent increased risk of dying. But that was only true for the people who also believed that stress is harmful for your health.

People who experienced a lot of stress but did not view stress as harmful were no more likely to die. In fact, they had the lowest risk of dying of anyone in the study, including people who had relatively little stress.

Now the researchers estimated that over the eight years they were tracking deaths, 182,000 Americans died prematurely, not from stress, but from the belief that stress is bad for you. That is over 20,000 deaths a year. Now, if that estimate is correct, that would make believing stress is bad for you the 15th largest cause of death in the United States last year, killing more people than skin cancer, HIV/AIDS and homicide.

You can see why this study freaked me out. Here I've been spending so much energy telling people stress is bad for your health.

So, this study got me wondering: Can changing how you think about stress make you healthier? And here, the science says yes. When you change your mind about stress, you can change your body's response to stress."

Analysis – How much stress have you experienced in the last year? Well, considering we've been living through a global pandemic since the beginning of 2020, my guess is that most people would say, a lot! Isolation, anxiety, loss of income, fear, and bereavement all contribute to our stress levels. Back in the '80s, there was a public service announcement on TV that you may remember. A man in a kitchen held up an egg and said, "This is your brain." Then cracked it into a hot frying pan. "This is your brain on drugs." I wonder what our brains look like almost two years into a global pandemic? Probably something like an egg sizzling in a hot pan. Motivation and efficiency are waning, and we are tired, defeated, and foggy. I wonder if we changed how we viewed the pandemic our collective sadness and anxiety would improve? What if we told ourselves that we don't have to be lonely or depressed—that we are just living through a pandemic? McGonigal suggests changing your mindset and making stress your friend—instead of looking for the good in the situation the key to dealing with stress is to look for the good in ourselves and our communities.

McGonigal references a study that she and her colleagues conducted with more than 30,000 people. The study participants were asked if they were stressed and if they believed that being stressed was harmful to their health. McGonigal believes how you think about stress matters and calls it the *stress mindset effect*. If you believe stress is bad for you, you are more likely to get sick and die from stress. If you believe stress is a toxic state, and your immediate thought when you get stressed is, "this is bad, this is poison," then it will be. McGonigal suggests adopting a mindset that stress happens in our minds and bodies only when we care about something. It is not a sign that we're not equipped to cope but a sign that we care deeply. Our body and brain are simply trying to push us toward a coping strategy. What a refreshing perspective!

McGonigal suggests that higher levels of stress correlate with how meaningful your life is. Meaningful careers, roles, goals, and relationships all contribute to higher stress levels. Stress is a human response when something you care about is at stake. It is an expression of who we are, and if we see meaning in our lives, we are by proxy more stressed.

Everyone experiences stress from time to time. McGonigal doesn't delineate between physical, mental, or emotional stress. We've all heard that not all stress is bad, but what McGonigal is suggesting is more significant in that how we think about and perceive stress can positively or negatively impact our body's reaction to it. McGonigal debunks that stress on its own can harm your health—you must believe it to be harmful for it to be harmful.

McGonigal talks about various hormones that are released during stress including, Oxytocin. I thought Oxytocin was the cuddle hormone, not a stress hormone! Oxytocin enhances empathy. It makes us crave physical contact with friends and family and makes us social. It's the hormone that wants you to be surrounded by people who care about you. "People who spent time caring for others showed absolutely no stress-related increase in dying. Zero," says McGonigal. Whoa, could that be right? Believing that stress is bad for you is the issue, not the stress itself. Stress gives us access to our hearts. The compassionate heart finds joy and meaning in connecting with others. Perhaps this is why so many people seem so sad right now. As we continue to navigate this global pandemic, we are touch-deprived due to countless lockdowns and quarantines. No handshaking, no hugging, no social gatherings. McGonigal's hypothesis proves true.

The topic is captivating for sure, but McGonigal's delivery is also worthy of note. She is relaxed, comfortable, funny and engages with her audience. I look at stress differently now because of this fourteen-minute talk, and isn't that what you want from your talk, to leave your audience transformed in some way?

Tip – Embrace the stress in your next talk and view it not as a danger but as a trigger to cope.

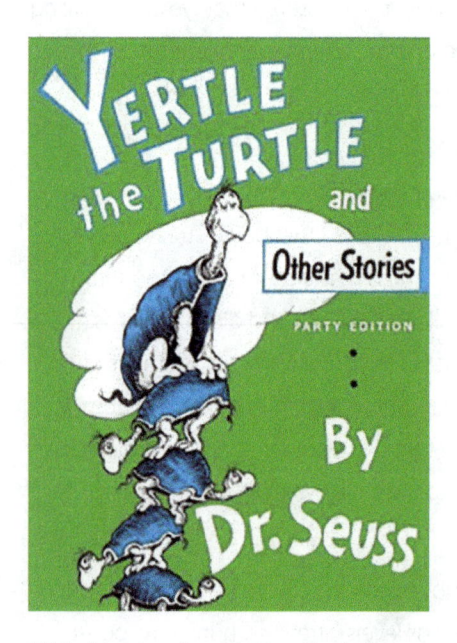

#215 – Dr. Seuss

1904–1991

Context – *Yertle the Turtle* written 1958

On the far-away island of Sala-ma-Sond,
Yertle the Turtle was king of the pond.
A nice little pond. It was clean. It was neat.
The water was warm. There was plenty to eat.
The turtles had everything turtles might need.
And they were all happy. Quite happy indeed.

They were… until Yertle, the king of them all,
Decided the kingdom he ruled was too small.
"I'm ruler", said Yertle, "of all that I see.
But I don't see enough. That's the trouble with me.

With this stone for a throne, I look down on my pond

*But I cannot look down on the places beyond.
This throne that I sit on is too, too low down.
It ought to be higher!" he said with a frown.
"If I could sit high, how much greater I'd be!
What a king! I'd be ruler of all that I see!"*

*So Yertle the Turtle King, lifted his hand
And Yertle, the Turtle King, gave a command.
He ordered nine turtles to swim to his stone
And, using these turtles, he built a new throne.
He made each turtle stand on another one's back
And he piled them all up in a nine-turtle stack.
And then Yertle climbed up. He sat down on the pile.
What a wonderful view! He could see 'most a mile!*

*"All mine!" Yertle cried. "Oh, the things I now rule!
I'm the king of a cow! And I'm the king of a mule!
I'm the king of a house! And, what's more, beyond that
I'm the king of a blueberry bush and a cat!
I'm Yertle the Turtle! Oh, marvelous me!
For I am the ruler of all that I see!"*

*And all through the morning, he sat up there high
Saying over and over, "A great king am I!"
Until 'long about noon. Then he heard a faint sigh.*

*"What's that?" snapped the king, and he looked down the stack.
And he saw, at the bottom, a turtle named Mack.
Just a part of his throne. And this plain little turtle
Looked up and he said, "Beg your pardon, King Yertle.
I've pains in my back and my shoulders and knees.
How long must we stand here, Your Majesty, please?"*

*"SILENCE!" the King of the Turtles barked back.
"I'm king, and you're only a turtle named Mack."
"You stay in your place while I sit here and rule.
I'm the king of a cow! And I'm the king of a mule!
I'm the king of a house! And a bush! And a cat!
But that isn't all. I'll do better than that!
My throne shall be higher!" his royal voice thundered,
"So pile up more turtles! I want 'bout two hundred!"*

"Turtles! More turtles!" he bellowed and brayed.

And the turtles 'way down in the pond were afraid.

They trembled. They shook. But they came. They obeyed.
From all over the pond, they came swimming by dozens.
Whole families of turtles, with uncles and cousins.
And all of them stepped on the head of poor Mack.
One after another, they climbed up the stack.

Then Yertle the Turtle was perched up so high,
He could see forty miles from his throne in the sky!
"Hooray!" shouted Yertle. "I'm the king of the trees!
I'm king of the birds! And I'm king of the bees!
I'm king of the butterflies! King of the air!
Ah, me! What a throne! What a wonderful chair!
I'm Yertle the Turtle! Oh, marvelous me!
For I am the ruler of all that I see!"

Then again, from below, in the great heavy stack,
Came a groan from that plain little turtle named Mack.
"Your Majesty, please… I don't like to complain,
But down here below, we are feeling great pain.
I know, up on top you are seeing great sights,
But down here at the bottom we, too, should have rights.
We turtles can't stand it. Our shells will all crack!
Besides, we need food. We are starving!" groaned Mack.

"You hush up your mouth!" howled the mighty King Yertle.
"You've no right to talk to the world's highest turtle.
I rule from the clouds! Over land! Over sea!
There's nothing, no, NOTHING, that's higher than me!"

But, while he was shouting, he saw with surprise
That the moon of the evening was starting to rise
Up over his head in the darkening skies.
"What's THAT?" snorted Yertle. "Say, what IS that thing
That dares to be higher than Yertle the King?
I shall not allow it! I'll go higher still!
I'll build my throne higher! I can and I will!
I'll call some more turtles. I'll stack 'em to heaven!
I need 'bout five thousand, six hundred and seven!"

But, as Yertle, the Turtle King, lifted his hand
And started to order and give the command,

That plain little turtle below in the stack,
That plain little turtle whose name was just Mack,

Decided he'd taken enough. And he had.
And that plain little lad got a bit mad.
And that plain little Mack did a plain little thing.
He burped!
And his burp shook the throne of the king!

And Yertle the Turtle, the king of the trees,
The king of the air and the birds and the bees,
The king of a house and a cow and a mule…
Well, that was the end of the Turtle King's rule!
For Yertle, the King of all Sala-ma-Sond,
Fell off his high throne and fell Plunk! in the pond!

And today the great Yertle, that Marvelous he,
Is King of the Mud. That is all he can see.
And the turtles, of course… all the turtles are free
As turtles and, maybe, all creatures should be.

Analysis – I'm a monster Dr. Seuss fan and read a Seuss book nearly every day. The above excerpt is from one of my favourites, *Yertle the Turtle*. This book illustrates how Seuss was a master of political satire. He wrote on so many levels and appealed to so many. For the wee ones there are great rhymes and rhythms, for the bigger wee ones there are moral messages, and for adults there is social commentary. None of it is condescending. Seuss' work is always smart and witty, and he appeals to all ages. Not many authors can do that.

I could deconstruct *Yertle the Turtle* and wax lyrical about rulership, ownership, dictatorship, and debate Yertle's place as a political figure in history, but I won't. Today, let's look at the appeal of this story to every reader. How can your presentations appeal to such a vast audience? What could you do so that your entire audience gets something (each person extracting something different, perhaps) from what you are *saying*?

Tip – Appeal to your entire audience.

#214 – David Byrne

(1952)

Context – David Byrne, most recognizable perhaps for his role in the band, Talking Heads, is credited with saying the below quote.

"Sometimes it's a form of love just to talk to somebody that you have nothing in common with and still be fascinated by their presence…you can be absolutely fascinated, even enamoured by others that you share nothing with."

Analysis – I once had a spate of people accuse me of having absolutely nothing in common with them! In each scenario, the inference was that because we lacked common ground, we should cease any attempt to develop, maintain, or enhance our relationship. I said to each person, "I didn't realize that one needed to have something in common with another to relate." I find this point of view inane. My life experiences inevitably creep into my work, and I am compelled to dissect them. I can't relate to a person who is deaf as I have my hearing. But does this mean then that I should not try to get to know this individual because I don't share this commonality? What about a blind person? An individual with a learning disability? An individual in a wheelchair? How about someone with different skin colour from my own? I don't have those things in common with them. In my work and personal life, I meet all types of people. Some of the people I meet are dramatically different in terms of personality and points of view, and some of these people are my best friends. I love that I can get together with a group of people and be able to share our different vantage points. Sometimes there will be heated debates as we struggle to get our messages across and be heard, but I wouldn't have it any other way. I don't want to live in a land of Carolines. Frankly, it would be plain boring, and I wouldn't learn anything. I want to live in a world filled with differences. Byrne nails it with his quote. It is your attitude as you enter into that exchange. When you are delivering a presentation or a talk, the people in your audience will bring with them different life experiences and different perspectives. If you are so narrowminded that you struggle to connect with people who you have little in common with, then how are you ever going to get your message across? Open yourself up to those around you, welcome them in, be interested in what they have to say, even debate with them if you choose, but don't refuse to enter into an exchange and don't judge a book by its cover. Talk to anyone for more than five minutes (this means listening too), and you will likely discover that you have more in common than you first thought. As Bryne says, it is a form of love to show everyone you meet the respect that they deserve. A great Indian philosopher by the name of Krishnamurti said, "It is the highest form of human intelligence to be able to observe yourself and not judge yourself." If you have identified yourself as someone who makes blanket statements about commonality, observe your behaviour and work on changing it. You will be amazed how your presentation skills improve.

Tip – Realize that you have something in common with everyone. It is up to you to seek it out.

#213 – Dan Pink

(1964)

Context – Former speechwriter for Al Gore, Dan Pink speaks on the surprising truth about what motivates us. Based on Pink's fourth non-fiction book, this animated talk was released in 2010. It illustrates the hidden truths behind what really motivates us in the workplace.

"Our motivations are unbelievably interesting, and I've been working on this for a few years, and I just find the topic still so amazingly engaging and interesting, so I want to tell you about that. The science is really surprising; the science is a little bit freaky, okay? If we are not as endlessly manipulable and as predictable as you would think. There's a whole set of unbelievably interesting studies. I want to give you two that call *into question this idea that if you reward something you get more of the behaviour you want; if you punish something you get less of it....What the science has taught us is that people don't do great things with simply a profit motive...As soon as the task permeates outside the boundaries of rudimentary cognitive skill, money isn't a motivator to elicit better or faster performance."*

Analysis – This is one of the finest presentations I've seen, and I'm thrilled to be able to share it with all of you! You won't see the presenter presenting. What you will see is an animated depiction of the presenter's words. You see, Pink's words so inspired the animator that he took his presentation and set live animation to the words. I love it! It is visually unique. As I watch it, I'm mesmerized both by the content and the animation. Pink doesn't waste a single word in the 11-minute talk. Each word has been chosen artfully to further solidify his message. If you manage people, are a leader of others, or want to understand motivation more fully, this is the presentation for you! Pink talks about several experiments that show people aren't as endlessly manipulatable, at least when it comes to money or compensation. When I managed people, I would often ask my direct reports to tell me what motivates them. I would set parameters around this question such as, what would motivate you if we took money out of the equation. The answers were fascinating. As soon as you remove money from the discussion, the answers become about the three things Pink talks about: autonomy, mastery, and purpose. At our foundation, we all want to have purpose in the world, and this is not motivated by financial gains. Many of the organizations that I observe, try to motivate their employees with money and profit, and they are often at a loss when this doesn't work. People like to feel that they are making a difference and that what they are contributing has value. Pink finishes by saying that what we need to do is start treating people like people and not horses; with carrots and sticks because that just doesn't work. Do you get the sense that I adore this talk? Yup, I could talk ad nauseam about it and its implications, but let's change the trajectory. Imagine if that presentation that you have coming up could make a real and profound difference in the lives of all the individuals listening to it. What if you were able to motivate them authentically and naturally? It doesn't take money. It takes inspiring others for a greater purpose.

Tip – Inspire your audience to reach their purpose.

#212 – Christopher Poole

(1988)

Context – Poole, an internet entrepreneur, talks about "The Case For Anonymity Online" in his 2010 TED Talk.

"When I was 15, I found this website called Futaba Channel. And it was a Japanese forum and imageboard. That format of forum, at that time, was not well-known outside of Japan. And so what I did is I took it, I translated it into English, and I stuck it up for my friends to use. Now, six and a half years later, over seven million people are using it, contributing over 700,000 posts per day. And we've gone from one board to 48 boards.

This is what it looks like. So, what's unique about the site is that it's anonymous, and it has no memory. There's no archive, there are no barriers, there's no registration. These things that we're used to with forums don't exist on 4chan. And that's led to this discussion that's completely raw, completely unfiltered. What the site's known for, because it has this environment, is it's fostered the creation of a lot of Internet phenomena, viral videos and whatnot, known as memes."

Analysis – In this talk, the founder of 4chan, an uncensored, often controversial online imageboard, discusses his company as a place and the need for anonymity. Let's not focus on the content of Poole's talk but on the delivery. Poole is the opposite of *acting hot*. Remember when you were in elementary school, and everyone ran around accusing others about acting hot, or was this just the arrogant and self-righteous kids I went to school with? So often, in a speech, you will find the speaker pretending to know more than they do and coming across unfavourably. Poole does the opposite, and this is why I've chosen to include his talk in my list. He is humble in every way. It's refreshing. It's also indicative of Generation Y (sometimes called Millennials—those born between 1981 and 1994/6). Many Gen Xers (1965 to 1979/80) and Boomers (1946 to 1964) don't understand Gen Yers, and part of the reason is what I'm touching on today. Gen Ys generally are not fans of putting on a show, whereas Boomers, and to some extent, Gen Xers, often feel the need to do so, especially in business environments. Gen Ys get a bad rap. They are considered the trophy generation or the Peter Pan generation because apparently, they have a failure to launch into adulthood. Supposedly, no one in this group ever failed at anything (think participation awards). Frankly, Xers and Boomers could learn a ton from this often-undervalued group. Like all generations, Millennials have been shaped by the developments and events of their time, and it's their Gen X and Boomer parents who throw the most sticks at them. Access to instant communication, email, texting, IM, YouTube, Facebook, LinkedIn, etc., have made Millennials rely on concise messaging. That is why I always enjoy watching a presentation from this age group. It is generally concise, intelligent, and doesn't contain an excess of pomp and ceremony. I like that, and I like Poole's presentation for these reasons.

Tip – Be humble and take out the pomp and ceremony.

#211- Mike Rowe

(1962)

Context – Mike Rowe, in his 2008 TED Talk, "Learning from *Dirty Jobs*." Rowe hosted *Dirty Jobs* a television series that saw Rowe performing difficult, messy, strange, and dirty jobs from 2012 to 2020.

"The Dirty Jobs *crew and I were called to a little town in Colorado, called Craig. It's only a couple dozen square miles. It's in the Rockies. And the job in question was sheep rancher.*

My role on the show, for those of you who haven't seen it – it's pretty simple. I'm an apprentice, and I work with the people who do the jobs in question. And my responsibilities are to simply try and keep up and give an honest account of what it's like to be these people for one day in their life. The job in question: herding sheep. Great. We go to Craig, and we check into a hotel, and I realize the next day that castration is going to be an absolute part of this work. Normally, I never do any research at all. But this is a touchy subject, and I work for the Discovery Channel, and we want to portray accurately whatever it is we do. And we certainly want to do it with a lot of respect for the animals. So I call the Humane Society and I say, 'Look, I'm going to be castrating some lambs. Can you tell me the deal?'

And they're like, 'Yeah, it's pretty straightforward.' They use a band, basically, a rubber band, like this, only a little smaller. This one was actually around the playing cards I got yesterday –

But it had a certain familiarity to it.

And I said, 'Well, what exactly is the process?'

And they said, 'The band is applied to the tail, tightly. And then another band is applied to the scrotum, tightly. Blood flow is slowly retarded; a week later the parts in question fall off.'

'Great – got it.' OK, I call the SPCA to confirm this. They confirm it. I also call PETA just for fun, and they don't like it, but they confirm it. OK, that's basically how you do it.

So, the next day I go out. And I'm given a horse and we go get the lambs and we take them to a pen that we built, and we go about the business of animal husbandry...."

Analysis – Talk in terms of pictures! You don't need video, you don't need PowerPoint slides, you don't need anything but the abilities of Rowe to tell a perfectly constructed tale. My favourite writing teacher would forever say to me and scribble in bright red letters on my short stories, "Caroline; show me, don't tell me." This is what Rowe does so well in his talk, he shows vivid pictures and you forget you are listening to a talk, as you are transported into a world of being a sheep rancher. You can see Rowe is transported in his mind as he is reliving this experience. This dirty job had a profound impact on him and as a result of sharing the story, it has a profound impact on the audience too. Brilliant, simply brilliant.

Tip – Talk in terms of pictures.

#210 – Jamiroquai

(Band formed in 1992)

Context – From the song, "Virtual Insanity" by British jazz-funk band Jamiroquai from their third studio album, *Travelling Without Moving* (1996).

Oh yeah, what we're living in (let me tell ya)
It's a wonder man can eat at all
When things are big, that should be small
Who can tell what magic spells we'll be doing for us
And I'm giving all my love to this world
Only to be told
I can't see
I can't breathe
No more will we be
And nothing's going to change the way we live
Cos' we can always take but never give
And now that things are changing for the worse,
See, it's a crazy world we're living in
And I just can't see that half of us immersed in sin
Is all we have to give these -

Futures made of virtual insanity now
Always seem to, be govern'd by this love we have
For useless, twisting, our new technology
Oh, now there is no sound – for we all live underground.

And I'm thinking what a mess we're in
Hard to know where to begin
If I could slip the sickly ties that earthly man has made
And now every mother can choose the colour
Of her child
That's not nature's way
Well, that's what they said yesterday
There's nothing left to do but pray
I think it's time I found a new religion
Waoh – it's so insane
To synthesize another strain
There's something in these
Futures that we have to be told.

Futures made of virtual insanity – now
Always seem to be govern'd by this love we have
For useless, twisting, our new technology
Oh, now there is no sound – for we all live underground.

Now there is no sound
If we all live underground

And now it's virtual insanity

Forget your virtual reality

Oh, there's nothing so bad.

I know yeah

Of this virtual insanity, we're livin in.

Has got to change, yeah

Things will never be the same.

And I can't go on

While we're livin' in oh, oh virtual insanity

Oh, this world has got to change

Cos I just, I just can't keep going on, it was virtual.

Virtual insanity that we're livin' in, that we're livin' in

That virtual insanity is what it is

Futures made of virtual insanity – now

Always seem to, be govern'd by this love we have

For useless, twisting, our new technology

Oh, now there is no sound – for we all live underground.

Living – Virtual Insanity

Living – Virtual Insanity

Living – Virtual Insanity

Living – Virtual Insanity

Virtual Insanity is what we're living in

Analysis – I'm a massive fan of Jamiroquai. Nothing can get me bopping around like the track "Feels So Good," but today I want to focus on "Virtual Insanity." Released in the late 90s, this song was then and continues to be an observant commentary on the state of the world. Technology, and our dependence on it, has continued to grow in the last couple of decades. I've chosen to include these lyrics on this list because it is refreshing to listen to lyrics or speeches that come from a person's truth. So often, in speeches, songs, poems, etc., people dilute aspects of themselves to make their message more digestible. Frankly, a hearty dose of truth now and then can be refreshing. I abhor the thought of not speaking my truth. So, when I watch others diluting or sugar coating their truths, I'm always a little puzzled. If you have an opinion, then state it (obviously stay within limits of ethical tastes, please). Perhaps this is why I adore Jamiroquai's lead vocalist Jay Kay, because he doesn't mince words (this track was written by Kay and fellow bandmate the late Toby Smith).

Why not give your truth a shot in your next presentation? You most likely will elicit a reaction from your audience and have them listening and interacting with you.

Tip – Speak your truth.

#209 – Ralph Waldo Emerson

1803–1882

Context – Ralph Waldo Emerson was an American philosopher. Emerson is perhaps best remembered for leading the Transcendentalist Movement in the mid 19th century.

"Self-trust is the first secret of success."

Analysis – Finding your own voice as a public speaker is not as difficult as you may think but it does hold the key to any form of success you will have as a presenter. All presenters have a unique rhythm and cadence to their voice. There is a pulse and breath to your words. For the presenter who is a novice, it is hearing your own voice over and over again that will develop self-trust. That comes with practice. Not the kind of practice that I see so many do with a glossy PowerPoint slide and a bunch of anecdote notes at the base. Sure, that is a small part of your preparation but the largest amount of time any presenter should spend in preparing for a talk is practicing out loud. When I began my career speaking in front of groups, I would lay all of my materials out on the dining room table and pretend that I had an audience sitting in the dining room seats. Sounds strange I'm sure. I have a professional public speaker friend that practices in front of a mirror and another that practices in front of her family so, there is no right way or wrong way to practice out loud, you simply have to find a way that you feel most comfortable, and do it. Through those many hours, that I'm sure turned into years of practicing at that dining room table with my 'ghost' audience members, I discovered my voice and to trust in that voice. I understand almost immediately through practicing out loud which sections of my presentation need to be reshaped, changed or even omitted. This could not be done had I not rehearsed out loud. You see, on paper they looked good, they made sense, but as soon as I spoke them, put shape to them, I recognized immediately that they didn't drive the message forward. As a novice writer, I've taken that learning to the written page as well. As soon as a section of a chapter is done, I will not go forward with the story that I'm writing until I read the entire content out loud. I am always shocked at what I thought intellectually made sense, but as I read it out loud, how it takes on a different meaning, how its context changes, or that it simply doesn't work. In writing or speaking it is imperative to know your voice and trust in that voice.

Tip – Trust your voice!

#208 – Mark Twain

1835–1910

Context – Samuel Langhorne Clemens was an American author and was well known by his pen name, Mark Twain. William Faulkner called Twain, "the father of American literature." That's quite a compliment from such an accomplished source. Twain's work includes *Adventures of Huckleberry Finn* and *The Adventures of Tom Sawyer*.

"There are two types of speakers: those that are nervous and those that are liars."

Analysis – Most, if not all, professional public speakers get nervous before giving their presentations.

Even those who garner an income from giving talks. If you followed my original blog or have been reading this book in a linear fashion, you'll know my opinion on nerves. To quote Martha Stewart, "it's a good thing." If you're nervous, it simply means you care. The professional speaker still gets nervous, albeit not (well, hopefully not anyway) to the extent as the novice speaker. Still, sometimes the nerves are a bit more voluptuous, grander, and more at the fore. I watched a friend of mine give a talk not too long ago, and having coached a few people in presentation skills, I saw all the tell-tale signs of nervousness just before she took to the stage. She demonstrated the typical physiological behaviours that coincide with nerves and public speaking: sweating, pacing, and blushing to name a few. As I've seen her give several talks, I didn't intrude. She always has these physiological reactions, and she always finds a way to calm down just before taking to the stage. She then spends her first few minutes on the stage finding what I like to call her "presentation legs." Most presenters have a routine to relax their nerves. For some, it takes just a few minutes before they go on stage, and for others, it is an all-day affair involving various relaxation techniques. There is no right or wrong way of calming yourself down just that you find your way. So, I watched my friend. She started talking quietly to herself off to the side of the stage where no one could see her. She started changing her body position—instead of pacing, she began a rigid stance, with some fist-pumping. I could see she was giving herself a pep talk. It was incredible to watch, and it made me wonder what I look like as I work through my calming routine before taking to the stage.

My friend pinched her legs gently a few times and then walked onto the stage with an air of calm and confidence. Because I know her well, I could still detect her nerves just underneath the surface (understandably so, as there were some 200 people in the audience). The secret to calming yourself down before launching into your talk is to throw it back out to the audience. Don't even introduce yourself. Introduce yourself later once you've calmed down and your audience has had a laugh or two. My friend throws it back to the audience by asking everyone to take out a pen and paper and imagine an apple. Not any apple, but a specific apple that they have thought about for an entire minute. She then asks each audience member to describe their apple in a new and unique way. She encourages them, to pick it up in their mind's eye, hold it in their palm, turn it around, notice the stem, and observe the bruising before writing down a single word. "Each apple," she says, "is like a snowflake, and no two are alike." So, the audience members are urged to use descriptors that are unique to describe the single best apple that ever existed. My friend is a writer and a writing teacher. So, her exercise looks like writing. My examples as a communication skills speaker look different. Some of my ice breakers include getting bums out of chairs and having people introduce themselves to one another or answering questions that relate to the topic at hand. These exercises buy the presenter a little time to ease into their role by diverting the audience's eyes off them for a moment so they can get a feel for the room and give their best while easing into their comfort zone. Additionally, it allows the audience to warm up and share an experience right off the bat. Some days, you don't need to do it, and you can throw in those exercises later on but some days you need a little more help in finding your legs. Get good at recognizing those days and adopt the professional speakers' tip of throwing it back to your audience.

Tip – Throw an exercise out to the audience when you feel the nerves washing over you.

#207 – Paulo Coelho

(1947)

Context – Coelho is a Brazilian lyricist and novelist. He has published 26 books.

"It's the possibility of having a dream come true that makes life interesting … Before a dream is realized, the Soul of the World tests everything that was learned along the way. It does this not because it is evil, but so that we can, in addition to realizing our dreams master the lessons we have learned as we have moved toward that dream. That's the point at which most people give up … [At this point] Tell your heart that the fear of suffering is worse than the suffering itself. And that no heart has ever suffered when it goes in search of its dreams, because every second of search is a second's encounter with God and with eternity."

Analysis – I immediately became enamoured with this quote the first time I read it. I encourage you to read it over and over until you embrace its whole, robust, and voluptuous meaning. It's pretty weighty. It's apparent that it is written by someone with great zest and zeal and *joie de vivre*. Presentation skills mirror this sentiment. It is the pursuit of delivering the perfect presentation that drives us to overcome all the obstacles this goal presents. It is the possibility of realizing this dream. Each skill needs to be learned one by one before you can level up. It is the pursuit, the lessons learned along the way that challenges us, and many people will give up. That internal voice of self-doubt pipes up with, "I can't do that!" "I suck." "This is too hard." "I have nothing of value to say!" The truth is in what Coelho says, that one needs to convince themselves, in their own heart, that the *fear* of the task is worse than the actual task. This is what I recommend to the novice presenter or those who feel as though they lack the confidence to tackle it. Tell others what you are planning to talk about. If you are planning a work presentation, start talking about it to your co-workers. Explain the goal of your presentation, and what you're aiming to achieve. You'd be surprised how supportive and helpful others can be. Some of my best presentations have stemmed from other people's contributions to my ideas. Be open to receiving new and exciting novel ideas but also be aware of the wacky ideas thrown down and learn how to distinguish one from the other. Be open to realizing your dreams by enjoying the journey and including others along the way.

Tip – Share your ideas and your presentation dreams with others.

#206 – Rory Sutherland

(1965)

Context – Rory Sutherland talks at TED London on "Sweating the Small Stuff."

"Those of you who may remember me from TEDGlobal remember me asking a few questions which still preoccupy me. One of them was: Why is it necessary to spend six billion pounds speeding up the Eurostar train when, for about 10 percent of that money, you could have top supermodels, male and female, serving free Chateau Petrus to all the passengers for the entire duration of the journey? You'd still have five billion left in change, and people would ask for the trains to be slowed down. Now, you may remember me asking the question as well, a very interesting observation, that actually those strange little signs that actually flash "35" at you, occasionally accompanying a little smiley face or a frown, according to whether you're within or outside the speed limit -- those are actually more effective at preventing road accidents than speed cameras, which come with the actual threat of real punishment.

So there seems to be a strange disproportionality at work, I think, in many areas of human problem solving, particularly those which involve human psychology, which is: The tendency of the organization or the institution is to deploy as much force as possible, as much compulsion as possible, whereas actually, the tendency of the person is to be almost influenced in absolute reverse proportion to the amount of force being applied. So there seems to be a complete disconnect here. So what I'm asking for is the creation of a new job title – I'll come to this a little later – and perhaps the addition of a new word into the English language. Because it does seem to me that large organizations including government, which is, of course, the largest organization of all, have actually become completely disconnected with what actually matters to people.

Let me give you one example of this. You may remember this as the AOL-Time Warner merger, okay, heralded at the time as the largest single deal of all time. It may still be, for all I know. Now, all of you in this room, in one form or other, are probably customers of one or both of those organizations that merged. Just interested, did anybody notice anything different as a result of this at all? So unless you happened to be a shareholder of one or the other organizations or one of the dealmakers or lawyers involved in the no-doubt lucrative activity, you're actually engaging in a huge piece of activity that meant absolutely bugger-all to anybody, okay? By contrast, years of marketing have taught me that if you actually want people to remember you and to appreciate what you do, the most potent things are actually very, very small. This is from Virgin Atlantic upper-class, it's the cruet salt and pepper set.

Quite nice in itself, they're little, sort of, airplane things. What's really, really sweet is every single person looking at these things has exactly the same mischievous thought, which is, "I reckon I can heist these." However, you pick them up and underneath, actually engraved in the metal, are the words, "Stolen from Virgin Atlantic Airways upper-class." Now, years after you remember the strategic question of whether you're flying in a 777 or an Airbus, you remember those words and that experience..."

Analysis – In this talk, Sutherland discusses how big, flashy, expensive fixes interfere with better and more straightforward answers. He discusses how the smallest details can have a massive impact. He uses two marketing examples that made me smile—the first was Virgin Airlines' adorable salt and pepper shakers that look like mini stainless-steel airplanes. Each passenger, he says, looks at them and thinks the same thing, "How am I gonna swipe these?" When you turn the shakers over, they are engraved with the words, *Stolen from Virgin Atlantic Airlines*. Cute. The second example takes place in an elevator at a hotel. The elevator has all the typical buttons you'd expect to see on its control panel; however, when you look more closely it also has options for garage, funk, rhythm, or blues because on this elevator ride, you get to choose the music for your journey. Do either of these examples cost a ton of money to implement? No, they don't. But they have a dramatic impact, and I'm sure people go home and share their experiences with their family and friends. These are great examples of fun creating free, word-of-mouth advertising. Sutherland uses less trivial marketing examples to illustrate his point further, but the two I've highlighted can be easily transferred to the topic of presentation skills. Often, presenters are so focused on the meat of presentations, the big stuff, that we fail to realize the power of the little stuff. The details that will compel your audience members to talk about your presentation long after you're done. For example, after a break, I always include brainteasers in my talks, to re-energize the group. It is one of those tiny things that people love. They'll talk about how many they got right or wrong days after the exercise. You can feel the energy heighten when you give them out, and people get jazzed to take their brain away to another dimension. Another thing I do is always bring some small giveaways such as books, CDs, items that relate to the topic I'm presenting. I use them as trivia, and the winners gets to take them away. I'll often include a handwritten quote as a reminder of where they acquired it. For some presentations with the budget, I have given away the same book to all the participants. One that had a profound impact on me and related to the topic at hand. In one instance, I did a workshop that lasted a week, so I got to know each of my 25 participants exceptionally well. On the last day, I gifted my participants with a book and inside I had written a strength specific to each participant. It was a personal touch. That workshop was some eight years ago now, and I happened to hear from one of those participants not too long ago. She remarked that she still looks at that comment in that book whenever she feels overwhelmed with constructive criticism and not enough appreciation. It is the small details that will often have the most significant impact on your audiences.

Tip - Small details are important.

#205 – Stefan Sagmeister

(1962)

Context – Sagmeister is a graphic designer and storyteller renowned for album covers, posters, and his book of life lessons, *Things I Have Learned In My Life So Far*. In his 2004 TED Talk, Stefan Sagmeister discusses "Happiness by Design."

"About 15 years ago, I went to visit a friend in Hong Kong. And at the time I was very superstitious. So, upon landing – this was still at the old Hong Kong *airport that's Kai Tak, when it was smack in the middle of the city—I thought, "If I see something good, I'm going to have a great time here in my two weeks. And if I see something negative, I'm going to be miserable, indeed.*

So, the plane landed in between the buildings and got to a full stop in front of this little billboard. (Laughter) And I actually went to see some of the design companies in Hong Kong in my stay there. And it turned out that—I just went to see, you know, what they are doing in Hong Kong.

But I actually walked away with a great job offer. And I flew back to Austria, packed my bags, and, another week later, I was again on my way to Hong Kong still superstitions and thinking, "Well, if that 'Winner' billboard is still up, I'm going to have a good time working here. But if it's gone, it's going to be really miserable and stressful." So, it turned out that not only was the billboard still up but they had put this one right next to it. On the other hand, it also taught me where superstition gets me because I really had a terrible time in Hong Kong.

However, I did have a number of real moments of happiness in my life – of, you know, I think what the conference brochure refers to as "moments that take your breath away." And since I'm a big list maker, I actually listed them all. Now, you don't have to go through the trouble of reading them and I won't read them for you. I know that it's incredibly boring to hear about other people's happinesses.

What I did do, though is, I actually looked at them from a design standpoint and just eliminated all the ones that had nothing to do with design. And, very surprisingly, over half of them had, actually, something to do with design.

So, there are, of course, two different possibilities. There's one from a consumer's point of view – where I was happy while experiencing design. And I'll just give you one example. I had gotten my first Walkman. This is 1983. My brother had this great Yamaha motorcycle that he was willing to borrow to me freely. And The Police's "Synchronicity" cassette had just been released and there was no helmet law in my hometown of Bregenz. So, you could drive up into the mountains freely blasting The Police on the new Sony Walkman. And I remember it as a true moment of happiness. You know, of course, they are related to this combination of at least two of them being, you know, design objects. And, you know, there's a scale of happiness when you talk about in design, but the motorcycle incident would definitely be, you know, situated somewhere here – right in there between Delight and Bliss…"

Analysis – What makes you happy? This is the profound question that Sagmeister tackles during his talk. He does it using a whimsy, clear and concise, and at times satirical, method. Presenting is not an activity limited to the time you are on stage or in front of an audience, but it is an ongoing process of how you view and digest the world. Sagmeister included a list of the things that brought him happiness in his life. His list looks different from my list, and my list will look different to yours. We all have different portals into the universe, and with that, we all digest the world in profoundly unique ways. It is these idiosyncratic differences that we need to bring to our presentations to make them unique and different from anyone else's. Sagmeister uses an example that is fun and distinctive. It involves billboards with empty speech bubbles for passers-by to write in their caption. One of the examples includes the iconic E.T. the Extra-Terrestrial poster and someone has written, "Please let me die in peace," in the speech bubble. Another poster with Piglet from Winnie-the-Pooh says, "Capitalism breeds poverty." I would never come up with those quotes. I thought of two very different ideas, and I'm sure you did too!

As you design your presentation, look at the world around you and bring your little notebook (I call them *learning journals*). Jot things down that are interesting to you. Go out to dinner alone and listen to the conversations of those around you. Take note of the cadence and the pretence if there is pretence. Or narcissism, shyness, whatever you observe around you. Take your world in and design your own experiences. Through those experiences, your unique presentation will be brought to the fore.

Tip – Be conscious of the world around you and bring your experiences into your presentations.

#204 – Baltasar Gracián

1601–1658

Context – Baltasar Gracián was a Spanish baroque prose writer and philosopher.

"A single lie destroys a whole reputation for integrity"

Analysis – I've devoted a great deal of time to the analysis of presenters. Most of my time is spent labouring through, and observing horrible presenters. We've all watched motivational speakers, and I use that term loosely, that shouldn't have the voice that they have. Why do so many horrendous public speakers have so many followers? These speakers talk about things they have no business speaking about, with half-truths and, at times, outright lies. The goal varies depending on whom we are discussing; it could be to drive their money-making schemes, or to drive their insatiable ego. Whatever the reason, it becomes obvious to me almost in the first minute. What is in a person's psyche that allows them to gravitate to someone who pontificates ad nauseam about having the answers (for life, for love, for business, parenthood, whatever)? It's human nature to look at the world around us and try to make sense of it and, for some, those answers may come from others. I'm sickened (and, no, that isn't too harsh a word) by speakers who take advantage of those on an honest quest for life's meaning. In my reflection, we can learn a lot by observing the bowels of the earth who have chosen the speaking profession as a form of money laundering. For those reading this who are in the honest pursuit of getting better at their craft, I encourage you to watch video clips (they are plentiful) of the wealth of horrendous speakers out there. Study them. Watch their eyes, their body language, their delivery. Is it slick? Is it ego-driven? Learn how to identify those signs and do the opposite when you are in front of a crowd. If you are deceitful when in front of a room, you will be found out. Is that the legacy you want to leave behind? Speak from what you know, speak from your truth, be yourself, everyone else is taken—that is all anyone can ask of you.

Tip – Speak from your truth.

#203 – Stephen King

(1947)

Context – Stephen King is an author of fiction often in horror and suspense. In Stephen King's book, *On Writing*, he shares his experiences that have shaped his work and life (pg. 155-156)

"When I'm asked why I decided to write the sort of thing I do write, I always think the question is more revealing than any answer I could possibly give. Wrapped within it, like the chewy stuff in the center of a Tootsie Pop, is the assumption that the writer controls the material instead of the other way around. The writer, who is serious and committed, is incapable of sizing up story material the way an investor might size up various stock offerings, picking out the ones which seem likely to provide a good return. If it could indeed be done that way, every novel published would be a best-seller, and the huge advances paid to a dozen or so "big-name writers" would not exist (publishers would like that).

John Grisham, Tom Clancy, Michael Crichton, and myself-among others are paid these large sums of money because we are selling uncommonly large numbers of books to uncommonly large audiences.
A critical assumption is sometimes made that we have access to some mystical vulgate that other (and often better) writers either cannot find or will not deign to use. I doubt if this is true. Nor do I believe the contention of some popular novelists that their success is based on literary merit-that the public understands true greatness in ways the tight-assed, consumed-by-jealously literary establishment cannot. This idea is ridiculous, a product of vanity and insecurity.

Book-buyers aren't attracted, by and large, by the literary merits of a novel; book-buyers want a good story to take with them on the airplane, something that will first fascinate them, then pull them in and keep them turn the pages. This happens, I think when readers recognize the people in a book, their behaviors, their surroundings, and their talk. When the reader hears strong echoes of his or her own life and beliefs, he or she is apt to become more invested in the story."

Analysis – I've been considering participating in a three-day novel contest for years, okay decades! It's a wonderfully insane contest that started in 1977 and takes place over 72 hours during September long weekend. Writers are pitted against the clock to draft an entire novel-length manuscript and submit it to a board of judges for review. A winner is announced, and according to friends I know who have participated previously, the judges will know if you cheat, although the contest runs on the honour system, likely they hinge on cheating only harms the cheater. I do buy that. The average novel is around 60,000 words. That would mean that you'd have to write 833 words per hour during the weekend. When I'm in a writing groove, I can hit about that, but never for more than three hours at a time. I usually log how much I write, so I looked back, and the most I've ever written in a day is roughly 5,000 words, and at least half of those words were later trashed in the editing process! So, with no interruptions, no outside distractions, and being completely immersed I can pen 5,000 word a day, so, how the heck do writers put together an entire novel in a weekend? Firstly, it should be noted that 60,000 words is simply an industry standard and that a novel (whether you call it a novella or novelette) can start at whatever number you deem appropriate. Most of the novels completed over the years are around 30,000 words. Funny to me, though, how my first thought was to do the math. How would I get to 50,000 or 60,000? Could I even hit 30,000? I've spent a good few mental vacations (those daydreams that permeate my mind now and again) thinking about these stupid number goals, and not on the more important question—would my novel be about the characters, the plot, the prose, the dialogue, the landscape? How would I move myself to want to spend that much continuous time without sleep, with no one else but me and my thoughts and these characters? Funny, I thought about completing the project, it didn't matter whether the content was good or bad, just that I had entered the contest and completed a novel. A bright light shone onto my thought process, and I realized in these situations I tend to visualize the result. I see the celebration and the jubilation. I see the bells and whistles, the flash, but is that what it takes to write a great novel?

A friend of mine and I were having a discussion the other day on whether a presentation is successful because of the presenter or the content. Initially I said, "If I had to choose one, it would be the presenter who makes a presentation successful." I went on a diatribe about how the content can be fantastic, but if the presenter is horrible, the audience will never hear or digest the material. My friend is a wise guy, and he said that he would be able to tell almost immediately if the presenter didn't know their content or if the content was crude or rudimentary or plain uninteresting. "But what if the presenter was able to make that content interesting?" I asked. "Nope," came his quick response. "Boring, uninteresting material is just that. You can throw bells and whistles all over that hot mess, and it still will be that. I had to agree. My answer is both. You need a great presenter delivering great content. It's impossible to choose one over the other.

My objective for today's post is to relay an analogy about writing a novel. The prose, the characters, the plot, and the cadence must draw the writer into the fictional world so that the reader will want to spend months, and many times years, enveloped in that world. The content must be good enough to sustain them in the face of no real end goal. Most writers never get published and many don't earn a penny for the countless hours and sacrifices they spend on their craft. They do it simply because they cannot imagine *not* doing it. Not all writers love to write. Many writers say they can't stand the process but have a compulsion to sit at their computer screen and type anyway. Any good writer will worry about the content and ensure that it delivers in the quest to suspend the belief of the reader and take on them on a journey through the imaginary world they've created. This is also true of presenters. Many presenters I meet spend most of their time on the bells and whistles, the flash, but don't step back to study their content. A presenter, too, must look at the prose, their cast of characters, the plot, and their cadence. Is your content new and unique? Has it been said before? How can you say something in your unique voice? How can you put your spin on what you are saying? Focus on developing brilliant content; do your research, study, be the subject matter expert in what you are about to present, and you may just be able to keep your audience members turning the pages of your metaphorical novel.

Tip – Focus on the content.

#202 – Napoleon Hill

1883–1970

Context – Napoleon Hill was a self-help author known best for his 1937 book, *Think and Grow Rich*, which is amongst the best-selling self-help books of all time. In a talk delivered shortly after publishing, *Think and Grow Rich,* Hill explores what the mind can conceive, believe, and achieve.

"Whatever your mind feeds upon is what your mind becomes."

Analysis – I finally read Napoleon Hill's great classic *Think and Grow Rich*. It's a rather cheesy title for such a fine and profound piece of literature. Yes, I suppose Hill tells you in the confines of the nearly 400 pages how to think and grow rich. But it is not just his views on the acquisition of money that wins him a place on my list. If you haven't read this book, I encourage you to get yourself a copy and read it. This is not a book to be skimmed but savoured. Today, the concepts in Hill's book aren't considered new news with many alternatives and self-help teachers out there who have devoted much of their lives to the pursuit and discussion of the same goal. Deepak Chopra comes to mind as one at the fore of these discussions recently. Chopra has written more than 50 books and conducts talks and workshops with the ideas of mindfulness as the nucleus. Hill talked about the mind-body connection in the early 1930s. It's no accident that many of his books continue to be reprinted for the next generation. What I'd like to focus on are two key components that Hill discusses in his book:

1. Get a notebook and write a clear description of your idea of success.

2. On page #2 of that notebook, write what you will give in return.

Memorize your idea of success and what you are willing to give in return and repeat at least a dozen times a day.

When I read this in his book, I thought, "Okay, this is simple! If I do these two things, then what? I become rich?" I guess I had a pessimistic view of what I was reading at the time, but I've since changed my mind (I allow my opinions to be tested and challenged daily!) What Hill is suggesting is simple: Give concrete form to intangible desires. Wishing upon something is just that. When you can put words and structure around a desire then it becomes real. By memorizing both statements (something, I consider to be near genius!), you begin the process of talking to yourself about your desires. Something you most likely wouldn't do a dozen times a day. Creating a ritual starts the process of altering your state of mind from wishing to attaining. This entire post can be placed into every aspect of your life. For my followers looking for a tip today on presentation skills, this is easily transferrable to that lofty goal too.

Tip – Memorize your ideas of success.

#201 – Monica Lewinsky

(1973)

Context – American activist, public speaker, writer, and the former White House intern who was catapulted into the public arena following her affair with former U.S. President Bill Clinton, Monica Lewinsky speaks about "The Price of Shame" in her 2015 TED Talk.

"You're looking at a woman who was publicly silent for a decade. Obviously, that's changed, but only recently.

It was several months ago that I gave my very first major public talk at the Forbes "30 Under 30 Summit"—1,500 brilliant people, all under the age of 30. That meant that in 1998, the oldest among the group were only 14, and the youngest, just four. I joked with them that some might only have heard of me from rap songs. Yes, I'm in rap songs.

Almost 40 rap songs.

But the night of my speech, a surprising thing happened. At the age of 41, I was hit on by a 27-year-old guy.

I know, right? He was charming, and I was flattered, and I declined. You know what his unsuccessful pickup line was? He could make me feel 22 again.

I realized, later that night, I'm probably the only person over 40 who does not want to be 22 again.

At the age of 22, I fell in love with my boss. And at the age of 24, I learned the devastating consequences.

Can I see a show of hands of anyone here who didn't make a mistake or do something they regretted at 22? Yep. That's what I thought. So, like me, at 22, a few of you may have also taken wrong turns and fallen in love with the wrong person, maybe even your boss. Unlike me, though, your boss probably wasn't the president of the United States of America.

Of course, life is full of surprises.

Not a day goes by that I'm not reminded of my mistake, and I regret that mistake deeply.

In 1998, after having been swept up into an improbable romance, I was then swept up into the eye of a political, legal and media maelstrom like we had never seen before. Remember, just a few years earlier, news was consumed from just three places: reading a newspaper or magazine, listening to the radio, or watching television. That was it. But that wasn't my fate. Instead, this scandal was brought to you by the digital revolution. That meant we could access all the information we wanted when we wanted it, anytime, anywhere. And when the story broke in January 1998, it broke online. It was the first time the Internet usurped the traditional news for a major news story—a click that reverberated around the world.

What that meant for me personally was that overnight, I went from being a completely private figure to a publicly humiliated one worldwide. I was patient zero of losing a personal reputation on a global scale almost instantaneously…"

Analysis – I've seen Lewinsky's TED Talk many times, and each time I'm left gobsmacked as I try to imagine what she must have gone through at the tender age of 22. Lewinsky asks her audience, "Can I see a show of hands of anyone here who didn't make a mistake or do something they regretted at 22?" Um, I hear ya, Sista! At 22, I was a heap of mistakes and throwing more onto the pile consistently. Lewinsky talks about the evolution of our media consumption from traditional news (print, TV, and radio) to the Internet. Back in 1998 the story of Lewinsky's affair with then U.S. President Bill Clinton broke online, and she was exposed and publicly humiliated worldwide.

Lewinsky says quite astutely, "I was seen by many but known by few." Cyberbullying and online harassment are so common nowadays that we almost forget how this started and continues. Lewinsky's talk reminds me of the dark side of the internet. Some dive into social media as voyeurs, seeing who's happy, who's amassed wealth, who's beautiful. Others, treat it as an itch they must scratch going after anyone who will engage in an online brawl, while hiding behind a screen. I read a study that suggests a strong link between heavy social media consumption and an increased risk for depression, anxiety, loneliness, self-harm, and even suicidal thoughts. Overindulging in social media content can promote a sense of inadequacy about one's life or appearance. It's no wonder why so many feel like an imposter in their own life. There are benefits to social media—it promotes networks and creates a sense of connectedness. Many of the talks I reference in this book are housed online. But this insatiable need for likes and social acceptance is fundamentally perplexing to me.

We're in a compassion deficit and empathy crisis. Lewinsky uses her story as a catapult for changing our perceptions of her and all those who have been caught in the eye of cyberbullying storms since her story broke. Lewinsky delivery is thoughtful, deliberate and surprisingly not fueled by anger but a deep desire to have her listeners change their behaviour, and think about how the audience may be perpetuating this culture of voyeurism.

As I watch this talk, I'm able to transport myself back to the scene of a beret-wearing Lewinsky pictured in a crowd as Clinton reached for her hand. It seemed innocent enough at the time, but this image was soon plastered on every news outlet around the world. We snooped into her life as though it was something she wanted and were complicit to her public humiliation without giving her a second thought or anything in return. I, too, judged her back then but we prefer to snoop than to be snooped on. The balance of power is out of whack and Lewinsky's talk has made me question social media. When we are given the privilege of speaking to groups we need to consider our role in society and ramp up our compassion and empathy at a visceral level.

Tip – Speak with intention rather than for attention.

#200 – Elizabeth Hardwick

1916–2007

Context – Elizabeth Hardwick was an American literary critic, novelist and short-story writer.

"Letters are above all useful as a means of expressing the ideal self; and no other method of communication is quite so good for this purpose. In letters we can reform without practice, beg without humiliation, snip and shape embarrassing experiences to the measure of our own desires…"

Analysis – Instead of giving just a public speaking tip today, I'd like to encourage you to do an exercise. Over the years, I've had the privilege of doing this exercise as a participant and as facilitator for leadership workshops. Write yourself a letter of inspiration. Tell yourself in this letter what aspirations and goals you have for your future, include specifics on the kind of presenter you will be in the future. Bring it to life. Give specifics on where you are, who else is there, and the content of your presentation. Bring your visualization to life by showing rather than telling. Look around the room. What does it feel like? The letter can be as long or as short as you wish, but I do have one caveat: do not allow any negative voices to get into your letter. Give the sealed letter to a friend and tell them that you would like this mailed to you in one year. It may even inspire your friend to do the same and they can provide you with a copy of their letter and trust you with the task of mailing it to them in a year. When I received my own letter one year after attending this workshop, I was astounded at how much I had accomplished. I had achieved many of my goals. I firmly believe that writing that letter was a process of designing my destiny. Control your destiny; start the process today.

Tip – Control your destiny.

#199 – Anish Kapoor

(1954)

Context – Anish Kapoor is an Indian sculptor born in Bombay in 1954.

"I've always felt that if one was going to take seriously this vocation as an artist, you have to get beyond that decorative facade."

Analysis – Through the grapevine today, I heard some startling news about a friend. It wasn't gossip, as it wasn't relayed to me in that way. The news was sad and factual. It was startling because the image this person presented to the world was one of sheer delight and almost euphoria about the life she was living. You'd ask her how she was doing, and her response would always be jubilant and upbeat. The illusion of perfection always made me leery. Perfection always does that to me. The tiny hairs on the back of my neck go up, my gut tells me something isn't congruent, something isn't right. People commonly put up a facade in their worlds and present a different perception of who they are, or what they want to be, or the life that they are living. Why? Is it ego? Jealousy or a need to be envied? Keeping up with the Joneses? What motivates people to pretend to be something more or less than who they are?

The other day someone said to me: "Boy, they must want for nothing!" They were referring to a couple who they perceived to be wealthy. You never know what is going on behind closed doors. Sure, those folks may not have money problems, heck, they could be billionaires, but does that mean that they, "want for nothing?" Material things, perhaps not, but life and the pursuit of happiness involve so much more than big fancy expensive things to fill the void. As presenters, this notion of presenting ourselves inauthentically is a big problem. One of the most common issues I encounter when I'm asked to review a presenter is the presenter not being genuine. It's almost like they are actors on a Broadway stage. They take the role of a character that is far removed from who they are naturally. I'm able to identify it quickly because I had the same traits back in the day, until I was called out by a mentor. I have been eternally grateful to this mentor ever since. Don't get me wrong, at the time, I didn't appreciate these notes at all, and it took me years to digest her honest comments. But I did eventually accept the feedback. So, it takes one to know one, and I can always pick out my presentation actors in a heartbeat. To the presentation actors out there reading this, it is almost embarrassing watching you take the stage. Have you ever watched a movie or TV show, and cringed at the actors' performance? You tried to avert your eyes but couldn't? That is what it is like watching someone doing a presentation who is mimicking and pretending to be someone they are not. We were all born with unique gifts and talents (cheesy but true); use the ones bestowed on you rather than trying to imitate somebody else's.

Tip – There is no room for a decorative facade when giving a presentation. Be who you are naturally!

#198 – Yogi Bear

Context – *Yogi Bear* is an animated television show that began in 1958 highlighting a funny bear whose personality was based on Art Carney a character in The Honeymooners. Here an excerpt from Episode #1.

"Every day it's the same old thing; 'Look at the bears; look at the bears!' I'm gonna get outta this park! I'll use strategy Boo Boo." When he does finally escape, he realizes it is hunting season, and rushes back to the gate, announcing, *"I've only been gone two minutes, and I already miss the park!"*

Analysis – Yogi Bear dresses up in disguises, uses a pole vault, plays dead, digs a hole, parachutes over the park wall, hitchhikes, shoots himself out of a cannon—all to avert Ranger Smith and escape the park. I've always adored Yogi Bear. It was one of my favourite cartoons as a kid. What I like about Yogi is a reoccurring theme during many of the episodes, and as Boo Boo states in this episode: "I gotta admit that you don't quit Yogi." Yogi never gives up; he is the opposite of a quitter. He continues until his task is accomplished, no matter the obstacles. Preparing for a presentation is much the same. How often do you procrastinate? How often do you quit in the prep and say, "I'll finish that tomorrow"? How often do you renege on your offer to do the presentation because it's turned out to be too much work? Like Yogi, you've got to try different strategies to accomplish your presentation prep goals. Don't be a procrastinator or a quitter!

Tip – Be smarter than the average bear, take a lesson from Yogi, and don't quit!

#197 – Wayne Dyer

1940–2015

Context – Wayne Dyer was an American self-help advocate, author and lecturer.

"All blame is a waste of time. No matter how much fault you find with another, and regardless of how much you blame him, it will not change you. The only thing blame does is to keep the focus off you when you are looking for external reasons to explain your unhappiness or frustration. You may succeed in making another

feel guilty about something by blaming him, but you won't succeed in changing whatever it is about you that is making you unhappy."

Analysis – I honestly have never understood the point of the blame game. It's just not something that comes naturally to me (I'm not being smug, I have plenty of other flaws that I need to work on, but this is not one of them). To point the finger at someone else to avert negative attention onto another person or thing is puzzling to me. In my practice, I'm confronted with the blame game much too often. "Well, the projector didn't work so I couldn't do the presentation very well," or "They put me on right before lunch, and everyone was tired and hungry, so I didn't do very well," or "So and so didn't give me enough time to practice or talk," or "They didn't give me all the necessary materials," or "They did a horrible job of introducing me." Dyer nails it when he says, "the only thing blame does is to keep the focus off you when you are looking for external reasons to explain your unhappiness or frustration." Instead of taking ownership of the situation, it is simply easier to look around and throw the liability onto someone or something else. The truth is if something goes wrong in a presentation and you are the presenter, with very few exceptions, it will be your fault. In my presentation skills workshops, I teach Murphy's Law. Murphy's Law states that if it can go wrong, it will go wrong. As a presenter, you must prepare accordingly. Ask yourself if you could do your presentation if there was a problem with the equipment, if the venue changed, or if you forgot your notes? Could you do your presentation if the venue changed? Could you do your presentation if you forgot your notes? And so on. The answer needs to be yes to all! You should know your presentation backwards, forwards, and inside out, and as a result, you will be equipped to handle any challenge that may arise before you take the stage. Take ownership of your presentations, and that includes taking responsibility for all facets. If you blame something or someone, then how will you ever learn from your mistakes? You need to own your mistakes before you can fix them.

Tip – Don't blame; take ownership.

#196 – Siegfried Woldhek

(1951)

Context – Siegfried Woldhek is an artist who specializes in drawing portraits. He has drawn over 1100 portraits over the course of 30 years and is well qualified to study them. In a 2008 TED Talk he explores "The Search For The True Face of Leonardo."

"Let's look for a minute at the greatest icon of all, Leonardo da Vinci. We're all familiar with his fantastic work – his drawings, his paintings, his inventions, his writings. But we do not know his face. Thousands of books have been written about him, but there's controversy, and it remains, about his looks. Even this well-known portrait is not accepted by many art historians. So, what do you think? Is this the face of Leonardo da Vinci, or

isn't it? Let's find out. Leonardo was a man that drew everything around him. He drew people, anatomy, plants, animals, landscapes, buildings, water, everything. But no faces? I find that hard to believe. So, surely a passionate drawer like Leonardo must have made self-portraits from time to time. So, let's try to find them. If we were to scan all his work and look for self-portraits, we would find his face looking at us. So, I looked at all of his drawings, more than 700, and looked for male portraits. There are about 120. Which ones of these could be self-portraits? Well, for that they have to be done as we just saw, en face (facing forward) or three-quarters. So, we can eliminate all the profiles. It also has to be sufficiently detailed. So, we can also eliminate the ones that are very vague or very stylized. And we know from his contemporaries that Leonardo was a very handsome, even beautiful man. So, we can also eliminate the ugly ones or the caricatures. And look what happens – only three candidates remain that fit the bill. And here they are. Yes, indeed, the old man is there, as is this famous pen drawing of the Homo Vitruvianus. And lastly, the only portrait of a male that Leonardo painted, "The Musician."

Analysis – There is much controversy about what Leonardo da Vinci looked like. There is the famous painting of an old man, which many believe to be the face of da Vinci, but not everyone is entirely convinced.

In this talk, Woldhek tried to uncover the mystery by analyzing all of da Vinci's drawings to see if there were self-portraits in his collection. He started with 700 drawings from which he was able to reduce to 120 male portraits. From there, he was able to home in again by removing side angles since a self-portrait must be a full-face depiction. Then, he removed all ugly portraits as da Vinci was well known as a handsome man. Woldhek narrowed it down to three portraits that fit his criteria. One, from 1485, another from 1490, and the last one from 1513. So, did these portraits correspond to da Vinci's age at the time each would have been painted? Yup, age 33, 38, then age 63. In the video clip, Woldhek proclaims, "Here is Leonardo da Vinci!" The truth is I have been saving this talk for some time. It is full of suspense and incredible slides. As presenters we need to borrow the techniques used by movie makers and novelists to build anticipation and create excitement. These creatives build the story artfully and don't give away the results until the viewer is on the edge of their seats. I adore this talk because it serves as a reminder to inject suspense into all your presentations.

Tip – Build suspense in your talks!

#195 – Malcolm X

1925–1965

Context – During the last tumultuous eight months of his life, Malcolm X gave numerous speeches in his quest to abolish racial inequality in the United States. The below is an excerpt from a speech entitled "By Any Means Necessary."

"We declare our right on this earth to be a man, to be a human being, to be respected as a human being, to be given the rights of a human being in this society, on this earth, in this day, which we intend to bring into existence by any means necessary."

Analysis – Malcolm X was considered to be far more radical than his contemporary, Dr. Martin Luther King. In contrast to King, Malcolm X advocated violence in the struggle for civil rights for African Americans. In 1964, he made a series of speeches criticizing Dr. King's non-violent approach, indicating that it had never worked in the past and calling for a revolution. Do I believe in violence? No, I do not. That said, I am not a black man or woman, I wasn't born in the 1920s, and I didn't live in the 50s and 60s, during a time of rampant racism. If I try to put myself in Malcolm's shoes for a moment (which is impossible, but I will try), I too might have a fervent fire in my belly that would have manifested toward unconventional methods. What we know for sure is Malcolm refused to sit on the sidelines. He didn't sit back and wait for others to make a difference. He made the difference. This is a man who speaks with great urgency, trying desperately to abolish racism. I think Dr. King's reaction to Malcolm X's assassination in 1965 says it best: "While we did not always see eye to eye on methods to solve the race problem, I always had a deep affection for Malcolm and felt that he had a great ability to put his finger on the existence and root of the problem. He was an eloquent spokesman for his point of view, and no one can honestly doubt that Malcolm had a great concern for the problems that we face as a race." Malcolm was a brilliant orator who could move his followers with both his words and his actions. When was the last time you spoke on a topic that you had a fervent passion for? A topic that could change the world. Do you have strong convictions? If not, why not? As Socrates said, "The unexamined life is not worth living." And I'm pretty sure that Malcolm X would agree with Socrates on this. Malcom X examined his life, his world, and others' reactions to this life. When he wasn't accepting of these truths, he did something about it. How about you? Get involved, get an opinion, change the world through your words.

Tip – Get off the sidelines and change the world with your words.

#194 – Marcus Aurelius

121 AD – 180 AD

Context – Marcus Aurelius was a Roman emperor from 161 AD to his death. He is widely considered to be the most important of all Stoic philosophers.

"It's time you realized that you have something in you more powerful and miraculous than the things that affect you and make you dance like a puppet."

Analysis – I recently worked one-on-one with an individual to improve his presentation skills. As we discussed his current skill set, I asked, "What is your biggest presentation challenge?" He replied, "I struggle to take out of my brain all the negative things that are going on in my day to day, to push that aside, and go forward with the focus and positivity I require in order to do the presentation." As a senior person in an organization, this individual does a lot of presentations. There are team meetings, business result meetings, vision meetings, etc. How do you put aside all the negative day-to-day stuff that you have to deal with so that you can inject the proper emotion into a talk? Two things immediately come to mind: movies and novels. When a screenwriter, director or producer is making a movie, how do they stay on task—making the movie and driving the script forward with its original intent without imparting their world? How does a novelist finish their manuscript without compromising the integrity of the project even though they may have significant personal dilemmas occurring in their own lives and finish it without compromising the integrity of the project? It really depends. Too wishy-washy? Perhaps, but it is true. If your challenges are such that they have no place in your presentation you must find a way to switch to the right state of mind. If your presentation can benefit from personal examples and analogies that draw on your current challenges and state of mind, then use them! My guess is that the storylines of most movies and novels are improved by their creators' negative and positive emotions. That said, there is a caveat I'd like to add: a presentation (in any form) is not a therapy session! I've seen that before, and this is not the time nor the place. Often, whatever you are going through can be used as a brilliant analogy that can further solidify your presentation's goals. If we analyze for a moment what Aurelius says in the quote above, he is beyond brilliant. So many of us become puppets to the circumstances in our lives. We get bad news, and we are in a bad mood. We get good news, and we are in a good mood. The pendulum swings from one side to the other in accordance with our current circumstances. The truth is we can learn something from Aurelius (and countless others who say the same thing) we must learn to stay neutral and allow life events to subtly influence our work. We all can do so, yet so many of us choose the bumpy responses to our environments. As a presenter, you need to learn the art of sucking it up. Believe me. There have been plenty of times I had bad news or unfortunate circumstances presented to me shortly before taking the stage. I have learned to compartmentalize those thoughts and emotions until I'm finished. Again, if warranted, I have countless times utilized those circumstances as examples and analogies, but they remain just that. I will not pontificate ad nauseam about these situations with my audience because that is not what they've come to hear. Like many of you, I am still learning the art of living in a state of mind as the Tao Te Ching states:

Being and non-being produce each other.
Difficulty and ease bring about each other.
Long and short delimit each other.
High and low rest on each other.
Sound and voice harmonize each other.
Front and back follow each other.
Therefore the sage abides in the condition of unattached action.
And carries out the wordless teaching.
Here, the myriad things are made, yet not separated.

Tip – Ride the highs and lows and control your emotions in your presentations.

#193 – James Lipton

1926–2020

Context – James Lipton was a writer, actor and dean of the Actors Studio, Drama school at Pace University in New York City. Lipton interviews Johnny Depp in Season 8 of *Inside the Actors Studio* in 2007.

James Lipton: *What is your favorite word?*

Johnny Depp: *Why.*

James Lipton: *Didn't that sound appropriate to you? It did to me. What is your least favorite word?*

Johnny Depp: *No.*

James Lipton: *What turns you on?*

Johnny Depp: *Breathing.*

James Lipton: *What turns you off?*

Johnny Depp: *Not breathing.*

James Lipton: *What sound or noise do you love?*

Johnny Depp: *My daughter's voice.*

James Lipton: *What sound or noise do you hate?*

Johnny Depp: *Vacuum cleaner.*

James Lipton: *What is your favorite curse word?*

Johnny Depp: *Boy. This is a real opportunity here. I don't want to mess this up. I think the most expressive would be shit. Yeah. Shit works a lot.*

James Lipton: *And it's just as good, maybe even better in French.*

Johnny Depp: *Yeah, yeah. And it's used a lot. It's said more in French than anywhere else.*

James Lipton: *Yes, it is. What profession, other than yours, would you like to attempt?*

Johnny Depp: *Writing, I think. Writing.*

James Lipton: *What profession would you absolutely not like to try?*

Johnny Depp: *President of the United States.*

James Lipton: *Johnny, if Heaven exists, what would you like to hear God say when you arrive at the Pearly Gates?*

Johnny Depp: *Wow.*

Analysis – Have you ever seen the TV show *Inside the Actors Studio*? It is one of my favourite shows in the entire world. I'll watch and re-watch the same episodes. If it's on and I'm there, I watch. I can't say that about that many TV shows. Sure, it's fun to see the big movie stars, and this particular episode features Johnny Depp, one of the biggest. But this is not why I adore this show so much. I adore James

Lipton. He is a prime example of being over-prepared. If you've ever seen this show, you know Lipton is famous for the stacks of blue cue cards that rest on his desk. He does an exorbitant amount of research on the actors that he interviews. His interviews personify what I would consider the blueprint of a superb presentation. There is a beginning, a journey to uncover a goal, culminating with a thought-provoking finish. Watch the beginning of this interview and watch how James sets up his interview with a fine introduction, one that more often than not has his interviewee saying, "Wow!" or "That was generous." or "You've done your research!" or "How did you know that?" I've not seen an episode where the actor doesn't proclaim something along these lines at some point. Simply, Lipton takes his job seriously and puts in hours of hard work. What you see may seem effortless, but it only appears that way because of the hours Lipton spends preparing. I read on Lipton's blog that he devotes two weeks of solid prep time to each guest. I wonder how much time the average host invests. I highly doubt it's two weeks. Lipton gets the biggest names in the movie business, people such as Johnny Depp don't give a ton of interviews, yet they come to this school. The fact that it is a master's degree program at a school that teaches acting is one reason they accept Lipton's invitation, but another reason, and perhaps the bigger reason, is Lipton's elevated interviewing skills. Although he is prepared, he can depart from that to be impromptu with his guests. You see, he has earned the right to leave the script and just chat. He knows far more about his topic than he could ever tell, discuss, or ask, and with that comes a man able to relax and exchange some banter. He shows us some of the wittiest banter on television. Do you see how this can translate to presentation skills? Prepare, prepare, and prepare. Then you've earned the right to relax and play. Another technique that I'd like to bring to the fore that Lipton utilizes in each episode is finishing the one-on-one interview with a questionnaire. French television personality Bernard Pivot originated the original questionnaire concept after the Proust Questionnaire. The ten questions Lipton asks are:

1. What is your favourite word?
2. What is your least favourite word?
3. What turns you on?
4. What turns you off?
5. What sound or noise do you love?
6. What sound or noise do you hate?
7. What is your favourite curse word? (always a hilarious response, by the way)
8. What profession other than your own would you like to attempt?
9. What profession would you not like to do?
10. If Heaven exists, what would you like to hear God say when you arrive at the pearly gates?

This set of ten questions are perhaps my favourite part of the entire show. It is telling, and if you didn't already have a better sense of Lipton's guest, you undoubtedly will after they have answered those ten questions. And the responses are just plain funny most of the time. In your presentations, are there some of these questions that could be injected? Maybe as part of an icebreaker or part of your talk. Don't use your platform to lecture. Yes, your job is to talk about what you've been asked to talk about, but you also need to interact and get to know your audience while you are on stage. Presentations are a full-contact sport.

Tip – Earn the right to relax and play with your presentations.

#192 – William Arthur Ward

1921–1994

Context – William Arthur Ward wrote more than 100 articles and poems. Ward is one of the most frequently quoted writers in the pages of *Quote*, the international weekly magazine for public speakers.

"The mediocre teacher tells. The good teacher explains. The superior teacher states.
The great teacher inspires."

Analysis – Hopefully we have all had at least one great teacher. But what is it that sets them apart from the dozens of other teachers you've had in your life? Is it what Ward says in his quote, that the great teachers inspire? Teaching and presenting are one in the same. Your job as a presenter is to teach others about the topic that you are presenting. You may inform, entertain, or persuade, but at the root of it, you are introducing something to your audience. So then, what is it to inspire? Wayne Dyer (Post #197) says that being inspirational is being in-spirit and connected to creativity. I agree with that. Inspiration is about creating an urgency in others to do or feel something. If that isn't what speaking to a group is about, I don't know what is! So, how do we not tell, explain or state (as in the quote) but *inspire* others to action. For most of us, inspiration shows up now and then, and just as mysteriously as it arrives, it vanishes. It's this mystical and intangible thing that we can't seem to lasso. Some days you may feel inspired to pick up the guitar collecting dust in the corner or to paint or sing or write. Many of us think that inspirational people are creative people who have learned to tap into their inspiration in every moment. This is not the case. The ability to inspire is within all of us, and the trick is to find a way to tap into this with more frequency so that you can transmit this energy to your audiences. As a presenter, you need to be impassioned, even enamoured with your topic to find your burst of inspiration. Think back to a teacher you loved. Did they love teaching, or did they love the subject? I bet they loved both, but the subject matter was most likely paramount. The teachers I know who sucked were the ones who may have adored teaching but had limited knowledge of the topic. It reminds me of my biology teacher in Grade 10. She had just left university and was assigned to our biology class. We later discovered that she actually wanted to teach English (being assigned a subject matter rather than being able to choose is undoubtedly a massive failing in our educational system! Whoops! I digress). Sure, she cared, she was articulate, organized, disciplined, but, respectfully, she was hands down one of the worst teachers I ever had. When you present, you must feel your topic; you must have a yearning to dig in and learn more even if you've never had the opportunity to speak to a group of people before? Some of you may not have a choice on what you are presenting, or it's a work thing or something along those lines. Too bad! It's still your job to figure it out and immerse yourself in researching and learning all you can about the subject material because only then will you get jazzed about it.. The only way you will inspire your audience to action or inspire a new way of thinking is to dig in, do your research, and then have fun with it.

Tip – Harness your ability to inspire through research and inject it into every single presentation.

#191 – Tina Turner

(1939)

Context – Tina Turner performs "Proud Mary" at the GelreDome in Arnheim (Netherlands) in 2009.

Left a good job in the city
Workin' for the man every night and day
I never lost one minute of sleep
Worryin' about the way things might have been
Big wheels Keep on turnin'
Proud Mary keeps on burnin'
And we're rollin'
Rollin', rollin' on the river
Cleaned a lot of plates in Memphis
and I pumped a lot of 'tane down in New Orleans
But I never saw the good side of the city until I hitched
a ride on the river boat Queen
Big wheels Keep on turnin'

Proud Mary keeps on burnin'
And we're rollin'
Rollin', rollin' on the river
And we're rollin'
Rollin', rollin' on the river
And we're rollin'
Rollin', rollin' on the river
And we're rollin'
Rollin', rollin' on the river
Cleaned a lot of plates in Memphis
and I pumped a lot of 'tane down in New Orleans
But I never saw the good side of the city until I hitched
a ride on the river boat Queen

Big wheels Keep on turnin'
Proud Mary keeps on burnin'
And we're rollin'
Rollin', rollin' on the river

Analysis – Every presentation requires an element of performance or an exaggerated version of yourself. If it doesn't, then why the heck wouldn't your audience just read about what you have to say versus coming to hear you speak? Performance is a requirement in any presentation, period. Well, one need not look any further for performance than Ms. Turner. Turner is the ultimate performer! She has millions of fans all over the world. Energy, exuberance, passion, fire; this is what she brings to the stage. Here is a woman who has overcome some serious obstacles in her life not least being a survivor of domestic abuse. With just 36 cents in her pocket, she set out to create a new life for herself, and boy did she ever. Many have said that watching Turner perform is a life-enhancing experience. To be honest, I had not paid Turner much mind, until I stumbled across this video, and not only do I get it, but I feel it! She cuts loose; she feels the music and encapsulates herself in it while never forgetting her audience. While you and I won't throw on a sequin number and dance to "Proud Mary" with a backup entourage for our presentations (well…maybe? heehee), we can learn from Turner's showmanship, delivering simply the best, most captivating concert one can put on. It is well thought out and well-executed, there great costumes, a brilliant light show, the band is tight and no detail is left unchecked. Her concerts are all wrapped up with a downpour of Turner's charisma, and you can't keep your eyes off her. At the time of this performance, Turner was 70 years old, and she has more energy than most 30-year-olds I know. Where does that come from? Having a desire is the first step. You simply have to want to put on the best performance you possibly can, every single time.

Tip – Find your inner Tina!

#190 – Stuart Brown

Context – Stuart Brown in his 2008 TED Talk says, "Play Is More Than Just Fun."

"So, here we go: a flyby of play."

It's got to be serious if the New York Times puts a cover story of their February 17th Sunday magazine about play. At the bottom of this, it says, "It's deeper than gender. Seriously, but dangerously fun. And a sandbox for new ideas about evolution." Not bad, except if you look at that cover, what's missing?
You see any adults?

Well, lets go back to the 15th century. This is a courtyard in Europe, and a mixture of 124 different kinds of play. All ages, solo play, body play, games, taunting. And there it is. And I think this is a typical picture of what it was like in a courtyard then. I think we may have lost something in our culture.

So, I'm gonna take you through what I think is a remarkable sequence. North of Churchill, Manitoba, in October and November, there's no ice on Hudson Bay. And this polar bear that you see, this 1200-pound male, he's wild and fairly hungry. And Norbert Rosing, a German photographer, is there on scene, making a series of photos of these huskies, who are tethered. And from out of stage left comes this wild, male polar bear, with a predatory gaze. Any of you who've been to Africa or had a junkyard dog come after you, there is a fixed kind of predatory gaze that you know you're in trouble. But on the other side of that predatory gaze is a female husky in a play bow, wagging her tail. And something very unusual happens. That fixed behavior – which is rigid and stereotyped and ends up with a meal – changes. And this polar bear stands over the husky, no claws extended, no fangs taking a look. And they begin an incredible ballet.

A play ballet. This is in nature: it overrides a carnivorous nature and what otherwise would have been a short fight to the death. And if you'll begin to look closely at the husky that's bearing her throat to the polar bear, and look a little more closely, they're in an altered state. They're in a state of play. And it's that state that allows these two creatures to explore the possible. They are beginning to do something that neither would have done without the play signals. And it is a marvelous example of how a differential in power can be overridden by a process of nature that's within all of us…"

Analysis – You only have to wait a few seconds into this talk for Brown to start telling an amazing story set in a place just north of Churchill, Manitoba. In the story, a polar bear and a husky play together. It's fall and there is no ice on the Hudson Bay. It's wild to see because both are probably quite hungry, but it seems that the husky initiates play, with a play signal, and the polar bear follows suit. Such a great series of pictures and a great reminder to us that you don't know what to expect from others, so approach all with an open heart. I'd give Brown's talk a 5 out of 10. If you've been following this project, you certainly don't need me to tell you why; you already know. If you don't know, start working your way through these pages and links and you'll figure it out. What is this talk doing on my list of *365 Must-Know Talks*? I am keen on the content, so this is one of the few times I will choose a talk due to its content and not its delivery. As presenters, we often take the task of presenting so seriously (hmmm, this post could be a case in point with a talk about play delivered in an academically unplayful approach). Why? Is it because we have too much riding on it, and we need to impress? Why aren't people naturally playful? Whatever the reason, it seems quite sad that we wouldn't enjoy the process more. Injecting play into your presentations will do what it does for all the examples Brown shows, such as the monkey rolling snowballs or the baby and mother, the children, or the dogs. Brown's theory is that play in childhood makes for happy, smart adults, and keeping it up can make us smarter at any age. I agree. Many of us have lost the ability to play. It's been so long we don't even know what it feels like anymore. So, what are you waiting for? Throw some play into your world and your presentations, and you may even increase your intelligence. Sounds good to me. Where's that ColecoVision video-game console I played with as a kid? Pac-Man anyone? Hmmm, I wonder how I can make a presentation out of that. Play is a state of mind.

P.S. Watch Brown in the Q&A, which starts at around 22 minutes. Can you see how he is far superior in this medium? Tone, body language, cadence, interest level, and even more playful! Much better.

Tip – Adopt a playful mindset.

#189 – Albert Einstein

1879–1955

Context – Albert Einstein talks about intuition. Although the below may have been paraphrased, Einstein has been widely quoted as saying the below.

"The intuitive mind is a sacred gift, and the rational mind is a faithful servant. We have created a society that honors the servant and has forgotten the gift."

Analysis – Have you ever thought about someone and then had the telephone ring only to find the person that you were just thinking about at the end of the line? It happens to me all the time. Honestly, it happens so frequently that I started to delve into a bit of research in this area. I'm fascinated with the brain, and so my research led me down that path. A study I read recently indicated that the two hemispheres of our brain function as two distinct and separate spheres of consciousness, each with its own personality and agenda. Whoa, read that again. Take the example of thinking of someone and then they show up either via phone or in person, it can be argued that the person who can access both hemispheres of their brain with great frequency is intuitive or more intuitive than if they lived on one side of their hemisphere with great frequency. Now, if you've ever taken any of the behavioural assessments out there, and they are plentiful (i.e., Myers Briggs, DiSC, Firo-B, CLI, EQ, etc.) most of them have a measurement on intuition. Mine is always off the charts. I don't need a test or an assessment to tell me this though, I already knew. I have always felt things in my gut. I will get a sensation in my stomach that will often, depending on the situation and emotion, elicit strong feelings. I can walk into a room and feel if something is off. You know, if you walk into a room and two people just argued, you can pick up on that negative energy. It's kind of like that, but I tend to feel it in my gut, even small emotions. It can be distracting, but it can also be beneficial, especially in a presentation scenario. I can sense when a concept I've presented hasn't been absorbed, or if I need to do a better job explaining something, or if we need to move on, even when the room isn't showing any physiological characteristics, such as body language cues. This is not unique to me. Any speaker will figure this out in due course, but it takes practice, and more importantly, it requires that speakers trust their inner voice, their intuition. Practice is simple.
Be attuned to what is going on around you and trust that what you're feeling is accurate. If you continue to develop your intuitive side, you will not only become a better speaker but a dramatically different one. It is the speakers who are insular or into themselves that cannot be intuitive. To be intuitive in the presentation room, you must be prepared to be somewhat relaxed so that you can tune into the room. Have you ever watched a presentation where the speaker can read the room at any given time? It's almost a sixth sense. The presenter will sense that the audience don't understand a concept or need a break or similar. It is a valuable tool to include in your presentation toolbox.

If you are hyper or nervous or in an ego-driven state, you will never be able to feel what is happening in the room. Frankly, that is why I wasn't very good in my early years as a public speaker. I was ego-driven, cared too much about how I was perceived, and couldn't relax enough to tune into the room and use my intuition. This skill takes time to develop. It takes hours in front of a group of people before you get good at it, although I have seen some do this rather naturally right out of the gate. So be patient, and it will come if you continue to work on it. Einstein, understood the importance of intuition. Your intuition really is one of the most valuable things you possess.

Tip – Home in on your intuition as part of your presentation process, and watch your skills improve dramatically.

#188 – Adam Grant

(1981)

Context – Adam Grant is a psychologist, author, and professor specializing in organizational psychology at the Wharton School of the University of Pennsylvania. In his 2021 TED Talk, "How to Stop Languishing and Start Finding Flow," Grant shares that if you are staying up late, joylessly bingeing TV shows and doom-scrolling through the news, or simply navigating your day uninspired and aimless you may be experiencing languishing—a psychic malaise that has become common after many months of the pandemic.

"I know you all have long to-do lists, but I hate wasting time so much that I have a to-don't list. Don't scroll on social media, don't check my phone in bed and don't turn on the TV unless I already know what I want to watch. But last year, I found myself breaking all of those rules. I was staying up way past midnight, doom-scrolling, playing endless games of online Scrabble and bingeing entire seasons of TV shows that weren't even good. The next morning I'd wake up in a daze and swear, "Tonight in bed by 10:00." But it kept happening night after night for weeks. What was I thinking?

As an organizational psychologist, I have spent my whole career studying motivation, so it really bothers me when I can't explain my own behaviour. I wasn't depressed; I still had hope. Wasn't burned out; had energy. Wasn't lonely; I was with my family. I just felt a little bit aimless and a little bit joyless. Eventually, I remembered there's a name for that feeling, languishing. Languishing as a sense of emptiness, stagnation, and ennui. It was coined by a sociologist Corey Keyes and immortalized by a philosopher, Mariah Carey.

When you're languishing, it just feels like you're muddling through your days, looking at your life through a foggy windshield. So, I'm curious how many of you have felt like that over the past few months. OK, those of you who didn't have the energy to raise your hands —you might be languishing right now. And you over here who didn't laugh, you're definitely languishing. Strangely enough, some of you passed the quiz. Strangely enough, what rescued me from that feeling was playing Mario Kart. But let's back up for a second.

In the early days of covid, a lot of us were struggling with fear, grief, and isolation. But as the pandemic dragged on with no end in sight, our acute anguish gave way to chronic languish. We were all living in Groundhog Day. It felt like the whole world was stagnating. So, I wrote an article to put languishing on the map. I called it "The Neglected Middle Child of Mental Health," and I suggested it might be the dominant emotion of our time. And soon, it was everywhere. I was seeing it all over the media, being discussed by celebrities, by royalty. I've never seen people so excited to talk about their utter lack of excitement.

And – I think – I think that naming languishing, helped people make sense of some puzzling experiences. Why, even after getting vaccinated, people were having trouble looking forward to the rest of the year. Why when National Treasure came on TV, my wife already knew all the words by heart. And why I was staying up way too late, falling victim to what's known as revenge bedtime procrastination.

We were looking for bliss in a blah day and purpose in a perpetual pandemic. But languishing is not unique to a pandemic. It's part of the human condition. Two decades of research show that languishing can disrupt your focus and dampen your motivation. It's also a risk factor for depression because languishing often lurks below the surface. You might not notice when your drive is dwindling, or your delight is dulling. You're indifferent to your own indifference, which means you don't seek help, and you might not even do anything to help yourself. Meh. Languishing isn't just hard to spot, though. In many cultures, it's hard to talk about, too. When people ask, "How are you?" you're expected to say, "Great!" or "Living my best life." That's called toxic positivity.

It's the pressure that we face to be optimistic and upbeat at all times. If you say, "You know, I'm just OK," then people might encourage you to look on the bright side or count your blessings, which isn't just annoying. It can actually be bad advice…"

Analysis – In 2020, we started to experience the unchartered territory of a global pandemic. With COVID-19, we have felt emptiness, stagnation, and listlessness. In Grant's talk, we uncover that most of us are feeling malaise. Before the pandemic, many started down this path of malaise, this *blah* feeling, no energy, no sense of purpose. The "I'm so busy" culture is bologna. Being a workaholic doesn't drive productivity. It's a recipe for languishing. We have it wrong. Having fun isn't an enemy of efficiency, it's fuel for finding flow. Play isn't a reward for finally making it through your to-do list.

Grant says the best predictor of well-being is not optimism but flow. It's total absorption in an activity where you lose track of time; you lose your sense of self. Peak flow is active participation in the real world. It has three conditions: mastery, mindfulness and mattering.

How to translate peak flow into preparing for a talk:

1. **Give yourself uninterrupted time to focus.** It's easy to fall prey to checking emails and switching tasks. In the past year and a half, many of us have also struggled with interruptions from kids around the house and bosses around the clock. Block off some uninterrupted time to find your flow and work on your talk.

2. **Tiny goals.** Create an outline, draft an opening sentence, and create the purpose of the talk. Getting into flow requires momentum sparked by small wins. You can't eat an elephant in a single bite, nor can you create an entire talk in one sitting. Break the task of creating a talk into small, achievable goals.

3. **A change of scenery can be refreshing and recharging.** If you're stuck, break out of where you typically work and go for a walk to get your endorphins pumping. Stop thinking so hard and inevitably, new creative ideas will begin to flow.

4. **Your voice matters.** Knowing that you make a difference to other people can help reinvigorate you in developing your talk. Your voice is unique; there is only one you, and we all have something to say that is through your eyes and is a gift to those listening.

The antidote for languishing doesn't have to be excessive productivity. It can be something joyful. Our peak moments of flow are often when we are having fun with the people we love, and this should be a daily task. Let go of the task of creating, writing, thinking, and go out and have some fun.

Tip – Find your peak flow by mixing up how you have traditionally developed talks.

#187 – Hippocrates

460–370 BCE

Context – Hippocrates writes the Hippocratic Oath. The original oath was written in Ionic Greek, between the fifth and third centuries BCE.

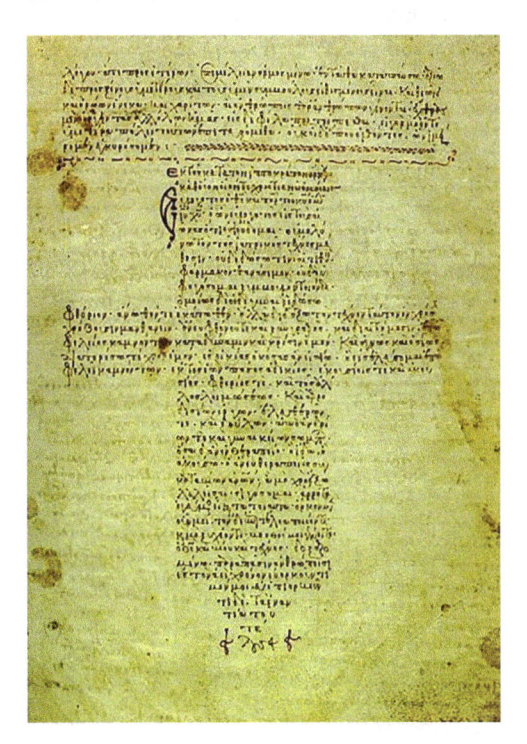

"I swear by Apollo, the healer, Asclepius, Hygieia, and Panacea, and I take to witness all the gods, all the goddesses, to keep according to my ability and my judgment, the following Oath and agreement:

To consider dear to me, as my parents, him who taught me this art; to live in common with him and, if necessary, to share my goods with him; To look upon his children as my own brothers, to teach them this art.

I will prescribe regimens for the good of my patients according to my ability and my judgment and never do harm to anyone.

I will not give a lethal drug to anyone if I am asked, nor will I advise such a plan; and similarly I will not give a woman a pessary to cause an abortion.

But I will preserve the purity of my life and my arts.

I will not cut for stone, even for patients in whom the disease is manifest; I will leave this operation to be performed by practitioners, specialists in this art.

In every house where I come I will enter only for the good of my patients, keeping myself far from all intentional ill-doing and all seduction and especially from the pleasures of love with women or with men, be they free or slaves.

All that may come to my knowledge in the exercise of my profession or in daily commerce with men, which ought not to be spread abroad, I will keep secret and will never reveal.

If I keep this oath faithfully, may I enjoy my life and practice my art, respected by all men and in all times; but if I swerve from it or violate it, may the reverse be my lot."

Analysis – Hippocrates is widely regarded as the father of Western medicine. If you've ever attended one of my workshops, you will have heard me pontificate about Hippocrates quite a lot. Hippocrates was the first to reject the idea that illness was caused by divine or magical intervention, instead, he favoured the theory that the body contained four fluids. These fluids could also be correlated with behaviours. So, when you look at all the behavioural profiles in the world, you can thank Hippocrates for being the originator. The four fluids that Hippocrates outlined were: blood, black bile, yellow bile, and phlegm. He indicated that when any of these elements were out of balance, sickness occurred.

The Hippocratic Oath is an oath sworn by doctors to practice medicine ethically. Does this mean that all do? Well, no, obviously, or there would be no such thing as medical malpractice. But I like the idea that there is a set of rules that follow a path of integrity for a profession. I wish all professions had their version of the Hippocratic Oath. It is a fine text, and one deserved to be on a list of must-know talks. I wondered what an oath for presentation skills would look like. What would it look like for you? I wrote my oath tonight and I suggest you do the same. Build and deliver a presentation that adheres to your values, integrity, and ethics, and stick to it.

Tip – Create your own presentation skills oath.

#186 – J.K. Rowling

(1965)

Context – Written by J.K. Rowling, the first in the series of seven Harry Potter novels, *The Philosopher's Stone*

"Not Slytherin, eh?" said the small voice [of the Sorting Hat]. "Are you sure? You could be great, you know, it's all here in your head, and Slytherin will help you on the way to greatness, no doubt about that–no? Well, if you're sure–better be GRYFFINDOR!" (Chapter 7)

Analysis – Unless you've been living under a rock, you must've heard about good ol' Harry Potter. Potter is an orphan who discovers that he is a wizard at the age of 11. Although the wizard ability is inborn, children are sent to a wizarding school (Hogwarts) to learn the magical skills necessary to navigate the wizarding world. I remember when the first book, *Harry Potter and the Philosopher's Stone*, came out in 1997 and I read through it in sheer delight. It is imaginative and a stunning piece of literature.

I love the first book in the series so much because it opens a portal into a universe I've never seen. It is fascinating, and like many great children's (or teens', I suppose) movies or novels, there are many messages aimed at the adults watching and reading along. The above quote is from the Sorting Hat who assigns each child who enters Hogwarts to one of four houses: Gryffindor, Hufflepuff, Ravenclaw, and Slytherin. Slytherin, the house that Harry doesn't want to be in, adopts the values of cunning, ambition, and most of all, pure wizard blood. Gryffindor's values: courage, bravery, loyalty, and chivalry. I like the above quote because it speaks to life in general as often, we have little control over the matters at hand and many choices are made for us. The same is sometimes true for presentation skills. Even though we may hope and pray, like Potter, for one thing, the opposite may be handed to us. We must learn to not only deal with our lot but also make it work in our favour. Now in Potter's case, he did get what he wanted. He was placed in Gryffindor house, but it could've been a natural crossroad for him had he been placed in Slytherin. Notice how the Sorting Hat could read Potter's thoughts? Interesting indeed. There are two things to glean from Potter's anxious moment that can be directly translatable to presentation skills

1. In order to steer the destiny of your presentation skills let the powers that be know what you are seeking! Harry Potter knew the Sorting Hat could read his thoughts. This is not the case in the real world, so you must speak up! if you want to present on a particular topic but haven't been asked, then ask! If you want to choose the topic instead of being assigned, then ask! If you want to design a presentation that is different from any others your organization has seen, then ask and you might get the opportunity.

2. If you find yourself at a crossroads not knowing where to start, continue or finish your presentation, channel your inner Harry Potter, and visualize your desired goal.

Tip – Design your own presentation skills destiny.

#185 – Daniel Goleman

(1946)

Context – Daniel Goleman, author of *Emotional Intelligence*, in his 2007 TED Talk talks about "Why Aren't We More Compassionate?"

"You know, I'm struck by how one of the implicit themes of TED is compassion, these very moving demonstrations we've just seen: HIV in Africa, President Clinton last night. And I'd like to do a little collateral thinking, if you will, about compassion and bring it from the global level to the personal. I'm a psychologist, but rest assured, I will not bring it to the scrotal.

There was a very important study done a while ago at Princeton Theological Seminary that speaks to why it is that when all of us have so many opportunities to help, we do sometimes, and we don't other times. A group of divinity students at the Princeton Theological Seminary were told that they were going to give a practice sermon and they were each given a sermon topic. Half of those students were given, as a topic, the parable of the Good Samaritan: the man who stopped the stranger in—to help the stranger in need by the side of the road. Half were given random Bible topics. Then one by one, they were told they had to go to another building and give their sermon. As they went from the first building to the second, each of them passed a man who was bent over and moaning, clearly in need. The question is: Did they stop to help?

The more interesting question is: Did it matter they were contemplating the parable of the Good Samaritan? Answer: No, not at all. What turned out to determine whether someone would stop and help a stranger in need was how much of a hurry they thought they were in—were they feeling they were late, or were they absorbed in what they were going to talk about. And this is, I think, the predicament of our lives: that we don't take every opportunity to help because our focus is in the wrong direction.

There's a new field in brain science called social neuroscience. This is the study of the circuitry in people's brains that activate when they interact. And the new thinking about compassion from social neuroscience is that our default wiring is to help. If we attend to the other person, we automatically empathize, and we automatically feel with them. There are these newly identified neurons, mirror neurons, that act like a neuro Wi-Fi, activating the same areas in our brain as those activated in the other person. We feel empathy automatically. And if a person is in need, if a person is suffering, we're automatically prepared to help. At least that's the argument.

But then the question is: Why don't we? And I think this speaks to a spectrum that goes from complete self-absorption, to noticing, to empathy and to compassion. And the simple fact is, if we are focused on ourselves, if we're preoccupied, as we so often are throughout the day, we don't fully notice the other. And this difference between the self and the other focus can be very subtle…"

Analysis – I must admit that I know a little something about Daniel Goleman as I've studied some of his materials at length, including his book *Emotional Intelligence*. There is another great book entitled *The EQ Edge* that I'd also recommend if you're interested in researching further.

Goleman asks a valid question: "What determines whether someone will stop to help a person or not?" Can you believe it's how much of a hurry a person is in? Sad really, because as I look at my city's downtown, or any street corner for that matter, every person is bustling by in a mad dash, busy, busy, busy. Even if they're not busy, at times some people pretend to be. Isn't that what cell phones are for? Really who can't wait until they reach their destination to make that call. The point is many of us pretend to be uber busy. It is this busyness that Goleman discusses in his talk. How we, with this view of ourselves, have a difficult time focusing on others. Goleman asks, "How long does it take for you to have a conversation where the other person uses the word *you*. The first time I watched this clip I thought I'd try an experiment. I wanted to test this hypothesis. How long would it take before someone asked me a question about me. I tried it on for a couple of weeks and was amazed at how infrequently someone asked a question about me. During this experiment, I made an enormous effort to throw out you statements to the person I was speaking with. Those who know me well know that I'm a better receiver of information than a provider of information (perhaps shocking to my blog friends as I pontificate ad nauseam. Maybe this is the reason an outlet such as this exists, hmm, I digress). So, I have learned the art of drawing out stories from the folks I'm speaking with. With Goleman's talk in mind, I found it fascinating how self-absorbed, dare I say narcissistic, some people are! But, and I say this without casting judgment, I do understand that everyone wants to be heard and feel valued. So, each of us turns from one person to the next, never really feeling heard, so we try a little harder with the next person and so on. And this perfectly illustrates the attitudes of many of the people we encounter.

Let's talk presentation skills and the importance of emotional intelligence. As an individual looking to develop a superb presentation skill set, it is imperative that you bake in time for your audience to contribute to your presentation so they, too, can be heard and afforded the luxury of contributing something of value. Your job, as Goleman says, is to "return their sentiment with compassion and empathy."

There is zero correlation between IQ (intelligence quotient) and EQ (emotional quotient or emotional intelligence), yet in our society, we are rewarded for having a high IQ. What Goleman is suggesting is to focus on your emotional intelligence and how you connect with people. If you open up to the emotional side of your presentations, inject a high level of integrity and allow your audience to interact, you will be successful.

Tip – Focus on your EQ not your IQ.

#184 – George Eliot

1819–1880

Context – English novelist George Eliot.

"It's never too late to be who you might have been."

Analysis – Do you have unrealized dreams? An unaccomplished goal? We all have something that we've wished for, hoped for, but for whatever reason, haven't yet realized. Instead of driving forward that dream, we let life get in the way and don't reach our full potential. Here is a true story about my mom that I know she won't mind me telling. This is a tale about setting goasl regardless of how the chips are stacked, the realization of a dream. It's a story about being persistent and diligent no matter what. My mom had always admired the dedication and form of bodybuilders—the chiseled, fitness-crazed folk who spend hours, days, years at the gym pumping iron when the rest of us can't seem to squeeze in an hour in a week. While researching for this entry I read an article that the average body builder spends five hours a day in the gym, six days a week, increasing to seven days a week in the weeks leading up to a competition. Let's break that down:

An average of 5 hours a day x 6 days a week = 30 hours per week x 6 months = 1,080 hours in training

I'm calculating it takes six months or so to prep adequately for a competition. Now, that is commitment! When was the last time, other than your day job, that you spent in excess of 1,000 hours trying to accomplish something?

So, back to my mom. Life squeaked on by, and although she was quite the aerobics queen, she hadn't set the goal (at least outwardly) of entering a bodybuilding competition. One day, she realized the true meaning of what George Eliot meant when he said, "It's never too late to be who you might have been." And with that, at the age of 54, my mom decides to enter a bodybuilding competition. Wouldn't you know it, after hours and months in the gym and following a strict diet, she gets to the bodybuilding competition and competes on stage in front of hundreds of people? She accomplished a lofty goal by putting in the hours, the dedication, and the discipline necessary to make it happen. It might have been easy for her to say, "I'm too old!" or "I'm too out of shape!" or "It will be too hard!" The truth is she may have said all those things, but she didn't sit and wallow. She pushed through to accomplish the goal and realized her dream. I've often told her that she should be teaching others this mindset, that it's never too late, based not only on this experience but plenty of others in her life.

We all know people like this in our lives. They are the doers. If they announce something or a goal, then it's as good as done. We also know people (probably more of these folks) that seem to be talkers. They rarely, if ever, accomplish anything they say they will. They talk about all the things they want to do but never do. Perhaps the reason I deplore the latter is because I was raised by my mom. What separates these two camps of people: the doers and the talkers? I believe it comes down to confidence. The doers have confidence and know that no matter the task, that they will accomplish it, period. There is an inherent faith, a belief that it will be done, and so they push forward and have the diligence to continue to pursue the goal. Even in the face of significant adversity, they'll adjust and figure it out. The talkers lack confidence, and they continue to talk about the goal or task at hand as they are trying desperately to convince themselves that they can do it, but they never quite get there, and then procrastination and laziness creeps in before they have even started the process. If they had started the process, they would begin to improve their confidence by celebrating the small wins and milestones along the way that propel the entire process forward.

Now, to presentation skills.

Consider how the following statements feel?

"I will never be a good public speaker."

"I am too old to learn how to give a superb presentation!"

"Who would want to listen to what I have to say?"

Now, how does this feel?

"I will be a superb public speaker!"

"It's never too late to learn how to give an amazing presentation. Bring it on!"

"I have learned a great deal in my life and I am looking forward to sharing some of it with others!"

Changing your language is the first step in realizing your goals. Try using positive statements instead of negative ones and begin writing down your goals. Whatever you do, start the process. It is the small milestones and wins that will propel you forward.

I'll leave you with two questions to ponder:

1. Can it ever be too late to do your best or try your best or make your dreams (including your presentation skills dreams) come true?

2. Where will you be in one year? Closer to your presentation skills goal or further away?

Tip – Be a doer, not a talker. It's never too late.

#183 – Ronald Reagan

1911–2004

Context – August 11, 1984, radio broadcast.

"My fellow Americans, I'm pleased to tell you today that I've signed legislation that will outlaw Russia forever. We begin bombing in five minutes."

Analysis – President Reagan was mic'd for a radio broadcast, unaware that his microphone and channel were live when he said the above quote. He was making a joke. This joke resulted in the Soviets claiming that the Americans had no intention of pursuing detente or peace. If you look at the fallout from an American perspective, it is interesting that there were no real ramifications for Reagan from the polls or the people. When asked, the majority chalked it up to another Reagan slip up. This reminded me of a talk I attended a few years back. We were on a ten-minute break, and I overheard the presenter comment while on his cell phone that he couldn't wait for the day to be over and how the participants weren't digesting what he was saying. He had this call where anyone could have heard, and I just happened to be within earshot. It gave me a valuable lesson, one that Reagan hopefully learned because of his mistake, that when you are giving a talk, you are always on. Always. Reserve those negative remarks and jokes if you must, until you have left the building!

Tip – As presenter, you are always on.

#182 – Douglas Englebart

1925–2013

Context – December 9, 1968 demonstration at the Fall Joint Computer Conference in San Francisco. This talk by Douglas Englebart is appropriately entitled "The Mother of All Demos."

"If in your office, you as an intellectual worker, were supplied with a computer display backed up by a computer that was alive for you all day and was instantly responsive to every action you have, how much value could you derive from that?" Engelbart asked. *"Well, this basically characterizes what we've been pursuing for many years in what we call augmented human intellect research center at the Stanford Research Institute."*

Analysis – Several experimental technologies were presented at this convention in 1968. This demo features the first computer mouse the public had ever seen and introduced interactive text, video conferencing, teleconferencing, email, hypertext, and a collaborative real-time editor. It is one old-school presentation! Is it the most exciting and passionate presentation I've ever seen? Absolutely not. It is rather dull, however, it earns a spot on my list of the *365 Must-Know Talks* because it was revolutionary. This talk was new and exciting in its day and created a massive buzz among the 1,000 attendees that permeated beyond the conference's boundaries. It reminded me that my presentations should always include something unique or new that my audience had not heard before. To create buzz with the attendees and possibly beyond that, the content must be pioneering. A friendly reminder to hit the books and do some research to uncover the next mouse (okay, maybe not the next mouse, but you know what I'm saying)!

Tip – Include cutting-edge content in all your presentations.

#181 – John Cleese

(1939)

Context – In 2009, John Cleese, comedian actor and co-founder of the Monty Python comedy troupe, visits a laughter club in Mumbai, India and talks to Dr. Madan Kataria, the founder of the Laughter Yoga Movement. The short video, "Why Laughter Is the Best Medicine" is taken from the BBC science show *The Human Face,* and is narrated by Cleese.

"We all know what a good laugh feels like," he tells the camera. "But what struck me was how easy it was to get started. When you have a lot of warm, friendly, funny faces coming at you, you respond very naturally…I'm struck by how laughter connects you to people. It's almost impossible to maintain any kind of distance or any sense of social hierarchy when you're just howling with laughter. Laughter is a force for democracy."

Analysis – Laughter. Who doesn't like to laugh? In this fun documentary, John Cleese investigates the Laughter Yoga Movement and a session in an Indian jail. If they can laugh, then surely we can too, can't we? Cleese uncovers the benefits of laughter. There are actual physiological benefits to laughing: you inhale more oxygen, it boosts your immune system, and it affords you the luxury of connecting with others regardless of social hierarchy. According to this documentary, the best part is that it can be a manufactured laugh or a real one. The body doesn't know the difference. What if you baked-in five to ten minutes to simply laugh as part of the preparation process? How would your mood be before you took to the stage? How would you feel? I bet that it would dissolve some of your nerves and put you in a good frame of mind. I'm going to try it!

Tip – Adopt a laughing ritual before taking to the stage.

#180 – Dale Carnegie

1888–1955

Context – Dale Carnegie was a writer and lecturer and developer of self-improvement courses. Below is an excerpt from the book *The Leader in You.*

"Charles Schwab was paid a salary of a million dollars a year in the steel business, and he told me that he was paid this huge salary largely because of his ability to handle people. Imagine that! A million dollars a year because he was able to handle people! One day at noontime, Schwab was walking through one of his steel mills when he came across a group of men smoking directly under a sign that said No Smoking.

Do you suppose that Charles Schwab pointed at the sign and said, "Can't you read?"

Absolutely not, not that master of human relations.

Mr. Schwab chatted with the men in a friendly way and never said a word about the fact that they were smoking under a No Smoking sign.

Finally he handed them some cigars and said with a twinkle in his eye, "I'd appreciate it, boys, if you'd smoke these outside."

That is all he said. Those men knew that he knew that they had broken a rule, and they admired him because he hadn't called them down. He had been such a good sport with them that they in turn wanted to be good sports with him."

Analysis – I read *The Leader in You* some 30 years ago, and I have always remembered this story, almost verbatim. First, Dale Carnegie writes as if he's having a conversation with his readers. It is much more impactful than choosing to tell rather than show through a story. Many new self-help writers could learn a thing or two from reading Carnegie's work on how to construct a compelling book. So, I've never forgotten this story and am often reminded of it when I give my presentations and observe others. I had the opportunity not too long ago to watch a presenter who was asking for my feedback. One of my first observations was how the presenter made her audience feel, particularly on occasions when there was a loss of control in the room. You know, when others are talking, or some other type of disruptive behaviour occurs. In this instance, two people were having a side conversation, and immediately the presenter stopped, looked at the two, and said, "Is there something you two would like to share with the group?" It reminded me of the countless teachers I had in high school, yet this was a group of highly skilled professionals in the room. The presenter used this technique of calling out disruptive audience members every time there was the slightest infraction. Each time, the individuals being called out were embarrassed and gradually became more and more disengaged. In my debrief with the presenter, I had asked her if there might be a different way to handle these situations so that the individuals weren't left embarrassed. When I asked her to provide examples of what an alternative reaction might look like, she gave me two that I think are far more appropriate and effective. The first was to leave her podium where she was speaking (oh yes, you can move out of the podium circle) and continue presenting but walking towards the individuals talking. Never calling them out but simply changing her presentation spot. Brilliant! The second was to ask a question back to the group such as, "I see there may be some questions or confusion on what we've just covered. What questions do you have?" Again, brilliant. I've personally learned a great deal from Carnegie. Always afford others the opportunity to save face, so never embarrass or put an individual in the audience on the spot. You will be left with an audience that is more likely to listen, be engaged, and feel comfortable. And that's exactly what you want from your audience.

Tip – Allow your audience to save face.

#179 – Julia Child

1912–2004

Context – Julia Child was an author, cooking teacher and television personality.

"I was 32 when I started cooking; up until then, I just ate."

Analysis – I adore Julia Child. She's funny, witty, and with her playful demeanor it's clear she doesn't take herself too seriously. Her show *The French Chef* launched in 1963 and turned Child into a household name. In one episode, she has six roast chickens lined up and with great simplicity, explains why one is different from the next. The above quote is a perfect illustration of giving an art form or a craft the respect it deserves. From this statement, I can infer that Child gained great respect and admiration for the ingredients and the product after learning how to construct a great meal. Isn't this true of so many things in life? Take public speaking as an example, you can watch someone live or on television give a talk and find all kinds of flaws and have comments and feedback that you would like to share with the presenter, but when the time comes for you to present you garner new respect for them and the art form.

If I converted Child's quote from cooking to public speaking, it may look something like this: "I was 32 when I started public speaking; up until then, I just talked." There is a vast difference between simply talking and public speaking. I like it, and I may adopt this quote as my own :) with acknowledgment to Child, of course.

Tip – Talking and public speaking are two very different things. Respect the difference!

#178 – William E. Hickson

1803-1870

Context – The short poem "Try Again" is attributed to Thomas H. Palmer and was often quoted in 19th century children's literature. William E. Hickson is credited with popularizing the poem, and quoted it in moral songs (1857).

'Tis is a lesson you should heed,
Try, try again;
If at first you don't succeed,
Try, try again;
Then your courage should appear,
For, if you will persevere,
You will conquer, never fear;
Try, try again.
Once or twice though you should fail,
Try, try again;
If you would at last prevail,
Try, try again;

If we strive, 'tis no disgrace
Though we do not win the race;
What should you do in the case?
Try, try again.
If you find your task is hard,
Try, try again;
Time will bring you your reward,
Try, try again.
All that other folks can do,
Why, with patience, should not you?
Only keep this rule in view:
Try, try again.

Analysis – I think I can safely say we have all heard this saying before. We use this phrase to motivate disheartened children as they take on learning new skills, but do we practice what we teach? I'm often reminded I will likely not be successful on the first go of a new task, and it will sometimes take several attempts before I master something new. As I reflect on my public speaking career, this is absolutely the case. If I had to fathom a guess, I'd say I delivered at least a hundred presentations before I felt I had delivered the message the way I had intended and elicited the desired response from the audience. A hundred times! I may have taken much longer than the average novice presenter, but that's okay because I loved every minute. I wanted to do it, and even though I wasn't very good at first, I didn't give up. Today, I still need to remind myself of this whenever I take on new tasks. There's always tomorrow, the next day, and the day after that, to continue to try.

Tip – Keep on trying.

#177 – Warren Buffett

(1930)

Context – Warren Buffett is an American investor, industrialist, and philanthropist. He is undoubtedly one of the most successful investors in the world. He is the CEO and primary shareholder of Berkshire Hathaway. In 2021 Buffet was ranked #6 among the world's wealthiest people. When giving a speech to the University of Georgia students many years ago, Buffet began with a question he is often asked: "Whom should I go to work for when I graduate college?"

"I've got a very simple answer…the real thing to do is to get going for some institution or individual that you *admire. I mean It's crazy to take little in-between jobs just because they look good on your resume, or because you get a little higher starting pay. I was up at Harvard a while back, and a very nice young guy picked me up at the airport, a Harvard Business School attendee. And he said, "Look, I went to undergrad here, and then I worked for X and Y and Z, and now I've come here." And he said, "I thought it would really round out my resume perfectly if I went to work now for a big management consulting firm." And I said, "Well, is that what you want to do?" And he said no, but he said, "That's the perfect resume." And I said, "Well, when are you going to start doing what you like." And he said, "Well, I'll get to that someday." And I said, "Well, you know, your plan sounds to me a lot like saving sex for your old age. It just doesn't make a lot of sense."*

Analysis – Do what you love and work for whom you admire the most, and you've given yourself the best possible chance in life. Start doing what you love today! As a corporate rat racer, I've held a sales bag slogging cereal, I've been a global sales trainer helping account managers figure out how to pump more gum into the world, I've led sales teams throughout Western Canada, I've consulted in pretty much every industry. I've led teams, I've worked on teams, I've had superb bosses, I've had horrible bosses, I've been highly engaged, and I've been actively disengaged at times too, I've had great teammates, and worked alongside some doozies too. I know what corporate life looks like inside out and upside down and I can say that finding the courage to do what you love is the greatest gift you can give yourself.

Speak about things that you love and subjects that elicit emotion. Surround yourself with mentors who live life to the full as these are undoubtedly the best public speakers out there.

Tip – Live and love life.

#176 – Theodore Roosevelt

1858–1919

Context – Roosevelt's robust attitude to foreign policy can be summed up in these two quotations from a speech he gave at the opening of the Minnesota State Fair in 1901, "Speak Softly and Carry a Big Stick."

"Speak softly, and carry a big stick".

"Right here let me make a vigorous plea as I know how in favor of saying nothing that we do not mean and of acting without hesitation up to whatever we say. A good many of you are probably acquainted with the old proverb, 'Speak softly and carry a big stick—you will go far.' If a man continually blusters, if he lacks civility, a big stick will not save him from trouble and neither will speaking softly avail, if back of the softness there does not lie strength, power. In private life there are few beings more obnoxious than the man who is always loudly boasting and if the boaster is not prepared to back up his words, his position becomes absolutely contemptible. So it is with the nation. It is both foolish and undignified to indulge in undue self-glorification and above all, in loose-tongued denunciation of other peoples. Whenever on any point we come in contact with foreign power, I hope that we shall always strive to speak courteously and respectfully of that foreign power…

"Let us make it evident that we intend to do justice. Then let us make it equally evident that we will not tolerate injustice being done us in return. Let us further make it evident that we use no words which we are not which

prepared to back up with deeds, and that while our speech is always moderate, we are ready and willing to make it good. Such an attitude will be the surest possible guarantee of that self-respecting peace, the attainment of which is must ever be the prime aim of a self-governing people."

Analysis – Teddy Roosevelt refers to the need to talk diplomatically to other governments and build-up and keep an effective Navy so that the ideas of the Monroe Doctrine (a doctrine that was aimed at preventing European interference in the Americas) could be implemented. I've chosen this quote more for the meaning of what is now a proverb, "Speak softly and carry a big stick." It is this notion that the tactic of caution and non-aggression is most effective if you can back it up. I like this notion as it relates to presentation skills too. No matter how verbally pushy or argumentative an audience member may get, it is best to proceed with caution and counteract aggression with non-aggression. Always. I've observed many heated debates between audience members and presenters, and it never goes well. Be the calm, cool-headed force in the room. As the presenter, you set the tone in the room for that moment so choose to lead with calm authority.

Tip – Counteract assertive behaviour with caution and non-aggression.

#175 – Michael Pollan

(1955)

Context – Michael Pollan, is an American author and journalist and is one of the writers and activists of the 2008 documentary *Food, Inc.*, an unflattering look inside America's corporate controlled food industry. He followed up with the documentary Cooked.

"The way we eat has changed more in the last 50 years than in the previous 10,000. But the image that used to sell the food, it is still the imagery of agrarian America. You going to the supermarket, and you see pictures of farmers, the picket fence in The Silo, in the 30s farmhouse in the green grass. It's the spinning of his past role fantasy. The modern American supermarket has on average 47,000 products. There are no seasons in the American supermarket.

Now there are tomatoes all year round, grown halfway around the world, picked when it was green and ripened with ethylene gas. Although it looks like it's tomato, it's kind of a notional tomato. I mean it's the idea of a tomato. In the meat aisle there no bones anymore.

There is this deliberate veil, that's dropped between us and where our food is coming from. The industry doesn't want you to know the truth about what you're eating because if you knew you might not want to eat it."

Analysis – I had an interesting discussion about the movie *Food, Inc.* I must admit that this was not the first film I've seen that discusses the perils of the food industry or Monsanto (the American agrochemical and agricultural biotechnology corporation acquired by Bayer in 2018) in particular. There have been plenty of documentaries on the food industry prior to and since *Food Inc*; *Supersize Me*, *What the Health*, *GMO OMG*, *Farmland*, *Eating you Alive*, *King Corn*, *Hungry for Change* etc. It. took me a long time to convert from what is widely considered the normal way of eating—buy food at the grocery store, go-to fast food joints occasionally, trust producers enough to not read every label, shop based on price not quality—and, by quality, I mean organic or free range, etc. It took me a solid few years to really buy into the concepts of eating clean. To really understand what this meant and make the necessary changes. I watched several documentaries and read countless books. I needed to be questioned on my choices because everything was so hard-wired and habitual. Frankly, it was just so much easier to shop in the normal way and to go outside that takes work, in terms of time and effort but it also changes your world view. You start to look more closely at how animals, farmers and individuals are treated, how individuals in the food industry system are treated, this is the real work—thinking before you act and making mindful decisions. Being well informed isn't easy. As I watched *Food, Inc.*, it made me think of presentation skills. Well, let's be honest. What doesn't? Changing or showcasing another opinion is a monumental task. I had the best intentions of changing my food buying habits, and I did, eventually. I intellectually understood the concepts and was horrified by the treatment of the animals, yet when it came time to put something in my cart, I was deterred by various factors. The next time you are doing a talk to persuade, where you are asking something of your audience, ask yourself what it will take for your audience to alter their behaviours? It's not an easy question. There is a farmer featured in the trailer for *Food Inc.* who says, "If you could grow a chicken in 49 days, why the heck would you raise one that grows in three months?" Ignorance is bliss. If you don't know about something or how something affects another thing, then you don't have to do anything about it. It may even be easier to stick your head in the proverbial sand. As a presenter, you do not have the luxury of being ignorant or lacking knowledge. You must know far more about your topic than you have the time to discuss. Understand, research, and learn all the layers of your topic. Force yourself to go beyond.

Tip – Ignorance is not bliss!

#174 – Matt Damon

(1970)

Context – Matt Damon's damning speech in the bar scene from the 1998 movie, *Good Will Hunting*.

"Will: Of course, that's your contention. You're a first-year grad student. You just got finished readin' some Marxian historian—Pete Garrison probably. You're gonna be convinced of that 'til next month when you get to James Lemon, and then you're gonna be talkin' about how the economies of Virginia and Pennsylvania were entrepreneurial and capitalist way back in 1740. That's gonna last until next year—you're gonna be in here regurgitating Gordon Wood, talkin' about, you know, the Pre-revolutionary utopia and the capital-forming effects of military mobilization.

Clark: Well, as a matter of fact, I won't, because Wood drastically underestimates the impact of social –

Will: Wood drastically—Wood 'drastically underestimates the impact of social distinctions predicated upon wealth, especially inherited wealth.' You got that from Vickers, 'Work in Essex County,' page 98, right? Yeah, I read that too. Were you gonna plagiarize the whole thing for us? Do you have any thoughts of your own on this matter? Or do you...is that your thing? You come into a bar. You read some obscure passage and then pretend...you pawn it off as your own idea just to impress some girls and embarrass my friend? See the sad thing about a guy like you is in 50 years you're gonna start doin' some thinkin' on your own and you're gonna come up with the fact that there are two certainties in life. One: don't do that. And two: You dropped a hundred and fifty grand on a f----n' education you coulda' got for a dollar fifty in late charges at the public library..."

Analysis – There are very few movie scenes that will bring an unrestrained grin to my face as much as this one. It wraps up so much of what I think about our educational system, particularly our post-secondary educational system. As presenters, you will almost always have a guy or gal strut in your class acting hot. By hot I mean they are elevating themselves so they can be condescending to others, including the presenter.

There are not many personality characteristics that make me feel queasy, but this one tops my short list. The only reason to be condescending, is to raise your poor self-esteem. It's that simple. When I observe this behaviour in the presentation room, I do everything in my power to stop it immediately and to gently open a portal into their self-esteem issues. Although I am not a fan of embarrassing anyone in the presentation room, I believe this is the one instance that needs to be addressed right away so that the person quickly understands that their behaviour is inappropriate. The unruly participant might not immediately understand what has occurred, but it will give them something to chew on for a few days. What Damon does in this clip is not so subtle, and at one time or another, we all may have wanted to put someone in their place when they've had such ill intentions. While I certainly don't advocate Damon's rebuttal, I can tell you that there have been plenty of times that I have been pretty close to sharing my own version of this diatribe.

Tip – Don't allow participants to be condescending during your presentation. Ever!

#173 – Ludwig van Beethoven

1770–1827

Context – Beethoven, was a German composer and pianist, and he remains one of the most influential composers of all time.

"Music is the one incorporeal entrance into the higher world of knowledge which comprehends mankind, but which mankind cannot comprehend."

Analysis – I once had the opportunity to participate in a music class that was fantastic. Sure, the music was amazing, but it was the two facilitators of the class that made the experience what it was. Each of them brought uniqueness to the class and welcomed people of all music levels and abilities. Their focus and mantra for the week-long course: "Let's focus on what you can do, not what you can't." For me, it was such an accepting and nurturing experience. Music is the perfect analogy for communication and presentation skills. There is a sender of information (the presenter, or the composer) and the receiver (the audience or the people tapping their toes to the beat). For a presentation to be truly successful, there needs to be a perfect connection between sender and receiver, just like a musician reading the notes on sheet music. When that happens, it feels like magic. One of the things that I thought about while in the class was utilizing music terms to describe presentation skills; like *a cappella*—where you perform solo without anyone assisting you. A cappella would be like a keynote talk where the presenter transmits their message to the audience. There can still be a great melody for the audience with an a cappella performance. Let's take *capriccio*—a lively piece of music that is usually short and free form. Capriccio could be compared to a short presentation where the presenter is there to entertain the audience. Whatever your musical style or taste, remember to play it the very best you can and focus on your strengths.

Tip – Think of your presentation as a well-crafted and executed piece of music!

#172 – Richard Dreyfuss

(1947)

Context – Alien and Human communication in the film *Close Encounters of the Third Kind*, 1977.

"I know this sounds crazy, but ever since yesterday on the road, I've been seeing this shape. Shaving cream, pillows... Dammit! I know this. I know what this is! This means something. This is important."

Analysis – For my younger blog followers, let me begin today by saying if you haven't seen *Close Encounters of the Third Kind*, run, don't walk, and watch it immediately. It is an excellent film on so many levels, but I want to focus on the final scene where the UFO lands and teaches the humans on Earth basic music patterns so that they may communicate. It's interesting because the humans think they are teaching the aliens, but they quickly realize that it is the aliens that are teaching them. Is this real language though and should it be included in a list of *365 Must-Know Talks*? Yes. Yes. And yes. When you meet someone for the first time, and they do not speak your language, what do you do? Do you say, "Oh, they don't speak English" and walk away? Of course not. You meander through a series of activities —think hand gestures, rapid pointing, google translate—until you find one that works. Such is the basic tonal vocabulary that the aliens in *Close Encounters* patiently teach the humans.

I had the opportunity to do several talks in several countries a good few years ago. I had translators at the back of the room who interpreted my words directly into the earphones worn by the participants. What was most interesting to me was how we communicated on breaks, and during lunches and dinners. We both had a deep desire to communicate with one another and used whatever resources we had to hand to converse. One lady in Mexico pulled out a piece of paper and drew stick figures to represent her family, an Italian gentleman played charades with me, another in Spain did a re-enactment with a colleague. What fun it was. The process of figuring out how to communicate broke down barriers in the spirit of doing whatever it took to get to know one another. Look at your presentation format from several angles to ensure that you are doing all that you can to share your message with your audience. Could you do more?

Tip – Enter your presentations with a deep desire to communicate.

#171 – The Fun Theory

Context – How do you get people to change their behaviour? The fun theory, an initiative of Volkswagen, attempted to tackle that question by staging four different public interventions: a piano staircase, a bin with a fifty-foot drop, fast lanes in supermarkets, the bottle-bank arcade, and subways with a speed camera lottery. Their hypothesis was that the easiest way to change people's behaviour for the better is to make whatever they need to do fun.

In the piano staircase, Volkswagen created stairs that looked and sounded like the keys to a piano. Alongside the piano stairs was an escalator—66% more people than normal chose the stairs over the escalator.

Analysis – Want to elicit change through your presentation? Inject fun! Okay, so maybe I'm stretching the boundaries of a talk. The Fun Theory served as a welcome reminder that so often, we take our presentations too seriously! Sometimes it is warranted to be serious, but we often miss the opportunity to inject fun as the catalyst for changing behaviour. Ice breakers are fun. Brainteasers are fun. There are so many exercises and activities out there that are tailor-made for presentations such as team-building exercises, quizzes, game show takeoffs (*Jeopardy* is a personal favourite) and many more. The purpose of these exercises is primarily to change up whatever is happening in the presentation room, to get people to use a different brain space, and learn by doing something different and often fun. One of my favourite websites, by the way, to get fun exercises is *businessballs.com*. There should always be at least one fun exercise in every talk simply because they ignite a new sense of learning.

Tip – Inject fun exercises into every talk.

#170 – Julie Andrews

(1935)

Context – Julie Andrews, alongside Dick Van Dyke singing "Supercalifragilisticexpialidoucious" in the classic 1964 musical fantasy film *Mary Poppins*.

Um diddle diddle diddle um diddle ay
Um diddle diddle diddle um diddle ay

Supercalifragilisticexpialidocious!
Even though the sound of it
Is something quite atrocious
If you say it loud enough
You'll always sound precocious
Supercalifragilisticexpialidocious!
Um diddle diddle diddle um diddle ay
Um diddle diddle diddle um diddle ay
Because I was afraid to speak
When I was just a lad
My father gave me nose a tweak
And told me I was bad
But then one day I learned a word
That saved me aching nose
The biggest word I ever heard
And this is how it goes:
Oh, supercalifragilisticexpialidocious!
Even though the sound of it
Is something quite atrocious
If you say it loud enough
You'll always sound precocious
Supercalifragilisticexpialidocious!
Um diddle diddle diddle um diddle ay
Um diddle diddle diddle um diddle ay
So when the cat has got your tongue
There's no need for dismay
Just summon up this word
And then you've got a lot to say
But better use it carefully
Or it may change your life
One night I said it to me girl
And now me girl's my wife!
She's supercalifragilisticexpialidocious!
Supercalifragilisticexpialidocious
Supercalifragilisticexpialidocious
Supercalifragilisticexpialidocious!

Analysis – Presenters sometimes get tongue-tied. We don't know what to say when we probably should. This is why Mary Poppins has a well-earned spot on the top *365 Must-Know Talks of All Time*. "Supercalifragilisticexpialidocious" is a nonsensical word uttered by Poppins in the 1964 movie. Poppins uses this word to impress others, "You'll always sound precocious," says Poppins or, as the young Jane Banks explains in the movie, "It's something to say when you don't know what to say." Funnily enough, as I began research this entry, there are all kinds of theories that the word does indeed mean something, one example I came across is, "atoning for educability through delicate beauty." Since this breakdown of the word doesn't follow typical English rules, I'm going stick to the nonsensical side. So, if you find yourself stuck for a word in a critical moment, take a deep breath and summon up, well, summon up any ol' word. Being hung up on our articulation is precisely why we get stuck for words in the first place. Who are you trying to impress? Don't concern yourself with $20 words, get the 20 cent words out, and the rest will follow. It's about getting your message across in a meaningful and perhaps entertaining way.

Tip – Summon those 20 cent words if you're tongue-tied.

#169 – Pericles
c. 495 – 429 BCE

Context – Pericles' *Funeral Oration* is a famous speech from Thucydides *History of the Peloponnesian War*. The speech was delivered by Pericles, a prominent politician in Athens, at the end of the first year of the Peloponnesian War as part of the annual public funeral for those who died during the war

"Most of those who have spoken here before me have commended the lawgiver who added this oration to our other funeral customs; it seemed to them a worthy thing that such an honour should be given at their burial to the dead who have fallen on the field of battle. But I should have preferred that, when men's deeds have been brave, they should be honoured in deed only; and with such an honour as this public funeral, which you are now witnessing…

"I will speak first of our ancestors, for it is right and seemly that now, when we are lamenting the dead, a tribute should be paid to their memory. There has never been a time when they did not inhabit this generation, and we have received from them a free state. But if they were worthy of praise, still more were our fathers, who added to their inheritance, and after many a struggle transmitted to us their sons this great empire…

"Our form of government does not enter into rivalry with the institutions of others. We do not copy our neighbours, but are an example to them. It is true that we are called a democracy, for the administration is in the hands of the many and not of the few. But while the law secures equal justice to all alike in their private disputes…and when a citizen is in any way distinguished, he is preferred to the public service, not as a matter of privilege, but as the reward of merit…

"I have dwelt upon the greatness of Athens because I want to show you that we are contending for a higher prize than those who enjoy none of these privileges, and to establish by manifest proof the merit of these men whom I am now commemorating. Their loftiest praise has been already spoken. For in magnifying the city I have magnified them, and men like them whose virtues made her glorious. And of how few Hellenes can it be said as of them, that their deeds when weighed in the balance have been found equal to their fame! Methinks that a death such as theirs gives the true measure of a man's worth; it may be the first revelation of his virtues,

but is at any rate their final seal. For even those who come short in other ways may justly plead the valour with which they fought for their country; they have blotted out the evil with the good and have benefited the state more by their public services than they have injured her by their private actions. None of these men were enervated by wealth or hesitated to resign the pleasures of life; none of them put off the evil day in the hope, natural to poverty, that a man, thou poor, amy one day become rich. But, deeming that the punishment of their enemies was sweeter than any of these things, and that they could fall in no nobler cause, they determined at the hazard of their lives to be honourably avenged, and to leave the rest. They resigned to hope their unknown chance of happiness, but in the face of death they resolved to rely upon themselves alone. And when the moment came they were minded to resist and suffer, rather than to fly and save their lives; they ran away from the word of dishonour, but on the battlefield their feet stood fast and in an instant, at the height of their fortune, they passed away from the scene, not of their fear, but of their glory...

Analysis – It would be utterly remiss of me not to include Pericles' *Funeral Oration* on any list of *365 Must-Know Talks*. It is significant because it departed from the typical formula of Athenian funeral speeches and was a glorification of Athens' achievements designed to resurrect the mood and spirits of a nation at war. The speech begins by praising the custom of the public funeral for those who had lost their lives. Pericles says, "the oration has the impossible task of satisfying the associates of the dead, who would wish that their deeds be magnified, while everyone else might feel jealous and suspect exaggeration." Honesty, while giving a talk, is paramount. Pericles says what the audience is perhaps already thinking and therefore quashes this train of thought by simply putting it out there. So often, when we give a presentation under stressful conditions, amid layoffs, salary freezes, considering some catastrophic event, etc., we try to mask the truth or maybe resist being transparent. Take a page out of Pericles' speech and say what your audience may already be thinking.

Tip – Be transparent. Address the elephant in the room, answer questions, and then move on.

#168 – Jeff Bezos

(1965)

Context – Amazon founder, Jeff Bezos delivers a Princeton University graduation address, "We Are What We Choose" in 2010.

"As a kid, I spent my summers with my grandparents on their ranch in Texas. I helped fix windmills, vaccinate cattle, and do other chores. We also watched soap operas every afternoon, especially Days of Our Lives. My grandparents belonged to a Caravan Club, a group of Airstream trailer owners who traveled together around the US and Canada and every few summers we'd join the caravan. We'd hitch up the Airstream to my grandfather's car and off we'd go and align with 300 other Airstream adventurers. I loved and worshiped my grandparents and I really looked forward to these trips.

On one particular trip I was about 10 years old, I was rolling around in the big bench seat in the back of the car. My grandfather was driving, and my grandmother had the passenger seat. She smoked throughout these trips, and I hated the smell. At that age, I'd take any excuse to make estimates and do minor arithmetic. I'd calculate our gas mileage, figure out useless statistics on things like grocery spending. I'd been hearing an ad campaign about smoking. I can't remember the details, but basically the ad said, "Every puff of a cigarette, take some number of minutes off of your life." I think it might've been two minutes per puff.

At any rate, I decided to do the math for my grandmother. I estimated the number of cigarettes per day, estimated the number of puffs per cigarette and so on. When I was satisfied that I'd come up with a reasonable number, I poked my head into the front of the car, tapped my grandmother on the shoulder and proudly proclaimed, "At two minutes per puff, you've taken nine years off of your life." I have a very vivid memory of what happened next, and it was not what I had expected. I expected to be applauded for my cleverness and my arithmetic skill. "Jeff, you're so smart. You had to have made some tricky estimates, figure out the number of minutes in a year and do some division." That's not what happened. Instead, my grandmother burst into tears.

I sat in the backseat. I Didn't know what to do while my grandmother was crying. My grandfather, who'd been driving in silence, pulled over onto the shoulder of the highway. He got out of the car and came around and opened my door and waited for me to follow. Was I in trouble? My grandfather was a highly intelligent, quiet man. He had never said a harsh word to me and maybe this was to be the first time. Or maybe he would ask that I get back in the car and apologize to my grandmother. I had no experience in this realm with my grandparents and no way to gauge what the consequences might be. We stopped beside the trailer. My grandfather looked at me and after a bit of silence he gently and calmly said, "Jeff, one day you'll understand that it's harder to be kind than clever."

Analysis – Let's tackle the pause. Pauses are an important component of any speech or presentation whether it's the well-timed pause, the pause to collect oneself, or the pregnant pause perfected by comedians or similar, silent time in presentations can be just as important as the spoken word. There is quite a bit of research on the positive effects of presenters pausing to allow time for the audience to absorb the material. At elevated levels, thinking demands processing time. There is undisputed research that indicates it can take three to five seconds to process more elevated or higher-level thoughts. This may not seem that long, a mere three to five seconds, but if you think about it, it is a significant amount of time when you are continuing to listen to and take on board more information. Another way to look at this is that a presenter, or anyone speaking for that matter, speaks at an average rate of 150 words per minute (wpm) and thinks at 450 wpm. So, we tend to think faster than we comprehend, and some may get overwhelmed. However, you want to look at it, and whatever study you choose to rely on, there can be no denying that a well-timed pause can help your audience understand the material. Bezos shows us the pause several times in his presentation given at Princeton. Bezos has a story-telling presentation style with a slower cadence and the skilled inclusion of pauses, some pauses are intentionally timed while others are required to help him find his way. From Bezos' delivery we learn that it's more than okay to take your time and include some well-timed pauses. It is a preferred delivery if you are feeling somewhat trepidatious, and more importantly, if you want to ensure that your audience has time to digest the contents of your presentation.

Tip – Include and be conscious of pauses in your presentations.

#167 – Carlos Castaneda

1925–1998

Context – Carlos Castaneda was an anthropologist and author. After writing *The Teachings of Don Juan*, Castaneda wrote a series of 12 books that describe his training in Mesoamerican shamanism. The below quote is from the 3rd book in the series *Journey to Ixtlan*, in which Castaneda's shaman-teacher don Juan Matus explains the role of strategy in the life of a warrior.

"All of us, whether or not we are warriors, have a cubic centimetre of chance that pops out in front of our eyes from time to time. The difference between an average man and a warrior is that the warrior is aware of this, and one of his tasks is to be alert, deliberately waiting, so that when his cubic centimetre pops out, he has the necessary speed, the prowess, to pick it up."

Analysis – Some may call Castaneda controversial, and some believe his works are fictional, while others (myself included) believe his writings are an accurate and true description of actual events. If you haven't read any of the Castaneda series, I won't attempt to decipher or provide a synopsis here as that would be hardy endeavour. But I believe that this series needs to be read by all. It is almost too profound a work to analyze. Alternatively, it should be experienced and felt. Heads-up, this is not light reading and Castaneda is not for the faint of heart. Castaneda's works tackle unbelievably earth-shattering and awe-inspiring content while he is under the tutelage of a Yaqui shaman, Don Juan Matus. Out of the 12 books in the series, I have read three. It has taken me nearly 23 years as I have needed space in between each book to fully grasp what I had read.

I know people who have read the entire series in a short time, but each time I've picked up the fourth in the series, I've gently put it back on the shelf, as I am not yet ready to absorb its contents.

I've known since this project's inception that I would include Carlos Castaneda in my list of *365 Must-Know Talks*. There are so many passages that resonate with me so profoundly, it was a challenge to narrow it down to the above excerpt. I admire the above quote because it is so true, but many don't even realize it. When I hear the phrase, "You're so lucky," uttered to another it always puts a smile on my face as I don't believe in luck. It is about understanding, as Castaneda says, "the cubic centimetre of chance" when it is placed in front of us. Most people don't recognize that it is there, and they allow it to slip away. It takes alertness to know when we should gather up our "cubic centimetre of chance." Such are presentation skills. So often, when we do a presentation, it is because we have been asked to do so. Let's say, for example, it is a work-type presentation, such as a budget re-cap and you've also been asked to act as MC for the meeting that the executive suite will attend. Because you've done this type of presentation before, you know the players, you do the presentation with minimal effort, and prepare very little for the MC component, figuring how hard could it be to introduce a few people. If this scenario rings true for you, then you have squandered your cubic centimetre of chance. You had it, and you probably won't get another opportunity to do it over, the *right* way with the due diligence, attention, alertness, preparedness required. Imagine what the cubic centimetre of chance could've been.

Tip – Recognize when your cubic centimetre of chance is in front of you!

#166 – Severn Cullis-Suzuki

(1979)

Context – 12-year-old Severn Suzuki spoke at the UN Earth Summit in 1992. At the age of nine, she started the Environmental Children's Organization (ECO.). ECO is a group of children committed to learning and teaching other kids about environmental issues.

"Hello, I am Severn Suzuki speaking for ECO – the Environmental Children's Organization. We are a group of 12- and 13-year-olds trying to make a difference, Vanessa Suttie, Morgan Geisler, Michelle Quigg and me. We've raised all the money to come here ourselves, to come 5,000 miles to tell you adults you must change your ways. Coming up here today, I have no hidden agenda. I am fighting for my future. Losing my future is not like losing an election, or a few points on the stock market." "I am here to speak for all generations to come. I am here to speak on behalf of the starving children around the world whose cries go unheard. I am here to speak for the countless animals dying across this planet, because they have nowhere left to go. I am afraid to go out in the sun now, because of the holes in our ozone. I am afraid to breathe the air because I don't know what chemicals are in it. I used to go fishing in Vancouver, my home, with my dad until, just a few years ago, we found a fish full of cancers. And now we hear of animals and plants going extinct every day, vanishing forever. In my life, I have dreamt of seeing the great herds of wild animals, jungles and rainforests full of birds and butterflies, but now I wonder if they will even exist for my children to see." "Did you have to worry of these things when you were my age? All this is happening before our eyes and yet we act as if we have all the time we want and all the solutions. I'm only a child and I don't have all the solutions, but I want you to realize, neither do you. You don't know how to fix the holes in our ozone layer. You don't know how to bring the salmon back up a dead stream. You don't know how to bring back an animal now extinct. And you can't bring back the forest that once grew where there is now a desert. If you don't know how to fix it, please stop breaking it." "Here you may be delegates of your governments, businesspeople, organizers, reporters or politicians. But, really, you're mothers and fathers, sisters and brothers, aunts and uncles and all of you are someone's child. I'm only a child, yet I know we are all part of a family, 5 billion strong, in fact 30 million species strong. And borders and governments will never change that. I'm only a child, yet I know we are all in this together and should act as one single world towards one single goal." "In my anger, I am not blind and in my fear, I am not afraid of telling the world how I feel. In my country we make so much waste, we buy and throw away, buy and throw away, buy and throw away and yet Northern countries will not share with the needy. Even when we have more than enough, we are afraid to share, we are afraid to let go of some of our wealth. In Canada, we live the privileged life. We've plenty of food, water and shelter. We have watches, bicycles, computers and television sets. The list could go on for 2 days. Two days ago, here in Brazil, we were shocked when we spent time with some children living on the streets. This is what one child told us, 'I wish I was rich and if I were, I would give all the street children food, clothes, medicines, shelter and love and affection'. If a child on the street who has nothing is willing to share, why are we who have everything still so greedy? I can't stop thinking that these are children my own age, that it makes a tremendous difference where you are born. And that I could be one of those children living in the favelas of Rio. I could be a child starving in Somalia, or a victim of war in the Middle East or a beggar in India. I am only a child, yet I know if all the money spent on war was spent on finding

*environmental answers ending poverty and in finding treaties, what a wonderful place this earth would be."
"At school, even in kindergarten, you teach us how to behave in the world. You teach us to not to fight with others, to work things out, to respect others and to clean up our mess, not to hurt other creatures, to share, not be greedy. Then, why do you go out and do the things you tell us not to do? Do not forget why you are attending these conferences, who you are doing this for. We are your own children. You are deciding what kind of a world we are growing up in. Parents should be able to comfort their children by saying 'Everything is going to be all right, it's not the end of the world, and we are doing the best we can'. But I don't think you can say that to us anymore.*

Are we even on your list of priorities? My dad always says, 'You are what you do, not what you say'. Well, what you do makes me cry at night. You grown-ups say you love us. But I challenge you, please, make your actions reflect your words. Thank you."

Analysis – If you want to know the definition of an inspirational talk then look no further. Long before Greta Thunberg, Cullis-Suzuki gave a talk at the U.N Summit in 1992 that one may conjecture inspired Greta on her own environmental journey. Cullis-Suzuki has what one would call, *Chutzpah*. She's indignant toward the attendees at this UN conference. She has a gutsy audacity, and I say that with a spirited grin. Age aside, Cullis-Suzuki asks some of the most intriguing and lionhearted questions I've ever heard. I encourage you to watch this talk at least twice; the first time you will be immersed in Cullis-Suzuki and her powerful delivery, the second time watch the delegates; they are moved and shocked. Her words are changing each of them, right then in the moment. Cullis-Suzuki quotes her dad as saying, "You are what you do, not what you say." I couldn't agree more and believe that is the perfect tip for today.

Tip – You are what you *do* and not what you *say*.

#165 – Muammar al-Gaddafi

1942–2011

Context – In the wake of the atrocious events of 9/11, world leaders shared their utter disgust. Even countries that had traditionally been tied to supporting terrorism and terrorists condemned al-Qaeda's actions. This included Libyan leader Muammar al-Gaddafi, who had previously provided liberation armies with terrorist funds.

"Irrespective of the conflict with America, it is a human duty to show sympathy with the American people and be with them at these horrifying and awful events which are bound to awaken human conscience. When I was five, my brother was shot by an Israeli soldier, since then I have been dedicated to uniting the Arab countries throughout the Middle East and retain a trade flow with the West."

Analysis – I will not claim to be an expert in international affairs but a developing connoisseur of what makes a great presentation. The above is undoubtedly a speech that deserves its place in the history books. Instead of focusing on the events or even the politics surrounding the events, I'd like to focus on when a leader must deliver a talk in the face of tragedy and adversity. Whether pro or con, it is a necessity that a leader comes forward to show, at the minimum, humanity and empathy with whatever tragedy has occurred and encourage their followers to do the same. When you are a leader in an organization or a political party or a community or whatever, others look to you for guidance on what to do next. In the case of al-Gaddafi, you can dispute his authenticity, but he did show his followers, at the very least, that outbursts outside the bounds of the solidarity would not be tolerated. You'll likely remember where you were when you heard the news on 9/11. I was at a conference in Toronto, and the President of the organization got up to speak following the news of the terrorist attacks. I vividly remember sensing that something was wrong as I watched his body language and saw the anguish in his eyes. All eyes were on him. Everyone in the audience sensed it, but we had no forewarning since we didn't have access to television, radio, or the Internet. When he got up to speak, he set the tone for how we would react. It was his delivery that set the tone for how we would conduct ourselves. He was calm but couldn't hold back his devastation. That is how we all spent the remainder of the day: calm and devastated. My tip today is if you are leading in the face of tragedy, remember that you will set the barometer of how your audience will react through your words and demeanor. Choose your words and the tone of your delivery carefully and thoughtfully.

Tip – Your words and conduct in tragedy will have a dramatic and lasting impression.

#164 – Eliezer Wiesel

1928–2016

Context – Writer, professor, political activist, and Holocaust survivor, Eliezer Wiesel, delivered "The Perils of Indifference" on April 12, 1999, in Washington D.C.

"Mr. President, Mrs. Clinton, members of Congress, Ambassador Holbrooke, Excellencies, friends:

"Fifty-four years ago, to the day, a young Jewish boy from a small town in the Carpathian Mountains woke up, not far from Goethe's beloved Weimar, in a place of eternal infamy called Buchenwald. He was finally free, but there was no joy in his heart. He thought there never would be again. Liberated a day earlier by American soldiers, he remembers their rage at what they saw. And even if he lives to be a very old man, he will always be grateful to them for that rage, and also for their compassion. Though he did not understand their language, their eyes told him what he needed to know—that they, too, would remember and bear witness.

"And now, I stand before you, Mr. President—Commander-in-Chief of the army that freed me and tens of thousands of others—and I am filled with a profound and abiding gratitude to the American people. "Gratitude" is a word that I cherish. Gratitude is what defines the humanity of the human being. And I am grateful to you, Hillary, or Mrs. Clinton, for what you said, and for what you are doing for children in the world, for the homeless, for the victims of injustice, the victims of destiny and society. And I thank all of you for being here.

"We are on the threshold of a new century, a new millennium. What will the legacy of this vanishing century be? How will it be remembered in the new millennium? Surely it will be judged, and judged severely, in both moral and metaphysical terms. These failures have cast a dark shadow over humanity: two World Wars, countless civil wars, the senseless chain of assassinations (Gandhi, the Kennedys, Martin Luther King, Sadat, Rabin), bloodbaths in Cambodia and Algeria, India and Pakistan, Ireland, and Rwanda, Eritrea, and Ethiopia, Sarajevo, and Kosovo; the inhumanity in the gulag and the tragedy of Hiroshima. And, on a different level, of course, Auschwitz and Treblinka. So much violence, so much indifference.

"What is indifference? Etymologically, the word means "no difference." A strange and unnatural state in which the lines blur between light and darkness, dusk and dawn, crime and punishment, cruelty, and compassion, good and evil. What are its courses and inescapable consequences? Is it a philosophy?
Is there a philosophy of indifference conceivable? Can one possibly view indifference as a virtue? Is it necessary at times to practice it simply to keep one's sanity, live normally, enjoy a fine meal and a glass of wine as the world around us experiences harrowing upheavals?

"Of course, indifference can be tempting—more than that, seductive. It is so much easier to look away from victims. It is so much easier to avoid such rude interruptions to our work, our dreams, our hopes. It is, after all, awkward, troublesome to be involved in another person's pain and despair. Yet, for the person who is indifferent, his or her neighbor are of no consequence. And, therefore, their lives are meaningless. Their hidden or even visible anguish is of no interest. Indifference reduces the Other to an abstraction.

"Over there, behind the black gates of Auschwitz, the most tragic of all prisoners were the "Muselmanner," as they were called. Wrapped in their torn blankets, they would sit or lie on the ground, staring vacantly into space, unaware of who or where they were—strangers to their surroundings. They no longer felt pain, hunger, thirst. They feared nothing. They felt nothing. They were dead and did not know it.

"Rooted in our tradition, some of us felt that to be abandoned by humanity then was not the ultimate. We felt that to be abandoned by God was worse than to be punished by Him. Better an unjust God than an indifferent one. For us to be ignored by God was a harsher punishment than to be a victim of His anger. Man can live far from God—not outside God. God is wherever we are. Even in suffering? Even in suffering.

"In a way, to be indifferent to that suffering is what makes the human being inhuman. Indifference, after all, is more dangerous than anger and hatred. Anger can, at times, be creative. One writes a great poem, a great symphony. One does something special for the sake of humanity because one is angry at the injustice that one witnesses. But indifference is never creative. Even hatred at times may elicit a response. You fight it. You denounce it. You disarm it.

"Indifference elicits no response. Indifference is not a response. Indifference is not a beginning; it is an end. And, therefore, indifference is always the friend of the enemy, for it benefits the aggressor—never his victim, whose pain is magnified when he or she feels forgotten. The political prisoner in his cell, the hungry children, the homeless refugees—not to respond to their plight, not to relieve their solitude by offering them a spark of hope is to exile them from human memory. And in denying their humanity, we betray our own.

"Indifference, then, is not only a sin, it is a punishment.

"And this is one of the most important lessons of this outgoing century's wide-ranging experiments in good and evil.

"In the place that I come from, society was composed of three simple categories: the killers, the victims, and the bystanders. During the darkest of times, inside the ghettoes and death camps—and I'm glad that Mrs. Clinton mentioned that we are now commemorating that event, that period, that we are now in the Days of Remembrance—but then, we felt abandoned, forgotten. All of us did.

And our only miserable consolation was that we believed that Auschwitz and Treblinka were closely guarded secrets; that the leaders of the free world did not know what was going on behind those black gates and barbed wire; that they had no knowledge of the war against the Jews that Hitler's armies and their accomplices waged as part of the war against the Allies. If they knew, we thought, surely those leaders would have moved heaven and earth to intervene. They would have spoken out with great outrage and conviction. They would have bombed the railways leading to Birkenau, just the railways, just once.

"And now we knew we learned, we discovered that the Pentagon knew, the State Department knew. And the illustrious occupant of the White House then, who was a great leader—and I say it with some anguish and pain, because today is exactly 54 years marking his death—Franklin Delano Roosevelt died on April the 12th, 1945. So, he is very much present to me and to us. No doubt, he was a great leader. He mobilized the American people and the world, going into battle, bringing hundreds and thousands of valiant and brave soldiers in America to fight fascism, to fight dictatorship, to fight Hitler. And so many of the young people fell in battle. And, nevertheless, his image in Jewish history—I must say it—his image in Jewish history is flawed.

"The depressing tale of the St. Louis is a case in point. Sixty years ago, its human cargo—nearly 1,000 Jews—was turned back to Nazi Germany. And that happened after the Kristallnacht, after the first state-sponsored pogrom, with hundreds of Jewish shops destroyed, synagogues burned, thousands of people put in concentration camps. And that ship, which was already in the shores of the United States was sent back. I don't understand. Roosevelt was a good man with a heart. He understood those who needed help. Why didn't he allow these refugees to disembark? A thousand people—in America, the great country, the greatest democracy, the most generous of all new nations in modern history. What happened? I don't understand. Why the indifference, on the highest level, to the suffering of the victims?

"But then, there were human beings who were sensitive to our tragedy. Those non-Jews, those Christians that we call the "Righteous Gentiles," whose selfless acts of heroism saved the honor of their faith. Why were they so few? Why was there a greater effort to save SS murderers after the war than to save their victims during the war? Why did some of America's largest corporations continue to do business with Hitler's Germany until 1942? It has been suggested, and it was documented, that the Wehrmacht could not have conducted its invasion of France without oil obtained from American sources. How is one to explain their indifference?

"And yet, my friends, good things have also happened in this traumatic century: the defeat of Nazism, the collapse of communism, the rebirth of Israel on its ancestral soil, the demise of apartheid, Israel's peace treaty with Egypt, the peace accord in Ireland. And let us remember the meeting, filled with drama and emotion, between Rabin and Arafat that you, Mr. President, convened in this very place. I was here, and I will never forget it.

"And then, of course, the joint decision of the United States and NATO to intervene in Kosovo and save those victims, those refugees, those who were uprooted by a man, whom I believe that because of his crimes, should be charged with crimes against humanity.

"But this time, the world was not silent. This time, we do respond. This time, we intervene.

"Does it mean that we have learned from the past? Does it mean that society has changed? Has the human being become less indifferent and more human? Have we really learned from our experiences? Are we less insensitive to the plight of victims of ethnic cleansing and other forms of injustices in places near and far? Is today's justified intervention in Kosovo, led by you, Mr. President, a lasting warning that never again will the deportation, the terrorization of children and their parents, be allowed anywhere in the world? Will it discourage other dictators in other lands to do the same?

"What about the children? Oh, we see them on television, we read about them in the papers, and we do so with a broken heart. Their fate is always the most tragic, inevitably. When adults wage war, children perish. We see their faces, their eyes. Do we hear their pleas? Do we feel their pain, their agony? Every minute one of them dies of disease, violence, famine.

"Some of them—so many of them—could be saved.

"And so, once again, I think of the young Jewish boy from the Carpathian Mountains. He has accompanied the old man I have become throughout these years of quest and struggle. And together, we walk towards the new millennium, carried by profound fear and extraordinary hope."

Analysis – To say that I am thrilled to present this speech to you would be an understatement. I have watched the clip and read the transcript more times than I can count. I've posted the entire transcript of Part One here and I encourage you to seek out Parts Two and Three, as Wiesel's delivery compels you to open your mind and ears. Each time I hear his speech, the tiny hairs on my arms stand straight up because his words come from truth, understanding and a deep desire to impact his audience through sharing his experiences. I love to be a participant in one of Wiesel's university classes in Boston. My hope for you today is that you will put down the remote control, delve into history, home in on an opinion, obtain a better understanding of the world and the injustices in them, get involved, and change people's lives. Inject what you uncover into all your presentations. Yes, even the most modest presentation on a random subject can affect an opinion and change how others view the world. It is your delivery that will determine whether people take you seriously or not. Take a page out of Wiesel's schooling and persuade your audience to open their minds and ears, and maybe, get the tiny hairs on their arms to stand up.

Tip – Inject meaning into all your presentations!

#163 – Elizabeth Barrett Browning

1806-1861

Context – Elizabeth Barrett Browning was certainly one of the most famous poets of the Victorian era. "How Do I Love Thee?" is most likely her most recognizable work. One of my favourite renditions of the poem is from *Be My Valentine, Charlie Brown* (1975), where the character of Sally reads the poem aloud while Snoopy mimes.

How do I love thee? Let me count the ways.
I love thee to the depth and breadth and height
My soul can reach, when feeling out of sight
For the ends of Being and ideal Grace.
I love thee to the level of every day's
Most quiet need, by sun and candlelight.
I love thee freely, as men strive for Right;
I love thee purely, as they turn from Praise.
I love with a passion put to use
In my old griefs, and with my childhood's faith.
I love thee with a love I seemed to lose
With my lost saints, I love thee with the breath,
Smiles, tears, of all my life! and, if God choose,
I shall but love thee better after death.

Analysis – These are some of the most beautiful words ever strung together to form a poem. It's interesting as Barrett Browning initially didn't want the poem to be published because she considered it too deeply personal. Her husband eventually persuaded her to share it and to him we are all forever grateful. Barrett Browning speaks from the heart, and when doing a presentation, that is all anyone can ask of you. There is so much energy wasted on nerves, anticipation and preparation where most of one's energy should be absorbed in honouring one's truth and speaking from a place of integrity.

If you've ever been a fan of Peanuts, the comic strip, and subsequent television specials—could we live without *A Charlie Brown Christmas*? I think not! It is beyond a classic and etched into my mind. You most likely have seen *Be My Valentine, Charlie Brown*, in which Sally recites Barrett Browning's poem. It is Snoopy rather than Sally that I'd like to channel your attention toward. Snoopy mimes each of the poem's words. So often, when we are giving a presentation, we deliver our words with the appropriate inflection and tone but fail to see the significance of our body language. Subconsciously, superb presenters will mime or use gestures, expressions and move to further punctuate their points.

Tip – Got mime? Channel your inner Snoopy and sprinkle some well-placed mime into your talk.

#162 – Sebastian Wernicke

(1983)

Context – Sebastian Wernicke, a Munich based data scientist, explains in his 2011 presentation, "1,000 TED Talks in Six Words" what good TED Talks have in common. This is a TED Talk on the ultimate TED Talk.

"There's currently over a thousand TED Talks on the TED website. And I guess many of you here think that this is quite fantastic, except for me, I don't agree with this. I think we have a situation here. Because if you think about it, 1,000 TED Talks, that's over 1,000 ideas worth spreading. How on earth are you going to spread a thousand ideas? Even if you just try to get all of those ideas into your head by watching all those thousand TED videos, it would actually currently take you over 250 hours to do so. And I did a little calculation of this. The damage to the economy for each one who does this is around $15,000. So having seen this danger to the economy, I thought, we need to find a solution to this problem.

Here's my approach to it all. If you look at the current situation, you have a thousand TED Talks. Each of those TED Talks has an average length of about 2,300 words. Now take this together, and you end up with 2.3 million words of TED Talks, which is about three Bibles-worth of content.

The obvious question here is, does a TED Talk really need 2,300 words? Isn't there something shorter? I mean, if you have an idea worth spreading, surely you can put it into something shorter than 2,300 words. The only question is, how short can you get? What's the minimum amount of words you would need to do a TED Talk?

While I was pondering this question, I came across this urban legend about Ernest Hemingway, who allegedly said that these six words here: "For sale: baby shoes, never worn," were the best novel he had ever written. And I also encountered a project called Six-Word Memoirs where people were asked, take your whole life and please sum this up into six words, such as these here: "Found true love, married someone else." Or "Living in existential vacuum; it sucks." I actually like that one. So, if a novel can be put into six words and a whole memoir can be put into six words, you don't need more than six words for a TED Talk. We could have been done by lunch here.

And if you did this for all thousand TED Talks, you would get from 2.3 million words down to 6,000. So I thought this was quite worthwhile.

So, I started asking all my friends, please take your favorite TED Talk and put that into six words. So here are some of the results that I received. I think they're quite nice. For example, Dan Pink's talk on motivation, which was pretty good, if you haven't seen it: "Drop carrot. Drop stick. Bring meaning." It's what he's basically talking about in those 18 and half minutes."

Analysis – This was one of the very first standing ovations I've seen resulting from a TED Talk. It is well earned! I have watched thousands of TED Talks, and this is reflective in this project, with nearly 40 percent of my entries coming from TED archives. I couldn't stop laughing during this talk—full-blown, hearty belly laughs. Good stuff. Wernicke is funny. Funny because boy, oh boy, does he know his topic. His quest is to create the ultimate TED Talk. He looks at the ideal topic to choose, the delivery, and the visuals one should use.

Some of Wernicke's tips include:

- Talk as long as they let you.
- Do not cite the *New York Times*.
- Fake intellectual capacity by saying et cetera et cetera.
- Let your hair grow a little longer than average.
- Make sure you wear your glasses.
- Slides are okay but you may want to consider props instead.
- Colour closely correlates with mood and the ratings on the TED website; fascinating talks contain blue, ingenious contain green, et cetera et cetera.

Wernicke created the TEDPad. It is a matrix of 100 specifically designed sentences that you can piece together to create your own TED Talk. The whole presentation is bloody hilarious. I adore it because while all his tips are so true, he delivers them in such a way that every person in the auditorium is listening with glee. Do you think he'll be invited back? Yup, that is guaranteed.

Tip – Use Wernicke's tips. My personal favourite is to fake intellectual capacity by peppering in the odd et cetera et cetera.

#161 – Antoine de Saint-Exupery

1900–1944

Context – Saint-Exupery was a French writer and aviator. He is likely best remembered for his novella, *The Little Prince*.

"Man imagines that it is death he fears, but what he fears is the unknown…"

Analysis – I have to say that there have only been a few occasions that I have experienced genuine fear: Childbirth and my first presentation. Childbirth most likely etches out my first presentation for the number one spot. There are many reasons why the baby takes nine months to incubate, and one of those is so that the soon-to-be Mom can prepare for and wrap her brain around the childbirth experience. As a bit of a hippie type, I didn't opt for an epidural, so most of my friends thought I was figuratively, metaphorically, and clinically insane. I remember committing to myself beforehand that no matter how bad the pain was, I would not take medication. There were a variety of reasons for that; one was the risk to the child, but the other robust reason was I wanted to have the experience and to be fully present in the moment. I knew the likelihood of dying was low, and women have been doing this since time immemorial, so why couldn't I? As I reflect on that experience, I can assure you that the fear I had leading up to the experience was much stronger than the actual event. I'm not going to say it didn't hurt a lot, because it did, but the fear of the unknown was much greater than the experience.

My first presentation happened during my second year of university, in a Political Geography class where we were informed in the first class that 100 percent of the final grade would come from a presentation on a country of our choice. When the second class rolled around, more than half the class had dropped out. To this day, I'm unsure why I too didn't drop the class as I had an immense fear of doing a presentation. Many of the class participants had never done a presentation before, so no one had a ton of experience under their belts. I was assigned South Africa and got lucky by having my name pulled to present later in the semester, so I had several months to prepare. I watched my classmates speak on their assigned countries in succession until finally it was my turn. I had done the work, and I had practiced, rehearsed, and had a brilliant presentation in my hands. But five minutes before the presentation was to begin, I was kissing the porcelain throne, because I had worked myself up into such a tizzy that I became physically ill. Somehow, I pulled myself together, walked on stage, and experienced every physiological reaction: sweating, blushing, stuttering. You name it, I did it. But I finished and scored an A-minus. It was the best A-minus I ever received. I won't lie, the next presentation I did was only slightly better than my first experience, but I learned a valuable lesson, the anticipation and fear of the unknown were much worse than the reality of the presentation. I learned by the third or fourth presentation that I needed to see the room before the presentation. I needed to feel the vibe before I walked on to do my thing. To this day, I still scout the room before the presentation. I see how I will set things up, and I envision my audience. I envision myself delivering the talk and practice aloud to get a feel for the acoustics in the room.

Tip – Lessen the fear of the unknown by familiarizing yourself with as much as you can before the presentation.

#160 – Clark Gable

Context – Clark Gable's closing scene in the 1939 movie, *Gone with the Wind*.

"Frankly, my dear, I don't give a damn."

Analysis – When we are talking about Must-Know Talks, which encapsulate all forms of the talking medium, it's only fair to include some of the greatest films of all time. *Gone with the Wind* features on many best movies lists. A while ago, I had the chance to blow four hours and sat down to watch this classic for the first time. Yup, it's good, and unlike so many movies today the story gets better as it progresses, and the ending, well the ending is infamous and classic, and this is the reason it's included on my list.

As Clark Gable's character Rhett Butler walks out of the door, planning to return to his hometown of

Charleston, Scarlett O'Hara, played by Vivian Leigh, pleads, "Rhett, if you go, where shall I go? What shall I do?" He famously answers, "Frankly, my dear, I don't give a damn," and walks away into the fog. O'Hara sits on her stairs and weeps in despair, "What is there that matters?" She then recalls the voices of her father Gerald, Ashley Wilkes (another of her love interests), and Butler, all of whom remind her that her strength comes from Tara, her father's plantation. Hope lights up O'Hara's face: "Tara! Home. I'll go home, and I'll think of some way to get him back! After all, tomorrow is another day!"

The ending of the film perfectly captures finality and new beginnings and is a stellar metaphor for presentations that is often overlooked. Leave your audience with a story, metaphor, or analogy that will have them sharing its meaning and implementing change or a new way of thinking immediately.

Tip – Pay special attention to the ending of your presentation. Be sure to mark finality and spark new beginnings.

#159 – William Shakespeare

1564–1616

Context – Shakespeare was an English poet and playwright. His surviving works consist of some 38 plays, 154 sonnets, and two long narrative poems.

"Hear the meaning within the word."

Analysis – The sound of the word will set the tone, mood, and feeling—this appears to be what Shakespeare is alluding to in the above quote. It goes beyond any of the posts we've tackled thus far on cadence or simply tone into the choice of word versus the inflection of the word. A cacophony is a harsh sound or a discordant mixture of sounds, but cacophony can also be used to describe word choice. For example, when explosive consonants, like T, P, K or B, and also C, CH, Q and X are used in prose. The word itself could be described as cacophonous because of its repetition of the "K" sound. They say that learning to speak French is one long exercise in the art of avoiding cacophony. On the contrary, euphony is a word, or more appropriately, a series of words that are pleasant to the ear. The famous monologue that starts, "To be, or not to be" in Shakespeare's *Hamlet* would be an example of euphony. Euphony is a mixture of harmonious words in arrangement, repetition, and flow of sound patterns. Shakespeare reminds us to take special care with our word choice, not only in written form, as he has so eloquently demonstrated many times, but also our spoken words. When was the last time that you thought about the words you would use to convey the message in your presentation? For me, I practice my thought process and the stories that I might tell, but they never sound the same twice. It's wise not to choose every word, as your presentation could become robotic. Instead, choose a few euphonious words that you know will make a dramatic impact.

Tip – Choose some euphony-inspired words before your presentation!

#158 – Oscar Wilde

1854–1900

Context – Oscar Wilde was an Irish writer and poet.

"Most people are other people. Their thoughts are someone else's opinions, their lives a mimicry, their passions a quotation."

Analysis – I wholeheartedly agree with Wilde on the above and this is the primary reason for including his quote today. Wilde was not a fan of mimicry, and neither am I, for the most part. In one of the first presentation skills classes I took in my early 20s, the facilitator encouraged us to think about a speaker we admired, or thought was particularly effective and imitate or mimic them. This exercise is a good one, but the challenge is when people get stuck with what works and lose themselves in the process. I have had great success and significant failure with this exercise. In my first position in sales, I found myself mimicking a popular self-help and self-anointed guru. That did not come across very well at all. I ended up looking like one of those jacked-up infomercial types. Nope, not good at all. In contrast, while I was struggling to find my presentation voice, I took on the personae of one of my mentors. I learned a great deal from that experience, as her personality type was the opposite to mine. I learned through that experience how to sit in silence, to be calmer in disposition, listen, answer questions appropriately, etc.

I quickly realized, though, that adopting that more successful disposition as my own would not be congruent with who I am, a rather boisterous and loud presenter. I do believe, however, that you must be able to come in and out of who you are naturally so that all personality types in your audience can hear you. As an example, if I stay as energetic and rowdy as I would naturally like to during a presentation, I will inevitably tick off my more introverted audience members. Being a presenter is much like being the conductor of a roller coaster ride; you go up and down your natural style, adopting opposite styles to your own so that you keep all members of your audience not only listening but truly digesting your message.

Tip – Find your own natural style through imitating others.

#157 – Jean-Jacques Rousseau

1712–1778

Context – Born in Switzerland but raised in France, Rousseau was a writer, musical theorist, composer, and philosopher. The below quote is from one of his writings: *The Discourse on Inequality*.

"The first man who, having fenced in a piece of land, said 'This is mine,' and found people naive enough to believe him, that man was the true founder of civil society. From how many crimes, wars, and murders, from how many horrors and misfortunes might not any one have saved mankind, by pulling up the stakes or filling up the ditch and crying to his fellows: Beware of listening to this impostor; you are undone if you once forget that the fruits of the earth belong to us all, and the earth itself to nobody."

Analysis – Rousseau discussed two types of inequality: natural or physical, and ethical or political. He is, as I am, more interested in looking at the topic of ethical or natural inequality. Rousseau says, "man has strayed from his natural state of isolation and consequent freedom to satisfy his individual needs and desires." He argues that moral inequality is endemic to civil society and is the reason for differences in power and wealth. Society is a bad influence and is corrupted by civilization, and man should remain in the natural state. He also believed that morals are innate and not resulting from society. So, the quote above is Rousseau's opinion that civilization has always been artificial, promoting inequality and envy. This is a brief synopsis indeed, but I'd like to extrapolate from it the idea of not adopting the points of view of others as your own, on the first merit. I believe this is the nucleus of why Rousseau is so darn cynical. Whether you're an audience member or the presenter, you should question new ideas and form your own opinions. Too often, we hear someone speak eloquently, and wrongly assume this equals truth. This is not always the case! Take in new information and form your own opinion. Do not regurgitate someone else's point of view while doing a presentation. Be unique!

Tip – Take in new information and form your own opinion.

#156 – Tony Robbins

(1960)

I Am Not Your Guru, a 2016 documentary, goes behind the scenes of Robbins' mammoth, "Date With Destiny," seminar is attended by over 2,500 people in Boca Raton, Florida, each year, gives an insider look at how one man can affect millions. This film provides never before seen access to the behind-the-scenes modus operandi of this enormous event and captures both the immense effort of producing this live seminar, as well as the life-changing transformations of the participants in real time.

Context – Tony Robbins speaks at TED in 2006 on "Why We Do What We Do, and How We Can Do It Better," in front of an audience that includes the former United States Vice President Al Gore. The below is taken from the 5-minute mark of the talk.

Tony Robbins: *"We've got to remind ourselves that decision is the ultimate power. When you ask people, have you failed to achieve something significant in your life?"*

Tony Robbins: *"Say, Aye."*

Audience: *"Aye."*

Tony Robbins: *"Thanks for the interaction on a high level there. But if you ask people, why didn't you achieve something? Somebody who's working for you, or a partner, or even yourself. When you fail to achieve, what's the reason people say? What do they tell you? Didn't have the knowledge, didn't have the money, didn't have the time, didn't have the technology. I didn't have the right manager."*

Al Gore (from the audience): *"Supreme Court"*

Tony Robbins: *"The Supreme Court. What do all those, including the Supreme Court, have in common?"*

Analysis – I'd like to draw your attention to the five-minute mark of this talk as it demonstrates an essential part of any presentation—audience interaction.

Do I think Tony Robbins is the best speaker out there? No, I don't. I'd love for him to hire me (this is tongue-in-cheek here, folks, but I think I could cast light on a few things and suggest ways to improve. To tell Robbins how to change some pretty darn annoying habits he has (insert "say Aye" here). But one of the reasons Robbins is so popular and has remained popular is his ability to be in the moment and interact with his audience. He does this exceptionally well. His 2010 television show *Breakthrough* with Tony Robbins, his Netflix film, *I Am Not Your Guru* saw Robbins interacting one-on-one with people to make dramatic changes in their lives. In terms of his TED Talk, he is very planned, and he knows his content so well that five minutes into his talk, when Robbins asks the audience what kinds of reasons people give for not achieving their goals, and Al Gore shouts out, "Supreme Court!" Robbins gets his butt off the stage and high fives Gore and follows up with some banter directed specifically at Gore. As a professional speaker, I hope Robbins reviews his clips to see that when he is at his best, he is lost in interaction; his speech slows down to a more manageable cadence and he's just more likable. Robbins teaches each of us a fundamental presentation skills lesson—the actual stage isn't your only stage! You can move around, even step into the audience to add excitement to your delivery. At around 19 minutes, Robbins further demonstrates my point: he stops his story short at a place where he has his audience in the palm of his hands listening intently and pretends to walk off stage as he is out of time. The audience bellows back with *oohs* and *ahhs*. That interaction shows that Robbins is not lecturing but forming stories and building experiences with his audience. His presentation becomes a collective experience instead of an individual one.

Tip – Form experiences with your audience during every single presentation.

#155 – Dr. Seuss

1904–1991

Context – Dr. Seuss (Theodor Seuss Geisel) wrote *The Sneetches and Other Stories,* which is a collection of stories that include *The Sneetches*, *The Zax*, *Too Many Daves* and *What Was I Scared of?*

But, because they had stars, all the Star-Belly Sneetches

Would brag, "We're the best kind of Sneetch on the Beaches."

With their snoots in the air, they would sniff and they'd snort

"We'll have nothing to do with the Plain-Belly sort!"

And whenever they met some, when they were out walking,

They'd hike right on past them without even talking.

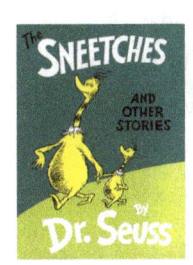

Analysis – This is probably one of Dr. Seuss's most unrecognizable books, but boy, oh, boy, it's good! If you haven't read *The Sneetches* or *The Zax*, then you need to now. *The Sneetches* is a story about prejudice, discrimination, and materialism. It is, as with all of Seuss' books, a great commentary on society, all wrapped up under the guise of a children's book. Seuss writes on so many levels; he's a poet, a philosopher, and he's whimsical and funny. In some of the best presentations I've encountered, the speaker delivers in a similar style. This, my friends, takes wit and intellect. It is like a living, breathing allegory—an allegory is a story with two meanings: a literal meaning and a symbolic meaning. This layering of meaning is what makes a book, a great book and it's what makes a talk, a great talk.

Tip – Use allegories and hidden meanings to convey your message.

#154 – Robin Williams

1951–2014

Context – Robin Williams as the energetic English teacher John Keating in the 1989 film, *Dead Poets Society.*

"Because, you see gentlemen, these boys are now fertilizing daffodils. But if you listen real close, you can hear them whisper their legacy to you. Go on, lean in. Listen, you hear it? – Carpe – hear it? – Carpe, carpe diem, seize the day boys, make your lives extraordinary."

Analysis – Oh, how I adore this movie especially the "Carpe Diem" scene , that introduces Keating and his very different teaching style to the young men in his class who are unaccustomed with and frankly, haven't a clue what to do in the situation. Imagine having a teacher like Keating. They have been told when and how to speak, what to wear and how to behave for so long that they don't know how to interact with their new teacher. "O captain, my captain" or "Mr. Keating" are the options he gives for how he would like to be addressed. Of course, the students opt for the fun and unique moniker. He mixes fun with calm, brilliant intellectual food for the poetic brain. He bridges the gap and breaks down the barriers between him and the students and lets them know that he is in no way shape or form superior to them. He bridges the gap to their ancestors who attended the school before them. He makes all equal. By making everyone equal, he opens all kinds of possibilities, and shatters the patterns to which the students have become accustomed. Keating wants them to seize the day and delivers a class or presentation that couldn't be rehearsed. Practiced yes, rehearsed no. You see, if it had been rehearsed, it would have been recited from a piece of paper or delivered robotically and without class interaction. Instead he knows the direction that he wants to take the class without necessarily knowing each word he will use to get them there. He knows the nucleus of his talk will be Carpe Diem and to teach it requires him to transmit real emotion with more than just words. He let the class's digestion of the information guide his teaching. Rare indeed. If you want to deliver a superb presentation in the real world, go ahead. Give this a try. I call it presenting on the fly. However, it takes some skill and only the most well-practiced individuals may enter this territory, for it requires the presenter to know their content to its core.

Tip – Present by creating an equal field and by shattering presentation patterns.

#153 – Al Pacino

(1949)

Context – Al Pacino in the 1999 sports film *Any Given Sunday*, depicting a fictional professional football team. Pacino plays Tony D'Amato, the coach.

"We can fight our way back, into the light, out of hell, one inch at a time. Now I can't do it for you; I'm too old. I look around, and I see these young faces and I think I made every wrong choice a young man can make. I lost all my money. I chased off anyone that loved me, and lately I can't even stand the face I see in the mirror…life is a game of inches. The margin for error is so small…the inches we need are everywhere around us…on this team, we fight for that inch…When we add up all those inches that is going to be the difference between winning or losing…Now, what are you going to do?"

Analysis – I'm not the biggest football fan out there, but I am a fan of this speech, delivered with nothing less than brilliance by Al Pacino. Watch it through once and notice how his delivery is like a great piece of classical music. It starts slow and quiet and builds to a crescendo until the audience is so filled with emotion that they must take action. Have you ever delivered a talk of inspiration? A talk in which you must find a way to inspire, motivate, encourage, influence, energize and spark action in your listeners? Usually, the inspirational talk will ask you to do something at the end, as Pacino does in his speech, inspiring his team to win. It is, in my estimation, one of the most challenging talks to do well. It takes the ability to tug on your audience members' emotions to be effective. It requires the speaker to be willing and able to open themselves up and tell stories about their struggle—Pacino talks about being broke and not having love—it takes courage to expose yourself in this way. For this type of talk to be successful, the speaker has to connect with their audience by sharing their struggles so that the audience are sufficiently moved to take action. Be courageous enough to share your story with others. You never know, you may help others going through a similar struggle in the process. Words, a talk, a speech can have far more impact than you may think.

Tip – In delivering the inspirational talk, connect with your audience by sharing your own struggles.

#152 – James Veitch

(1980)

Context – Writer and comedian James Veitch's 2015 TED Talk, "This Is What Happens When You Reply to Spam Email" recounts a weeks-long exchange with a spammer who offered to cut Veitch in on a hot gold deal.

"A few years ago, I got one of those spam emails. And it managed to get through my spam filter. I'm not quite sure how, but it turned up in my inbox, and it was from a guy called Solomon Odonkoh.

I know.

It went like this: it said, 'Hello James Veitch, I have an interesting business proposal I want to share with you, Solomon.' Now, my hand was kind of hovering on the delete button, right? I was looking at my phone. I thought I could just delete this. Or I could do what I think we've all always wanted to do.

And I said, 'Solomon, your email intrigues me.'

And the game was afoot.

He said, 'Dear James Veitch, we shall be shipping Gold to you. You will earn 10% of any gold you distributes.'

So, I knew I was dealing with a professional…"

Analysis – The entertaining talk should be captivating and maintain the audience's attention with every word. Veitch's talk delivers! His message is simple. It amuses and tickles the funny bone and puts the audience in his shoes as he does what many of us have always wanted to do when we receive a spam email.

An entertaining talk is a little different from other talks. Veitch's talk is funny, no question. His deadpan delivery is brilliant. His well-timed pauses, body language, the cadence of his sentence structure and gentle smirks are what make his talk unique. There is a natural mystique about Veitch that has his audience intrigued about what is coming next.

When I looked at the words on the page and, in the absence of James' delivery, it's not that funny. It's his delivery that makes it truly entertaining. When Veitch gets to the part of the exchange with the spammer when he convinces him to use code words because he is concerned about security, the audience is beside themselves with laughter.

The visuals Veitch uses in his talk are impressively simple. He shows the email exchanges and a straightforward graph. Veitch has a light in his eyes right before delivering each punchline, and he knows he has his audience in the palm of his hands immediately. I'd want to invite Veitch to my next dinner party. You know that he has an arsenal of humorous stories and that he'd wait for just the right moment to share.

Tip – Bake mystery into your talks to make your audience eager for more.

#151 – Lia Mills

(1996)

Context – In 2009, in front of a crowd of more than 10,000, 12-year-old Lia Mills delivered a pro-life speech on Parliament Hill in Ottawa, Canada.

"What if I told you that, right now, someone was choosing if you were going to live or die?...

Thousands of children are right now in that very situation, that someone is their mother. And that choice is abortion...

Fetuses are definitely human beings, knit together in the womb by their wonderful creator."

Analysis – It is no wonder this video went viral. Let's remove the debate component entirely and look at Mills as a speaker. Firstly, bravo to Mills' parents. Bravo! Here is a girl who has developed a firm opinion on a controversial issue. I wish most people I encounter had the same resolve to read into, source out information, and make a compelling argument on any one point, let alone one surrounded by such intense debate. For those who are cynical and say Mills has been force-fed this information by her parents, this doesn't appear to be the case based on my research. It also seems that Mills is a very bright, thoughtful, and articulate young girl in her own right. But this is not my focus. My focus is on the quality of Mills' delivery, and this is the reason the speech has hit my list of *365 Must-Know Talks*. I want to highlight two things that you can take into your next presentations from Mills' speech—the beginning and the end. In the beginning, Mills asks several times, "What if I told you…" in quick succession. She doesn't introduce herself, doesn't banter, she gets right down to it. Her talk is filled with facts, figures, stories, analogies, and definitions, all intended to build her argument. The succession of questions right at the fore is incredibly effective, and I encourage you to weave this technique into your upcoming presentations. Asking questions in this way stops the audience in their tracks and makes them think about their opinion on the subject, which is precisely what you want your audience to do—to think about and mull over what you are saying. Now, the end. Mills finishes by quoting Dr. Seuss, "Even though you can't see them at all, a person's a person no matter how small." Ending with a quote is a highly effective way to wrap up her eight-minute speech. Mills has been delivering her talk much as an adult would, so to hear a little Seuss from a 12-year-old seems appropriate. This technique is also effective because Seuss is so famous and *Horton Hears a Who* was popular with its movie release a few years previously. Most people will be familiar with the story and can immediately think about the book and movie and bridge it to her content. Very effective. Finally, finishing any talk with a quote is one of my little secrets. One can practice beforehand, and it ends a talk with polish instead of a hollow "Thank You."

Tip – Start with a question, end with a quote.

#150 – Spider-Man

Context – Known as the Peter Parker principle, the quote originates and popularized from the Spider-Man Marvel comic series.

Peter snaps at Uncle Ben as he tries to impart some wisdom onto his nephew: "With great power comes great responsibility."

Analysis – I have always remembered this quote from my youth, Spider-Man's Uncle Ben imparting these words of wisdom. You don't need me to decipher what that meant in relation to the comic. It's obvious. But as it relates to presentation skills, it isn't as obvious. Every time you do a presentation, realize that you are in a position of power; no matter what type of presentation you are delivering, people listen to you. You are in a position to influence your audience. There is responsibility with that position, and you need to act and behave accordingly. Many years ago, I had the opportunity to hire a speaker to come to one of my leadership workshops. He was to impart his life story to inspire an audience that was filled with people who held senior positions in an international organization. There was the CEO and regional presidents and vice presidents within the company. The speaker came in, delivered his hour-long keynote address, and did a fabulous job. Each of the attendees was energized, inspired, and motivated, following his address. That evening we all went out for dinner, and the speaker joined us. After a few too many cocktails, he said and did some things that I'm sure he regretted later. The following day we had a full program of workshop material and exercises to cover. Several of the attendees commented on the keynote speaker's behaviour from the previous night. One person said what many others were no doubt feeling, "His conduct last night lessened my opinion of him and thus made the contents of his speech less valuable." I couldn't have agreed more. It was disappointing. You have a great responsibility when you've been asked to do a talk, behave professionally with integrity, honesty, and respect both on and off stage.

Tip – Remember your audience is watching you both on and off stage, so behave accordingly.

#149 – Anthony Michael Hall

(1968)

Context – From the 1985 film, *The Breakfast Club*, where five high school students from different walks of life endure a Saturday detention. Here brainy Brian played by Anthony Michale Hall, writes an essay on behalf of the group to the school's principal.

"Dear Mr. Vernon, we accept the fact that we had to sacrifice a whole Saturday in detention for whatever it was we did wrong, but we think you're crazy to make us write an essay telling you who we think we are. You see us as you want to see us: in the simplest terms and the most convenient definitions. But what we found out is that each one of us is a brain … and an athlete … and a basket case … a princess … and a criminal. Does that answer your question? Sincerely yours, the Breakfast Club."

Analysis – I have quoted the above more times than probably any other movie quote I have in the corners of my brain. This quote and scene from the movie are fabulous on so many levels. If, like me, you were an angsty teenager in the 80s, this quote will likely have been your anthem. If you look at the words and the delivery, if would be fair to assume that it would be much more assertive and bolder than the way Hall delivers it—Hall gives the words an eerie and thoughtful approach. I enjoy when a speaker turns a line on its head and delivers it in an unexpected or unconventional way. By delivering a line that isn't congruent with the words, you create a different mood, and the vibe changes. Often, you get a fantastic result as the audience will lean in to hear, especially if the delivery has been chosen to be soft and overly annunciated, as is the example here.

Tip – Turn the delivery of your presentation on its head and deliver its components in an unconventional way.

#148 – Conan O'Brien

(1963)

Context – Conan O'Brien's 2000 Harvard class day speech.

"I'd like to begin by thanking the class marshals for inviting me here today. The last time I was invited to Harvard it cost me $110,000. So, I was reluctant to show up.

I'm going to start before I really begin by announcing my one goal this afternoon. I want to be half as funny as tomorrow's commencement speaker, moral philosopher and economist Amartya Sen. That's the job. Must get more laughs than seminal wage-price theoretician. By the way, enjoy that. Bring a calculator. It's going to be a nerd fest.

Students of the Harvard Class of 2000, 15 years ago I sat where you sit now. And I thought exactly what you are now thinking. What's going to happen to me? Will I find my place in the world? Am I really graduating a virgin? Still have 24 hours. Roommate's mom very hot. Swear she's checking me out. There was that Rob Lowe movie.

Being here today, on a sincere note, is very special for me. I do miss this place. I especially miss Harvard Square.

Let me tell you, you don't know this, Harvard Square is extremely unique. Nowhere else in the world will you find a man wearing a turban and a Red Sox jacket working in a lesbian bookstore. I'm just glad my dad's working.

It's particularly sweet for me to be here today because—this is true—when I graduated, I wanted very badly to be a Class Day speaker. Unfortunately, my speech was rejected. So, if you'll indulge me I'd like to read a portion of that speech. This is the actual speech from 15 years ago. "Fellow students, as we sit here today listening to that classic A-ha tune which will definitely stand the test of time, I would like to make several predictions about what the future will hold. I believe that one day a simple governor from a small southern state will rise to the highest office in the land. He will lack political skill but will lead on the sheer strength of his moral authority. I believe that justice will prevail and one day the Berlin Wall will crumble, uniting East and West Berlin forever under Communist rule. I believe that one day a high-speed network of interconnected computers will spring up worldwide, so enriching people that they will lose their interest in idle chitchat and pornography. And finally, I believe that one day I will have a television show on a major network seen by millions of people at night which I will use to re-enact crimes and help catch at-large criminals.

Then I had a section on the death of Wall Street, but you don't need to hear about that…"

Analysis – You may think, "Yeah, this is a funny speech, but I'm no comedian so what does this have to do with me and the presentation I have tomorrow?" Whether you are launching into your first presentation or your thousandth, we all can learn valuable lessons by watching stand-up comedians before giving a talk. The delivery; yes, the cadence; yes, the well-timed pauses; yes. But I got to thinking, what is it about the comedian that makes us watch? I mean, in the belly of it all, why do we watch them? And can that trait be transferred to the public speaker arena, one that isn't particularly or naturally funny? Then I came across something the famous radio comedian and entertainer Jack Benny said, "There has to be something more than just getting laughs. Laughs are not everything. People can scream at a comedian and yet can't remember anything afterwards to talk about. To become successful, they must like you very much —they must have a feeling, like, 'Gee, I wish he was a friend of mine. I wish he was a relative.'" Boom. That's it! I read this and had the realization that this is exactly what a public speaker needs to do. Whether you are doing a corporate speech, an inspirational speech, a sales speech, an entertaining speech, an informative speech, a persuasive speech, a demonstrative speech, or whatever type of speech: the audience must like you, I mean really like you as Benny says, "they should want to be your friend and to hang out with you." How do you do that? You watch lots of comedians in action as they do it best.

Tip – Be likeable. The goal is for your audience to want to be your friend.

#147 – Voltaire

1694–1778

Context – The first appearance of this quote is in a 1906 book, *The Friends of Voltaire*, by Evelyn Beatrice Hall in 1906.

"I disapprove of what you say, but I will defend to the death your right to say it."

Analysis – This is a great, fabulous, amazing quote! Voltaire was widely known in the enlightenment circles of his time for his defense of civil liberties. As a presenter, never forget that your audience is made up of individuals with their very own ideas, points of view, and opinions. Presenters should welcome opposing views. Maybe you'll learn something new. Many presenters that I work with forget it is not necessarily your job to change, alter or convert your audience's point of view to your message, but to shine a light on your point of view. If you've done your job properly, you won't come across as arrogant but instead as someone with a fresh vantage point. If you've done your job properly, the person in your audience who may have an opposing view may say, "I never thought of it that way." And if you've listened to your audience, you may say the same thing in return. I like to think of it as 'an open-door policy on a grand scale where everyone feels they can share their opinion, knowing they will not be judged but will be listened to and heard. Isn't that what we are all here for?

Tip – Have an open-door policy in your presentations.

#146 – John Mayer

(1977)

Context – John Mayer on *VH1 Storytellers* in 2010.

"You know it's hard to talk about songs without talking about relationships. And that's what people like to talk about. And I sing about relationships, and I have to talk about them since this is called Storytellers. I loved a girl a lot. And I had an experience that a lot of guys have. I loved the girl a lot, but she couldn't trust man and if you traced it back as to why it was the first man in her life that she couldn't trust. And I know this song Daughters sounds a lot like I'm just sitting around the house spit balling, but it really is as result of trying to figure out how to love this person, but you can't…."

Analysis – There was a television show on VH1 called *Storytellers*. It was a great show where music artists talk intimately with their audience and their fans in a relaxed setting. The artists tell stories and take questions. In my estimation, Mayer is the most adept at being himself (there are six episodes on YouTube if you're interested). Now, someone out there in blog land may say, "Well, Caroline, have you met John Meyer, and do you know definitively that he is being himself?" Well, no, I've not met Meyer, but yes, after watching all six parts of the series, I feel like we are on a first-name basis. Here's the deal, you can just tell when someone is being authentic, and you can tell when someone is putting on an act. There are 1,000 gradients in between, and most people are pretty good at deciphering where someone fits on the authenticity scale. Being yourself comes with practice and to do so in front of such a crowd is a skill. Take Meyer's ability to tell a story. He does this very well, it's not rehearsed, or driven from any other place but to convey the inspiration behind some of his songs. Notice how he uses his guitar to show something he calls "liquidy." What this shows is his desire to use his own prop to develop and enhance the story. I've written about this countless times, but it is shown here perfectly. The other reason why I've chosen this clip is the fact that he restarts his song, not once but twice, and not only gets away with it but comes across as endearing. You can't do this if you are constantly striving for perfection. To seek perfection in any performance, whether performing as an artist or a keynote speaker, would manifest into a stiff, robotic, type-A-style delivery. When you loosen up you allow yourself to make mistakes and that creates the kind of an environment that I like to be in—creative, non-judgmental, and fun.

Tip – Loosen up, embrace imperfections, and roll with your mistakes.

#145 – Steve Ballmer

(1956)

Context – Steve Ballmer at the Microsoft convention in 2011 going crazy on stage.

Steve Ballmer (screaming and sweating profusely): *"Get up, get up, getup, let's go, come on, woohoo, woohoo, come on, who said sit down! I have four words for you. I love this company! Yaaaasssss."*

Analysis – So far I've only mentioned one other talk that I absolutely, 100 percent cannot advocate or promote or celebrate. I'm including this entry as another firm example of what *not* to do in your presentations as sometimes this is the best way to demonstrate the point. My list of Must-Know Talks is not necessarily made up entirely of ones that I love. In your search browser, just type in "Steve Ballmer goes crazy," there are many examples. How does it make you feel? I feel anxiety and pity for Ballmer because he feels the need to pretend that he is pumped up to motivate his audience of employees. I fear he may have a heart attack (I'm not kidding, this thought crossed my mind several times). When I watched this talk for the first time, I kept asking, "Why is he behaving like this? Does he think that putting on this act will translate into true and real energy?" We've talked a lot about being authentic and finding a way to do that while on stage, and we've devoted plenty of time to exploring this area. When you put on a show, and don't act within the bounds of who you naturally are, it comes across as fake and it's really difficult to watch.

That said, I know Ballmer was trying to get the audience's energy up, and trying to get his employees genuinely excited, trying to motivate them for a long day of talks, new learnings, exercises, etc. I understand all this. If I were to be hired to work with Ballmer, the very first thing I'd do is make him watch this talk ten times in a row, with no discussion or comment and ask him at the end of that exercise: "Now, how do you feel after watching that clip?" I guarantee he would express some of the similar emotions I have above. After reviewing his own performance, he may not even need my coaching in terms of tools and techniques for his presentation skills. This is why there is so much importance on having your presentations videotaped. You are the best person to provide yourself with feedback. That is, if you're prepared to be honest with yourself.

Tip – Record and review your presentations so you can provide yourself with honest feedback.

#144 – Robert Pio Hajjar (1977)

Context – Robert Pio Hajjar is a motivational speaker. He founded of the charity *Ideal-Way.ca* in 2006 with his life savings of $62.05.

"31 years ago, I was born, and the doctors told my parent to put me away. Bye. And from then they said I would not walk, or talk, or do what other kids do, they painted a very sad picture of my life and my future. My parents said I was a gift from God, and they would never give me away. I took a little longer to do things, but each step was a victory for me. DS does not stop me from living a happy and meaningful life. I have done so many things in my life. I will forgive me if you call me handicapped or retarded. Because you didn't know me. As the philosopher Eric Fromm "Men are born equal, but they are also born different…"

Analysis – Pio Hajjar quotes Erik Fromm, a German sociologist, humanistic philosopher, psychologist, psychoanalysts, sociologist, in his talk: "Men are born equal, but they are also born different." And to that I say, "Hallelujah!" This post is everything #145 is not: it is controlled, authentic, and fun, and it has a profound and lasting message. Pio Hajjar started the charity Ideal-Way in 2006 to give a voice to the people who cannot speak. His mission is for people with disabilities to feel IDEAL: Included, Deserving, Equal, Appreciated and Loved. It's a pretty awesome goal if you ask me and it's a goal that we should have for ourselves, and for those around us.

Pio Hajjar was born with Down syndrome in 1977, and doctors told his parents they should put him into an institution. His parents were told he wouldn't be able to walk, talk, or do what other kids do, as if those are the only characteristics of value in a person. I hope that Pio Hajjar's parents sent the doctors a copy of this clip. Pio Hajjar learned to walk and talk, which are great skills, but the most crucial skill that Pio Hajjar possesses is his kind, nurturing, and caring nature. His message is love, inclusion, equality, encouraging others and that it is possible to beat the odds if you have the right attitude. A great presentation should get you out of, or at least to the edge of your seat. It should take you on a roller-coaster ride of emotion, it should compel you to take action and to use positivity to accomplish your goals. As a virtual member of Pio Hajjar's audience, I certainly feel energized to do just that. Bravo, Robert! Bravo.

Tip – Take your audience on a roller-coaster ride of emotion and motivate them to do what you are asking of them.

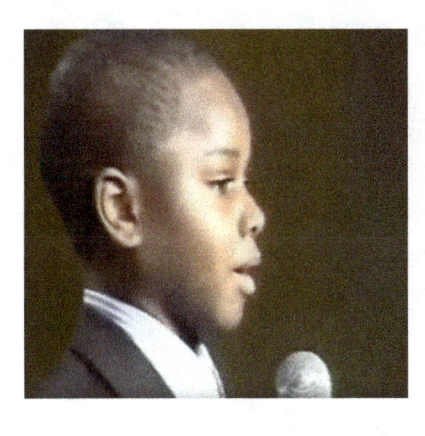

#143 – Jonathan McCoy

(1997)

Context – In 2009, 11-year-old Jonathan McCoy, delivered a speech to a congregation of more than 1,500 at the Empowerment Temple in Balitmore, MD on eliminating the n-word.

"According to the definition of the n-word, an n-word will never be a lawyer, a doctor, or a teacher…It is implausible that 40 years after the assassination of Dr. Martin Luther King Jr., that we still use this word that holds no worth in our lives and our future"

Analysis – After watching this video I came to a new realization; anyone over the age of ten can learn a thing or two or maybe even a thousand from this talk. I do enjoy watching children give speeches. They are often better at it than adults are, as they haven't been indoctrinated with social filters. Sure, they may sound rehearsed, but they are able to pull themselves out of that container fast, way faster than the rest of us. McCoy is simply awesome! This is what you call an amazing, well-rehearsed, deeply moving speech. Period. In your next presentation, take a page from McCoy's presentation book and use history as the foundation of your presentation. Lay each block carefully, allowing each to grow bigger and bigger until your presentation's crescendo. Notice how you've heard of the individuals he mentions, but he makes them sound bolder, bigger, and more impactful when pulled together as a cohesive unit. Heck, you may even want to throw in a song at the end as McCoy does, if you are so inclined. I will forget many talks over my time I'm sure, as I've watched 1,000s on video and in person, but I guarantee I will never forget this one.

Tip – Use history as the building blocks of your presentation.

#142 – George H.W. Bush

1924–2018

Context – George H. W. Bush Sr. and George W. Bush are the first father and sons to attain the Presidency since John Quincy and John Quincy Adams. Bush Sr. delivered this talk at the 1988 Republican National Convention known as the "Thousand Points of Light" speech.

"And I'm the one who will not raise taxes. My opponent now says he'll raise them as a last resort or a third resort. But when a politician talks like that, you know that's one resort he'll be checking into. My opponent, my opponent won't rule out raising taxes. But I will. And the Congress will push me to raise taxes and I'll say no. And they'll push, and I'll say no, and they'll push again, and I'll say, to them, 'Read my lips: no new taxes."

Analysis – This speech is monotone and lackluster, but the contents are what make it a must on any list of Must-Know Talks including my own. This speech lifted the presidential candidate's poll ratings while on the campaign trail. If you've been following me at all, you'll know that with very few exceptions, I highlight talks from people who I consider to have mentorship skills and strength of character, the kind of traits we should aspire to develop. This is not the case with this entry. Once again, I'm providing an example of what not to do in a speech. Here, Bush promises the world as it relates to taxes (in the same speech, he drones on about his support for gun rights and the fact that the Pledge of Allegiance in schools should be mandatory amongst other nonsensical commitments). The above quote has become a defining soundbite to Bush's entire presidency because, once elected, he raised taxes. The Bill O'Reilly's of the world might be able to build some lame argument as to why, but no matter how you look at it, he did exactly what he said he wouldn't do, period. This parlays nicely into all presentations that you may have on the horizon. It's easy to overcommit or promise more than you can deliver in the heat of the moment, but this is not the legacy you want to leave behind. Think before you speak, and, if anything, under-promise, and over-deliver. Keep your integrity in check.

Tip – It's always best to under promise and over deliver so be sure to say what you mean and mean what you say.

#141 – Abraham Lincoln

1809–1865

Context – Abraham Lincoln delivers The Gettysburg Address, November 19, 1863.

"Fourscore and seven years ago our fathers brought forth, on this continent, a new nation, conceived in liberty, and dedicated to the proposition that all men are created equal. Now we are engaged in a great civil war, testing whether that nation, or any nation so conceived, and so dedicated, can long endure.

We are met on a great battlefield of that war. We have come to dedicate a portion of that field, as a final resting-place for those who here gave their lives, that that nation might live. It is altogether fitting and proper that we should do this. But, in a larger sense, we cannot dedicate, we cannot consecrate—we cannot hallow—this ground. The brave men, living and dead, who struggled here, have consecrated it far above our poor power to add or detract. The world will little note, nor long remember what we say here, but it can never forget what they did here. It is for us the living, rather, to be dedicated here to the unfinished work which they who fought here have thus far so nobly advanced. It is rather for us to be here dedicated to the great task remaining before us—that from these honored dead we take increased devotion to that cause for which they here gave the last full measure of devotion—that we here highly resolve that these dead shall not have died in vain—that this nation, under God, shall have a new birth of freedom, and that government of the people, by the people, for the people, shall not perish from the earth."

Analysis – During the dedication ceremony for the Soldiers' National Cemetery, President Lincoln gave a two-minute talk, which has become one of the best known and most influential in American history. In that two-minute speech he eloquently pays tribute to the thousands of men who had died during the Civil War battle at Gettysburg. He redefined the war as one with the goal of freedom, rather than a struggle between states. He reignited the Declaration of Independence, and finally he inspired his listeners to increase their devotion and commitment so that the deaths of so many would not be in vain. And he managed to so this in just two minutes. 120 seconds. In one of my workshops on presentation skills, I have an exercise where the participants present a two-minute speech to the group. Someone will always say, "That isn't nearly enough time! Are you crazy?" And I always respond by citing Lincoln's Gettysburg address, in full. How many times have you bore witness to a presentation and the presenter went on and on. It takes wisdom and great restraint to do what Lincoln does. So, I challenge you today to get a stopwatch, and time yourself doing your next talk. Can you whittle down the crescendo of your talk to two minutes? How about the introduction? The conclusion? How about the entire presentation? This two-minute exercise is difficult, but difficult does not mean impossible. If you take a few minutes and jot down your own list of must-know talks or favourite speeches, I can almost guarantee that at least half of them will be delivered in under five minutes. One doesn't need to talk ad nauseam, or have verbal diarrhea to make an impact, in fact the reverse is true.

Tip – Practice being short and succinct.

#140 – Jennifer Buchanan

Context – Jennifer Buchanan is the president and founder of JB Music Therapy, an organization established in 1991 to provide music therapy for those with brain injuries.

In this short documentary, we get a portal into how Buchanan and her team use music to allow those with brain injuries to find their own unique voice even in the absence of language.

"Are you ready, what Lisa and I are going to do we are going to come around and sing your song that you've written. Music is a message; it is a message of your past and a message of your present. We are going to bring your words to life for you."

Singing: *"I didn't used to have a care in the world, family and friends have always been there. Well now the most important thing is to walk, walk and family and friends well they're still there..."*

"So the process we request from the participants their thoughts on what's important to them. Mike hadn't written anything but was able to get an F out and that was a challenge. Let to the assumption that Fishing was meaningful and blinking his eyes once said yes. Singing Mike's song... Fishing is something I love to do, Fishing brings such good memories of the time I used to sit in the boat relax my legs, pull on the rope, Fishing brought so much hope..."

Analysis – Jennifer Buchanan is a music therapist based in Calgary, Alberta, Canada. You will see in the belly of her talk, Buchanan, speaks and then sings. In a word, Buchanan is brilliant! I am overwhelmed by her and found myself in tears as she finds her way to Mike, not tears of pity, but tears of inspiration. (Mike is a capable and extraordinary person). Buchanan is observant and compassionate enough to understand what her student is saying. She removes herself from the equation altogether and in the moment is able to find Mike's voice. His visceral reaction is because someone has chosen to take the time to de-code, what he wanted desperately to say. Notice how she is not the center of attention, her words and the emotion and caring behind her words are much bigger. Her goal is to discover what her audience wants to say and simply become a vehicle to deliver their message.

For all the arrogant, self-righteous speakers I've observed over the years, this is the video I have on hand to show them. Any talk at the nucleus should rarely be about you, unless you have been asked to share your own life story. You have been asked to help convey something in your talk, and that needs to be the overriding purpose. Up to this point, we haven't seen a more thoughtful, or flawless example of someone showing authenticity in a talk. You can almost see Buchanan's emotion through her delivery, and she becomes secondary to the story. This is incredibly difficult to do, as any superb facilitator or public speaker will tell you. I proudly post this as one of my *365 Must-Know Talks*. Buchanan is, without question, one of the best facilitators I've ever seen. She gives her all to her audience with genuine affection and gentleness. I cannot offer a more resounding applause for the work she does and the person she is. While words and song are her venue this is also simply a splendid demonstration of the power of the human spirit. Bravo, Jennifer!

Tip – Allow the emotion of your words to be bigger than your ego.

#139 – Barack Obama

(1961)

Context – Illinois State Senator and the United States Senate candidate, Barack Obama delivers his first national speech at the 2004 Democratic National Convention.

"On behalf of the great state of Illinois, crossroads of a nation, land of Lincoln, let me express my deep gratitude for the privilege of addressing this convention. Tonight, is a particular honor for me because, let's face it, my presence on this stage is pretty unlikely. My father was a foreign student, born and raised in a small village in Kenya. He grew up herding goats, went to school in a tin-roof shack. His father, my grandfather, was a cook, a domestic servant.

But my grandfather had larger dreams for his son. Through hard work and perseverance my father got a scholarship to study in a magical place; America which stood as a beacon of freedom and opportunity to so many who had come before. While studying here, my father met my mother. She was born in a town on the other side of the world, in Kansas. Her father worked on oil rigs and farms through most of the Depression. The day after Pearl Harbor he signed up for duty, joined Patton's army and marched across Europe. Back home, my grandmother raised their baby and went to work on a bomber assembly line. After the war, they studied on the G.I. Bill, bought a house through FHA, and moved west in search of opportunity.

And they, too, had big dreams for their daughter, a common dream, born of two continents. My parents shared not only an improbable love; they shared an abiding faith in the possibilities of this nation. They would give me an African name, Barack, or "blessed," believing that in a tolerant America your name is no barrier to success. They imagined me going to the best schools in the land, even though they weren't rich, because in a generous America you don't have to be rich to achieve your potential. They are both passed away now. Yet, I know that, on this night, they look down on me with pride.

I stand here today, grateful for the diversity of my heritage, aware that my parents' dreams live on in my precious daughters. I stand here knowing that my story is part of the larger American story, that I owe a debt to all of those who came before me, and that, in no other country on earth, is my story even possible. Tonight, we gather to affirm the greatness of our nation, not because of the height of our skyscrapers, or the power of our military, or the size of our economy. Our pride is based on a very simple premise, summed up in a declaration made over two hundred years ago, "We hold these truths to be self-evident, that all men are created equal. That they are endowed by their Creator with certain inalienable rights. That among these are life, liberty and the pursuit of happiness.

That is the true genius of America, a faith in the simple dreams of its people, the insistence on small miracles. That we can tuck in our children at night and know they are fed and clothed and safe from harm. That we can say what we think, write what we think, without hearing a sudden knock on the door. That we can have an idea and start our own business without paying a bribe or hiring somebody's son. That we can participate in the political process without fear of retribution, and that our votes will be counted—or at least, most of the time…"

Analysis – Obama was relatively unknown on the political stage when he gave this speech, and it launched his run for the presidency and the start of his successful journey to the White House.

How can one speech have such a huge impact? The answer to this question has several components.

- I don't believe in luck per se. It is about taking the reins when opportunity knocks and Obama understood this and harnessed it at the right moment.

- This speech includes strong personal stories that allow the audience to get to know Obama on a more intimate level. This is important as, at the time, Obama was running for Senate but had his eye on the presidency. A presidential candidate must open themselves up to their audience so that the audience can understand not just their politics but also their moral and ethical leanings. The brief autobiographical sketch starts with Obama paying homage to his Kenyan grandfather, who was a domestic servant, then to his father, who obtained a scholarship to come to the U.S., then to his mother's side of the family.

- This speech is well thought out. Obama began drafting it as soon as he was invited to do the speech. He spent many weeks and countless hours preparing. He had not used a teleprompter prior to this speech, so he held three one-hour practice sessions. The speech is 17 minutes long and has 2,297 words. It's amazing that in such a relatively short time, one's world can change so dramatically.

Tip – When opportunity presents itself in the form of a speech invitation, harness it and give it the time, energy, and attention it deserves.

#138 – Pablo Picasso

1881–1973

Context – Pablo Picasso was a Spanish painter and sculptor. He is best known for the wide variety of styles symbolized in his work and for co-founding the Cubist movement..

"Nothing can be created without loneliness. I have created a loneliness for myself which nobody can comprehend. It is very difficult to be alone! There are clocks and watches."

Analysis – Some may think that a professional speaker's life is filled with meeting interesting people, and engaging in lively discussion and extroverted banter. To some degree, that is correct, but for most of us, only a small percentage of time is spent in front of groups espousing our philosophies. But the most superb speakers I have encountered know what Picasso is referring to in the above quote. Time alone is needed to tap into one's creative prowess. Time to think, time to ruminate, time to contemplate. It is through this disproportionately large sum of time that the speaker is able to focus on honing the wisdom and introspection required to become an expert in their chosen field. If you've been asked to deliver a talk, the theory is that you are the expert. So, rise to the occasion by shutting the door, turning off your phone, switching off the television, and being alone with your thoughts.

Tip – Take the much-needed time to become introspective and focus on your topic before delivering your talk.

#137 – Oprah Winfrey

(1954)

Context – Oprah Winfrey accepted the Lifetime Achievement Award in 1998 at the 25th Daytime Emmy Awards held at Radio City Music Hall in New York City.

"Thank you. This is certainly one of life's full circle moments for me. We are all beacons of light for each other. And I'm grateful that Barbara Walters was there for me to see that beacon of life. Thank you Ms. Barbara….
"From the beginning, being colored, then negro then black, then African American child. Growing up in Mississippi my prayer was, for as long as I could remember, God use me. Use me. Use this life. I don't know what the future holds for me. But I know that there is a vision for my life that is greater than my imagination can hold, use me, what would you have me to do? And that dream, that desire that prayer, brought me somehow to television. And to be able to use this tremendous vehicle of television to go into people's homes, and somehow be able to touch their lives, and be the beacon that Barbra was for me. To be a light of hope and understanding, to share some sense of the illumination that maybe sometimes reflects people's lives, and

sometimes opens them up to themselves is the greatest blessing God could have given me. And I want to continue to use television as we become more polarized in this medium,
I choose to use it in whatever way I can, we can, to make people lead better lives. To lead them to the highest vision possible for themselves. That is the goal. I thank you for this award because it encourages me to run on and see what the end will be. Thank You!"

Analysis – This is a beautiful acceptance speech on so many levels. Firstly, it is short at about three minutes. The talk of acceptance should never be any longer than five minutes. Winfrey also shows us how to collect ourselves. Giving an acceptance speech can be overwhelming. Winfrey is overwhelmed with emotion, but she pulls it together and takes an exaggerated deep breath so that she can get share her carefully chosen words. It would be a disservice to all if she could not be understood because she was bawling, so she is consciously composing herself as she approaches the stage.

The talk has a well-formed speech arc. It has a beginning, a middle, and an end. It includes important Thank yous, a nod to her background and history and her vision for the future. She starts strong and finishes strong. There are no details that have been left to chance. Winging it is never the best way to accept an award. You are receiving an award and it is an opportunity to extend gratitude to all those in your inner and outer circle who have supported, mentored and championed you. You will likely forget someone or something if you wing it so plan ahead.

Winfrey thanks Barbara Walters, who presented her with the award, and generously gives Walters recognition for being one of her mentors. She speaks from her heart and when they pan to the audience, you see many are in tears as they are so moved by her words. This is a great gift to her audience.

Tip – Spend as much time preparing an acceptance speech as you would any other talk.

#136 – Simone De Beauvoir

1908–1986

Context – Simone de Beauvoir was a French writer, existentialist, philosopher, feminist, Marxist, and social theorist.

"…only a fool would assert that there is no more on Rembrandt's canvas than paint, nothing on Mozart's music paper than notes."

Analysis – This has been a quote I've kept to myself for a long time. It's a little treasure that sits alongside some of my favourite quotes. I'm known for quoting others when I do workshops or keynote talks, but there are some that I hold only for myself, and this is one of them. This isn't a careless quote, rather it's for the person who sits and contemplates. It seems almost an injustice to try to explain or justify the quote.

But if the truth is the point of this project, then this quote must find its way onto the list. In its simplest terms, this quote is about being more than what you produce, and what you produce is a by-product of who you are. Even for great artists such as Rembrandt or Mozart, an entire life goes into creating every piece. The same is true for any great painter, artist, musician, sculptor, inventor, creator and even public speaker. What you show as your desired end-product is only the tip of the proverbial iceberg. What lies beneath is what makes that iceberg magical. The challenges, the hardships, the happiness, the exuberance is you, but what you choose to reveal on your metaphorical canvas is a conscious choice. Picking the colours, the notes, the words, is a painstaking process that requires a great eye, a great ear, and great compassion. Your end product is art. It may be difficult for novice public speakers to digest this post, but I hope to convey the importance of taking the task at hand seriously, while adding humour and throwing your entire being into the process; much like Rembrandt or Mozart might do.

Tip – Your presentations are merely the tip of the iceberg when it comes to sharing your life experience and expertise with your audience. Choose what you say and how you say it wisely.

#135 – Bob Geldof

(1951)

Context – During the 1985 Live Aid concert at Wembley Stadium in London, England, Bob Geldof asked the TV audience for money and subsequently raised $127 million for famine relief in Africa. This concert was a follow up to the successful charity single "Do They Know It's Christmas?" another of Geldof's ideas to raise money for famine in Africa.

"Fuck the address. Don't go to the pub tonight. There are people dying, now! So please, stay in and give us the money."

Analysis – Those who were teenagers or older in 1985, will remember Live Aid—the birth child of musician Bob Geldof. In 1984, a year before the Live Aid concerts, Geldof along with the rest of the world, watched horrific televised images of men, women and children starving in east Africa, particularly Ethiopia, as a result of drought and wars. Geldof was fed up with watching people dying on his TV screen and decided to do something. He, alongside Midge Ure, the front man of the 80s band, Ultravox, bullied almost every musician they knew into using their talents to make music, which culminated in the release of two charity singles, "Do they know it's Christmas?" and "Feed the World." The duo then spent months organizing the Live Aid concerts, held at Wembley Stadium. People of all ages from across the globe were glued to their television screens. The concerts brought awareness to an important issue. In this quote, Geldof gets rather peeved at presenter David Hepworth who is trying to give a mailing address rather than a phone number so the public can call in and donate immediately. Geldof has conviction and purpose; he's more concerned with getting the information to the people than following the protocols and procedures of television interviews and he doesn't care if he offends anyone in the process. As a presentation tip this is a difficult one for me, as I wouldn't recommend demonstrating this level of bravado on stage in any one of my classes, but I love when I see it. Frankly,

I love to see anyone showing real emotion and allowing it to overcome them regardless of the delivery.

Tip – Speak with conviction on the topics you are passionate about.

#134 – Richard Nixon

1913–1994

Context – On November 3, 1969, President Nixon gave a television broadcast to the nation explaining, in the face of demonstrations and violent protests, why it would be wrong for the U.S. to pull out troops from the Vietnam War.

"Good evening, my fellow Americans:

Tonight I want to talk to you on a subject of deep concern to all Americans and to many people in all parts of the world the war in Vietnam.

I believe that one of the reasons for the deep division about Vietnam is that many Americans have lost confidence in what their Government has told them about our policy. The American people cannot and should not be asked to support a policy which involves the overriding issues of war and peace unless they know the truth about that policy.

Tonight, therefore, I would like to answer some of the questions that I know are on the minds of many of you listening to me.

How and why did America get involved in Vietnam in the first place?

How has this administration changed the policy of the previous administration?

What has really happened in the negotiations in Paris and on the battle-front in Vietnam?

What choices do we have if we are to end the war?

What are the prospects for peace?

Now, let me begin by describing the situation I found when I was inaugurated on January 20.

- *The war had been going on for four years.*
- *31,000 Americans had been killed in action.*
- *The training program for the South Vietnamese was behind schedule.*
- *540,000 Americans were in Vietnam with no plans to reduce the number.*
- *No progress had been made at the negotiations in Paris and the United States had not put forth a comprehensive peace proposal.*
- *The war was causing deep division at home and criticism from many of our friends as well as our enemies abroad.*

In view of these circumstances there were some who urged that I end the war at once by ordering the immediate withdrawal of all American forces.

From a political standpoint this would have been a popular and easy course to follow. After all, we became involved in the war while my predecessor was in office. I could blame the defeat which would be the result of my action on him and come out as the peacemaker. Some put it to me quite bluntly: This was the only way to avoid allowing Johnson's war to become Nixon's war.

But I had a greater obligation than to think only of the years of my administration and of the next election. I had to think of the effect of my decision on the next generation and on the future of peace and freedom in America and in the world.

Let us all understand that the question before us is not whether some Americans are for peace and some Americans are against peace. The question at issue is not whether Johnson's war becomes Nixon's war.

The great question is: How can we win America's peace?

Well, let us turn now to the fundamental issue. Why and how did the United States become involved in Vietnam in the first place?

Fifteen years ago North Vietnam, with the logistical support of Communist China and the Soviet Union, launched a campaign to impose a Communist government on South Vietnam by instigating and supporting a revolution.

In response to the request of the Government of South Vietnam, President Eisenhower sent economic aid and military equipment to assist the people of South Vietnam in their efforts to prevent a Communist takeover. Seven years ago, President Kennedy sent 16,000 military personnel to Vietnam as combat advisers. Four years ago, President Johnson sent American combat forces to South Vietnam.

Now, many believe that President Johnson's decision to send American combat forces to South Vietnam was wrong. Any many others I among them have been strongly critical of the way the war has been conducted.

But the question facing us today is: Now that we are in the war, what is the best way to end it?

In January I could only conclude that the precipitate withdrawal of American forces from Vietnam would be a disaster not only for South Vietnam but for the United States and for the cause of peace.

For the South Vietnamese, our precipitate withdrawal would inevitably allow the Communists to repeat the massacres which followed their takeover in the North 15 years before.

-They then murdered more than 50,000 people and hundreds of thousands more died in slave labor camps.

-We saw a prelude of what would happen in South Vietnam when the Communists entered the city of Hue last year. During their brief rule there, there was a bloody reign of terror in which 3,000 civilians were clubbed, shot to death, and buried in mass graves.

-With the sudden collapse of our support, these atrocities of Hue would become the nightmare of the entire nation and particularly for the million and a half Catholic refugees who fled to South Vietnam when the

Communists took over in the North.

For the United States, this first defeat in our Nation's history would result in a collapse of confidence in American leadership, not only in Asia but throughout the world.

Three American presidents have recognized the great stakes involved in Vietnam and understood what had to be done…"

Analysis – You can't have a list of *365 Must-Know Talks* and not mention Nixon. The above quote comes from a speech often called Vietnamization. It's a fascinating speech, particularly if you can watch and read it as an impartial third party and not stake a claim on either side of the argument. This speech was not successful in altering the minds of those who were opposed to the Vietnam War, but Nixon (or at least his speechwriter) does a noble job of designing a speech that addresses many questions and concerns. You'll notice, Nixon starts with a bang by addressing the big questions and going back into history:

How and why did America get involved in Vietnam in the first place?

How has this administration changed the policy of the previous administration?

What has really happened in the negotiations in Paris and on the battlefront in Vietnam?

What choices do we have if we are to end the war?

What are the prospects for peace?

The fallout from the speech was in large part unsuccessful, but Nixon shows us how to build the arc in a challenging speech.

1. Deconstruct the history
2. At the start of the speech, address the questions that your audience is likely thinking
3. Use facts and figures to support your views
4. Motivate your audience to action change

Tip – Build a presentation arc when preparing and giving difficult talks.

#133 – Harry S. Truman

1884–1972

Context – President Truman, 33rd President of the United States, was on his way back to the U.S. from the Potsdam Conference when he made this radio speech in 1945 aboard the USS *Augusta*.

"Sixteen hours ago an American airplane dropped one bomb on Hiroshima, an important Japanese army base. That bomb had more power than 20,000 tons of TNT. It had more than 2000 times the blast power of the British 'Grand Slam,' which is the largest bomb ever yet used in the history of warfare.

The Japanese began the war from the air at Pearl Harbour. They have been repaid manyfold. And the end is not yet. With this bomb we have now added a new revolutionary increase in destruction to supplement the growing power of our armed forces. In their present form these bombs are now in production, and even more powerful forms are in development.

It is an atomic bomb. It is a harnessing of the basic power of the universe. The force from which the sun draws its power has been loosed against those who brought war to the Far East.

Before 1939, it was the accepted belief of scientists that it was theoretically possible to release atomic energy. But no on knew any practical method of doing it. By 1942, however, we knew that the Germans were working feverishly to find a way to add atomic energy to the other engines of war with which they hoped to enslave the world. But they failed. We may be grateful to Providence that the Germans got the V-1s and V-2s late and in limited quantities and even more grateful that they did not get the atomic bomb at all."

Analysis – When Truman became president, on the death of President Roosevelt he did not know about the Manhattan Project—a project to develop atomic and nuclear weapons. Negotiations with the Japanese had been underway, but they did not agree to unconditional surrender demands. Unconditional surrender dictates that those surrendering make no requirements during the surrender proceedings. Truman had to decide on costly fighting or a quick strike. He chose a quick strike and dropped an atomic bomb on the city of Hiroshima, Japan on August 6, 1945.

Whether or not you fully understand the bombing of Hiroshima and all the details and politics that surround it, know that Truman needed to act quickly and make some pretty major decisions. I've chosen this speech as one of my Must-Know Talks because it is a classic. You can almost feel the power in Truman's words, and because of that, he becomes firmly implanted in this list. Nicknamed Little Boy, the bomb leveling more than 60 percent of the city. Seventy thousand residents died instantly in a searing flash of heat. Three days later, on August 9, a second nuclear bomb, nicknamed Fat Man was dropped on Nagasaki. Over 20,000 people died instantly. In the coming weeks, thousands more died from the after-effects of the radiation exposure from the blast. It was a horrific display, but Truman said, "The World will note that the first atomic bomb was dropped on Hiroshima, a military base. That was because we wished in this first attack to avoid, insofar as possible, the killing of civilians." Truman felt that he needed to use soldiers and sailors as the target and not women and children. But is that really what happened? Well, I won't go into a long diatribe of my beliefs, but Truman's speech can teach us something when applied to presentation skills. He does a good job of stating the facts in his radio address, and he doesn't lace them with niceties and bulls**t. Truman simply states the facts. If you are ever asked to give a talk on a difficult subject, stick to the facts.

Tip – In the most difficult talks, stick to the facts.

#132 – Dean Furness

Context – Dean Furness is a data and analytics professional. In 2011, an accident left him without the use of his legs. In his 2020 TED Talk, "To Overcome Challenges, Stop Comparing Yourselves with Others," Furness shares how after becoming a person living with paraplegia, he discovered a powerful new mindset and redefined his personal average in his recovery by getting to work.

"It seems we have been measured almost all of our lives, when we are infants, with our height and our weight, and as we grew, it became our speed and our strength. And even in school, there are test scores and today with our salaries and job performance. It seems as if those personal averages are almost always used to measure where we are in comparison to our peers. And I think we should look at that a little differently. That personal average is just that, it's something very personal, and it's for you, and I think if you focus on that and work to build that, you can really start to accomplish some really amazing things.

This idea started for me on a December evening in 2011. I had just stepped outside to do our evening chores to feed our horses. I hopped into our tractor, and a few minutes later, a five-foot tall, 700-pound bale of hay fell from the loader, crushing me in the seat of the tractor and in the process shattering my T5 and T6 vertebrae. I didn't lose consciousness, but I felt this buzz throughout my body, and I knew what had happened right away. My hands were reaching for my legs, but my legs didn't recognize anything touching them. And in fact, I couldn't feel anything from the center of my chest down.

So, there I was, about 100 feet from the house, with my arms wrapped around the steering wheel, trying to hold myself up, waiting for help. And unlike what you see in TV and the movies, as much as I tried to get the dogs to go to the house and get help—(laughter)

They just stared at me. Well, 45 minutes later, my wife came home, and I heard her step out of the house and, like, normal, if I needed help, 'Hey, do you need help?'" And I said, 'Yes.' And there was a brief pause and then I heard her yell, 'Do you need 9/11 help?' And again, I yelled, 'Yes.' Well, not long after I was enjoying my very first helicopter ride all the way to the hospital.

Now, the injury wasn't very dramatic or graphic. I simply broke a bone or two. And in the process, I was told I'd probably never walk again. It became very normal for me to use a rope to sit up in bed because my abdominal muscles no longer work. Or to use a board to slide out of bed into a wheelchair, or to even wait for people to reach things for me. Everything that I had learned and had known about my height and my strength, and my balance and my mobility was blown away. My entire personal average had been reset.

Now you could be sure in those days I was being measured more than ever, by the doctors and nurses for sure but maybe more so in my own mind, and I found myself comparing what I thought I was going to be able to do going forward with what I once was able to do. And I became frustrated. It took some very consistent prodding from my wife, who kept saying, 'Get your eyes up,' before I could get moving forward. And I soon realized that I almost had to forget about the person I was before and the things I was able to do before. I almost had to pretend it was never me. And I'm afraid if I had not made that realization, my frustration would have turned into something much harder to recover from…

…What I found out is that good and bad really didn't have a lot of meaning unless I had the context of knowing what my average was. It was really up to me to decide if something was bad or good based on where I was at that point in time, and it was in my control to determine if it really was a bad day. In fact, it was my decision on whether or not I could stop a streak of bad days. And what I found during that time away from home is I never had a bad day, even with everything going on. There were parts of my day that were certainly not as pleasant as they could be, but it was never an entirely bad day."

Analysis – Is this talk inspirational and emotional and soul-stirring? Absolutely. But, for me, it is also refreshing. I'm in an exclusive group that can view this talk a little differently. My son is in a wheelchair, not from an accident like Furness but due to an undiagnosed genetic condition.

Furness' talk struck a chord with me. Shortly after my son's birth, he lost weight and never fit in any of the height and weight charts associated with his age group. At the time, his father and I didn't know what the future would hold for him or if he even had a disability, but we knew by the countless physician appointments that the search was on to unearth his underlying condition. Nearly 15 years later, and despite consulting with various specialists, we are no further ahead in determining a prognosis. I am a self-anointed Google physician with files upon files of research. So, I can relate to Furness' compare and contrast sentiment. I compared my son in those early days because that's what the physicians were doing, but thankfully I soon got over that. Hand on heart, I do not ever compare him to his peers. So, this talk made me think, "Why do I continue to compare myself to others when I know that it is futile and detrimental to my progress?" As you're reading this, having read or watched Furness' 12-minute talk, is the same thought surfacing for you? Why are we brought up and socialized to compare ourselves to others?

I recently found my old report cards from junior high and high school. They are hilarious! My teachers thought by curbing my in-class talking and socializing, that they would somehow build me into a better student. They didn't know that I was the type of learner who needed to use words to learn. I was being compared to others in my class. A good student, in my teachers' minds, was someone who sats politely, attentive, notepaper and pen in hand, absorbing their every word. What those teachers didn't know is that I would become a lifelong learner, in the classroom or through a concept known as autodidactic—a Greek-derived word that means a self-taught person who learns things at their own pace.

Later, in the corporate world, my worth was measured through performance reviews. I can vividly remember the only poor performance review I received during my entire 26-year sales career, and the kicker was that it wasn't even accurate, not one bit. The leader didn't recognize my accomplishments outside the bounds of their sales targets and profitability comparables. Those equally important but difficult to measure components such as teamwork, quality client work, calibration and developing relationships didn't make the scale. By comparing one employee to the next, leaders overlook individual skillsets and risk triggering negativity and poor performance in addition to spreading resentment, rivalry, and self-doubt throughout their teams. Instead, leaders need to look for unique qualities and find alternate ways to motivate their employees. Whether it's a report card or a performance review, leaders need to stop measuring by comparison.

When Furness tells us about competing in wheelchair marathons, he highlights how we an accomplish so much more attacking things in a new way—looking at new challenges as getting to work and that by uncovering our individual averages, rather than comparing ourselves to the averages of others. Bravo, Dean! This is a talk delivered with such wisdom that I find myself mesmerized by Furness' experience, knowledge, and humanity. Like many of the talks that we've reviewed in this book, the core of Furness' talk stems from his life experience and helps his audience on their journey. It is refreshing and simply beautiful.

While Furness' and my son's challenges may be visible, we need to recognize that many are navigating life with invisible challenges. Your invisible challenge may be giving a talk! Maybe one of the biggest keys is not only, as this book suggests, studying the craft of public speaking; watching TED Talks, reading speeches, and being inspired by books and movies but ultimately finding your own voice and no longer comparing yourself to other. You have a unique story to share, and your audience needs and wants to hear your distinctive take on the subject material.

Tip – Get to work in preparing for your talk and stop comparing yourself to others.

#131- Leon Trotsky

1879–1940

Context – The October Revolution of 1917 was a significant phase in the Russian Revolution (fun fact: it actually took place in November, but the Russians used the Julian Calendar, rather than the Gregorian Calendar used in the West, so it became known as the October Revolution). Leon Trotsky shouted at the Mensheviks, and the large numbers of delegates from the socialist revolutionaries who were beginning to walk out of the grounds, starting the second congress of the Soviets from whom Lenin and Trotsky had illegally seized power.

"You are pitiful isolated individuals, you are bankrupts; your role is played out. Go where you belong from now on—into the dustbin of history!"

Analysis –This little list of mine will hit some major speeches at times, and this is one of them. I won't go into great detail as it won't mean much unless you are familiar with the Russian Revolution. Cliff Notes: After three years of war, the starving soldiers of the Russian army were leaving, and the workers began to do the same. The February Revolution had deposed the Tsar, but the interim government was just as incapable of ending the food shortages or implementing land reform. Workers' Soviet's councils began forming, among them Trotsky's Bolshevik Soviet Petrograd. After the near bloodless takeover of the Winter Palace, the interim government collapsed, and the Soviets staged a takeover. Suffice to say, Trotsky was eventually expelled from the Communist Party and deported from the Soviet Union and was later assassinated in Mexico by a Soviet agent. Whew! Trotsky philosophy became known as Trotskyism to distinguish it from Marxism and to introduce his massive opposition to the theories of

Stalinism. Okay, so I will shy away from throwing my two political cents in here and instead concentrate only on his words. Words can dramatically impact individuals, small groups, large groups, and if you get enough press, entire countries and even the world. Be cautious of your word choice, particularly harsh words. When you are giving a presentation, or a talk, you are always in a power position so be cautious of the impact your words will have not only on you, but also on others.

Tip – Be aware that your words, good or bad, have the potential to create a far-reaching ripple effect.

#130 – Tom Lehrer

(1928)

Context – Tom Lehrer is a singer-songwriter, satirist, pianist and mathematician. Lehrer is best known for the forcefully expressive and often humorous songs he recorded in the 1950s and 1960s. "Be Prepared," was very risqué for the time.

"Life is like a sewer–what you get out of it depends on what you put into it. It's always seemed to me that this is precisely the sort of dynamic, positive thinking that we so desperately need today in these occasionally trying times of crisis and universal brouhaha."

Analysis – I do enjoy when someone wraps honesty in a crisp crust of sarcasm. There are some who are just naturally better at sarcasm than others. I can occasionally bat that ball around, but certainly am no master. I find it refreshing, funny and enlightening when I'm an audience member with someone who has studied their neighbourhood, their country, their world and have come up with some solid opinions on how things should be run. As it relates to presentation skills and you…who the hec wants to listen to the same old monologue over and over? Whatever you've been asked to talk about, put your own spin, your own j'oie de vivre, your own *you* into it…and hey, if that includes a crisp crust of sarcasm then so be it, we'll enjoy it as your audience.

(cartoon as it appears on the album *An Evening Wasted*, by Tom Lehrer)

Tip – Throw your own spin on all your talks, and don't emulate others!

#129 – Eldridge Cleaver

1935–1998

Context – As a writer, political activist and a leading member of the Black Panther Party, Eldridge Cleaver had a history of crime and a prison record. After the assassination of Martin Luther King Jr., Cleaver addressed a rally against the Vietnam War. This speech spurred a highly visible collection of speeches on the radical left. Cleaver later turned to the right after spending some time in Algeria, North Africa and became a born-again Christian and a member of the Republic Party.

"There is no more neutrality in the world. You either have to be part of the solution, or you're going to be part of the problem."

Analysis – Who hasn't heard the latter part of this quote before? You've likely not only heard it but said it at some point. I know I have, but until recently, I never knew its origins came from an African proverb before it was said by Cleaver. I believe that Cleaver didn't come to this conclusion without encountering some hardcore life experiences. Having had my share of not so easy experiences, and I'm sure there are more ahead of me, I can appreciate what Cleaver is saying. It is one thing to pontificate ad nauseam about what needs to be done, who should do it, and how it should be done—but it takes a different mindset to address a problem head on, take ownership of what has been presented to you and actually do something tangible to rectify, modify or help with the resolution of the situation.

Looking at your presentations with the same mindset is integral in the success of its delivery, but more importantly, in relation to the follow-up. One might think that the presentation is from the time the stopwatch starts your talk to the time the stopwatch indicates your time is up. Nope. A talk goes far beyond those parameters. There is a before (the preparation, the practice, the discussion), the during (the time you spend delivering your talk), and the aftermath, which, for some, is one of the most important aspects of any talk. The aftermath follows up on all the stuff you've heard while conducting your presentation. You may have heard objections, positive or negative feedback, opinions from disgruntled people and whatever else. You cannot stop there! You must position yourself as part of the solution. Consider it your job to follow up, and work towards finding a solution. This, too, is part of a presenter's role.

Tip – The aftermath of a presentation is equally as important as the actual talk.

#128 – Eric Miller

Context – "Love Hurts" is Eric Miller's story told at the 2019 The Moth StorySLAM. A story slam is an open microphone event where you drop your name in a hat and if you get picked, you climb up onstage and tell a true story about yourself, in five minutes or less. The Moth is one of the most popular organizations in this genre and "celebrates the ability of storytelling to honour both the diversity and commonality of human experience and satisfy a vital human need for connection. It seeks to present recognized storytellers among established and emerging writers, performers and artists and encourage storytelling among communities whose stories often go unheard."

"I was married. I was in love. I was resigned to staying married. We had kids. We had issues. We worked them out until we couldn't. And now, 20 years later, after marriage, I'm a single guy. 48. The last time I dated prior to marriage, there was no cell phones, there was no digital, and I come out of this coma of a relationship into this new world, and I'm intimidated. I was confused. I'm in a place that I was always trying to avoid.

I've got some friends, and they know me. And we were out one night, and this woman approached them. Do you know where we can meet some guys? We know a guy. They gave her my number. I got her number. I texted her. This is terrible. Rambling thing. She thought it was kinda cute. So, we started to text. Then we had a conversation with our voices. I was way better doing that. Hey, I know this is kinda quick, but I'm desperate for a coffee. Would you like to meet? Sure. Great, Starbucks. Put the phone down. This is happening. The phone vibrates. And it's her, and she sends me a picture. She sends me a picture a picture of black shirt on a couch. I don't know what this means, not at all. She sends me another picture of contact lenses next to a bottle of saline solution on a bathroom counter. That made no more sense than the shirt did. Then she says, well, you're gonna have to come back, look at all the stuff you left here.

For those of you who are not moaning, let me explain what is happening. A woman asks me for a date but then immediately sends pictures to the guy that slept over the other night, except she sent them to me. And then she goes, OMG, can't believe I just did that, sad face.

And then she goes, I guess you can judge me now. And I didn't need her permission to do that. So, I guess I have to come back, but I don't wear contacts. We had a little laugh and I decided to meet her anyway. So, we went out for coffee, and we had a nice time. It was uncomfortable at first, but you know, she's active; she's sexual. I want to be sexual, so we had that in common.

Then we have another date that week. We had a nice dinner, it went really well. We didn't agree to monogamy, so cool.

So, that weekend, it was off-season but I'm a surfer, so I was going to the Jersey Shore to my happy place. Off season when I go to the beach, I've got my wetsuit on and I'm on the beach for like five minutes and I'm doing my warmups and I'm very focused on the water. And I see in the distance a couple on the beach—the only other people on the beach. And I've been on the beach literally five minutes. And I squint and I see them coming and it looks like a woman I used to work with, nah that's not her and I totally forget about them. And they get closer and I'm like, are you fucking kidding me? It's the same woman with another guy. She looks appalled; he looks confused. Well, we never agreed to monogamy, and I don't know how all this works. So, I go out and I surf. Come back in, grab my phone. There is a diatribe message. She is apologizing. She really likes me, but this was a guy that she met, and she had this set up before we met—(to the audience) yeah, I know, that's kinda how I felt.

So, what would you do if you were in my position? We dated for a year."

Analysis – I believe this is the first time I've explored a story slam with you. The Moth is a non-profit group based in New York City dedicated to the art and craft of storytelling. I've attended several events since its inception in 1997. Real people, telling real stories, in five minutes or less. It's true stories, told live and without notes. It reminds me of poetry readings in the hippy days. Poetry has slams too if you're so inclined. If your name is picked from the hat, you get up, share your story, and instead of poetry snapping, you hope for a solid clap at the end. I've never done one, but my editor gently suggested that we need a slam event on the list in our re-edit, and well, if that isn't a sign, then what is? So, not only am I going to include a story slam here but I've also signed up to take part in a live story slam. I can't believe I haven't done this before.

Miller's talk is a blend of interesting staccato delivery, sarcasm and self-deprecating humour. It is brutally honest, and you're sucked in immediately. If you only read the written word of Miller's speech, you are missing out. You'll miss his body language, which acts as another character in his story of meeting a woman through a blind date. His pauses are natural, and you have a sense watching him that he has completely transported himself back in time as he recounts how his date screws up several times. Firstly she sends texts to the wrong date and then she shows up on a beach with yet another guy. Miller's start is brilliant, but the end of his talk is spectacular.

"So, what would you do if you were in my position? We dated for a year."

In 5 minutes and 42 seconds, Miller delivered a funny, vulnerable and memorable story.

So, here are some of my tips as I prepare for my first story slam:

1. Instead of practising in the mirror, try a slam.
2. Rehearse at least ten times.
3. Try to inject some humour.
4. As my writing teacher said to me many times, "show me, don't tell me."
5. You only have 5 minutes, so get into the story immediately.
6. Do no harm. Never embarrass or hurt someone in telling your story. Change names and be vague with the details, if needed. And, never take your audience to a turbulent place without bringing them home safely.

There are many platforms on which to play when storytelling, even as a novice. Look up "Story Slam" online and you'll get lots of hits. The Moth is one of my favourites story slam organizations.

Tip – Instead of practising in the mirror, try a story slam.

#127 – Henry Miller

1891–1980

Context – Henry Miller was an American novelist and painter. His most famous works include: *Tropic of Cancer*, *Tropic of Capricorn* and *Black Spring*.

"After all, most writing is done away from the typewriter, away from the desk. I'd say it occurs in the quiet, silent moments, while you're walking or shaving or playing a game, or whatever, or even talking to someone you're not vitally interested in. You're working, your mind is working, on this problem in the back of your head."

Analysis – I enjoy everything this sentiment brings to the fore. To be introspective, contemplative, calm, and, most importantly, perhaps, to be aware. Awareness is a phenomenon that many people don't tap into. That's why a writer has written this quote. Not that others can't be aware, but a writer's job is to soak it all in and be hyper aware of their surroundings so that they can bring that richness to their work. A writer may have to take a longer time with a piece, to allow the details to marinate and age. Writing a great novel may have to be put to the side for a moment if more information is needed from the world and the writer may need to ruminate on things for a while before resuming the project.

Actors will read a script, make notes, do a bunch of preparation, but it is often in the stillness that they'll find inspiration. There are a lot of professions like this. A mathematician will often be more extraordinary if they back away from their work and absorb their surroundings. And the same can be said of the presenter. When I work with novice presenters, most want everything fast, fast, fast. I'll admit to chuckling inside as I too was once that person wanting everything now. You can certainly be pretty good now, but more often, you must wait for your skills to mature and to guide you to be better than simply good. When I look back at my speeches over the years, the ones I'm most proud of—the ones with the best analogies, story ideas, and exercises—came when I was anywhere other than sitting at my desk plugging away at a PowerPoint presentation. More often great ideas come to me while I am out enjoying, loving, hating, or agonizing over life. It is those experiences that make a talk good, not the monotone copycat delivery.

Just like a fine wine maturing in an oak barrel, presenters who take in their surroundings, become introspective, and take a step back, will often get better, later. If anything, it is something for us all to aspire to, no?

Tip – Be aware of your surroundings.

#126 – Jeremy Rifkin

(1945)

Context – Jeremy Rifkin is president of the Foundation on Economic Trends and a bestselling author. In this animated talk, "The Empathic Civilization" Rifkin investigates the evolution of empathy and the profound ways it has shaped society through the RSA Animate series.

"In the last ten years there's been some very interesting developments in evolutionary biology, neuro? Science, child development, research and many other fields which is beginning to challenge some of these long-held shibboleth that we've had about human nature and the meaning of the human journey. But there is another frame of reference emerging in the sciences which is quite interesting, it really challenges these assumptions and with that the institutions that we have created based on those assumptions: our educational institutions, our business practices, our governing institutions etc. Let me take you back to the early 1990s sleepy little laboratory in Parma, Italy and scientists had an MRI brain scanning machine on a Macaw monkey as the Macaw monkey was trying to open a nut - they wanted to see how the neurones would light up. So, the monkey's trying to open up the nut the neurones light up, and just by serendipity, and this is how science sometimes happens, a human being walked in the laboratory, I don't know if it was by mistake, and he was hungry he saw the nuts and opened up one of the nuts and tried to crack it open. The Macaw monkey was totally shocked because who was this invader in his laboratory, and he didn't move he just gazed at this human trying to open up the nut, just like he had done a few seconds earlier, and then the scientists looked on the MRI brain scan and the same exact neurones were lighting up when he observed the human being opening the nut as when the monkey opened the nut, and the scientists had not a clue as to what this was, they thought the MRI machine had broken. They then began to put MRI brain scanning machines on other primates, especially chimpanzees with our big neocortex. Then they went to humans, and what they found over and over again is something called mirror neurons, and that is we are apparently soft wired some of the primates, all humans, we suspect elephants, we're not sure about dolphins and dogs we've just begun, but all humans are soft wired with mirror neurons; so that if I'm observing you - your anger, your frustration, your sense of rejection, your joy whatever it is, and I can feel what you're doing the same neurones will light up in me as if I'm having that experience myself. Now this isn't all that unusual. We know if a spider goes up someone's arm and I'm observing it going up your arm I'm going to get a creepy feeling. We take this for granted but we're actually soft wired to actually experience another's plight as if we're experiencing it ourselves. But mirror neurones are just the beginning of a whole range of research going on in neuro psychology and brain research and in child development that suggest that we are actually soft wired not for aggression and violence and self-interest and utilitarianism that we are actually soft wired for sociability, attachment, as John Bowlby might have said, affection, companionship and that the first drive is the drive to actually belong - it's an empathic drive. What is empathy—very complicated. When little babies in a nursery and one baby cries the other babies will cry in response they just don't know why, that's empathic distress it's built into their biology. Around two and a half years of age a child actually can begin to recognise himself in a mirror, that's when you began to mature empathy as a cultural phenomenon. And that is once a child who can identify themselves then they know that if they're observing someone else have a feeling, they know that if they feel something it's because they're feeling it because someone else has it, they're two separate things. Selfhood goes together with *empathic development, increasing selfhood, increasing empathic development. Around eight years of age a child learns about birth and death. They learn where they came from. ... So a child learns that life is vulnerable and fragile, and every moment is precious."*

Analysis – Not familiar with the RSA Animated series? Stop right now and search for one. RSA Animate clips are pictorial genius and an essential guide for all presenters.

The talk becomes increasingly more complex over time, but a rudimentary synopsis would be this: empathy breeds empathy.

So often, when I'm asked to evaluate someone giving a talk, empathy is the missing link. The presenter has prepared, is armed with a sexy PowerPoint presentation, has fantastic gesturing, handles questions like a pro, may even be funny and witty, etc., but the missing component is mirroring what the audience is putting forth by providing a response that has empathy at its nucleus—to truly understand and share the feelings of another. What does this have to do with being an accomplished presenter? In a word, everything. Throughout this list, I've talked about connecting with one's audience, but as I reflect, merely connecting doesn't get to the root of my intention. As Rifkin so eloquently points out, empathy is at the core of human nature. We lose the ability to be empathetic as we become socialized. We need to extend our empathetic identities to the world, we need to remove our masks and show our humanity, including empathy to others. So many of us have become me-centered and we have lost our innate ability to feel for one another. The good news is we all have the ability. There are plenty of cultures, religions, and societies that have empathy imbedded as part of their core values, but somehow here in the West, we've lost it. Bringing us back to presentation skills, I'm not suggesting, that as a presenter or as a human being, you sit in the pissing hole bucket when someone is complaining and bellyaching about something they have control over. What I am suggesting is that every reaction comes from a deeper place, and as a presenter, your role is to connect with the individuals in your audience on their level. Presenting well is no easy feat and the skills needed reach far beyond the boundaries of a simple presentation checklist.

Tip – Be empathetic when you give a presentation.

#125 – Kelli Jean Drinkwater

(1983)

Context – In her 2016 Sydney TED Talk, Kelli Jean Drinkwater discusses a society obsessed with body image and marked by a fear of fat. She encourages us to rethink our biases. Drinkwater is an artist, filmmaker, educator, and activist. She is recognized internationally for her creative practice and voice in radical body politics.

"I'm here today to talk to you about a very powerful little word, one that people will do almost anything to

avoid becoming. Billion-dollar industries thrive because of the fear of it, and those of us who undeniably are it are left to navigate a relentless storm surrounding it.

I'm not sure if any of you have noticed, but I'm fat. Not the lowercase, muttered-behind-my-back kind, or the seemingly harmless chubby or cuddly. I'm not even the more sophisticated voluptuous or curvaceous kind.

Let's not sugar-coat it. I am the capital F-A-T kind of fat. I am the elephant in the room. When I walked out on stage, some of you may have been thinking, 'Aww, this is going to be hilarious because everybody knows that fat people are funny.'

Or you may have been thinking, 'Where does she get her confidence from?' Because a confident fat woman is almost unthinkable. The fashion-conscious members of the audience may have been thinking how fabulous I look in this Beth Ditto dress – thank you very much. Whereas some of you might have thought, 'Hmm, black would have been so much more slimming.'

You may have wondered, consciously or not, if I have diabetes or a partner or if I eat carbs after 7 p.m.

You may have worried that you ate carbs after 7 p.m. last night and that you really should renew your gym membership.

These judgments are insidious. They can be directed at individuals and groups, and they can also be directed at ourselves. And this way of thinking is known as fatphobia.

Like any form of systematic oppression, fatphobia is deeply rooted in complex structures like capitalism, patriarchy, and racism, and that can make it really difficult to see, let alone challenge. We live in a culture where being fat is seen as being a bad person—lazy, greedy, unhealthy, irresponsible, and morally suspect. And we tend to see thinness as being universally good—responsible, successful, and in control of our appetites, bodies, and lives. We see these ideas again and again in the media, in public health policy, doctors' offices, in everyday conversations and in our own attitudes. We may even blame fat people themselves for the discrimination they face because, after all, if we don't like it, we should just lose weight. Easy. This anti-fat bias has become so integral, so ingrained to how we value ourselves and each other that we rarely question why we have such contempt for people of size and where that disdain comes from.

But we must question it because the enormous value we place on how we look affects every one of us. And do we really want to live in a society where people are denied their basic humanity if they don't subscribe to some arbitrary form of acceptable?"

Analysis – I have great reverence for Drinkwater and am in awe as I watch this talk. She describes how society views her and how she feels about it and shares her experiences of being openly laughed at and "receiving violent death threats for daring to make work that centers around fat people's bodies and lives and treats us as worthwhile human beings with valuable stories to tell."

Fat is a powerful word. "Not chubby or cuddly or voluptuous or curvaceous, I am the elephant in the room," says Drinkwater as she invites us to explore our own complex relationship with our bodies and how that defines the world in which we live. "Fatphobia describes a culture where being fat equates to being a bad person. Fat people are viewed as lazy, greedy, unhealthy, irresponsible, and morally suspect.

Being thin is seen as universally good. Thinness is seen as responsible, successful and in control of our appetite's bodies and minds. Media, doctors' offices, everyday conversations create reinforcements for this idea. Why do we have such contempt for people of size? The value we place on what people look like affects every one of us. People are denied basic humanity if they don't subscribe to some arbitrary form of acceptable," says Drinkwater.

Drinkwater goes on to say, "There are fatshionistas who reclaim their bodies and beauty by wearing fatkinis and crop tops, exposing the flesh that we're all taught to hide. Some fat athletes run marathons, teach yoga, or do kickboxing, all done with a middle finger firmly held up to the status quo. These people have taught me that radical body politics is the antidote to our body-shaming culture."

Our culture remains obsessed with controlling our bodies. The media pepper our social platforms with diet systems, exercise regimes, and new shapewear that promises to compress our rolls. One might say that we've come a long way. We claim to celebrate all bodies. But do we really? For many, the desperation to change our bodies, verges on an obsession. I feel terrible for the generation that has grown up with social media, filters, Botox, lip-plumping and spending money they don't have, and valuable time and energy in the pursuit of something shallow and superficial.

As the world reexamines what we perceive to be normal in the wake of yet another wave of the pandemic, somehow, we still have a moral obligation to watch our weight. This year, myself and many of my friends turn 50, and with that, there are parties, remember those? So, I've attended many parties this past year to celebrate as each of my friends reaches this milestone age and the opening remark from many women and men that I've chatted with at these gatherings has been some iteration of, "'Oh don't mind me, I gained the COVID-19 pounds." What the hell are we apologizing for? I have no clue if I've gained weight since the world shut down because I don't weigh myself. This was a decision I made many years ago to get off the proverbial treadmill of obsessing about my weight. Even when I go to the doctor, I turn around and tell the person weighing me that I don't need to know, because outside of a medical environment, I refused to be measured by something as arbitrary and inconsequential as where the pin settles when I step onto a scale.

This talk also made me think of how many of us are prohibiting ourselves from delivering a talk because of the negative narrative, both internal and external, about how we look. There have been plenty of times in my speaking career that I changed outfits dozens of times, rolled my eyes in disgust as I inspected my reflection in the mirror before going on stage. Let's be conscious of the biases we have toward each other and with ourselves. Let's extend some kindness since everyone has a story that you know nothing about and boomerang that kindness to ourselves.

Tip - Reclaim your body as the brilliant vessel it is, fully commit to being comfortable in your own skin, and then go out and deliver your talk.

#124 – Derek Sivers

(1969)

Context – Derek Sivers in his 2010 TED Talk: "Keep Your Goals to Yourself."

"Everyone, please think of your biggest personal goal. (For real) – you can take a second. You've got to feel this to learn it. Take a few seconds and think of your personal biggest goal, okay? Imagine deciding right now that you're going to do it. Imagine telling someone that you meet today what you're going to do. Imagine their congratulations, and their high image of you. Doesn't it feel good to say it out loud? Don't you feel one step closer already, like it's already becoming part of your identity?

Well, bad news: you should have kept your mouth shut, because that good feeling now will make you less likely to do it. The repeated psychology tests have proven that telling someone your goal makes it less likely to happen. Any time you have a goal, there are some steps that need to be done, some work that needs to be done in order to achieve it. Ideally you would not be satisfied until you'd actually done the work. But when you tell someone your goal and they acknowledge it, psychologists have found that it's called a "social reality." The mind is kind of tricked into feeling that it's already done. And then because you've felt that satisfaction, you're less motivated to do the actual hard work necessary.

So, this goes against conventional wisdom that we should tell our friends our goals, right? So, they hold us to it.

So, let's look at the proof. 1926: Kurt Lewin, founder of social psychology, called this "substitution." 1933: Wera Mahler found when it was acknowledged by others, it felt real in the mind. 1982, Peter Gollwitzer wrote a whole book about this, and in 2009, he did some new tests that were published.

It goes like this: 163 people across four separate tests. Everyone wrote down their personal goal. Then half of them announced their commitment to this goal to the room, and half didn't. Then everyone was given 45 minutes of work that would directly lead them towards their goal, but they were told that they could stop at any time. Now, those who kept their mouths shut worked the entire 45 minutes on average, and when asked afterward, said that they felt that they had a long way to go still to achieve their goal. But those who had announced it quit after only 33 minutes, on average, and when asked afterward, said that they felt much closer to achieving their goal.

So, if this is true, what can we do? Well, you could resist the temptation to announce your goal. You can delay the gratification that the social acknowledgment brings, and you can understand that your mind mistakes the talking for the doing. But if you do need to talk about something, you can state it in a way that gives you no satisfaction, such as, "I really want to run this marathon, so I need to train five times a week and kick my ass if I don't, okay?"

So, audience, next time you're tempted to tell someone your goal, what will you say?"

Analysis – I find this clip fascinating! Is it better to share your goals with others, or keep them to yourself? This is agreat question and there isn't a definitive answer. I'm familiar with people from all camps; those who tell anyone who will listen about what they will do in the future, those who never say a word but make things happen and those who fit somewhere in between. I fit in the in-between category. The theory that Sivers puts out there is that if you tell others of your intentions, then you prematurely feel the satisfaction that goes along with completing the task, and the motivation needed to stay on track wanes. Sivers refers to a study of 164 people where half were told to announce their goals, and the other half were told to withhold sharing their goals. Those who announced their goals became overconfident and didn't work as hard as those who kept their goals to themselves. It made me think about my own experiences, particularly recent ones. I continue to plug along with the big goals I've set for myself. My motivation has waned, and an awkwardness arises when I'm asked how a particular goal is progressing. "Yup, I'm still working on that," or "Yeah, seems to be taking a long time, eh?" The truth is that procrastination has set in with some of those big goals. In contrast, the goals I've set and kept quiet about, those have been accomplished. I've learned my lesson here. As it relates to presentation skills, I heartily suggest that you come up with some tangible goals for yourself, write them down, then stick them in your desk drawer only to be revisited by you. Unless, of course, you are attending a presentation skills course, then you'll have to, at the very least, inform your facilitator where you're headed so that he or she can help build an appropriate road map for you.

Tip - Delay gratification and keep your presentation goals to yourself.

#123 – Charles Darwin   1809–1882

Context – An excerpt from an *Autobiography of Charles Darwin*.

"…poetry of many kinds…gave me great pleasure and even as a schoolboy I took intense delight in Shakespeare, especially in the historical plays. I have also said that formerly pictures gave me considerable, and music very great, delight. But now for many years I cannot endure to read a line of poetry: I have tried lately to read Shakespeare, and found it so intolerably dull that it nauseated me. I have also lost almost any taste for pictures or music…My mind seems to have become a kind of machine for grinding general laws out of large collections of fact, but why this should have caused the atrophy of that part of the brain alone, on which the higher tastes depend, I cannot conceive…The loss of these tastes is a loss of happiness, and may possibly be injurious to the intellect, and more probably to the moral character, by enfeebling the emotional part of our nature."

Analysis – Charles Darwin understood so well that using both sides of one's brain is an integral component to happiness and fulfillment. It is a rather sad quote as he recounts his atrophy in one area of his brain. What he may not have realized is that he could've regained it.

Some neuroscientists don't believe in narrowing the brain's function into two hemispheres; the right and left. I am on the other side of this and believe that there are two brain centres that house different tasks. This is an oversimplification but for the sake of this entry, it will suffice. The left hemisphere controls, for the most part reading, speaking, writing, and thinking in numbers. The right hemisphere controls, for the most part spatial perception, mental map-making, geometry, and the ability to rotate shapes in our mind. We could break the brain into quadrants or even break it into physiological components, but for today, let's stick to two hemispheres. An example to support the localization of hemispheres is solid and robust. Research indicates that if one hemisphere is damaged, the other side can be re-wired to compensate, something called neuroplasticity. This ability to re-wire is easier for children than adults, but it is feasible for both, and it has been shown time and time again. *The Creative Brain*, by Ned Hermann includes a section on the lateralization of the brain and Hermann refers to people who stutter. Hermann's theory is that some people stutter because "…a competing verbal capability from the right hemisphere comes and interferes with the left-hemisphere expression. This could explain why some stutterers can sing without stuttering and also why therapists have been able to reduce stuttering in some cases by tranquilizing patients' right hemispheres."

This is of paramount importance to the presenter. Studying and understanding the brain, our behaviours, and our responses is critical in becoming a superb presenter. By understanding your dominant hemisphere, you can change your presentations to honour your strengths and also tap into the psyches of those in your audience! If you are left-hemisphere dominant, how will you talk in a way that will resonate with the folks in your audience who are right dominant and vice versa? One needs to extend out of their comfort zones to do this effectively. Most of my favourite presentations arise because the presenter has the capacity to seamlessly move from the right to the left, back and forth, over and over again. Now that takes practice and talent!

Tip – Speak from both hemispheres of your brain to both hemispheres of your audience's brain.

#122 – Isaac Newton

1642–1727

Context – Sir Isaac Newton was a physicist, astronomer, philosopher, mathematician, chemist, and theologian. He is considered by many to be one of the most influential people in history having discovered the laws of gravity and motion and invented calculus.

"If I have seen further, it is by standing on the shoulders of giants."

Analysis – It's common to think of the theory of gravitation when you think of Newton. But in doing so you may forego some of his most important works that go beyond the boundaries of gravity. His theory of light, differential and integral calculus, Newtonian telescope or reflector, and the Principia are amongst hundreds of other theories, inventions and writings that Newton left behind and others have since built upon. What he knew and what he advocates in the above quote, is that none of his work would have been possible without building on the work of his predecessors.

For those seeking input on how to conduct a fantastic presentation, I advise you watch as many presenters as possible! I have learned so much by observing others and often integrate new ideas into my presentations after having had the privilege of watching others talk. Everything I've learned has come from watching others, integrating it, tweaking it, and finding a balance that works for me. I give all the credit to these fabulous people who have allowed me the honour of observing and learning.

If you've been invited to another's presentation, go! If you haven't been invited, but know of a presentation occurring, ask if you can go for the learning opportunity. You'd be amazed at how thrilled people will be by your interest.

Tip – Watch as many presentations as you possibly can and integrate what you've learned into your talk.

#121 – Patrick Henry

1736–1799

Context – May 23, 1775, American attorney and politician Patrick Henry gave a speech to the Virginia Convention on May 23, 1775, which ends with the famous line, "Give Me Liberty or Give me Death!"

"No man thinks more highly than I do of the patriotism, as well as abilities, of the very worthy gentlemen who have just addressed the house. But different men often see the same subject in different lights; and, therefore, I hope it will not be thought disrespectful to those gentlemen if, entertaining as I do opinions of a character very opposite to theirs, I shall speak forth my sentiments freely and without reserve. This is no time for ceremony. The question before the house is one of awful moment to this country. For my own part, I consider it as nothing less than a question of freedom or slavery; and in proportion to the magnitude of the subject ought to be the freedom of the debate. It is only in this way that we can hope to arrive at the truth, and fulfill the great responsibility which we hold to God and our country. Should I keep back my opinions at such a time, through fear of giving offence, I should consider myself as guilty of treason towards my country, and of an act of disloyalty toward the Majesty of Heaven, which I revere above all earthly kings?

Mr. President, it is natural to man to indulge in the illusions of hope. We are apt to shut our eyes against a painful truth, and listen to the song of that siren 'til she transforms us into beasts. Is this the part of wise men, engaged in a great and arduous struggle for liberty? Are we disposed to be of the numbers of those who, having eyes, see not, and, having ears, hear not, the things which so nearly concern their temporal salvation? For my part, whatever anguish of spirit it may cost, I am willing to know the whole truth, to know the worst, and to provide for it.

I have but one lamp by which my feet are guided, and that is the lamp of experience. I know of no way of judging of the future but by the past. And judging by the past, I wish to know what there has been in the conduct of the British ministry for the last ten years to justify those hopes with which gentlemen have been pleased to solace themselves and the House. Is it that insidious smile with which our petition has been lately received?

Trust it not, sir; it will prove a snare to your feet. Suffer not yourselves to be betrayed with a kiss. Ask your-selves how this gracious reception of our petition comports with those warlike preparations which cover our waters and darken our land. Are fleets and armies necessary to a work of love and reconciliation? Have we shown ourselves so unwilling to be reconciled that force must be called in to win back our love? Let us not deceive ourselves, sir. These are the implements of war and subjugation; the last arguments to which kings resort. I ask gentlemen, sir, what means this martial array, if its purpose be not to force us to submission? Can gentlemen assign any other possible motive for it? Has Great Britain any enemy, in this quarter of the world, to call for all this accumulation of navies and armies? No, sir, she has none. They are meant for us: they can be meant for no other. They are sent over to bind and rivet upon us those chains which the British ministry have been so long forging. And what have we to oppose to them? Shall we try argument? Sir, we have been trying that for the last ten years. Have we anything new to offer upon the subject? Nothing. We have held the subject up in every light of which it is capable; but it has been all in vain. Shall we resort to entreaty and humble supplication? What terms shall we find which have not been already exhausted? Let us not, I beseech you, sir, deceive ourselves. Sir, we have done everything that could be done to avert the storm which is now coming on. We have petitioned; we have remonstrated; we have supplicated; we have prostrated ourselves before the throne, and have implored its interposition to arrest the tyrannical hands of the ministry and Parliament. Our petitions have been slighted; our remonstrances have produced additional violence and insult; our supplications have been disregarded; and we have been spurned, with contempt, from the foot of the throne! In vain, after these things, may we indulge the fond hope of peace and reconciliation.

There is no longer any room for hope. If we wish to be free–if we mean to preserve inviolate those inestimable privileges for which we have been so long contending–if we mean not basely to abandon the noble struggle in which we have been so long engaged, and which we have pledged ourselves never to abandon until the glorious object of our contest shall be obtained–we must fight! I repeat it, sir, we must fight! An appeal to arms and to the God of hosts is all that is left us! They tell us, sir, that we are weak; unable to cope with so formidable an adversary. But when shall we be stronger? Will it be the next week, or the next year? Will it be when we are totally disarmed, and when a British guard shall be stationed in every house? Shall we gather strength but irresolution and inaction? Shall we acquire the means of effectual resistance by lying supinely on our backs and hugging the delusive phantom of hope, until our enemies shall have bound us hand and foot? Sir, we are not weak if we make a proper use of those means which the God of nature hath placed in our power. The millions of people, armed in the holy cause of liberty, and in such a country as that which we possess, are invincible by any force which our enemy can send against us. Besides, sir, we shall not fight our battles alone. There is a just God who presides over the destinies of nations, and who will raise up friends to fight our battles for us. The battle, sir, is not to the strong alone; it is to the vigilant, the active, the brave. Besides, sir, we have no election. If we were base enough to desire it, it is now too late to retire from the contest. There is no retreat but in submission and slavery! Our chains are forged! Their clanking may be heard on the plains of Boston! The war is inevitable– and let it come! I repeat it, sir, let it come.

It is in vain, sir, to extenuate the matter. Gentlemen may cry, Peace, Peace–but there is no peace. The war is actually begun! The next gale that sweeps from the North will bring to our ears the clash of resounding arms! Our brethren are already in the field! Why stand we here idle? What is it that gentlemen wish? What would they have? Is life so dear, or peace so sweet, as to be purchased at the price of chains and slavery? Forbid it, Almighty God! I know not what course others may take; but as for me, give me liberty or give me death!"

Analysis – Patrick Henry, in his famous speech, urges the American colonies to revolt against England. In fact, Henry's speech was given only a few weeks before the Revolutionary War began. Powerful words, not only in writing, but you can imagine the gusto with which they were delivered. It is harsh, bold, brazen language and could only be delivered with vigour. How could you possibly deliver the sentiment of opting for death, rather than live under tyranny and oppression? This speech rallied the convention's spirit of resistance, the resolution passed, and the state of Virginia took a significant step toward independence.

When was the last time you were able to believe in something so much that you spoke with intense vigour and gusto? When was the last time you talked about something that you were so passionate about, any sacrifices seemed meaningless? When was the last time you spoke and moved thousands of people to action? The truth is, you may not think you are able to make a monumental change in history, but that is not always the case. Each of us could answer yes to one or more of the above questions but we rarely do. Today's tip is simple. Find a cause or a topic that you are passionate about, and, without question, you'll be able to deliver an outstanding, history-shattering presentation. The key to any great presentation is a burning nucleus that erupts from genuine and grand emotion.

Tip – Find a cause or topic that creates within you a burning desire to share your message with an audience.

#120 – Franklin D. Roosevelt

1882–1945

Context – Franklin D. Roosevelt was the 32nd President of the United States. In 1933 he delivered his first inauguration address. The address was 27 minutes long and opened with his famous quote, "the only thing we have to fear is fear itself."

"So, first of all, let me assert my firm belief that the only thing we have to fear… is fear itself—nameless, unreasoning, unjustified terror which paralyzes needed efforts to convert retreat into advance. In every dark hour of our national life a leadership of frankness and vigor has met with that understanding and support of the people themselves which is essential to victory. I am convinced that you will again give that support to leadership in these critical days."

Analysis – Obviously, Roosevelt, in his famous words, was talking about fear as it relates to a nation but can also apply to an individual who is navigating the art of presentations. Giving a presentation ranks above death and disease as the number one fear in North America. But does it need to be feared? I've shared some of my embarrassing examples of fear before, during, and after a presentation in this project so I can relate but the more I consider fear, as it relates to presentations skills, the more I realize it is quite the tangled web. People often find themselves paralyzed by anticipation, a lack of knowledge on a subject, anxiety over how they will be perceived by the audience, and embarrassment of physiological reactions (i.e., blushing, sweating, shaking, etc.) or a combination of these factors, and the list goes on. Roosevelt is right though. It is the anticipation of the fear, not the fear itself, that is paralyzing. If you were to stop someone about seven minutes into their talk, and ask them where they would rank their fear, it would likely hover around a three out of ten—I've tested this theory in my workshops countless times. If you were to stop someone seven minutes before a presentation and ask them to rank their fear, it would likely be around an eight or nine. It's simple. The act of giving a presentation isn't frightening but the anticipation beforehand can be debilitating. There are lots of things you can do, but for today, I'd like you to focus on the opening and the closing of your presentation. Much like taking off and landing a plane these are the two sections of a talk that generate and demonstrate the most nerves and are the times most prone to things going awry.

You have between four and seven seconds to make a positive first impression. That said, remember those stress hormones I've talked about before? Your cortisol and adrenaline level will be off the charts in the first four to seven seconds. Often the stress hormones take over completely, the primitive brain shuts down, and the fight or flight response takes over. If you've ever experienced fuzzy head, my technical term for this condition, then you can relate. The only way to get through this gracefully, is to know your opening so well that you could recite it backwards, forwards, inside out, and in your sleep. I'm not kidding. Prolonged repetition is a requirement. Rehearse and then rehearse some more.

By the time the close of your presentation comes along, you will be feeling more like yourself. You will most likely have found a rhythm. Quite possibly, you'll be down to minimal stress hormones. The close needs to be crisp and crystal clear. If there is something you want your audience to do differently as a result of listening to your presentation, tell them clearly so there is no room for misinterpretation.

Tip – Instead of focusing and anticipating fear in your upcoming presentation, focus your energy on expertly landing your opening and your close.

#119 – 14th Dalai Lama of Tibet

(1935)

Context – Born Lhamo Dhondup, is a spiritual leader revered by Tibetan Buddhists. The 14th Dalai Lama and current leader is often referred by and called His Holiness.

"If science proves some belief of Buddhism wrong, then Buddhism will have to change. In my view, science and Buddhism share a search for the truth and for understanding realism. By learning from science about aspects of reality where its understanding may be more advances, I believe
that Buddhism enriches its own worldview."

Analysis – Under Buddhist belief, Dalai Lamas are enlightened beings who choose rebirth to benefit humanity and are considered to be manifestations of Avalokiteshvara or Chenrezig, the Bodhisattva of Compassion and the patron saint of Tibet. His Holiness the 14th Dalai Lama is thought of as the latest reincarnation whose spirit has chosen to be reborn to enlighten others. His Holiness continues to be a thorn in the side of the Chinese government, often criticizing its human rights abuses. He is known for his work and words on nonviolence, his philosophy, but probably, even more, his cheerful disposition and eternal and contagious optimism. He co-wrote the aptly named book *The Art of Happiness* with psychiatrist Howard Cutler. The book blends science and philosophy to explore such ideas as compassion, the meaning and purpose of life, anger, pain, loneliness, relationships, and understanding the meaning of suffering. I'd like you to focus on your openness to new ideas. If you've ever watched an interview with the Dalai Lama, he is a beautifully engaging man filled with a joy. His introspection and inner exploration of everything has brought him to a place of tranquility. It is only when one is firmly planted in the pursuit of new learning that they become open to changing their opinions, much like a wind changing direction.

Exploration is key to becoming a skilled presenter. Whether you draw on outer or inner world perspectives it is absolutely necessary to chase dreams and work to become the best you can be at whatever profession you choose. If nothing else, simply work on becoming a decent human being. It is through exploration that one can be open to new ideas, broadening horizons, adopting new techniques, and ultimately embracing a new and improved way of being.

Tip – Use exploration as a portal to learning.

#118 – James (Jimmy) Stewart

1908–1997

Context – In the film *Mr. Smith Goes to Washington* (1939), Stewart plays Jefferson Smith, a naïve man who is appointed to fill a vacancy in the US Senate. In his monologue, he doesn't back down from the rampant political corruption.

"You think I'm licked? You all think I'm licked? Well, I'm not licked! And I'm going to stay right here for this lost cause, even if this room gets filled with lies like these; and the Taylors and all their armies come marching into this place. Somebody will listen to me. Som…(Smith collapses)."

Analysis – You've gotta love Jimmy Stewart! He is in some of my favourite movies. It seems interesting to me that many of the characters he portrays deal with issue of morality and cynicism. In this clip, Stewart, who plays Jefferson Smith, has been sent letters and telegrams from people in his home state demanding his expulsion. Stewart is nearly broken by this news and finds a friendly smile in his audience—that of the President of the Senate—and this smile gives him a glimmer of hope, it raises his spirit, and allows Stewart to launch into his vow to press on until all the people believe him, and then, overcome with emotion, he faints. I could pick a plethora of things to translate into tips for presentation skills, but what I'd like to focus on today is finding positive listener support from your audience. This is a secret of many professional speakers. Look for people in the audience who are nodding their heads, smiling, and providing you with body language that demonstrates that they are listening. Lock eyes with them if you find yourself getting nervous or if you are faced with communicating difficult news, or when you are receiving a difficult response. If you are given positive reinforcement that what you are saying is having an impact, this can change your mood instantly. On the flip side, if you are in the audience, show the speaker that you understand what is being said by providing them with all the appropriate body language in return.

Tip – Seek positive listener support from your audience.

#117 – Charles Spencer, 9th Earl Spencer

(1964)

Context – On September 6, 1997, Earl Spencer, the younger brother of the late Diana, Princess of Wales, pays tribute to his sister as she was laid to rest in a public televised funeral watched by more than 2.5 billion people worldwide.

"…There is a temptation to rush to canonize your memory, there is no need to do so. You stand tall enough as a human being of unique qualities not to need to be seen as a saint. Indeed, to sanctify your memory would be to miss out on the very core of your being, your wonderfully mischievous sense of humor with a laugh that bent you double. Your joy for life transmitted wherever you took your smile and the sparkle in those unforgettable eyes. Your boundless energy which you could barely contain.

But your greatest gift was your intuition, and it was a gift you used wisely. This is what underpinned all your other wonderful attributes and if we look to analyze what it was about you that had such a wide appeal, we find it in your instinctive feel for what was really important in all our lives.

Without your God-given sensitivity we would be immersed in greater ignorance at the anguish of AIDS and H.I.V. sufferers, the plight of the homeless, the isolation of lepers, the random destruction of landmines.

Diana explained to me once that it was her innermost feelings of suffering that made it possible for her to connect with her constituency of the rejected. And here we come to another truth about her. For all the status, the glamour, the applause, Diana remained throughout a very insecure person at heart, almost childlike in her desire to do good for others so she could release herself from deep feelings of unworthiness of which her eating disorders were merely a symptom.

The world sensed this part of her character and cherished her for her vulnerability whilst admiring her for her honesty.

…Someone with a natural nobility who was classless and who proved in the last year that she needed no royal title to continue to generate her particular brand of magic"

…I pledge that we, your blood family, will do all we can to continue the imaginative and loving way in which

you were steering these two exceptional young men so that their souls are not simply immersed by duty and tradition, but can sing openly as you planned.

…The unique, the complex, the extraordinary and irreplaceable Diana whose beauty, both internal and external, will never be extinguished from our minds."

Analysis – A eulogy or funeral oration is unquestionably the most difficult speech of all. Here, Diana's brother, Earl Spencer, does a brilliant job and takes his audience (not only those present inside London's Westminster Abbey but the millions of people watching on television) on an intimate journey of the Diana he knew. He acknowledges not only the insurmountable grief felt by her family but also those around the world grieving the loss of someone they had never met. Rather than focusing on her public image, Earl Spencer offers an emotionally driven, raw and heartfelt account of Diana's life as a mother, a daughter, a sister, an aunt, and a friend. Typically, a eulogy is not the place to be controversial or to cast aspersions, but here it is absolutely called for and Earl Spencer does it carefully and with grace but it is clearly pointed. Apparently, the Queen was rather angered by some of the lines in his eulogy such as, "Someone with a natural nobility who was classless and who proved in the last year that she needed no royal title to continue to generate her particular brand of magic." Ouch! The fact that he did it whilst the world watched shows his intense desire to show the world who she really was.

Additionally, Earl Spencer does not shy away from Diana's less favourable characteristics such as her eating disorders, insecurities, and self-esteem challenges. He draws attention to a story arc filled that often misinterpreted and fabricated aspects of her life, so in his final tribute to his sister, he shines a bright light onto her real life.

Tip – In the face of a challenging talk, speak from your heart.

#116 – Sylvester Stallone

(1946)

Context – Sylvester Stallone stars as Rocky in the 2006 eponymous film, *Rocky Balboa*.

"Let me tell you something you already know. The world ain't all sunshine and rainbows. It's a very mean and nasty place, and I don't care how tough you are it will beat you to your knees and keep you there if you let it. You, me or nobody is gonna hit as hard as life. But it ain't about how hard you hit. It's about how hard you can get hit and keep moving forward."

Analysis – Rocky shares the above advice with his son, Robert Balboa Jr., in the sixth installment of the Rocky franchise. Initially Balboa Jr. is arrogant but his entire demeanor changes as his father proves he knows a thing or two about life and all that it encompasses. As the writer and director of the movie, Stallone does a fine job of building up the scene so that you can empathize with both characters. It's worth considering that there will always be people who won't like you. The naysayers will hit you hard because no matter how good you are, no matter how great your intentions, and no matter how much you practice, you have no control over some people criticizing, condemning and complaining about your efforts. There are plenty of things you can do to duck and weave and avoid this negativity, but let's focus on the two main counter moves:

1. If you notice an unhappy camper in your audience and you can schedule a break, do so, and address it with the audience member privately. Be honest. I'll usually start by saying, "I've noticed that you may not agree with some of the points of view in my presentation. What can I do to help?" Always take ownership and take responsibility for finding a resolution. Open the dialogue and ask the audience member for input on how to find a solution, and hopefully, it can be addressed. If not, commit to following up after the presentation, but whatever you do, offer them a platform to voice their opinions as this may sway them from being a negative distraction in the room.

2. Evaluate the feedback that has been provided to you. Can you learn from it? If yes, well, best be getting on the fact that change is in order and start. If the feedback is not valid, then throw it out! Some participants will come to your presentation with a chip on their shoulder, and deliberately try to provoke you. If you are confident in your abilities, you won't take it personally. If you've done the pre-work and post-work and have given your all during the talk then allow the negative comments to be tossed aside. This gets easier with practice. You'll eventually get to a place where you no longer need positive affirmation. Negative feedback will not impact you in the slightest, as you will be well-versed in providing self-feedback.

The true measure of any form of success is to keep trying regardless of how many times you get knocked down. Get up, brush yourself off, and try again.

Tip – Keep moving forward no matter how many times you get knocked down.

#115 – John Keats

1795–1821

Context – John Keats was an English Romantic poet who died at just 25 years of age. His "Ode on a Grecian Urn" written in 1819, is one of his "Great Odes of 1819," which includes "Ode on Indolence," "Ode on Melancholy," "Ode to a Nightingale," and "Ode to Psyche."

Thou still unravish'd bride of quietness,
Thou foster-child of silence and slow time,
Sylvan historian, who canst thus express
A flowery tale more sweetly than our rhyme:
What leaf-fring'd legend haunt about thy shape
Of deities or mortals, or of both,
In Tempe or the dales of Arcady?

What men or gods are these? What maidens loth?
What mad pursuit? What struggle to escape?
What pipes and timbrels? What wild ecstasy?
Heard melodies are sweet, but those unheard
Are sweeter: therefore, ye soft pipes, play on;
Not to the sensual ear, but, more endear'd,
Pipe to the spirit ditties of no tone:
Fair youth, beneath the trees, thou canst not leave
Thy song, nor ever can those trees be bare;
Bold lover, never, never canst thou kiss,
Though winning near the goal – yet, do not grieve;
She cannot fade, though thou hast not thy bliss,
For ever wilt thou love, and she be fair!

Ah, happy, happy boughs! that cannot shed
Your leaves, nor ever bid the spring adieu;
And, happy melodist, unwearied,
For ever piping songs for ever new;
More happy love! more happy, happy love!
For ever warm and still to be enjoy'd,
For ever panting, and for ever young;
All breathing human passion far above,
That leaves a heart high-sorrowful and cloy'd,
A burning forehead, and a parching tongue.
Who are these coming to the sacrifice?
To what green altar, O mysterious priest,
Lead'st thou that heifer lowing at the skies,
And all her silken flanks with garlands drest?
What little town by river or sea shore,
Or mountain-built with peaceful citadel,
Is emptied of this folk, this pious morn?
And, little town, thy streets for evermore
Will silent be; and not a soul to tell
Why thou art desolate, can e'er return.

O Attic shape! Fair attitude! with brede
Of marble men and maidens overwrought,
With forest branches and the trodden weed;
Thou, silent form, dost tease us out of thought
As doth eternity: Cold Pastoral!
When old age shall this generation waste,

Thou shalt remain, in midst of other woe
Than ours, a friend to man, to whom thou say'st,
"Beauty is truth, truth beauty," – that is all
Ye know on earth, and all ye need to know.

Analysis – There is quite a bit of debate as to whether the final lines of this poem increase or diminish its overall beauty. I say, "who cares?" If you think it sounds beautiful, then it is! This is one of my favourite poems, it has so many layers to it, and I wouldn't be surprised if there are university courses that lead students through months of deciphering its contents. We won't do that here, but I do encourage you to read it a few times. I've included a reading of it that breathes new air into the words. This is what today's post is about. When we build our presentations, we write down notes and do fancy slides, but often don't say the words aloud in preparation, which is essential to do before the presentation. Several years ago, I worked with a client who didn't feel comfortable speaking out loud to herself or to a mock audience when practicing her presentation. One of the assignments I gave her was to go to a local bookstore that was hosting an open mic poetry reading. She had a great love of poetry, so I asked her to pick her favourite (which just so happens to be this Keats poem) and to recite it to the audience. She came alive as she delivered it. I was thrilled to see this performance. It was a great first experience for her in front of an audience (of more than fifty people, by the way!) She was able to shield herself behind the words of another author but pull her personality forward in the narration. We used that experience as the springform for her upcoming presentation, where she would be showcasing her own words. Her first presentation was undoubtedly one of my all-time favourites. Part of the reason is that she found a way to practice expressing herself.

Tip – Set yourself up for success by getting comfortable with the sound of your own voice during practice sessions.

#114 – Nahda Media

Context – Nahda Media is a 14-year-old Muslimah (Muslim woman). She spoke on the Gaza conflict at a Da'wah event in the city of Adana, in southern Turkey. The event was organized by Hizb ut-Tahrir, a group that considers itself a non-violent political party and seeks to unite Muslims under one Islamic caliphate.

(TRANSLATION)

I am a Palestinian child.

I have been left hungry for days and now for weeks. I hear in other places children sleep in their warm beds. Their mothers are by their side singing to them songs. Their fathers would kiss them once they wake up in the morning from their beds. They have games and toys to play with… But I, I play and wait for death.

I am a Palestinian child.

My mother always cries, she wears black because she faces darkness everyday. The enemies of the sun…the children of those oppressors. When they first hit our house with their bombs my father became a shahid. Just like the other Palestinian fathers.

Now I am all alone. Without an Owner, just like the other Palestinian children.

I am an orphaned Palestinian young girl. I have brothers and sisters; Azra and A'ishah, five year old Mohammad and Zeyneb which is nine years old. We sleep in one bed together, the five of us because we have no other bed.

I am a Palestinian child but I, I haven't been able to sleep from the sounds of planes and bombs. In times like this we would hug each other and cry. On a night like this we were struck with fire from the bombs. I screamed out and Cried: "Mother, Mother, Mother!"

My mother did not reply to me for she was covered in red but red did not have a voice.

My mother who always used to wear black was now covered in blood. My mother had become a shahid. Ai'shah's cradle was covered in blood, Mohammad and rest of my sisters had become shahids.

I am a Palestinian child, orphaned.

I could not get up then because I had lost a leg. I cried out asking, what was my crime? They said your name is Summaya. This is your crime. Just like those named A'ishah, Fatima and Mohammad. It is because you are a Shahids child like all the rest of the Palestinian children.

They told me it's because I am a palestinian child, 'don't bother' they said to me… 'no one can hear you'. I asked them, 'isn't there anyone else in this world who is just like me', they said '1.5 billion, among them named A'ishah and Ahmad'. I couldn't believe it. 'Where are they? Show me, where are they? Where are the Muslims?. Have they abandoned us for a handful of Yahoud?!'"

So I raise my hands and seek refuge in My Rabb!!

"O Allah, I believe in You and I see refuge in You. I depend on You and trust in You. You are my protector and the Owner of everything. You are the Lord of the Universe and You are my Lord. Oh Allah, Destroy them!

I am a Palestinian child, an orphaned child."

Analysis – I struggle to analyze this moving talk. I don't speak Media's language, but it doesn't matter. This is one of the most awe-inspiring, beautiful, painful, sad, frustrating and moving talks I've ever heard. Her pain is palpable, and I feel compelled to help, to take action and to share these words far and wide. I feel compelled to find out more. I feel the need to say a prayer for Media even though I don't pray. I feel like crying. These are the types of feelings that a talk should inspire.

Tip – Share your story with passion and you will have a monumental and profound effect on your listeners.

#113 – Confucius

551 BCE – 479 BCE

Context – Confucius was a Chinese thinker and social philosopher. Hundreds, if not thousands, of intensely profound and often witty sayings are attributed to him, and the below is but one.

"By three methods, we may learn wisdom: First, by reflection, which is noblest; Second, by imitation, which is easiest; and Third by experience, which is the bitterest."

Analysis – I gave myself the gift of reflection this morning. I ruminated on my public speaking career—teaching workshops, coaching and delivering keynote talks. Anyone who knows me knows that I adore what I do. After reading the Confucius quote, I reflected on the path that brought me to where I am today. Some of it was intentional, and some of it was not. I've met some phenomenal people along the way, and some of these people have been instrumental in my journey. There were real crossroads at times, choices that needed to be made, and I wonder if I had made even a slightly different choice, how that may or may not have impacted my life today. I believe that part of wisdom is the ability to sit in stillness and silence when faced with choices and recognize that however small the choice, it can have a monumental impact on the present, and ultimately the future. I have to give credit to the people who have graced my path, as I know with certainty that they came into my life at the right time and place to change the trajectory and course for the better. So today, I reached out to three of people who were pivotal in steering my career in the right direction to say, "Thank you." What a fun exercise that was! How often do you receive appreciation from old colleagues or friends for having had a positive impact in their life?

Presentation skills need to follow the same thought process. There are people who will help you become a great speaker, people who will give you opportunities, people who will provide you with honest feedback—it's a winding and unpredictable path. Take some time to reflect on the individuals who have helped you thus far, then reach out to them and let them know the dramatic impact they have had and that you are grateful for their help in the pursuit of your goals. Additionally, why not commit to help others, no strings attached, today and in the future? Teaching others is one of the best ways to teach yourself.

Tip – Reflect on those who have helped you develop your presentation skills and reach out to them personally to thank them and then commit to helping others!

#112 – Bill Clinton

(1946)

Context – Archbishop Desmond Tutu introduces the phrase *Ubuntu*, and former President Bill Clinton expands upon the word's meaning and significance during the Clinton Global Initiative (CGI) annual meeting in 2006. This speech has become known as "I Am Because You Are."

"Bishop Tutu reminded us that the essential wisdom of Africa about the human condition is captured in the word Ubuntu, he didn't give you the literal translation because it is almost mystical. The literal

translation of Ubuntu in English is, 'I am, because you are.' Now, when we finish sequencing the human genome, we discovered the astonishing fact that genetically every breathing human being on the planet is more than 99.9% ithe same, you think about your life is organized around that one 10th of one percent. You have better grades than someone else, you are better looking than someone else, we're arrogant enough to think that those who have a lot of money are so much better than that poor girl growing up in that village…"

Analysis –The art of listening to what a speaker says and then integrating those ideas and messages into your introduction takes great confidence to do well. You must get outside of your own head for long enough to digest what is happening before you take the stage. Bill Clinton is a masters at this. There are a ton of clips showing the ease with which he is able to digest what someone else has said and then integrate those thoughts into his introduction and talk. Why is this an important skill? It allows for a seamless transition from one speaker to the next. You might not be following another speaker, but perhaps you are being introduced. This is an often overlooked but critical step in the presentation process. Listen to the introduction and comment on it in some way. The person who has introduced you has most likely spent some time building that talk, and it deserves to be acknowledged in some way

Tip – Acknowledge and comment on what has been said before you when you take to the stage.

#111 – Jason Sudeikis (1975)

Context – Starring Jason Sudeikis, *Ted Lasso* is an award-winning comedy series that premiered on Apple TV+ in 2020. The eponymous Ted Lasso is an American football coach hired to train a premier league soccer team in England. Lasso brings along his best friend and co-coach, Coach Beard and the pair try and improve the fractured team while the club's manager is going through a terrible divorce from her husband, the owner of the football team.

"You know, Rupert, guys have underestimated me my entire life. And for years, I never understood why. It used to really bother me. But then, one day, I was driving my little boy to school, and I saw this quote by Walt Whitman, and it was painted on the wall there. It said, 'Be curious, not judgmental.' I like that.

[throws a dart and hits his first triple 20]

So, I get back in my car, and I'm driving to work, and all of a sudden, it hits me. All them fellas that used to belittle me, not a single one of them, were curious. You know, they thought they had everything all figured out. So, they judged everything, and they judged everyone. And I realized that their underestimating me… who I was had nothing to do with it. Cause if they were curious, they would've asked questions. You know? Like, 'Have you played a lot of darts, Ted?' [throws another dart and hits his second triple 20]

To which I would've answered, 'Yes, sir. Every Sunday afternoon at a sports bar with my father, from age 10 until I was 16 when he passed away.'

Barbecue sauce.

[throws his third dart and hits the bullseye; crowd cheers wildly]

Good game, Rupert."

Analysis – I have played in the leadership arena for more than 25 years. I conduct leadership workshops, I'm an executive coach to leaders who want to improve, and leaders entrust me with their teams to develop their leadership skills.

I've yet to come across a character who embodies leadership as well as Lasso. Lasso defines so many of the qualities needed to be an outstanding leader. Watching Lasso in the show is like being handed a cheat sheet on how to be a good leader.

The show's writing is sharp, optimistic, and hilarious without being cheesy. Each character is flawed and that keeps them from becoming caricatures. Many lessons emerge from the show that can easily translate to the art of public speaking:

- **Believe.** A sign with the word Believe hangs proudly—secured with duct tape—above Lasso's office door. It's a reminder of the team's goals. In the pilot episode, it is pointed out to Lasso that the sign is crooked, but the sign is left as it is after it's decided that beliefs don't have to be perfect they just have to exist.

- **Kindness matters.** The characters on *Ted Lasso* are beautifully imperfect, but the one constant is that good things happen whenever a character demonstrates kindness.

But my all-time favourite leadership lesson from the show is this:

- **Be curious.** During a high-stakes game of darts with his boss's ex-husband, (Spoiler: he loses the soccer club in the divorce settlement) Lasso uses the famous quote, "Be curious, not judgmental," to explain why curiosity is more effective than closed-minded judgment. Our internal dialogues are filled with biases, which can be self-destructive. What if instead of judgment we approached new, unfamiliar, or unexpected experiences with curiosity? We have so much to learn from one another and being judgmental prevents us from exploring and developing wisdom. What if we tackled our talks from a place of genuine curiosity, tamed our judgmental internal dialogue and immersed ourselves in the process of exploration?

Tip – Be curious, not judgmental.

#110 – Steven Johnson

(1968)

Context – Steven Johnson is an author of six books on the intersection of science, technology, and personal experience. This talk is based on his 2010 book *Where Good Ideas Come From: The Natural History of Innovation*.

"Fifty-two minutes ago, I took this picture about 10 blocks from here. This is the Grand Café here in Oxford. I took this picture because this turns out to be the first coffeehouse to open in England, in 1650. That's its great claim to fame. And I wanted to show it to you, not because I want to give you the Starbucks tour of historic England – but rather because the English coffeehouse was crucial to the development and spread of one of the great intellectual flowerings of the last 500 years, what we now call the Enlightenment.

And the coffeehouse played such a big role in the birth of the Enlightenment in part because of what people were drinking there. Because, before the spread of coffee and tea through British culture, what people drank – both elite and mass folks drank – day in and day out, from dawn until dusk, was alcohol. Alcohol was the daytime beverage of choice. You would drink a little beer with breakfast and have a little wine at lunch, a little gin, particularly around 1650, and top it off with a little beer and wine at the end of the day. That was the healthy choice, because the water wasn't safe to drink. And so, effectively, until the rise of the coffeehouse, you had an entire population that was effectively drunk all day.

And you can imagine what that would be like in your own life—and I know this is true of some of you—if you were drinking all day, and then you switched from a depressant to a stimulant in your life. You would have better ideas. You would be sharper and more alert. So, it's not an accident that a great flowering of innovation happened as England switched to tea and coffee.

But the other thing that makes the coffeehouse important is the architecture of the space. It was a space where people would get together, from different backgrounds, different fields of expertise, and share. It was a space, as Matt Ridley talked about, where ideas could have sex. This was their conjugal bed, in a sense; ideas would get together there. And an astonishing number of innovations from this period have a coffeehouse somewhere in their story.

I've been spending a lot of time thinking about coffeehouses for the last five years because I've been kind of on this quest to investigate this question of where good ideas come from. What are the environments that lead to unusual levels of innovation, unusual levels of creativity? What's the kind of environmental -- what is the space of creativity? And what I've done is, I've looked at both environments like the coffeehouse, I've looked at media environments like the World Wide Web, that have been extraordinarily innovative; I've gone back to the history of the first cities; I've even gone to biological environments, like coral reefs and rain forests, that involve unusual levels of biological innovation. And what I've been looking for is shared patterns, signature behavior that shows up again and again in all of these environments. Are there recurring patterns that we can learn from, that we can take and apply to our own lives or our own organizations or our own environments to make them more creative and innovative? And I think I've found a few…"

Analysis – This talk is brilliant and dazzling and can be used as inspiration. The content is intriguing and exciting. The delivery is even better. In terms of content, Johnson spends nearly 20 minutes discussing where ideas come from and how best to create environments (Fun fact: ideas often emerge in chaotic environments with lots of people) that will hone, nurture and birth new ideas. Johnson builds a good argument for why ideas flourish in fast-paced environments, as traditionally we think we need to sit in quiet solitude to generate genius. Johnson bridges between what we traditionally think of as deep thought by utilizing the image of Newton as the deep thinker whose theory of gravity is sparked in a moment of inspiration when he gets hit on the head by an apple and he juxtaposes this with William Hogarth's famous painting of a political dinner at a tavern where there are lots of people huddled in a small space talking, laughing, and playing music. Johnson suggests the latter, more chaotic environment is the type of space we should aspire to create in our offices. Now, at the time of this talk, Johnson couldn't have known a global pandemic was headed our way and the ramifications this would have on our home and working environments, but I do think he is onto something. Ideas that are stitched or cobbled together in non-linear and unexpected ways don't always come from the types of environments favoured by the likes of Newton or Socrates.

Johnson also discusses that ideas that percolate over time are great examples of how the concept of natural selection emerged gradually, instead of during a single day. I would, however, like to focus on the delivery of this talk as it relates to today's tip. Yes, Johnson can do articulation gymnastics. He's pretty confident, and he's done his homework and is well-read, etc. The two things I especially enjoy are his conversational delivery style and his ability to bring the nearly 20-minute presentation full circle, finishing with the same topic as he began: the coffee house.

We've yet to touch on one aspect of presentation skills, finishing where you began.

This relatively simple technique reminds the audience of the journey that they've taken with you during the course of your talk. As a reviewer of presentation skills I always appreciate the effort it takes to bring the talk back to the beginning. It feels more professional, well thought out. Give it a try! When you are giving your next presentation, finish the talk by weaving in a throwback to the story you started with and show your audience how much they've learned during your time together.

Tip – Bring your presentation full circle by referencing the story you shared in the opening of your talk.

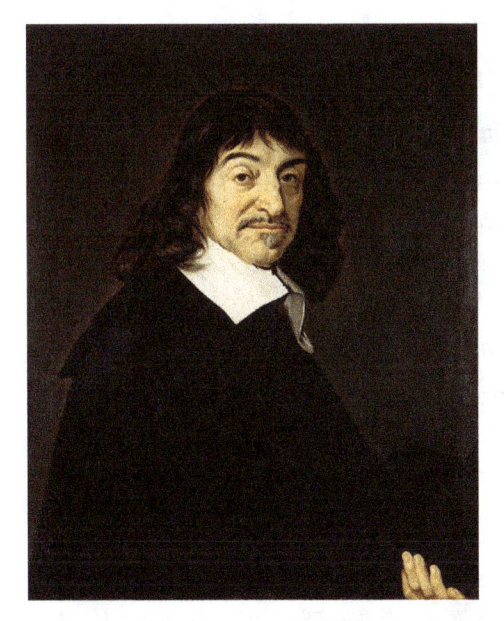

#109 – Rene Descartes

1596–1650

Context – Descartes is regarded as the founder of modern Western philosophy.

"Je pense donce je suis." (I think, therefore I am.)

Analysis – This simple saying is one of Descartes' founding arguments, published in his *Discourse on Method*. This quote is fascinating to me. If someone doubts whether he or she exists, these words provide proof that they do! I am able and capable of thinking; therefore, I am alive. The quote hits my list of the *365 Must-Know Talks* for several reasons: Firstly, it was revolutionary. Descartes's work alongside this quote developed Western philosophy. Secondly, Descartes work is still discussed, contemplated, argued and agreed with, and pondered upon. This is why I've chosen to include it on this list. As we draw our attention to presentation skills, I've often thought to myself, how long will this presentation stay in the minds of my audience? Most presentations and training, if done well, will only stay with the participant/audience for a few hours. If it has been a particularly influential talk, it will sometimes stay with that individual for a few days, perhaps even a few weeks. Rarely, however, will a talk stay with someone for months, years, and gulp, even a lifetime.

People forget presentations and talks because they are not original. They are, in simplest terms, regurgitations of what someone else has said. Now, sometimes that is okay! A friend of mine told me the other day, "There is nothing new to say; it has all been said before!" I disagree with that statement but understand the thinking behind it. Much of what is said today in talks has been said before. But, if you're anything like me, an old theory delivered in a new way is refreshing and a great reminder. That said, I do believe there are new ideas out there to lay down. It is a question of finding them. Once found, it is having the courage, as Descartes repeatedly did, to voice and defend them.

Tip – Find presentation topics that will keep your audience thinking, discussing, and sharing for days, months, and maybe even a lifetime!

#108 – Sebastian Seung

(1966)

Context – Multi-disciplinary scientist, Sebastian Seung is mapping a new model of the brain that focuses on the connections between each neuron. According to Seung, understanding the connectome could open a new way to understanding our brains and our minds. Our connectome is as individual as our genome is explored in his 2010 Ted Talk, "I Am My Connectome."

SS: *"We live in in a remarkable time, the age of genomics. Your genome is the entire sequence of your DNA. Your sequence and mine are slightly different. That's why we look different. I've got brown eyes; you might have blue or gray. But it's not just skin-deep. The headlines tell us that genes can give us scary diseases, maybe even shape our personality, or give us mental disorders. Our genes seem to have awesome power over our destinies. And yet, I would like to think that I am more than my genes. What do you guys think? Are you more than your genes?" (Audience: Yes.) "Yes? I think some people agree with me. I think we should make a statement. I think we should say it all together. All right: I'm more than my genes—all together. "Everybody:"I am more than my genes." (Cheering) "What am I?" (Laughter) "I am my connectome. Now, since you guys are really great, maybe you can humor me and say this all together too." (Laughter) "Right. All together now." Everybody: "I am my connectome." SS: "That sounded great. You know, you guys are so great, you don't even know what a connectome is, and you're willing to play along with me. I could just go home now"*

"Well, so far only one connectome is known, that of this tiny worm. Its modest nervous system consists of just 300 neurons. And in the 1970s and '80s, a team of scientists mapped all 7,000 connections between the neurons. In this diagram, every node is a neuron, and every line is a connection. This is the connectome of the worm C. elegans. Your connectome is far more complex than this because your brain contains 100 billion

neurons and 10,000 times as many connections. There's a diagram like this for your brain, but there's no way it would fit on this slide. Your connectome contains one million times more connections than your genome has letters. That's a lot of information.

What's in that information? We don't know for sure, but there are theories. Since the 19th century, neuroscientists have speculated that maybe your memories—the information that makes you, you—maybe your memories are stored in the connections between your brain's neurons. And perhaps other aspects of your personal identity—maybe your personality and your intellect—maybe they're also encoded in the connections between your neurons. And so now you can see why I proposed this hypothesis: I am my connectome. I didn't ask you to chant it because it's true; I just want you to remember it. And in fact, we don't know if this hypothesis is correct, because we have never had technologies powerful enough to test it. Finding that worm connectome took over a dozen years of tedious labor. And to find the connectomes of brains more like our own, we need more sophisticated technologies, that are automated, that will speed up the process of finding connectomes. And in the next few minutes, I'll tell you about some of these technologies, which are currently under development in my lab and the labs of my collaborators…"

Analysis – You've picked up this book perhaps to find some tips on how to present more effectively. This presentation by Seung is one of the finest examples I've included yet. In his fascinating talk, he utilizes most of the ideas and techniques we've talked about up until this point. He takes the topic of connectomes, which is difficult to digest by all intents and purposes. He is a neuroscientist after all and isn't science in any capacity hard to digest? This is why I spend hours on the TED site as, if done well, the presenter can distill an awe-inspiring, challenging topic into one that is accessible to all. If you're going to give a talk to a group outside of your peers (in this case, the audience isn't filled with other neuroscientists), it has to be relatable, and it has to be digestible and interesting to the audience so that they can participate. Here, Seung is exemplary at getting audience participation, and he uses a technique called mirroring, whereby he gets his audience to agree and repeat his words. Evidence suggests that if a person says something aloud, their ability to recall the information and surrounding content increases exponentially. Notice how Seung does it, though. He is enthusiastic and excited, with not a hint of condescension. I've seen countless others try, but they often come across as patronizing and arrogant.

Seung also injects humour, and well-crafted 3D slides into his presenation—after watching the clip even I understand what a neuron is! The last quality I'd like to highlight is Seung's capacity to sit with questions. His audience doesn't always answer immediately, and the natural reaction is to jump in and answer for them. But Seung allows the audience several seconds to sit in reflection and come up with an answer. This is not easy to do, but it is a highly effective technique that encourages your entire audience to think.

Tip – Utilize as many presentation techniques as possible when presenting difficult-to-digest topics.

#107 – Archimedes

287 – 212 BCE

Context – Archimedes was most likely the world's greatest engineer, astronomer, mathematician, and physicist. The below quote was written in AD 340 and was found to be attributed to Archimedes through the pages of Pappus' Synagogue collection.

"Give me a lever, a fulcrum, and a firm place to stand, and I will move the world."

Analysis – Archimedes came up with the saying, "Eureka!" and it is still used today when finding the solution to a problem. It is said that this exclamation came from the completion of understanding how to weigh objects through the displacement of water. He also was the first to calculate Pi with great accuracy. Archimedes also demonstrated the principle of the lever—the relationship between the distance and weight of an object from the lever's fulcrum and those of the counterweight at the other end of the lever—which led to the above quote. The reason I have chosen Archimedes and this quote today is simple. Archimedes put each one of his many inventions and explorations to practical use. As I reflect on presentation skills, I am somewhat astounded at how few presentations I can think of, that I've seen first-hand, where the audience or participant could put what they learned in the talk into immediate and practical use. Most presentations are there to teach the audience to do something. Yet, how the presenter presents makes it nearly impossible to leave the presentation, go home and immediately use whatever has been presented with success. When you are preparing to give a talk, go back, reread and rereview. Is your presentation relevant to your audience? If you're in sales, is the presentation designed so that your audience can take techniques away and apply them immediately? The same can be said for IT, human resources, engineering, or whatever the profession or industry. One of the best ways to transfer practical use of content is to insert exercises into your talk. Exercises allow your audience to play with the content. Roleplaying is one of my favourites techniques to use with small groups. A great resource for designing role play content is *businessballs.com*.

Tip – To be an effective and superb public speaker make your presentations real-world applicable.

#106 – J.K. Rowling

(1965)

Context – J. K. Rowling was born Joanne or Jo but is better known by her pen name. Rowling is a British author and the creator of the *Harry Potter* series. The *Harry Potter* books have sold more than 400 million copies and have been adapted into seven movies.

"It is impossible to live without failing at something, unless you live so cautiously that you might as well not have lived at all, in which case you fail by default."

Analysis – I saw Rowling in an interview once, and she references the above quote. I had seen the interview before and had already chosen it for this list of *365 Must-Know Talks*. Rowling spoke about her intense fear of and physiological reactions to public speaking. But, as I watch her presenting in these clips, I am challenged to see it. She does a brilliant job at starting out by being brutally honest of her fear and nervousness, the opening is funny, it breaks the ice and creates a comfortable setting not only for her audience, but more importantly for herself, as she has another 30 minutes or so to go.

Rowling's talk is, at its core, about the benefits of failure and I've extracted the above quote because it made me think. We talk so much about success whether it's how to get it, where to find it, or what it feels like to have it, but rarely do we highlight and celebrate failure. Failure, as Rowling says, "Strips away the unessential." In essence, it makes you authentically you. You cannot pretend in times of failure. You only have the time and energy to be who you are. I like that. I've had too many presentation failures to count, but it is those experiences that taught me what not to do or how to do things differently in the future. More importantly, as I reflect on those failures, standing in front of an audience is how I learned to be me. Whether you are a novice or a professional public speaker, failure is a part of the travel plan in becoming superb and you cannot get to the pot of gold without carving a trail on the rainbow, which occasionally may include some thunderstorms and rain.

Tip – Nurture and embrace your failures, learn from them, and use those experiences to hone your craft.

#105 – Caecilius Statius

220 BCE – 166 BCE

Context – Caecilius Statius was a Roman comic poet. Forty-two play titles are associated with Statius.

"There is often wisdom under a shabby cloak."

Analysis – In my humble estimation and my years of studying, reading, and researching Socrates, he immediately came to mind as I read this famous sentiment from Statius. Socrates has been compared to Silenus (a Greek mythological deity), whom it is said had both "an ugly exterior and a beautiful interior." What is fascinating to me if you've read about Socrates is that he was very much someone who adored aesthetics. It is said over and over that he was a lover of the beautiful ones, yet in all the literature I've poured through, he was not described as beautiful himself. As I consider this quote from Statius, I think this is true of nature and true of people. Caterpillars and butterflies can best illustration this sentiment in nature. People too are often judged only on their exterior appearance. I give a keynote entitled "The Practice of Confidence" and I use a clip that I'd like to share with you. It is a clip of the popular show *Britain's Got Talent* from several years ago, highlighting the operatic singer, Paul Potts. Whether one is talking about wisdom, as Statius does, or talent, this quote is transferrable. The body language of the three judges as Potts walks onto the stage is palpable. They look at each other in disbelief as if to say,

"Let's get this over with." Simon Cowell is chewing on his pen and looks bored as he sighs deeply. The judges have no confidence that Potts will be able to sing, let alone sing opera! But mere seconds into Potts' performance of "Nessun Dorma" the judges are converted into believers. It cannot be disputed that Potts has a fantastic voice and that he is brilliant. And the judges are left ashamed and embarrassed for having judged Potts so harshly by his exterior cloak. My tip as it relates to presentation skills is simple: when you are in the presenter's audience, keep an open mind as you look at the people around you and be respectful, as if you do, you may be fortunate to uncover wisdom and talent right beside you. With that, I always believe that being in the presence of wisdom and talent is contagious and those two attributes can only help with your presentation.

Tip – Wisdom and talent are contagious, open your mind to better receive them.

#104 – Saint Augustine

354 AD – 430 AD

Context – Saint Augustine, also known as Augustine of Hippo (Bishop of Hippo Regius) was a Latin-speaking philosopher and theologian who lived in the Roman Africa Province. His writings, it is said, were rather influential in the development of Western Christianity.

"Be always displeased at what you are, if you desire to attain what you are not."

Analysis – I talked to a friend the other day, and she shared how incredibly bored she was at her job. "Incredibly bored," I asked. Honestly, I have never been incredibly bored, and certainly, never in any position that I've held! How do some people have this mindset and others not? It made me think of this quote by Augustine immediately. So, allow me to play philosopher for a moment and dissect two thoughts: the dissatisfaction of acquisition and the dissatisfaction of aspiration, which I give full credit to my adored *Philosophy for Dummies* book. The discontent of acquisition is almost always unhealthy. For example, you buy yourself a new Mercedes SUV, but you live in squalor, so you buy stuff to fulfill a need to be the centre of attention, and it works, until a Lamborghini pulls up beside you. Then you feel inferior, and so the cycle begins again. Some call this philosophy Keeping up with the Joneses. The dissatisfaction of aspiration is very different. Wanting the future to be different from the reality of the present. So, the trick is to be content (a state of peaceful happiness) with today but have ambition for the future. The dissatisfaction of aspiration is healthy, as it can propel one to further personal growth. I believe this is what Augustine is talking about in the above quote.

In this world, one cannot be incredibly bored because there is always a desire for more, not necessarily more things but more knowledge and a drive to acquire talent. So, in those lulls, the person with the dissatisfaction of aspiration will fill those periods almost immediately with something to propel them in their desired direction. This is all so easily converted to presentation skills improvement. As you continue on the path of attaining presentation skills and achieving *superb-dom* (you know what I mean) choose to fill those lulls with the pursuit of knowledge and talent.

Tip – Fill life's lulls with the attainment of knowledge and talent.

#103 – Michelangelo di Lodovico Buonarroti Simoni

1475–1564

Context – Michelangelo was an Italian Renaissance painter, sculptor, architect, engineer and poet.

"If you knew how much work went into it, you wouldn't call it genius."

Analysis – I adore the quote that we are highlighting here today from Michelangelo because it calls upon my firm belief system that there is no luck and no genius. Sure, I believe that some people are born with predispositions to a certain talent, but little will come of it unless one puts in some hardcore effort. So many people squander their predispositions due to a lack of complex, often painstaking, work. A close second to my time spent studying Socrates is my love of learning about Leonardo da Vinci and one cannot read about da Vinci without hearing about and studying Michelangelo. Why? Because these two were archrivals (for those with similar interests I recommend *The Science of Leonardo*, by Fritjof Capra). Competition isn't always a negative attribute. Healthy competition can bring out a great work ethic, new learning, and an increased talent. This, in my estimation, is what happened to Michelangelo. Both da Vinci and Michelangelo were clearly talented, but I do believe that their work was elevated because they lived at the same time and played in the same metaphorical sandbox. It has been well documented that Michelangelo had a relatively low opinion of painting, but I believe da Vinci drove him to create some of his most widely recognized, beautiful, and stunning masterpieces such as the scenes from Genesis, the first book of the Bible, on the ceiling and The Last Judgement on the altar wall of the Sistine Chapel in Rome. This brings us to presentation skills. I will occasionally encounter someone who, upon hearing what I do professionally, will say, "Oh, good Gawd, I could never do that!" or "I'm horrible at public speaking!" The truth is it has taken years of hard, difficult, arduous, and joyful work to becomes skilled at what I do. If you were to ask my mom, she would say that I had a natural disposition for public speaking because as a child I liked to take center stage.I was incredibly talkative and liked to role play (I'm thankful we didn't have video back then because I have a feeling footage of a certain dance recital would find its way to be included here). Those attributes didn't ensure any success in the public speaking realm, but they certainly gave me a gentle nudge in this direction. I've worked my butt off to execute talks and workshops that I would be proud of, and I continue to work on it every single day. I think Michelangelo would agree when I say, "There is no perfection, rather perfection in the pursuit."

Tip – Work hard every single day in the pursuit of great presentation skills.

#102 – William Lyon Phelps

1865–1943

Context – William Lyon Phelps was an American author, critic, and scholar. He taught English at Yale University for 41 years. This speech was entitled, "The Pleasure of Books" (1933).

"The habit of reading is one of the greatest resources of mankind, and we enjoy reading books that belong to us much more than if they are borrowed. A borrowed book is like a guest in the house; it must be treated with

punctiliousness, with a certain considerate formality. You must see that it sustains no damage; it must not suffer while under your roof. You cannot leave it carelessly; you cannot mark it; you cannot turn down the pages; you cannot use it familiarly. And then, someday, although this is seldom done, you really ought to return it.

But your own books belong to you; you treat them with that affectionate intimacy that annihilates formality. Books are for use, not for show; you should own no book that you are afraid to mark up or afraid to place on the table, wide open and face down. A good reason for marking favorite passages in books is that this practice enables you to remember more easily the significant sayings, to refer to them quickly, and then in later years, it is like visiting a forest where you once blazed a trail. You have the pleasure of going over the old ground and recalling both the intellectual scenery and your own earlier self.

Everyone should begin collecting a private library in youth; the instinct of private property, which is fundamental in human beings, can here be cultivated with every advantage and no evils. One should have one's own bookshelves, which should not have doors, glass windows, or keys; they should be free and accessible to the hand as well as to the eye. The best of mural decorations is books; they are more varied in color and appearance than any wallpaper, they are more attractive in design, and they have the prime advantage of being separate personalities so that if you sit alone in the room in the firelight, you are surrounded with intimate friends. The knowledge that they are there in plain view is both stimulating and refreshing. You do not have to read them all. Most of my indoor life is spent in a room containing six thousand books, and I have a stock answer to the invariable question that comes from strangers.

'Have you read all of these books?'

'Some of them twice.' This reply is both true and unexpected.

There are, of course, no friends like living, breathing, corporeal men and women; my devotion to reading has never made me a recluse. How could it? Books are of the people, by the people, for the people. Literature is the immortal part of history; it is the best and most enduring part of personality. But book-friends have this advantage over living friends; you can enjoy the most truly aristocratic society in the world whenever you want it. The great dead are beyond our physical reach, and the great living are usually almost as inaccessible; as for our personal friends and acquaintances, we cannot always see them. Perchance they are asleep or away on a journey. But in a private library, you can at any moment converse with Socrates or Shakespeare or Carlyle or Dumas or Dickens or Shaw or Barrie or Galsworthy. And there is no doubt that in these books, you see these men at their best. They wrote for you. They "laid themselves out," they did their ultimate best to entertain you, to make a favorable impression. You are necessary to them as an audience is to an actor; only instead of seeing them masked, you look into their innermost heart of heart."

Analysis – I thought of this classic speech many months ago as a catalyst for this entry, and a spark for an exercise, or perhaps a mission, if you choose to accept it! A few days ago, I had the opportunity to watch a series of presentations in the corporate world. They were okay. Nothing overly horrible, nothing wildly grand about any of them. As the fourth presenter wrapped up their talk, I had jotted down copious notes and scribbled in the margin, *The Pleasure of Books*, Phelps. If any of those four presenters who had given those stuffy corporate presentations had talked about their hobbies or something that they adore, the talks would've been something very different indeed. It's fair to assume that a business presentation should be just that, business! But why can't you insert the same joie de vivre that you would if you were speaking about your hobby? It is possible. It simply takes an understanding of how you would present if you were jazzed about the topic. So, this is your mission: Construct a short presentation, a maximum of two minutes, on a topic that you have a great fondness for. As Phelps has done here, it could be anything from books, skiing or writing to pets, Christmas, or photography. You get the idea. Tell your audience, as Phelps does here, why it is so important to you and how by listening to your presentation, they too can feel the same exuberance. Practice aloud.

Tip – Practice feeling your natural presentation style when you delight in your topic matter and then, inject that same feeling into every single presentation, no matter the topic.

#101 – Charles Dickens

1812–1870

Context – Except from Charles Dickens' classic 1860 novel, *Great Expectations*. It's a coming-of-age story of Pip Pirrip, an orphan adopted by a poor family in England. Pip grows up finding friendship and love rather than money and social status.

"My father's family name being Pirrip, and my Christian name Philip, my infant tongue could make of both names nothing longer or more explicit than Pip."

Analysis – I recall my first writing teacher saying to the class, "The first line of your novel is the most important sentence you will ever construct. You may have to write it more than one thousand times to get it to a place where it feels just right!" Take Dickens' classic, *Great Expectations*, as an example, and you'll see the painstaking effort that went into the opening sentence. If you've read *Great Expectations*, you know that the story centers on a young man's attempt to establish an identity, so it is appropriate and fitting that the first line begins with a relatively plain statement about his name and nickname. Pip, a nickname for Philip, is a small, undistinguished name, and the novel is the story of Pip attempting to become Philip, distinguished, influential, wealthy, and to transcend the social class into which he was born. It made me think of first impressions and the first words that fall from our mouths as we give presentations. Sure, we've talked about the introduction a few times and the need to know it backward, forwards, and inside out. However, we've tackled the as it relates to overcoming nerves. Now, I'd like to talk about the first minute and how it can make a profound and lasting impression on your entire presentation. Let's look at two examples:

Person A: Starts their presentation with, "I must begin with an apology. I haven't spent as much time on this presentation as I would have liked. As you know, we've been swamped, and unfortunately, something had to give in terms of my time allocation. Let's start with some sales numbers. Hopefully, Barb updated these numbers, so they are accurate…"

Person B: Starts their presentation with, "I made my first sale when I was eight years old. I knocked on the neighbours' door, string bracelets that my sister had made in hand, feeling nervous and not knowing if I had priced my wares appropriately. The door started to open, and my pulse skyrocketed. I would like to tell you one technique that I learned from that sale that I continue to use some 30 years later...."

Hopefully, you can see how Person A's opening is inferior in every way. Starting with an apology, and blaming others is no way to start a presentation yet, it is something I see repeatedly. Person B begins with a story, with a great first line that grabs the audience's attention immediately and makes them wonder where the story is going and how it relates to the topic at hand. They are both sales presentations, but one grips the audience, and the other leaves the audience feeling tired and bored.

Tip - Take the time to invest in a great first line. It will set the tone of the entire presentation regardless of length or content.

#100 – Meryl Streep

(1949)

Context – Actress Meryl Streep delivers a commencement speech at Columbia University, 2010.

(4 min. 31sec) "…Hello I'm Meryl Streep, and today, Class of 2010 I am really, I am very honored, and I am humbled to be asked to pass on tips and inspiration to you for achieving success in this next part of your lives.

President Spar, when I consider the other distinguished medal recipients and venerable Board of Trustees, the many accomplished faculty and family members, people who've actually done things, produced things, while I have pretended to do things, I can think about 3,800 people who should have been on this list before me, and you know since my success has depended wholly on my putting things over on people. So, I'm not sure parents really think I'm that great a role model anyway.

I am, however, an expert in pretending to be an expert in various areas, so just randomly like everything else in this speech, I am, or I was an expert in kissing on stage and on screen. How did I prepare for this? Well, most of my preparation took place in my suburban high school or rather behind my suburban high school in New Jersey. One is obliged to do a great deal of kissing in my line of work. Air kissing, ass-kissing, kissing up and of course actual kissing, much like hookers, actors have to do it with people we may not like or even know. We may have to do it with friends, which is, believe it or not particularly awkward, for people of my generation, it's awkward.

My other areas of faux expertise, river rafting, miming the effects of radiation poisoning, knowing which shoes go with which bag, coffee plantation, Turkish, Polish, German, French, Italian, that's Iowa-Italian from the bridges of Madison county, bit of the Bronx, Aramaic, Yiddish, Irish clog dancing, cooking, singing, riding horses, knitting, playing the violin, and simulating steamy sexual encounters, these are some of the areas in which, I have pretended quite proficiently to be successful, or the other way around. As have many women here, I'm sure.

Women, I feel I can say this authoritatively, especially at Barnard where they can't hear us, what am I talking about? They professionally can't hear us. Women are better at acting than men. Why? Because we have to be, if successfully convincing someone bigger than you are of something he doesn't want to know is a survival skill, this is how women have survived through the millennia. Pretending is not just play. Pretending is imagined possibility. Pretending or acting is a very valuable life skill and we all do it all the time. We don't want to be caught doing it but nevertheless it's part of the adaptations of our species, we change who we are to fit the exigencies of our time, and not just strategically, or to our own advantage, sometimes sympathetically, without our even knowing it for the betterment of the whole group…"

Analysis – It takes four minutes and 31 seconds for Meryl Streep to introduce herself in this speech. Four minutes and 31 seconds! Love it! This method creates great anticipation and she starts the presentation immediately with a story. Streep tells a series of brilliant stories that are so engaging I was a little shocked and saddened when the 28 minutes came to a close. This is why…tone. You'll notice that Streep has notes, and you may be aware that I am not a huge fan of notes., that I'm not a huge fan of. Notice that the notes are not being read and how she lives each and every word. She feels each word, she is reliving her stories as she tells them. It reminds me of a story I read about Mark Twain. Twain had what one would call a potty mouth, he had an affinity for swearing, a lot. This apparently bothered his wife a great deal and she would scold him each time a profanity escaped his mouth. One morning, after he cut himself while shaving he ran through a string of swear words. His wife listened from the next room and wrote each word down before meeting him in the bathroom. She threw each of these words out to him in succession, and he responded, "That's very good, honey. You've got the words, you just don't have the tune." Speaking is like constructing a great tune, you need to have the *oomph* behind each and every one of them to elicit a response from your audience. I really encourage you to watch Streep in action here as she is magnificent at singing the presentation tune with skill and zest.

Tip – Think of your presentation as singing your favourite tune.

#99 – Jesse Jackson

(1941)

Context – "I am Somebody" is a poem performed by Jesse Jackson on *Sesame Street*, 1971. "I Am – Somebody" was written in the 1950s by Reverend William Holmes Borders, Sr., senior pastor at Wheat Street Baptist Church and civil rights activist in Atlanta, Georgia.

I am Somebody
I may be poor
But I am Somebody
I may be young
But I am somebody
I may be on the street
But I am somebody

I may be small
But I am somebody
I may make mistakes
But I am somebody
My clothes are different, my face is different, my hair is different
But I am somebody
I am black, brown, white
I speak a different language
But I must be respected, protected, never rejected
I am a child
I am somebody

Analysis – Three words are the basis for what amounts to a total of a few dozen words in the entirety of this poem. The reading totals one minute and 25 seconds. It is superb and memorable because of its powerful language, the character of the presenter, which is evident during the reading, and the affect the words have on the audience.

Presenters inspire, they tug at our heartstrings, announce innovations, start and stop wars, create laughter, indoctrinate belief systems, teach, and lecture and any presenter worth their salt will moved their audience in some way. The clip from Jackson on *Sesame Street* is perhaps the most moving I have seen to date. "I am Somebody" is recited in a call and response fashion by Jackson to the children. During the clip, children of all races are scattered throughout Sesame Street. The purpose of the poem is to promote cultural understanding and it succeeded. This poem is a cultural mainstay. This poem has inspired songs from Carlos Santana to the Black Eyed Peas. It has been published in books and showcased in film. Those few words, delivered in a big way, have a massive impact. This talk made me think about my presentations and others that I've observed. Like many, I tend to have verbal diarrhea and talk ad nauseam when the content could be more concise. Longer doesn't necessarily mean better. Although I adore Leo Tolstoy, 560,000 words clocked for *War and Peace* may have been a touch too many (oh, no, she didn't!)

Tip – You don't need an excess of words to have a deep, lasting, and profound impact on the audience or even on a generation.

#98 – Charlie Chaplin

1889–1977

Context – Actor, filmmaker and composer Charlie Chaplin gives a speech in the 1940 film *The Great Dictator*.

"I'm sorry, but I don't want to be an emperor. That's not my business. I don't want to rule or conquer anyone. I should like to help everyone if possible – Jew, Gentile – black man—white. We all want to help one another. Human beings are like that. We want to live by each other's happiness—not by each other's misery. We don't want to hate and despise one another. In this world, there's room for everyone, and the good earth is rich and can provide for everyone."

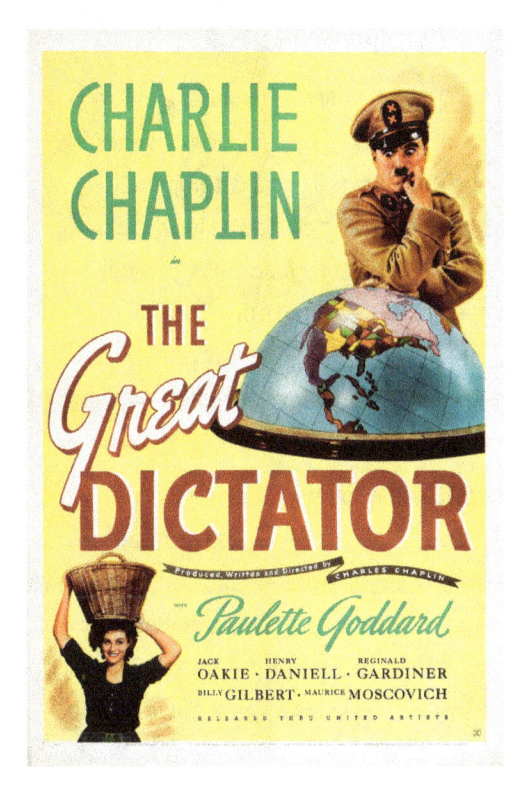

Analysis – *The Great Dictator* was Charlie Chaplin's first talking picture. It is a film about defiance against Nazism. Hands down, the above is one of my favourite speeches of all time, and that is why it's found its way onto this list of *365 Must-Know Talks*. Its content is perfection, and its delivery is the *crème de la crème*.

A fellow by the name of William Jennings Bryan (an American politician and orator) said it best, "As long as there are human rights to be defended; as long as there are great interests to be guarded; as long as the welfare of nations is a matter for discussion, so long will public speaking have its place." Public speaking or delivering a speech is not simply for the corporate world where business professionals endorse and promote their interests. It is so much more than that. Well thought out words change the world. Bravo, Charlie, bravo!

Tip – Use your words to change the world for the better.

#97 – Naguib Mahfouz

1911–2006

Context – Naguib Mahfouz was an Egyptian novelist and screenplay writer. He won the Nobel Prize for Literature in 1988. Mahfouz wrote more than 50 novels, 350 short stories, five plays and dozens of screenplays.

"You can tell whether a man is clever by his answers. You can tell whether a man is wise by his questions."

Analysis – As a presenter, you will likely receive lots of questions from your audience, but let's focus on the questions you as a presenter should be asking. One of the first things I look for when evaluating a presenter is the quality and quantity of their questions. If there is low group interaction with your presentation, part of this is an inability to properly drive questions to your audience. Your questions as a presenter are the bread and butter of your talk. It is a check system to see if what you're saying is being understood. I worked with an individual many years ago that was a trainer who worked in a large organization. He complained that every time he conducted mandatory training the audience "never wanted to participate, they were quiet, and they were slugs!" Gulp, slugs. But if your audience is silent and not participating, the only person at fault is you! Harsh? Perhaps, but the truth hurts sometimes. Content and delivery aside, your ability to ask the right questions at the right time, in the right cadence and tone, is essential to keeping your participants engaged in what you're saying.

There are several techniques that a presenter can use in delivering questions. Today we will focus on five:

1. The Guided Technique: this technique suggests you ask a specific audience member a question such as, "Tom, tell me about your experience with…?" When I attend a presentation or workshop, I'm astounded at how many presenters use this technique, without realizing it is completely ineffective. Never single out a participant and put them on the spot. They may be in with a group of their peers or people reporting to them or with people they report to. It doesn't allow the participant to put their best foot forward. Participants need to be given the opportunity to think through what they are going to say. If you use this technique, you will alienate much of your audience who will be sitting in fear that you are going to prey on them next rather than listening to what you are saying. They will shut down, stop listening and look for ways to exit the building.

2. The Group Technique: This technique allows you to ask a question to the group as a whole. It is much more challenging to navigate than the guided technique because you have to be aware of the people who always respond versus those who never respond. Any presentation aims to elicit as many opinions as possible from as many people as possible. It is *your* job to create an environment where the audience feels comfortable brainstorming and spitballing ideas and sharing opinions. I like to say in my presentations, "What happens in Vegas stays in Vegas," as a metaphor for the upcoming presentation. People laugh. They understand that they are in a safe environment where all opinions are nurtured and appreciated.

3. Smaller Group Technique: If you notice several people not responding and would like to elicit more responses and participation, you can break the audience down into tables or rows (depending on how your audience is situated). "I haven't heard from table #2 yet. What are your thoughts on…?" You may have to sit in silence but if you're patient, someone will share something, eventually. In countless presentations, I've never been left hangin' indefinitely and neither will you.

4. Bouncing Back: This is a technique where the participant asks you a question, and instead of answering you ask them what they think. This is one of my personal favourites because more often than not, the participant knows the answer and is eager to share. By using this technique carefully and without condescension, you can give members of your audience a platform to share their knowledge with their peers.

5. Another way to get group participation is to break your audience out into groups, ask them to do

something (perhaps play with a concept you've just presented) appoint a presenter to present back to the group. This one is a great icebreaker, and I like to recommend doing this at the beginning of your presentation, as it does metaphorically 'thaw' your audience.

Tip – Use a variety of questioning techniques to get your audience involved.

#96 – Frank Morgan

Context – Frank Morgan plays the Wizard in the classic 1939 film, *The Wizard of Oz*.

To the Scarecrow, a Brain:

("Why, anybody can have a brain. That's a very mediocre commodity. Every pusillanimous creature that crawls on the Earth or slinks through slimy seas has a brain. Back where I come from, we have universities, seats of great learning, where men go to become great thinkers. And when they come out, they think deep thoughts and with no more brains than you have! But they have one thing you haven't got—a diploma. Therefore, by virtue of the authority vested in me by the Universitatus Committeatum E Pluribus Unum, I hereby confer upon you the honorary degree of Th. D…that's Doctor of Thinkology.")

To the Cowardly Lion, Courage:

("As for you, my fine friend, you're a victim of disorganized thinking. You are under the unfortunate delusion that simply because you run away from danger, you have no courage. You're confusing courage with wisdom. Back where I come from, we have men who are called heroes. Once a year, they take their fortitude out of moth balls and parade it down the main street of the city and they have no more courage than you have. But they have one thing that you haven't got—a medal. Therefore, for meritorious conduct, extraordinary valour, conspicuous bravery against Wicked Witches, I award you the Triple Cross. You are now a member of the Legion of Courage.")

To the Tin Woodsman, a Heart:

("…Back where I come from, there are men who do nothing all day but good deeds. They are called phila-, er, er, philanth-er, yes, er, good-deed doers, and their hearts are no bigger than yours. But they have one thing you haven't got – a testimonial. Therefore, in consideration of your kindness, I take pleasure at this time in presenting you with a small token of our esteem and affection. And remember, my sentimental friend, that a heart is not judged by how much you love, but by how much you are loved by others.")

Analysis – The Wizard is sought after by the characters in the Wizard of Oz as the only man skillful enough to solve their problems. It is eventually revealed that the Wizard is not all powerful as his reputation suggests, but rather an ordinary man from Kansas who has been using embellished tricks and props to make him appear great and all powerful. He came to be the supreme ruler of Oz by chance. He was working as a magician for a circus and wrote Oz on the side of his hot air balloon, strictly for promotional purposes, when one day his balloon sailed into the Land of Oz, and he found himself being admired as a great sorcerer. He tried his best to sustain this myth while never disclosing his real self until he is forced to by Dorothy, the Scarecrow, the Cowardly Lion, and the Tin Man.

This movie is perfection. I cannot find a singular flaw. It has a great story filled with analogies, metaphors, and double talk. Today's post is about being who you are and not emulating something or someone else. When we think of presentation skills, authenticity is one of the biggies. So many people, while doing a presentation, go into another personae. While on some level this is a good attribute (i.e., punching up one's enthusiasm, being animated, etc.) more often than not, it is off-putting. Like the Wizard who found himself in a situation where he felt the need to assume a character, he eventually found that he could not sustain this persona and was exposed as a fraud. Such is the case with presentation skills. As a presenter, you are looked upon as the one with knowledge and power, but the individuals in your audience also have these attributes. To play the role of the presenter as superior or all knowing is arrogant, self-important, and ego driven, and these traits will alienate your audience. Instead, present authentically by developing true confidence, which comes from actually knowing something. This confidence comes from self-reflection and being comfortable with who you are. Most importantly, it comes from understanding that you are a student of your audience before you are a teacher. In your next presentation, be open and willing to learn from others, even on the presentation platform.

Tip – Be confident and unleash your authentic self in front of your audience.

#95 – Louis Armstrong

1901–1971

Context – Louis Armstrong was an American jazz trumpeter and singer from New Orleans, Louisiana. "What a Wonderful World" was written by written by Bob Thiele (as George Douglas) and George David Weiss, and was first recorded by Armstrong and released as a single in 1967.

I see trees of green, red roses too
I see them bloom for me, and you
And I think to myself, what a wonderful world.
I see skies of blue and clouds of white
The bright blessed day, the dark sacred night
And I think to myself, what a wonderful world.
The colors of the rainbow so pretty in the sky
Are also on the faces of people going by
I see friends shaking hands saying how do you do
They're really saying I love you.
I hear babies crying; I watch them grow
They'll learn much more than I'll never know
And I think to myself, what a wonderful world
Yes, I think to myself what a wonderful world.

Analysis – A big part of being a superb presenter is getting into the right headspace before taking to the stage. We've talked about pep talks before, but this is not what I'm referring to here. One of my mentors taught me something some 25 years ago that I still rely on today. Once you've done the prep work and given yourself a pep talk you need to get into a relaxed and calm headspace by doing something that has nothing to do with your presentation. Otherwise your audience will take on your tension and be so mesmerized by your anxiety, they will be unable to listen to what you have to say. My mentor encouraged me to do something one to two hours beforehand that has nothing to do with the presentation. I asked what she did to relax before giving a presentation, and she said she listens to Louis Armstrong's "What a Wonderful World." She shared with me that the beauty within Armstrong's rendition of the song embedded into her soul, and this is what she wanted to give to her audience.

Tip – Relax into a calm and beautiful frame of mind before taking the stage.

#94 – Linus Van Pelt (Charles Schulz)

1922–2000

Context – The character Linus Van Pelt in the episode "You're not Elected" from Charles Schulz's classic cartoon series, *Charlie Brown*.

"Mr. Chairman, teachers and fellow students, this will be my last speech before our election. I want you to know that I have enjoyed this campaign and it has been a pleasure to meet so many of you and I have appreciated your support. Therefore, I have a little surprise for you. And as a change of pace, rather than campaign talk, I decided to say a few words about the great pumpkin. Halloween will soon be with us, and on Halloween night the great pumpkin rises out of the pumpkin patch and brings toys to all the good little children...

(walking off stage..."I've blown the election")

Analysis – In this episode, Linus gives two speeches; one is what everyone expects, it's got everything an election speech is supposed to have. In the second speech, he talks from the heart about the great pumpkin and his audience laughs at him and mocks him. Even though he is laughed at and all his friends, including Charlie Brown, thinks he's lost the election, he goes on to win. This shows us that when we speak about the things that mean something to us, the results can surprisingly work in our favour. This made me think of my own little world. Most of my friends don't always agree with everything that I say, or everything I believe, and vice versa. But thank goodness! We are friends because we respect and encourage each other, even when our opinions differ, and our paths are divergent. Such is the case for Linus. He is bold enough to share his beliefs even when he knows his theories will be met with mockery. I admire this and certainly admire this quality when a speaker shows it in their presentation. Be bold, be fearless, be brave enough to speak your truth. You never know, you may come out a winner!

Tip – Be fearless in delivering talks and express your truth vehemently.

#93 – Alec Baldwin

(1958)

Context – Alec Baldwin, an actor on stage, screen, and television, speaks at New York University's 2010 Commencement held on May 12th in Yankee Stadium about commitment.

"You know, California and Florida may have the sunshine, but they don't have New York University, am I right? I'd rather get my degree in the rain in New York any day.

Several years have gone by since I was where you are today; there's that phrase when I was where you are today. Today I can only remember three things at any one time, so there are three things I want to share with you today, and they are all about commitment. Today ends the successful fulfillment of one commitment you have made that begins the consideration of others you will be asked to make.

I would like you to consider that when you commit to something or someone, and it proves to be unfulfilling by your measure, that is painful. But in my life, I have learned that when you do not commit, and when you do not risk, and you discover you should have, that is even more consequential. The myth of a risk-free life is just that—myth.

First, I believe you must commit to loving and caring for the people in your lives with real respect and compassion. Commit to your family and your friends. Commit to marriage and having children. Families, whatever their composition in our society today, are where we all come from. Share the best of who you are with the next generation and the next. Commit to your parents. One day, you will fully understand what your parents did for you, and you will want to thank them while they can still see you and hear you.

Second, I want you to commit to yourselves, to your health, your opinions and creative self-expression, your spiritual growth and/or religious devotion, and to your own joy. For example, only recently, I became serving as the radio announcer for the New York Philharmonic here in New York. An opportunity that has provided me with more satisfaction than I ever imagined.

For some, commit to further education. I once dreamed of attending law school but took another path. Many here are eager to enter the job market, to put on their skates, and hit the ice. And I know today you can never go wrong with more school, especially when that school is New York University.

And lastly, I want you to commit to our society whether you one day run for president of the United States or president of your book club, whether you serve as secretary of education or serve on the local school board. The systems and organizations that operate our increasingly complex nation and the world require the efforts of all of you sitting here today. America runs on capitalism and democracy in an often-conflicting arrangement. The success of that arrangement requires the work of dedicated and honorable Americans who will aggressively protect what we have in this country and when you look at the world today, even considering American problems, we still have a great deal to protect. Protecting what we have means giving back while we are striving to get ahead. I am deeply honoured to be presented with this degree from my alma mater, and I am very happy and touched to be able to share this experience with all of you here today."

Analysis – Before I launch into the analysis of Baldwin's speech, let's give a shout out to the introducers. The Dean does an exemplary job of sharing who Baldwin is, and how appreciative she is for having him attend and give the speech. You can see that Baldwin appreciates being given such a fine introduction. Want to know how to introduce a speaker? Watch this Dean. Okay, now on to Baldwin. We've touched on this before, but it's worth repeating that a talk does not need to be long in order to be impactful. This speech is about seven minutes long. Baldwin has three takeaways he gives to the graduating class. He doesn't go on some long diatribe, he gets to the point, and what great points they are. His take-aways all fall within the umbrella of commitment:

1. To commit to those around us.

2. To commit to oneself.

3. To commit to our society.

As I watch this talk, I get a real sense that Baldwin put a great deal of effort into distilling down what he believes is the best advice to pass on to this graduating class. I wonder how often those who are presenting have their own takeaways that they can pass along. A presentation at its core—for the most part—is about helping others, counselling them, guiding them, providing information, and inserting your point of view. It is your point of view that will erupt stories, analogies, and metaphors and bring your talk to life. So, your task, if you choose to accept it, is to write down three pieces of advice you'd give to your younger self about how to live life. How would you weave those three pieces of advice into your public speaking role? These three pieces of advice are the core of who you are, and I would guess are a huge part of who you are. If that is the case, then these three pieces of advice must be a set of guiding principles in all you do, including public speaking.

Tip – Uncover your guiding principles as the foundation for your presentations.

#92 – Bono

(1960)

Context – Bono (born Paul David Hewson), is the lead singer of the band U2. Bono spoke at the prayer breakfast hosted by the United States President, George W. Bush in February 2006.

"Thank you. Mr. President, First Lady, King Abdullah, other heads of State, Members of Congress, distinguished

guests…Please join me in praying that I don't say something we'll all regret. That was for the FCC.

If you're wondering what I'm doing here, at a prayer breakfast, well, so am I. I'm certainly not here as a man of the cloth, unless that cloth is leather. It's certainly not because I'm a rock star. Which leaves one possible explanation: I'm here because I've got a messianic complex.

Yes, it's true. And for anyone who knows me, it's hardly a revelation. Well, I'm the first to admit that there's something unnatural… something unseemly… about rock stars mounting the pulpit and preaching at presidents, and then disappearing to their villas in the South of France. Talk about a fish out of water. It was weird enough when Jesse Helms showed up at a U2 concert… but this is really weird, isn't it?

You know, one of the things I love about this country is its separation of church and state. Although I have to say: in inviting me here, both church and state have been separated from something else completely: their mind.

Mr. President, are you sure about this? It's very humbling and I will try to keep my homily brief. But be warned— I'm Irish.

I'd like to talk about the laws of man, here in this city where those laws are written. And I'd like to talk about higher laws. It would be great to assume that the one serves the other; that the laws of man serve these higher laws… but of course, they don't always. And I presume that, in a sense, is why you're here.

I presume the reason for this gathering is that all of us here—Muslims, Jews, Christians—all are searching our souls for how to better serve our family, our community, our nation, our God.

I know I am. Searching, I mean. And that, I suppose, is what led me here, too.

Yes, it's odd, having a rock star here—but maybe it's odder for me than for you. You see, I avoided religious people most of my life. Maybe it had something to do with having a father who was Protestant and a mother who was Catholic in a country where the line between the two was, quite literally, a battle line. Where the line between church and state was… well, a little blurry, and hard to see.

I remember how my mother would bring us to chapel on Sundays…and my father used to wait outside. One of the things that I picked up from my father and my mother was the sense that religion often gets in the way of God. For me, at least, it got in the way. Seeing what religious people, in the name of God, did to my native land… and in this country, seeing God's second-hand car salesmen on the cable TV channels, offering indulgences for cash…in fact, all over the world, seeing the self-righteousness roll down like a mighty stream from certain corners of the religious establishment…

I must confess, I changed the channel. I wanted my MTV.

Even though I was a believer.

Perhaps because I was a believer.

I was cynical… not about God, but about God's politics. (There you are, Jim.)

Then, in 1997, a couple of eccentrics, septuagenarian British Christians went and ruined my shtick—my reproachfulness. They did it by describing the Millennium, the year 2000, as a Jubilee year, as an opportunity to cancel the chronic debts of the world's poorest people. They had the audacity to renew the Lord's call—and were joined by Pope John Paul II, who, from an Irish half-Catholic's point of view, may have had a more direct line to the Almighty.

'Jubilee'—why 'Jubilee'?

What was this year of Jubilee, this year of our Lords favor?

I'd always read the Scriptures, even the obscure stuff. There it was in Leviticus (25:35)

'If your brother becomes poor,' the Scriptures say, 'and cannot maintain himself… you shall maintain him… You shall not lend him your money at interest, not give him your food for profit.'

It is such an important idea, Jubilee, that Jesus begins his ministry with this. Jesus is a young man, he's met with the rabbis, impressed everyone, people are talking. The elders say, he's a clever guy, this Jesus, but he hasn't done much… yet. He hasn't spoken in public before…

When he does, is first words are from Isaiah: 'The Spirit of the Lord is upon me,' he says, 'because He has anointed me to preach good news to the poor.' And Jesus proclaims the year of the Lord's favour, the year of Jubilee. (Luke 4:18)

What he was really talking about was an era of grace—and we're still in it.

So fast-forward 2,000 years. That same thought, grace, was made incarnate—in a movement of all kinds of people. It wasn't a bless-me club… it wasn't a holy huddle. These religious guys were willing to get out in the streets, get their boots dirty, wave the placards, follow their convictions with actions… making it really hard for people like me to keep their distance. It was amazing. I almost started to like these church people.

But then my cynicism got another helping hand…"

Analysis – Honest, humorous, intelligent, and significant, Bono is a person with intense and bold opinions. He is an activist, and with that label comes extremism. Bono knows this and spends a considerable portion of the beginning of his presentation, putting his audience at ease. This is what I'd like to focus my energy on for today, although I do encourage you to watch the entire 21-minute clip for, amongst other things, the content.

I had several meetings this week. This is the nature of what I do. I meet individuals and companies, find out what kind of workshop or keynote talk they are seeking, and customize an itinerary. Generally, several months after that initial meeting I'll deliver the program. Sometimes there are a couple of weeks that separate that first meeting and the delivery, but sometimes it is a year. One thing I noticed while I hopped from one appointment to the next, is the importance of putting people at ease in a first encounter. In a meeting, it is often a bunch of strangers sitting around a table in a boardroom, and all parties may put up walls. What I've learned is that it takes incredible perception, intuition, and an ability to read nonverbal cues, to understand and to deploy techniques that will put everyone at ease and create a productive space. You cannot be effective in a meeting if you or the person across the table from you is simply masquerading as themselves. Sorry, it just can't be done. It is a delicate balance of figuring out what type of personality is seated across from you and gently easing out their authenticity by using what I call the push/pull technique. This technique involves probing into business space, then pulling out some personal detail and going back and forth. Now, how this is done is entirely dependent on the individual in front of you. How I do this with a loud extrovert personality looks dramatically different from my approach with a softly spoken introvert. This takes practice. Making individuals comfortable becomes even more challenging when you stand at the front of the room in a presentation format. How can you ensure everyone in your audience is comfortable? Bono is a fine example of someone who has mastered this technique. Watch the first two minutes of his talk, go back and watch it again, and you'll get the answer. He uses self-deprecation, humour, and honesty. He exposes his nerves, which makes him human, and completes his introduction by asking, "Mr. President, are you sure about this?" It's funny, and at the end of two minutes, the audience is no longer thinking, "What is this rock star doing here with all his pomp? What does he know about the world? What can he possibly contribute?" They don't ask those questions because he's already answered them. He's anticipated the audience's skepticism and used that skepticism to put his audience at ease with laughter.

Tip – Read the room. Tune into how those around you are feeling and take the time to put them at ease so that your message will be heard.

#91 – Gerald Huther

(1951)

Context – Gerald Huther is head of the Department of Fundamental Neurobiological Research at the psychiatric clinic of Gottingen, Germany. His research concerns the effects of fear, stress, psychological addiction, and the nourishment of the brain. The below excerpt is from his book, *The Compassionate Brain*.

"…I still find it fascinating how much there is to dissect, measure, and study in such a brain. But by now, I no longer believe that we can succeed in this way in understanding how any brain, so say nothing of a human brain, functions. On the contrary, this kind of research leads us to regard whatever can be especially easily dissected, measured, and studied as being of particular importance in the functioning of the brain. And because researchers are quite happy to talk about that which seems particularly important to them, and because the media are quite delighted to publicize these kinds of new developments, more and more people have gradually come to believe, for example, that happiness results from heightened endorphin secretion, that harmony is produced by plenty of serotonin, and that love comes from particular peptides in the brain. They think that the amygdala is the source of fear, the hippocampus is the source of learning, and the cerebral cortex is the source of thinking. Now in case you have heard of any of this stuff, you can just go ahead and forget and forget about it. The same goes for any claims that particular genetic configurations are responsible for what goes on in your brain. There are no genes for laziness, intelligence, melancholy, addiction, or egotism. What do exist are different basic tendencies, characteristic predispositions, and specific vulnerabilities. But what ultimately becomes of these depends on the conditions for development each of them encounter." (pg. 4, *The Compassionate Brain – How Empathy Creates Intelligence*)

Analysis – I bought Huther's book some fifteen years ago, and I take it with me to every one of my workshops or keynote talks. The truth is there is an evolving stack of books that come with me on my professional excursions as I always set up a resource table. At any given time in a workshop or talk, when I feel inspired or when it has been pre-planned, I refer to or quote from one of my favourite books and have found that at breaks the participants enjoy flipping through my magnificent ten. They enjoy discussing whichever one strikes their fancy, and so, unwittingly, I have them learning on the breaks too!

My ten books are:

1. *The Compassionate Brain* – Gerald Huther Ph.D
2. *How to Think Like Leonardo da Vinci* – Michael J. Gelb
3. *Who Are You? 101 Ways of Seeing Yourself* – Malcolm Godwin
4. *The Creative Brain* – Ned Herrman
5. *The Quick and Easy Way to Effective Speaking* – Dale Carnegie
6. *The EQ Edge: Emotional Intelligence and Your Success* – Steven J. Stein Ph.D and Howard E. Book, M.D.
7. *The Death of Ivan Ilyich* – Leo Tolstoy
8. *The Power of Moments* – Heath & Heath
9. *The 5 Dysfunctional Behaviors* – Patrick Lencioni
10. *Mindset* – Carol Dweck

It is a varied list, that ebbs and flows over time, from fiction to self-help, to philosophy, to medicine. Depending on the workshop or talk I'll add to the mix, but those ten books are my mainstays (they are dog-eared, worn, sorry looking books that I love). So, I start today's entry with a tangible technique that you too can use for your next presentation. Amass a collection of books, articles, props that you can set up as a resource at the back of the room. It shows your audience that you adore whatever you are presenting, and you would be thrilled to discuss it even outside of the presentation arena. There is something about a resource table that calms people. Especially if it is a room of people that don't know one another. It's a place for everyone to go and engage in discussion. A resource table does wonders for the room's vibe. Even if you don't want to truck along books, another idea is to screen shot the book covers and display them on a screen and have a variety of quotes from each at the ready on cue cards or notes. It can and will spark discussion.

Okay, now back to Huther for a moment. I won't spend an exorbitant amount of time deciphering this excerpt for you, but I would like to bring to the fore the very end: *"There are no genes for laziness, intelligence, melancholy, addiction, or egotism. What does exist are different basic tendencies, characteristic predispositions and specific vulnerabilities."* Be honest with yourself for a moment as you read this; are you the type of person who plays the blame game? Seriously? Do you blame everyone else around you for your shortcomings, failures, procrastination? Have you ever stood at the front of the room and begun with an apology that sounded something like: *"I'm sorry, but I just didn't have the time to invest in this presentation, so I am not as prepared as I would like."* Huther discusses in his book that what happen in your life depends on the conditions you create for yourself.

Tip – Never begin a presentation with an apology.

#90 – Chesley Sullenberger, Jeffrey Skiles and Patrick Harten

Chesley Sullenberger 1951, Jeffrey Skiles 1958, Patrick Harten 1974

Context – On January 15, 2009, pilot Chesley (Sully) Sullenberger, first officer Jeffrey Skiles and air traffic controller Patrick Harten successfully landed an Airbus A320 on the Hudson River following a bird strike shortly after takeoff that blew out both engines. The skills and quick thinking of the crew and ground control saved the lives of the 155 people on board. This is an excerpt from the air traffic control audio U.S. Airways flight 1549 as it crash-lands in the Hudson River.

Capt. Chesley Sullenberger: Uh, what a view of the Hudson today.

First Officer Jeffrey Skiles: Yeah.

Skiles: Flaps up please. After takeoff checklist.

Sullenberger: Flaps up.

Sullenberger: After takeoff checklist complete.

Sullenberger: Birds.

Skiles: Whoa.

(Sound of thump/thud(s) followed by shuddering sound.)

Skiles: Oh, (expletive).

Sullenberger: Oh, yeah.

(Sound similar to decrease in engine noise/frequency begins.)

Skiles: Uh, oh.

Sullenberger: We got one rol—both of 'em rolling back.

(Rumbling sound begins.)

Sullenberger: Ignition, start.

Sullenberger: Mayday. Mayday. Mayday. Uh, this is, uh, Cactus fifteen thirty-nine hit birds, we've lost thrust (in/on) both engines we're turning back towards LaGuardia.

LaGuardia departure control: Ok, uh, you need to return to LaGuardia? Turn left heading of uh, two two zero.

(Sound similar to electrical noise from engine igniters begins.)

Skiles: Airspeed optimum relight. Three hundred knots. We don't have that.

Sullenberger: We don't.

Departure control: Cactus fifteen twenty-nine, if we can get it for you do you want to try to land runway one three?

Skiles: If three nineteen…

Sullenberger: We're unable. We may end up in the Hudson.

Departure control: Alright Cactus fifteen forty-nine it's gonna be left traffic for runway three one.

Sullenberger: Unable.

Departure control: Okay, what do you need to land?

Skiles: (He wants us) to come in and land on one three … for whatever.

Skiles: FAC (Flight Augmentation Computer) one off, then on.

Departure control: Cactus fifteen (twenty) nine runway four's available if you wanna make left traffic to runway four.

Sullenberger: I'm not sure we can make any runway. Uh what's over to our right anything in New Jersey maybe Teterboro?

Departure control: Ok yeah, off your right side is Teterboro airport.

Skiles: No relight after thirty seconds, engine master one and two confirm …

Departure control: You wanna try and go to Teterboro?

Sullenberger: Yes.

Sullenberger (over public address system): This is the Captain brace for impact.

Departure control: Cactus fifteen twenty-nine turn right two eight zero, you can land runway one at Teterboro.

Skiles: Is that all the power you got? … (Wanna) number one? Or we got power on number one.

Sullenberger: We can't do it.

Sullenberger: Go ahead, try number one.

Departure control: Kay which runway would you like at Teterboro?

Sullenberger: We're gonna be in the Hudson.

Departure control: I'm sorry say again Cactus?

Departure control: Cactus fifteen forty-nine radar contact is lost you also got Newark airport off your two o'clock in about seven miles.

Skiles: Got flaps out.

Skiles: Two hundred fifty feet in the air.

Skiles: Hundred and seventy knots.

Skiles: Got no power on either one? Try the other one.

Skiles: Hundred and fifty knots.

Skiles: Got flaps two, you want more?

Sullenberger: No let's stay at two.

Sullenberger: Got any ideas?

Departure control: Cactus fifteen twenty-nine if you can uh, …. you got, uh, runway, uh, two nine available at Newark it'll be two o'clock and seven miles.

Skiles: Actually not.

Sullenberger: We're gonna brace.

Analysis – Let's talk air traffic control for a moment. An air traffic controller needs to be aware of dozens of planes simultaneously, with each aircraft denoted on a radar screen by a squawk code. That code, in turn, refers to a progress strip sometimes electronically displayed but often literally consisting of a strip of paper bearing relevant information that cannot easily fit on screen, such as the type of plane, its radio signal, its destination, the assigned route and altitude and so on. The complexity of handling air traffic is staggering! Traffic control mistakes are surprisingly rare but catastrophic when they do occur. In 1996, a Saudi Arabian jumbo jet collided with a Kazakh-owned cargo plane near New Delhi, killing 349 people in the world's worst mid-air accident. There have been on-ground collisions too. So how do a pilot and an air traffic controller with all the cards stacked against them manage to land smoothly enough to get 155 people out alive when birds blow out both the aircraft's engines? Communication. Listen or read this exchange between Sully, Skiles and Departure Control or Harten. I'm sure, by now, you've all heard it before. But really, listen to what is happening. Sullenberger gets a lot of credit, as he should, but how about Skiles and Harten. All are calm, which is a part of the training but no matter how much training you've had, staying calm in a situation as unprecedented as this is beyond impressive. In an interview I watched, Sully's initial reaction was "This can't be happening" as he recounts the physiological reactions of increased blood pressure and tunnel vision he experienced as both engines lost all power. Sully had never trained for a water landing, they didn't have flight simulations for such things, the only training he had was theoretical discussions of what one might do in a water landing situation. He'd never experienced anything like this in his four-decade long aviation career, so he needed to rely on his training and his years in the industry and focus on only the clear, immediate and highest priority items. He said in the interview that multi-tasking is a myth and that he needed to focus only on those items that were necessary. Sully has short staccato like communication. He distills the content into necessary information, so clearly, he can focus on the aircraft and flying it. Notice Harten is willing to do whatever it takes to get the plane landed safely. You can feel it in his voice. Both incredible. Harten later recounted his utter disbelief that Sully had chosen to land on the Hudson, believing that would be the aircraft's demise…you cannot hear it in his voice, but he does retort, "I'm sorry, say again Cactus?" Right before impact, as Sully thinks about his broadcast message to the passengers, he recounts that courage can be contagious as he took an extravagant amount of time, a 3-4 second pause to think before saying, "Brace for impact" to give the crew and passengers a vivid image of what was about to happen.

Skiles and Sully were able to work wordlessly according to Sully. Using as few words as possible to maintain focus. Right before impact, Sully says to Skiles, "Got any ideas?" and Skiles responds, "Actually not." Knowing they had both done everything in their power, they had exhausted all their means to land safely. When they eventually landed, they said to one another; "Well that wasn't as bad as I thought." An agonizing 4 hours post evacuation followed to ensure that everyone was accounted for and safe.

I thought of this incident repeatedly as I compiled this list of *365 Must-Know Talks* because it perfectly illustrates the need for effective and succinct communication in a crisis. A presentation is not always one that you have been given time to prepare for, it may arise out of a tragedy. If you are the one asked to speak, or you have volunteered in a difficult circumstance, take a page out of Sullenberger's, Skiles and Harten's exchange; remain unflappable, distill your language down to what is necessary and do whatever it takes to land your plane safely.

Tip – Remain unflappable and calm in your language when speaking in times of crisis.

#89 – Godfrey Hardy

1877–1947

Context – Godfrey Hardy was an English mathematician known for his achievements in number theory and mathematical analysis. He is best known by those outside the field of mathematics for his essay in 1940 on the *Aesthetics of Mathematics, A Mathematician's Apology*. This essay is considered one of the best insights into the mind of a mathematician, written for the amateur of mathematics.

"Beauty is the first test. There is no permanent place in this world for ugly mathematics."

Analysis – I must admit before I had heard of Hardy and his essay, *A Mathematician's Apology*, I had not given much thought to math as analogous to painting or poetry. Sure, I felt at some level math could be creative for those whose minds are numerically inclined, but now that I've devoted days to studying Hardy and specifically this essay, I'm 100 percent converted. I believe that math can be beautiful even if I don't completely understand, and the minds of pure mathematicians, or at least the ones who don't force a practical application out of all the math that they do, are, in particular, a thing of wondrous beauty. It is astounding to me as I write and reflect on math how very little insight into math as an artform I was given as a child in school. Not one teacher in my 13 years of elementary, junior high, and high school found a way to generate a notion of math being beautiful, balanced, harmonious and aesthetically pleasing or even awoke a desire for me to learn outside of the standard applied set of mathematics? Let's come back to these questions, but first.

In the 1800s Carl Friedrich Gauss said, "mathematics is the queen of the sciences, and the number theory is the queen of mathematics." Hardy further explains Gauss' statement by saying that the number theory, has extreme un-applicability, but that alone is not what makes it queen. It is because the concepts that constitute the number theory are more elegant compared to those of any other branch of mathematics. For Hardy, real mathematics was a creative activity and shouldn't require an explanation in the same way a person observing the Mona Lisa at the Louvre, doesn't need for an explanation or discussion (although her smile is something of a da Vinci trademark of 'self-amusement'), but can simply soak up the piece's beauty and stand in awe of its composition.

My pursuit in truly digesting the concept that mathematics has beauty led me to the human brain. The brain is acclimatized to natural orderliness for good reason—evolution. An unbruised pear is better than a bruised one because bruising and bumps signify disease. Well-balanced features even influence our selection of partners. I watched a TED video the other day on the symmetry of our bodies and faces and how to others, this unconsciously signifies healthy genes. Balance, beauty, and harmony are driven by evolutionary reasons. These reasons ensure that we continue as a species.

So, this is where the math comes in, and my theory that balance, beauty, and harmony were first driven by survival. Once survival was destined, scientists could start extending that theory of aesthetics toward equations and working on them. If something feels right or fits nicely, I believe it comes from an unconscious observation of symmetry and harmony. Stay with me. I'm still working on this theory, and it has plagued me for a few days as I funneled it down to apply it to presentation skills. Let's go back to the questions I had for my schoolteachers. Why didn't they teach the notion that math is beautiful, balanced, harmonious and aesthetically pleasing? Why didn't they show me this or encourage a desire to learn outside of the applied set of mathematics? Either they didn't understand what Hardy's essay discussed, or they sought no value in teaching it, perhaps they didn't fully grasp the concept because math had never been presented to them as an artform. One thing is for sure that they were indeed taught Hardy's concept, or if the essay came out after their schooling (the essay was published in the 1940s), then certainly they were taught the concepts by Einstein, who said, "It is possible to know when you are right, way ahead of checking all the consequences. You can recognize truth by its beauty and simplicity." So, either they didn't understand, or they thought it had no value. What I'm saying is, this concept introduced at the right stage of my math journey could've made a monumental difference to me and countless others trying to embrace the joys of mathematics. That said, I don't think my career in mathematics would've surfaced either way as it's not my natural disposition, but it would've likely sparked an interest in an arena that was completely void for my entire educational career. So many hours were wasted when they could've been spent in enlightened learning. If taught with a zest and zeal, including these theories of the beauty of math, it likely would've captured my attention. Isn't that the purpose of teaching, to capture attention, spark interest, plant concepts?

As we've discussed, most presentations are about teaching or translating knowledge to your audience. If you are not fully absorbed in your topic and don't understand it completely, or you see no value in what you are sharing, please stop and take another path. Allow someone else who has devoted the time, energy, and intellect to the topic to put it forward in a presentation format. Harsh? Perhaps, but it needs to be said.

Tip – Teach and present your content with zest and zeal or don't teach it at all.

#88 – Barbara Charline Jordan

1936–1996

Context – Barbara Charline Jordan was an American politician from Texas. From 1973–1979 she also served as a congresswoman in the U.S. House of Representatives. Here, Jordan gives a keynote address at the 1976 Democratic National Convention.

"…I, Barbara Jordan, am a keynote speaker. When—a lot of years passed since 1832, and during that time, it would have been most unusual for any national political party to ask a Barbara Jordan to deliver a keynote address. But tonight, here I am. And I feel—I feel that notwithstanding the past that my presence here is one additional bit of evidence that the American Dream need not forever be deferred." And at the end of her speech, "Now I began this speech by commenting to you on the uniqueness of a Barbara Jordan making a keynote address. Well, I am going to close my speech by quoting a Republican President, and I ask you that as you listen to these words of Abraham Lincoln, relate them to the concept of a national community in which every last one of us participates:

"As I would not be a slave, so I would not be a master." "This—This—This expresses my idea of Democracy. Whatever differs from this to the extent of the difference, is no democracy."

Analysis – This is one of the most powerfully confident deliveries of a speech that I've ever seen! Notice the rhythm, the pulse, the beat of the line, "I Barbara Jordan am a keynote speaker." I love it! The content of Jordan's talk is exemplary and historically noteworthy given that in 1976, as Jordan herself points out, one may not automatically assume that she would be asked to give such a necessary talk. And boy, does she ever! The speech itself is artfully crafted as it covers so much ground gracefully and boldly. For today's post, though, I want to focus on Jordan's delivery, because in my estimation, you will not find another speech as good at showcasing the artfulness of modulation. In this book of *365 Must-Know Talks* we've covered intonation and cadence many times, which are umbrella terms that describe what one does with their voice in a presentation. Here, let's narrow the funnel of that definition and talk about modulation. Modulation is defined in a collection of ways:

a. A change in stress, pitch, loudness, or tone of the voice; an inflection of the voice.

b. An instance of change or inflection.

c. The harmonious use of language, as in poetry or prose.

d. A transition from one key to another in a musical score.

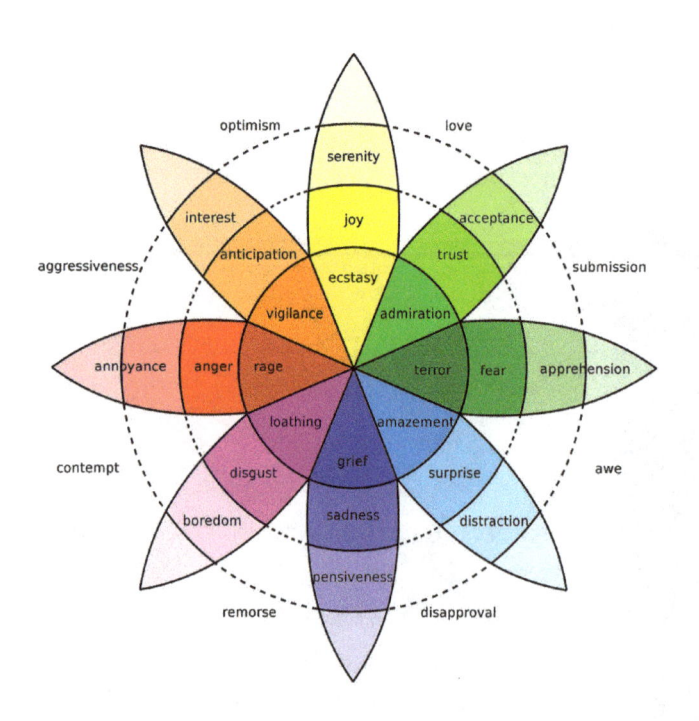

Modulation is not simply stressing a singular word but looking at the feeling of an entire sentence or thought and putting extra emphasis (including pace, pitch, power, and volume) on that section. Simply put, appropriately modulating your voice is more appealing to the ear. That's it! Modulation is a way to emote the emotional aspect of your words, and it injects some zeal and spirit into your delivery. This is an area that I spend a reasonable amount of time on in my presentation classes because, for many people, this task of modulating is quite tricky. How you would modulate your voice in regular one-on-one conversation looks very different from how you'd modulate in a speech. One of the things I do in these classes is present Robert Plutchiks' eight classified primary emotions:

- Anger
- Fear
- Sadness

- Disgust
- Surprise
- Anticipation
- Trust
- Joy

These primary emotions intermix with one another to form the full spectrum of human emotional experiences much the same way that primary colours work together to make all colours. In my classes, I'll often get participants to try on each of these primary emotions through game-type exercises. Most people know how to do each of the eight pretty easily, and it becomes a question of amplification and animation. Here's an example: Let's say you have a dog. When you come home from a long day of work, which of the eight primary emotions do you use to greet your dog? Hopefully, it's joy. How does that sound? Most likely, your voice will escalate up, and the words will match the emotion with kindness. What if you maintained the same modulation (higher-pitched, happy voice) but replaced the words with angry ones telling your dog that he was the most useless animal that ever lived and that you hated him? Well, he would most likely still come running to you, tail wagging. The effects of proper modulation are amazing. Now, the real skill is to match the words with the emotion and demonstrate the fitting modulation.

Tip - Take a page from Jordan's speech and embrace, nurture and use modulation to display the emotions behind your words.

#87 – A.A. Milne

1882–1958

Context – A.A. Milne was an author best known for his books that center on the character, Winnie-the-Pooh.

"When you wake up in the morning, Pooh," said Piglet at last, "what's the first thing you say to yourself?"

"What's for breakfast?" said Pooh. "What do you say, Piglet?"

"I say, I wonder what's going to happen exciting today?" said Piglet.

Pooh nodded thoughtfully.

"It's the same thing," Pooh said."

Analysis – As a child, I must confess, I was not a fan of Winnie-the-Pooh at all. I didn't own a single Winnie-the-Pooh book and when Winnie-the-Pooh television specials would come on, I would initially be excited because it was a cartoon (this, my youngin' readers was before any cartoon channels and one would have to wait for a cartoon to surface on the boob tube) but after a few minutes, I would become bored and switch the channel (and that meant getting up and walking to the television set to manually change the channel —I may have just outed myself as Gen X!)

I've since been converted and am now quite the fan, which isn't surprising since Milne has been rather boisterous about indicating that he didn't write the Pooh books for children in the first place. To me, they are adult reading material. I was shown the way of the Pooh through a book called *The Tao of Pooh* (written by Benjamin Hoff) which explains Taoism by Winnie-the-Pooh. There are some interesting principles nestled in the book's contents, such as "P'U, the Uncarved Block." The Uncarved Block states that things and people in their original simplicity contain their own natural power. When changed, as simplicity is so often done, this innate power is damaged. Pooh is this Uncarved Block (my opinion anyway) and acts as the epitome of simplicity and happiness. The other characters: Piglet, Owl, Eeyore, Rabbit, Tigger, Kanga, Roo and Christopher Robin too represent deviations from Pooh's simplicity and shine a light onto characteristics in various personalities.

Most of us overcomplicate almost everything in life, and presentations are no exception. How many times have you been asked to do a presentation and immediately go into the Owl mode and immediately start seeking knowledge so that you may *appear* wise (maybe not necessarily so)? Perhaps you channel your inner Eeyore and promptly begin complaining about the upcoming task, or perhaps you are an overexcited Tigger (I think I'm a Tigger) and take on everything with an I-can-do-it-all-and-then-some attitude even when you can't. Maybe you embody Rabbit, and immediately show everyone how busy you are with the task at hand, but along the way you miss critical elements that should've been included. Perhaps you are Piglet who, after accepting the task, start feeling scared and hesitant and because of this, get very little done.

Pooh doesn't hesitate. He just does. Things always work out for Pooh, and I don't think it was coincidental in Milne's mind-eye that this is so. Pooh works alongside his inner nature and doesn't interfere with it. He lives a simple life, in mind and spirit. I think we can all learn a thing or two from good ol' Winnie-the-Pooh when it comes to presentation skills:

1. Don't hesitate, make a start!
2. Work with your inner nature to uncover your presentation's content.
3. Live with an uncluttered mind so that you may live a life of simplicity.
4. Be open to everyone.
5. The simplest solution is often the best solution.

Tip – Adopt the philosophy behind simplicity and your presentations will soar.

#86 – Blake Mycoskie

(1976)

Context – Blake Mycoskie, is the founder of TOMS shoes, known as the shoe CEO with a soul. Here Mycoskie visits Georgia Southern University in February 2010 and addresses the student population.

"Heard of TOMS shoes? With every pair you purchase, TOMS will give a pair of new shoes to a child in need. One for One."

Analysis – I have no affiliation or commission by doing so, but go here, *tomsshoes.ca* and buy some shoes. My interest with this book is to list the best of the best as it relates to presentation skills. As has happened innumerable times during my pursuit of the *365 Must-Know Talks*, I encounter an individual who uses their cause as a platform to transmit an idea or product in the format of a presentation and they do so brilliantly. Such is the case with Mycoskie. Here is a guy from Texas, who aspired to be a tennis player, but his tennis career was cut short due to an injury, and instead he goes to Argentina on vacation, and after talking to some people on a volunteer shoe-drive mission in a café, comes up with the idea for TOMS. Not only does he come up with the idea, but he executes it in February 2006 and achieved the goal of providing the company's one-millionth pair of shoes to a child in need in September of 2010. To date, the company is worth nearly 400 million dollars. Wow!

What an eclectic mix of presenters this list of talks includes, and I'm thrilled to give Mycoskie a mention. There is an absence of pomp and ceremony. Mycoskie utilizes the platform of giving a presentation to drive the cause. He does so with great storytelling, superb body language, and impressive delivery. It is refreshing to see the owner of a company, that has its foundation in philanthropy, fulfill a need. When you believe in what you are presenting, people will listen and take action when you propose an action plan i.e., buying some shoes or sunglasses. If you appeal to your audience through noble motives, you will have a relaxed and interesting delivery, and they will be compelled to help.

Tip – Believe in what you are presenting, and your audience will too.

#85 – Seth Godin

(1960)

Context – Marketing guru, Seth Godin talks at TED 2013 about why bad or bizarre marketing ideas are more successful than boring ones in his talk entitled, "How To Get Your Ideas to Spread."

"I'm going to give you four specific examples; I'm going to cover at the end about how a company called Silk tripled their sales; how an artist named Jeff Koons went from being a nobody to making a whole bunch of money and having a lot of impact; to how Frank Gehry redefined what it meant to be an architect. And one of my biggest failures as a marketer in the last few years—a record label I started that had a CD called Sauce.

Before I can do that, I've got to tell you about sliced bread, and a guy named Otto Rohwedder. Now, before sliced bread was invented in the 1910s, I wonder what they said? Like the greatest invention since the telegraph or something. But this guy named Otto Rohwedder invented sliced bread, and he focused, like most inventors did, on the patent part and the making part. And the thing about the invention of sliced bread is this—that for the first 15 years after sliced bread was available no one bought it; no one knew about it; it was a complete and total failure. And the reason is that until Wonder came along and figured out how to spread the idea of sliced bread, no one wanted it. That the success of sliced bread, like the success of almost everything we've talked about at this conference, is not always about what the patent is like, or what the factory is like—it's about can you get your idea to spread, or not. And I think that the way you're going to get what you want, or cause the change that you want to change, to happen, is to figure out a way to get your ideas to spread.

And it doesn't matter to me whether you're running a coffee shop or you're an intellectual, or you're in business, or you're flying hot air balloons. I think that all this stuff applies to everybody regardless of what we do. That what we are living in is a century of idea diffusion. That people who can spread ideas, regardless of what those ideas are, win. When I talk about it, I usually pick business, because they make the best pictures that you can put in your presentation, and because it's the easiest sort of way to keep score. But I want you to forgive me when I use these examples because I'm talking about anything that you decide to spend your time to do.

At the heart of spreading ideas is TV and stuff like TV. TV and mass media made it really easy to spread ideas in a certain way. I call it the TV-industrial complex. The way the TV-industrial complex works, is you buy some ads, interrupt some people, that gets you distribution. You use the distribution you get to sell more products. You take the profit from that to buy more ads. And it goes around and around and around, the same way that the military-industrial complex worked a long time ago. That model of, and we heard it yesterday—if we could only get onto the homepage of Google, if we could only figure out how to get promoted there, or grab that person by the throat, and tell them about what we want to do. If we did that then everyone would pay attention, and we would win. Well, this TV-industrial complex informed my entire childhood and probably yours. I mean, all of these products succeeded because someone figured out how to touch people in a way they weren't expecting, in a way they didn't necessarily want, with an ad, over and over again until they bought it.

Analysis – Seth Godin is an author and is considered one of the best speakers in the corporate world. I'd agree with that. He's smart, he's interesting, his content is captivating. This talk is a must-see on so many levels. From a content perspective, Godin's bestowal of the term *Otaku*—a Japanese term used to refer to people with obsessive interests—is rather skillful in bridging an analogy to marketing. I won't forget that term or his story about the rise of Apple or Silk or the lava lamp. Honestly, I feel I could recite much of this talk from memory. Hold on, I'm going to try.

Insert final Jeopardy music. Total time-lapse 33 minutes.

So, I retold the presentation to a friend (it took about seven minutes, not the 18 or so minutes that it took Godin) and I asked her if she would watch the clip to see if I did the speech justice (full disclosure, I did watch the talk twice, a few months apart before I recounted it to my friend). I asked her to rate me on having the basic crux of the message and also my ability to re-count most of the examples. My friend gave me a score of eight out of ten (probably a little generous, as I'd have given myself a 6.5). The point is when a talk is delivered well, it is easy to recount much of the detail, and oodles of fun to share it over and over again with others, long after the talk has reached its end. I encourage you to give this experiment a try. Start with a talk you adore (I'm sure you can find at least one between the pages of this book), and then try to do the same exercise with a presentation you attend in person, maybe at work. What's the difference, if any?

There are many aspects of Godin's presentation that I enjoy, but I would like to showcase one final attribute that we've yet to discuss in this list of *365 Must-Know Talks*—roadmaps. Not the kind of roadmaps that are used to navigate actual roads but the sort of map that outlines to your audience the trajectory of your talk. In so many presentations that I observe, this is a much needed component. If you have in your audience anyone like me, someone who needs to understand the motivation of the talk and how you are going to get there, then including a presentation road map is critical to keeping type A's happy and engaged. It should be a given that everyone in your audience will want to know who you are and why you're there. By establishing a road map, you let your audience know what they can expect. Godin does the road map brilliantly, with words. In about 20 seconds he walks you through what is going to unfold: "I'm going to give you four specific examples—and I'm going to cover at the end—how a company called Silk tripled their sales by doing one thing. How an artist named Jeff Koons went from being a nobody to making a whole bunch of money and having a lot of impact, how Frank Gehry redefined what it meant to be an architect. And one of my biggest failures as a marketer in the last few years, a record label I started that had a CD called "Sauce." Godin's road map is enticing, it lures you into wanting to hear more.

Another road map that I use is an actual map that I draw on flip chart paper. This works well for a presentation, a workshop, and even a keynote address. There isn't a talk I give where I don't prepare a flip chart road map. They are all customized to what the upcoming talk covers. I draw a car on a road, and there are pit stops, and those pit stops are the key components or objectives of the talk. As the car travels on the flip chart road, we go through all of the major objectives of our time together. By the way, particularly for longer talks or doing workshops, theroad map is awesome for recapping the day and bringing the beginning of the day full circle with the end.

Tip – Leave your audiences fascinated with your presentation so they are excited to re-tell it! And use roadmaps to set up for your audience the route your presentation will take.

#84 – Cinderella

Context – Cinderella is a classic folk tale, and the popular Disney 1950's version is just one adaptation. At its core, the story is about uncovering unjust oppression, emerging triumphant, and then reaping the reward. The woes of the title character can be seen in thousands of variations throughout the world, all with the same theme—a young woman living in pitiful circumstances that are abruptly changed to astonishing fortune.

A dream is a wish your heart makes

When you're fast asleep

In dreams, you lose your heartaches

Whatever you wish for, you keep

Have faith in your dreams, and someday

Your rainbow will come smiling thru

No matter how your heart is grieving

If you keep on believing

the dream that you wish will come true.

Analysis – A Cinderella song making its way onto my list of *365 Must-Know Talks* may be a little unexpected. But a song is just a talk, with a melody attached. A poem is perhaps one of the most well-thought-out and well-composed talks there is. That is, in my humble estimation anyway, why people connect so emotionally and veraciously to songs and poetry. Think about your favourite song. What is the song's message? Why do you connect to it? Often it comes down to the lyrics and the message.

In this Disney classic Cinderella says to her mouse friends, "They can't order me to stop dreaming!" and this is the core of the song's message. Cinderella takes a dreadful circumstance and uses the pep talk presentation technique to aid in the process. Does Cinderella seem angry, depressed, or vengeful to you? Nope. Instead, she takes her situation and talks to herself in a kind way, and in a way that is sprinkled with hope and dreams. We should talk to ourselves thoughtfully, honestly, and peacefully. Our own pep talk should bolster our enthusiasm and morale, and not bring us down. What can you glean from Cinderella that you can use in your presentation skills preparation checklist and beyond that in your own lives? I hope you see it is all about attitude. Launch into every new experience, every difficult challenge with a Cinderella-like attitude. It does a world of good.

Tip – Channel an inner Cinderella-like attitude into all you do.

#83 – William Boughton Pitkin

1878–1953

Context – William Pitkin was an author and a publisher, literary agent and university professor. Through a series of lectures, Pitkin explored the implications of increasing life expectancy in his book, *Life Begins at Forty*.

"Every day brings forth some new thing that adds to the joy of life after forty. Work becomes easy and brief. Play grows richer and longer. Leisure lengthens. Life's afternoon is brighter, warmer, fuller of song, and long before shadows stretch, every fruit grows rife…Life begins at forty."

Analysis – Life begins at forty has become a part of our regular vernacular here in North America. Although Pitkin's book was written in 1932, it seems that social culture has brought this sentiment to the fore more and more. This made me think of presentation skills (imagine that?). How many times have you attended or participated in a presentation on a subject that had nothing to do with you, nothing that you were interested in, and was ultimately a waste of time? My guess is probably at least a few times. Part of being a superb presenter is understanding who is in your audience, what they want/need to learn, what will make them listen, and then encouraging and giving them the tools, they need to take action, if appropriate. I once watched a sales presentation at a large corporation here in Calgary. The speaker presented to the organization's human resources department, intending to help the HR department understand the current sales. I gleaned that the root of the presentation was a high-level transfer of sales numbers with the hope of shedding light on where the current sales numbers were and where they needed to be for the next quarter, the next year and a five-year projection. The presenter (the salesperson) talked for nearly 45 minutes to a room of ten HR professionals ranging from the VP to the payroll administrator. The first slide that sprung up was littered with numbers; sales numbers, forecasts, budget numbers, year-ago numbers, percentages. It was overwhelming. About three minutes into the presentation the audience had already completely checked out. This was the problem. Although the content of the presentation was quite good, it was designed for other salespeople, not human resource professionals. What tends to happen when we have been in a position for some time is we begin to think that everyone understands our department's lingo, but nothing could be further from the truth. VYAG, prospect, closing, velocity, probing, opening, a need behind the need, all of these sales terms may not mean a whole lot unless you're in sales, so remove the lingo entirely from the presentation or be ready to explain the concepts in layman's terms. Think of it like being the author of one of those …*For Dummies* books. A presenter has to distill their information to be accessible to their audience. It would've been far more appropriate for the presenter in the above example to sit back and ask the following questions:

1. If I was in HR, what type of information would I want to hear? (i.e., the bottom line.)

2. In what format would I like to see this information—what props or visual aids could I use to help the process? (i.e., uncluttered PowerPoint slides, handouts, takeaways, audience participation group activities.)

3. How could my key message be digested by those not in sales? (i.e., we need more sales, and this is how much.) Perhaps it would be beneficial to have the audience analyze the information through activities, etc.

For the record, I believe that life does unfold more vibrantly once you reach the age of forty. I believe that wisdom and natural confidence emerge when one has continued to be introspective and reflective. Think about the people you most admire. I'd bet many of them are over the age of 40 😊.

Russian-born American singer, Sophie Tucker said it best, "The secret of longevity is to keep breathing!"

Tip – Tailor your presentation to fit your audience's needs.

82 – Anna Quindlen

(1953)

Context – Anna Quindlen is an American author, journalist, and columnist. Three of her five best-selling novels have been made into films, including *One True Thing*, for which Meryl Streep won an Academy Award. The following speech transcript was delivered at a graduation ceremony where Quindlen was awarded an honorary Ph.D.

"I'm a novelist. My work is human nature. Real life is all I know.

Don't ever confuse the two, your life and your work. You will walk out of here this afternoon with only one thing that no one else has. There will be hundreds of people out there with your same degree: there will be thousands of people doing what you want to do for a living.

But you will be the only person alive who has sole custody of your life. Your particular life. Your entire life. Not just your life at a desk or your life on a bus or in a car or at the computer. Not just the life of your mind, but the life of your heart. Not just your bank accounts but also your soul.

People don't talk about the soul very much anymore. It's so much easier to write a resume than to craft a spirit. But a resume is cold comfort on a winter's night, or when you're sad, or broke, or lonely, or when you've received your test results and they're not so good.

Here is my resume: I am a good mother to three children. I have tried never to let my work stand in the way of being a good parent. I no longer consider myself the centre of the universe. I show up. I listen. I try to laugh. I am a good friend to my husband. I have tried to make marriage vows mean what they say. I am a good friend to my friends and them to me. Without them, there would be nothing to say to you today, because I would be a cardboard cut out. But I call them on the phone and I meet them for lunch.

I would be rotten, at best mediocre, at my job if those other things were not true.

You cannot be really first rate at your work if your work is all you are. So here's what I wanted to tell you today: Get a life. A real life, not a manic pursuit of the next promotion, the bigger pay cheque, the larger house. Do you think you'd care so very much about those things if you blew an aneurysm one afternoon or found a lump in your breast?

Get a life in which you notice the smell of salt water pushing itself on a breeze at the seaside, a life in which you stop and watch how a red-tailed hawk circles over the water, or the way a baby scowls with concentration when she tries to pick up a sweet with her thumb and first finger.

Get a life in which you are not alone. Find people you love, and who love you. And remember that love is not leisure, it is work. Pick up the phone. Send an email. Write a letter. Get a life in which you are generous. And realize that life is the best thing ever, and that you have no business taking it for granted. Care so deeply about its goodness that you want to spread it around. Take money you would have spent on beer and give it to charity. Work in a soup kitchen. Be a big brother or sister. All of you want to do well. But if you do not do good too, then doing well will never be enough.

It is so easy to waste our lives, our days, our hours, and our minutes. It is so easy to take for granted the colour of our kids' eyes, the way the melody in a symphony rises and falls and disappears and rises again.

It is so easy to exist instead of to live.

I learned to live many years ago. I learned to love the journey, not the destination.

I learned that it is not a dress rehearsal, and that today is the only guarantee you get.

I learned to look at all the good in the world and try to give some of it back because I believed in it, completely and utterly. And I tried to do that, in part, by telling others what I had learned. By telling them this: Consider the lilies of the field. Look at the fuzz on a baby's ear. Read in the back yard with the sun on your face.

Learn to be happy. And think of life as a terminal illness, because if you do, you will live it with joy and passion as it ought to be lived".

Analysis – I've been searching for the video counterpart to this transcript for a while now and haven't been able to uncover it. You know what? It doesn't matter. I've never met Quindlen, I've never heard her speak, but I can envision the delivery by the nature of her finely chosen words. Words are an interesting phenomenon, aren't they? As a novice writer myself with the first draft of a manuscript containing some 85,000 words that is waiting to be massaged, edited, and mothered, I know that meticulously choosing the right word can make the sentence jump from the page. String enough of those sentences together, and the story will leap from the page, and you'll have at your fingertips an artfully constructed, complete piece that can impact other's lives. Isn't that what writing is about? Isn't that too what being a public speaker is also about? Constructing words that funnel into sentences that flow into concepts that create a whole presentation ultimately has an impact and meaning on others. So, why did I choose this speech from Quindlen? Simply because it had a profound effect on me. It has meaning, and it is alive and vibrant. I understand its meaning, and I connect with it profoundly. I aspire to it and I've learned from it. What more can you ask for from a talk?

While you're preparing your own presentations, why not ask yourself a crucial question in the preparatory phase, "Will these words, these sentences, this message have an impact on others?" If the answer is no, ask yourself, why not?

Tip – With every presentation you give, make sure to have an impact on your listeners.

#81 – Jill Tarter

(1944)

Context – Astronomer Jill Tarter is awarded the TED Prize One Wish to Change the World in 2009 for her talk, "Why the Search for Alien Intelligence Matters."

"So, my question: are we alone? The story of humans is the story of ideas—scientific ideas that shine light into dark corners, ideas that we embrace rationally and irrationally, ideas for which we've lived and died and killed and been killed, ideas that have vanished in history, and ideas that have been set in dogma. It's a story of

nations, of ideologies, of territories, and of conflicts among them. But, every moment of human history, from the Stone Age to the Information Age, from Sumer and Babylon to the iPod and celebrity gossip, they've all been carried out—every book that you've read, every poem, every laugh, every tear—they've all happened here. Here. Here. Here. Perspective is a very powerful thing. Perspectives can change. Perspectives can be altered. From my perspective, we live on a fragile island of life, in a universe of possibilities. For many millennia, humans have been on a journey to find answers, answers to questions about naturalism and transcendence, about who we are and why we are, and of course, who else might be out there. Is it really just us? Are we alone in this vast universe of energy and matter and chemistry and physics? Well, if we are, it's an awful waste of space. But, what if we're not?"

Analysis – This is one of my favourite talks, ever! Obviously, or it wouldn't be on this list of the *365 Must-Know Talks*. This talk is 21 minutes long, so if you are genuinely seeking counsel on how to become a better speaker, then take the time to watch it in its entirety. Sure, Tarter is articulate, intelligent, qualified, engaging, but the sheer beauty in how she has constructed this talk is what my focus will be on today. This talk is so aesthetically appealing from a visual and auditory perspective that you get sucked in, much like watching your favourite film for the first time.

I felt transported while watching Tarter speak, and that is one of the biggest compliments I can bestow. Let's be honest, the topic matters; aliens and intelligent life is an incredibly difficult topic for most to absorb, but I walked away having understood her message and wanting to learn more. It is no wonder that Tarter won the TED prize that year.

From a visual perspective: Tarter's slides are stunning, and she uses them brilliantly. Not a single string of words in bullets, instead she uses graphics to illustrate her words. There are at least a dozen examples, but the cluster of slides right at the beginning—when she shows us how small earth is, *"it all happened, here, here, here, here, here,"*—are so powerful that you can hear the audience's emotion.

From an auditory perspective: Tarter's style of presenting this topic is not by ramming her ideas and opinions down her audience's throat, but rather to use a questioning technique throughout. She begins her presentation by jumping right into a question, "Are we alone?" Her voice is commanding, yet soft, articulate, and accessible. She is passionate about her topic, and it emanates from her every pore. When I first watched this talk, I found Tarter's communication style so incredibly mesmerizing that I watched it five times over to try to figure out exactly what her secret was. It is her, and that is all. She is authentic, and she is herself. There is no incongruence, so her message flows like a melody flowing out of a singer who has practiced relentlessly to hit the right notes. I'm a fan, Jill, a huge fan. Finally, I'd like to point out a vital component of this talk. At the very end, notice how her tone and delivery becomes quiet, and how she leans in to give the illusion of being closer to her audience. She finishes with how we can all share her vision. This is possibly the most convincing last minute of a talk I've ever seen.

Tip – Create a presentation that is both visually and acoustically beautiful.

#80 – Harvey Milk

1930–1978

Context – In 1977, Harvey Milk became the first openly gay man to be elected to public office in the U.S. This speech entitled You Cannot Live on Hope Alone was given in 1978. Milk was assassinated shortly after delivering this speech. *Milk*, the film starring Sean Penn, was released in 2008.

"Somewhere in Des Moines or San Antonio, there is a young gay person who all the sudden realizes that he or she is gay; knows that if their parents find out, they will be tossed out of the house; their classmates will taunt the child; and the Anita Bryant's and John Briggs' are doing their part on TV. And that child has several options: staying in the closet, and suicide. And then one day that child might open the paper that says "Homosexual elected in San Francisco" and there are two new options. The option is to go to California, or stay in San Antonio and fight.

"Two days after I was elected, I got a phone call, and the voice was quite young. It was from Altoona, Pennsylvania. And the person said, "Thanks".

"And you've got to elect gay people, so that thousands upon thousands like that child know that there is hope for a better world; there is hope for a better tomorrow. Without hope, not only gays, but those blacks, the Asians, the disabled, the seniors; the "us's". The "us's": without hope the "us's" give up. I know that you can't live on hope alone, but without it, life is not worth living. And you, and you, and you… have got to give them hope."

Analysis – Create a vision of 1977. Sit back and think about North American culture, what was accepted, and what wasn't. Almost 45 years later, I wonder what Harvey Milk's speech would look like.
I would fathom that it would not be that different from the original. This is, in my estimation, one of the best speeches of all time. It is short, it has impact, and it creates a vision. It leaves us with hope. You can feel Milk's desire to change the world. And he did. When I think about presentation skills and giving talks that motivate others to action, one key component is to leave your audience with the confidence that things will change and with the hope for a better tomorrow and a better future. I believe Milk accomplishes this goal and has had a profound, far-reaching impact with his words. Thank you, Harvey Milk.

Tip – Transmit hope in your talks to motivate others to action.

#79 – Bill Stewart

1952–2012

Context – West Virginia Head Coach Bill Stewart rallies his team in the locker room prior to the 2008 Fiesta Bowl football game in a speech that has been titled, "Leave No Doubt."

"We got a great opportunity. We got a dandy waiting for us out there.

Offense. Play fast. Assignment free, man.

Defense. Swarm. Swarm and tackle. Punch that ball any chance you get and keep bustin' them.

Special teams: Lay it on the line and attack your responsibility. Attack.

We can out-block them. We can out-tackle them. We can out-hit 'em and hustle.

It's real simple. You out-block them. You out-tackle them. You out-hit 'em. You out-hustle 'em.

And you stay within the legal limits of the game!

It's Mountaineer pride! Nothing cheap! From the heart! Strain them!

Damn. I'm proud to be a Mountaineer! I picked you a good one, didn't I? Huh?

We got a good one. We are going to out-strain and out-hit these guys.

Let' em know. Leave no doubt tonight! Leave no doubt tonight! No doubt!

They shouldn't have played the old gold and blue. Not this night! Not this night!

Don't ever leave your wingman. Never, ever, ever bail out on your brother! You help. You strain and you fight!"

Analysis – I've been holding onto this pep talk for quite some time, waiting patiently to find the perfect place for it on this list of *365 Must-Know Talks*. Alright, confession, I am not the biggest sports fan, okay, I'm not a fan at all, but I am a monster fan of watching coaches, well, coach. It is fascinating to me and, this pep talk given by Stewart garners all of my interest and respect. I'd say a small fraction of all public speakers could pull this off as successfully as Stewart. I was reading some of the comments under the YouTube clip (as I always do) and found some of the negative comments he receives rather interesting. "Loudmouth" is the general comment from a negative nature, and I couldn't disagree more. Would this mode of delivery work for a president to rally their team? No! But that isn't what this talk is about. This talk has one singular purpose and that is to get the player's adrenaline pumping so that they will believe that they *will* win. Stewart tugs at every emotion in this short two-minute rally: anger, joy, pride, brotherhood, and fun, all wrapped up with some obvious direction of how to make it all happen. The two minutes play out like a great tune, with the crescendo billowing out of his every word…Bill believes they will win, and as an observer, so do I.

What can you take and learn from this talk, that can apply to your presentations?

Tip – Believe what you are saying in the talk to rally team.

#78 – Luc de Clapiers, marquis de Vauvenargue

1715–1747

Context – Luc de Clapiers, marquis de Vauvenargues, was a French writer, essayist and moralist.

"It is a great sign of mediocrity to praise always moderately."

Analysis – It's fair to say that most, if not all, human beings gravitate toward doing what they get attention for, and to be praised. Praise, in our culture, seems to come from some pretty odd places:

- A child gets good grades simply for regurgitation and memorization and is praised generously by both the institution and their parents but is not encouraged to learn independently.

- An adult is adored and praised for being physically beautiful even though they don't appear to possess any conceivable talent.

These are only two examples, but as a culture we seem to revere the wrong person, object, or idea when it comes to providing applause for a job well done. When I talk about praise, it is with the intent of appropriate praise. Praise that is warranted and necessary and needed. Not inappropriate praise that is based on vacant qualities.

I adopted as my mantra a Dale Carnegie quote that comes from *How to Win Friends and Influence People*: "Praise the slightest improvement and praise every improvement. Be hearty in your approbation and lavish in your praise." When I first read Carnegie's book some 25 years ago and started the process of instructing the program, it would fall on this section that talked about praise more often than any other component of the book. I remember thinking that it made sense to me but noted how often people don't praise lavishly. I have continued as part of my professional life to utilize this mantra. In workshops, I highlight only the positives, and the improvements I see. Rarely do I highlight the negatives or provide even constructive criticism. I believe that if I consistently provide criticisms, that is all the individual will remember. Think about a performance review that you've received in the past, I bet you remember the constructive bits far more readily than the criticism, it's human nature. So, with this method, if I highlight the improvements and provide praise along the way, those behaviours will be nurtured, and the behaviour that may need some work will naturally be replaced with positive ones. I believe that, and after years of adopting this method, I know it works. However, people are so used to receiving criticism they will often ask you for it, and at times beg you for it. They soon figure out as the workshop or presentation goes on what my method is, and I also explain it and I would encourage you to do the same. Whether you are about to launch into a presentation or conduct a workshop, remember that praise, as Vauvenargues says, should not be limited to a moderate plateau but should, as Carnegie says, be lavish. Your participants, and your audience will absorb and learn what you are teaching much more aptly than any alternate method.

Tip – Praise lavishly.

#77 – Jimmy Carter

(1924)

Context – President Jimmy Carter was the 39th President of the United States from 1977 to 1981. Carter was also the recipient of the 2002 Nobel Peace Prize, the only president to have received this prize after leaving office. He gave his "Crisis of Confidence" Speech, in 1979.

"First of all, I got a lot of personal advice. Let me quote a few of the typical comments that I wrote down.

This from a southern governor: "Mr. President, you are not leading this nation—you're just managing the government."

"You don't see the people enough anymore."

"Some of your Cabinet members don't seem loyal. There is not enough discipline among your disciples."

"Don't talk to us about politics or the mechanics of government, but about an understanding of our common good."

"Mr. President, we're in trouble. Talk to us about blood and sweat and tears."

"If you lead, Mr. President, we will follow."

…I want to talk to you right now about a fundamental threat to American democracy.

I do not mean our political and civil liberties. They will endure. And I do not refer to the outward strength of America, a nation that is at peace tonight everywhere in the world, with unmatched economic power and military might.

The threat is nearly invisible in ordinary ways.

It is a crisis of confidence.

It is a crisis that strikes at the very heart and soul and spirit of our national will. We can see this crisis in the growing doubt about the meaning of our own lives and in the loss of a unity of purpose for our nation.

The erosion of our confidence in the future is threatening to destroy the social and the political fabric of America."

Analysis – In this famous speech from President Jimmy Carter, delivered in 1979, he asks the question, "Why have we not been able to get together as a nation to resolve our serious energy problem?" Like peeling away layers of an onion to get to the meat of his speech, Carter realizes it is not merely a question of energy but a question of confidence. The United States of America had just lived through the famous Watergate Scandal and the country was in need of a leader who would be honest. And boy, did they get it in droves from the following president. It is a profound speech. I've now seen most presidential and prime ministerial speeches, at least in North America, both historical and current. This one is undoubtedly the most thought-provoking speech on many levels. Carter attempts to get at the root of what is plaguing the energy crisis by suggesting and doing a few things, but the two that strike me as most effective are: Being brutally honest and offering a significant challenge to his audience.

The crisis of confidence is suggested as it relates to the government, its values, and its way of life. Carter challenges the people of America to unite. What strikes me about President Carter is he tells the truth even though the truth is somewhat melancholy. Most public figures try to spin their language, so the truth gets muddled, and the outcome gets muddled too because the urgency of the issue doesn't surface. There is no real direction, or they blatantly lie (insert Nixon here). Carter doesn't do this. He acknowledges the elephant in the room. He tells the people to curb self-absorption for the good of the country: "…too many of us now tend to worship self-indulgence and consumption. Human identity is no longer defined by what one does, but by what one owns. But we've discovered that owning things and consuming things does not satisfy our longing for meaning. We've learned that piling up material goods cannot fill the emptiness of lives which have no confidence or purpose…And I'm asking you for your good and for your Nation's security to take no unnecessary trips, to use carpools or public transportation whenever you can, to park your car one extra day per week, to obey the speed limit, and to set your thermostats to save fuel. Every act of energy conservation like this is more than just common sense— I tell you it is an act of patriotism…."

Did his speech work? No, it didn't. But whether a speech achieves its objectives does not always determine its worth. I believe if the people watching this speech that day in 1979 had implemented much of what Carter was suggesting, we would be in a very different predicament both as a North American entity and as it relates to energy. In the end, my own belief is that Carter was too principled for the masses, and the audience didn't understand the severity of the issues. But I'm not sure if Carter could have done anything differently in this speech. As I sum up a tip for today, I reflect on Carter's speech. When someone offers knowledge and expertise to you, as an audience member, digest it, ruminate on it, and think about it. Ask yourself if you should change based on what you've heard and how you should go about changing. If you are the presenter offering this knowledge and expertise, allow it to be an exchange with those around you, find the best way to gain momentum so that the metaphorical train can continue and not come to a crashing halt.

Tip – Exchange knowledge and expertise with your audience.

#76 – Brothers Grimm

Wilhelm Carl Grimm 1786–1859 and Jacob Grimm 1785–1863

Context – *Hansel and Gretel* is a story written by the famous Brothers Grimm—Wilhelm Carl Grimm, a German author and anthropologist, and his younger brother of Jacob Grimm. It is a story published in 1812 in Grimm's Fairy Tales. Hansel and Gretel are brother and sister are abandoned in a forest where they encounter a witch who prepares to fatten them up prior to eating them.

"…Suddenly the door opened, and a woman as old as the hills, who supported herself on crutches, came creeping out. Hansel and Gretel were so terribly frightened that they let fall what they had in their hands.

The old woman, however, nodded her head, and said, "Oh, you dear children, who has brought you here? Do come in, and stay with me. No harm shall happen to you."

She took them both by the hand, and led them into her little house. Then good food was set before them, milk and pancakes, with sugar, apples, and nuts. Afterwards two pretty little beds were covered with clean white linen, and Hansel and Gretel lay down in them, and thought they were in heaven.

The old woman had only pretended to be so kind. She was in reality a wicked witch, who lay in wait for children, and had only built the little house of bread in order to entice them there. When a child fell into her power, she killed it, cooked and ate it, and that was a feast day with her. Witches have red eyes, and cannot see far, but they have a keen scent like the beasts, and are aware when human beings draw near. When Hansel and Gretel came into her neighbourhood, she laughed with malice, and said mockingly, "I have them, they shall not escape me again."

Early in the morning before the children were awake, she was already up, and when she saw both of them sleeping and looking so pretty, with their plump and rosy cheeks, she muttered to herself, that will be a dainty mouthful."

Analysis – Did you know that fairytales have existed in every corner of the world within every culture and are most likely, the strongest and oldest tradition of oratory? Fairytales were originally told out loud and were written with that intent. To think, back in the day, that a fairytale was to be read aloud would have seemed preposterous. It is also why when one begins trying to uncover the original transcripts, it proves challenging since many of the versions were only ever spoken aloud. The Brothers Grimm were the first to begin the process of recording them in the 1800s.

I knew many moons ago that *Hansel and Gretel* would make it onto my list of *365 Must-Know Talks* particularly the highlighted excerpt above, because the language and message are so fascinating to me. What a spellbinding fairytale. The story's main characters, Hansel and Gretel, are a brother and sister who discover a house of candy and cake in the forest that is owned by a cannibalistic witch! They have an awful stepmother and a spineless father, and that is why they find themselves in the black forest. In that black forest, they feast on the house made of candy but it was a scheme to trap the children so the witch could devour them! It is dark, and many of the newer versions of the story water down the original version.

So, what does *Hansel and Gretel* have to do with presentation skills? A few things—we could talk about the power of a positive attitude, which is a significant moral component of this tale, or we could talk about making the best of a horrendous situation, or we could talk about the same actions and how they will produce the same results. But let's focus on the overall, original intent of this fairytale and that is to have it told out loud. While preparing for any presentation, how often do you focus on the oratory skills required to deliver your presentation? Words are but words when written on a slide or in your notes but think of them and how they will sound when spoken aloud. Consider the rise and fall of your voice when creating suspense, the artful pause, the happy cadence of joy. Next time you are preparing a presentation, develop your oratory skills by always practicing your speech out loud, much like the telling of a fairytale. Your exercise for today, if you choose to accept it, is to read aloud the above quote until you get the delivery just right and make the Grimm brothers proud.

Tip – Practice your presentations aloud, much like fairytales were originally intended to be shared.

#75 – Alfred Adler

1870–1937

Context – Alfred Adler was an Austrian doctor, psychiatrist, and the founder of the school of individual psychology. His influential system of individual psychology introduced the term *inferiority feeling*, later widely and often inaccurately called the *inferiority complex*. Adler along with Sigmund Freud and Carl Jung, are considered to be the three founding figures of depth psychology, which emphasizes the unconscious and psychodynamics.

"What do you first do when you learn to swim? You make mistakes, do you not? And what happens? You make other mistakes, and when you have made all the mistakes you possibly can without drowning—and some of them many times over—what do you find? That you can swim? Well – life is just the same as learning to swim! Do not be afraid of making mistakes, for there is no other way of learning how to live!"

Analysis – There is this notion that one needs to reach perfection the first time they attempt anything. I see it time and time again in my consulting practice, particularly as it relates to presentation skills. An individual attends one of my workshops and expects that they will present flawlessly the first time they stand in front of the audience! Nothing could be further from the truth. I despise the word perfection because it does not exist. Practice does not make perfect as I've yet to meet a perfect human being and have yet to find perfection in any one discipline. I prefer to say, practice makes permanent. If we look at Adler's quote above, he is not suggesting that the swimmer is now ready and able to join the Olympic swim team. He is saying that by practicing and continuing to try, even when milestones aren't achieved in the expected time frame. The goal isn't perfection, the goal is to continue to grow and get better and maybe even achieve excellence, but perfection is a pipe dream. Adler says that mistakes are a part of the excursion. Those mistakes are how you learn and get closer to your goal. Did Thomas Edison invent the light bulb on his first try? Was Leonardo da Vinci a brilliant artist the first time he held a paintbrush? How about Alexander Graham Bell, was he able to invent the telephone the first time? Of course not! I could produce thousands of examples of individuals who would be considered experts in their chosen craft, and not one of them was superb or successful one the first or even the thousandth attempt. Continue to be kind to yourself when mistakes are made but learn from those mistakes and apply those learnings the next time. Just keep trying!

Tip – Learn from each presentation, apply those learnings to the next attempt and keep trying.

#74 – Benjamin Franklin

1706–1790

Context – Benjamin Franklin was a scientist, inventor, diplomat, publisher, and one of the Founding Fathers of America, as one of the signatories of the Declaration of Independence. Franklin recited the following quote just before signing the Declaration of Independence in 1776.

"We must indeed all hang together, or, most assuredly, we shall all hang separately."

Analysis – All of the signatories to the Declaration of Independence knew that the country's future was at risk by signing the document. This quote responded to John Hancock's remark that the revolutionaries should be unanimous in their actions. A little history lesson in case you've forgotten :) the Declaration of Independence announced that the 13 American colonies then at war with Great Britain were now independent states. He made this statement to rally the signers and the states they represented to stick together against Great Britain. As a result, Britain denounced the entire population as rebels and sentenced them all to death by hanging.

This speech is a requirement on a list of the *365 Must-Know Talks*. It shows us that to make a change, we will often face opposition, but our response to this negative energy will have an everlasting impact. In this book, we have yet to tackle presentation skills related to delivering a talk amid substantial change. This can be one of the most challenging talks to deliver. While Franklin and the signatories were in the midst of change related to a country, perhaps you are in the midst of change at work or home. At work, this can look like mergers or acquisitions in your company. It could be a new role, it could be a recent layoff, it could be a vast number of things, but if you have found yourself in a leadership role, most assuredly, you have found yourself delivering the talk of change. This is one of the singular talks that if done correctly can act as a catalyst for making a real and tangible difference. In times of change, we have the power to alleviate fear and uncertainty, and move and motivate those around us. We can create unity. If we look at Franklin's quote, he creates unity, solidifies and reassures those around him that it is a time to create one path to the future and leave the fragmented one behind. So, if you are talking about change, remember Franklin and create a keen sense of unity with your words, establish a solid team environment, be nurturing and kind in your delivery, empathize with your audience. If you do this, then the power in that talk has the potential to last forever.

Tip – Use your words to create unity in your talk on change.

#73 – Heribert Watzke (1954)

Context – Food scientist Heribert Watzke studies the brain in our gut. He works to develop new kinds of food that will satisfy our bodies and minds. In his 2010 TED Talk, "The Brain in Your Gut" tells us about the 'hidden brain' in our gut and the surprising things it makes us feel.

"This technology made a very important impact on us. It changed the way our history developed. But it's a technology so pervasive, so invisible, that we, for a long time, forgot to take it into account when we talked about human evolution. But we see the results of this technology, still. So, let's make a little test. So everyone of you turns to their neighbor please. Turn and face your neighbors. Please, also on the balcony. Smile. Smile. Open the mouths. Smile, friendly. (Laughter) Do you – Do you see any Canine teeth? (Laughter) Count Dracula teeth in the mouths of your neighbors? Of course not. Because our dental anatomy is actually made, not for tearing down raw meat from bones or chewing fibrous leaves for hours. It is made for a diet which is soft, mushy, which is reduced in fibers, which is very easily chewable and digestible. Sounds like fast food, doesn't it?"

…I cook; therefore, I am… cooking is linked to improved cognition as we have evolved over the years and… achieving a balance between the big brain and the gut brain…"

Analysis – Here Watzke's theory is distilled into one line. This is why I've chosen to include this talk in my list of *365 Must-Know Talks*. This talk has a beautiful conversational presentation style. The content is exciting, but if we move beyond the scope of content for a moment and focus on delivery, I was enamoured by this presentation. Watzke is controlled, he uses his slides beautifully, creates superb analogies and stories ("cat in the gut" is something I'll never forget!), and he creates audience involvement all while creating the feeling that he is sitting with you enjoying a glass of Merlot at your kitchen table.

His delivery is informal but structured, and this is something of a rarity in the presentation community.

For today's tip, I'd like to highlight the 40 second mark of the talk, Watzke involves his audience by having each of them look at their neighbour. I love when a presenter does this, especially in a room with a large audience, as is the case here. Listen to the energy of the room. He's got each one of them tuning in with all their senses. He can even demand that they smile at one another, and they do! There is great power in getting your audience involved in your presentations right at the beginning, they feel like they are a part of the talk and that they are creating the presentation with you.

Tip – Get your audience involved from the very beginning of your presentation.

#72 – David Icke

(1952)

Context – David Icke is an English writer, public speaker, and media personality. He has written 20 books, one of which is a 533-page epic entitled, *The Biggest Secret* and has been called the conspiracy theorists' Rosetta Stone.

Analysis – The fundamental question Icke is obsessed with is who and what is controlling the world? For those who are familiar with Icke's work, let me begin by saying I am not agreeing or disagreeing with his content. This book of *365 Must-Know Talks* does not necessarily mirror my political slate or opinions, that is not my role (okay, perhaps a few of my opinions have snuck in here and there, haha). This time, I'm distancing myself because reptiles, aliens, and Zion are just too controversial for a book on presentation skills. I do encourage you to read up and develop your own opinion, however. One of the central components of becoming a superb public speaker is having vast knowledge of a vast number of topics. The more you read on a broad range of topics, the more interesting a human being you will become. Keep working hard to acquire and digest knowledge. Those are the people that are thought-provoking and engaging. Those are the ones you want to listen to. So yes, the idea of delving into various topics is undoubtedly a part of this post's tip. The other component of today's tip that I'd like to highlight is Icke's delivery style.

This speech is nearly 30 years old. I watched a more recent Icke clip, and except for a few more grey hairs and a few more wrinkles, the body language and delivery is almost identical. The cadence and gusto of his voice, the internal drive to deliver his message, and his passion and zeal remain the same. His delivery in whatever method you observe him (TV, speech, radio) reads like a great science fiction novel, and I say that as a compliment. He consistently asks questions as part of his delivery style, and you can almost envision the *Star Trek* theme song playing in the background. What he proposes is so bizarre, and so peculiar that it is tough to comprehend, yet his delivery style sucks you in so you want to hear more. It is because of his delivery style that people will listen to his content, and that is undoubtedly one of the highest compliments a public speaker can acquire.

Tip – Seek knowledge in a vast range of topics and create a delivery style that makes your audience sit up and listen.

#71 – Gerda Weissmann Klein

(1924)

Context – Gerda Weissmann Klein, Holocaust survivor and the subject of Best Documentary Short at the 68th Academy Awards, "One Survivor Remembers", an autobiographical account of the holocaust adapted from her book *All But My Life*. Here is an excerpt from her acceptance speech.

"I have been in a place for six incredible years, where winning meant a crust of bread and to live another day …. In my mind's eye I see those years and faces of those who never knew the magic of a boring evening at home…. Each of you who knows the joy of freedom is a winner."

Analysis – You'll need to skip to one minute, 39 seconds, to get to Klein's speech. "Why Am I Here? I Am No Better?" I cannot produce a more fruitful example of extending gratitude in any speech I've featured in this book so far. Klein, a Holocaust survivor and the subject of the short documentary film, "One Survivor Remains," speaks for about a minute in an acceptance speech at the Oscars. Her words are chosen carefully and deliberately, and her heart is on her sleeve as gratitude booms from her every pore. "Thank you on their behalf and with all my heart," are her parting words. I cannot think of ten words I've heard delivered by another human being that I felt more. Speak from your heart, and your audience will be transported to the contents of your content, and it will be implanted in the emotion you are feeling. Your audience will want to learn more as a result and will continue to pursue your topic long after you've left the stage. The reverberations of your words will be felt for days, weeks, and years, perhaps even a lifetime. This can only be achieved when you speak with authenticity, speak from the heart, speak without vanity, and speak from a place of truth.

Tip – Remove all vanity and speak your truth.

#70 – Bert Lahr

1895–1967

Context – Bert Lahr plays the Cowardly Lion in the classic, Frank Baum's, *The Wizard of Oz*.

Lion
Yeh, it's sad, believe me, Missy, When you're born to be a sissy
Without the vim and verve.
But I could show my prowess, be a lion not a mou-ess
If I only had the nerve.
I'm afraid there's no denyin' I'm just a dandelion,
A fate I don't deserve.

I'd be brave as a blizzard….
Tin Man
I'd be gentle as a lizard….
Scarecrow

I'd be clever as a gizzard....

Dorothy

If the Wizard is a Wizard who will serve.

Scarecrow

Then I'm sure to get a brain,

Tin Man

a heart,

Dorothy

a home,

Lion

the nerve!

Analysis – This is the third time *The Wizard of Oz* has hit this list of *365 Must-Know Talks* (and it won't be the last!) I adore this film, it has so many messages, and today I've chosen to highlight the Cowardly Lion's message: Nerve! Of all the characters that could be transported into the topic of presentation skills, the Lion serves the best. The parallels to presentation skills are unbounded. Regardless of how long they have been delivering talks, most presenters will feel nervous at some point either before, during, or after a presentation. And, in some cases, all three! What the Cowardly Lion uncovers in *The Wizard of Oz* is that he always had it within him to be brave, gutsy, and fearless. It is that he didn't believe he could! We have covered handling our nerves several times in this list, but we have yet to tackle the question of nerves as it relates to belief. In his famous book, *The Quick and Easy Way to Effective Speaking*, Dale Carnegie says, "If you act enthusiastic, you will be enthusiastic." This is something I adopted some 25 years ago now, and I have taken some liberties with this line in my workshops changing to it, "If you act confident, you will be confident." At the core, I believe that is what Carnegie meant. You can inject any emotion into that statement, it is transferrable to anything you fear. You may be familiar with the phrase, fake it until you make it. But here is the caveat, I wouldn't suggest that you pretend to be something you are not, but rather you adopt the feeling of what it would be like to be confident or have the nerve. So, sit back and envision yourself delivering your talk with confidence, poise, and getting your message across. How does that feel? What does that look like? Do a trial run many, many times before your actual talk. Get into the headspace of believing you will deliver your speech confidently. Go through every minute detail—no detail is too small—from walking into the room and scanning the faces of your audience, to what you have in your hands and your body language. Every detail is essential as you visualize being confident and being successful. Believe that this is how you will deliver your talk. If you've done your due diligence (preparation and practice), then it will be so. Believing that you can deliver your speech well is the best way to overcome your nerves. Take a page out of the Cowardly Lion's book and apply the wisdom to believe in yourself enough to make it so.

Tip – Believe and visualize success.

#69 – Melinda French Gates

(1964)

Context – Melinda French Gates is the co-chair of the Bill and Melinda Gates Foundation. In this TED Talk, Gates explores what nonprofits can learn from Coca-Cola.

"Analyze it, learn from it, then save lives."

Analysis – The above quote is how French Gates begins her talk. I don't necessarily agree with all of the content in her talk (Coke, as with other organizations answer to shareholders, and even with the most robust philanthropic spirit, they are still a multi-billion-dollar company that has to turn a profit to satiate the appetites of those holders—but I digress—this is not about my opinion on content.) However, I do agree with her thought process. If we utilize her core message to analyze, learn, and then save lives, it can be nicely transferrable to presentation skills.

One aspect of presentation skills that we have yet to tackle is the necessity to observe as many presentations and talks as possible. In your company, ask to be invited to presentations, join networking organizations where you can observe others, and watch the millions of talks out there on the Internet. Find interesting websites (clearly, I'm a lover of TED) and watch its video content. I mean, watch what those speakers are doing. Whether watching presentations in person or on the screen, if you view enough talks, you will naturally find what appeals to you and what works. Watch some more, and you can start to weave some of the techniques in your presentations. I cannot overemphasize the importance of observing and analyzing others on the journey to becoming a superb public speaker.

As speakers we may not save lives with our words, as French Gates suggests in her analogy, but wouldn't it be an extraordinary pursuit to be ready and capable of transferring your message to an audience in such a way that you will be genuinely heard and leave a lasting impact. Perhaps it is your destiny to save another life with your words. Today is the day to prepare.

Tip – Analyze it, learn and maybe, just maybe, your words will save lives!

#68 – Richard St. John

(1947)

Context – Author Richard St. John is the founder of the marketing company, The St. John Group. He has spent more than a decade interviewing 500 people he defines as successful. From those interviews, erupts a book entitled *Spike's Guide to Success: Stupid, Ugly, Unlucky and Rich: Spike's Guide to Success*. The below is a excerpt from another of St. John's books, *The 8 Traits Successful People Have in Common: 8 To Be Great*.

"This is really a two-hour presentation I give to high school students, cut down to three minutes. And it all started one day on a plane, on my way to TED, seven years ago. And in the seat next to me was a high school student, a teenager, and she came from a really poor family. And she wanted to make something of her life, and she asked me a simple little question. She said, "What leads to success?" And I felt really badly, because I couldn't give her a good answer.

So, I get off the plane, and I come to TED. And I think, jeez, I'm in the middle of a room of successful people! So why don't I ask them what helped them succeed, and pass it on to kids? So here we are, seven years, 500 interviews later, and I'm going to tell you what really leads to success and makes TEDsters tick.

And the first thing is passion. Freeman Thomas says, "I'm driven by my passion." TEDsters do it for love; they don't do it for money…"

Analysis – St. John's first words are that he has condensed a two-hour talk into a three-minute presentation. Yes, you read that correctly, two hours of content into three minutes and this is my sole reason for choosing this talk to hit my list of *365 Must-Know Talks*. Concise, compact, and possible! So often in my workshops people say, "Caroline! They told me that I had an hour for my presentation but because the person before me is running long now I only have ten minutes to speak!" The devastation in the presenter's voice is palpable and believe me, I can understand it. You've taken all the proper and necessary preparatory plans, you've rehearsed, you've practiced, you didn't sleep the night before, and now you don't even get to show your audience. Well, my friends this is life. I cannot tell you how many times this has happened to me. So, the truth is you've got to be ready to roll with the punches, be like water—ride the wave and take advantage of the opportunity put in front of you. Be unshakable, unnerved, and unflustered. If you've done your due diligence, you'll know how to condense that hour-long sucker into ten minutes on the fly. If you've done your slides properly, if you know your presentation backwards, forwards and inside out you'll be able to glide through ten minutes while still being engaging, interesting and even funny, if that is what you've planned. This is my tip for you today. For every presentation you prepare, prepare an abridged version, either mentally or even physically, with condensed PowerPoint slides. Too much preparation? Where will you find the time? Be ready for every possible scenario and you will thank yourself because at some point in your presentation career, you'll need to be prepared for the unexpected.

Tip – Prepare an abridged version of your presentation, every single time.

#67 – Wayne Gretzky

(1961)

Context – Canadian Wayne Gretzky is a former professional ice hockey player. Nicknamed The Great One, Gretzky is often regarded as the best player in the history of the National Hockey League (NHL).

"You miss 100 percent of the shots you never take."

Analysis – Call it the Canadian in me, but Wayne Gretzky was a staple character in my youth. My dad, an avid hockey fan, would watch, good ol' number 99 score over and over again and since I was my dad's side kick, I too would watch, even though no one ever considered me a sports fan by any stretch of the imagination. But I vividly remember the sheer excitement that would erupt when 99 set foot on the ice. There was something very palpable about his presence, and it most assuredly had something to do with the great deal of effort, muscle, toil, blood, sweat, tears, elbow grease that Gretzky put into his craft. He worked hard, and yes, there's no doubt he had a natural talent for the sport as many athletes do, but natural talent is nothing without hard work. This is why I've chosen Gretzky's quote to hit my list of *365 Must-Know Talks*. If you never work hard and try, then you will never accomplish anything. Seriously, it's that simple. If you acquiesce, if you submit to this notion that you can't then you most assuredly will live up to your expectations. In fact, you will live up to any expectation you put out to the ether, good or bad.

So, take a page out of Gretzky's book when it comes to presentation skills. Keep on trying, you'll reach that goal eventually. It might even be a wicked slap shot.

Tip – Keep on trying.

#66 – Scott Berkun

(1973)

Context – Scott Berkun is a writer and public speaker. His book, *Confessions of a Public Speaker* is the foundation of his 2009 talk that includes the below quote.

"1. All good communication is storytelling. You can tell good/bad stories through any technology.

2. Our failures to connect will never be solved by technology alone.

3. You must transcend your technology."

Analysis – Today I have picked a professional public speaker to hit my list of *365 Must-Know Talks*. Berkun describes himself as a writer first, then a public speaker to support that writing habit. I would say most professional public speakers find themselves in that category. They write and their way of selling that product is to deliver keynote addresses, workshops or presentations. I'm always keenly interested in observing other speakers who make a career of it. I use it as a barometer. Can they really garner the fees that they are asking? Do they have something in their delivery that I can learn from? Is their content of value? The answer is a resounding yes when it comes to Berkun. I've watched several clips of Berkun in action and I enjoy his delivery and content. He is relaxed, he is conversational, and he has a definitive opinion. I'd like to highlight two aspects of Berkun's talk. First is Berkun's discussion on miscommunication. He uses an illustration of sending an email and having it be misinterpreted by the receiver, something most of us can relate to. The same can be said when addressing a group of people in a presentation format. As presenter, if you don't have an ardent attitude of wanting to communicate with your audience, you simply won't. Such is the case with technology. For example, in a lecture format where there is only one-way communication—you are addressing your audience—then that isn't really communicating. There needs to be a check and balance in place to ensure that your message is being received and understood, even with the position you hold at the front of the room. Asking questions and eliciting head nods is an important component of ensuring two-way communication with your audience.

The second aspect of this talk that I'd like to highlight is the sales ingredient. Berkun starts with introducing his book and he reminds his audience about his book at the end of his presentation, and he asks for the sale. For those who are reading this and are in sales, you can learn a great deal by this technique. Berkun does his selling, and it doesn't seem forced or salesy (insert the metaphorical used-car salesman here).

If you are in sales and you are doing a sales presentation, then my goodness, you had better ask for the sale. I'd suggest, like Berkun, you do this at the end of your talk.

Tip – Elicit two way communication with your audience and ask for the sale.

#65 – Pat Carroll

(1927)

Context – Pat Carroll sings "Poor Unfortunate Souls" as the character of Ursula in the Disney 1989 classic, *The Little Mermaid*.

…You'll have your looks, your pretty face.
And don't underestimate the importance of body language, ha!
The men up there don't like a lot of blabber
They think a girl who gossips is a bore!
Yet on land it's much prefered for ladies not to say a word
And after all dear, what is idle babble for?
Come on, they're not all that impressed with conversation
True gentlemen avoid it when they can
But they dote and swoon and fawn
On a lady who's withdrawn
It's she who holds her tongue who get's a man
Come on you poor unfortunate soul
Go ahead!
Make your choice!
I'm a very busy woman and I haven't got all day
It won't cost much
Just your voice!
You poor unfortunate soul

It's sad but true
If you want to cross the bridge, my sweet
You've got the pay the toll
Take a gulp and take a breath
And go ahead and sign the scroll
Flotsam, Jetsam, now I've got her, boys
The boss is on a roll
This poor unfortunate soul…"

Analysis – I read an article the other day that said that there are between 25–33 million business presentations in North America every day. If this is the case then most of us, at some point in time, will deliver at least one presentation, and more often than not, dozens, if not hundreds. It made me think, of those 25–33 million presentations, how many were good? I mean, how many engaged their audiences? How many were interesting and elicited changed behaviour as a result? How many were entertaining? How many had people in the audience falling asleep? My guesstimate is that fifty percent were considered pretty good, 45 percent scored a horrible or unbearable rating, and five percent were considered superb, interesting, or exciting. Now, these numbers are only a ballpark, but they are a pretty educated guess, considering the number of companies I work with on presentation skills improvement. It is a rare day indeed for a participant or audience member to show up to a presentation, workshop or keynote and be re-energized and stimulated enough to do whatever the presenter is asking. Very rare.

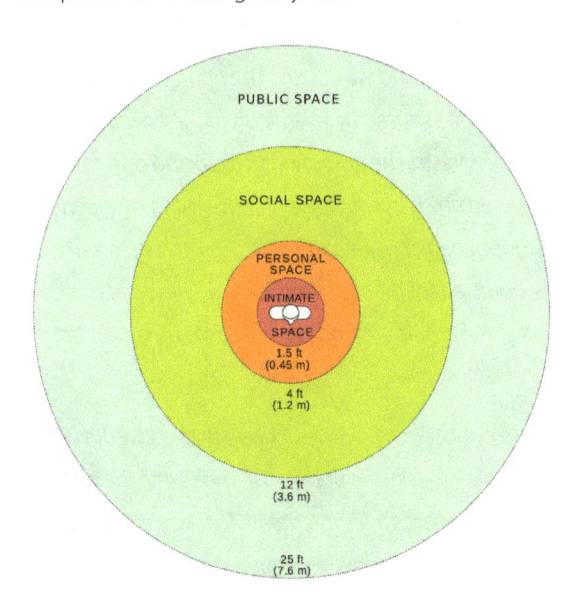

I was once asked by a client, "If you had to share one delivery technique that sets apart a mediocre presenter from a spectacular one, what would it be?" There are many answers to this question, but without missing a beat, I said, "Body language." You cannot underestimate the importance of the presenter understanding the body language cues of their audience and being aware of the body language cues they are giving. Now I know I've previously talked robustly about body language, but today I'd like to take it from a different angle. As it impacts real space, not simply metaphorical space. This relates to how you move through the world as a form of communication without words. Anthropologist Edward T. Hall was deeply interested in exploring cultures. In 1959 he wrote the classic book, *The Silent Language*, in which he described the study of space as proxemics and indicated that there are four zones of space between people.

Much of Hall's work was based on understanding cross-cultural differences, but I believe that this idea can be used in the realm of presentation skills. When I conduct a workshop, I rarely stand at the front of the room and anyone who has attended one of my workshops will be able to attest to this. I organize a workshop space to facilitate and present from any given corner of the room. I set up flip charts stations in different areas of the room, and if there are white boards, I make sure that there are markers available. I do this to get closer to my audience, into that personal space you see on the above Hall chart. I read a study many years ago that said there was a neurological reaction when people were close to one another. So, if someone was telling a story or teaching in close proximity, then the neurons of the audience would fire faster, and in essence, there was an increased chance that the listeners would feel what the presenter was feeling. Amazing. I've never forgotten that, and it is why I'll move about whether I do a workshop or a keynote talk. The keynote talk is a little more challenging in terms of getting up close because often, the presenter is on a stage with a larger audience. Sometimes, if my microphone is hooked up and it can be done (this is where scoping out your space beforehand can be beneficial) I do step down from the stage and get closer to the audience. However, sometimes it isn't possible, so moving about the stage, making eye contact, and leaning in acts as a significant modification to the issue of proximity.

Tip – The closer you are to your audience, the more they will digest what you are saying.

#64 – Matt Ridley

(1958)

Context – At TED 2010, author Matt Ridley shows how human progress has occurred by the mating of ideas and morphing those ideas into new ideas. His talk is entitled, "When Ideas Have Sex."

"When I was a student here in Oxford in the 1970s, the future of the world was bleak. The population explosion was unstoppable. Global famine was inevitable. A cancer epidemic caused by chemicals in the environment was going to shorten our lives. The acid rain was falling on the forests. The desert was advancing by a mile or two a year. The oil was running out, and a nuclear winter would finish us off. None of those things happened, (Laughter) and astonishingly, if you look at what actually happened in my lifetime, the average per-capita income of the average person on the planet, in real terms, adjusted for inflation, has tripled. Lifespan is up by 30 percent in my lifetime. Child mortality is down by two-thirds. Per-capita food production is up by a third. And all this at a time when the population has doubled.

How did we achieve that, whether you think it's a good thing or not? How did we achieve that? How did we become the only species that becomes more prosperous as it becomes more populous? The size of the blob in this graph represents the size of the population, and the level of the graph represents GDP per capita. I think to answer that question you need to understand how human beings bring together their brains and enable their *ideas to combine and recombine, to meet and, indeed, to mate. In other words, you need to understand how ideas have sex. …"*

Analysis – I'm excited to have the opportunity to share with you another of my favourite TED Talks! Ridley does an exemplary job explaining why the collective mind is far superior to the individual mind. Watch this talk, and you will learn that cumulation is an evolutionary process. The habit of exchanging one idea for another is a human process and this process has enabled us to create a better quality of life year after year. Ridley uses a fun example of light and asks, "How long would you have to work to earn an hour of reading light?" Around half a second in 2021, eight seconds in 1950, 15 minutes in 1880, 16 hours in 1800. Think about it, in 1800, what would you need to do and acquire to be able to open a book in the evening with enough light to last an hour?

His point is that exchanging goods and services over the years has raised the standard of living for everyone. Ridley asks, "Who knows how to make a computer mouse? Nobody?" or "Who knows how to make a pencil? Nobody?" And this is true, even the president of the organization that produces the mouse doesn't know all of the intricate facets of making a computer mouse, from the manufacturing of the plastic to perhaps the wiring inside. The same is true of a pencil. In order to produce that from scratch, for starters you'd have to have a working and applicable knowledge of how to extract lead from the ground.

I adore this talk because it demonstrates what presentation skills development is all about. Often presenters believe they have to produce from scratch, and they have to have the highest IQ. They have to be able to re-invent the most spectacular slides. But this couldn't be further from the truth. There is a collective brain out there as it relates to presentation skills. Hey, you've found your way to this book, and by doing so, we are sharing ideas, or in Ridley's words, we are "mating our ideas'" to create the process of an exchange of ideas. Any of the content in this book, approximately 235,000 words, has been a process of adopting and sharing ideas from and with others, making them my own, testing them in the real world then sharing them with you. This is no different from the hunter sharing his meat with the gatherer who exchanges or adds to the protein with vegetation. The exchange of ideas will make us all become better presenters, and I hope that you will exchange and share your learnings with others so that we can continue to evolve into a spectacular public speaking community.

(To leave your exchange of ideas, go to *talktalk.ca* and send me a note. I look forward to the exchange.)

Tip – Exchange and harvest your presentation skill ideas with others.

#63 – Carl Jung

1875–1961

Context – Carl Gustav Jung was a Swiss psychiatrist and the founder of what has been termed analytical psychology.

"Everything that irritates us about others can lead us to an understanding of ourselves."

Analysis – If you've ever taken an introductory psychology class in university, no doubt you've heard of

Carl Jung or Jungian psychology. I vividly remember being exposed to the notion of archetypes in my intro psychology class and to the notion of individuation—the process of forming a stable personality. The Myers-Briggs Type Indicator (or MBTI) personality test was principally developed from Jung's theories. It is a self-report questionnaire that indicates differing psychological preferences in how people perceive the world and make decisions. For those who are interested,: I'm an ENFJ (Extraverted, Intuitive, Feeling, and Judging personality).

In my workshops, I often begin with what I call a foundational skill knowledge exercise during which I utilize some type of behavioural or psychological profile. It often takes the form of William Mouton Marston's DiSC profile, which is my favourite, but truthfully, it can be any of the countless behavioural/psychological assessments out there (Firo B, CLI, HBDI, EQi to name just a few!). The function of these assessments is to become introspective, to figure out where our natural styles rests, understand our strengths and challenges within that context, and then to start the process of understanding others. That's it. I've taken all types of certification classes in a variety of these assessments. I've been a participant in a lot of these classes, and it comes down to introspection. It is a process of self-evaluation, reflection, contemplation, and self-observation. The theory is that if you understand yourself fully, you can better relate to others, both professionally and personally, and fulfill your destiny by understanding your natural desires and strengths. So, I begin with this foundational exercise to have the participants understand themselves first because, it's impossible to teach or be taught any skill without first having that knowledge.

If you have an audience member or participant who is irritating you, it most assuredly is based on your actions. Yup, I said it! When I coach others on presenting, at some point, someone will say something like, "My audience was tiresome (or maddening, trying, annoying, infuriating, etc.) and they didn't want to listen to anything I had to say!" This frame of mind should be turned inward. What could you have done differently? Why do you find this behaviour so annoying? What could you do differently in the future? Use the opportunity to turn inward so you can understand yourself better.

Tip – Be introspective and understand yourself fully before hitting the presentation stage.

#62 – Tiffany Shlain

(1970)

Context – Tiffany Shlain was honoured by Newsweek as one of the "Women Shaping the 21st Century." Shlain is a filmmaker (*Life, Liberty and The Pursuit of Happiness, The Tribe*), an artist and founder of the Webby Awards. Here, Shlain delivers the UC Berkeley Keynote Commencement Speech, 2010. Below are her last words of advice to the graduating students.

"Have moxie

Think Big

Love deeply

Fail big

Pay your dues

Take risks

Laugh at yourself

Make a difference

Whatever you think you can do or believe you can do, begin it. Action has magic, grace, and power in it."

Analysis – There are 11,500 people in the audience at this commencement address and Shlain had a real impact on much of her audience. Bravo! It is a talk that sparks every emotion: joy, happiness, sadness, anxiety, devastation. I've picked this talk because it speaks tthe art of reflection. As part of this project, I have watched thousands of talks, many of which have been commencement addresses. At some point in their life everyone should prepare a talk that espouses what they've learned in life thus far and what they have learned in the hopes of benefitting others. Take some time to think about what your commencement speech would look like. How could your life's journey be translated to an audience to inspired them to go out and conquer the world? What does your autobiography look like? I consider myself to be a person who contemplates quite a lot, so it surprised me that had never thought of doing this before. The truth is we all have a story that needs to be told. All of us have a life story that could inspire and motivate others. Knowing this can make a monumental difference in every single presentation you do moving forward. What facets of your autobiography can you use as illustrations, analogies, metaphors in the belly of your talks? Start the process of outlining your life, in words, in pictures, or whatever creative venue works best for you. What a gift it will be for those around you and, if you have children, Shlain says, "When you teach your children, you teach your children's children."

Tip – Use your life story to impact, inspire and motivate those around you.

#61 – Lewis Carroll

1832–1898

Context – Lewis Carroll was a writer best known perhaps for his 1865 novel, *Alice's Adventures in Wonderland*. Lewis Carroll was a pen name for writer Charles Lutwidge Dodgson.

"Cheshire Puss," she began, rather timidly, as she did not know at all whether it would like the name: however, it only grinned a little wider. Come, it's pleased so far, thought Alice, and she went on. *"Would you tell me please, which way I ought to go from here?"*

"That depends a good deal on where you want to get to," said the cat.

"I don't much care where," said Alice.

"Then it doesn't matter which way you go," said the cat.

"… So long as I get somewhere," Alice added as an explanation.

"Oh, you're sure to do that," said the cat, *"if you only walk long enough."*

Analysis – *Alice's Adventures in Wonderland* has been popularized under the title *Alice in Wonderland* and is possibly the best example of the literary nonsense genre. It is a story of Alice who falls down a rabbit hole into a fantasy world filled with strange and peculiar creatures. It is a much-revered work and, as such, has been adapted countless times in film. If you haven't read it in a while, I encourage you to do so (the original only, please). Carroll's writing style plays with logic in the most beautiful ways, and even if the children reading it don't fully feel the weight of its message, the adults reading it to them likely will (hopefully!).

One of the biggest issues I encounter in my consulting world is that organizations and the people within those organizations don't know where they are going. When I ask, "Where do you see you and your business today, three years from now and ten years from now?" I'm usually met with a dramatic gesture, arms raised to the air, and an answer along the lines of, "I want to be rich; I want my company to be profitable!" These answers are horrible! They are far too vague. Let's say you want to take a vacation. You might first go to a travel agency and say, "I'd like to take a vacation!" The travel agent will probably reply, "Great! Where would you like to go?" and if your response is, "I don't know," then the agent will likely tell you to come back when you have a destination in mind or they may ask specific questions to help you narrow down your choices:

When would you like to go?

Would you like to go somewhere hot?

Would you like to go somewhere you've never been?

What mode of transportation? Car? Bus? Train? Plane? Boat?

How long would you like to go for?

What is your budget?

And so on until the destination was chosen. I often think of myself as a travel agent, but a travel agent for organizations. When the response is too vague, it is as if the CEO is wandering aimlessly, hoping that they'll arrive at their destination, but have no real plan in place to get them there. Many people and companies have no real, tangible road map to get them to where they want to be. And their goals certainly aren't measurable—such as S.M.A.R.T goals meaning the goals are Specific, Measurable, Achievable, Realistic, and Timely). Having measurable goals is incredibly important. The same can be said for doing a presentation. You must begin with the end in mind. Decide on the outcome or goal you want to achieve by giving a particular presentation? Then work backward from there. Beginning with the end in mind starts with visualizing the end. What does it look like? Is the goal to have your audience buy something, be inspired, be persuaded or be entertained? How will you make that happen in your presentation?

One of my tricks for developing a road map for my presentations is to draw it out. I create some type of pictorial of my presentation. Sometimes it looks like a circle at the center of the page with a large illustration or collection of words that outline the goal or the outcome; from there, prongs extend out of that inner nucleus to the key points that will support the goal. Sometimes, I draw a map with a car at the beginning taking the presentation on long and winding roads, through the forest, and the signs that would traditionally be stop signs or speed limit signs are replaced with key topics that need to be covered. At the very end, a finish line is complete with a black and white checkered flag with the outcome goal. Whatever method you choose to plan out the road map for your presentations doesn't matter but you must undertake the exercise for every presentation!

Tip – Start all presentations with the end goal in mind.

#60 – Barack Obama

(1961)

Context – In 2009, Barack Obama addresses school kids at Wakefield High school in Arlington, Virginia at the start of a new school year.

"You won't click with every teacher that you have. Not every homework assignment will seem completely relevant to your life right at this minute. And you won't necessarily succeed at everything the first time you try. That's okay.

Some of the most successful people in the world are the ones who've had the most failures. J.K. Rowling, who wrote Harry Potter, *her first Harry Potter, book was rejected 12 times before it was finally published. Michael Jordan was cut from his high school basketball team. He lost hundreds of games and missed thousands of shots during his career. But he once said, 'I have failed over and over and over again in my life. And that's why I succeed.' These people succeeded because they understood that you can't let your failure define you, you have to let your failure teach you. You have to let them show you what to do differently the next time."*

Analysis – First, let us applaud the fine gentleman, Tim Spicer, senior class president, that introduces the President of the United States. What a fine job he does! Next time you are doing the introductory talk, think of this boy who was tasked with introducing the President of the United States!

All right, Obama is a pretty darn good orator, however, he isn't the best in the world, but what he does well—and the reason I've chosen to highlight this talk—is modify and customize his talks and his delivery to his audience. This is a magnificent example. It is not just his tailored words, but his entire delivery: cadence, enthusiasm, body language. It's everything. In a sea of politicians who appear unable to do this, Obama stands outs as a refreshing change, and I believe this is partly why he can connect with so many people; young, old, and in every profession. He mirrors whatever demographic he is facing.

When you are preparing for a presentation, do you think of your audience first, and prepare from that vantage point? If you're like most presenters, the answer is, sadly, no. In your preparatory phase and your road map phase (see post #85) think about who your audience is and how you should deliver and construct your presentation. One of the exercises I do in my workshops is to assign the participants an audience demographic. So, on three by five index cards, the participant is given a selected audience group that might include:

- A group of 25 senior executives ranging from CEOs, CIOs, presidents, vice presidents and shareholders
- A group of 100 high school students
- A group of 50 recently laid-off people
- A group of ten salespeople
- A group of 200 senior citizens
- A group of 75 people for whom English is a second language
- A group of 20 entrepreneurs

The participant has already prepared a presentation in an earlier part of the workshop, and now it is time for delivery. I firmly believe that a talk needs to be reworked when you understand who is in your audience. Looking at some of the above examples, we can see how our delivery would need to change to cater to each group. Depending on the demographic, everything would need to be customized to the specific audience. I was watching a popular comedian on television the other day and was amazed at how she had customized her entire act for her audience. She had researched the pop culture of the city and integrated that knowledge into her act. Did she re-write her entire routine? Of course not, but she took the time to find out about her host city and the types of people likely to be in her audience and tailored her routine to suit. Where did she get the best laughs? Of course, in the sections where she addressed, specific examples of the city.

If you want to connect with your audience, if you want to have your audience digest the contents of your presentation, then customize it!

Tip – Customize your presentations to fit the needs of your audience.

#59 – Ryan Hreljac

(1991)

Context – Ryan Hreljac is the founder of Ryan's Well Foundation, a Canadian water charity providing access to clean water, sanitation services, and hygiene education in developing countries.

"Some people become activists. Some people are born activists."

Analysis – In 1998, six-year-old Grade One student Ryan Hreljac learned that some children in Africa had to walk a significant distance every single day to get water. So, Hreljac decided to build a well for a village in Uganda, Africa, with the money he had saved from his chores. The well was completed in 1999 in a northern Ugandan village. Hreljac founded Ryan's Well Foundation, which has since contributed to 1,531 water and sanitation projects, and 1,267 latrines in 16 developing countries. This results in 1,109,193 people having been provided with clean, fresh, water. Hreljac is 30 years old and is the executive director of the foundation.

There are lots of reasons I chose Hreljac to be a part of the *365 Must-Know Talks* on this list. I adore what Hreljac has achieved, and his age was not a barrier in his determination to accomplish a monumental task, and he continues to head the foundation to this day. From a presentation skills perspective, I have chosen Hreljac for another reason—his mom has previously said that Hreljac was a deeply shy child, but he pushed those fears aside because the cause was bigger than his shyness. I have met many shy people over the years, and for them standing in front of a group of people may be the last activity they want to engage in. Shyness or introversion is one of the most misunderstood personality characteristics out there. From my vantage point, introversion and extraversion relate to where you get your energy from. While an extravert may attain their energy from others, an introvert gathers their energy stores in a more contemplative manner. So even though Hreljac was (and probably still is) a person who is more on the introverted side, he found himself in a peculiar position of wanting and needing to tell others of the water plight in Africa. I suppose he could have written an article or a book or started a blog perhaps, something less nerve-racking, but is that all that would be required? Of course not! Hreljac put a face and a voice behind his cause, and he did so by overcoming his shyness, standing up in front of others and persuading them to take action. I'd say they listened.

Less nerve-racking, but is that all that would be required? Of course not! He needed to put a face and a voice behind his cause, and to do so would need to stand up in front of others in the hopes of persuading them to action.

Tip – When you have a deep desire to change the world, trust that you will find your voice!

#58 – Leonardo da Vinci

1452–1519

Context – Leonardo da Vinci was an Italian painter, sculptor, architect, musician, scientist, engineer, mathematician, polymath, inventor, geologist, cartographer, botanists, anatomist and writer.

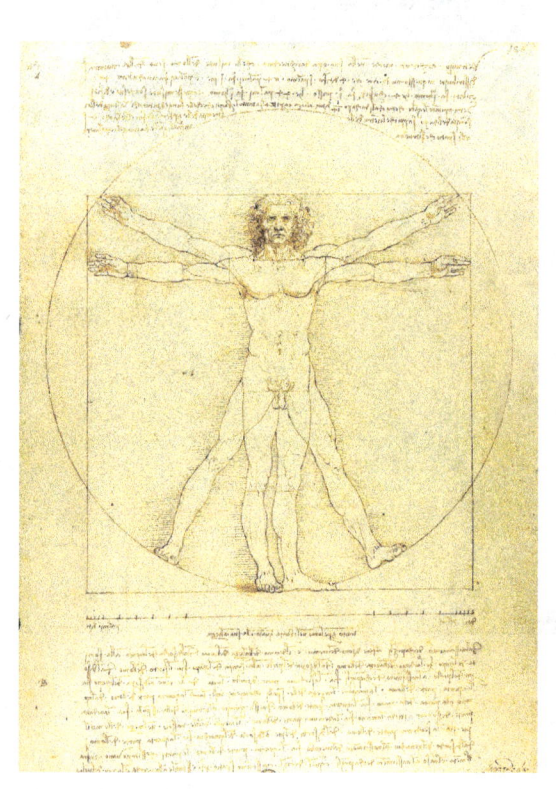

"Just as eating contrary to the inclination is injurious to the health, so study without desire sports the memory, and it retains nothing that it takes in."

Analysis – Leonardo da Vinci, that great mind of the renaissance, continues to influence people around the world even today. As modern-day people, we can learn a lot from da Vinci about how to live a better, more fulfilling life. A ton has been written about da Vinci, and I have poured over many of these publications and found myself lost in his notebooks. For years now, I've been fascinated by him, and just recently, having put down a book that centred on the science of his developments, I was struck by the teachings on the pursuit of a better way to live. The following four ideas have been distilled from thousands of pages of text and are my own, but I hope da Vinci would have been in agreement with me if he were alive today. My admiration for da Vinci does border on obsession. I suppose there could be far worse things than to be consumed with such a tremendous historical figure! I think everyone should have somebody in history that they are obsessed with, someone they can learn from and who can be a historical mentor. Okay, so, the four ideas that I have for living life more robustly and with greater depth and meaning from the portal of da Vinci are:

1. **Be Curious** – Clearly da Vinci was Curiosita which is defined by a great book, How to Think Like

Leonardo da Vinci: "An insatiably curious approach to life and an unrelenting quest for continuous learning." Da Vinci had curiosity in such a vast number of topics; it is almost staggering! Think about when you were a child and you had innumerable questions, such as "Why was I born?" "What is this?" "How does this work?" "Why? Why? Why?" Somewhere along the way, those questions fall to the wayside, and we begin to accept what is. Da Vinci never lost his insatiable quest, and neither should you!

2. **Be multi-talented** - Look at the long list of professions da Vinci has alongside his name.

3. **Take your time** – I can assure you that the *Vitruvian Man*, the *Mona Lisa*, *The Last Supper*, the innumerable inventions, the analysis and drawings of anatomy and all of da Vinci's explorations, interests, and final products took time. I can assure you da Vinci sought perfection. He sought a refined and deliberate approach to all that he did, and as such, there was no speedy conclusion. In fact, many of his paintings were abandoned as he was never really happy with his art for the most part. All his work took time and exhaustive energy to produce.

4. **Strive for quality not quantity** - Surprisingly, da Vinci finished only 31 paintings in his life. Obviously, he was one to strive for excellence in lieu of mass production.

So, what does all of this da Vinci exploration have to do with presentation skills? Everything. Let's look at the above quote. A desire to do well in any vocation is of primary importance or the mind will not absorb what is needed to excel. Think about a time in your educational career where you crammed for a test. I know I did that many times. How much can you recollect from that test today? If your memory is anything like mine, absolutely nothing. That crammed information would simply have been stored in your short-term memory reserve. There was no desire to learn but rather to simply regurgitate. Desire is key in preparing for any talk as are all four key ideas that I've illustrated above. These ideas can be implanted into the belly of giving a superb presentation. Now get out there, be curious, be multi-talented, take your time striving for quality, and your presentations will be stored in the long-term memories of your audience.

Tip – Adopt these four ideas from da Vinci to produce a superb presentation ever, one that will be stored in the long term memory of your audience.

#57 – Richard Bach

(1936)

Context – Richard Bach wrote *Jonathan Livingston Seagull* in 1970. Below is a collection of quotes from that work. I've also attached a clip from the ending of the film by the same name highlighting singer-songwriter Neil Diamond.

1. *"Your whole body, from wingtip to wingtip,"* Jonathan would say, other times, *"is nothing more than your thought itself, in a form you can see. Break the chains of your thought, and you break the chains of your body, too."*

2. *"Instead of our drab slogging forth and back to the fishing boats, there's reason to live. We can lift ourselves out of ignorance, we can find ourselves as creatures of excellence and intelligence and skill. We can learn to be free! We can learn to fly!"*

3. *"I want to learn to fly like that," Jonathan said, and a strange light glowed in his eyes. "Tell me what to do."*

Chiang spoke slowly and watched the younger gull ever so carefully. "To fly as fast as thought, to anywhere that is," he said, "you must begin by knowing that you have already arrived ...The trick, according to Chiang, was for Jonathan to stop seeing himself as trapped inside a limited body with a forty-two inch wingspan.... The trick was to know that his true nature lived, as perfect as an unwritten number, everywhere at once across space and time."

Analysis – *Jonathan Livingston Seagull* by Richard Bach is one of those classic reads that everyone should pick up at some point in their lives. I read it many years ago and read it again this morning. It is a 127-page novella (short novel), and includes several pages of pictures, so it's a quick read, a story about seagulls, but the undercurrent is that the seagulls represent humans. At the nucleus, it is a story about flying, and I learnt that while seagulls can fly, they don't enjoy flying; they do so only to obtain food. Jonathan's father reminds him that, "the reason you fly is to eat." Truth is, I couldn't pick just one quote, but I've chosen three to showcase as today's entry. Each quote represents the vibe that I want to convey, which is that we already have all we need within ourselves. It is tapping into those reserves, unleashing the power within us all, recognizing that our thoughts are manifestations of our reality.

As I think of presentation skills, I am reminded of another one of my favourite Bach quotes—you teach best what you need to learn. I'm not sure if I've ever given a workshop where I have not offered up this quote at some point. It is a humble admission to the participants in the workshop, that I do not know everything. I, too, am on the quest for what Bach calls freedom. I, too, am on a journey of altering my thought process consistently to transform my own reality into one filled with joy, fulfillment, and happiness. And that even though I'm leading the workshop, I am also still learning. In fact, I took a few minutes this morning to go through my file archives and document all of the PowerPoint slides, articles, workshops, and keynote talks I've done over my career so far and I had an epiphany. With few exceptions, the subjects that I've taught over the years have been the subjects that I needed to learn. It took painstaking effort to research those subjects in my search for answers. Truthfully, I'm not sure if any answers were ever revealed, but the result was an act of exploration. Diving into a topic soothes my soul and is probably the reason I continue to pick challenging subject matter because I am driven by exploration and a need to find meaning.

When you are preparing your own presentations, pick topics that puzzle and challenge you. The exploration phase will be a great gift to yourself.

Tip – Everything you need to deliver informative and meaningful presentations can be found within you. Start the process of exploration, today.

#56 – Pema Chödrön

(1936)

Context – Pema Chödrön (formerly known as Deirdre Blomfield-Brown) has been a Buddhist nun since 1981. With two failed marriages behind her, she found the path to Buddhism in her late 30s. She is currently the resident teacher of Gampo Abbey, a monastery in rural Cape Breton, Nova Scotia. Here is an excerpt from her book, *When Things Fall Apart: Heart Advice for Difficult Times*.

"Instead of making others right or wrong, or bottling up right and wrong in ourselves, there's a middle way, a very powerful middle way...... Could we have no agenda when we walk into a room with another person, not know what to say, not make that person wrong or right? Could we see, hear, feel other people as they really are? It is powerful to practice this way...true communication can happen only in that open space."

Analysis – I spent the better part of this morning pouring over talk after talk delivered by Chödrön. Every single talk is honest, humble, funny, energetic, wise and engaging. I first heard of Chödrön when a friend sent me one of her quotes. To understand the gravity of the content, I've had to read and reread the quotes again. It is a powerful collection, one that I can learn from and aspire to as a writer, and I hope you find the same. I'm an over-preparer in every way. When it comes to presentation skills this project has showcased my thoughts on preparing, preparing, preparing! If we were to convert what Chödrön is saying here into a presentation skills exercise, it would be to visualize all the things that will happen in the presentation room and prepare in all the ways we've discussed. But once you arrive on stage, allow yourself the freedom to let go. Remove all pre-conceived notions of your audience, whether you know them or not, and allow each of them to simply be. Create an open space where you don't arrive with judgment, and you don't stay in judgment; move with no hidden agenda but behave in a space of acceptance. Accept what is occurring, what is being said, what rebuttals may occur with the movement of wind—allowing it to move with you without destabilizing your stance.

Tip – Create a space of open communication in the presentation room!

#55 – Harry S. Truman

1884–1972

Context – Harry S. Truman was the 33rd President of the United States of America (1945-1953).

"It is amazing what you can accomplish if you do not care who gets the credit."

Analysis – There is another quote in a similar vein by Dwight Morrow (1935) that says, "The world is divided into people who do things, and people who get the credit. Try, if you can, to belong to the first class. There's far less competition." This notion of giving credit is something that comes up over and over in my own consulting practice. People are ticked off when someone takes more credit than they deserve or when people take credit entirely from another. This is what I've learned over my years. Seriously, who cares! Eventually credit where credit is due will rise to the surface. It may not be on the one project or task you are agitated about, but eventually the appropriate credit will surface. I'm always intrigued when this credit issue arises and is a source of gossip and angst. It is human nature to want to be revered for what we do, but as long as the task at hand has been accomplished, it has been done well, and the goal is achieved, that is really what should be the focus. I have not been shielded from the credit bandit either and, earlier in my career, it did agitate me beyond belief. It was the source of a lot of venting with my co-workers. But as I have aged, I recognize why someone would take credit which is not due. Each situation is different, but it often comes down to feeling inferior in some way, and the need to piggyback on the credit of others to further their career and perhaps even mask a lack of skill, which is nothing more than a lack of work ethic (skill can only surface from hard work).

Time and time again you will find someone in your audience who will grasp onto one of your ideas as their own. They will take it back to their work teams or wherever and embrace it as though they had conceived it. I honestly can tell you when this happens to me, I am flattered. It means that I have made my audience think that my idea is their own, and they have not only understood the idea but valued its enough to teach it to others. Can you get a better compliment than that?

Tip – Be flattered when others adopt your ideas as their own.

#54 – Lucius Annaeus Seneca

c. 4 BCE – 65 AD

Context – Lucius Annaeus Seneca, often known simply as Seneca, was a Roman philosopher, statesman, tutor, and advisor to emperor Nero. The below quote is from *On The Shortness of Life & other life lesson for the 21st Century*. Seneca's concepts are timeless but were written in Latin over 2,000 years ago. Even with English translation some of his work is incredibly difficult to follow.

"You can tell the character of every man when you see how he receives praise."

Analysis – In my world, the annual Giller Prize ceremony is up there with great weddings, holidays at home, friend's milestone birthday parties, listening to and watching Tchaikovsky's Nutcracker Symphony, and hearing my son giggle in delight. The Giller Prize is a big deal in my world. Perhaps you are not as obsessed with the prize as I am, so you may be wondering what the heck it is. The Giller Prize is a Canadian literary fiction award. It was founded by Jack Rabinovitch in 1994 to honour the memory of his late wife, Doris Giller. Doris was a literary journalist who died of cancer in 1993. Hundreds of literary authors submit entries each year. The entries are judged by a five-member jury panel who long list the entries, then short list, and then narrow it down to the top five literary fiction author nominees. The winning book is sought after by readers across Canada. It's all Canadian, and it's all sublime. There are a ton of literary awards out there; the Booker, the Nobel Prize in Literature, the Pulitzer Prize, the Quill, and more, but for me, the Giller is the most prestigious, most authentic, and the most fun. My world stops for an hour or so each fall as I sit with a big ol' bowl of popcorn and watch the one-hour television broadcast announcing the finalists. I then buy all five books and try desperately to finish them all by the time the winner is announced at a gala ceremony, which takes place in the winter. So, what do literary awards have to do with presentation skills? It's about how one accepts the praise. Each year the Giller Prize winner comes forward and gives a short speech, and some years the speeches are better than others. Sometimes the author could have used a bit more practice and a better plan. But they're writers, not speakers. Writers, engineers, IT professionals, architects, NASA astronauts, your profession doesn't matter, there will be a time in your career when you are offered praise, and you must stand up and graciously accept it.

How you choose to accept praise is, as Seneca says, a very telling component of one's character. You might bask in the limelight or brag about other accomplishments or treasure the moment, breathe it in and enjoy it, or you may kick your toe on the floor and mumble a quick thank you, become so embarrassed that you have a physiological reaction (i.e., blushing, sweating, tremors, etc.) or become self-deprecating. How you accept praise has a direct correlation to your true self-confidence. I have a friend who, when you pay her a compliment, looks you square in the eye, and with gusto, says, "Thank you." I have another friend who when paid a compliment, will inevitably downplay it and say something like, "Oh that, that's nothing." In both examples, you are given a direct portal into how each of those individuals feels about themselves. In the first example, the person is confident and accepting. In the second example, the person yearns for a compliment but ultimately feels inadequate and that the compliment isn't earned or deserved. Accepting praise well is a skill I continue to work on. I instinctively I begin self-deprecating because I don't want to appear arrogant. So, I work hard on being mindful and matching my internal confidence with accepting praise comfortably and graciously.

Here are a few techniques to include in your acceptance speech:

1. Begin with a big, heartfelt, "Thank you!" before anything else leaves your mouth. Thank your support network, perhaps your spouse, children, parents, publisher, your editor etc. Rarely are any of these works created in a vacuum.

2. Accept the praise as you would a gift. Give thanks graciously, fervently, and sincerely (if you become

emotional, that's okay, it means that you've allowed yourself to be in the moment).

3. Be specific. Explain why your work has such a deep impact on you and *how* the recognition will impact your future.

4. Wrap up your speech with another heartfelt thank you!

5. Follow up with a handwritten note of thanks to the organizers, judges, etc.

Maybe one of the Giller Prize finalists next year will stumble upon this book, follow this simple five-step process above and give an impactful and memorable acceptance speech.

Tip – Follow this five-step formula and accept praise with confidence.

#53 – Ellen DeGeneres

(1958)

Context – Comedian, TV host, and actress Ellen DeGeneres at Tulane's 2009 Commencement Speech. The Ellen DeGeneres Show wrapped up its 19th and final season in 2022. Maybe that was always the plan or perhaps the decision to cancel the show was brought about by the allegations of a "toxic work environment" from various crew members and guests. The allegations certainly tainted the friendly and charming, "Be kind" persona DeGeneres put forward on the air. But DeGeneres is no stranger to the wrath of the press, so we'll have to wait and see how her next chapter unfolds.

"Oh boy, thank you so much, thank you so much. Thank you, President Cowan, Mrs. President Cowen; distinguished guests, undistinguished guests, you know who you are, honored faculty and creepy Spanish teacher. And thank you to all the graduating Class of 2009, I realize most of you are hungover and have splitting headaches and haven't slept since Fat Tuesday, but you can't graduate 'til I finish, so listen up.

When I was asked to make the commencement speech, I immediately said yes. Then I went to look up what commencement meant, which would have been easy if I had a dictionary, but most of the books in our house are Portia's, and they're all written in Australian. So, I had to break the word down myself, to find out the meaning.

Commencement: common, and cement, common cement. You commonly see cement on sidewalks. Sidewalks have cracks, and if you step on a crack, you break your mother's back. So, there's that. But I'm honored that you've asked me here to speak at your common cement.

I thought that you had to be a famous alumnus, alumini, aluminum, alumis; you had to graduate from this school. And I didn't go to college here, and I don't know if President Cowan knows, I didn't go to any college at all, any college. And I'm not saying you wasted your time, or money, but look at me, I'm a huge celebrity.

Although I did graduate from the school of hard knocks, our mascot was the knockers. I spent a lot of time here growing up. My mom worked at Newcomb, and I would go there every time I needed to steal something out of her purse.

But why am I here today? Clearly not to steal, you're too far away and I'd never get away with it. I'm here because of you. Because I can't think of a more tenacious, more courageous graduating class. I mean, look at you all, wearing your robes. Usually when you're wearing a robe at 10 in the morning, it means you've given up...."

Analysis – As you watch the clip, keep your eyes on the white-haired gentlemen sitting to the right of DeGeneres. Man, he is enjoying her talk. You can tell a ton about how well a speaker by looking at the audience around them. I do this a lot when I'm asked to observe and give pointers to a speaker. Sure, I look at the speaker, but I spend more time looking at the audience. Are they engaged, interested, and having fun? That is part of the point of DeGeneres' standup performance.

DeGeneres delivery is unmistakably superb. She gives a talk almost every single day and it shows. She is at ease, she is funny, and she is inspiring. What I'd like to highlight today is a story she shares that surfaced from tragedy. When DeGeneres was 19 years old her girlfriend died in a car accident and, in desperation, DeGeneres started writing to God in the hopes that she would find answers. In one of her letters to God, she wrote about being on *The Tonight Show* with Johnny Carson. She penned that she'd be the first woman invited to sit down on *The Tonight Show*. The letter, she says, is what started her path to standup. It made me think about life and the importance of writing down your aspirations such as what kind of presenter you want to be. So, I wrote down my aspirations because I won't ask you to do something I wouldn't or couldn't do myself. And it was a very difficult but rather enlightening task. I learned that I wanted to have a more significant and profound influence on my audience by being less corporate and more personable. The document ended up being many pages long, so that is a synopsis, but it's a terrific exercise and I encourage you to try it. I believe that thoughts are true and living energy. What you think inevitably becomes who you are. Why not take your thoughts, as DeGeneres did and make them whole, rich, and robust. (Oh, by the way, my synopsis included $9.6 million dollars in revenue.) If you dream it then it will be.

Tip – Dream big, aloud and on paper. Your thoughts are living energy with the power to manifest your reality!

#52 – Aristotle

384 BCE – 322 BCE

Context – Aristotle was a Greek philosopher, a student of Plato, and the teacher of Alexander the Great. With Plato and Socrates (Socrates is Plato's teacher), Aristotle is unquestionably one of the most important founding figures in Western philosophy. His writings cover vast topics: physics, poetry, music, logic, theatre, politics, ethics, biology, zoology, and more. The below quote is taken from *The Art of Rhetoric* (sect. 6, ch. 2.11.).

"Jealousy is both reasonable and belongs to reasonable men, while envy is base and belongs to the base, for the one makes himself get good things by jealousy, while the other does not allow his neighbour to have them through envy. "

Analysis – Imagine you are Plato for a moment. You are heading up the now-famous Academy. You are basking in the glory of a reputation whereby you are revered by both your students and the larger Athenian population. You are reaching the end of your years, and faintly hear the whisper and eventual boom of a young chap who all refer to as the Reader or the Mind of the Academy. A boy of 17 years old has joined the Academy and is quickly becoming prolific in the halls of the Academy, both with the students and faculty. His name is Aristotle. Although you have enjoyed a remarkable career, you feel green with envy.

Aristotle remained at the school for 20 years, first as a student, then a teacher. He did depart for one year, which coincided with the year of Plato's death—there is no documentation as to why he left, but I believe his departure was a sign of loyalty and respect to Plato. Today's topic on the list of *365 Must-Know Talks* highlights jealousy and the role it plays in presentation skills.

Vain people, those who are in love with a grandiose image of themselves, or in extreme cases, those with narcissistic personality disorder can become envious of those, more intelligent, educated, or successful. But what Aristotle uncovered is the difference between jealousy and envy—while jealousy can drive a person to do better and succeed, envy stirs up pain at another's good fortune. Kate Barros said, "Envy always involves a comparison—we envy that which we lack." Envy then is an extremely damaging emotion whereby one desires to have something that is possessed by another. Jealousy is predominantly concerned with the fear of losing something one already possesses, while envy is driven by the wish to own something another possesses.

Aristotle thought jealousy motivated man to obtain good things. On the other hand, envy was base because it didn't allow others to have good things. I couldn't agree more. If we turn our attention to presentation skills, then jealousy can drive us to continue to learn, have new aspirations, and new goals. While envy will only halt our progress.

The truth is no one knows who was jealous or envious of who back then, but it made me contemplate the notion of all the students in Greek philosophical times and all the teachers. You have Plato, who was the teacher to Aristotle, you have Socrates, who taught Plato. I don't believe Socrates would have fallen prey to this thought process, based on my research, but Plato and Aristotle struggled. Aristotle was undoubtedly Plato's prized student, but they did have well-documented disagreements. I think those disagreements, to some degree, were based on jealousy and that jealousy drove both of them to achieve higher knowledge and this further punctuates Aristotle's point that jealousy is a reasonable attribute. So, my advice is to seek out a teacher and mentor with whom you can have robust and rich disagreements.

(The fresco by Raphael depicts Plato on the left and Aristotle on the right and it is loaded with metaphors…stunning!)

Tip – A healthy dose of jealously can be useful but keep your envy in check.

#51 – Ho Chi Minh

1890–1969

Context – Ho Chi Minh was the president of North Vietnam from 1946 to 1969.

"If the tiger ever stands still, the elephant will crush him with his mighty tusks. But the tiger will not stand still. He will leap upon the back of the elephant, tearing huge chunks from his side, and then he will leap back into the dark jungle. And slowly the elephant will bleed to death. Such will be the war in Indochina."

Analysis – Vietnam, during World War II, was occupied by the Japanese, and after their defeat, the Viet Minh—Viet Minh translates to The League for the Independence of Vietnam. The Viet Minh were determined not to allow the former colonial power, France, to reassert control. After the August revolution of 1945, Emperor Bao Dai relinquished control, Ho Chi Minh declared independence, and the Viet Minh emerged as the most powerful party. The quote above indicates the tactics and force used over the next eight years against the French and later against The American army between 1965 and 1975.

This is a giant beast of a topic, so let's not delve too vastly into the history but rather the reason for choosing the above quote to be included in this list of *365 Must-Know Talks*—the use of an analogy. I'm not going to lie, as I was prepping this entry, I referenced my Grade nine grammar. I got monumentally confused by the difference between an analogy, a metaphor, and a simile. This is what you need to know:

- an analogy is showing a similarity between two things on which a comparison may be based

- a simile is an expressed analogy

- a metaphor is an implied analogy

Whether you failed Grammar 101 or not, all you need to know is expressed wholly in the belly of Ho Chi Minh's quote. Transferring boring words and converting them into another idea brings the words to life and creates a new meaning behind what you are saying. When you are engaged in a presentation, it is the analogies, the metaphors, and the similes that will bring your words to life. You can't just string one to the next, because your talk will end up sounding like a jig-saw puzzle but, placed appropriately, analogies can solidify your subject matter in such a way that your ideas become more visual and tangible to your audience.

One dollar would buy a taco for everyone living in the town of New Amsterdam, Indiana (population 1)

241,114 is the population of Jersey City, New Jersey, in the USA in 2008

243,100 educational, vocational, and school counsellors employed in the USA.

10,000 McDonald's Big Macs laid next to each other would reach as far as 9.84 American football fields.

You can fit 35 million London Buses between the Earth and Moon and you would need to run nine thousand marathons to get there.

Used sparingly, word and number analogies, metaphors, and similes bring your presentations to life.

Tip – Use analogies, metaphors and similes in your presentations.

#50 – George Berkeley

1685–1753

Context –George Berkeley was a philosopher who advanced the theory he called immaterialism. Born in Kilkenny Berkeley attended Kilkenny College and Trinity College in Dublin. He was ordained into the Anglican Church.

"If a tree falls in a forest and no one hears it, does it make a sound?"

Analysis – Objects exist only when they are perceived by someone or something else, and the observer cannot know whether something exists, only that it is perceived. Read that again. This idea, first presented by Berkeley, in the 1700s, was met with mockery, disdain, and contempt. In 1713, Berkeley published a defense of his argument in Esse est percipi (Translation: To be is to be perceived) and said, "because God is all-seeing and all-hearing, there is always someone to hear it fall."

If I had to distill Berkeley's philosophies down, he was consumed with this notion of the inner world vs. the external world. Does internal perception match one's external reality? How do we even know if an external world exists at all? This philosophical problem of the external world is much of Berkeley's work and writing. Berkeley's principles were largely ignored in his lifetime, and even today, philosophers and novices alike read him with great skepticism. This skepticism is why Berkeley has earned a spot on this list of *365 Must-Know Talks*.

Skepticism is good! Don't be concerned if your ideas are met with doubt, cynicism, disbelief, hesitation, uncertainty, and apprehension—this means you are choosing thought-provoking subject matter. If you are presenting topics that are met with ovation, adulation, and admiration, then the topics you are choosing are likely uninteresting. Obviously, there are some great topics out there that should be met with positivity—for example those that affect charities, children, illness, injustice, etc. But there are times when a presentation should allow some inner exploration, some inner introspection and where we should uncover new and perhaps controversial new ways of looking at the world that will elicit skepticism. Think about how inventors at some point have to describe their inventions to others and how they are probably met with suspicion. How about the people who invented toothpaste or the submarine, or the gun or the television or the fax machine or the hula hoop? These inventors likely didn't receive resounding applause initially. You need to continuously figure out how to represent an idea a second time, a third time and over again until your vision becomes clear. If you believe in your content as Berkeley did, you will write and speak about it for an entire lifetime, hoping that it will eventually be embraced. When you believe so much in your product or your idea, you will do whatever it takes to share it with the masses. Now that is what you call tenacity.

German philosopher Friedrich Wilhelm Nietzsche said, "All great intellects are skeptical." And, for me, all great presentations should evoke skepticism.

Tip – Strive to evoke skepticism in your presentations.

#49 – Moses

c.1527 BCE– c.1407 BCE

Context – Moses was a Hebrew born during the Jewish enslavement in Egypt when Pharaoh decreed that all male Hebrew infants were to be drowned at birth. In an effort to save him, Moses' mother put him in a basket and hid him in the reeds on the Nile where he was found by the Pharaoh's daughter and raised at the court of Pharaoh. Later, God commanded Moses to lead the Hebrew slaves to freedom. At Mount Sinai in Palestine, God delivered the Ten Commandments to Moses.

1. I am the Lord your God, who brought you out of the land of Egypt, out of the house of slavery; you shall have no other gods before me.

2. You shall not make for yourself an idol, whether in the form of anything that is in heaven above, or that is on the earth beneath, or that is in the water under the earth. You shall not bow down to them or worship them; for I the Lord your God am a jealous God, punishing children for the iniquity of parents, to the third and the fourth generation of those who reject me, but showing steadfast love to the thousandth generation of those who love me and keep my commandments.

3. You shall not make wrongful use of the name of the Lord your God, for the Lord will not acquit anyone who misuses his name.

4. Remember the sabbath day and keep it holy. Six days you shall labor and do all your work. But the seventh day is a sabbath to the Lord your God; you shall not do any work—you, your son or your daughter, your male or female slave, your livestock, or the alien resident in your towns. For in six days the Lord made heaven and earth, the sea, and all that is in them, but rested the seventh day; therefore the Lord blessed the sabbath day and consecrated it.

5. Honor your father and your mother, so that your days may be long in the land that the Lord your God is giving you.

6. *You shall not murder.*

7. *You shall not commit adultery.*

8. *You shall not steal.*

9. *You shall not bear false witness against your neighbour.*

10. *You shall not covet your neighbor's house; you shall not covet your neighbor's wife, or male or female slave, or ox, or donkey, or anything that belongs to your neighbour.*

Analysis – The Ten Commandments are recognized in Judaism, Christianity, and Islam as a summary of the central rules of behaviour that God expects of humankind. The Old Testament (the Book of Exodus) says that God gave the Ten Commandments to Moses after he led the Israelites to freedom from slavery in Egypt.

The first five commandments focus on duties toward God while the next five relate to duties toward other people.

Whether you are religious or not, you've most likely heard of the Ten Commandments. And, once again, it is not my role as the author of this list of *365 Must-Know Talks* to offer an opinion on the content, but to look at talks from the perspective of transferring tangible presentation tools, techniques, skills, and knowledge. The Ten Commandments are a list of central rules of behaviour that are used as a moral compass for humankind. It is a fascinating notion that these rules are still taught and preserved today.

I compare this notion of adopting and perpetuating new rules to flocking, bird-like behaviour. Stay with me for a second. If you look at birds or fish or insects or a herd of animals, and even humans, one can see great similarities. Flocking is the collective motion of a large number of entities (birds, fish, insect, humans, whatever) that emerges from simple rules.

If we look at birds, there are three flocking rules (Wikipedia):

1. Separation – avoid crowding neighbours (short range repulsion)

2. Alignment – steer towards the average heading of neighbours

3. Cohesion – steer towards average position of neighbours (long range attraction)

Without these rules, a flock of birds would not be able to fly together. It would be mayhem. So, whether you are talking birds, fish, insects, or a herd of animals, a set of spoken or unspoken rules are needed to prevent chaos. The same can be said for the human race, and the Ten Commandments. What about presentation skills? Is there a set of rules for presentation skills? I believe there are.

Rules of Superb Presenters:

#1. The Golden Rule: Treat others as you wish to be treated and operate with integrity and humility.

#2. Prepare…and prepare…and prepare.

#3. Adopt Level 1 listening skills (see entries #359 and #251 for further discussion on Level 1 listening.)

#4. Don't include too much detail in your presentation. Too much detail will leave the content flat and dull.

#5. Be introspective and understand who you are before hitting centre stage.

#6. Create uncluttered visual aids that drive the message forward rather than complicate it.

#7. Understand nonverbal and body language cues, both the ones you are giving and those you receive from your audience.

#8. Be prepared for the question-and-answer period.

#9. Check the vitals—who, what, when, where and why—before stepping onto the presentation stage.

#10. Have a deep desire to communicate your message to an audience with enthusiasm and passion.

Tip – Create and follow a set of central rules to deliver a superb presentation and follow them.

#48 – Clarence Darrow

1857–1938

Content – Clarence Darrow was an American lawyer and civil libertarian. This text comes from the transcript published in 1927, which had underwritten the defence of Henry Sweet (1926). Please note, this speech (or closing argument) in its entirety is seven hours long; this is the concluding section of a speech that is titled, "I Believe in the Law of Love."

"Now, gentlemen, just one more word, and I am through with this case. I do not live in Detroit. But I have no feeling against this city. In fact, I shall always have the kindest remembrance of it, especially if this case results as I think and feel that it will. I am the last one to come here to stir up race hatred or any other hatred. I do not believe in the law of hate. I may not be true to my ideals always, but I believe in the law of love, and I believe you can do nothing with hatred. I would like to see a time when man loves his fellow man and forgets his color or his creed. We will never be civilized until that time comes.

I know the Negro race has a long road to go. I believe the life of the Negro race has been a life of tragedy, of injustice, of oppression. The law has made him equal, but man has not. And, after all, the last analysis is, what has man done? And not what has the law done? I know there is a long road ahead of him before he can take the place which I believe he should take. I know that before him, there is suffering, sorrow, tribulation, and death among the blacks and perhaps the whites. I am sorry. I would do what I could to avert it. I would advise patience; I would advise toleration; I would advise understanding; I would advise all of those things which are necessary for men who live together.

Gentlemen, what do you think is your duty in this case? I have watched, day after day, these black, tense faces that have crowded this court. These black faces that now are looking to you twelve whites, feeling that the hopes and fears of a race are in your keeping.

This case is about to end, gentlemen. To them, it is life. Not one of their colour sits on this jury. Their fate is in the hands of twelve whites. Their eyes are fixed on you, their hearts go out to you, and their hopes hang on your verdict.

This is all. I ask you, on behalf of this defendant, on behalf of these helpless ones who turn to you, and more than that, on behalf of this great state, and this great city which must face this problem, and face it fairly, I ask you, in the name of progress and of the human race, to return a verdict of not guilty in this case!"

Analysis – If you have not heard of Clarence Darrow before, I urge you to watch and review this real-life Atticus Finch in action! In this case, a white mob in Detroit attempted to drive a black family out of the home they purchased in a white neighbourhood. A white man was killed in the struggle, and the 11 blacks in the house were charged with murder. Darrow insisted that the entire mess was nothing but prejudice and if the colour of their skin was reversed (white men in the house and a black mob) that they would have been given medals instead of a prison sentence. Darrow would defend Henry Sweet first (three family members were brought to trial, 11 in total). In the end, Sweet was found not guilty on the grounds of self defence, and the prosecution dropped the charges against the others.

Darrow's closing statement lasted seven hours. His ardent pleas and well-constructed arguments are a masterpiece. In 1927, how would you convince this jury that what has occurred is unjust, wrong, and prejudice? How would you appeal to an all-white jury, while defending a black person? Would you wing it and hope for the best? Of course not! You'd need to be very thoughtful and do an exorbitant amount of research. I'm no lawyer, but presenters can certainly glean some essential techniques by studying how Darrow sums up the case in his closing argument.

When preparing for the persuasive talk:

1. Gather all the facts (in this case, what happened on that day).

2. Understand the facts (it's not enough to pull a bunch of numbers and statistics. Distill the facts down so you can explain what they mean and the implications.)

3. Utilize the facts to make your point (Darrow shows how it would have been impossible for Sweet to commit the crime).

4. Use history (Darrow talks about racial history and how much further we must go to attain equality).

5. Appeal to the moral fibre of your audience. Darrow refers to the fate of these men being in the hands of the jury.

Darrow argues these points with such incredible skill that it makes me well up. As I read the entirety of the closing statement again today, I realized that if someone gave a presentation, and they put forth as much effort and skill as Darrow, what a different world we would live in. Granted, not all presentations deal with life or death or freedom or imprisonment issues, but many significant and profound presentations, talks, and speeches worldwide involve serious topics. If speeches are done well, they can have a monumental impact and change the future.

Tip – Ensure you research and do your due diligence with each and every presentation.

#47 – Mother Teresa

1910–1997

Context – In 1979, Mother Teresa delivers her Nobel prize speech, "Love Begins at Home."

"As we have gathered here together to thank God for the Nobel Peace Prize, I think it will be beautiful that we pray the prayer of St. Francis of Assisi, which always surprises me very much. We pray this prayer every day after Holy Communion because it is very fitting for each one of us.

And I always wonder that 400-500 years ago, when St. Francis of Assisi composed this prayer, they had the same difficulties that we have today as we compose this prayer that fits very nicely for us also. I think some of you already have got it—so we pray together: Let us thank God for the opportunity that we all have together today, for this gift of peace that reminds us that we have been created to live that peace and that Jesus became man to bring that good news to the poor.

He, being God, became man in all things like us except in sin, and he proclaimed very clearly that he had come to give the good news. The news was peace to all of good will, and this is something that we all want—the peace of heart. And God loved the world so much that he gave his son—it was a giving:

it is as much as if to say it hurt God to give because he loved the world so much that he gave his son.

He gave him to the Virgin Mary, and what did she do with him?

As soon as he came in her life, immediately she went in haste to give that good news, and as she came into the house of her cousin, the child—the child in the womb of Elizabeth, leapt with joy. He was, that little unborn child was, the first messenger of peace. He recognized the Prince of Peace; he recognized that Christ had come to bring the good news for you and for me.

And as if that was not enough—it was not enough to become a man—he died on the cross to show that greater love and he died for you and for me and for that leper and for that man dying of hunger and that naked person lying in the street not only of Calcutta, but of Africa, and New York, and London, and Oslo – and insisted that we love one another as he loves each one of us.

And we read that in the Gospel very clearly: "love as I have loved you; as I love you; as the Father has loved me, I love you." And the harder the Father loved him, he gave him to us, and how much we love one another, we too must give to each other until it hurts. It is not enough for us to say: "I love God, but I do not love my neighbour." Saint John says that you are a liar if you say you love God and you don't love your neighbor.

How can you love God whom you do not see if you do not love your neighbor whom you see, whom you touch, with whom you live? And so, this is very important for us to realize that love, to be true, has to hurt. It hurt Jesus to love us. It hurt him. And to make sure we remember his great love, he made himself the bread of life to satisfy our hunger for his love – our hunger for God – because we have been created for that love. We have been created in His image.

We have been created to love and to be loved, and he has become man to make it possible for us to love as he loved us. He makes himself the hungry one, the naked one, the homeless one, and he says, "You did it to me." He is hungry for our love, and this is the hunger that you and I must find. It may be in our own home. I never forget an opportunity I had in visiting a home where they had all these old parents of sons and daughters who had just put them in an institution and forgotten, maybe.

And I went there, and I saw in that home they had everything, beautiful things, but everybody was looking towards the door. And I did not see a single one with a smile on their face. And I turned to the sister, and I asked: How is that? How is that these people who have everything here, why are they all looking towards the door? Why are they not smiling? I am so used to see the smiles on our people, even the dying ones smile. And she said: "This is nearly every day."

They are expecting; they are hoping that a son or daughter will come to visit them. They are hurt because they are forgotten." And see – this is where love comes. That poverty comes right there in our own home, even neglect to love. Maybe in our own family, we have somebody who is feeling lonely, who is feeling sick, who is feeling worried, and there are difficult days for everybody. Are we there?

Are we there to receive them? Is the mother there to receive the child? I was surprised in the West to see so many young boys and girls given into drugs. And I tried to find out why. Why is it like that? And the answer was: "Because there is no one in the family to receive them." Father and mother are so busy they have no time. Young parents are in some institution, and the child goes back to the street and gets involved in something.

We are talking of peace. These are things that break peace. But I feel the greatest destroyer of peace today is abortion because it is a direct war, a direct killing, direct murder by the mother herself. And we read in the scripture, for God says very clearly: "Even if a mother could forget her child, I will not forget you. I have curved you in the palm of my hand." We are curved in the palm of his hand, so close to him, that unborn child has been curved in the hand of God.

And that is what strikes me most, the beginning of that sentence, that even if a mother could forget, something impossible – but even if she could forget – I will not forget you. And today, the greatest means, the greatest destroyer of peace, is abortion. And we who are standing here – our parents wanted us.

We would not be here if our parents would do that to us. Our children, we want them, we love them.

But what of the other millions. Many people are very, very concerned with the children of India, with the children of Africa where quite a number die, maybe of malnutrition, of hunger, and so on, but millions are dying deliberately by the will of the mother. And this is what is the greatest destroyer of peace today. Because if a mother can kill her own child, what is left for me to kill you and you to kill me? There is nothing between. And this I appeal in India, I appeal everywhere – "Let us bring the child back" – and this year being the child's year: What have we done for the child?

At the beginning of the year, I told, I spoke everywhere, and I said: let us ensure this year that we make every single child born, and unborn, wanted. And today is the end of the year. Have we really made the children wanted? I will tell you something terrifying. We are fighting abortion by adoption. We have saved thousands of lives. We have sent word to all the clinics, to the hospitals, police stations: "Please don't destroy the child; we will take the child."

So, every hour of the day and night there is always somebody – we have quite a number of unwedded mothers – tell them: "Come, we will take care of you, we will take care of the child from you, and we will get a home for the child." And we have a tremendous demand for families who have no children; that is the blessing of God for us. And also, we are doing another thing which is very beautiful. We are teaching our beggars, our leprosy patients, our slum dwellers, our people of the street, natural family planning.

And in Calcutta alone in six years – it is all in Calcutta – we have had 61,273 babies less from the families who would have had them because they practice this natural way of abstaining, of self-control, out of love for each other. We teach them the temperature method, which is very beautiful, very simple. And our poor people understand. And you know what they have told me? "Our family is healthy, our family is united, and we can have a baby whenever we want."

So clear – those people in the street, those beggars – and I think that if our people can do like that, how much more you and all the others who can know the ways and means without destroying the life that God has created in us. The poor people are very great people. They can teach us so many beautiful things. The other day one of them came to thank us and said: "You people who have evolved chastity; you are the best people to teach us family planning because it is nothing more than self-control out of love for each other."

And I think they said a beautiful sentence. And these are people who maybe have nothing to eat, maybe they have not a home where to live, but they are great people. The poor are very wonderful people.

One evening we went out, and we picked up four people from the street. And one of them was in a most terrible condition. And I told the sisters: "You take care of the other three; I will take care of this one that looks worse." So, I did for her all that my love can do. I put her in bed, and there was such a beautiful smile on her face.

She took hold of my hand, as she said one word only, "Thank you" – and she died. I could not help but examine my conscience before her. And I asked, "What would I say if I was in her place?" And my answer was very simple. I would have tried to draw a little attention to myself. I would have said, "I am hungry, I am dying, I am cold, I am in pain", or something. But she gave me much more – she gave me her grateful love.

And she died with a smile on her face – like that man who we picked up from the drain, half-eaten with worms, and we brought him to the home – "I have lived like an animal in the street, but I am going to die like an angel, loved and cared for." And it was so wonderful to see the greatness of that man who could speak like that, who could die like that without blaming, without cursing anybody, without comparing anything. Like an angel – this is the greatness of our people.

And this is why we believe what Jesus has said, "I was hungry; I was naked, I was homeless; I was unwanted, unloved, uncared for – and you did it to me." I believe that we are not really social workers.

We may be doing social work in the eyes of people. But we are really contemplatives in the heart of the world. For we are touching the body of Christ twenty-four hours. We have twenty-four hours in his presence, and so you and I, too, must try to bring that presence of God into your family, for the family that prays together stays together.

And I think that we in our family, we don't need bombs and guns, to destroy or to bring peace – just get together, love one another, bring that peace, that joy, that strength of presence of each other in the home. And we will be able to overcome all the evil that is in the world. There is so much suffering, so much hatred, so much misery, and we, with our prayer, with our sacrifice, are beginning at home. Love begins at home, and it is not how much we do but how much love we put in the action that we do.

It is to God almighty – how much we do does not matter because he is infinite, but how much love we put in action. How much we do to him in the person that we are serving. Some time ago, in Calcutta, we had great difficulty in getting sugar. And I don't know how the word got around to the children, and a little boy of four years old, a Hindu boy, went home and told his parents: "I will not eat sugar for three days.

I will give my sugar to Mother Teresa for her children." After these three days, his father and mother brought him to our house. I had never met them before, and this little one could scarcely pronounce my name. But he knew exactly what he had come to do. He knew that he wanted to share his love. And this is why I have received such a lot of love from all. From the time that I have come here, I have simply been surrounded with love and with real, real understanding love.

It could feel as if everyone in India, everyone in Africa is somebody very special for to you. And I felt quite home; I was telling Sister today. I feel in the convent with the Sisters as if I am in Calcutta with my own Sisters. So completely at home here, right here. And so here I am talking with you. I want you to find the poor here, right in your own home first. And begin love there. Be that good news to your own people. And find out about your next-door neighbour.

Do you know who they are? I had the most extraordinary experience with a Hindu family who had eight children. A gentleman came to our house and said, "Mother Teresa, there is a family with eight children; they have not eaten for so long; do something." So, I took some rice, and I went there immediately. And I saw the children – their eyes shining with hunger. I don't know if you have ever seen hunger. But I have seen it very often.

And she took the rice, she divided the rice, and she went out. When she came back, I asked her, "Where did you go, what did you do?" And she gave me a very simple answer, "They are hungry also." What struck me most was that she knew – and who are they? A Muslim family – and she knew. I didn't bring more rice that evening because I wanted them to enjoy the joy of sharing. But there were those children radiating joy, sharing the joy with their mother because she had the love to give.

And you see, this is where love begins – at home. And I want you – and I am very grateful for what I have received. It has been a tremendous experience, and I go back to India – I will be back by next week, the 15th, I hope, and I will be able to bring your love. And I know well that you have not given from your abundance, but you have given until it has hurt you. Today the little children, they gave – I was so surprised – there is so much joy for the children that are hungry.

That the children like themselves will need love and get so much from their parents. So let us thank God that we have had this opportunity to come to know each other and that this knowledge of each other has brought us very close. And we will be able to help the children of the whole world because, as you know, our Sisters are all over the world. And with this prize that I have received as a prize of peace, I am going to try to make the home for many people that have no home.

Because I believe that love begins at home, and if we can create a home for the poor, I think that more and more love will spread. And we will be able through this understanding love to bring peace, be the good news to the poor. The poor in our own family first, in our country, and in the world. To be able to do this, our Sisters, our lives have to be woven with prayer. They have to be woven with Christ to be able to understand, to be able to share. Today, there is so much suffering, and I feel that the passion of Christ is being relived all over again.

Are we there to share that passion, to share that suffering of people – around the world, not only the poor countries? But I found the poverty of the West so much more difficult to remove. When I pick up a person from the street, hungry, I give him a plate of rice, a piece of bread, I have satisfied. I have removed that hunger. But a person that is shut out, that feels unwanted, unloved, terrified, the person that has been thrown out from society – that poverty is so hurtful and so much, and I find that very difficult.

Our Sisters are working amongst that kind of people in the West. So, you must pray for us that we may be able to be that good news. We cannot do that without you. You have to do that here in your country.

You must come to know the poor. Maybe our people here have material things, everything, but I think that if we all look into our own homes, how difficult we find it sometimes to smile at each other, and that the smile is the beginning of love.

And so let us always meet each other with a smile, for the smile is the beginning of love, and once we begin to love each other, naturally we want to do something. So, you pray for our Sisters and for me and for our Brothers, and for our Co-Workers that are around the world. Pray that we may remain faithful to the gift of God, to love Him and serve Him in the poor together with you.

What we have done we would not have been able to do if you did not share with your prayers, with your gifts, this continual giving. But I don't want you to give me from your abundance. I want you to give me until it hurts. The other day I received $15 from a man who has been on his back for twenty years, and the only part that he can move is his right hand. And the only companion that he enjoys is smoking.

And he said to me, "I do not smoke for one week, and I send you this money." It must have been a terrible sacrifice for him but see how beautiful, how he shared. And with that money, I brought bread, and I gave to those who are hungry with joy on both sides. He was giving, and the poor were receiving.

This is something you and I can do – it is a gift of God to us to be able to share our love with others.

And let it be able to share our love with others. And let it be as it was for Jesus. Let us love one another as he loved us. Let us love him with undivided love. And the joy of loving him and each other – let us give now that Christmas is coming so close. Let us keep that joy of loving Jesus in our hearts and share that joy with all that we come in touch with.

That radiating joy with all that we come in touch with. That radiating joy is real, for we have no reason not to be happy because we have Christ with us. Christ in our hearts, Christ in the poor that we meet, Christ in the smile that we give and the smile that we receive. Let us make that one point – that no child will be unwanted and also that we meet each other always with a smile, especially when it is difficult to smile.

I never forget some time ago about fourteen professors came from the United States from different universities. And they came to Calcutta to our house. Then we were talking about the fact that they had been to the home for the dying. (We have a home for the dying in Calcutta, where we have picked up more than 36 000 people only from the streets of and out of that big number more than 18 000 have died a beautiful death. They have just gone home to God). And they came to our house, and we talked of love, of compassion.

And then one of them asked me, "Say, Mother, please tell us something that we will remember." And I said to them, "Smile at each other, make time for each other in your family. Smile at each other." And then another one asked me, "Are you married?" and I said, "Yes, and I find it sometimes very difficult to smile at Jesus because he can be very demanding sometimes." This is really something true. And there is where love comes – when it is demanding, and yet we can give it to him with joy.

Just as I have said today, I have said that if I don't go to heaven for anything else, I will be going to heaven for all the publicity because it has purified me and sacrificed me and made me ready to go to heaven. I think that this is something that we must live life beautifully, we have Jesus with us, and he loves us. If we could only remember that God loves us, and we have an opportunity to love others as he loves us, not in big things, but in small things with great love, then Norway becomes a nest of love.

And how beautiful it will be that from here, a center for peace from war has been given. That from here, the joy of life of the unborn child comes out. If you become a burning light of peace in the world, then really, the Nobel Peace Prize is a gift of the Norwegian people.

God bless you! You will get credit for it."

Analysis – I read this speech many years ago and I am thrilled to share it with you here. I'm not a religious person, but I do consider myself to be spiritual. There is a distinct difference between the two, but occasionally you encounter words that transcend both and are just pure, beautiful, and intentionally loving. You might be thinking, "Well, it's Mother Teresa, so this is no surprise."
But how did Mother Teresa embody these qualities? Was she born this way? How did she come to minister to the poor, sick, orphaned, and dying? In one of her biographies, it is said that Mother Teresa

received her calling to commit herself to a religious life at the age of 12 and immersed herself completely when she left home at age 18. She began her missionary work in 1948, commencing with an experience she had that she later described as, "the call within the call." While traveling by train one day, she describes what she felt and heard and says, "I was to leave the convent and help the poor while living among them. It was an order. To fail would have been to break the faith."

Was it easy for her? Absolutely not! Her first year was laden with difficulties. She found herself with no income and begging for food and supplies. She had constant doubt. She wrote in her diary:

"Our Lord wants me to be a free nun covered with the poverty of the cross. Today I learned a good lesson. The poverty of the poor must be so hard for them. While looking for a home, I walked and walked 'til my arms and legs ached. I thought how much they must ache in body and soul, looking for a home, food, and health. Then the comfort of Loreto [her former order] came to tempt me. 'You have only to say the word, and all that will be yours again,' the Tempter kept on saying … Of free choice, my God, and out of love for you, I desire to remain and do whatever be your Holy will in my regard. I did not let a single tear come."

Always listen to your inner voice. It can be God; it can be instinct; it can be whatever you choose to call it. One of the best attributes a presenter can have when delivering a talk is allowing their voice to guide them. Mother Teresa's speech is, by far, the best example of a speech that is driven by a strong, determined, and loving inner voice.

Tip – Let your inner voice guide you.

#46 – Ronald Reagan

1911–2004

Context – Ronald Reagan was the 40th President of the United States (1981-1989). He began his career as an actor in films and television. His political career began during his work for General Electric. Interestingly, he switched political parties from being a Democrat to a Republican in 1962. This speech entitled, "Tear Down This Wall" takes place on June 12, 1987, near the Berlin Wall in front of 45,000 people.

"We welcome change and openness; for we believe that freedom and security go together, that the advance of human liberty can only strengthen the cause of world peace. There is one sign the Soviets can make that

would be unmistakable, that would advance dramatically the cause of freedom and peace. General Secretary Gorbachev, if you seek peace, if you seek prosperity for the Soviet Union and eastern Europe, if you seek liberalization, come here to this gate. Mr. Gorbachev, open this gate.

"Mr. Gorbachav, tear down this wall!"

Analysis – As I begin the countdown of my final 50 talks on this list of 365 Must-Know Talk, I notice a common theme amongst many of them is that they changed the world somehow. Here, Reagan changed the world rather significantly with this speech. Reagan challenged Soviet leader and General Secretary of the Communist Party, Mikhail Gorbachev, to destroy the Berlin Wall. The speech takes place by the Berlin Wall at the Brandenburg Gate, commemorating the 750th anniversary of Berlin. Here's the history in a nutshell; the Berlin Wall was built in 1961 and became a symbol of communism. The wall was constructed as a barrier to restrict movement from the East side of Germany to the West side of Germany. The two countries forced its people to choose sides. The United States, under Kennedy showed support for the Western side (the democratic side) while the Soviet Union pledged their support to the Eastern side (the Communist side). The location of Reagan's speech, at the Brandenburg Gate (on the West), was artfully chosen to highlight the United States' conviction for Western democracy. It is also worth noting that the speech was delivered from behind two panes of bulletproof glass.

Today I'd like to highlight the lasting impact of a few choice words in one's delivery. Reagan's speech for the most part doesn't need vast and profound explanation. Most people know exactly what those last four words of Reagan's speech were referring to. Now that is impact!

The fascinating thing is that this speech didn't receive a ton of press when it was delivered; it did receive some momentum some two years later, when they finally did tear down the Berlin Wall. This speech is arguably one of the most remembered and most important of Cold War history. I believe it is because of the strength, the gusto, and the significance of those four little words. When giving a presentation to elicit change, remember short, direct words can have a significant impact!

Tip – Choose short and direct words for a long-lasting impact.

#45 – George W. Bush

(1946)

Context – George Walker Bush was the 43rd President of the United States from 2001 to 2009. Bush Junior is one of only two American presidents to be the son of a preceding president.

"Today, our fellow citizens, our way of life, our very freedom came under attack in a series of deliberate and deadly terrorist acts. The victims were in airplanes or in their offices: secretaries, businessmen and women, military and federal workers, moms and dads, friends and neighbors. Thousands of lives were suddenly ended by evil, despicable acts of terror. The pictures of airplanes flying into buildings, fires burning, huge – huge structures collapsing have filled us with disbelief, terrible sadness, and a quiet, unyielding anger. These acts of mass murder were intended to frighten our nation into chaos and retreat. But they have failed. Our country is strong.

A great people has been moved to defend a great nation. Terrorist attacks can shake the foundations of our biggest buildings, but they cannot touch the foundation of America. These acts shatter steel, but they cannot dent the steel of American resolve. America was targeted for attack because we're the brightest beacon for freedom and opportunity in the world. And no one will keep that light from shining. Today, our nation saw evil —the very worst of human nature—and we responded with the best of America. With the daring of our rescue workers, with the caring for strangers and neighbors who came to give blood and help in any way they could.

Immediately following the first attack, I implemented our government's emergency response plans. Our military is powerful, and it's prepared. Our emergency teams are working in New York City and Washington D.C. to help with local rescue efforts. Our first priority is to get help to those who have been injured, and to take every precaution to protect our citizens at home and around the world from further attacks. The functions of our government continue without interruption. Federal agencies in Washington which had to be evacuated today are reopening for essential personnel tonight and will be open for business tomorrow. Our financial institutions remain strong, and the American economy will be open for business as well.

The search is underway for those who were behind these evil acts. I have directed the full resources of our intelligence and law enforcement communities to find those responsible and to bring them to justice. We will make no distinction between the terrorists who committed these acts and those who harbor them.

I appreciate so very much the members of Congress who have joined me in strongly condemning these attacks. And on behalf of the American people, I thank the many world leaders who have called to offer their condolences and assistance. America and our friends and allies join with all those who want peace and security in the world, and we stand together to win the war against terrorism.

Tonight, I ask for your prayers for all those who grieve, for the children whose worlds have been shattered, for all whose sense of safety and security has been threatened. And I pray they will be comforted by a Power greater than any of us, spoken through the ages in Psalm 23:

Even though I walk through the valley of the shadow of death, I fear no evil for you are with me.

This is a day when all Americans from every walk of life unite in our resolve for justice and peace. America has stood down enemies before, and we will do so this time. None of us will ever forget this day, yet we go forward to defend freedom and all that is good and just in our world.

Thank you. Good night. And God bless America."

Analysis – On September 11, 2001, a series of terrorist attacks occurred in the United States just eight months into Bush's first term as president. On that morning, 19 al-Qaeda terrorists hijacked four commercial passenger jet airliners. Planes were deliberately flown into the Twin Towers of the World Trade Center in New York City and The Pentagon in Arlington, Virginia. The passengers of the fourth plane, suspected to be headed toward Washington, DC, thwarted the hijackers plan and, in attempted to retake control of the cockpit, crashed landed into a field in rural Pennsylvania. There were no aircraft survivors.

That evening, in a televised broadcast, Bush announced a global War on terrorism, and ordered an invasion of Afghanistan and invaded Iraq in 2003. In August 2021, 18 years after that invasion, Joe Biden, the 46th and residing president, pulled those troops out of Afghanistan.

For the sake of today's entry, let us put politics aside and observe the speech that George W. Bush delivered on the evening of 2001. This speech was always going to rear its head in the top 50 of my *365 Must-Know Talks*. This speech was critically important on the evening of September 11, 2001, as it set the tone for the people of the United States and the world following the attack. This speech, lasting just four minutes, 24 seconds, needed to comfort and instill confidence in the masses, show the people of the world the plan, and send a firm message to the perpetrators of the attack.

Let's talk pressure! The melting pot of emotions Bush must've been feeling would have included anger, fear, frustration, confusion, and devastation. And he was still very new to his job. As the commander in chief, he would have been pulled in a million directions by the military, his White House team, the media, and his family. His security detail would have wanted him and his family down in the bunkers throughout that evening. As I reflect on this speech, I am astounded at Bush's ability to appear calm even as everything was crumbling around him. No doubt, he was coached, and probably pretty intensely, but still, it is rather impressive that he injected tranquility as he delivered what was one of the most challenging speeches of the century. Interestingly, the tone and delivery change rather dramatically just nine days later when he addressed Congress on September 20th. That later speech is fraught with pathos and an urgent tone. It shows a strong and defined action plan, and at the belly, hostility and anger. This speech here is somber and reverent, and in a macro way, stresses the need to bring the enemy to justice. As I stand back and do an amateur analysis, Bush did this well. In the hours after the attacks, four minutes of somber and reverent mood was what people around the world needed to feel less alone. At that point in time, I don't think anyone needed minute detail of how justice would be served, only to know that the atrocities of that day would not go unpunished. Nine days later, when Bush gave his speech to congress, all the details surfaced, and that was appropriate, as it gave the government time to gather more intelligence. Too bad much of that information proved to be incorrect, but I digress. The point is, when you are giving a talk that is stressful (and it's likely never to be *this* stressful), keep it short, keep it macro, and commit to coming back with more details when you have had time to unpackage the full extent of the events.

Tip – When giving a presentation laden with stress, keep it short and macro.

#44 – Queen Elizabeth I

1523–1603

Context – In 1558, at the age of 25, Queen Elizabeth I became Queen of England and ruled until her death in 1603. Elizabeth's reign is known as the Elizabethan era and was marked by emerging drama and playwrights including, William Shakespeare. Below is the famous speech she gave to the troops at Tilbury in 1588 as England prepared to battle the Armada, a sizable fleet of warships sent by King Philip II of Spain.

"My loving people, we have been persuaded by some that are careful of our safety, to take heed how we commit ourselves to armed multitudes, for fear of treachery; but I assure you I do not desire to live to distrust

my faithful and loving people. Let tyrants fear, I have always so behaved myself that, under God, I have placed my chiefest strength and safeguard in the loyal hearts and good-will of my subjects, and therefore I am come amongst you, as you see, at this time, not for my recreation and disport, but being resolved, in the midst and heat of the battle, to live and die amongst you all; to lay down for my God, and for my kingdom, and my people, my honour and my blood, even in the dust. I know I have the body but of a weak and feeble woman; but I have the heart and stomach of a king, and of a king of England too, and think foul scorn that Parma or Spain, or any prince of Europe, should dare to invade the borders of my realm; to which rather than any dishonour shall grow by me, I myself will take up arms, I myself will be your general, judge, and rewarder of every one of your virtues in the field. I know already, for your forwardness, you have deserved rewards and crowns; and We do assure you in the word of a prince, they shall be duly paid you. In the meantime, my lieutenant-general shall be in my stead, than whom never prince commanded a more noble or worthy subject; not doubting but by your obedience to my general, by your concord in the camp and your valour in the field, we shall shortly have a famous victory over those enemies of my God, of my kingdom, and of my people."

Analysis – Elizabeth I doesn't mince words as she rallies her troops before they go to war against the Armada. There was no time or energy for that. She knew that a female monarch would be looked upon as less suited to lead a nation in wartime than a man. This speech has garnered tremendous popularity because it addresses gender inequality. Elizabeth I was an interesting character. She was known as a person with a short temper who most say enjoyed a lot of luck in her reign. I don't believe in luck, so I don't think Elizabeth I's success was down to luck. Based on what I've read, she was a charismatic individual with much tenacity and *chutzpah*. At a time when monarchies in neighbouring countries were facing collapse, Elizabeth I reigned for 44 years. This was not luck. Sure, she may have come across as demanding and even a little bitchy (she had her cousin, Mary Queen of Scots, beheaded for treason) but would the same be said if she were a man? Elizabeth I gets a bad rap for being short-tempered, and was not perceived as an equal during these times.

Elizabeth I teaches us a valuable presentation lesson by putting forward what everyone is already thinking. Regarding her gender, she addresses the elephant in the room directly as it's likely that her troops were thinking she was ill-equipped to teach them how to launch into war. So, she admits, *"I have the body of a weak and feeble woman,"* then adds, *"…but I have the heart and stomach of a King."* She turns a negative into a positive. She shows the troops she is a strong and King-like leader. The next time you are giving a presentation and recognize the elephant in the room, whether it relates to yourself or someone or something else, call it out and turn it into a positive.

Tip – Address the elephant in the room.

#43 – George Washington

1732–1799

Context – George Washington was an American soldier, statesman, Founding Father, and the first President of the United States of America to serve two terms. He gave his farewell address on September 17, 1796 and emphasized the importance of the Union.

"Friends and Citizens:

The period for a new election of a citizen to administer the executive government of the United States being not far distant, and the time arrived when your thoughts must be employed in designating the person who is to be clothed with that important trust, it appears to me proper, especially as it may conduce to a more distinct expression of the public voice that I should now apprise you of the resolution I have formed, to decline being considered among the number of those out of whom a choice is to be made.

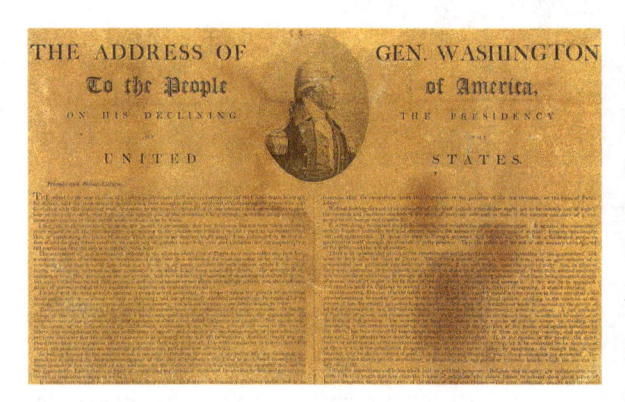

I beg you, at the same time, to do me the justice to be assured that this resolution has not been taken without a strict regard to all the considerations appertaining to the relation which binds a dutiful citizen to his country; and that in withdrawing the tender of service, which silence in my situation might imply,

I am influenced by no diminution of zeal for your future interest, no deficiency of grateful respect for your past kindness, but am supported by a full conviction that the step is compatible with both.

The acceptance of and continuance hitherto in, the office to which your suffrages have twice called me have been a uniform sacrifice of inclination to the opinion of duty and to a deference for what appeared to be your desire. I constantly hoped that it would have been much earlier in my power, consistently with motives which I was not at liberty to disregard, to return to that retirement from which I had been reluctantly drawn. The strength of my inclination to do this, previous to the last election had even led to the preparation of an address to declare it to you; but mature reflection on the then perplexed and critical posture of our affairs with foreign nations, and the unanimous advice of persons entitled to my confidence impelled me to abandon the idea.

I rejoice that the state of your concerns, external as well as internal, no longer renders the pursuit of inclination incompatible with the sentiment of duty or propriety, and am persuaded, whatever partiality may be retained for my services, that, in the present circumstances of our country, you will not disapprove my determination to retire….

Your Union ought to be considered as a main prop of your liberty, and that the love of the one ought to endear to you the preservation of the other. Interwoven as is the love of liberty with every ligament of your hearts, no recommendation of mine is necessary to fortify or confirm the attach independence.

The unity of government, which constitutes you one people, is also now dear to you. It is justly so; for it is a main pillar in the edifice of your real independence, the support of your tranquility at home, your peace abroad, of your safety, of your prosperity, of that very Liberty, which you so highly prize...Citizens, by birth or choice of a common country that country has a right to concentrate your affections. The name of American, which belongs to you, in your national capacity, much always exalt the just pride of patriotism, more than any appellation derived from local discriminations. With slight shades of difference, you have the same religion, manners, habits, and political principles. You have in a common cause fought and triumphed together, the Independence and Liberty you possess are the work of joint counsels, and joint efforts, of common dangers, sufferings, and success....

...A passionate attachment of one nation for another produces of variety of evils. Sympathy for the favourite nation, facilitating the illusion of an imaginary common interest in cases where no real common interest exists and infusing into one the enmities of the other, betrays the former into a participation in the quarrels and wars of the latter, without adequate inducement or justification. It leads also to concessions to the favourite nation of privileges denied to others, which is apt doubly to injure the Nation making the concessions, by unnecessarily parting with what ought to have been retained, and by exiting jealously, ill-will, and a disposition to retaliate, in the parties from whom equal privileges are withheld. And it gives to ambitious, corrupted, or deluded citizens (who devote themselves to the favourite nation) facility to betray or sacrifice the interest of their own country, without odium, sometimes even with popularity; gilding, with the appearances of a virtuous sense of obligation, commendable deference for public opinion, or laudable zeal for the public good, the base or foolish compliances of ambition, corruption or infatuation..."

Analysis – This is a rather lengthy speech, so I haven't copied it in its entirety but have instead included the highlights. The speech was addressed to the people of the United States near the end of Washington's second and final term. It was initially published on September 19, 1796 in the *American Daily Advertiser* and was immediately reprinted in newspapers across the country. After almost 45 years of service (Army and presidency), Washington retired as the President of the United States. Interestingly, Washington only ever planned to be in office for one term, but his staff persuaded him to stay for an additional term. He had already written this speech after completing the first term but put it away for four more years. He revised the original draft and announced his intention to decline a third term in office.

My first observation as I read Washington's speech—and perhaps because I've been reading speeches from hundreds of years ago for several days—is that the English language has taken an interesting turn. The language in use today is far more straightforward compared to what was used in Washington's time. Since there is no video footage of these older speeches being given, I repeat the sentences aloud until I come up with what might have been the cadence and tone of the person and the time. Sometimes I wish there was a camera on me so that you could see me try to reenact what the delivery may have looked like (insert; flailing arms, stomping feet, and in the case of Socrates' posts...finger lodged under the chin in a *thinking* pose). Line by line, I envy the English language that we used to speak. Back in the day it was a beautiful language held up to a very high standard back in the day. If we come across someone that has command of language now, we should compliment them on being articulate. I suspect that almost everyone back in Washington's time was articulate, chose their words with care and held themselves and those around them up to high standard as it relates to language. I hope that this standard for language will permeate the boundaries of this century. You don't have to be articulate when you are giving a presentation, but if you want to show command of your topic, reflect some semblance of interest, and arouse curiosity, then having a solid command of language is a good place to start. Develop a robust vocabulary and choose your words with care.

Tip – Develop a vast vocabulary and choose descriptive language to keep your audience engaged.

#42 – Nelson Mandela

1918–2013

Context – Nelson Rolihlahla Mandela was a South African civil rights advocate and political activist who helped topple apartheid and went on to become the first president of South Africa to be elected in fully representative democratic elections. Mandela's inauguration brought together the largest number of Heads of State since the funeral of the US President, John F. Kennedy. Mandela retired in 1999 from office but continued his advocacy for human rights. Here is his speech from May 2, 1994, entitled "Free at Last."

"This is one of the most important moments in the life of our country. I stand here before you filled with deep pride and joy:—pride in the ordinary, humble people of this country. You have shown such a calm, patient determination to reclaim this country as your own—and joy that we can loudly proclaim from the rooftops—free at last!"

Analysis – Nelson Mandela made many speeches during his life. His speeches are often quoted, and there are books written exclusively on the topic. What is it about his speeches that elicit such exquisite listening power? It's simple. He is compassionate, intelligent, and wrought with conviction and kindness, purpose and meaning. He is a man filled with forgiveness and a desire for change. After twenty-seven years of imprisonment and a long struggle to make democracy a reality in South Africa, he finally stood with his supporters free at last.

Mandela forgives the political system that held the people of South Africa down for too long. He forgives those who imprisoned him and shares the joy of victory in this speech. If you listen to the speech and read the transcript, you can feel the weight of his words. He is not but one man; he is but every man and he is humble.

The truth is no one can ever truly understand the extent of Mandela's struggles even those who have studied Mandela in depth. While his suffering was significant, he never abandoned hope and chose to forgive and live his life with determination and conviction. Mandela serves as a catalyst for change and was an expert teacher in the art of breathing your convictions into your presentations. He charmed his enemies and adversaries with his smile, high level of forgiveness and selflessness and positivity. Mandela showed us how to project authenticity into your presentations. Let there be no difference in your convictions and the person you put forward in your presentations. If you do so, your words and the person you have become will undoubtedly have a profound and lasting impact.

Tip – Project your convictions on the presentation stage.

#41 – James Carville

(1944)

Context – In additional to being a prominent liberal, James Carville is a political consultant, commentator, actor, attorney, and media personality. Carville is most recognized for gaining national attention for his work as the lead strategist of the Bill Clinton presidential campaign, as well as being married to Mary Matalin, who is a Republican political consultant. Below is a quote from Carville's 2008 Tulane Commencement Address entitled, "Failure is to success as oxygen is to life."

"As you see, my speech will be awfully short on advice, but I do advise you that when you pick a spouse, pick one – be as lucky as I did, and pick one that fascinates you, and challenges you, and entertains you, that you enjoy like so much, as I do with Mary, and we're delighted to be returned to the city that we fell in love in, and we got married in, and now we're going to live in.

Now, I want to welcome all you old school fans—I left Louisiana in 1986 and returned in 2008, which is 22 years. To give you some idea of 22 years—that was how long it took me to get out of undergraduate school—or it's how long it took FEMA to get to New Orleans. I don't know which one, but...

All of these commencements, and I've – from everywhere – from Pala Alto to Princeton, from Boulder to Boston, from Athens to Ann Arbor, all have a certain tenor, and that is that a commencement speaker is supposed to deliver some wisdom or observation, something about what they've learned, to you, and that's what's supposed to take you forward in life—and you will get no such thing here in New Orleans. (Laughter) I'll promise you. The May air is full of such nauseating bunk.

But when you listen to what Dr. Cowen said – and I did the research – I thought I might use this, as the rabbis would say, as a teaching moment. And a teaching moment is not what I have to teach you. It's what "you" have taught "me," and what you have taught the world. That's right. This is about you giving me and the world an education.

The first thing you taught me – I suspected this was true, but I didn't know it. I now know it. The age of cynicism is dead. You drove a stake right through the heart of it. (Applause) Your fingerprints are all over it. You heard it. You left because of the storm. You had to disperse all over the country – 600 different schools. You heard about, "Oh, the heat, the humidity, the corruption, the crime," the this, "the geographics" – whatever -- you heard every reason that you shouldn't come back, and you did. Every cynic had every reason for you.

I want to remind you of what C.S. Lewis said in the 1943 essay. He said, "You can't go on seeing through things forever. The whole point of seeing through something is to see something through it. If you see through everything, then everything is transparent. But a wholly transparent world is an invisible world. To see through all things is to say is not to see." And every cynic, every person, could see through everything, but you felt – you felt that -- you felt it. And your feelings are much, much more important to you than your sight. Those are the most important things they have. And you saw it. And when this history of his generation is written – and Dr. Cowen is right, you are going to be the next-greatest generation. At the top – at the very top of this generation is going to be the Tulane Class of 2008.

Lesson Number 2 – in this teaching moment we're having here is: You did not fear failure. And I want to talk to you a little bit about failure. Failure is to success what oxygen is to life. You say, "Wait a minute. That sounds absurd. How can – "Failure is to success what oxygen is to life." There can be no success without failure. You instinctively understood that. Because in September of 2005, this was not an assured thing – not at all. In order to succeed you have to fail.

Let me give you an example. Now you say, "I'm a little bit skeptical of this. I need some proof." Okay. Who is the most successful American ever? Who is the person that – okay, I'll throw a name out just for the hell of it. How about Abe Lincoln, Springfield, Illinois? Pretty stout, wasn't he? Pretty stout. Who is the greatest failure in American history? Abraham Lincoln…"

Analysis – One might ask why James Carville is placed above historical icons such as Washington or Reagan or Mother Teresa in this list of great speeches? The truth is no one on the list is superior to the next. These contributors are interchangeable in terms of their brilliance. So please look less at the number that each speech holds, and more at the list as a collective whole of superb and brilliant talks. This one, given by James Carville is spilling over with passion, emotion, and great nuggets of wisdom. Carville uses the platform of his commencement speech for what he calls a teaching moment and distills three lessons into his talk in a unique way. Instead of pontificating his own lessons, he shares what the graduating class has taught him. An excellent, appropriate, and humble approach.

Lessons that James Carville has learned from the 2008 graduating class at Tulane:

1. The age of cynicism is dead.

2. You didn't fear failure. Failure is to success what oxygen is to life. There cannot be success without failure. Abraham Lincoln is the greatest failure in American history. You're not going to fail as much as Lincoln, so don't worry about it.

3. If you build it, they will come. It is appropriate that you graduate in this building.

There are many reasons why I adore this talk, and at the fore is Carville's use of multiple examples.

First he runs through a list of all of Abraham Lincoln's failures to support his point that Lincoln was the greatest failure in the United States' history. He uses examples to support why the building they are standing in has such reverence and power. He uses many examples throughout his nearly ten minutes on stage. It is the examples in a speech that bring it to life, and I can remember each of them. So, fill your talks to the brim with support, through tangible examples, and your audience will remember your talk.

Tip – Use plenty of examples in all of your talks.

#40 – Jesse Jackson

(1941)

Context – Jesse Jackson is a civil rights activist and Baptist minister. Jackson was a candidate for the Democratic presidential nomination in 1984 and 1988. Here, Jackson speaks at a rally during the 1984 run for President. He beat out candidates future Vice President Al Gore, and future Vice President and President Joe Biden amongst others. Jackson came in second in delegates behind Michael Dukakis.

"Tonight, we come together bound by our faith in a mighty God, with genuine respect and love for our country, and inheriting the legacy of a great Party, the Democratic Party, which is the best hope for redirecting our nation on a more humane, just, and peaceful course.

This is not a perfect party. We are not a perfect people. Yet, we are called to a perfect mission. Our mission: to feed the hungry; to clothe the naked; to house the homeless; to teach the illiterate; to provide jobs for the jobless; and to choose the human race over the nuclear race.

We are gathered here this week to nominate a candidate and adopt a platform which will expand, unify, direct, and inspire our Party and the nation to fulfill this mission. My constituency is the desperate, the damned, the disinherited, the disrespected, and the despised. They are restless and seek relief. They have voted in record numbers. They have invested the faith, hope, and trust that they have in us. The Democratic Party must send them a signal that we care. I pledge my best not to let them down…

Young America, dream. Choose the human race over the nuclear race. Bury the weapons and don't burn the people. Dream -- dream of a new value system. Teachers who teach for life and not just for a living; teach because they can't help it. Dream of lawyers more concerned about justice than a judgeship. Dream of doctors more concerned about public health than personal wealth. Dream of preachers and priests who will prophesy and not just profiteer. Preach and dream!

…Our time has come. Our time has come. Suffering breed's character. Character breeds faith. In the end, faith will not disappoint.

Our time has come. Our faith, hope, and dreams will prevail. Our time has come. Weeping has endured for nights, but now joy cometh in the morning.

Our time has come. No grave can hold our body down. Our time has come. No lie can live forever.

Our time has come. We must leave racial battle ground and come to economic common ground and moral higher ground. America, our time has come. We come from disgrace to amazing grace.

Our time has come. Give me your tired, give me your poor, your huddled masses who yearn to breathe free and come November, there will be a change because our time has come."

Analysis – Hands down, this is another of my favourite speeches. I know I say that a lot but this speech is especially good. In it, Jackson compares the election in 1984 to the story of David and Goliath, with Reagan as Goliath and the liberal coalition as David.

There are many reasons this talk stands out for me, but at the fore is that Jackson talks with a cadence and tone that is mesmerizingly devoid of the pomp, ceremony, and arrogance of the typical politician.

Jackson oozes charisma from every pore. His talk feels like a poem, each word artfully placed. The cadence rises and falls just in the right places, and because of that, he has his audience deeply engaged, hanging on his every word. Jackson dispels some of the myths in the political arena on topics such as foreign policy, race, sex, and choice.

Watch the speech. There is no doubt in my mind that Jackson is speaking with conviction and because of this he holds the world's attention. Beyond holding the attention of the world, I can assure you that had I been living in the United States in 1984 and had seen this speech, I would have voted. Jackson's plea to his audience to vote is unparalleled.

Tip – Believe in what you say, and your audience will hang on your every word.

#39 – William Faulkner

1897–1962

Context – William Faulkner was an author of novels, novellas, and short stories. *The Sound and the Fury* (1929) is considered his most famous work. Though Faulkner's books were initially published in 1919 and during the 20s and 30s, he was relatively unknown until receiving the 1949 Nobel Prize in Literature. Here is his acceptance speech:

"I feel that this award was not made to me as a man, but to my work–a life's work in the agony and sweat of the human spirit, not for glory and least of all for profit, but to create out of the materials of the human spirit, something which did not exist before. So, this award is only mine in trust. It will not be difficult to find a dedication for the money part of it commensurate with the purpose and significance of its origin. But I would like to do the same with the acclaim too, by using this moment as a pinnacle from which I might be listened to by the young men and women already dedicated to the same anguish and travail, among whom is already that one who will someday stand where I am standing.

Our tragedy today is a general and universal physical fear so long sustained by now that we can even bear it. There are no longer problems of the spirit. There is only one question: When will I be blown up? Because of this, the young man or woman writing today has forgotten the problems of the human heart in conflict with itself, which alone can make good writing because only that is worth writing about, worth the agony and the sweat. He must learn them again. He must teach himself that the basest of all things is to be afraid: and, teaching himself that, forget it forever, leaving no room in his workshop for anything but the old verities and truths of the heart, the universal truths lacking which any story is ephemeral and doomed love and honour and pity and pride and compassion and sacrifice. Until he does so, he labours under a curse. He writes not of love but of lust, of defeats in which nobody loses anything of value, and victories without hope and worst of all, without pity or compassion. His griefs grieve on no universal bones, leaving no scars. He writes not of the heart but of the glands.

Until he learns these things, he will write as though he stood among and watched the end of man.

I decline to accept the end of man.

It is easy enough to say that man is immortal because he will endure; that when the last ding-dong of doom has clanged and faded from the last worthless rock hanging tideless in the last red and dying evening, that even then there will still be one more sound: that of his puny inexhaustible voice, still talking. I refuse to accept this.

I believe that man will not merely endure; he will prevail. He is immortal, not because he alone among creatures has an inexhaustible voice, but because he has a soul, a spirit capable of compassion and sacrifice and endurance. The poet's, the writer's, duty is to write about these things. It is his privilege to help man endure by lifting his heart, by reminding him of the courage and honour and hope and pride and compassion and pity and sacrifice which have been the glory of his past. The poet's voice need not merely be the record of man; it can be one of the props, the pillars to help him endure and prevail."

Analysis – William Faulkner received the 1949 Nobel Prize for Literature for "his powerful and artistically unique contribution to the modern American novel." Faulkner was a man who avoided speeches throughout his life. But he couldn't avoid the spotlight when he was awarded the Nobel Prize and gave this short but immensely influential speech. He insisted that he was, "just a farmer who likes to tell stories." This is a brilliant acceptance speech, partly due to Faulkner's humble and modest nature.

From a man who avoided speaking in front of groups, his acceptance speech is aspirational. He could've talked about his work, novels, short stories, and how he came up with his clever, thoughtful, and artful prose. Instead, he shares his thoughts on life and all that it entails. He talks about the human spirit and, in the end, talks about a writer's duty to write about these sorts of things. It made me think of presenters, what is our duty? Is it to pontificate ad nauseam about sales numbers or policies or corporate mumbo jumbo? I think not. The task at hand may be to communicate those things, but that is the packaging. It's what's inside that matters. So that presentation on HR policy can be delivered from an angle that contains the human spirit, it can contain "love and honour and pity and pride and compassion and sacrifice." The trick is to carry those characteristics with you always so that they are simply channeled into everything you do.

I adore the speaking profession; I really do. So, as I start the process of grieving the end of this list of *365 Must-Know Talks*, I'm struck by the thought that the topic of presentation skills is far more important than it is given credit. Faulkner, more than any other speaker I have analyzed, seems to understand this. Whether one is talking about a writer, a poet, an artist, an engineer, a sales professional, a mechanic, or a public speaker, public speaking is about communicating and connecting with the human spirit.

Tip – You are capable of compassion, sacrifice, and endurance. Be sure to weave those characteristics into your presentations and share them with your audience.

#38 – Edward "Teddy" Kennedy

1932–2009

Context – Senator Edward "Teddy" Kennedy was a U.S. Senator from Massachusetts, a prominent member of the Democratic Party.and the 4th longest-serving senator in U.S. history, serving nearly 47 years. He was the youngest brother of President John F. Kennedy. "The Dream Shall Never Die" was his concession speech given in 1980.

"And someday, long after this convention, long after the signs come down and the crowds stop cheering, and the bands stop playing. May it be said of our campaign that we kept the faith.

May it be said of our Party in 1980 that we found our faith again.

And may it be said of us, both in dark passages and in bright days, in the words of Tennyson that my brothers quoted and loved, and that have special meaning for me now:

"I am a part of all that I have met

Too [sic] much is taken, much abides

That which we are, we are –

One equal temper of heroic hearts

Strong in will

To strive, to seek, to find, and not to yield."

For me, a few hours ago, this campaign came to an end. For all those whose cares have been our concern, the work goes on, the cause endures, the hope still lives, and the dream shall never die."

Analysis – Charisma and oratorical skills come to mind when I think of Ted Kennedy, and there are plenty of speeches from which to choose. His 1968 eulogy honouring his brother Robert, and his 1980 rallying cry for modern American liberalism are amongst his most recognizable speeches. Today, however, I have chosen to highlight his 1980 speech entitled, "The Dream Shall Never Die."

Ted teaches us to accept defeat with grace and take the opportunity to inspire and rally others to victory. This speech was his concession speech, but of all the defeated political speeches out there (and there are tons), this is by far superior. Why? Because quite simply, you believe that Ted believes what he is saying. Have you ever watched a speech, or someone talk after they have failed at something? They are so often filled with excuses or blame. The person listening hears the excuses but will often agree with the argument to make the espouser feel better in their time of defeat. The political world is littered with these speeches. But Teddy Kennedy's speech contains no excuses or fuss, just honest and true optimism. It's refreshing.

Tip – Accept defeat with grace and offer genuine optimism to your audience.

#37 – Steve Jobs

1955–2011

Context – Steve Jobs, was the CEO of Apple and Pixar. Here Jobs addresses the graduating class at Stanford University in June 2005.

"I am honored to be with you today at your commencement from one of the finest universities in the world.

I never graduated from college. Truth be told, this is the closest I've ever gotten to a college graduation. Today I want to tell you three stories from my life. That's it. No big deal. Just three stories.

The first story is about connecting the dots.

I dropped out of Reed College after the first 6 months, but then stayed around as a drop-in for another 18 months or so before I really quit. So why did I drop out?

It started before I was born. My biological mother was a young, unwed college graduate student, and she decided to put me up for adoption. She felt very strongly that I should be adopted by college graduates, so everything was all set for me to be adopted at birth by a lawyer and his wife. Except that when I popped out they decided at the last minute that they really wanted a girl. So my parents, who were on a waiting list, got a call in the middle of the night asking: "We have an unexpected baby boy; do you want him?" They said: "Of course." My biological mother later found out that my mother had never graduated from college and that my father had never graduated from high school. She refused to sign the final adoption papers. She only relented a few months later when my parents promised that I would someday go to college.

And 17 years later I did go to college. But I naively chose a college that was almost as expensive as Stanford, and all of my working-class parents' savings were being spent on my college tuition. After six months, I couldn't see the value in it. I had no idea what I wanted to do with my life and no idea how college was going to help me figure it out. And here I was spending all of the money my parents had saved their entire life. So I decided to drop out and trust that it would all work out OK. It was pretty scary at the time, but looking back it was one of the best decisions I ever made. The minute I dropped out I could stop taking the required classes that didn't interest me, and begin dropping in on the ones that looked interesting..."

Analysis – This talk is one of the most vivid I've ever heard. It is bright, clear, mesmerizing, and makes me think in a new and refreshing way. Steve Jobs was known for his keynote talks. I'm team Apple Mac but would not consider myself a computer person. When Jobs was at the helm, the world would become abuzz whenever a new Mac product was launched, and computer professionals, particularly those who work with and for Mac, would get into a frenzy. I would get hyped for Jobs' presentation delivery more than the product. Sure, I was interested in the new product, but I'd be more jazzed to watch Jobs taking centre stage and launching the new product. If you haven't seen this address before, I am thrilled to put it on your radar.

Jobs talks about three stories to this Stanford graduation class:

1. Connecting the dots
2. Love and Loss
3. Death

These are all stories that are personal to Jobs. There is no exaggerated sense of importance of one over another. There is a humble disclosure of how Jobs became one of the wealthiest people on the planet and not simply with his finances. From dropping out of university and dropping into classes that he enjoyed, getting fired from Apple Macintosh in 1985, and being diagnosed with pancreatic cancer, Jobs shares the arc of his life story that often leaves a dramatic impact on those who that watch it. But how do I distill this talk down into a piece of advice or a singular tip? It's simple, look back at your own life and connect your dots. From there, have a deep desire to want to help others with your own story and you will.

Tip – Connect your dots and utilize your life story to help others.

#36 – Sir Winston Churchill

1874–1965

Context – Sir Winston Churchill was a British politician known for his leadership of the UK during WWII. He was the country's prime minister twice (1940-45 and 1951-55). Churchill was the only British prime minister to receive the Nobel Prize in Literature "for his mastery of historical and biographical description as well as for brilliant oratory in defending exalted human values." Churchill's *A History of the English-Speaking Peoples* is a four-volume history of Britain published between 1956-1958.

Below is an excerpt from a speech entitled, "We Shall Fight on the Beaches," given to the House of Commons on June 4, 1940.

"We shall go on to the end, we shall fight in France,

we shall fight on the seas and oceans,

we shall fight with growing confidence and growing strength in the air, we shall defend our Island, whatever the cost may be,

we shall fight on the beaches,

we shall fight on the landing grounds,

we shall fight in the fields and in the streets,

we shall fight in the hills;

we shall never surrender, and even if, which I do not for a moment believe, this Island or a large part of it were subjugated and starving, then our Empire beyond the seas, armed and guarded by the British Fleet, would carry on the struggle, until, in God's good time, the New World, with all its power and might, steps forth to the rescue and the liberation of the old."

Analysis – On the last day of the rescue where the Navy was protecting British, French, and Canadian soldiers from the German Navy, Churchill addressed the House of Commons. He was trying to get the help of the American government and to instill a grave sense of danger into the British public. His speech is 34 minutes long and ends with a call to arms.

This speech was not broadcast at the time and the rendition we are familiar with was recorded some nine years later when Churchill was persuaded to record it for prosperity. This speech was certainly not selected for this list for its delivery—Churchill is famous for his British mumble-jumble way of speaking—but rather for its impact and significance on the world and how his rhetoric turns into precise crystal delivery when he needs to be forceful. It should be noted that Churchill had a significant speech impediment, which he worked tirelessly to overcome. He even had his dentures specially designed to lessen his lisp. He did at one point say that his speech impediment is no hindrance anymore, which I believe is less about the improvement of his speech and more of his acceptance.

This was a defining speech given during the Second World War. This speech was given as Churchill prepared his country to save Europe, and ultimately the world, from Nazi control. It is one of the most recognized, and influential speeches of the 20th century.

As it relates to presentation techniques, Churchill utilizes a technique I call conscious repetition. I've included the transcript of the speech above to highlight it best. He repeats, 'We shall…" eight times in succession. I'm a fan of this technique, especially the talk to garner support, rouse enthusiasm, and encourage solidarity. In your next talk, use conscious repetition if your goal is to ignite unity within your audience. You'll be pleasantly surprised by how effective simple repetition can be.

Tip – Utilize conscious repetition.

#35 – Susan B. Anthony

1820–1906

Context – Susan B. Anthony was a prominent civil rights leader who played a central role in the 19th century Women's Rights Movement. Anthony was fined $100 for casting a ballot in the 1872 presidential election. At the time, it was illegal for women to vote. She was furious. That fury turned to action as she undertook a vast speaking tour supporting female voting rights. During this tour as she averaged 75–100 speeches per year, she delivered the below speech.

"Friends and fellow citizens: I stand before you tonight under indictment for the alleged crime of having voted at the last presidential election, without having a lawful right to vote. It shall be my work this evening to prove to you that in thus voting, I not only committed no crime, but instead, simply exercised my

citizen's rights, guaranteed to me and all United States citizens by the National Constitution, beyond the power of any state to deny.

The preamble of the Federal Constitution says:

"We, the people of the United States, in order to form a more perfect union, establish justice, ensure domestic tranquility, provide for the common defence, promote the general welfare, and secure the blessings of liberty to ourselves and our posterity, do ordain and establish this Constitution for the United States of America."

It was we, the people; not we, the white male citizens; nor yet we, the male citizens; but we, the whole people, who formed the Union. And we formed it, not to give the blessings of liberty, but to secure them; not to the half of ourselves and the half of our posterity, but to the whole people—women as well as men. And it is a downright mockery to talk to women of their enjoyment of the blessings of liberty while they are denied the use of the only means of securing them provided by this democratic-republican government—the ballot.

For any state to make sex a qualification that must ever result in the disfranchisement of one entire half of the people, is to pass a bill of attainder, or an ex post facto law, and is therefore a violation of the supreme law of the land. By it the blessings of liberty are forever withheld from women and their female posterity.

To them, this government has no just powers derived from the consent of the governed. To them, this government is not a democracy. It is not a republic. It is an odious aristocracy; a hateful oligarchy of sex; the most hateful aristocracy ever established on the face of the globe; an oligarchy of wealth, where the rich govern the poor. An oligarchy of learning, where the educated govern the ignorant or even an oligarchy of race, where the Saxon rules the African, might be endured; but this oligarchy of sex, which makes father, brothers, husband, sons, the oligarchs over the mother and sisters, the wife, and daughters, of every household—which ordains all men sovereigns, all women subjects, carries dissension, discord, and rebellion into every home of the nation.

Webster, Worcester, and Bouvier all define a citizen to be a person in the United States, entitled to vote and hold office.

The only question left to be settled now is: Are women persons? And I hardly believe any of our opponents will have the hardihood to say they are not. Being persons, then, women are citizens, and no state has a right to make any law or to enforce any old law that shall abridge their privileges or immunities. Hence, every discrimination against women in the constitutions and laws of the several states is today null and void, precisely as is every one against Negroes."

Analysis – Anthony never paid that $100 fine and paragraph four of the above speech says it best, "It was we, the people; not we, the white male citizens; nor yet we, the male citizens; but we, the whole people, who formed the Union. And we formed it, not to give the blessings of liberty, but to secure them; not to the half of ourselves and the half of our posterity, but to the whole people—women as well as men." You can imagine in 1873 how this sentiment was received. Anthony was and still is a hero. She devoted her life to equality for all. She advocated for anti-slavery and rights for women throughout her life and put her beliefs into action. She taught at an all-female academy and organized civil-rights movements. She was boisterous about her point of view. The venue that she used to try to convert others to her way of thinking was public speaking. She had an exhaustive tour of speeches she did every year for many years. She used that platform to showcase injustices relating to race and gender.

Public speaking, regardless of your platform, really can transform lives. Without speaking in public, Anthony would not have garnered the attention she did. She was relentless in the pursuit of justice. If you are passionate about something, then this is what you should be talking about in your presentations. I firmly believe that no matter what you are presenting, there is almost always an opportunity to change the world by sharing what you believe with others. Look back on the last 15 entries on this list of *365 Must-Know Talks*, and you'll notice that each speaker is impassioned, sincere, and earnest. They believed with their entire being and when given the presentation platform, used it to empower, enlist and motivate others. I'd say that is a noble attribute. Don't squander your presentation platform opportunities, instead, use them to motivate real and lasting change not only in your audience and participants but possibly, even the world.

Tip – Don't squander your presentation platform opportunities.

#34 – Margaret Thatcher

1925–2013

Context – Margaret Thatcher served as Prime Minister of the United Kingdom from 1979 –1990. Thatcher was the first woman to hold this position—she would later earn the nickname, the Iron Lady for her uncompromising politics and leadership style. The below speech was delivered on May 4th, 1979, her first day and her first address to the nation.

"That where there is discord, I may bring harmony;
that where there is error, I may bring truth;
that where there is doubt, I may bring faith;
that where there is despair, I may bring hope"

Analysis – This is a relatively simple but well-thought-out speech. Thatcher had just become prime minister, and you can see her nerves as she begins walking through her well-rehearsed speech outside 10 Downing Street, the residence of the Prime Minister of the UK. She chooses a very informal setting outside her new residence, which is a common and traditional venue for PMs to give speeches. Thatcher shares that she understands what is expected of her and that building and maintaining the trust and confidence of the British people is of paramount importance. What I enjoy so much about this speech is its simplicity. Often when embarking on preparing and executing a presentation, we overcomplicate the delivery and make it more complex, wordy, challenging, and lengthy than it needs to be (do you see what I did there?). Sure, sometimes hammering home a point is needed, but some of my favourite speeches are short, awkward, easy to follow, and spoken from the heart. I like those ones the best. Here, Thatcher delivers on all these aspects and her words, as a result, are not only practical but memorable. She finishes with an excerpt from the Prayer of Saint Francis that is fitting given the circumstances. She reminds me (and hopefully you too) that finishing a talk with a fitting quote or analogy is one of the most effective ways to wrap up a speech.

Tip – Keeping your talks simple will make them more memorable.

#33 – Sidney Poitier

1927–2022

Context – Sidney Poitier was a retired actor, film director, activist, and ambassador. In 1964 he won the Academy Award for best actor in the film *Lilies of the Field*, becoming the first black male to win the award. Here he accepts the Honorary Oscar for his body of work at the 74th annual Academy Awards held in 2002.

"I arrived in Hollywood at the age of 22, at a time that was different than today's, a time in which the odds against me standing here tonight 53 years later would not have fallen in my favour. Back then no route had been established for where I was hoping to go, no pathway left in evidence for me to trace, no custom for me to follow. Yet, here I am this evening at the end of a journey that in 1949 would have been considered almost impossible and in fact might never have been set in motion were there not an untold number of courageous, unselfish choices made by a handful of visionary American filmmakers, directors, writers and producers; each with a strong sense of citizenship responsibility to the times in which they lived; each unafraid to permit their art to reflect their views and values, ethical and moral, and moreover, acknowledge them as their own. They knew the odds that stood against them and their efforts were overwhelming and likely could have proven too high to overcome. Still those filmmakers persevered, speaking through their art to the best in all of us. And I've benefited from their effort. The industry benefited from their effort. America benefited from their effort. And in ways large and small the world has also benefited from their effort.

Therefore, with respect, I share this great honor with the late Joe Mankiewicz, the late Richard Brooks, the late Ralph Nelson, the late Darryl Zanuck, the late Stanley Kramer, the Mirisch brothers, especially Walter whose friendship lies at the very heart of this moment, Guy Green, Norman Jewison, and all others who have had a hand in altering the odds for me and for others. Without them this most memorable moment would not have come to pass and the many excellent young actors who have followed in admirable fashion might not have come as they have to enrich the tradition of American filmmaking as they have. I accept this award in memory of all the African-American actors and actresses who went before me in the difficult years, on whose shoulders I was privileged to stand to see where I might go…"

Analysis – This speech is commanding, and in control. It is reflective, thankful, and it resonates. It's a speech that you can learn so much from simply by watching it. Poitier is a man of great juxtaposition, extraordinary humbleness, and is exceedingly self-assured. He is one of the most genuinely confident people I've ever observed. Confidence comes from his every pore, from the depths of his being and from a lifetime of living. it's a joy to watch this speech from every angle, but particularly to observe Poitier's confidence.

If you are seeking to acquire skills in the art of presenting, then watch this clip repeatedly and you will learn how humbleness and confidence can translate into a superb talk of acceptance. Bravo Sidney!

Tip – Juxtapose various presentation characteristics to create a rich delivery.

#32 – Demosthenes

384 BCE – 322 BCE

Context –Demosthenes was a prominent Greek orator, politician, and statesman in ancient Athens, Greece (not to be confused with Demosthenes, who was the general who fought in the Peloponnesian War).

""Many speeches are made, men of Athens, at almost every meeting of the Assembly, with reference to the aggressions which Philip has been committing, ever since he concluded the Peace, not only against yourselves but against all other peoples.

And I am sure that all would agree, however little they may act on their belief, that our aim, both in speech and in action, should be to cause him to cease from his insolence and to pay the penalty for it. And yet I see that in fact the treacherous sacrifice of our interests has gone on, until what seems an ill-omened saying may, I fear,

be really true—that if all who came forward desired to propose, and you desired to carry, the measures which would make your position as pitiful as it could possibly be, it could not, so I believe, be made worse than it is now.

It is this fate, I solemnly assure you, that I dread for you when the time comes that you make your reckoning and realize that there is no longer anything that can be done. May you never find yourselves, men of Athens, in such a position! Yet, in any case, it were better to die ten thousand deaths than to do anything out of servility towards Philip [or to sacrifice any of those who speak for your good]. A noble recompense did the people in Oreus receive for entrusting themselves to Philip's friends and thrusting Euphraeus aside! And a noble recompense the democracy of Eretria, for driving away your envoys and surrendering to Cleitarchus! They are slaves, scourged and butchered! A noble clemency did he show to the Olynthians, who elected Lasthenes to command the cavalry, and banished Apollonides!

It is folly, and it is cowardice, to cherish hopes like these, to give way to evil counsels, to refuse to do anything that you should do, to listen to the advocates of the enemy's cause, and to fancy that you dwell in so great a city that, whatever happens, you will not suffer any harm….

This then is my proposal and this I move. If the proposal is carried out, I think that even now, the state of our affairs may be remedied. But if anyone has a better proposal to make, let him make it, and give us his advice. And I pray to all the gods that whatever be the decision that you are about to make, it may be for your good."

Analysis – Demosthenes was against a peace treaty with Phillip II, the King of Macedonia. Because of this conflict, Demosthenes delivered his *Philippics* (a fancy way of saying, diatribe or lecture). There was a series of four Philippics that Demosthenes delivered before the Athenian people and it is the third of those, delivered in 341 BCE, that I've highlighted in today's entry. The third Philippics is widely considered the best, and having read them all, I agree. In it, Demosthenes demands action against Phillip II and calls for the Athenian people to erupt with newfound energy.

Demosthenes was significant in creating a portal into the culture and politics of ancient Greece during the 4th century BCE. It is his speeches that give us a view into what was happening at that time. Even back then, Demosthenes was known as a superb public speaker among those who observed him. He studied robustly, both modern orators and those who predeceased him and delivered his first speech at the age of 20, which was a resounding success. Later, he made his living as a professional speechwriter, including writing speeches for lawyers in private legal suits. So, I wondered how I would understand this because obviously, there would be no video and I would have to infer the delivery based on transcripts. So, once again, I am standing in my office, looking out onto a pretend audience, and trying desperately to bring the words of Demosthenes to life. I'm doing a pretty good job! Demosthenes was a master orator for several reasons: he constructs his prose much like that of an eloquent lawyer, he has thought of every angle, every rebuttal and he tackles them head-on. As I read the third Philippic transcript, I can almost hear his eloquence. His speech is articulate, potent, persuasive, fluid and fluent, but this is not what I'd like to highlight. All these attributes are fantastic, but beyond those characteristics it is his pure and straightforward research.

I can see what influences his words, the other ancient Greek orators who impacted him, and how he has extracted the qualities that best suited him into his content and delivery. This is what sets Demosthenes apart. As Cicero said (another ancient Greek cat), "Demosthenes is the perfect orator, one that lacks nothing." I believe that the success he achieved directly correlates to the research, analysis, and studying of those he admired.

Tip – Research your peers and weave the qualities of those you admire into your speeches.

#31 – Alexander the Great

356 BCE – 323 BCE

Context – Alexander III of Macedon aka 'Alexander the Great' was a Greek, King of Macedon. Alexander was a member of the Argead dynasty (the ancient Greek ruling house of Macedon).

"I observe, gentlemen, that when I would lead you on a new venture you no longer follow me with your old spirit. I have asked you to meet me that we may come to a decision together: are we, upon my advice, to go forward, or, upon yours, to turn back?

If you have any complaint to make about the results of your efforts hitherto, or about myself as your commander, there is no more to say. But let me remind you: through your courage and endurance you have gained possession of Ionia, the Hellespont, both Phrygias, Cappadocia, Paphlagonia, Lydia, Caria, Lycia, Pamphylia, Phoenicia, and Egypt; the Greek part of Libya is now yours, together with much of Arabia, lowland Syria, Mesopotamia, Babylon, and Susia; Persia and Media with all the territories either formerly controlled by them or not are in your hands; you have made yourselves masters of the lands beyond the Caspian Gates, beyond the Caucasus, beyond the Tanais, of Bactria, Hyrcania, and the Hyrcanian sea; we have driven the Scythians back into the desert; and Indus and Hydaspes, Acesines and Hydraotes flow now through country which is ours. With all that accomplished, why do you hesitate to extend the power of Macedon–your power– to the Hyphasis and the tribes on the other side ? Are you afraid that a few natives who may still be left will offer opposition? Come, come! These natives either surrender without a blow or are caught on the run–or leave their country undefended for your taking; and when we take it, we make a present of it to those who have joined us of their own free will and fight on our side.

For a man who is a man, work, in my belief, if it is directed to noble ends, has no object beyond itself; none the less, if any of you wish to know what limit may be set to this particular camapaign, let me tell you that the area of country still ahead of us, from here to the Ganges and the Eastern ocean, is comparatively small. You will undoubtedly find that this ocean is connected with the Hyrcanian Sea, for the great Stream of Ocean encircles the earth. Moreover I shall prove to you, my friends, that the Indian and Persian Gulfs and the Hyrcanian Sea are all three connected and continuous. Our ships will sail round from the Persian Gulf to Libya as far as the Pillars of Hercules, whence all Libya to the eastward will soon be ours, and all Asia too, and to this empire there will be no boundaries but what God Himself has made for the whole world.

But if you turn back now, there will remain unconquered many warlike peoples between the Hyphasis and the Eastern Ocean, and many more to the northward and the Hyrcanian Sea, with the Scythians, too, not far away; so that if we withdraw now there is a danger that the territory which we do not yet securely hold may be stirred to revolt by some nation or other we have not yet forced into submission. Should that happen, all that we have done and suffered will have proved fruitless–or we shall be faced with the task of doing it over again from the beginning. Gentlemen of Macedon, and you, my friends and allies, this must not be. Stand firm; for well you know that hardship and danger are the price of glory, and that sweet is the savour of a life of courage and of deathless renown beyond the grave.

Are you not aware that if Heracles, my ancestor, had gone no further than Tiryns or Argos–or even than the Peloponnese or Thebes–he could never have won the glory which changed him from a man into a god, actual or apparent? Even Dionysus, who is a god indeed, in a sense beyond what is applicable to Heracles, faced not a few laborious tasks; yet we have done more: we have passed beyond Nysa and we have taken the rock of Aornos which Heracles himself could not take. Come, then; add the rest of Asia to what you already possess– a small addition to the great sum of your conquests. What great or noble work could we ourselves have achieved had we thought it enough, living at ease in Macedon, merely to guard our homes, accepting no burden beyond checking the encroachment of the Thracians on our borders, or the Illyrians and Triballians, or perhaps such Greeks as might prove a menace to our comfort ?

I could not have blamed you for being the first to lose heart if I, your commander, had not shared in your exhausting marches and your perilous campaigns; it would have been natural enough if you had done all the work merely for others to reap the reward. But it is not so. You and I, gentlemen, have shared the labour and shared the danger, and the rewards are for us all. The conquered territory belongs to you; from your ranks the governors of it are chosen; already the greater part of its treasure passes into your hands, and when all Asia is overrun, then indeed I will go further than the mere satisfaction of our ambitions: the utmost hopes of riches or power which each one of you cherishes will be far surpassed, and whoever wishes to return home will be allowed to go, either with me or without me. I will make those who stay the envy of those who return."

Analysis – As I ponder this list of *365 Must-Know Talks*, I see a variety of motivational talks, whereby the presenter is rallying the troops either metaphorically or literally. Coaches are enlisting their teams to win, politicians are attempting to sway the public one way or another on a vast array of topics, authors are inspiring generations, but few come close to how I envision this speech delivered by Alexander the Great. He uses his aptitude for speaking to breathe new life into his army. This was not an easy feat for Alexander as his army had been fighting for over ten years. But Alexander's zeal to recapture former Greek cities and to take on new cities to add to his blooming empire triumphed. At the time of this speech, Alexander's empire included Greece, Egypt, and Persia, but that wasn't enough, so he set his sights on India, and ten years later, his troops are bruised, tired and homesick.

Alexander repeatedly uses the power of a empathy (*"You and I, gentlemen, have shared the labour and shared the danger and the rewards are for us all."*) and autonomy (*"are we, upon my advice, to go forward, or, upon yours, to turn back?"*) to motivate his troops and re-energize his vision. Could using genuine empathy in your talks motivate your audience into action?

Showing others that you understand where they are and what they are experiencing is incredibly powerful. It is consoling and comforting to know that you are not alone, that others acknowledge and appreciate your efforts. If you are a leader in an organization or someone who has people management responsibility, I suggest you adopt this speech as part of your management repertoire.

Tip – Using genuine empathy in your presentation will motivate your audience.

#30 – John F. Kennedy

1917–1963

Context – John F. Kennedy was the 35th President of the United States and served from 1961 until his assassination in 1963. In 1962, President Kennedy visited Rice University in Houston, Texas, on a sweltering summer's day. This speech, affectionately titled "The Moon Speech", is one of the world's most important regarding space and discusses the need to solve the mysteries of the moon and the universe.

"…We choose to go to the moon. We choose to go to the moon in this decade and do the other things, not because they are easy, but because they are hard because that goal will serve to organize and measure the best of our energies and skills because that challenge is one that we are willing to accept, one we are unwilling to postpone, and one which we intend to win, and the others, too.…

…Many years ago, the great British explorer George Mallory, who was to die on Mount Everest, was asked why did he want to climb it. He said, "Because it is there." Well, space is there, and we're going to climb it, and the moon and the planets are there, and new hopes for knowledge and peace are there. And, therefore, as we set sail, we ask God's blessing on the most hazardous and dangerous and greatest adventure on which man has ever embarked."

Analysis – Sit back and soak in the words of John F. Kennedy as he finally hits this list. JFK was a fine orator without question, and you can understand why his legacy is so unyielding. He was a natural born leader, and you would have wanted to join in whatever cause he was backing. He was charismatic, intelligent, and had the ability to communicate on various levels, including the art of public speaking. I do admire anyone who takes on the challenge for knowledge and betterment. And JFK did just that. At the time, many held the opinion that government funding could be used for something other than the pursuit of exploration and knowledge. And, they weren't necessarily wrong, but JFK recognized the necessity to make a difficult decision for the benefit of the future.

On a smaller scale, taking the leap to volunteer to give your next presentation or continuing to operate outside of your comfort zones, will certainly bring knowledge in the art of public speaking, but it can also serve as an investment in your public speaking future.

Tip – Continue in your pursuit for knowledge throughout your presentation career.

#29 – William Shakespeare

1564–1616

Context – William Shakespeare was an English poet and playwright. In Shakespeare's play, *Julius Caesar*, originally published in 1599, "Friends, Romans, countrymen, lend me your ears" is the first line of a famous and often quoted speech spoken by Mark Antony. The speech is written in iambic pentameter and is taken from Act III, Scene II.

Friends, Romans, countrymen, lend me your ears;
I come to bury Caesar, not to praise him.
The evil that men do lives after them,
The good is oft interred with their bones,
So let it be with Caesar. The noble Brutus

Hath told you Caesar was ambitious:
If it were so, it was a grievous fault,
And grievously hath Caesar answer'd it …
Here, under leave of Brutus and the rest,

(For Brutus is an honourable man.
So are they all, all honourable men)
Come I to speak in Caesar's funeral.
He was my friend, faithful and just to me:
But Brutus says he was ambitious;
And Brutus is an honourable man….
He hath brought many captives home to Rome,
Whose ransoms did the general coffers fill:
Did this in Caesar seem ambitious?
When that the poor have cried, Caesar hath wept:
Ambition should be made of sterner stuff:
Yet Brutus says he was ambitious;
And Brutus is an honourable man.
You all did see that on the Lupercal
I thrice presented him a kingly crown,
Which he did thrice refuse: was this ambition?
Yet Brutus says he was ambitious;
And, sure, he is an honourable man.
I speak not to disprove what Brutus spoke,
But here I am to speak what I do know.
You all did love him once, not without cause:
What cause withholds you then to mourn for him?
O judgement! thou art fled to brutish beasts,
And men have lost their reason…. Bear with me;
My heart is in the coffin there with Caesar,
And I must pause till it come back to me.

Analysis – This is the third time Shakespeare has hit this list and this entry reigns preeminent. I hadn't really paid Shakespeare any mind until I began compiling this list. I was the kid in high school with a wad of Bubblicious gum in my cheek, rolling my eyes at the English teacher, who had no interest in teaching English. This is the reason I didn't feel jazzed about Shakespeare. I didn't get what he was saying, and I had little ambition back then to figure it out. Today, however, is a different story, and I pour over and dive into Shakespeare's words as I would tackle a bowl of pumpkin pie loaded to the hilt with whipped cream. His words are a thing of beauty, and his composition is pure genius.

Shakespeare wrote Mark Antony's speech in iambic pentameter, a classic poetry technique that describes the rhythm establish by the words in a particular line. It is beautiful to listen to, if a little awkward to read with my inside voice. I understand Shakespeare with greater depth when I read his work aloud. So, as I have mentioned before, when you are preparing a speech or presentation, it is crucial to practice reading aloud. Many people don't see the importance of this, so it's worth repeating. Having taught more presentation skills workshops that I am able to count, this is one of the main areas that I struggle to spark genuine and tangible interest. Shakespeare is the perfect illustration of why you would need to practice aloud since Shakespeare wrote his plays not to be read silently by candlelight, but for the words to be powerfully projected aloud by actors on a grand stage. Whether you care to admit this or not, you become actors to some degree when you take on the task of public speaking. You need to balance being authentically you, while portraying all the attributes needed to keep your audience engaged and interested in what you have to say. How you would *write* out your speech should look dramatically different than how you would *vocalize* your talk. For example, as I finished writing this paragraph, I stopped to read it aloud. It sounds different to the words on the page when I read aloud. The essence is the same, the message is the same, but what comes out of my mouth takes on new meaning. It's like my external iambic pentameter. How you write and how you speak should be dramatically different.

Tip – Take a page out of Shakespeare book and practice reading your work aloud. Find a natural rhythm to your speaking voice that sounds and feels different to the written word.

#28 – Sally Field

(1946)

Context – Actress Sally Field stars in *Norma Rae*, a 1970 film that tells the story of a factory worker from a small town in Alabama, who becomes involved in the labour union activities at the textile factory where she works. The film is an adaptation of the book, *Crystal Lee, a Woman of Inheritance* and is based on a true story.

"I'm staying put, right where I am. It's gonna take you and the police department and the fire department to get me out of here. I'll wait for the sheriff to take me home and I ain't gonna budge until he takes me."

(Writes on a cardboard box) UNION.

Analysis – Inspired by hearing a speech by the union organizer, factory worker Norma Rae decides to join the effort to unionize her shop. The conditions in the minimum wage cotton mill are bleak and have taken a toll on the health of Rae and her family. Field's performance is superb, and you can see why she won an Academy Award for Best Actress. See post #352 for Field's equally eloquent acceptance speech.

Here, Rae goes beyond passion, encompassing fervour, spirit, animation, and fieriness. Watch her eyes, watch the powerful stance she assumes. Read her words aloud. It's impossible to say them without getting jacked. You believe every one of her words; you root for her, understand her plight, and feel her pain. This is a speech that I've go over and over whenever I want to feel what it is like to fight for something. Take out the cause (Rae's effort to unionize) and simply feel the words. Think about believing you would do anything to fulfill a goal. Beyond the zeal of this speech, I've chosen it for the #28 spot because living in a vanilla world, we rarely encounter a person willing to step out of their comfort zone and take on a more robust, commanding role in order to have their message heard.

Tip – Go beyond passionate into the corners of fieriness to enlist others to join your cause!

#27 – Malcolm X
1925–1965

Context – Malcolm X, born Malcolm Little, was an African American human rights activist, a Muslim minister, and a public speaker. The below is an excerpt from Malcolm's speech, "You Can't Hate the Roots of a Tree and not Hate the Tree," which was given on February 14, 1965, at the Ford Auditorium in Detroit the night after Malcolm's home was firebombed. This was to be the last speech he delivered as he was assassinated the following week as he prepared to address a crowd at the Audubon Ballroom in Upper Harlem, New York.

"You have to realize that up until about 1959, Africa was dominated by the colonial powers. And by the colonial powers of Europe having complete control over Africa, they projected the image of Africa negatively. They projected Africa always in a negative light—jungles, savages, cannibals, nothing civilized. And, naturally, it was so negative; it was negative to you and me. And you and I began to hate it. We didn't want anybody to tell us anything about Africa, and much less call us an African. And in hating Africa and hating the Africans, we end up hating ourselves, without even realizing it.

Because you can't hate the roots of a tree and not hate the tree. You can't hate Africa and not hate yourself. You show me one of those people over here who has been thoroughly brainwashed, who has a negative attitude toward Africa, and I'll show you one who has a negative attitude toward himself. You can't have a positive attitude toward yourself and a negative attitude toward Africa at the same time.

To the same degree, your understanding of and your attitude toward Africa becomes positive; you'll find that your understanding of and your attitude toward yourself will also become positive. ..."

Analysis – There are all kinds of controversy surrounding Malcolm X—to his supporters, he was a fearless advocate for the civil rights of African Americans. To his critics, he was a racist, black supremacist and an advocate for violence in the fight for black empowerment. My role is to curate a list of speeches that I believe are influential and are delivered with power, so I won't distract from this objective by weighing with my political views. I will say that this speech changed the world. It was that big. It is perhaps lesser known than some of the speeches coming up in my top ten, but it stands as one of the speeches that changed the trajectory of the civil rights movement. Malcolm X used racially charged language and the listener may be alarmed at what is being said regardless of their stance on the subject. But there are times when it is warranted for a speech to shock the audience to get their attention and prompt action.

The shock factor does not necessarily need to mirror Malcolm X's language or tone but interjecting a shock into your presentation can be a good way to get your audience to sit up and take notice. Let's say you are doing a speech on child poverty in Canada. You may start with a statistic such as one in nine Canadian children, live below the poverty line. Or perhaps you are doing a speech on communication, and you start by sharing that more than 500 million active Facebook users spend more than 700 billion minutes a month logging on and perusing the site. Whatever your subject, find a way to shock or provide a revelation to your audience early on in your presentation, and you'll immediately garner your audience's attention. If you continue to weave in surprising facts, you will keep their attention right to the end.

Tip – Utilize the shock and revelation technique to get your audience's attention.

#26 – Pierre Elliot Trudeau

1919–2000

Context – Pierre Elliot Trudeau was the 15th Prime Minister of Canada (1968–1979 and 1980–1984). Trudeau delivered the below speech during what is now known as the October Crisis of 1970 and informed citizens that the War Measures Act had been invoked to combat the FLQ (Quebec Liberation Front) and a series of terror attacks in Montreal.

I am speaking to you at a moment of grave crisis when violent and fanatical men are attempting to destroy the unity and the freedom of Canada. One aspect of that crisis is the threat which has been made on the lives of two innocent men. These are matters of the utmost gravity, and I want to tell you what the Government is doing to deal with them.

What has taken place in Montreal in the past two weeks is not unprecedented? It has happened elsewhere in the world on several recent occasions; it could happen elsewhere within Canada.

But Canadians have always assumed that it could not happen here and as a result we are doubly shocked that it has.

Our assumption may have been naive, but it was understandable; understandable because democracy flourishes in Canada understandable because individual liberty is cherished in Canada.

Notwithstanding these conditions—partly because of them – it has now been demonstrated to us by a few misguided persons just how fragile a democratic society can be, if democracy is not prepared to defend itself, and just how vulnerable to blackmail are tolerant, compassionate people.

Because the kidnappings and the blackmail are most familiar to you, I shall deal with them first.

The governments of Canada and Quebec have been told by groups of self-styled revolutionaries that they intend to murder in cold blood two innocent men unless their demands are met. The kidnappers claim they act as they do in order to draw attention to instances of social injustice. But I ask them whose attention are they seeking to attract. The Government of Canada? The Government of Quebec? Every government in this country is well aware of the existence of deep and important social problems. And every government, to the limit of its resources and ability, is deeply committed to their solution. But not by kidnappings and bombings. By hard work.

And if any doubt exists about the good faith or the ability of any government, there are opposition parties ready and willing to be given an opportunity to govern. In short, there is available everywhere in Canada an effective mechanism to change governments by peaceful means. It has been employed by disenchanted voters again and again.

Who are the kidnap victims? To the victims' families, they are husbands and fathers. To the kidnappers, their identity is immaterial. The kidnappers' purposes would be served equally well by having in their grip you or me, or perhaps some child. Their purpose is to exploit the normal, human feelings of Canadians and to bend those feelings of sympathy into instruments for their own violent and revolutionary ends.

What are the kidnappers demanding in return for the lives of these men?

Several things. For one, they want their grievances aired by force in public on the assumption, no doubt, that all right-thinking persons would be persuaded that the problems of the world can be solved by shouting slogans and insults.

They want more; they want the police to offer up as a sacrificial lamb, a person whom they assume assisted in the lawful arrest and proper conviction of certain of their criminal friends.

They also want money. Ransom money.

They want still more. They demand the release from prison of 17 criminals and the dropping of charges against six other men, all of whom they refer to as "political prisoners." Who are these men who are held out as latter-day patriots and martyrs? Let me describe them to you. Three are convicted murderers; five others were jailed for manslaughter; one is serving a life imprisonment after having pleaded guilty to numerous charges related to bombings; another has been convicted of 17 armed robberies; two were once paroled but are now back in jail awaiting trial on charges of robberies.

Yet we are being asked to believe that these persons have been unjustly dealt with, that they have been imprisoned as a result of their political opinions, and that they deserve to be freed immediately, without recourse to due process of law.

The responsibility of deciding whether to release one or other of these criminals is that of the Federal Government. It is a responsibility that the Government will discharge according to law. To bow to the pressures of these kidnappers who demand that the prisoners be released would be not only an abdication of responsibility, it would lead to an increase in terrorist activities in Quebec. It would be as well an invitation to terrorism and kidnapping across the country. We might well find ourselves facing an endless series of demands for the release of criminals from jails, from coast to coast, and we would find that the hostages could be innocent members of your family or mine.

At the moment, the FLQ is holding hostage two men in the Montreal area, one a British diplomat, the other a Quebec cabinet minister. They are threatened with murder.

Should governments give in to this crude blackmail, we would be facing the breakdown of the legal system and its replacement by the law of the jungle. The Government's decision to prevent this from happening is not taken just to defend an important principle; it is taken to protect the lives of Canadians from dangers of the sort I have mentioned. Freedom and personal security are safeguarded by-laws; those laws must be respected in order to be effective.

If it is the responsibility of government to deny the demands of the kidnappers, the safety of the hostages is without question the responsibility of the kidnappers. Only the most twisted form of logic could conclude otherwise. Nothing that either the Government of Canada or the Government of Quebec has done or failed to do, now or in the future, could possibly excuse any injury to either of these two innocent men. The guns pointed at their heads have FLQ fingers on the triggers. Should any injury result, there is no explanation that could condone the acts. Should there be harm done to these men, the Government promises unceasing pursuit of those responsible.

During the past 12 days, the governments of Canada and Quebec have been engaged in constant consultations. The course followed in this matter had the full support of both governments and of the Montreal municipal authorities. In order to save the lives of Mr. Cross and Mr. Laporte, we have engaged in communications with the kidnappers.

The offer of the federal government to the kidnappers of safe conduct out of Canada to a country of their choice, in return for the delivery of the hostages, has not yet been taken up, neither has the offer of the Government of Quebec to recommend parole for the five prisoners eligible for parole.

This offer of safe conduct was made only because Mr. Cross and Mr. Laporte might be able to identify their kidnappers and to assist in their prosecution. By offering the kidnappers safe exit from Canada, we removed from them any possible motivation for murdering their hostages. Let me turn now to the broader implications of the threat represented by the FLQ and similar organizations.

If a democratic society is to continue to exist; it must be able to root out the cancer of an armed, revolutionary movement that is bent on destroying the very basis of our freedom. For that reason, the Government, following an analysis of the facts, including requests of the Government of Quebec and the City of Montreal for urgent action decided to proclaim the War Measures Act. It did so at 4:00 a.m. this morning, in order to permit the full weight of Government to be brought quickly to bear on all those persons advocating or practicing violence as a means of achieving political ends.

The War Measures Act gives sweeping powers to the Government. It also suspends the operation of the Canadian Bill of Rights. I can assure you that the Government is most reluctant to seek such powers and did so only when it became crystal clear that the situation could not be controlled unless some extraordinary assistance was made available on an urgent basis.

The authority contained in the Act will permit Governments to deal effectively with the nebulous yet dangerous challenge to society represented by the terrorist organizations. The criminal law as it stands is simply not adequate to deal with systematic terrorism. The police have therefore been given certain extraordinary powers necessary for the effective detection and elimination of conspiratorial organizations which advocate the use of violence. These organizations, and membership in them, have been declared illegal. The powers include the right to search and arrest without warrant, to detain suspected persons without the necessity of laying specific charges immediately, and to detain persons without bail.

These are strong powers, and I find them as distasteful as I am sure do you. They are necessary, however, to permit the police to deal with persons who advocate or promote the violent overthrow of our democratic system. In short, I assure you that the Government recognizes its grave responsibilities in interfering in certain cases with civil liberties and that it remains answerable to the people of Canada for its actions. The Government will revoke this proclamation as soon as possible.

As I said in the House of Commons this morning, the government will allow sufficient time to pass to give it the necessary experience to assess the type of statute which may be required in the present circumstances.

It is my firm intention to discuss then with the leaders of the Opposition parties the desirability of introducing legislation of a less comprehensive nature. In this respect, I earnestly solicit from the leaders and from all honourable members constructive suggestions for the amendment of the regulations. Such suggestions will be given careful consideration for possible inclusion in any new statute.

Analysis – Pierre Elliot Trudeau was a leader! Love him or hate him, Trudeau stayed true to who he was, always. A true leader understands the truly lost art of communication, that communication is active, constant, and open to interpretation.

Of all the speakers I've seen, Trudeau best illustrates these three attributes:

1. **Active** – This means that there is a responsibility between the sender and the receiver that the message is understood and equal from both sides. The sender's responsibility is to be complete, clear, and concise. The receiver's responsibility is to listen, to ask questions, to confirm (or to restate). Trudeau fulfills his duty as the sender and is complete, clear, and concise.

2. **Constant** – Content, tone, and body language. When a message is received, 55 percent of the message is dependent on the sender's body language. Body language is the most critical attribute when delivering a message! Tone and inflexion count for 38 percent, and content comes in at just 7 percent. Often presenters spend most of their time constructing the script of their talk when it has the least impact on the delivery.

3. **Open to interpretation** – There are two types of words that should be removed from everyone's vocabulary: time descriptor weasel words and corporate buzzwords. Both sets of weasel words

have different interpretations from the sender and receiver. If I said, "I might attend your meeting," what percentage of likelihood that I will attend the meeting would you attach to that statement? 50 percent likelihood or maybe 30 percent, or 80 percent? The word "might" can be interpreted in so many different ways depending on who you are (other examples of time descriptor weasel words are: sometimes, maybe, rarely, occasionally, etc.) Corporate buzzwords such as synergy, commoditize, cross-functional, deploy, enabling, fast track, gap analysis, mission-critical, on the same page, pipeline, push the envelope, realignment, ramp up... Oh, I could go on... These words can also mean something different to every person, and thus they're open to interpretation and can lead to confusion and a poor understanding of the information being presented.

A true leader understands that listening is paramount and that you must never surround yourself with yes-people. To be a great leader, you should always seek adequate counsel and make the best decisions based on your research. If you watch Trudeau's interview, he answers questions on the fly, meaning there is no script, it is simply him and a reporter having an exchange and you get a real sense of this man. Watch as he listens to comprehend, not to respond

Tip – Study the art of active listening and communication to be a superb presenter.

#25 – St. Francis of Assisi

1181–1226

Context – Saint Francis of Assisi was the founder of the Franciscan monastic order and the patron saint of Italy and animals. Here is his speech entitled "Sermon to the Birds" (1220).

My little sisters, the birds, much bounden are ye unto God, your Creator, and always in every place ought ye to praise Him, for that He hath given you liberty to fly about everywhere, and hath also given you double and triple rainment; moreover He preserved your seed in the ark of Noah, that your race might not perish out of the world; still more are ye beholden to Him for the element of the air which He hath appointed for you; beyond all this, ye sow not, neither do you reap; and God feedeth you, and giveth you the streams and fountains for your drink; the mountains and valleys for your refuge and the high trees whereon to make your nests; and because ye know not how to spin or sow, God clotheth you, you and your children; wherefore your Creator loveth you much, seeing that He hath bestowed on you, so many benefits; and therefore, my little sisters, beware of the sin of ingratitude, and study always to give praises unto God.

Analysis – Saint Francis of Assisi was the son of a cloth merchant in Assisi, Italy. His family was considered wealthy. He renounced his wealth after he went to war with the city of Perugia, where he had volunteered. Before his service, Francis was a fun-loving man with few cares, but he was captured shortly after the first battle in the war and imprisoned for many months. After falling ill in prison, his life took on a dramatic change because of those experiences. Francis began the arduous process of questioning life and sought prayer and solitude. Francis' affinity with animals arose during this time when he came to believe that nature was the mirror of God and referred to all creatures as brothers and sisters. He had a particular affection for birds and is captured in the above speech and in a painting by Giotto.

Francis soon attracted followers and requested the Pope's permission to find a new religious order. The message was simple: seek an uncomplicated, simple lifestyle based on the ideals of Christ. The Franciscan movement spread rapidly throughout Europe until Francis sought out solitude and isolation in his retirement. The Franciscan movement still exists today, and its followers care for the poor, educate and continue with Francis' ideals.

St. Francis of Assisi's speech is simple and sincere. You can feel his gentleness and wholeheartedness. So often, when we prepare for a speech, we overcomplicate the entire process, from the slides to the content to the delivery. We can learn from Saint Francis that the simplest messages can often last the longest.

Tip – The simplest messages are often the most memorable.

#24 – Virginia Woolf

1882–1941

Context – Virginia Woolf was a British writer who is considered one of the foremost modernists and feminist literary figures of the twentieth century. Below is an excerpt from *A Room of One's Own*, an extended essay published in 1929. The essay is based on a series of lectures Woolf delivered in 1928.

"It would have been impossible, completely and entirely, for any woman to have written the plays of Shakespeare in the age of Shakespeare.

Let me imagine, since the facts are so hard to come by, what would have happened had Shakespeare had a wonderfully gifted sister, called Judith, let us say. Shakespeare himself went, very probably—his mother was an heiress—to the grammar school, where he may have learnt Latin – Ovid, Virgin, and Horace – and the elements of grammar and logic. He was, it is well known, a wild boy who poached rabbits, perhaps shot a deer, and had, rather sooner than he should have done, to marry a woman in the neighborhood, who bore him a child rather quicker than was right. That escapade sent him to seek his fortune in London. He had, it seemed, a taste for the theatre; he began by holding horses at the stage door. Very soon, he got work in the theatre, became a successful actor, and lived at the hub of the universe, meeting everybody, knowing everybody, practicing his art on the boards, exercising his wits in the streets, and even getting access to the palace of the queen.

Meanwhile, his extraordinarily gifted sister, let us suppose, remained at home. She was as adventurous, as imaginative, as agog to see the world as he was. But she was not sent to school. She had no chance of learning grammar and logic, let alone of reading Horace and Virgil. She picked up a book now and then, one of her brother's perhaps, and read a few pages. But then her parents came in and told her to mend the stockings or mind the stew and not moon about with books and papers. They would have spoken sharply but kindly, for they were substantial people who knew the conditions of life for a woman and loved their daughter – indeed, more likely than not, she was the apple of her father's eye. Perhaps she scribbled some pages up in an apple loft on the sly but was careful to hide them or set fire to them. Soon, however, before she was out of her teens, she was to be betrothed to the son of a neighbouring wool-stapler. She cried out that marriage was hateful to her, and for that, she was severely beaten by her father. Then he ceased to scold her. He begged her instead not to hurt him, not to shame him in this matter of her marriage. He would give her a chain of beads or a fine petticoat, he said; and there were tears in his eyes. How could she disobey him? How could she break his heart? The force of her own gift alone drove her to it. She made up a small parcel of her belongings, let herself down by a rope one summer's night and took the road to London. She was not seventeen. The birds that sang in the hedge were not more musical than she was. She had the quickest fancy, a gift like her brother's, for the tune of words. Like him, she had a taste for the theatre. She stood at the stage door; she wanted to act, she said. Men laughed in her face. The manager – a fat, loose-lipped man – guffawed. He bellowed something about poodles dancing and women acting – no woman, he said, could possibly be an actress. He hinted – you can imagine what. She could get no training in her craft. Could she even seek her dinner in a tavern or roam the streets at midnight? Yet her genius was for fiction and lusted to feed abundantly upon the lives of men and women and the study of their ways. At last – for she was very young, oddly like Shakespeare the poet in her face, with the same grey eyes and rounded brows—at last Nick Greene the actor-manager took pity on her; she found herself with child by that gentleman and so—who shall measure the heat and violence of the poet's heart when caught and tangled in a woman's body?—killed herself one winter's night and lies buried at some crossroads where the omnibuses now stop outside the Elephant and Castle.

That, more or less, is how the story would run, I think, if a woman in Shakespeare's day had had Shakespeare's genius.

But for my part, I agree with the deceased bishop, if such he was—it is unthinkable that any woman in Shakespeare's day should have had Shakespeare's genius. For genius like Shakespeare's is not born among labouring, uneducated, servile people. It was not born in England among the Saxons and the Britons. It is not born today among the working classes. How, then, could it has been born among women whose work began, according to Professor Trevelyan, almost before they were out of the nursery, who were forced to it by their parents and held to it by all the power of law and custom? Yet genius of a sort must have existed among women as it must have existed among the working classes. Now and again, an Emily Bronte or a Robert Burns blazes out and proves its presence. But certainly, it never got itself on to paper. When, however, one reads of a witch being ducked, of a woman possessed by devils, of a wise woman selling herbs, or even of a very remarkable man who had a mother, then I think we are on the track of a lost novelist, a suppressed poet, of some mute and inglorious Jane Austen, some Emily Bronte who dashed her brains out on the moor or mopped and mowed about the highways crazed with the torture that her gift had put her to. Indeed, I would venture to guess that Anon, who wrote so many poems without signing them, was often a woman. It was a woman Edward Fitzgerald, I think, suggested who made the ballads and the folksongs, crooning them to her children, beguiling her spinning with them, on the length of the winter's night.

This may be true, or it may be false—who can say?—but what is true in it, so it seemed to me, reviewing the story of Shakespeare's sister as I had made it, is that any woman born with a great gift in the sixteenth century would certainly have gone crazed, shot herself, or ended her days in some lonely cottage outside the village, half-witch, half wizard, feared and mocked at. For it needs little skill in psychology to be sure that a highly gifted girl who had tried to use her gift for poetry would have been so thwarted and hindered by other people, so tortured and pulled asunder by her own contrary instincts, that she must have lost her health and sanity to a certainty. No girl could have walked to London and stood at a stage door and forced her way into the presence of actor-managers without doing herself a violence and suffering and anguish which may have been irrational—for chastity may be a fetish invented by certain societies for unknown reasons—but were nonetheless inevitable. Chastity has then, it has even now, a religious importance in a woman's life and has so wrapped itself round with nerves and instincts that to cut it free and bring it to the light of day demands courage of the rarest. To have lived a free life in London in the sixteenth century would have meant for a woman who was a poet and playwright a nervous stress and dilemma which might well have killed her. Had she survived, whatever she had written would have been twisted and deformed, issuing from a strained and morbid imagination. And undoubtedly, I thought, looking at the shelf where there are no plays by women, her work would have gone unsigned. That refuge she would have sought certainly. It was the relic of the sense of chastity that dictated anonymity to women even so late as the nineteenth century. Currer Bell, George Eliot, George Sand, all the victims of inner strife as their writings prove, sought ineffectively to veil themselves by using the name of a man. Thus, they did homage to the convention, which if not implanted by the other sex was liberally encouraged by them, that publicity in women is detestable. Anonymity runs in their blood…."

Analysis – *A Room of One's Own* is an essay based on a series of lectures. The essay, as well as the series of lectures, are generally seen as feminist works. At the nucleus, the essay deals with the concept that a woman needs to have her own money and a room of her own if she is to write. Woolf's point is that women are kept from writing by poverty, and financial freedom affords women the freedom to write.

It is a brilliant piece that Woolf put forward some 90 years ago. Woolf's writing explores the limitations, both past and present, faced by women writers. Possibly inspired by her father reluctance to invest money into her education. But this was the norm at the time. So, Woolf did not receive formal education and spent much of her time thinking about improving her plight and the need to inform other women about the importance of education.

In her essay, Woolf invents a sister for Shakespeare, named Judith. Judith is denied the same opportunities as her brother, William, simply because she is a girl. William goes to school while Judith stays at home, mirroring Woolf's upbringing. "She was as adventurous, as imaginative, as agog to see the world as he was. But she was not sent to school." It is a story of being trapped, of inequality, and of suicide. Judith kills herself, and her creativity is lost, and her talents unexpressed. At the same time, William lives the life of the great William Shakespeare who enjoyed great success and adoration during his lifetime.

I came across this essay many years ago and was astounded that a person's creativity could be stifled based solely on their gender. Perhaps it is the novice writer in me, but the notion that someone, anyone, could prohibit me from exploring my creative side would be a cruel punishment. What I adore about Woolf is that she did something about it. It is one thing to think a noble thought; it is quite another to act on it. Although Woolf lived in a time when she wasn't afforded the luxuries available to her male counterparts, she still pushed on and took her truth and taught others. She taught others, especially women, how to take command of their own life regardless of their circumstances. To be a more effective speaker, channel your hardships, your life's struggles into teaching others the lessons you've learned. Share your knowledge with the world, as Woolf did, so that the world can change for the better.

Tip – Channel your struggles into teaching others how to live.

#23 – Aristotle

384 BCE – 322 BCE

Context – Aristotle was a Greek philosopher, the prized student of Plato and teacher of Alexander the Great. He wrote and spoke on a vast array of topics: poetry, theatre, music, logic physics, metaphysics, politics, rhetoric, government, ethics, biology, and zoology. Aristotle is amongst the greats (Plato and Plato's teacher, Socrates, are part of that bubble too) in terms of philosophy.

"Book 1: Chapter 3

Rhetoric falls into three divisions, determined by the three classes of listeners to speeches. For of the three elements in speech-making—speaker, subject, and person addressed—it is the last one, the hearer, that determines the speech's end and object. The hearer must be either a judge, with a decision to make about things past or future, or an observer. A member of the assembly decides about future events, a juryman about past events: while those who merely decide on the orator's skill are observers.

From this, it follows that there are three divisions of oratory—(1) political, (2) forensic, and (3) the ceremonial oratory of display.

Political speaking urges us either to do or not to do something: one of these two courses is always taken by private counsellors, as well as by men who address public assemblies.

Forensic speaking either attacks or defends somebody: one or other of these two things must always be done by the parties in a case.

The ceremonial oratory of display either praises or censures somebody.

These three kinds of rhetoric refer to three different kinds of time. The political orator is concerned with the future: it is about things to be done hereafter that he advises, for or against. The party in a case at law is concerned with the past; one man accuses the other, and the other defends himself, with reference to things already done. The ceremonial orator is, properly speaking, concerned with the present, since all men praise or blame in view of the state of things existing at the time, though they often find it useful also to recall the past and to make guesses at the future.

Rhetoric has three distinct ends in view, one for each of its three kinds. The political orator aims at establishing the expediency or the harmfulness of a proposed course of action; if he urges its acceptance, he does so on the ground that it will do good; if he urges its rejection, he does so on the ground that it will do harm; and all other points, such as whether the proposal is just or unjust, honourable or dishonourable, he brings in as subsidiary and relative to this main consideration. Parties in a law case aim at establishing the justice or injustice of some action and they too bring in all other points as subsidiary and relative to this one. Those who praise or attack a man aim at proving him worthy of honour or the reverse and they too treat all other considerations with reference to this one."

Analysis – Aristotle asks, "What is the difference between eloquence and rhetoric?" Oratory is the art of public speaking, and the quest is that the orator delivers his oration with eloquence. Here is something that I learned today, the word eloquence comes from the Latin term eloquentia, which refers to speech readiness, elegance, fluency, and persuasiveness. If you can deliver a pompous speech that is verbose and ostentatious, you are considered grandiloquent.

The word rhetoric is equivalent to the Greek word ritoriki, which in turn stems from the Greek term ritoras, meaning orator. Rhetoric, therefore, is the art, skill, or method of an orator. A master of rhetoric is also called a rhetor or a rhetorician.

At the end of your oration, you'll probably want to sum your message up in a nutshell and combine it with a call to action. This concluding part of your speech is called peroration. So then, this entire list of *365 Must-Know Talks* has been a quest to unleash Masters of Rhetoric! It is no wonder that this list has been generous with the ancient Greeks, as that community respected rhetoric as an artform.

I will not, nor can I detail in full Aristotle's *Rhetoric* as it is made up of three books and many, many chapters. I have included *Book 1*, Chapter 3, in my list of the *365 Must-Know Talks*. If you know anything about those Greek cats, you'll know that *Book 2* is much more popular, but I delight in going against the grain at times. *Book 1* of Aristotle's *Rhetoric* is about what he calls lexis or delivery style. The other two books address ethos, logos, and pathos (spirit of the character, appeal to emotion, reasoned discourse). So, *Book 1* addresses the way one says something or the arrangement of words. I find it fascinating!

In a nutshell, you need to understand your audience. Aristotle came up with three orators who had separate and different motivations for delivering their talks. He explored how each orator should understand whether they talked about a future, present or past goal. Outline at the fore your audience and your desired end goal, and the result will be eloquence.

Tip – Define your audience and your end goal.

#22 – Ray Nagin

(1956)

Context – Ray Nagin is the former mayor of New Orleans, Louisiana. Nagin gained notoriety in 2005 in the wake of Hurricane Katrina. Chocolate City is a nickname that some people have given to the Martin Luther King, Jr. Day speech given by Ray Nagin, on January 16, 2006, which is highlighted below.

"I greet you all in the spirit of peace this morning. I greet you all in the spirit of love this morning, and more importantly, I greet you all in the spirit of unity. Because if we're unified, there's nothing we cannot do.

Now, I'm supposed to give some remarks this morning and talk about the great Dr. Martin Luther King Jr. You know, when I woke up early this morning, and I was reflecting upon what I could say that could be meaningful for this grand occasion. And then, I decided to talk directly to Dr. King.

Now you might think that's one Katrina post-stress disorder. But I was talking to him, and I just wanted to know what would he think if he looked down today at this celebration. What would he think about Katrina? What would he think about all the people who were stuck in the Superdome and Convention Center, and we couldn't get the state and the federal government to come do something about it? And he said, "I wouldn't like that."

And then I went on to ask him, I said, "Mr. King when they were marching across the Mississippi River bridge, some of the folks that were stuck in the Convention Center, that were tired of waiting for food and tired of waiting on buses to come rescue them, what would he say as they marched across that bridge? And they were met at the parish line with attack dogs and machine guns firing shots over their heads?" He said, "I wouldn't like that either."

Then I asked him to analyze the state of black America and black New Orleans today and to give me a critique of black leadership today. And I asked him what does he think about black leaders always or most of the time tearing each other down publicly for the delight of many? And he said, "I really don't like that either."

And then finally, I said, "Dr. King, everybody in New Orleans is dispersed. Over 44 different states. We're debating whether we should open this or close that. We're debating whether property rights should trump everything or not. We're debating how should we rebuild one of the greatest cultural cities the world has ever seen. And yet still yesterday we have a second line, and everybody comes together from around this and that, and they have a good time for the most part, and then knuckleheads pull out some guns and start firing into the crowd, and they injure three people." He said, "I definitely wouldn't like that."

And then I asked him, I said, "What is it going to take for us to move and live your dream and make it a reality?" He said, "I don't think we need to pay attention anymore as much about the other folk and racists on the other side." He said the thing we need to focus on as a community, black folks I'm talking to, is ourselves.

What are we doing? Why is black-on-black crime such an issue? Why do our young men hate each other so much that they look their brother in the face, and they will take a gun and kill him in cold blood?

He said we as a people need to fix ourselves first. He said the lack of love is killing us. And it's time, ladies and gentlemen.

Dr. King, if he was here today, he would be talking to us about this problem, about the problem we have among ourselves. And as we think about rebuilding New Orleans, surely God is mad at America, he's sending hurricane after hurricane after hurricane, and it's destroying and putting stress on this country. Surely, he's not approving of us being in Iraq under false pretense. But surely, he's upset at black America, also. We're not taking care of ourselves. We're not taking care of our women. And we're not taking care of our children when you have a community where 70 percent of its children are being born to one parent.

We ask black people: it's time. It's time for us to come together. It's time for us to rebuild a New Orleans, the one that should be a chocolate New Orleans. And I don't care what people are saying Uptown or wherever they are. This city will be chocolate at the end of the day.

This city will be a majority African American city. It's the way God wants it to be. You can't have New Orleans no other way; it wouldn't be New Orleans. So, before I get into too much more trouble, I'm just going to tell you in my closing conversation with Dr. King, he said, "I never worried about the good people—or the bad people I should say—who were doing all the violence during civil rights time." He said, "I worried about the good folks that didn't say anything or didn't do anything when they knew what they had to do."

It's time for all of us good folk to stand up and say, "We're tired of the violence. We're tired of black folks killing each other. And when we come together for a second line, we're not going to tolerate any violence." Martin Luther King would've wanted it that way, and we should. God bless all."

Analysis – This is the speech Nagin gave at a Martin Luther King Jr. Day celebration at City Hall in New Orleans. The speech is laced with controversy. Much of it derives from the occurrence of the phrase Chocolate City, which Nagin used repeatedly. The history of the term Chocolate City should be outlined as a positive one in African American culture. It refers to a city with a predominantly African American population. It was popularized by pop culture over the years. But his use of the term caused Nagin considerable trouble in the days following his speech. The speech starts with the values of peace, love, and unity. Then it goes through an engaging, imagined conversation that he has with Martin Luther King Jr., regarding the Katrina crisis and the modern problems faced by black Americans. The speech generates intense negative feedback, partly because of the Chocolate City reference and what others deemed racist behaviour toward whites.

I've chosen this talk because it ignited something within me. People tend to be so scripted, rehearsed, and censored that you rarely hear their actual opinion. Whether you agree with that opinion or not is an entirely different conversation, but why do people elicit such ravenous reactions simply for saying what they think? Those who understand the history behind what Nagin was saying, would likely not see his words as controversial. But that isn't our society. We assume that someone will say something offensive, so without doing any research, we jump all over them without understanding the nucleus of the message. I never want to live in a world where everyone pontificates bland, regurgitated, reality-based type word vomit. I want to live in an un-censored world, one where people can speak their truth. And others can choose to agree or disagree—that to me is real freedom. So, this speech has been chosen as a bold reminder that when we are given a platform to speak to others, we must speak our truth. Please, do not use others' words, do not pretend to be someone else, find your voice, so that you may awaken a desire in others to change something in their own lives for the better.

Tip – Speak your truth.

#21 – Marie Curie

1867–1934

Context – Marie Curie was a Polish-born French physicist and chemist, famous for her work on radioactivity. She was the first person to be honoured with two Nobel prizes in chemistry and physics. She was also the first female professor at the University of Paris. The speech below is on the discovery of radium given May 14, 1921, entitled "The Scientific History of Radium."

"I could tell you many things about radium and radioactivity, and it would take a long time. But as we cannot do that, I shall only give you a short account of my early work about radium. Radium is no more a baby; it is more than twenty years old, but the conditions of the discovery were somewhat peculiar, and so it is always of interest to remember them and to explain them.

We must go back to the year 1897. Professor Curie and I worked at that time in the laboratory of the school of Physics and Chemistry, where Professor Curie held his lectures. I was engaged in some work on uranium rays which had been discovered two years before by Professor Becquerel.

I spent some time in studying the way of making good measurements of the uranium rays, and then I wanted to know if there were other elements giving out rays of the same kind. So, I took up a work about all known elements and their compounds and found that uranium compounds are active and also all thorium compounds, but other elements were not found active, nor were their compounds. As for the uranium and thorium compounds, I found that they were active in proportion to their uranium or thorium content.
The more uranium or thorium, the greater the activity, the activity being an atomic property of the elements, uranium, and thorium.

Then I took up measurements of minerals and I found that several of those which contain uranium or thorium, or both were active. But then the activity was not what I could expect; it was greater than for uranium or thorium compounds like the oxides, which are almost entirely composed of these elements.

Then I thought that there should be in the minerals some unknown element having a much greater radioactivity than uranium or thorium. And I wanted to find and to separate that element, and I settled to that work with Professor Curie. We thought it would be done in several weeks or months, but it was not so. It took many years of hard work to finish that task. There was not one new, lenient; there were several of them. But the most important is radium, which could be separated in a pure state.

Now, the special interest of radium is in the intensity of its rays which is several million times greater than the uranium rays. And the effects of the rays make the radium so important. If we take a practical point of view, then the most important property of the rays is the production of physiological effects on the cells of the human organism. These effects may be used for the cure of several diseases. Good results have been obtained in many cases. What is considered particularly important is the treatment of cancer. The medical utilization of radium makes it necessary to get that element in sufficient quantities. And so, a factory of radium was started to begin with in France, and later in America where a big quantity of ore named carnotite is available. America does produce many grams of radium every year, but the price is still very high because the quantity of radium contained in the ore is so small. The radium is more than a hundred thousand times dearer than gold.

But we must not forget that when radium was discovered no one knew that it would prove useful in hospitals. The work was one of pure science. And this is a proof that scientific work must not be considered from the point of view of the direct usefulness of it. It must be done for itself, for the beauty of science, and then there is always the chance that a scientific discovery may become like the radium a benefit for humanity.

The scientific history of radium is beautiful. The properties of the rays have been studied very closely.

We know that particles are expelled from radium with a very great velocity near to that of the light.

We know that the atoms of radium are destroyed by expulsion of these particles, some of which are atoms of helium. And in that way, it has been proved that the radioactive elements are constantly disintegrating and that they produce at the end ordinary elements, principally helium and lead. That is, as you see, a theory of transformation of atoms which are not stable, as was believed before, but may undergo spontaneous changes.

Radium is not alone in having these properties. Many having other radio elements are known already, the polonium, the mesothorium, the radiothorium, the actinium. We know also radioactive gases, named emanations. There is a great variety of substances and effects in radioactivity. There is always a vast field left to experimentation, and I hope that we may have some beautiful progress in the following years. It is my earnest desire that some of you should carry on this scientific work and keep for your ambition the determination to make a permanent contribution to science…

…But we must not forget that when radium was discovered no one knew that it would prove useful in hospitals. The work was one of pure science. And this is a proof that scientific work must not be considered from the point of view of the direct usefulness of it. It must be done for itself, for the beauty of science, and then there is always the chance that a scientific discovery may become like the radium, a benefit for humanity."

Analysis – This is a very famous speech, and if you haven't heard of it, drop everything, and give it a read. If you haven't heard of Marie Curie, stop, and do a bit of research. Curie was knowledgeable and changed the world of science, and that change created a snowball effect regarding the treatment of cancer. I've been waiting to include this gem of a talk in my list of *365 Must-Know Talks* and I am thrilled to be presenting it to you today. I encourage you to read the transcript aloud, as doing so makes the words leap off the page and come alive. You can see what a great teacher Curie is from her carefully chosen, crystal clear dialogue. Curie is talking about uranium rays, thorium compounds, polonium, and, even though I dropped out of chemistry in high school, I can understand and am driven to learn more!

Why? Again and again, it is the individuals with a thirst for knowledge who choose to share their insatiable hunger to learn and engulf themselves in their field of study who give the most meaningful speeches. It is like the famous question what came first the chicken or the egg? In this sense, it is what came first the speech or the topic? The topic should always come first. The individual who spends an inordinate amount of time losing themselves in their field of study has earned the right to teach others what they've learned. It is no wonder that Curie became the first woman professor at the University of Paris!

Giving a speech is about transferring your knowledge to those who need to learn it whether the subject is polonium, organizational reviews, salary structures, or constructing a sales process, etc.

Tip – Use crystal clear dialogue in transferring your knowledge to others.

#20 – Maya Angelou

1928–2014

Context – Maya Angelou was an American poet and autobiographer. Below is her recitation of a poem, "On the Pulse of the Morning," which she wrote for the 1993 inauguration of President Bill Clinton.

A Rock, A River, A Tree
Hosts to species long since departed,
Marked the mastodon,
The dinosaur, who left dried tokens
Of their sojourn here
On our planet floor,
Any broad alarm of their hastening doom
Is lost in the gloom of dust and ages.

But today, the Rock cries out to us, clearly, forcefully,
Come, you may stand upon my
Back and face your distant destiny,
But seek no haven in my shadow.
I will give you no hiding place down here.

You created only a little lower than
The angels have crouched too long in
The bruising darkness
Have lain too long
Face down in ignorance.
Your mouths spilling words

Armed for slaughter.
The Rock cries out to us today, you may stand upon me,
But do not hide your face.

Across the wall of the world,
A River sings a beautiful song. It says,
Come, rest here by my side.

Each of you, a bordered country,
Delicate and strangely made proud,
Yet thrusting perpetually under siege.
Your armed struggles for profit
Have left collars of waste upon
My shore, currents of debris upon my breast.
Yet today I call you to my riverside,
If you will study war no more. Come,
Clad in peace, and I will sing the songs
The Creator gave to me when I and the
Tree and the rock were one.
Before cynicism was a bloody sear across your
Brow and when you yet knew you still
Knew nothing.
The River sang and sings on.

There is a true yearning to respond to
The singing River and the wise Rock.
So say the Asian, the Hispanic, the Jew
The African, the Native American, the Sioux,
The Catholic, the Muslim, the French, the Greek
The Irish, the Rabbi, the Priest, the Sheik,
The Gay, the Straight, the Preacher,
The privileged, the homeless, the Teacher.
They hear. They all hear
The speaking of the Tree.

They hear the first and last of every Tree
Speak to humankind today. Come to me, here beside the River.
Plant yourself beside the River.

Each of you, descendant of some passed
On traveler, has been paid for.
You, who gave me my first name, you,
Pawnee, Apache, Seneca, you
Cherokee Nation, who rested with me, then
Forced on bloody feet,
Left me to the employment of

Other seekers—desperate for gain,
Starving for gold.
You, the Turk, the Arab, the Swede, the German, the Eskimo, the Scot,
You the Ashanti, the Yoruba, the Kru, bought,
Sold, stolen, arriving on the nightmare
Praying for a dream.
Here, root yourselves beside me.
I am that Tree planted by the River,
Which will not be moved.
I, the Rock, I the River, I the Tree
I am yours—your passages have been paid.
Lift up your faces, you have a piercing need
For this bright morning dawning for you.
History, despite its wrenching pain
Cannot be unlived, but if faced
With courage, need not be lived again.

Lift up your eyes upon
This day breaking for you.
Give birth again
To the dream.

Women, children, men,
Take it into the palms of your hands,
Mold it into the shape of your most
Private need. Sculpt it into
The image of your most public self.
Lift up your hearts
Each new hour holds new chances
For a new beginning.
Do not be wedded forever
To fear, yoked eternally
To brutishness.

The horizon leans forward,
Offering you space to place new steps of change.
Here, on the pulse of this fine day
You may have the courage
To look up and out and upon me, the
Rock, the River, the Tree, your country.
No less to Midas than the mendicant.
No less to you now than the mastodon then.

Here, on the pulse of this new day.
You may have the grace to look up and out
And into your sister's eyes, and into
Your brother's face, your country
And say simply
Very simply
With hope—
Good morning.

Analysis –I find it fascinating how I used to view poems. When I started this list, I didn't pay the poet any mind. But that is the beauty of studying a subject matter diligently. Eventually, you open all kinds of new worlds in the pursuit of understanding and acquiring new knowledge and perhaps even greater wisdom. Such is the case with the poet and me. Truthfully, I don't think I understood poetry until I started compiling this list of *365 Must-Know Talks* and it has opened this astonishingly sublime art to me. Perhaps it is that poetry previously felt unattainable. I thought there was a specific way to read it, speak it, and write it, and the meat of it was lost. I feel differently about poetry today. It is in 'the eye of the beholder.

As David Hume said:

"Beauty in things exists merely in the mind which contemplates them"

or Shakespeare:

"Good Lord Boyet, my beauty, though but mean
Needs not the painted flourish of your praise:
Beauty is bought by judgement of the eye,
Not utter'd by base sale of chapmen's tongues

Now, if I think a poem is beautiful, it is so. I don't need to explain it, I don't need to analyze it, I let the words wash over me, and that is the only barometer I use. When reading this poem by Maya Angelou, I feel hope and happiness. I could talk in detail about her measurements of pause (a poetry term) the pause frequency, pause location, pause duration, phrase length, speech rate, articulation rate and percentage of pause time, but I won't. It seems ridiculous to appoint a test to such a thing of beauty. As public speakers seeking advice on improving their oratory skills, this is what today's post is about. Listen, and allow the words to wash over you, don't try to discern why you like it or don't, just listen. The more you read, the more you listen to the art of public speaking, including poetic prose, the more naturally the process of presentation osmosis will occur.

Tip – Open up your world of public speaking by exploring all oratory prose.

#19 – Rudolph the Red-Nosed Reindeer

Context – Rudolph the Red-Nosed Reindeer is a fictional reindeer with a glowing red nose. He is popularly known as Santa's 9th reindeer and he leads the team of reindeer, pulling Santa's sleigh on Christmas Eve. There are many depictions of Rudolph. The below example is from the Stop Motion animation by Rankin/Bass. It first aired on December 6, 1964.

Young doe: *(to Rudolph)* Nice day?

Rudolph: *(coy)* Yup...

Young doe: For takeoff practice, I mean.

Rudolph: Yup...

Young doe: I bet you'll be the best.

Rudolph: *(blushed)* Well, I don't know.

Young doe: Something wrong with your nose? I mean, you talk kind of funny.

Rudolph: What's so funny about the way I talk?

Young doe: Don't get angry. I don't mind.

Rudolph: You don't?

Young doe: My name's Clarice. Hi.

Rudolph: My name's Rudolph. Hi.

Clarice: Hi.

Rudolph: Hey, Clarice... after practice, would you–would you–?

Comet: *(calling)* Rudolph, you get back here! It's your turn, you know?

Rudolph: Gee, I got to go back. *(starts to run off, but then runs back)* Would you walk home with me?

Clarice: Uh-huh...Rudolph. *(to his ear)* I think you're cute.

Rudolph: *(joyfully jumps and begins to float up to the air for his first flight; to himself)* I'm cute! I'm cuuuuute!! *(lands on the ground in front of Comet)*

Comet: Magnificent!

Rudolph: I'm cute! I'm cute! She said I'm cuuuuute!! *(again, floats up to the air, much to the other fawns, his parents and Santa's amazement and awe)*

Analysis – You've likely been living under a rock or in a monastery if you haven't seen the movie *Rudolph the Red-Nosed Reindeer* at least once during the holiday season. This popular animation highlights the notion of being a misfit. When Rudolph is born with a glowing nose, his father, Donner, who is Santa's lead reindeer, feels ashamed and uses a special cover of mud to hide Rudolph's bright red nose so Rudolph can go to take-off practice. There is also Hermey, the misfit elf, who prefers studying dentistry to making toys. The elf foreman tries to get Hermey to focus on making toys, but Hermey refuses to change his interests.

Most people can relate to feeling like a misfits at times. And even more so when it comes to delivering a presentation. We want to be more of this or less of that. We want to be extroverted, animated, articulate, authentic, the list is endless, but like Rudolph, we are all born with inherent skills. It is up to you to figure out what they are. All the workshops and training sessions on presentation skills will never help unless you learn this art. At first blush, you may think that you have a hindrance (glowing nose, or say, overly technical lingo aptitude) but viewing that hindrance as a positive can dramatically alter how you deliver your talks (glowing nose becomes the guiding light for Santa, and that overly technical lingo becomes clear oratory instruction).

It is how you view your impediments that will determine success. Oh, and by the way, we all have flaws. Mine, in the spirit of full disclosure, is my natural and strong extraversion, also known as being loud (no, this is not the definition of extroversion for those who study introversion/extroversion, this is my attempt at being funny) so, I am naturally loud. This could be seen as a hindrance, and I allow it to be so, but I have learnt the art of curbing that loudness while doing presentations to appeal to all personality types in my audience. This introspection has aided me tremendously in being an effective speaker who understands how to convert what I may initially deem a presentation obstruction into an attribute.

Tip – How you view your perceived flaws is crucially important in determining your presentation skills success.

#18 – Colin Powell

(1937)

Context – Colin Powell is a retired U.S. Army general and was the 65th U.S. Secretary of State (2001-2005) serving under President George W. Bush. Below is the speech Powell gave at Colgate University on the topic of leadership.

" Look out the front windshield of life, never look behind"

Analysis – Colin Powell is a fantastic speaker. I may not always agree with his views, but I always enjoy his delivery. I have included this speech as it perfectly highlights a few presentation wins:

1. A natural delivery style: Notice no notes, but a clear direction. Powell has a solid grasp on the goal of the talk.

2. Natural body language: Powell's arms and disposition naturally punctuate his points, and the real reason this talk has been chosen.

3. Look forward: It was the above quote that inspired me to take on the task of blogging every day for a year. It forced me to look forward, generate new knowledge, find new purpose, and improve my writing skills, with the added bonus of having a sense of accomplishment and pride in the final result. If I only look back on my career, I'd get stuck. Have you ever worked with someone who says,

"When I worked at (insert company) we did it this way." These people are stuck in the past, holding on to the way things used to be, instead of looking forward.

No one cares that you've never done a presentation before, or if your previous presentations were dreadful or embarrassing or difficult or mediocre. Looking forward and acquiring new skills changes the shape of your future. You've found your way to this list, and I'd say, that's a great first step.

Tip – Look forward, not backwards when working on becoming a superb presenter.

#17 – Graeme Taylor

(1996)

Context – Graeme Taylor speaks at a public school board meeting in November 2010 in Michigan. Graeme Taylor was just 14-years-old when he gave this speech at a public-school board meeting in Michigan in November 2010. In his speech, the openly gay student offered his support to a teacher who was suspended after he dismissed two students from his class for saying they did not accept gays. Taylor tells the board how he attempted suicide at 9 years old after being bullied and urges the board to reverse the disciplinary action toward the teacher.

"…And when you hear of things like Dr. King's speech that one day he wanted his grandchildren, his posterity to not be judged on the color of their skin but the content of their character, I hope that one day we too can be judged on the content of our character, and not who we love…

This teacher who I firmly support, finally stood up and said something. I've been in rooms, in classrooms where children have said the worst kinds of things, kinds of things that helped lead me to a suicide attempt when I was only 9 years old.

These are things that hurt a lot. There is a silent holocaust out there in which an estimated six million gay people every year kill themselves. Is this really the environment you want for a school? Do we really want this on our record?"

Analysis – Graeme Taylor speaks with eloquence, reverence, and confidence and it's evident why his speech has been included on this list. Taylor was an openly gay student who spoke out at a public-school board meeting to support his high school economics teacher in Ann Arbor, Michigan. His teacher was suspended without pay for removing a student from the classroom for making anti-gay statements. Taylor supports his plea to the board members by saying, "These are the things that hurt a lot. There is a silent holocaust out there, in which an estimated six million gay people every year kill themselves." Powerful language, honest delivery, as Taylor admits to a suicide attempt at the age of nine. Taylor makes a profound impact in his one minute and 48 second address by reminding us to always stay true to ourselves, stand up for what we believe in and never hide behind a facade.

Tip – Be true to yourself and stand up for what you believe in.

#16 – Frederick Douglass

1818–1895

Context – Frederick Douglass was an orator, a writer, a social reformer, and a statesman. The below speech entitled "The Hypocrisy of American Slavery" was delivered in 1852 as part of the Rochester 4th of July celebrations. Douglass accepted the invitation to speak, but I must glean the citizens were surprised with the curt language, as Douglass delivered an attack on the hypocrisy of a nation celebrating freedom and independence when nearly four million people were still enslaved.

"Fellow citizens, pardon me, and allow me to ask, why am I called upon to speak here today? What have I or those I represent to do with your national independence? Are the great principles of political freedom and of natural justice embodied in that Declaration of Independence extended to us? And am I, therefore, called upon to bring our humble offering to the national altar, and to confess the benefits, and express devout gratitude for the blessings resulting from your independence to us?

Would to God, both for your sakes and ours, that an affirmative answer could be truthfully returned to these questions. Then would my task be light and my burden easy and delightful? For who is there so cold that a nation's sympathy could not warm him? Who so obdurate and dead to the claims of gratitude that would not thankfully acknowledge such priceless benefits? Who so stolid and selfish that would not give his voice to swell the hallelujahs of a nation's jubilee when the chains of servitude had been torn from his limbs? I am not that man. In a case like that, the dumb might eloquently speak, and the "lame man leap as an hart."

But such is not the state of the case. I say it with a sad sense of disparity between us. I am not included within the pale of this glorious anniversary! Your high independence only reveals the immeasurable distance between us. The blessings in which you this day rejoice are not enjoyed in common. The rich inheritance of justice, liberty, prosperity, and independence bequeathed by your fathers is shared by you, not by me. The sunlight that brought life and healing to you has brought stripes and death to me. This Fourth of July is yours, not mine. You may rejoice; I must mourn. To drag a man in fetters into the grand illuminated temple of liberty and call upon him to join you in joyous anthems, were inhuman mockery and sacrilegious irony. Do you mean, citizens, to mock me by asking me to speak today? If so, there is a parallel to your conduct. And let me warn you that it is dangerous to copy the example of a nation (Babylon) whose crimes, towering up to heaven, were thrown down by the breath of the Almighty, burying that nation in irrecoverable ruin.

Fellow citizens, above your national, tumultuous joy, I hear the mournful wail of millions, whose chains, heavy and grievous yesterday, are today rendered more intolerable by the jubilant shouts that reach them. If I do forget, if I do not remember those bleeding children of sorrow this day, "may my right hand forget her cunning, and may my tongue cleave to the roof of my mouth!"

To forget them, to pass lightly over their wrongs and to chime in with the popular theme would be treason most scandalous and shocking and would make me a reproach before God and the world.

My subject, then, fellow-citizens, is "American Slavery." I shall see this day and its popular characteristics from the slave's point of view. Standing here, identified with the American bondman, making his wrongs mine, I do not hesitate to declare, with all my soul, that the character and conduct of this nation never looked blacker to me than on this Fourth of July.

Whether we turn to the declarations of the past, or to the professions of the present, the conduct of the nation seems equally hideous and revolting. America is false to the past, false to the present, and solemnly binds herself to be false to the future. Standing with God and the crushed and bleeding slave on this occasion, I will, in the name of humanity, which is outraged, in the name of liberty, which is fettered, in the name of the Constitution and the Bible, which are disregarded and trampled upon, dare to call in question and to denounce, with all the emphasis I can command, everything that serves to perpetuate slavery—the great sin and shame of America! "I will not equivocate – I will not excuse." I will use the severest language I can command, and yet not one word shall escape me that any man, whose judgment is not blinded by prejudice, or who is not at heart a slaveholder, shall not confess to be right and just.

But I fancy, I hear some of my audience say it is just in this circumstance that you and your brother Abolitionists fail to make a favourable impression on the public mind. Would you argue more and denounce less, would you persuade more and rebuke less, your cause would be much more likely to succeed. But I submit, where all is plain, there is nothing to be argued. What point in the anti-slavery creed would you have me argue? On what branch of the subject do the people of this country need light? Must I undertake to prove that the slave is a man? That point is conceded already. Nobody doubts it. The slaveholders themselves acknowledge it in the enactment of laws for their government. They acknowledge it when they punish disobedience on the part of the slave. There are seventy-two crimes in the State of Virginia, which, if committed by a black man (no matter how ignorant he be), subject him to the punishment of death; while only two of these same crimes will subject a white man to like punishment.

What is this but the acknowledgement that the slave is a moral, intellectual, and responsible being?

The manhood of the slave is conceded. It is admitted in the fact that Southern statute books are covered with enactments, forbidding, under severe fines and penalties, the teaching of the slave to read and write. When you can point to any such laws in reference to the beasts of the field, then I may consent to argue the manhood of the slave. When the dogs in your streets, when the fowls of the air, when the cattle on your hills, when the fish of the sea, and the reptiles that crawl shall be unable to distinguish the slave from a brute, then I will argue with you that the slave is a man!

For the present it is enough to affirm the equal manhood of the Negro race. Is it not astonishing that, while we are ploughing, planting, and reaping, using all kinds of mechanical tools, erecting houses, constructing bridges, building ships, working in metals of brass, iron, copper, silver, and gold; that while we are reading, writing, and ciphering, acting as clerks, merchants, and secretaries, having among us lawyers, doctors, ministers, poets, authors, editors, orators, and teachers; that we are engaged in all the enterprises common to other men—digging gold in California, capturing the whale in the Pacific, feeding sheep and cattle on the hillside, living, moving, acting, thinking, planning, living in families as husbands, wives, and children, and above all, confessing and worshipping the Christian God, and looking hopefully for life and immortality beyond the grave—we are called upon to prove that we are men?

Would you have me argue that man is entitled to liberty? That he is the rightful owner of his own body? You have already declared it. Must I argue the wrongfulness of slavery? Is that a question for republicans? Is it to be settled by the rules of logic and argumentation, as a matter beset with great difficulty, involving a doubtful application of the principle of justice, hard to understand? How should I look today in the presence of Americans, dividing and subdividing a discourse, to show that men have a natural right to freedom, speaking of it relatively and positively, negatively, and affirmatively? To do so would be to make myself ridiculous and to offer an insult to your understanding. There is not a man beneath the canopy of heaven who does not know that slavery is wrong for him.

What! Am I to argue that it is wrong to make men brutes, to rob them of their liberty, to work them without wages, to keep them ignorant of their relations to their fellow-men, to beat them with sticks, to flay their flesh with the lash, to load their limbs with irons, to hunt them with dogs, to sell them at auction, to sunder their families, to knock out their teeth, to burn their flesh, to starve them into obedience and submission to their masters? Must I argue that a system thus marked with blood and stained with pollution is wrong? No – I will not. I have better employment for my time and strength than such arguments would imply.

What, then remains to be argued? Is it that slavery is not divine, that God did not establish it, that our Doctors of Divinity are mistaken? There is blasphemy in the thought. That which is inhuman cannot be divine. Who can reason on such a proposition? They that can, may – I cannot. The time for such argument is past.

At a time like this, scorching irony, not convincing argument, is needed. Oh! had I the ability, and could I reach the nation's ear, I would today pour out a fiery stream of biting ridicule, blasting reproach, withering sarcasm, and stern rebuke. For it is not light that is needed, but fire; it is not the gentle shower, but thunder. We need the storm, the whirlwind, and the earthquake. The feeling of the nation must be quickened; the conscience of the nation must be roused; the propriety of the nation must be startled; the hypocrisy of the nation must be exposed, and its crimes against God and man must be denounced.

What to the American slave is your Fourth of July? I answer, a day that reveals to him more than all other days of the year, the gross injustice and cruelty to which he is the constant victim. To him, your celebration is a sham; your boasted liberty an unholy license; your national greatness, swelling vanity; your sounds of rejoicing are empty and heartless; your shouts of liberty and equality, hollow mock; your prayers and hymns, your sermons, and thanksgivings, with all your religious parade and solemnity, are to him mere bombast, fraud, deception, impiety, and hypocrisy – a thin veil to cover up crimes which would disgrace a nation of savages. There is not a nation of the earth guilty of practices more shocking and bloody than are the people of these United States at this very hour.

Go search where you will roam through all the monarchies and despotisms of the Old World, travel through South America, search out every abuse and when you have found the last, lay your facts by the side of the everyday practices of this nation, and you will say with me that, for revolting barbarity and shameless hypocrisy, America reigns without a rival."

Analysis – Born into slavery in Maryland, Frederick Douglass escaped in 1838 and became a leader of the abolitionist movement. Douglass' oratory skills have been described as dazzling and he was known for using piercing language in his antislavery writings and speeches. He earned praise for his 1845 autobiography, *Life and Times of Frederick Douglass*, in which he describes his own life as a slave.

As I read this speech aloud, as I do with all the speeches that don't have an accompanying video, I feel myself delivering it with as much force and gusto that I can conjure. If you don't have time to read the entire transcript aloud, then try just this short section:

"Whether we turn to the declarations of the past, or to the professions of the present, the conduct of the nation seems equally hideous and revolting. America is false to the past, false to the present, and solemnly binds herself to be false to the future."

Check in with how you are feeling after reading those words aloud. I felt outraged, indignant, and vexed. It is apparent that Douglass is beyond pissed at the state of the country at the time, and I say, "Hallelujah!" The world needed a Frederick Douglass to showcase the complete moronic behaviour of the slave masters. I cannot claim to even come close to understanding the depths of Douglass' plight, but his speech offers a portal into his world and his autobiography gives an even bigger gateway.

This esteemed speech stands alone and doesn't require a lot from me in terms of analysis. What I'd like to highlight, as you seek advice on improving your public speaking abilities, is that you are allowed to get hot and bothered and pissed off, if the subject material warrants it. Get busy doing something about the injustices you see around you. When you observe others living and doing something with their life, you can better understand your role in this universe. Take that role seriously and use your words. The aim is to leave this world better than when we entered? Frederick Douglass did just that.

Tip – Use your words to right the injustices you see around you.

#15 – Rosa Parks

1913–2005

Context – Rosa Parks was a civil rights activist who was known as the first lady of civil rights. On December 1st, 1955, in Montgomery, Alabama, Parks disobeyed the bus driver and refused to give up her seat for a white passenger. It's worth noting that Parks was not the first person to push back; both Sarah Louise Keys and Irene Morgan won rulings before the Supreme Court for the same issue in 1955 and 1946 respectively.

"I don't think I should have to stand up."

Later, Parks said:

"People always say that I didn't give up my seat because I was tired, but that isn't true. I was not tired physically or no more tired than I usually was at the end of a working day. I was not old, although some people have an image of me as being old then. I was forty-two. No, the only tired I was, was tired of giving in."

Analysis – Quite possibly the shortest talk I've included on this list, but one that had an impact of gargantuan proportions. These nine words resonated within the vernacular of North America and the world. After a hard day's work at Montgomery Fair department store, Parks boarded the bus at 6 p.m. She paid her fare and sat in an empty seat in the first row of seats reserved for black passengers that were located near the middle of the bus. In 1900 the city had passed a law to segregate passengers by race, and the drivers were given the power to assign seats to that end. When Parks refused to get up, she was arrested, asking the officer, "Why do you push us around?" That evening the Women's Political Council (WPC) was the first group to officially endorse a bus boycott to which many other individuals and groups followed.

If you are seeking advice on improving your public speaking skills, then remember that your words can have a lasting effect on the people listening. At the time, Rosa Parks did not know that her nine-word refusal to give up her seat would have the impact that it did.

I am always intrigued at the presenter who talks in an incongruent way, with respect to how to speak in front of a group compared to behind the scenes. I once observed an individual giving a presentation as part of a one-on-one coaching session. I was asked to provide feedback on what worked well and areas for improvement. The speech began, and the presenter was fantastic. He had full command of the large audience from every angle, and I had to search for my improvement feedback. But I was shocked to see how he interacted with the audience during the breaks. His professional, articulate, witty demeanor transformed into a Popeye-like character, during the breaks. It was so incongruent, and I didn't know what to make of it. When I called him out on it, he explained that he was trying to connect with all members of his audience. By speaking in a different vernacular, he felt he became more accessible to specific audience members. I can see where he was going with this, but it was the wrong way to connect. You must still be you at the end of the day and find a way to do that while appealing to your entire audience, whether on or off stage.

Tip – Be authentic both on and off the presentation stage.

#14 – Carrie Fisher

1956–2016

Context – Carrie Fisher was an actress, novelist, screenwriter, and lecturer. Her most famous role was as Princess Leia Organa in the original *Star Wars* trilogy. In 2005, The American Film Institute awarded the Life Achievement Award to the film's writer, and director, George Lucas and Fisher paid tribute to Lucus in the form of a tongue-in-cheek roast.

"Hi, I'm Mrs. Hans Solo and I'm an alcoholic. I'm an alcoholic because George Lucas ruined my life. 57 years ago, I did his little Star Wars film a cult film that later came to be known as the face of cinema. Now 65 years later people often ask me if I knew it was going to be a hit. Yes, I knew. We all knew, the only one that didn't know was George. We kept it from him because we all wanted to see what his face looked like when it changed expression. George is a sadist. But like any of your child wearing a metal bikini chained to a giant slug about to die, a I keep coming back for more. Only a man like George could bring us a whole new world...."

Analysis – The *roast* is a type of speech that honours a person with good-natured ridicule. As I review my list of *365 Must-Know Talks* this type of talk has yet to hit this list. Carrie Fisher roasting George Lucas is perhaps one of her finest moments. In a sea of serious talks, I'm reminded that Randy Pausch (don't worry, you'll be hearing from him shortly) stresses the importance of having a bit of fun and says, "Never underestimate the importance of having fun. I'm dying, and I'm having fun. And I'm going to keep having fun every day because there's no other way to play it." So, let's have a bit of fun and watch the magic of Carrie Fisher's dazzling performance as she honours *Star Wars* writer and director George Lucas.

I've said many times during this list that presenters seeking advice and wisdom on how to improve presentation skills can learn mountains of techniques from comedians. Comedians are skilled in comedic delivery, timing, writing comedy sketches and feeling the vibe in the room and these are also the attributes that public speakers need. Fisher is beyond witty. Sure, she has a teleprompter that she is following, but she is reading the room—she's in tune with the audience, the pulse of the laughter, the silence, the reaction to her words. This is a difficult technique to perfect and it's even more difficult to teach as it takes confidence, a keen sense of being in the moment and a desire to impact your audience. If you are new to injecting wit into your talks, do so in small doses so that you can get a feel for what works and what bombs. Fisher's roast of Lucas lasts four minutes. I recommend you try a few seconds on for size and see how it feels. Be forewarned, this technique and style are very addictive once learned!

Tip – Pepper a few seconds of clever wit into your presentation before launching into a full-blown roast.

#13 – Barack Obama

(1961)

Context – Barack Obama was the 44th President of the United States and the first African American to hold the office. Obama previously served as a Senator from Illinois (1997–2004). He was inaugurated on January 20th, 2009, in Washington, D.C. Below is an excerpt from his speech on that occasion.

"For us, they packed up their few worldly possessions and traveled across oceans in search of a new life. "For us, they toiled in sweatshops and settled the West; endured the lash of the whip and plowed the hard earth. "For us, they fought and died in places like Concord and Gettysburg; Normandy and Khe Sahn. Time and again, these men and women struggled and sacrificed and worked till their hands were raw so that we might live a better life. They saw America as bigger than the sum of our individual ambitions, greater than all the differences of birth or wealth or faction. "

Analysis – This is the third time Obama makes an appearance on this list of *365 Must-Know Talks* because he is such a natural orator. I must confess, of the three entries (#60 and #139) this is probably my least favourite in terms of delivery, but I am in awe of the pressure that it takes to deliver an inaugural address. Approximately four million people were in Obama's audience—can you imagine? Think of Obama as just another human being and not a president. Think of him like you. Can you imagine the pressure, teleprompter or not, to have to live up to your predecessors? I marvel at how he must've been feeling waiting in the wings before he came outside. The nervous energy must have been palpable.

You can have a rich debate about the quality of this speech with all who have an opinion. Many say it lacks the weight of JFK's and Reagan's speeches—lines from their speeches are still quoted to this day, such as, "Ask not what your country can do for you, but what you can do for your country" and "We have nothing to fear but fear itself," respectively. But I believe that the above section is deeply powerful and memorable, and given time, will find its way into everyday vernacular.

My tip for today is to use repetition. Repetition in a speech is incredibly powerful and allows a speech to become memorable. And if you get butterflies before doing a speech, remember that Obama held it together in front of an audience of around four million, so you've got this! That should put your nerves into perspective. Having a perspective is a valuable tool in managing one's confidence.

Tip – Repetition is vital in delivering a memorable speech.

#12 – Judy Garland

1922–1969

Context – Judy Garland was an actress and singer. Here, Garland stars as Dorothy Gale in The Wizard of Oz (1939), which is the MGM film adaptation of the 1900 book *The Wonderful Wizard of Oz*, written by L. Frank Baum.

"There's no place like home."

Analysis – This is the fourth and final time *The Wizard of Oz* hits this list (#70, #96 and #328). And the above quote is taken from Garland's last scene.

There are few films that are perfect in every way, but the *Wizard of Oz* really does have it all. The music the performances from the perfectly cast actors, but, most importantly, the implicit (hinted at) and explicit (clear) meanings behind each scene. There are so many ways to interpret the film, every scene, and every actor, that it unfolds like one of the best novels I've ever read. It is the viewer who decides what the film is about and its underlying meaning.

In the buildup to this scene, The Wizard reveals that he too was born in Oz and was brought to the Emerald City by a runaway hot air balloon. The Wizard thinks that the balloon could work to get Dorothy home. Dorothy says her goodbyes to the Tin Man, the Cowardly Lion, and her beloved Scarecrow. Just at that moment, Toto, her dog, jumps out of the balloon to chase a cat. Dorothy follows Toto, and the Wizard, who is still in the balloon and unable to control it, leaves without her. Saddened at the thought that she will never see her family again and that she will have to live her entire life in Emerald City, she begins to cry, and just then, Glinda, the Good Witch, appears and tells her that she has always had the power to return home. Glinda explains that she did not tell Dorothy this at the beginning because it was something she had to figure out on her own. So, upon Glinda's instruction, Dorothy closes her eyes and taps her famous red-sequined shoes together three times, exclaiming and believing: "There's no place like home." I swear I'm getting choked up just typing this because it is the most powerful line in any film, ever. (Okay, maybe it's just me because I'm such a huge *Wizard of Oz* junky).

So, Dorothy wakes up in her home in Kansas (the film reverts to black and white denoting that we have left the fantasy land—directorial brilliance!) with her family and friends. Dorothy tells them all about what has happened to her, but her Aunt Em insists it was all a dream, even with Dorothy's persistent denial. Dorothy's final line is the culmination of it all and she announces once again, "There's no place like home." Ahhh! What a great line! So, Dorothy, who we saw at the beginning of the film, is bored by her drab life on a farm and runs away for something more, but in the end, she realizes that it is her family and friends who add meaning to her life and all she wants is to go home. Who hasn't felt like that before?

Many of us dream and aspire to be and do something bigger, and more adventurous. We want a new job, a higher salary, a bigger house, a different friend group, a new life. But, as Dorothy shows us, only you have the power to change your world and it is necessary to relish in your current life, despite your thoughts. You must alter those thoughts so that they are filled with positivity and optimism, not hoping for a change in the future. You may be preparing for a presentation today and hoping that something new and exciting will happen to you. Here's the difference, if you know that you are the controller of your destiny, then it will be so. Stop hoping and start knowing that you have the power to change the course of your destiny.

Tip – Be confident in the knowledge that you are the navigator of your destiny.

#11 – Plato

427 BCE – 348 BCE

Context – Plato's philosophical text, *Symposium*, was written in c.385 – 380 BCE. It is a text about love and its purpose and nature.

1. "And the true order of going, or being led by another, to the things of love, is to begin from the beauties of earth and mount upwards for the sake of that other beauty, using these steps only, and from one going on to two, and from two to all fair forms to fair practices, and from fair practices to fair notions, until from fair notions, he arrives at the notion of absolute beauty, and at last, knows what the essence of beauty is.

Sec. 211

2. Socrates informs the guests that he had sought out Diotima of Mantinea (lit. "honored by Zeus") for her

knowledge. Socrates then proceeds to relate her story of Love's genealogy, nature, and purpose (201d).

"Diotima explains that Love is the son of "Resource" (father) and "Poverty" (mother). Love has attributes from both parents. Love is beggarly, harsh and a master of artifice and deception (203d) and is delicately balanced and resourceful(204c). Diotima states that humans have the yearning to procreate, mentally and physically; this desire is the expression of humanity's desire for immortality (207a-b). Diotima's explanation of Love entails how to become a philosopher, or a Lover of wisdom, and by doing so one will give birth to intellectual children of greater immortality than any conceived through procreation."

Analysis –Plato's *Symposium* is a narrative and description of what happened at a party. He wasn't even there! It was re-told to him by Socrates, and Plato put it into writing. Socrates didn't scribe a single word of his own, and all that we know of him is down to Plato's diligent work. The party was attended by Athens leading cultural classical figures. The *Symposium* examines love in a sequence of speeches delivered by these men. From what I can glean, it is a dinner party/drinking party. The Greek word symposium means a convivial evening of drinking and intellectual conversation.

Each man in attendance is asked to deliver a speech in praise of love (or Eros, the God of Love). The party takes place at the house of the tragedian, Agathon, in Athens. Socrates (Plato's teacher) in his speech, says that the highest purpose of love is to become a philosopher or a lover of wisdom. Seven participants give speeches in the *Symposium*:

Phaedrus

Pausanias

Eryximachus

Aristophanes

Agathon

Socrates

Alcibiades

So, why has Plato's *Symposium* been chosen to be included in this list of *365 Must-Know Talks*? Because the notion of the *Lover of Wisdom* fits into the notion of being a superb public speaker. Without a constant and persistent pursuit of knowledge, you cannot be a great speaker. If you only know what you are presenting on, and don't have a foundation of general knowledge in all other areas, then there is no resource to pool from when the topic pivots, as a result of a question, or as a result of your thought process. A superb public speaker knows they must be able to draw from a breadth of knowledge in a vast number of areas to be an effective speaker. It comes down to being interesting from loving the pursuit of knowledge and wisdom.

Tip – Be a lover of wisdom.

#10 – John F. Kennedy

1917–1963

Context – John F. Kennedy was the 35th President of the United States, serving from 1961 until his assassination in 1963. At 43 years of age, he was one of the youngest president elected only preceded by 42-year-old Theodore Roosevelt.

"My fellow Americans: ask not what your country can do for you—ask what you can do for your country."

Analysis – John F. Kennedy spent more than two months writing this speech. Two months for about 15 minutes of talk time! This is a fascinating speech, and upon deeper reflection, I can see why. For me, the speech doesn't say a whole lot. His speech intends to get the nation on board with a new, fresh, and positive start. He chooses his words carefully so as not to offend anyone. He pleases everyone and ensures there is no controversy with his words. Kennedy uses *phatic* function of language and those seeking advice on improving their presentation skills can learn much from this technique.

The phatic function of language is the notion that content and meaning are less important than the act of communicating. An example would be the response, "You're welcome." This statement is not intended to convey the message that the hearer is welcome. It is instead a phatic response to being thanked, a polite response to a gift. Here's another example, "How are you?" This phrase can be said in a sincere, concerned manner, or it can be delivered in such a way that it doesn't even require a response and becomes part of an everyday exchange. At the core, phatic language performs a social task instead of conveying information (think small or elevator talk). The Kennedy speech is phatic brilliance. And it's why I believe everyone who hears it comes away feeling good. There is an excellent place for this type of language in presentations, particularly the talks that set out to encourage and motivate others.

Tip – Include phatic language in your motivational talks!

#9 – Leonardo da Vinci

1452–1519

Context – Leonardo da Vinci was an Italian painter, sculptor, architect, musician, scientist, engineer, mathematician, polymath, inventor, geologist, cartographer, botanist, anatomist, and writer. This isn't his first appearance on this list as he is mentioned within many other entries and was featured previously at #58. I struggled to choose one excerpt or quote for this post, so I have highlighted five of my favourites.

1. *"Man has great power of speech, but the greater part thereof is empty and deceitful. The animals have little, but that little is useful and true, and better is a small and certain thing than a great falsehood."*

2. *"The noblest pleasure is the joy of understanding."*

3. *"It had long since come to my attention that people of accomplishment rarely sat back and let things happen to them. They went out and happened to things."*

4. *"Learning never exhausts the mind."*

5. *"Learning how to learn is life's most important skill."*

Analysis –There isn't another individual that I have studied more than da Vinci (even my beloved Socrates plays second fiddle to Leo 1.0). As I look at my bookshelf, it is crammed with texts about da Vinci. I even have a transcript of his notebooks that is dog-eared, highlighted, and riddled with copious notes in the margins. It's probably time for a new copy. I study da Vinci because he fascinates me. He is a profoundly unique and spellbinding individual who I can never seem to fully understand, so I continue to try. His notebooks cover a vast number of topics from philosophy, anatomy, physiology, human proportions, medicine, optics, acoustics, astronomy, botany, geography, atmosphere, flight, mathematics, hydraulics, inventions, music, fables, and many, many more. Some 6,000 pages of notes have been collected and these notebooks are filled with pictures, drawings, equations, and every other type of visual interpretation. It is as if da Vinci, with each of his new ideas or explorations, tried desperately to bring it alive in every way imaginable. Da Vinci had a deep respect for and an insatiable curiosity about life. He was compassionate toward animals and was in awe of nature. Da Vinci appeared to believe that human design was far inferior to nature's ingenuity, and I believe that his attempts at inventions and design were based on nature's mimicry.

Da Vinci was troubled deeply by any form of deceit, and this is why I have included him on this list. Words are powerful, and da Vinci recognized this. Perhaps those seeking to become more effective presenters can learn from da Vinci's pessimistic view on speech. I think da Vinci tried to find combinations in all that he did. It was his way of creating a more robust and deeply intimate account of whatever he was exploring. So, words were not enough of an explanation, nor was sculpting, but if you combine the two or more, you could create something that didn't exist before and do so in a highly effective way. An uncluttered and robust imagination is required to do this well. Gelb's book *How to Think Like Leonardo da Vinci* (a must read for anyone interested in da Vinci) points out that it's human nature to seek connection, which is ultimately da Vinci's quest. I agree with this assessment. On page 220 of his book, Gelb asserts a concept he calls *Connessione,* which he defines as, "a recognition of and appreciation for the interconnectedness of all things and phenomena. Systems thinking."

Being creative and seeking connectedness is how we connect with the world (a tad existentialist, perhaps). From a presentation aspect, it is about looking at your presentation topic, and finding seemingly unrelated issues that can be related. You could try to find a connection between the World Wide Web and sales training or between a donkey and an HR policy. This sort of practice helps you add depth to your talks. It shows that everything is connected to everything. It brings a richness of dialogue and an ability to relate any topic to anything and anybody.

Tip – Immerse yourself in the study of someone you admire and seek out areas of interconnectedness to give your presentation's dimension and depth.

#8 – Helen Keller

1880–1968

Context – Helen Keller was an author, activist and lecturer. She was the first deaf-blind person to earn a Bachelor of Arts degree and wrote a total of 12 books and many articles. The film, *The Miracle Worker*, tells Keller's story and how her teacher, Anne Sullivan, broke through Keller's immense language barrier, and thus allowed her to have a voice. With that voice she did much. She spoke out against war and campaigned tirelessly for women's rights. The below clip is not a speech, but more for those who are interested in how Keller learned to speak.

"The only thing worse than being blind, is having sight but no vision."

Analysis – Helen Keller wasn't born blind or deaf. At 19 months old, she contracted an illness described by doctors as an acute congestion of the stomach and the brain (possibly scarlet fever or meningitis). The illness didn't last long but Keller lost her hearing and her sight as a result. By the age of six she had learned how to communicate with the daughter of the family's cook. A 49-year relationship with her teacher, Anne Sullivan, began after an exhaustive effort by her mother to help Keller communicate with not just a select few but with everyone. Keller's mother discovered the Perkins Institute for the Blind and 20-year-old Sullivan, who was visually impaired herself, became Keller's teacher. In 1888, Sullivan brought Keller to Perkins School for the Blind where Keller was delighted to make many new friends..

If you have ever taken one of my workshops, you have undoubtedly heard me quote Keller especially the above as her words are profound and rich. Many people simply meander through life and any given task, without an end goal or clearly laid vision in mind, and this is what Keller is saying. To have vision, you need a healthy imagination, and not simply imagination for the sake of imagination, but an ability to visualize the future.

As I continue to reflect on the previous entries in this list, I see many themes. One recurring theme is how important creativity and imagination are in becoming a superb public speaker. Today, we take it from the angle of pretending you have a crystal ball and seeing the future before you even start the process of preparing. You need to understand where you want to take your speech, the vibe you want to send out, the message you have and what you want from your audience. As the speaker, you should have a very clear end in mind and be crystal clear in your motive throughout your talk. It's like going on a vacation but having no destination in mind, you need the road map to get there.

Tip – Ensure you evaluate, understand, and think about your presentation's vision before you even begin.

#7 – Martin Luther King Jr.

1929–1968

Context – Martin Luther King, Jr. was an activist and leader in the African American Civil Rights Movement. In 1964 King was the youngest man to win the Nobel Peace Prize at the age of 35. King gave speech entitled "I Have a Dream," on August 28,1963. King was assassinated on April 4, 1968, in Memphis, Tennessee.

Here are some of my favourite highlights from the speech:

"Five score years ago…" (alluding to Abraham Lincoln's Gettysburg Address)

"This sweltering summer of the Negro's legitimate discontent will not pass until there is an invigorating autumn…" (referring to Shakespeare's Richard III)

"Now is the time…" and "I have a dream" (a great example of Anaphora or the repetition of a phrase at the beginning of a sentence)

"We have also come to this hallowed spot to remind America of the fierce urgency of Now. This is no time to engage in the luxury of cooling off or to take the tranquilizing drug of gradualism. Now is the time to make real the promises of democracy."

"Free at last…"

Analysis – From the steps of the Lincoln Memorial during the March on Washington for Jobs and Freedom, on August 28, 1963, Martin Luther King Jr. outlines his vision of racial harmony. Delivered to more than 200,000 people, the speech is a mere 17 minutes long but in those 17 minutes, King calls for racial equality and the end to discrimination in a moving sermon that is a masterpiece of rhetoric. It is a defining moment in the American Civil Rights Movement. As I whittle down the top ten talks on this list, this entry could just as easily have taken the number one spot—each of these talks has merit when learning how to become a superb speaker.

While all these talks are interchangeable, I love so many things about this one. And It comes down to the words, "I have a dream," that King does not utter until the latter part of the speech. These four words, that are culturally tattooed in the minds of so many, were improvised. For those of you seeking advice on improving your presentation skills, sit with that notion for a moment. Mahalia Jackson (a gospel singer) was in the audience and shouted onto the stage, "Tell them about the dream, Martin!" When you speak from your heart, when you have something profound to say, your words will have everlasting power.

If you want to be schooled in how to deliver a superb speech, watch King in action.

Tip – When you speak from the depths of your being, you can change the world, and your words will live on for infinity.

#6 – Aristotle

384 BCE – 322 BCE

Context – Aristotle was a Greek philosopher, a student of Plato, and the teacher of Alexander the Great.

"Happiness does not consist in pastimes and amusements, but in virtuous activities."

Analysis – Success and happiness are deeply interrelated. Success is often related to wealth and fame and power and social status, when it should be related to an entirely different set of values such as fulfilment, accomplishment, and the pursuit of excellence and happiness. The question of happiness and success is the one that plagued Aristotle. Not simply his own happiness but happiness for as many as possible. For Aristotle, happiness comes from discovering who you are, developing that essence, and applying it to benefit yourself and others. There are innumerable quotes and texts related to happiness, but the one highlighted above is my favourite. It talks about virtuous or moral activities. Aristotle defined morality as the pursuit of goodness or becoming a good person and on morality as it relates to happiness. This stuff is deep but that doesn't mean that it is unattainable. If you need to, go back and reread it, until you understand, or dig deep and do your own research. We all learn differently, and the world isn't always easy to follow, and perhaps the reason that I adore the Greek philosophers is because they can be challenging to digest.

Let's look at it from a more modern angle:

In his book, *True Success: A New Philosophy of Excellence*, philosopher and pioneering business thinker, Tom Morris, outlines what he calls the seven Cs of success:

- A clear conception of what we want, a vivid vision, a goal clearly imagined
- A strong confidence that we can attain that goal
- A focused concentration on what it takes to reach the goal
- A stubborn consistency in pursuing our vision
- An emotional commitment to the importance of what we're doing
- A good character to guide us and keep us on a proper course
- A capacity to enjoy the process along the way

I adore these seven Cs, not because they are earth-shatteringly brilliant, because they serve as a great reminder of what success is, and what it should be and how to attain it. If you have found yourself reading between the pages of this book, it's likely you are seeking advice on how to improve your public speaking skills. So, if success and happiness are intertwined, then what is Aristotle saying in the above quote? Is it that success and happiness cannot be attained through the past or squandering time, but in actual and real activities? It is the act of participating in something of worth and being creative that brings fulfilment? Could it be that happiness is derived from being productive? A friend once complained that she was bored. When I asked what was boring her, she said, "Everything! I'm bored with life!" I can't think of anything worse than that. To seek and be happy, one needs to participate and be productive in life! So, seeking advice on improving your presentation skills, this entry is not cookie-cutter but more profound in its application. Produce great content and delivery in your presentations, get your audience to participate in what you are saying, attain participation in all aspects of your life. What one realizes in this pursuit is that engaging in activities, including a presentation for the sheer pursuit of joy and virtue, may not bring money, or fame, or improved social status but will likely bring forth the ownership of happiness.

Tip – Participate and be productive to deliver meaningful presentations that make you happy.

#5 – Socrates

c. 469 BCE – 399 BCE

Context – Socrates was a Greek philosopher and one of the founding members of Western philosophy. Our knowledge of Socrates stems from the writings of his students, Plato, Xenophon, and Aristophanes. Plato was undoubtedly the most prominent of the three.

"How you have felt, O men of Athens, at hearing the speeches of my accusers, I cannot tell, but I know that their persuasive words almost made me forget who I was—such was the effect of them, and yet they have hardly spoken a word of truth. But many as their falsehoods were, there was one of them which quite amazed me;

—I mean when they told you to be upon your guard and not to let yourselves be deceived by the force of my eloquence. They ought to have been ashamed of saying this because they were sure to be detected as soon as I opened my lips and displayed my deficiency; they certainly did appear to be most shameless in saying this, unless by the force of eloquence they mean the force of truth; for then I do indeed admit that I am eloquent.

But in how different a way from theirs! Well, as I was saying, they have hardly uttered a word, or not more than a word, of truth; but you shall hear from me the whole truth: not, however, delivered after their manner, in a set oration duly ornamented with words and phrases. No indeed! but I shall use the words and arguments which occur to me at the moment; for I am certain that this is right, and that at my time of life I ought not to be appearing before you, O men of Athens, in the character of a juvenile orator—let no one expect this of me. And I must beg of you to grant me one favor, which is this—If you hear me using the same words in my defence, which I have been in the habit of using, and which most of you may have heard in the a gora, and at the tables of the money-changers, or anywhere else, I would ask you not to be surprised at this, and not to interrupt me….

For I am more than seventy years of age, and this is the first time that I have ever appeared in a court of law, and I am quite a stranger to the ways of the place; and therefore I would have you regard me as if I were really a stranger, whom you would excuse if he spoke in his native tongue and after the fashion of his country; — that I think is not an unfair request. Never mind the manner, which may or may not be good, but think only of the justice of my cause, and give heed to that: let the judge decide justly, and the speaker speak truly.

…Someone may wonder why I go about in private, giving advice and busying myself with the concerns of others, but do not venture to come forward in public and advise the state. I will tell you the reason of this. You have often heard me speak of an oracle or sign which comes to me and is the divinity which Meletus ridicules in the indictment. This sign I have had ever since I was a child. The sign is a voice which comes to me and always forbids me to do something which I am going to do, but never commands me to do anything, and this is what stands in the way of my being a politician. And rightly, as I think. For I am certain, O men of Athens, that if I had engaged in politics, I should have perished long ago and done no good either to you or to myself. And don't be offended at my telling you the truth: for the truth is that no man who goes to war with you or any other multitude, honestly struggling against the commission of unrighteousness and wrong in the state will save his life; he who will really fight for the right, if he would live even for a little while, must have a private station and not a public one…

…Wherefore, O judges, be of good cheer about death and know this of a truth—that no evil can happen to a good man, either in life or after death. He and his are not neglected by the gods, nor has my own approaching end happened by mere chance. But I see clearly that to die and be released was better for me, and therefore the oracle gave no sign. For which reason also, I am not angry with my accusers or my condemners; they have done me no harm, although neither of them meant to do me any good; and for this, I may gently blame them.

Still, I have a favor to ask of them. When my sons are grown up, I would ask you, O my friends, to punish them; and I would have you trouble them, as I have troubled you if they seem to care about riches, or anything, more than about virtue; or if they pretend to be something when they are really nothing—then reprove them, as I have reproved you, for not caring about that for which they ought to care and thinking that they are something when they are really nothing. And if you do this, I and my sons will have received justice at your hands.

The hour of departure has arrived, and we go our ways—I to die, and you to live. Which is better, God only knows."

Analysis – In 357 posts, Socrates finally enters this list with his own spot. I've talked about him numerous times, as he is by far my favourite philosopher, and like Plato, I think of myself as one of his students—I'm just hundreds of years late for class! Socrates is the last of the ancient Greek philosophers discussed in this list, so I'll try to do them all justice and give them a worthy send off.

There is a story that Plato tells about Socrates and how he learned that the Oracle at Delphi had proclaimed him to be the wisest man in Athens. Socrates, who liked to question everything, took to the streets to determine if this was true. He questioned every man he could find and figured out rather quickly that even on basic questions and issues of life, most had not given it much thought, nor had they formulated any type of point of view, even in the areas they thought they were knowledgeable. Socrates realised, slowly and methodologically, that he knew very little, and what mattered most was the constant pursuit of knowledge, genuine curiosity and what Socrates called truth. One of Socrates' best and most famous sayings is, "I only know that I know nothing."

I cannot possibly unearth all that there is to know about Socrates, but my hope is that you will be compelled by my intense passion to seek out your truth as it relates to this great philosopher. There is a genuine reason that all who came before Socrates were dubbed Pre-Socratic as Socrates ideas and interests were so unique. He was the first to be able to "call philosophy down from the heavens" as Cicero once said. Socrates' concerns are not for the sake of philosophizing but for practical reasons—he wants to know the very best way to live. The famous Socrates quote, "the unexamined life isn't worth living," is a good foundation for all his philosophical thought and so the Socratic problem and method comes to be. Problem and method are a clever way of asking a series of questions to uncover underlying beliefs and the actual amount of knowledge a person holds on the topic at hand. Socrates designed this method of questions and answers, so the individual he was applying this method to would ultimately be forced to examine their own beliefs and validity. Socrates said, "I know you won't believe me, but the highest form of human excellence is to question oneself and others."

Socrates believed self-development was more critical than acquiring material wealth. Hence, the *Apology of Socrates* is included in this list of *365 Must-Know Talks*. In the *Apology of Socrates*, written by Plato, is a Socratic dialogue of a speech of legal self-defence, which Socrates gave at his trial for corruption in 399 BCE. Socrates faced charges of corrupting youth. He believed that one should focus on community and friendships. The speech proved unsuccessful, and he was ultimately convicted by a jury of his peers. And because he believed in accepting his peers' point of view, he subsequently killed himself by swallowing hemlock (a poisonous plant). "The hour of departure has arrived, and we go our ways—I to die, and you to live. Which is better, God only knows." Upon his last moments of life, he uttered this line that has propelled if not plagued philosophy. Human knowledge is woefully limited in effect.

Of all these entries, this is the one I've thought about most in terms of how it relates to improving public speaking attributes. I've come up with this, "The unexamined life is not worth living" and is certainly not worth speaking about. If you are going to take the presentation position, you'd have better examined it.

Tip – The unexamined life and unexamined presentation topic isn't worth executing!

#4 – Gandhi

1869–1948

Context – Mohandas Karamchand Gandhi was a lawyer and the political and ideological leader of India during the Indian independence movement. This speech, often referred to as the "Quit India" speech, was delivered to India Congress Committee on August 8, 1942, at Gowalia Tank Maidan, a park in Bombay (now Mumbai). Gandhi was assassinated on January 30, 1948.

'Before you discuss the resolution, let me place before you one or two things; I want you to understand two things very clearly and to consider them from the same point of view from which I am placing them before you. I ask you to consider it from my point of view because if you approve of it, you will be enjoined to carry out

all I say. It will be a great responsibility. There are people who ask me whether I am the same man that I was in 1920 or whether there has been any change in me. You are right in asking that question.

Let me, however, hasten to assure that I am the same Gandhi as I was in 1920. I have not changed in any fundamental respect. I attach the same importance to non-violence that I did then. If at all, my emphasis on it has grown stronger. There is no real contradiction between the present resolution and my previous writings and utterances.

Occasions like the present do not occur in everybody's and but rarely in anybody's life. I want you to know and feel that there is nothing but purest Ahimsa1 in all that I am saying and doing today. The draft resolution of the Working Committee is based on Ahimsa, the contemplated struggle similarly has its roots in Ahimsa. If, therefore, there is any among you who has lost faith in Ahimsa or is wearied of it, let him not vote for his resolution.

Let me explain my position clearly. God has vouchsafed to me a priceless gift in the weapon of Ahimsa. I and my Ahimsa are on our trail today. If in the present crisis, when the earth is being scorched by the flames of Himsa and crying for deliverance, I failed to make use of the God-given talent, God will not forgive me, and I shall be judged un-wrongly of the great gift. I must act now. I may not hesitate and merely look on when Russia and China are threatened.

Ours is not a drive for power, but purely a non-violent fight for India's independence. In a violent struggle, a successful general has been often known to affect a military coup and to set up a dictatorship. But under the Congress scheme of things, essentially non-violent as it is, there can be no room for dictatorship. A non-violent soldier of freedom will covet nothing for himself; he fights only for the freedom of his country. The Congress is unconcerned as to who will rule when freedom is attained. The power, when it comes, will belong to the people of India, and it will be for them to decide to whom it placed in the entrusted. May be that the reins will be placed in the hands of the Parsis, for instance-as I would love to see happen-or they may be handed to some others whose names are not heard in the Congress today. It will not be for you then to object, saying, 'This community is microscopic. That party did not play its due part in the freedom's struggle; why should it have all the power?' Ever since its inception, the Congress has kept itself meticulously free of the communal taint. It has thought always in terms of the whole nation and has acted accordingly.

I know how imperfect our Ahimsa is and how far away we are still from the ideal, but in Ahimsa, there is no final failure or defeat. I have faith, therefore, that if, in spite of our shortcomings, the big thing does happen. It will be because God wanted to help us by crowning with success our silent, unremitting Sadhana1 for the last twenty-two years.

I believe that in the history of the world, there has not been a more genuinely democratic struggle for freedom than ours. I read Carlyle's French Resolution while I was in prison, and Pandit Jawaharlal has told me something about the Russian revolution. But it is my conviction that inasmuch as these struggles were fought with the weapon of violence, they failed to realize the democratic ideal. In the democracy which I have envisaged, a democracy established by non-violence, there will be equal freedom for all. Everybody will be his own master. It is to join a struggle for such democracy that I invite you today.

Once you realize this, you will forget the differences between the Hindus and Muslims, and think of yourselves as Indians only, engaged in the common struggle for independence.

Then, there is the question of your attitude towards the British. I have noticed that there is hatred towards the British among the people. The people say they are disgusted with their behaviour. The people make no distinction between British imperialism and the British people. To them, the two are one. This hatred would even make them welcome the Japanese. It is most dangerous. It means that they will exchange one slavery for another. We must get rid of this feeling. Our quarrel is not with the British people; we fight their imperialism. The proposal for the withdrawal of British power did not come out of anger. It came to enable India to play its due part at the present critical juncture. It is not a happy position for a big country like India to be merely helping with money and material obtained willy-nilly from her while the United Nations are conducting the war. We cannot evoke the true spirit of sacrifice and velour so long as we are not free. I know the British Government will not be able to withhold freedom from us when we have made enough self-sacrifice. We must, therefore, purge ourselves of hatred. Speaking for myself, I can say that I have never felt any hatred. As a matter of fact, I feel myself to be a greater friend of the British now than ever before. One reason is that they are today in distress. My very friendship, therefore, demands that I should try to save them from their mistakes. As I view the situation, they are on the brink of an abyss.

It, therefore, becomes my duty to warn them of their danger even though it may, for the time being, anger them to the point of cutting off the friendly hand that is stretched out to help them. People may laugh; nevertheless, that is my claim. At a time when I may have to launch the biggest struggle of my life, I may not harbour hatred against anybody."

Analysis – Gandhi pioneered something called *satyagraha*, which is defined as the resistance to tyranny through mass civil disobedience, a philosophy firmly founded upon ahimsa or total nonviolence. It was this singular idea put forward by one man that propelled India to independence. Allow the former statement to sink in for a moment before reading on.

Gandhi is often referred to as Mahatma Gandhi, which means great soul in Sanskrit, an ancient Indo-European language of India. I encourage you to study Gandhi on your own, read what interests you, perhaps watch the film, it is quite moving. Gandhi humbles me in every way, a leader is not enough of a descriptor, so I too shall revere him as Mahatma—a human being with powers that seem supernatural.

In this speech, Gandhi appeals for a mass civil disobedience movement supporting India's freedom from British imperialism. Earlier that day, the All-India Congress Committee (AICC), endorsed the Quit India Resolution which demanded an immediate end to British rule in India. It was this approval that allowed Gandhi's speech to go ahead. What is quite remarkable is that almost the entire Indian National Congress leadership was put into confinement less than 24 hours after this speech, and most of the Congress leaders spent the rest of World War II in jail. It is not the time nor place to go into monumental historical detail here, suffice to say that the history of Gandhi is incredibly complex, and I will mirror the sentiments of the filmmakers with their opening remarks from the movie:

"No man's life can be encompassed in one telling… least of all Gandhi's, whose passage through life was so entwined with his nation's struggle for freedom. There is no way to give each year its allotted weight, to recount the deeds and sacrifices of all the great men and women to whom he and India owe such immense debts. What can be done is to be faithful in spirit to the record of his journey, and to try to find one's way to the heart of the man…" (source: Wikipedia)

And that is my task, to translate the heart of Gandhi from his awe-inspiring speech, into something tangible that you can implement. Now there's a task! There are similarities between Gandhi's speech and Martin Luther King, Jr., "I Have a Dream" address (#7), and it comes down to nonviolence and equality. Gandhi's speech came first (1942) vs King's (1963). This is my point, showing others through your actions can have an immediate and lasting impact. Perhaps even on the great Martin Luther King, Jr.

There is a famous quote from Gandhi: "Be the change you wish to see in the world." He was exactly the person needed to lead the Indian revolution. He was a person who embodied the love of oneself and others and one who promoted nonviolence protest, and persistence beyond measure. Gandhi showed his soul to the world when he spoke, and it was indeed significant with lasting reverberations. Before you take the presentation stage, check if you are driving your agenda and ego or if you are showing your audience the change you wish to see in them and the world. Be the change you aspire to be, and your audience will not only hang on your every word, but they will aspire to be more too. Isn't that why we ultimately do what we do?

Tip – Be the change you wish to see in the world and bring that to life in your presentations.

#3 – Leo Tolstoy

1828–1910

Context – Leo Tolstoy was a Russian writer who many consider to be the world's greatest novelist. Some of his novels include *War and Peace* and *Anna Karenina*.

First published in 1886, *The Death of Ivan Ilych* is considered a novella (shorter than a novel but longer than a short story). Of note, it is widely known that Tolstoy published this piece after a three-year stint of depression and what some might consider personal intellectual turmoil. It was after this time that Tolstoy converted to Christianity. I could post the entire contents of *The Death of Ivan Ilych*, but I have chosen instead to select these words:

"Ivan Ilych's life had been most simple and most ordinary, and therefore most terrible."

"'Maybe I did not live as I ought to have done,' it suddenly occurred to him. 'But how could that be, when I did

everything properly?' he replied, and immediately dismissed from his mind this, the sole solution of all the riddles of life and death, as something quite impossible."

Analysis – Without question, this is the finest piece of novella fiction that has ever existed. I remember taking a class in Banff many years ago. It was a fascinating leadership class, like no other I had taken before, and believe me, I have participated in many workshops. But this one was unique. It was a week-long introspective journey to discover one's natural leadership style and how we adapt our styles to fit the organizations we work for. Hands down, this is the best workshop I have ever taken (if you're interested, drop me a note, and I'll give you the details). Part of it was due to the content. It was a whole week of well-thought-out exercises, pre-work, and comfort zone stretching exercises—but it was the two facilitators who really brought the workshop alive. One of whom, I will never forget. Doug was a gentleman with grey hair and a professional look, a rounded belly and wisdom beyond his already bloomed age. He commanded attention, not because of his loud and boisterous voice, but because of his storytelling ability. He would suck you into his story by word three. I'd never seen someone do this so well before, or since, and I was mesmerized. On the last day of the workshop, just as all the participants were readying ourselves to go home, we all expected some closing remarks, some phatic chit-chat such as, "Thanks for coming, it's been a hoot," kind of stuff, but that didn't happen. In the final ten minutes were spent listening to Doug telling the story of Ivan Ilych. At the time, while I certainly had heard of Leo Tolstoy's *War and Peace* and all that, I had not heard of this novella. So, Doug pulls up a chair in the middle of a U-shaped room, hunches down and begins—this is not verbatim but as I close my eyes, I can transport myself to 4:15 p.m., September 20, 2002, so it's pretty close:

"There was this man named Leo Tolstoy who thought his entire life was a big mistake. You see, Leo, at the age of 45, is on his death bed. Weeks before, he panics, knowing his demise; he cries relentlessly, screams, and runs through all possible emotions. However, a mere two hours before his death, he finds clarity. He sees that he has lived a life of terrible disappointment and tragedy. He realizes that his entire life has been a mistake, who he married, his chosen career, how he parented, who he considered his friends. He deeply regrets how he has lived his life and sees only emptiness and abandonment. He sees compassion as the key to living and asks his wife for forgiveness. He no longer feels visceral hatred but only compassion. He retreats into his world of introspection to spend his last few moments digesting his newfound fact. He dies..."

Doug then took a long deep pause, that seem to drag on for what felt like five minutes, but probably wasn't any more than a few seconds. We all waited on his next word. And he finished with this, "We've done a ton of great work this week, soul searching, hard introspective work. The question then becomes, as I leave you here today, will you wait to learn your life lesson two hours before death, or will you choose to learn your life lesson today?"

And with that, Doug, left the building, head bowed with a swift and gentle glide. We gave a standing ovation, awestruck and most of us had tears welling in our eyes.

This is what great literature, great workshop facilitators, and great presenters can achieve. They can move others to contemplate their existences. All these years later, I'm still talking about Doug, in every single one of my classes and I still I talk about *The Death of Ivan Ilych*. I mean it, I haven't given a single talk without discussing this fine piece and the impact it has had on me, in the hopes that it will be contagious, and that one day, I will be someone's Doug, and they will teach others what they have learned from me and so on. On the idea of contagious learning, it is Tolstoy's work on nonviolence, as expressed within a piece entitled, *The Kingdom of God is Within You*, that is said to have a profound impact on Mahatma Gandhi (#4) and Martin Luther King, Jr. (#7).

Tip – Find the extraordinary life within so that it may be translated into all your talks.

#2 – Randy Pausch

1960–2008

Context – Randy Pausch was an American professor of computer science and human-computer interaction and design at Carnegie Mellon University in Pittsburgh, Pennsylvania. Pausch learned he had pancreatic cancer in 2006, and in 2007 was given a terminal diagnosis of three to six months of good health. Below is Pausch's speech/lecture entitled, "The Last Lecture: Really Achieving Your Childhood Dreams," which he gave on September 18, 2007, at Carnegie Mellon. The talk discusses everything he wanted his children to know after his cancer had taken his life including stories from his childhood, lessons he wanted them to know and things he wanted his children to know about him. He wrote a book, *The Last Lecture*, which follow the theme of his Carnegie Mellon lecture. He died on July 25, 2008.

"It's wonderful to be here. What Indira didn't tell you is that this lecture series used to be called the Last Lecture. If you had one last lecture to give before you died, what would it be? I thought, damn, I finally nailed the venue and they renamed it. So, you know, in case there's anybody who wandered in and doesn't know the back story, my dad always taught me that when there's an elephant in the room, introduce them. If you look at my CAT scans, there are approximately 10 tumors in my liver, and the doctors told me 3-6 months of good health left. That was a month ago, so you can do the math. I have some of the best doctors in the world. Microphone's not working. Then I'll just have to talk louder. [Adjusts mic] Is that good? All right. So that is what it is. We can't change it, and we just have to decide how we're going to respond to that. We cannot change the cards we are dealt, just how we play the hand. If I don't seem as depressed or morose as I should be, sorry to disappoint you. [laughter] And I assure you I am not in denial. It's not like I'm not aware of what's going on. My family, my three kids, my wife, we just decamped. We bought a lovely house in Virginia, and we're doing that because that's a better place for the family to be, down the road. And the other thing is I am in phenomenally good health right now. I mean it's the greatest thing of cognitive dissonance you will ever see is the fact that I am in really good shape. In fact, I am in better shape than most of you. [Randy gets on the ground and starts doing push-ups] [Applause] So anybody who wants to cry or pity me can get down and do a few of those, and then you may pity me. [laughter] All right, so what we're not talking about today, we are not talking about cancer, because I spent a lot of time talking about that and I'm really not interested. If you have any herbal supplements or remedies, please stay away from me. [laughter] And we're not going to talk about things that are even more important than achieving your childhood dreams. We're not going to talk about my wife, we're not talking about my kids. Because I'm good, but I'm not good enough to talk about that.

Without tearing up. So, we're just going to take that off the table. That's much more important. And we're not going to talk about spirituality and religion, although I will tell you that I have achieved a deathbed conversion. [dramatic pause] … I just bought a Macintosh. [laughter and clapping] Now I knew I'd get 9% of the audience with that … All right, so what is today's talk about then? It's about my childhood dreams and how I have achieved them. I've been very fortunate that way. How I believe I've been able to enable the dreams of others, and to some degree, lessons learned. I'm a professor, there should be some lessons learned and how you can use the stuff you hear today to achieve your dreams or enable the dreams of others. And as you get older, you may find that "enabling the dreams of others" thing is even more fun. So, what were my childhood dreams? Well, you know, I had a really good childhood. I mean, no kidding around. I was going back through the family archives, and what was really amazing was, I couldn't find any pictures of me as a kid where I wasn't smiling. And that was just a very gratifying thing. There was our dog, right? Aww, thank you. And there I actually have a picture of me dreaming. I did a lot of that. You know, there's a lot of wake ups! I was born in 1960. When you are 8 or 9 years old and you look at the TV set, men are landing on the moon, anything's possible. And that's something we should not lose sight of, is that the inspiration and the permission to dream is huge. So, what were my childhood dreams? You may not agree with this list, but I was there. [laughter] Being in zero gravity, playing in the National Football League, authoring an article in the World Book Encyclopedia—I guess you can tell the nerds early. [laughter] Being Captain Kirk, anybody here have that childhood dream? Not at CMU, nooooo. I wanted to become one of the guys who won the big stuffed animals in the amusement park, and I wanted to be an Imagineer with Disney. These are not sorted in any particular order, although I think they do get harder, except for maybe the first one…"

Analysis – The "Last Lecture" is a tradition of many universities and colleges, in which a professor is asked to prepare a lecture guided by the question, "If it was your last chance to give a lecture to students, what would you say?"

The video is one hour and sixteen minutes. If you haven't seen it; watch it. If you have seen it before; watch it again. From an analysis of technique, this presentation is superb.

- Randy's slides are precisely what slides should be! Uncluttered, minimal words, and filled with graphics.

- His introduction to the elephant in the room and close are well thought out, practiced and robust.

- He inserts video into his presentation that is effective and supports his point.

- The topic, achieving your childhood dreams, is innovative, creative, and relatable.

- His delivery is the kind that only comes from someone who has spent hours, if not years presenting in front of others. Pausch is one of the best storytellers I've ever heard.

- He uses props with ease to punctuate a point and intersperses them throughout the presentation.

Toss all of this aside because those techniques are nothing without Pausch's lessons on seeking advice on improving our presentation skills. And that is emotion. I've seen this talk at least a dozen times, and each time, I am astounded at how I lose track of time, how I am completely immersed into Pausch's world. His life's journey is mesmerizing, and his storytelling ability is one of the best I've ever heard. You can tell Pausch has spent a lot of time on this talk, as he should. He knew it would likely be his last. He wanted to do his life justice and impart what he's learned along the way, and he does that ten-fold. He has the audience, tapping into every single one of their senses to ensure they will remember it.

It is certainly one that I will never forget.

When is the last time you invested that kind of energy into developing a presentation? Some of you may say, "Well, Caroline, I'm not dying, so I don't need to!" I couldn't disagree more. Now is the perfect time. Invest the required amount of energy to transfer what you've learned in life, from childhood to adulthood, and impart that knowledge to your listeners. It is the only way your talks will ever be superb. We started with talks that focused on technique, strategies, tactics, methods of delivering a talk, but as we've progressed up the list, there has been far less emphasis on those aspects, and far more emphasis on the more difficult and onerous skills to teach such as emotion, introspection, authenticity, and the meaning of life. One might think these aren't essential attributes in delivering a great talk, but without them, one really shouldn't ever step foot on a stage. I feel very strongly about this.

I completed an exercise today as a homage to Randy Pausch. I wrote my own presentation on the same topic. It was one of the best exercises I've undertaken this year. I decided on Pausch for the #2 spot on this list around entry #363. It took me a solid year to complete this project, and this was the best way to bring the year to a close. It was a way to get out from under the weight of the intellectual, philosophical, and analytical angles and bring it down to what really matters: the emotion, who you love, and who loves you. Some of you have provided me with feedback that the content is too deep or difficult to understand because of its historical and philosophical nature. I welcome feedback but those entries were simply stepping stones on the journey to reaching this plateau. All the entries up to this point have simply constructed a solid foundation and built the house and now we get to focus on adding the finishing touches that make a house a home. This post is not esoteric or mysterious. It is simply pure emotion.

Emotion is the glue that brings a talk together. It is what makes the content of a talk leap from the stage and into the minds of the audience and it connects the presenter with the audience. Without it, a talk will come off as robotic, bland, and boring.

It is the emotional connection with your topic that makes it interesting, makes it easy to absorb, hypnotic, charming. Pausch's talk has this in abundance. In his talk, I am moved to tears, moved to laugh, and moved to be introspective and to cherish my own life. Pausch's talk was not delivered for his colleagues, but for his children: ages five, two and one at the time. And because of this motivation, this talk is superior to any before. It's interesting what happens when your motivation is fueled by love alone.

So, if you happen to attend one of my workshops or talks, you will know why I hand out the book, *The Last Lecture*. I have purchased cases of this book. It is a reminder that attaining presentation success is not about presentation technique. Instead, it is all about presentation emotion.

Tip – Be emotionally connected to all aspects of your presentations.

#1 – Atticus Finch

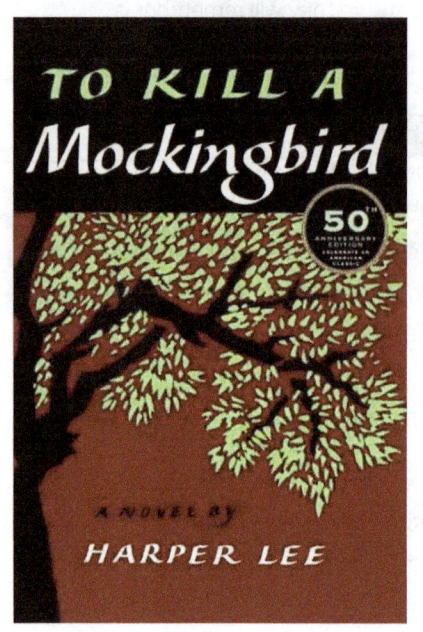

Context – Harper Lee is an author best known for her 1960s Pulitzer Prize-winning, *To Kill a Mockingbird*. It is a novel that deals with the topic of racism. This is Harper Lee's only published piece, and it took her two and half years to write. As a result of writing this book, she has won countless prizes and was awarded the Presidential Medal of Freedom for her contribution to literature in 2007. Lee has said that she was stunned by the novel's success and was simply hoping that a few would give her some encouragement after publishing. She has respectfully declined to make a speech at all awards ceremonies and has refused any type of personal publicity for her novel.

Who is being honoured here? Harper Lee or Atticus Finch, the character in Harper's book? Character or author? The initial working title of Lee's book was simply Atticus so, we shall celebrate both as we highlight our **#1 MUST-KNOW TALK OF ALL TIME** Atticus Finch, in *To Kill a Mockingbird*.

Atticus is a lawyer and resident of the fictional Maycomb County in Alabama and a single father to Jem and Scout Finch. Below is the audio of Gregory Peck, who played Atticus Finch in the 1962 film adaptation.

In a recent article published by British librarians *To Kill a Mockingbird* was ranked ahead of the Bible as a book that "every adult should read before they die."

"Shoot all the blue jays you want, if you can hit 'em, but remember it's a sin to kill a mockingbird."

Analysis – The above quote is the advice Atticus Finch gives to his children, Jem and Scout, as he defends the real mockingbird of Harper Lee's classic novel, Tom Robinson—a black man charged with the rape of a young white woman in the deep south in the 1930s.

The book is narrated by six-year-old, Scout Finch, who lives with her brother, Jem and her widowed father, Atticus, a lawyer. If you have not read this novel, I hope you will after reading this. This novel is funny and warm, despite the serious underpinnings of racial inequality and rape.

The story takes place in the fictional tired old town of Maycomb, Alabama. Jem and Scout befriend Dill, who has come to town to stay with his aunt for the summer. The three are frightened but strangely fascinated by Boo, their elusive neighbour. The town hasn't seen Boo in years, and his reclusion spurs all types of imaginative play for the three children.

Scout is a feisty tomboy-like character, and when Atticus agrees to defend Tom Robinson, who has been accused of raping a young white woman, Scout stands up for her father's honour by fighting, even though she's been told not to. Atticus is berated by the townspeople for being "a nigger-lover." The trio of Scout, Jem and Dill are forbidden to watch the trial, but they sneak in anyway and watch it all unfold from the balcony filled with Robinson's friends and family. Atticus establishes that the accusers are lying during the trial, yet the jury still convicts Robinson and when he tries to escape from prison he is shot and killed.

The accuser's father is enraged, despite his win. He intimidates Robinson's wife. He spits in Atticus' face and attacks Jem, Atticus' son. Jem breaks his arm in the attack. Someone scoops in amidst the struggle and brings Jem home. Scout realizes it is her reclusive neighbour, Boo and has an epiphany when she realizes what life looks like from Boo's perspective.

Atticus Finch is the moral hero of the book. He is a loving father and an overall good citizen. His closing argument is possibly the best speech ever given. It is well thought out, well written, filled with impassioned pleas and arguments and serves its purpose, which is to defend. Atticus has an unwavering dedication to defend and protect Robinson, who he knows is innocent.

"The witnesses for the state…have presented themselves to you gentlemen, to this court, in the cynical confidence that their testimony would not be doubted, confident that you gentlemen would go along with them on the assumption—the evil assumption—that all Negroes lie, that all Negroes are basically immoral beings, that all Negro men are not to be trusted around our women, an assumption one associates with minds of their caliber. Which, gentlemen, we know is in itself a lie as black as Tom Robinson's skin, a lie I do not have to point out to you. You know the truth, the truth is this: some Negroes lie, some Negroes are immoral, some Negro men cannot be trusted around women, black or white.

But this is a truth that applies to the human race and to no particular race of men…."

Despite the absence of evidence and this fantastic speech, Robinson is still convicted of a crime he did not commit. It is not fair, it is not just, yet these are two concepts that Atticus believes in fully. Society, or any civil society for that matter, needs to believe them too.

When I set out on my journey of blogging every day for a year to uncover the best speeches, talks, monologues, quotes and any other forms of the spoken word, I knew immediately that Atticus Finch's closing argument would take the #1 spot. I knew it because this speech encompasses every aspect of every post that has come before, but it also adds a new dimension: to defend those who cannot defend themselves. Lee's story is about racial discrimination and prejudice and the pursuit of honour and character, despite what everyone else thinks. Atticus uses his words to do what is right. Presentation skills often come down to knowing who you are, having a solid moral compass and using your voice in the pursuit of justice, regardless of whether the backdrop is a boardroom or a courtroom.

So, whether we are debating the philosophies of Socrates, laughing with Tina Fey, exploring the worlds created by C.S. Lewis, or fist-pumping alongside Martin Luther King, Jr., every single post has been designed to hold this one monumental post. No one is perfect and Atticus is equally flawed, but it is the pursuit of doing better that leads to greatness. Waking each day ready to learn more while using your words and platform to make a real and lasting difference will give your life meaning and perhaps one day result in you defending your own mockingbird, whoever or whatever that may be.

I named my son Atticus after this brave, honourable, and compassionate character. I can't think of a greater compliment to give a writer than to name a child after one of their characters and I cannot imagine a more noble or worthy character in real life or fiction.

Tip – Learn more, be more, so that you can use your words to make a real and lasting difference.

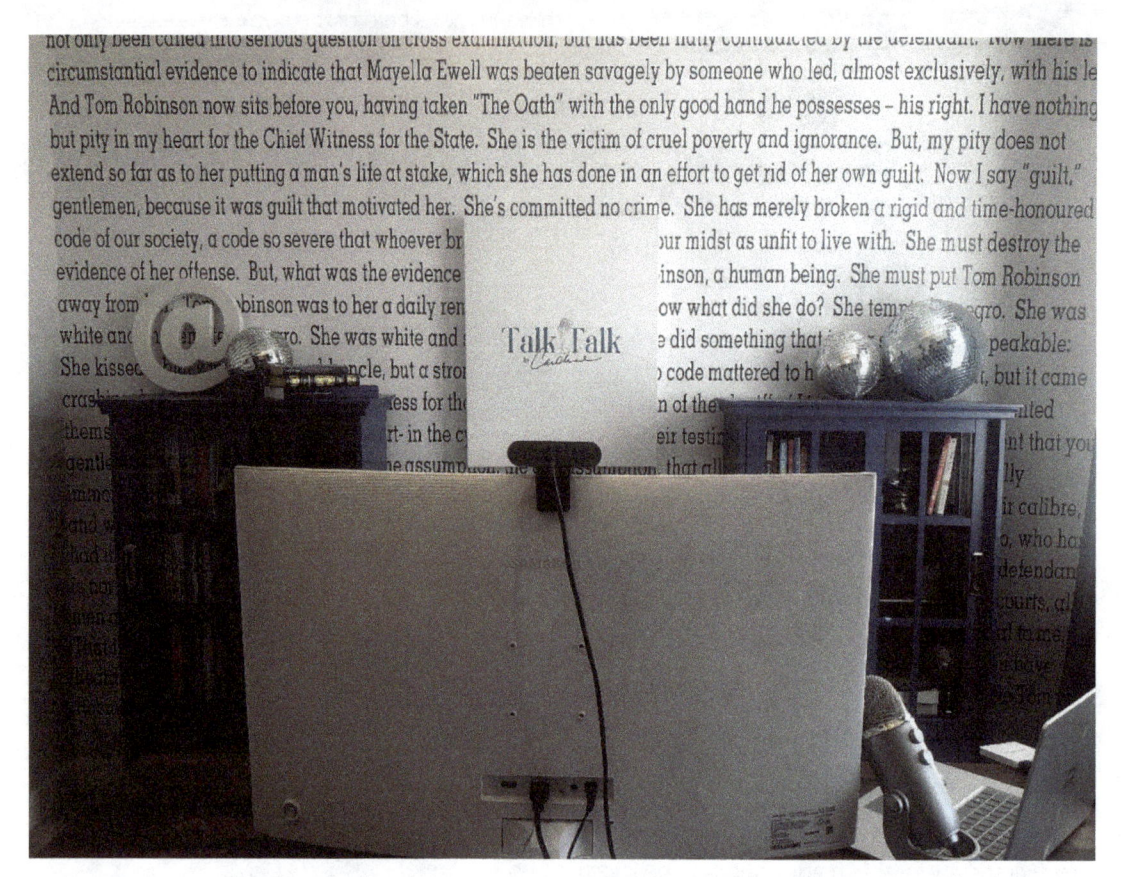

The backdrop to my office is a floor to ceiling mural of Atticus Finch's closing argument.

Web Links to Video References - reference links correct and active at the time of publication.

323. https://www.youtube.com/watch?v=TQMbvJNRpLE

316. https://www.ted.com/talks/isabel_allende_how_to_live_passionately_no_matter_your_age

311. https://www.ted.com/talks/frances_frei_how_to_build_and_rebuild_trust/transcript?language=en

310. https://www.americanrhetoric.com/speeches/jonstewart911firstresponders.htm

309. https://www.npr.org/2019/09/23/763452863/transcript-greta-thunbergs-speech-at-the-u-n-climate-action-summit

297. https://www.ted.com/talks/susan_blackmore_memes_and_temes/transcript

291. https://vimeo.com/325113231

289. https://www.ted.com/talks/tim_urban_inside_the_mind_of_a_master_procrastinator?language=en

288. http://www.ted.com/talks/shekhar_kapur_we_are_the_stories_we_tell_ourselves.html

286. https://www.ted.com/talks/robert_waldinger_what_makes_a_good_life_lessons_from_the_longest_study_on_happiness/transcript?language=en

282. https://www.ted.com/talks/apollo_robbins_the_art_of_misdirection

279. https://www.youtube.com/watch?v=sR6UeVptzRg

272. https://www.ted.com/talks/susan_cain_the_power_of_introverts

271. https://www.ted.com/talks/julian_treasure_the_4_ways_sound_affects_us?language=en

256. https://www.youtube.com/watch?v=g1KYKXS0Hls

255. https://www.youtube.com/watch?v=NQvMQEB0j_A

230. https://www.youtube.com/watch?v=u4taz6dfPQc

220. https://www.ted.com/talks/amy_cuddy_your_body_language_may_shape_who_you_are?language=en

216. https://www.ted.com/talks/kelly_mcgonigal_how_to_make_stress_your_friend?language=en

201. https://www.ted.com/talks/monica_lewinsky_the_price_of_shame/transcript?language=en

188. https://www.ted.com/talks/adam_grant_how_to_stop_languishing_and_start_finding_flow/transcript?language=en

170. https://www.youtube.com/watch?v=UR4uLNFEauw

163. https://holidayfilmreviews.blogspot.com/2013/02/be-my-valentine-charlie-brown.html

160. http://www.youtube.com/watch?v=CTz7yRzeu5g

152. https://www.ted.com/talks/james_veitch_this_is_what_happens_when_you_reply_to_spam_email?language=en

149. http://www.youtube.com/watch?v=Sv1I4q6lOpo

146. https://www.youtube.com/watch?v=HAA8JWC6lgU

135. https://www.youtube.com/watch?v=t_6SaRWdJMc

132. https://www.ted.com/talks/dean_furness_to_overcome_challenges_stop_comparing_yourself_to_others?referrer=playlist-the_most_popular_talks_ "f_2020

128. https://www.youtube.com/watch?v=kgGz7Ds0j6w

125. https://www.ted.com/talks/kelli_jean_drinkwater_enough_with_the_fear_of_fat

115. https://www.youtube.com/watch?v=vinFtnfObCM

111. https://www.youtube.com/watch?v=5x0PzUoJS-U

105. http://www.youtube.com/watch?v=1k08yxu57N

102. http://www.youtube.com/watch?v=0M_mTxEQ85I

101. https://www.youtube.com/watch?v=HeYodU8Gwik

96. http://www.youtube.com/watch?v=ky7DMCHQJZY

95. https://www.youtube.com/watch?v=rBrd_3VMC3c

92. http://il.youtube.com/watch?v=gUdrYDk8rVA

85. https://www.ted.com/talks/seth_godin_how_to_get_your_ideas_to_spread?language=en

84. https://www.youtube.com/watch?v=1i8XVQ2pswg

81. https://www.ted.com/talks/jill_tarter_join_the_seti_search/transcript?language=en

79. https://www.youtube.com/watch?v=URI0u5lR36g

73. https://www.ted.com/talks/984/transcript?language=en

72. https://archive.org/details/BitChute-TUMkjJ0LCfw

71. https://www.youtube.com/watch?v=5zn-fPM4KS0

70. https://www.youtube.com/watch?v=Pdh9JhwZ8nc

68. https://www.ted.com/talks/richard_st_john_8_secrets_of_success

66. https://www.youtube.com/watch?v=yhA04D_xfp8

65. https://www.youtube.com/watch?v=lOyy887d4vs

62. https://www.youtube.com/watch?v=ybwjB64xuaM

60. https://www.youtube.com/watch?v=-uWxdTxBi2g

59. https://www.youtube.com/watch?v=1cpBpIxYh7M

57. http://www.youtube.com/watch?v=L4eOIS9DFm4&p=4FCB02E3981F0246&playnext=1&index=3

53. https://www.youtube.com/watch?v=0e8ToRVOtRo

45. https://www.youtube.com/watch?v=WA8-KEnfWbQ

41. https://speakola.com/grad/james-carville-tulane-university-2008

40. https://www.c-span.org/video/?124303-1/jackson-campaign-rally

37. https://news.stanford.edu/2005/06/14/jobs-061505/

34. https://www.youtube.com/watch?v=UhXlAGmUitU

33. https://www.youtube.com/watch?v=mnjTANhBu3k

30. https://www.youtube.com/watch?v=TuW4oGKzVKc

28. https://www.youtube.com/watch?v=X8ulYIVcCeY

26. https://www.youtube.com/watch?v=Mbdsn_sp0Vw

19. https://www.youtube.com/watch?v=YmEUiHk_Uu8

18. https://www.youtube.com/watch?v=T21HBWxBd-U

17. https://www.queerty.com/graem-taylor-14-is-sticking-up-for-michigan-high-school-teacher-jay-mcdowell-and-he-is-the-awesome-20101113

14. https://www.youtube.com/watch?v=lZ97s396kb0

12. https://www.youtube.com/watch?v=zJ6VT7ciR1o

8. https://www.youtube.com/watch?v=XdTUSignq7Y

7. https://www.youtube.com/watch?v=vP4iY1TtS3s

2. https://www.ted.com/talks/randy_pausch_really_achieving_your_childhood_dreams

1. https://www.youtube.com/watch?v=tNxrnOC_WTs

Photo Sources - reference links correct and active at the time of publication.

365. ALBERT EINSTEIN
Library of Congress's Prints and Photographs division, Wikipedia Commons

364. AL GORE
By Alex de Carvalho - https://www.flickr.com/photos/adc/406859008/, CC BY 2.0, https://commons.wikimedia.org/w/index.php?curid=5407913

360. STEPHEN HAWKING
By ²º¹ºº - Photo created by ²º¹ºº, as documented at Wikipedia fr, Public Domain, https://commons.wikimedia.org/w/index.php?curid=802513

357. BILL CLINTON
Harry Hamburg, https://www.nydailynews.com/news/politics/clinton-admits-relationship-lewinsky-1998-article-1.817191

354. ANN RICHARDS
AP photo, https://www.texasmonthly.com/politics remembering-the-last-texan-to-deliver-the-dnc-keynote-address/

352. SALLY FIELD
Credit Image: Â© Phil Roach/Globe Photos/ZUMAPRESS.com, ALAMY STOCK PHOTO

350. STEVE JOBS
https://www.somagnews.com/steve-jobs-launches-first-macintosh-36-years-ago-today/

347. PETER PAN kobo.com

343. GEORGE BERNARD SHAW
By Alvin Langdon Coburn - Illustrated London News, p. 575 (subscription required), PD-US, https://en.wikipedia.org/w/index.php?curid=49887931

339. MICHEL DE MONTAIGNE
By Unknown author - http://www.archivio.formazione.unimib.it/DATA/Insegnamenti/11_2349/materiale/2.pdf, Public Domain, https://commons.wikimedia.org/w/index.php?curid=72061920

337. LAO TSU
By Zhang Lu - http://tech2.npm.gov.tw/cheschool/zh-tw/index.aspx?content=e_1_58, Public Domain, https://commons.wikimedia.org/w/index.php?curid=9846913

33. ELIZABETH GILBERT
By Erik Charlton from Menlo Park, USA - Eat, Pray, Love, CC BY 2.0, https://commons.wikimedia.org/w/index.php?curid=8026339

333. WILLIAM SHAKESPEARE
John Taylor, Public domain, via Wikimedia Commons

332. MARGARET THATCHER Chronicle / Alamy Stock Photo

330. CHIP N DALE.2021
https://www.dailymotion.com/video/x2bgfrk

327. PAUL POTTS one eye / Alamy Stock Photo

321. ROMEO AND JULIET
Artist: Ford Madox Brown, Photo Credit: Samuel and Mary R. Bancroft Memorial, 1935, Wikipedia Commons

318. JUDSON HAIMMLY
https://www.prweb.com/releases/evolution_of_dance/viral_video/prweb1767934.htm

315. HANS ROSLING
https://www.gatesnotes.com/About-Bill-Gates/Remembering-Hans-Rosling

306. DUKE ELLINGTON
https://www.britannica.com/biography/Duke-Ellington#/media/1/185019/242914

304. TEMPLE GRANDIN Wikipedia Commons

302. ARTHUR BENJAMIN
https://www.britannica.com/biography/Duke-Ellington#/media/1/185019/242914

299. BOBBY MCFERRIN
https://www.youtube.com/watch?v=S0kCUss0g9

298. TOM WUJEC
https://www.emeroleary.com/sketchnote-three-ways-the-brain-creates-meaning/

293. MATTHIEU RICAR
By Jon Schmidt - Jon Schmidt, photographe, collaborateur de Matthieu Ricard (sujet de la photo) au sein de l'association Karuna-Shechen, résidant en Suisse., CC BY-SA 4.0, https://commons.wikimedia.org/w/index.php?curid=58958315

292. STUART BROWN
https://www.optimize.me/authors/stuart-brown/

290. GARY VAYNERCHUCK
https://en.wikipedia.org/wiki/Gary_Vaynerchuk#/media/File:Gary_Vaynerchuk_public_domain.jpg

287. LAKSHMI PRATURY
https://commons.wikimedia.org/wiki/File:Girl_Power_at_TED_conference_2007_by_jurvetson.jpg

287. LAKSHMI PRATURY2
https://shenomics.com/lakshmi-pratury/

285. JAMIE OLIVER shutterstock.com

283. BENJAMIN ZANDER shutterstock.com

278. KIRAN BIR SETHI youtube.com

277. POET RIVES
https://www.ted.com/talks/rives_the_4_a_m_mystery

276. AL PACINO youtube.com

270. DALAI LAMA By Salvacampillo Shutterstock.com

269. ALAIN DE BOTTON
https://commons.wikimedia.org/w/index.php?curid=51560717

268. CARMEN AGRA DEEDY
https://www.blogtalkradio.com/akindvoice/2016/06/11/a-kind-voice-radio--carmen-agra-deedy

267. ERIN MCKEAN
By Erin McKean (Esperluette) - Own work, CC BY-SA 3.0, https://commons.wikimedia.org/w/index.php?curid=1614243

265. MALCOLM GLADWELL
https://medium.com/40fathoms/malcolm-gladwells-spaghetti-sauce-theory-applied-to-presidential-candidates-55479155807b

263. BECKY BLANTON
https://www.sparefoot.com/self-storage/blog/4656-living-in-a-storage-unit/

262. DAN ARIELY
Photographer: Chris Goodney/Bloomberg via Getty Images

260. SARAH JONES
By Вени Марковски - Own work, CC BY 3.0, https://commons.wikimedia.org/w/index.php?curid=5919595

259. SIR JOHN MORTIMER.2021
Fair use, https://en.wikipedia.org/w/index.php?curid=51816641

257. ANTHONY BOURDAIN shutterstock.com

255. EVEN ENSLER shutterstock.com

254. HILLARY CLINTON PIXABAY.COM

250. JIMI HENDRIX shutterstock.com

247. CHEVY CHASE shutterstock.com

246. NATALIE MERCHANT Wikipedia Commons

245. MARCUS DU SAUTOY
https://www.cbc.ca/radio/spark/spark-444-1.5178304/new-book-explores-ai-and-the- secrets-of-human-creativity-1.5178307

243. SIMON SINEK
https://www.ted.com/talks/simon_sinek_how_great_leaders_inspire_action

241. DIANA, PRINCESS OF WALES
Wikipedia Commons
By Nick Parfjonov - Own work, Public Domain, https://commons.wikimedia.org/w/index.php?curid=7366693

235. VIKTOR FRANKL
By Prof. Dr. Franz Vesely, CC BY-SA 3.0 de, https://commons.wikimedia.org/w/index.php?curid=15153593

231. GEORGE CLOONEY shutterstock.com

229. MICHELLE OBAMA
By flickr user Ava Lowery - https://www.flickr.com/photos/avalowery/2893907715/, CC BY 2.0, https://commons.wikimedia.org/w/index.php?curid=5211410

226. NEIL ARMSTRONG By Ms S. Ann, shutterstock.com

224. AMY TAN
https://www.ted.com/talks/amy_tan_where_does_creativity_hide?utm_campaign=tedspread&utm_medium =referral&utm_source=tedcomshare

222. GOLAN LEVIN
Flickr: Golan Levin at (Rocky Mountain College of Art and Design), October 2010
Wikipedia Commons

217. SOJOURNER TRUTH
By Randall Studio - This is a retouched picture, which means that it has been digitally altered from its original version. Modifications: Cropped. Cleaned image of spots and other imperfections. Adjusted levels and exposure to reduce overblown highlights. The original can be viewed here: Sojourner Truth, 1870.tif: . Modifications made by Coffeeandcrumbs., Public Domain, https://commons.wikimedia.org/w/index.php?curid=86793423

213. DAN PINK Getty Images/Riccardo S. Savi

211. MIKE ROWE
https://speaking.com/speakers/mike-rowe/

207. PAULO COELHO
By Ricardo Stuckert/PR - Agência Brasil [1], CC BY 3.0 br, https://commons.wikimedia.org/w/index.php?curid=1602560

205. STEFAN SAGMEISTER
By Merinda123 - Own work, CC BY-SA 4.0, https://commons.wikimedia.org/w/index.php?curid=98537581

202. NAPOLEON HILL
By New York World-Telegram and the Sun Newspaper staff photographer. - This image is available from the United States Library of Congress's Prints and Photographs division under the digital ID cph.3c36395.

201. GIRL FROM YOUTUBE (JESSICA) Youtube.com

199. ANISH KAPOOR
By Vogler - Own work, CC BY-SA 4.0, https://commons.wikimedia.org/w/index.php?curid=64752092

198. YOGI BEAR
By Source (WP:NFCC#4), Fair use, https://en.wikipedia.org/w/index.php?curid=39715110

196. SIEGFRED WOLDHEK
Wikipedia Commons for photo of Woldhek and drawing of Leonardo da Vinci

193. JAMES LIPTON
By David Shankbone - Own work, CC BY-SA 3.0, https://commons.wikimedia.org/w/index.php?curid=2010520

191. TINA TRUNER
Philip Spittle, CC BY 2.0 <https://creativecommons.org/licenses/by/2.0>, via Wikimedia Commons

187. HIPPOCRATES
By manuscript: Unknown authors can use in book: Foto de la Biblioteca Vaticanascan from book: User:Rmrfstar - page 27 of Surgery: An Illustrated History by Ira M. Rutkow, M.D. published in 1993: ISBN 0801660785., Public Domain, https://commons.wikimedia.org/w/index.php?curid=1446714

185. DANIEL GOLEMAN Robert Leslie | CREDIT: TED

182. DOUGLAS ENGLEBART SRI International

177. WARREN BUFFET shutterstock.com

173. LUDWIG VAN BEETHOVEN Wikipedia Commons

171. THE FUN THEORY Facebook, The Fun Theory / Rolighetsteorin

167. CARLOS CASTANEDA
By Source, Fair use, https://en.wikipedia.org/w/index.php?curid=12765330

164. ELIE WEISEL Getty Images/Chris Hondros

163. ELIZABETH BARRETT BROWNING
Snoopy: https://holidayfilmreviews.blogspot.com/2013/02/be-my-valentine-charlie-brown.html

163. ELIZABETH BARRETT BROWING 2
Public Domain, https://commons.wikimedia.org/w/index.php?curid=230346

161. ANTONE DE SAINT-EXUPÉRY Roger Viollet/Getty Images/Albert Harlingue

158. OSCAR WILDE
By Napoleon Sarony - Library of Congress, Public Domain, https://commons.wikimedia.org/w/index.php?curid=9816614

156. TONY ROBBINS
Randy Stewart, (CC) blog.stewtopia.com

155. DR. SEUSS
By Source, Fair use, https://en.wikipedia.org/w/index.php?curid=34952540

154. ROBIN WILLIMAS
Getty Images, https://daily.jstor.org/how-carpe-diem-got-lost-in-translation/

151. LIA MILLS
Courtesy of the Mills Family, https://torontolife.com/city/fetal-position/

147. VOLTAIRE
By Nicolas de Largillière - This file has been extracted from another file: Nicolas de Largillière, François-Marie Arouet dit Voltaire (vers 1724-1725) -001.jpg, Public Domain, https://commons.wikimedia.org/w/index.php?curid=80206718

145. STEVE BALLMER
By Jesús Gorriti - originally posted to Flickr as Le Ballmer, CC BY-SA 2.0, https://commons.wikimedia.org/w/index.php?curid=7920311

143. JONATHAN MCCOY youtube.com

140. JENNIFER BUCHANAN
Speakers Bureau of Canada www.speakerscanada.com. youtube.com

139. BARRACK OBAMA
Center for American Progress AP/Ron Edwards

138. PABLO PICASSO shutterstock.com

137. OPRAH WINFREY
https://twitter.com/CBS/status/1276691656029335552

134. RICHARD NIXON Wikipedia Commons

130. TOM LEHRER
Photo of Tom Lehrer. Wikipedia Commons.
Cartoon as it appears on the album An Evening Wasted, by Tom Lehrer

129. ELDRIDGE CLEAVER
By U.S. News & World Report Magazine staff photographer: Marion S. Trikosko - This image is available from the United States Library of Congress's Prints and Photographs divisionunder the digital ID ppmsc.01265.This tag does not indicate the copyright status of the attached work. A normal copyright tag is still required. See Commons:Licensing for more information., Public Domain, https://commons.wikimedia.org/w/index.php?curid=5817705

127. HENRY MILLER
By Wim van Rossem / Anefo - http://proxy.handle.net/10648/a9943796-d0b4-102d-bcf8-003048976d84, CC0, https://commons.wikimedia.org/w/index.php?curid=73707800

126. JEREMY RIFKIN
www.thersa.org/comment/2010/05/rsa-animate---empathic-civilisation

124. DEREK SIVERS
Creator: James Duncan Davidson | Credit: TED, https://www.npr.org/2015/08/14/431540456/what-s-the-best-way-to-achieve-a-new-goal

121. PATRICK HENRY
By Popular Graphic Arts - Library of CongressCatalog: http://lccn.loc.gov/2001700209Image download: https://cdn.loc.gov/service/pnp/cph/3a00000/3a04000/3a04000/3a04017r.jpgOriginal url: http://hdl.loc.gov/loc.pnp/pga.08961, Public Domain, https://commons.wikimedia.org/w/index.php?curid=65583755

119. DALAI LAMA
By *christopher* - Flickr: dalailama1_20121014_4639, CC BY 2.0, https://commons.wikimedia.org/w/index.php?curid=22580076

118. JAMES STEWART
By Columbia Pictures - National Board of Review Magazine for November 1939, Volume XIV, Number 8, page 14, Public Domain, https://commons.wikimedia.org/w/index.php?curid=63681673

115. JOHN KEATS
By William Hilton - one or more third parties have made copyright claims against Wikimedia Commons in relation to the work from which this is sourced or a purely mechanical reproduction thereof. This may be due to recognition of the "sweat of the brow" doctrine, allowing works to be eligible for protection through skill and labour, and not purely by originality as is the case in the United States (where this website is hosted). These claims may or may not be valid in all jurisdictions. As such, use of this image in the jurisdiction of the claimant or other countries may be regarded as copyright infringement. Please see Commons: When to use the PD-Art tag for more information., Public Domain, https://commons.wikimedia.org/w/index.php?curid=6370362

110. STEVEN JOHNSON
https://www.npr.org/2014/06/27/322920914/where-do-good-ideas-come-from

109. RENE DESCARTES
By After Frans Hals - André Hatala [e.a.] (1997) De eeuw van Rembrandt, Bruxelles: Crédit communal de Belgique, ISBN 2-908388-32-4., Public Domain, https://commons.wikimedia.org/w/index.php?curid=2774313

106. JK ROWLING
https://www.cnbc.com/2019/03/28/harry-potter-novelist-jk-rowling-famous-advice-to-harvard-students-is-dark-but-so-brilliant-and-true.html

100. MERYL STREEP Everett Collection Inc / Alamy Stock Photo

99. JESSE JACKSON Everett Collection Inc / Alamy Stock Photo

98. CHARLIE CHAPLIN
Wikipedia. https://en.wikipedia.org/wiki/The_Great_Dictator#/media/File:The_Great_Dictator_(1940)_poster.jpg. By Trailer screenshot - The Great Dictator trailer, Public Domain, https://commons.wikimedia.org/w/index.php?curid=8971703

93. ALEC BALDWIN
Credit: Jemal Countess; Photos: Getty, http://www.justjared.com/photo-gallery/2449915/alec-baldwin-nyu-commencement-speaker-04/fullsize/

90. CHESLEY SULLENBERGER
By Greg L - cropped from File: Plane crash into Hudson River.jpg (originally posted to Flickr as Plane crash into Hudson River), CC BY 2.0, https://commons.wikimedia.org/w/index.php?curid=5733716

89. GODFREY HARDY Wikipedia Commons

88. BARBARA CHARLINE JORDAN Circa Images, Alamy Stock Photo

88. PLUTCHIK'S WHEEL OF EMOTION
By Machine Elf 1735 - Own work, Public Domain, https://commons.wikimedia.org/w/index.php?curid=13285286

87. AA MILNE
By Brewster Publications; photograph by E. O. Hoppé, London - Shadowland, September 1922 (page 62), Public Domain, https://commons.wikimedia.org/w/index.php?curid=58472213

85. SETH GODIN
TED Talks, https://www.ted.com/talks/seth_godin_how_to_get_your_ideas_to_spread

83. WILLIAM PITKIN / SOPHIE TUCKER
Sophie Tucker image. https://www.amazon.com/DAYS-LIFE-BEGINS-RECORD-PICTURE-SLEEVE/dp/B0714M8FSD

81. JILL TARTER Wikipedia Commons

77. JIMMY CARTER
https://longtailpipe.com/2017/09/04/jimmy-carters-crisis-of-confidence-speech-was-political-disaster-but-oh--if-wed-only-stuck-to-his-plan/

76. BROTHERS GRIMM
By http://www.mythfolklore.net/3043mythfolklore/reading/grimm/images/rackham_hansel.htm and http://www.surlalunefairytales.com/illustrations/hanselgretel/rackhamhansel.html, Public Domain, https://commons.wikimedia.org/w/index.php?curid=1057110

75. ALFRED ADLER Science History Images / Alamy Stock Photo

74. BENJAMIN FRANKLIN
By Joseph Duplessis - ZgEyj5EEKdux-g at Google Cultural Institute maximum zoom level, Public Domain, https://commons.wikimedia.org/w/index.php?curid=21880454

72. DAVID ICKE
By Tyler Merbler - Flickr, CC BY 2.0, https://commons.wikimedia.org/w/index.php?curid=49917369

67. WAYNE GRETZKY
By Kris Krüg, CC BY-SA 2.0, https://commons.wikimedia.org/w/index.php?curid=36257814

65. PAT CARROLL
https://www.reddit.com/r/OldSchoolCool/comments/fodzpo/pat_carroll_singing_poor_unfortunate_souls_in_the/

63. CARL JUNG
By Unbekannt - This image is from the collection of the ETH-Bibliothek and has been published on Wikimedia Commons as part of a cooperation with Wikimedia CH. Corrections and additional information are welcome., Public Domain, https://commons.wikimedia.org/w/index.php?curid=94177705

62. TIFFANY SHLAIN
VIMEO, http://www.tiffanyshlain.com/speaking

61. LEWIS CARROLL amazon.ca

60. BARACK OBAMA
AP Photo/Gerald Herbert. Gerald Herbert / The Spokesman-Review

59. RYAN HRELJAC
https://www.youtube.com/watch?v=ZXDOxPiDyzc&list=PLF740C0F60EFFBB9E
https://www.youtube.com/watch?v=1cpBpIxYh7M

58. LEONARDO DAVINCI
   By Leonardo da Vinci - Leonardo Da Vinci - Photo from www.lucnix.be. 2007-09-08 (photograph). Luc Viatour, https://lucnix.be

56 PEMA CHODRON
   By https://www.flickr.com/people/64954998@N00 - https://www.flickr.com/photos/64954998@N00/520966065/, CC BY-SA 2.0, https://commons.wikimedia.org/w/index.php?curid=21100125

55. HARRY TRUMAN
   By National Archives and Records Administration. Office of Presidential Libraries. Harry S. Truman Library. Wikipedia Commons

53. ELLEN DEGENERES
   https://mediakron.bc.edu/profiles/profiles/ellen

52. ARISTOTLE
   By Raphael - Web Gallery of Art: Image Info about artwork, Public Domain, https://commons.wikimedia.org/w/index.php?curid=75881

51. HO CHI MINH
   By Unknown author - This file has been extracted from another file: Ho Chi Minh 1946 and signature.jpg, Public Domain, https://commons.wikimedia.org/w/index.php?curid=25126454

49. HO CHI MINH
   By Guido Reni - Web Gallery of Art: Image Info about artwork, Public Domain, https://commons.wikimedia.org/w/index.php?curid=15885392

47. MOTHER THERESA
   By Manfredo Ferrari - Own work, CC BY-SA 4.0, https://commons.wikimedia.org/w/index.php?curid=35010569

46. RONALD REAGAN Wikipedia Commons

45. GEORGE W BUSH
   The George W. Bush Presidential Library and Museum, https://www.marketwatch.com/story/newly-released-photos-capture-george-w-bush-in-the-moments-after-911-attacks-2016-05-09

44. QUEEN ELIZABETH I
   Formerly attributed to George Gower - http://www.luminarium.org/renlit/elizarmada.jpg, Public Domain, https://commons.wikimedia.org/w/index.php?curid=28313

43. GEORGE WASHINGTON
   By George Washington - This image is available from the United States Library of Congress; Religion and the Founding of the American Republic exhibition, https://www.loc.gov/exhibits/religion/rel06.html#obj156, Public Domain, https://commons.wikimedia.org/w/index.php?curid=11148207

40. JESSE JACKSON Mark Reinstein, shutterstock.com

38. EDWARD KENNEDY
   By Stevan Kragujevic - Transferred from sr.wikipedia to Commons., CC BY-SA 3.0, https://commons.wikimedia.org/w/index.php?curid=53532403

36. WINSTON CHURCHILL
   https://winstonchurchill.org/publications/churchill-bulletin/bulletin-084-june-2015/churchill-when-britain-said-no/

35. SUSAN B ANTHONY
   By Unknown author - [1], Public Domain, https://commons.wikimedia.org/w/index.php?curid=96243738

33. SIDNEY POITIER
   © Danial A. Anderson/KRT/ABACA. 33370-7. Los Angeles-CA-USA, 24/3/2002, Abaca Press / Alamy Stock Photo

32. DEMOSTHENES
   Bust of the Greek orator Demosthenes. Marble, Roman artwork, inspired from a bronze statue by Polyeuctos (ca. 280 BCE). Found in Italy. By Sting, CC BY-SA 2.5, https://commons.wikimedia.org/w/index.php?curid=295989

30. JOHN F. KENNEDY
    https://en.wikipedia.org/wiki/John_F._Kennedy#/media/File:JFKRiceUniversity.jpg

29. WILLIAM SHAKESPEARE
    By John Taylor - Official gallery link, Public Domain, https://commons.wikimedia.org/w/index.php?curid=5442977

27. MALCOM X
    Ed Ford, World Telegram staff photographer, Wikipedia Commons

26. PIERRE ELLIOT TRUDEAU
    Canadian Press, https://www.wsws.org/en/articles/2020/10/23/wmat-o23.html

25 ST. FRANCIS OF ASSISI
    By Master of St Francis - http://www.wga.hu/frames-e.html?/html/m/master/francis/index.html, Public Domain, https://commons.wikimedia.org/w/index.php?curid=3973175

24. VIRGINIA WOOLF
    By George Charles Beresford - Filippo Venturi Photography Blog, Public Domain, https://commons.wikimedia.org/w/index.php?curid=50293324

21. MARIE CURIE
    By Henri Manuel - Christie's, Public Domain, https://commons.wikimedia.org/w/index.php?curid=32735756

20. MAYA ANGELOU
    By Clinton Library - William J. Clinton Presidential Library, Public Domain, https://commons.wikimedia.org/w/index.php?curid=67072902

16. FREDERICK DOUGLASS https://vimeo.com/1275332

15. ROSA PARKS
    By Unknown author - USIA / National Archives and Records Administration Records of the U.S. Information Agency Record Group 306, Public Domain, https://commons.wikimedia.org/w/index.php?curid=4344206

12. JUDY GARLAND
    By CBS Television Network - Public Domain, https://commons.wikimedia.org/w/index.php?curid=20838645

9. LEONARDO DAVINCI
    By Leonardo da Vinci - www.vivoscuola.it : Home; Picture, Public Domain, https://commons.wikimedia.org/w/index.php?curid=109273

8. HELEN KELLER Everett Collection Historical / Alamy Stock Photo

5. SOCRATES
    https://commons.wikimedia.org

4. GANDHI
    By Kanu Gandhi - gandhiserve.org, Public Domain, https://commons.wikimedia.org/w/index.php?curid=171654

3. LEO TOLSTOY
    By F. W. Taylor - This image is available from the United States Library of Congress's Prints and Photographs division under the digital ID ppmsca.37767. Public Domain, https://commons.wikimedia.org/w/index.php?curid=39880503

1. ATTICUS FINCH
    Gregory Peck photo by Universal Pictures - eBay, Public Domain, https://commons.wikimedia.org/w/index.php?curid=67270089. To Kill a Mocking Bird book cover by Nate D. Sanders auctions, Wikipedia

DECEMBER: TIP:

30 JOHN F. KENNEDY   KNOWLEDGE!
29 WILLIAM SHAKESPEARE   IAMBIC PANTAMETER
28 SALLY FIELD   FIERINESS!
27 MALCOLM X   SHOCK/REVELATION!
26 PIERRE TRUDEAU   'ART'!
25 ST. FRANCIS OF ASSISI.   SIMPLEST!
24 VIRGINIA WOOLF   CHANNEL STRUGGLE
23 ARISTOTLE   WHO/WHAT!
22 RAY NAGIN   OWN TRUTH!
21 MARIE CURIE   CRYSTAL CLEAR!
20 MAYA ANGELOU   ORATORY PROSE
19 RUDOLPH   VIEW HINDERANCE
18 COLIN POWELL   FORWARDS!
17 GRAEME TAYLOR   BE WHO YOU ARE!
16 FREDERICK DOUGLASS.   RIGHT INJUSTICES
15 ROSA PARKS   CONSCIOUS!
~~14~~ CARRIE FISHER   WIT!
✓13 BARACK OBAMA (INAUGRAL ADDRESS) REPETITION!
✓12 WIZARD OF OZ   NAVIGATE DESTINY!
✓11 PLATO   LOVE WISDOM!
✓10 JOHN F. KENNEDY   PHATIC LANG.!
✓9   LEONARDO DA VINCI   STUDY LIFETIME
✓8   HELEN KELLER   VISION!
✓7   ~~SOCRATES (APOLOGY)~~ MARTIN LUTHER KING JR /time.com   CHANGE THE WORLD!
✓6   ~~MARTIN LUTHER KING JR.~~ ARISTOTLE / NELSON MANDELA   PRODUCTIVE!
✓5   ~~GANDHI~~ SOCRATES   UNEXAMINED!
✓4   ~~ROSA PARKS~~ GANDHI   BE THE CHANGE!
✓3   LEO TOLSTOY   EXTRA ORDINARY!
✓2   RANDY PAUSH   EMOTIONALLY CONNECTED!
*(#1) ATTICUS FINCH (courtroom scene)   LEARN MORE
                                                         BE MORE!!!

Hilroy

CPSIA information can be obtained
at www.ICGtesting.com
Printed in the USA
LVHW060435140522
718732LV00024B/1783